CNE Training Guide: NetWare 4.1 Update

Karanjit Siyan, Ph.D

New Riders

New Riders Publishing, Indianapolis, IN

CNE Training Guide: NetWare 4.1 Update

By Karanjit Siyan

Published by:
New Riders Publishing
201 West 103rd Street
Indianapolis, IN 46290 USA

Printed in the United States of America 1 2 3 4 5 6 7 8 9 0

CIP data available upon request

Warning and Disclaimer

This book is designed to provide information about the NetWare computer program. Every effort has been made to make this book as complete and as accurate as possible, but no warranty or fitness is implied.

The information is provided on an "as is" basis. The author and New Riders Publishing shall have neither liability nor responsibility to any person or entity with respect to any loss or damages arising from the information contained in this book or from the use of the disks or programs that may accompany it.

Publisher	Don Fowley
Associate Publisher	Tim Huddleston
Marketing Manager	Ray Robinson
Acquisitions Manager	Jim LeValley
Managing Editor	Tad Ringo

Product Development Specialist
Emmett Dulaney

Acquisitions Editor
Alicia Buckley

Production Editor
John Sleeva

Copy Editors
Geneil Breeze, Laura Frey,
Howard Pierce, Cliff Shubs,
Lisa Wilson, Lillian Yates

Technical Editors
Brian Benson
Tim Petru

Assistant Marketing Manager
Tamara Apple

Acquisitions Coordinator
Tracy Turgeson

Publisher's Assistant
Karen Opal

Cover Designer
Jay Corpus

Book Designer
Kim Scott

Production Team Supervisor
Laurie Casey

Graphics Coordinator
Dennis Clay Hager

Graphic Image Specialists
Clint Lahnen
Dennis Sheehan

Production Analysts
Angela D. Bannan
Bobbi Satterfield
Mary Beth Wakefield

Production Team
Gary Adair, Angela Calvert,
Dan Caparo, Nathan Clement,
Kim Cofer, Jennifer Eberhardt,
Rob Falco, Dave Garratt,
Aleata Howard, Erika Millen,
Beth Rago, Regina Rexrode,
Erich J. Richter, Christine
Tyner, Karen Walsh, Robert
Wolf

Indexer
Chris Cleveland

About the Author

Karanjit S. Siyan is president of Kinetics Corporation. He has authored international seminars on Solaris & SunOS, TCP/IP networks, PC Network Integration, Novell networks, Windows NT, and Expert Systems using Fuzzy Logic. He teaches advanced technology seminars in the United States, Canada, Europe, and the Far East. Karanjit is actively involved in Internet research and holds a Ph.D in Computer Science. He has published articles in *Dr. Dobb's Journal*, *The C User's Journal*, and *Databased Advisor*.

Before working as an independent consultant, Karanjit worked as a senior member of the technical staff at ROLM Corporation. As part of his consulting work, Karanjit has written a number of custom compiler and operating system development tools. Besides his interest in network security, his other interests include Unix-based, Novell-based, Windows NT-based, and OS/2 networks. Karanjit holds the ECNE certification for Novell-based networks and the Microsoft Certified Professional for Windows NT. His current book titles are *Internet Firewalls and Network Security*, *NetWare: The Professional Reference*, *Windows NT Server: The Professional Reference*, *NetWare TCP/IP and NFS*, *NetWare 4 Administration*, and *NetWare 4 Update*. He has also coauthored *LAN Connectivity*, *Banyan Vines: The Professional Reference*, *NetWare 4 for Professionals*, *Implementing Internet Security*, and *Down-sizing to NetWare*. Karanjit is based in Motana where he lives with his wife, Dei. He can be reached through the Internet at karanjit@siyan.com.

Trademark Acknowledgments

All terms mentioned in this book that are known to be trademarks or service marks have been appropriately capitalized. New Riders Publishing cannot attest to the accuracy of this information. Use of a term in this book should not be regarded as affecting the validity of any trademark or service mark. NetWare is a registered trademark of Novell, Inc.

Dedication

In dedication to the man who knew infinity:

Srinivasa Ramanujan 1887-1920

for his dazzling mathematical genius that showed the potential of the human mind.

Acknowledgments

One of the most pleasurable tasks of being an author is to thank the people responsible for the success of a book. My heartfelt thanks to my wife Dei for her love and support. I wish to thank my father, Ahal Singh, and my mother, Tejinder; my brothers, Harjit and Jagjit; my sisters, Kookie and Dolly. Thanks also to Margaret Cooper Scott, Cathryn and Bob Foley, Craig and Lydia Cooper,

Robert and Janie Cooper, Heidi and Steve Bynum, Barbara and Edward L. Scott (Scotty) for their love and support. Special thanks to Mother. Without her spiritual support, this book would not have been possible.

I would like to thank Learning Tree International for rekindling my interest in teaching and writing. For readers interested in additional information on seminars taught by the author, call 800-421-8166 (U.S.), 800-267-1696 (Canada), 0800282353 (U.K.). I wish to thank Bob Sanregret and Anders Amundson, who had no idea what they were starting when one fine day in July '90, they innocently asked me the question "Would you like to write a seminar on Novell networking?"

I wish to acknowledge the many people who have helped me along the way: Edward and Mary Kramer, Harpreet Sandhu, Bill Duby, Angela, Michael Anaast, Janice Culliford, my students Lisa, Debi, Sheri, Rondi; Daniel Gottsegen, David Stanfield, Jeffrey Wintroub, Dr. Wagner, Bill Joy, Professor Ramamoorthy, Professor G. S. Sanyal, Professor "M," Professor Kumar Subramaniam, Sunil Padiyar, Dwayne Walker, Rex Cardinale, mathematician D. R. Kaprekar, Mr. Gadre, Brad Koch, John Moriarty (Professor Moriarty!), Rick Adamson, Richard Beaumont, Rick Otto, Eric Garen, David Collins, Yo Amundson, Anders Amundson, Kristina Steeg, Mark Drew, Nancy Harrison, John Rutkai, David O'Neal, Doug Northcutt, Marti Lichtanski, Karen Snyder, Hy Yarchun, Hal Kane, Patrick Wolfe, Steve Blais, Susan Schneider, Beverly Voight, Marilyn Hilliard, Leslie Mezirow, Mike Murray, Stu Ackerman, Bruce Wadman.

I especially wish to thank my friends John Moriarty, Bob Sanregret, Rick Adamson, Marti Lichtanski, Terry Young, and Farshad Nowshadi for their fine company and interesting dinner conversations on several continents. Terry Young and Farshad Nowshadi provided many stimulating discussions on the topic of NetWare 4.x. Special thanks go to Farshad for his delightful company, his helping hand with some of the NetWare 4.x Update questions, his teaching me some fine points on "sharing," and the importance of creating backups!

I wish to thank Novell for its technical innovation and leadership in defining and creating the popular PC-based network computing market, and for having the vision to create NetWare Directory Services. Credit must also be given to Novell for popularizing professional certification in the computing industry through their CNE/ECNE/CNA programs. Special thanks to Rose Kearsley of Novell for her tremendous help and support.

I wish to also thank Watcom, creators of the professional Watcom C++ 32-bit compiler that is used for developing NLMs for NetWare. Special thanks to Chris, who was instrumental in providing the author with a copy of the Watcom compilers that the author used for exploring the NLM architecture.

Many thanks to the staff of Macmillan Computer Publishing. In particular, I wish to thank Emmett Dulaney, the Product Director, for his zeal and attention to the creation of this edition. I also wish to thank Drew Heywood for his many suggestions, encouragement, and his friendship. Thanks also to John Sleeva and all the editors for their editorial skills.

Contents at a Glance

Table of Contents

3 Implementing NetWare Security   149

INTRODUCTION

This book is designed for users and system administrators with NetWare 3.x experience. It covers the topics on the NetWare 4 operating system for administrators already familiar with NetWare 3.x. It also points out the many areas NetWare 4 is different from NetWare 3.x.

How This Book Helps You

Each chapter is made up of a comprehensive discussion of the subject material being studied, as well as an extensive selection of sample test questions. This two-fold approach is designed to give you, the reader, the most thorough textual training in NetWare 4 possible.

Chapter 1 introduces you to the network services that are available on a NetWare 4 based network. It gives you an overview of the features available with NetWare 4, and also which of these features are *new* to NetWare 4.

Chapter 2 introduces you to NetWare Directory Services (NDS) concepts and how NDS can be used to access and manage network resources. An understanding of NDS services is fundamental to managing NetWare 4, because access of network resources revolves around how the NDS is represented, accessed, and managed. Many of the changes in NetWare 4 utilities have been done to facilitate an easier and more logical way of managing network resources by using the NDS representation.

Chapter 3 discusses how NetWare 4 security is implemented. It discusses similarities and differences between NetWare 3.*x* and NetWare 4 security. This chapter discusses NDS security in detail.

Chapter 4 discusses NetWare 4 workstation architecture and client components. It introduces you to the concepts behind NetWare 4 client software support and how it is used to provide connection to the network.

Chapter 5 discusses client utility changes and differences in the login script processing mechanisms. It discusses the Novell Menu utilities and other NetWare 4 utilities. It also discusses the changes that have been made in login script processing and the new login script processing commands.

Chapter 6 discusses the new NetWare 4 auditing features and how they can be used to augment the existing NetWare security. It shows you the different scenarios in which auditing can be useful and explains how auditing is implemented.

Chapter 7 discusses NetWare 4 printing issues. It covers how NetWare 4 printing is implemented and the differences from NetWare 3.*x* printing. It also examines the new NetWare 4 printing concepts and the NetWare 4 printing tools.

Chapter 8 describes the changes that have taken place for managing the NetWare 4 server. It discusses the new and enhanced NetWare console utilities.

Chapter 9 discusses backup services in NetWare 4. It discusses the NetWare 4 backup services that are available with NetWare 4 and the features of SMS.

Chapter 10 discusses management of NetWare 3.*x* servers from NetWare 4 Directory Services. It discusses the use of Bindery Synchronization.

Chapter 11 discusses design and troubleshooting for NetWare Directory Services. The use of utilities such as DSREPAIR and DSMERGE are discussed.

Chapter 12 discusses the management of supplementary network services. It discusses MHS services for NetWare and the use of the NetWare MultiProtocol Router.

Appendix A contains the answers to the questions at the end of each chapter.

Appendix B contains hints and tips on preparing for exams. It also includes the procedures for registering for a test, not only in the United States and Canada, but also in other parts of the world.

The book has a two-fold purpose. It not only prepares you to pass the CNE NetWare 4 Update exams, but it also gives you practical information to perform system administration and installation and upgrade to a NetWare 4 network.

The book has extensive practice test questions that will be valuable not only to those preparing for CNE exams, but also for those who want to acquire practical skills. The NetWare 4 tests have a slightly different style from the questions in the NetWare 3.x tests. A question can have more than one possible correct answer. If there is a single correct answer, it is indicated by a circle (○) placed next to each answer. If there are several correct answers, the choices have a box (□)next to them. To get you used to this style, these circle and box icons are used with the test questions in this book. Some of the questions on the NetWare 4 test require you to type in the answer, instead of selecting from a number of alternatives. Also, the number of alternatives for a question can vary.

NetWare 3.11 to 4 Update Object Report

To meet the goals as a book for preparing you for the CNE exams, the book covers the following test objectives. These test objectives are from Novell and are listed here as an aid to prepare you for the CNE exams.

1. Organize your network resources using NetWare Directory Services (NDS) in NetWare 4.

2. Manage objects in NetWare Directory Services (NDS) that have been migrated from the NetWare 3 bindery. Such objects include users, groups, servers, and volumes.

3. Manage the file system using the Volume object in the NetWare Administrator utility.

4. Control file system security using NetWare Administrator. View effective rights, assign rights to users and groups, and modify the Inherited Rights Filter (IRF).

5. Create and modify user and container login scripts.

6. Create and compile menus.

7. Identify the procedures for converting NetWare 3.x menus using MENUCNVT.

8. Identify and explain the need for NDS security.

9. Identify the default object and property rights using NetWare Administrator.

10. Perform steps to assign additional object and property rights.

11. Set up an auditor User object and enable auditing.

12. Move a container object and its subordinate objects within the Directory tree.

13. Create a detailed design of the Directory tree that provides for securing NDS, partitioning the Directory, replicating partitions of the Directory, and synchronizing time.

14. Identify NDS inconsistencies.

15. Execute the procedures to prepare an NDS server for downtime. Note: This objective may have been changed to Move an NDS container from one context to another.

16. Execute the procedures to recover from a failed Master replica.

17. Perform the steps to remove a server from the Directory tree.

18. Define the purpose of the NetWare 4 MultiProtocol Router (MPR) 3.0 and give an example of its function within a network.

19. Determine appropriate use of messaging services through MHS Services for NetWare 4.

20. Create a Distribution List object and assign members.

21. Assign mailboxes to User, Group, Distribution List, and Organizational Role objects.

22. Enable Internationalization.

23. Interpret the MONITOR Statistics screen.

24. Monitor and modify file and directory cache performance.

25. View and modify server buffer and packet parameters.

26. Define and enable memory suballocation.

27. List the steps to enable file compression.

28. Enable and manage the Packet Burst protocol.

29. Enable and manage Large Internet Packets (LIP).

Special Reference Points

Several icons are used throughout the book to help you use the book as a quick reference.

 The Study Note icon is used to point out the specific areas of knowledge you are most likely to be tested on. Some tables in the book, for example, are referenced by the Study Note icon with the statement that you should be familiar with the contents of that table. It is generally a good idea to be familiar with all the information in the book, but when a piece of information is specifically referenced in a Study Note, it means you should review the contents of the table before taking your exams, as you are quite likely to be tested on it. A quick way to review the material in the book for preparing for the CNE exams is to browse through the book and study the Study Notes.

 The Practical Tip icon is used to point out information that you can apply directly in administering a NetWare 4 network. These are items of information that you normally acquire after working with NetWare 4 networks for some time.

 The Author's Note icon comments on or offers insight into the workings of NetWare that the author wants to share with you. You are not likely to be tested on this information. The Author's Note is meant to provide additional understanding into the workings of NetWare 4 that will help your understanding of the inner workings of NetWare 4.

 The Note icon is used for occasional expansion on a point made in the regular text.

New Riders Publishing

The staff of New Riders Publishing is committed to bringing you the very best in computer reference material. Each New Riders book is the result of months of work by authors and staff who research and refine the information contained within its covers.

As part of this commitment to you, the NRP reader, New Riders invites your input. Please let us know if you enjoy this book, if you have trouble with the information and examples presented, or if you have a suggestion for the next edition.

Please note, though: New Riders staff cannot serve as a technical resource for NetWare or for related questions about software- or hardware-related problems.

If you have a question or comment about any New Riders book, there are several ways to contact New Riders Publishing. We will respond to as many readers as we can. Your name, address, and phone number will never become part of a mailing list or be used for any purpose other than to help us continue to bring you the best books possible. You can write us at the following address:

New Riders Publishing
Attn: Associate Publisher
201 W. 103rd Street
Indianapolis, IN 46290

If you prefer, you can fax New Riders Publishing at (317) 581-4670.

You can send e-mail to New Riders at the following Internet address:

edulaney@newriders.mcp.com

NRP is an imprint of Macmillan Computer Publishing. To obtain a catalog or information, or to purchase any Macmillan Computer Publishing book, call (800) 428-5331.

Thank you for selecting *CNE Training Guide: NetWare 4.1 Update*!

Introduction to NetWare 4

In this chapter, you get an overview of the features that make NetWare 4 an interesting contribution to network computing technology. You also learn about the motivation for some of the NetWare 4 features that are beneficial in building secure large-scale, enterprise-wide networks. NetWare 4 is in many ways very similar to the architecture of the earlier NetWare 3.x operating system, and in other ways represents a radical departure in terms of how the network can be viewed and managed.

Motivation for New NetWare 4 Features

A network can consist of several LANs tied together with wide area links as shown in figure 1.1. For a user to use printer or network volume storage resources, the user has to know the location of the resources. In the example shown in figure 1.1, the user, in earlier versions of NetWare, would have to know the names of the file servers to which the printer and volume resources are attached. Before accessing a resource on a server, the user would have to log on to that server. If the user needed to access

a volume resource on another server, the user would have to attach to that server and then create a separate drive mapping. Attaching to a server implies that the user needs an account on each server that the user needs access to. This approach works well in small networks that have a workgroup orientation (called *workgroup networks*); but on large networks that have many servers, it is not easy for the user to remember what resources are available on each of the servers. It would be much easier for the user to have a logical view of the network that hides non-essential physical details of the network. Figure 1.2 shows a logical view of the network illustrated in figure 1.1.

Figure 1.1

An example of a NetWare-based network.

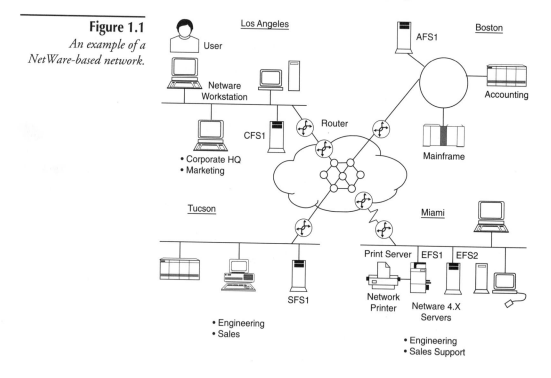

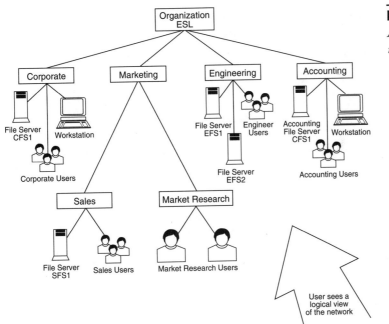

Figure 1.2
A logical view of a network.

In the logical view of the network, resources are organized into groups that are in turn organized into a hierarchy that reflects their usage, function, or geographical location. For the user to use the resources on this network, the user logs on to this logical view of the network. Access to resources on the network can be controlled by security mechanisms that are global in scope and apply to the entire network. In NetWare 3.*x* and NetWare 2.2 networks, access to resources is controlled by security mechanisms local to each server (called the *bindery*). The bindery did not have network-wide significance. The bindery-based services were therefore *server-centric*. To provide a single access to the network, the designers of NetWare 4 created a global database called the *NetWare Directory Services* (NDS). The NetWare Directory Services is the mechanism used in NetWare 4 to provide a logical view of the network.

The NetWare Directory Services provide a *global database* service that is not confined to a single server and represents network-wide resources. This is the single most important difference between NetWare 4 and NetWare 3.*x* and NetWare 2.2. It is also the feature that affects many network administration tasks and network utilities. Many of the pre-NetWare 4.0 network administration and utilities modified the network information in the bindery. The NetWare v3.*x*/v2.2 utilities cannot be used for NetWare 4 because the information in a global database needs to be modified, and the older utilities understand the bindery but have no concept of a global database. Because of this, several of the older utilities have been consolidated into newer utilities that need to have the understanding of how to correctly modify the global database.

Overview of NetWare 4 Features

Some of the more significant NetWare 4 features are as follows:

- NetWare Directory Services (NDS)

- Improvements in NetWare File System support

- Improved file system security and management

- Support for network auditing

- Simplified and more efficient memory management architecture

- Improvements in client networking services

- Integrated Storage Management Services (SMS)

- Improvements in network print services architecture

- Multiple language support (Internationalization)

- Simplified installation and upgrade procedures

- Online NetWare manuals via DynaText

These features are discussed in greater detail in the following sections.

NetWare Directory Services

NetWare Directory Services is perhaps the most distinct feature of NetWare 4. It provides the network administrator and the user with a logical view of a network that hides the sometimes bewildering complexity of the actual physical topology and configuration. The logical view of the network can be organized into what makes sense for the organization and what is easily recognizable to the users of the network. In figure 1.3, for instance, the view of the network is hierarchical and reflects the organization chart of the company, which can be expected to be recognized by the users in that organization. The physical details of the network such as the type of cabling or interconnecting devices such as routers and bridges, are hidden away in figure 1.3. In other words, the network administrator and the user does not need to be aware of the physical nature of the network in order to use the network.

Figure 1.3

A Logical network reflecting the hierarchy of an organization.

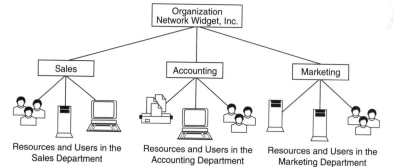

The logical view is possible because of the Network Directory Services. NDS provides a *distributed* database that can act as a repository of information on all the shared resources on the network. The database is distributed because it does not physically reside on any single server on the network. The database is *hierarchical* because it provides a convenient grouping of resources by function, location, or organization structure.

NDS is essentially a replacement for the *bindery* services that were part of the pre-NetWare 4.0 product line. The bindery in the earlier NetWare release was also a way of organizing resources, but the resources were specific to the server on which the bindery resided. The bindery could not easily support information on other nodes on the network, and because it was organized as a *flat* database rather than a hierarchical database, it did not have any natural way of representing usage or organizational relationships between resources.

If you were to categorize some of the benefits of using NDS, they would include the following:

- Logical organization of the network

- Single login to the network

- Global network management view

- Independence from physical location of resources

 The following statements about NDS are true:

- NDS is a NetWare 4 feature that is a replacement for NetWare 3.*x* bindery services.

- NDS structure is hierarchical, whereas the NetWare 3.*x* bindery structure is flat.

- NDS is a *distributed database* of network resources and services that are represented as objects (records).

- NDS advantages include logical organization, single network login, global network management, and location-independent resources.

Logical Organization of the Network

The logical organization of the network is a benefit that derives directly from the way the resources can be grouped in a hierarchical fashion in the NetWare Directory Service representation for an organization (see fig. 1.3). This grouping is done to reflect the way users would want to use the network. This makes it easy for users and network administrators to find the network resources without knowing the physical details of network connectivity, and this is a primary benefit. A user who needs to use a network resource has a *logical pointer* to the NDS database. These pointers are called *objects*, and they contain information on the resource. In NetWare 4 all network resources that can be accessed by a NetWare user are represented by objects.

An example of a network resource is a file server, which can be modeled as a file server object. Inside this file server object (see fig. 1.4) is information such as the name of the file server and its network address, location, and so on. Information about the file server is called the *properties* of the file server object.

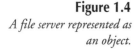

Figure 1.4

A file server represented as an object.

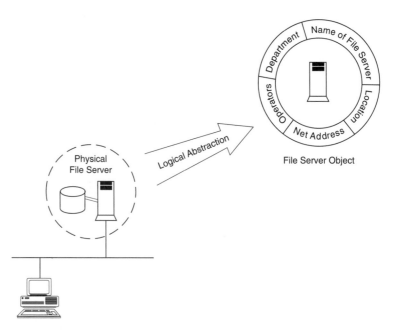

Single Login to the Network

A *single login* to a network (see fig. 1.5) allows a user to be authenticated just once to access all the resources on the network. After a user logs in, the network administrator can limit access to resources on the network. For example, all users, by default, are allowed to see the structure of an organization's directory, even though they cannot access all the objects in this directory unless explicitly given this access by a network administrator. A single login to a network can also simplify the use of the network, because a user does not need to have separate logins to multiple servers on the network.

In pre-NetWare 4.0, the user had to log in (or attach) explicitly by supplying a user name and password for every server that the user wanted to access. Also, the number of such concurrent connections was limited to eight. In addition, the network administrator had to create separate accounts on each server that the user needed access to. This could easily become burdensome on a large network.

The single login to a network is possible because the user authentication takes place against a global network directory that is not specific to a server. In figure 1.6, you can see that the first step to logging on to a network is authentication of the user against information in the global directory. When the user authentication is successful, the user is granted access to any resource on the network. The maximum number of concurrent connections to different NetWare servers is now increased to 50; in pre-NetWare 4.0, this limit was eight.

 NDS controls access to objects and resources on the network. NDS also eliminates redundant tasks such as adding a user account to multiple servers on the network.

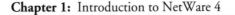

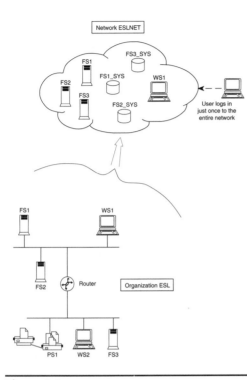

Figure 1.5

A single login to the network.

Global Network Management

In pre-NetWare 4.0, the network management tasks had to be performed separately on each NetWare server because network management usually resulted in a modification of the bindery, and the bindery was specific to each server. The bindery, a local database of network resources on a specific server, had to modified on each server.

Because the NDS is a global database, *global network management* is possible where information about network resources can be changed by the network administrator from any place on the network (see fig. 1.7). Also, as you learn later, the network administrator can delegate responsibility to other users, who serve as network administrators. In pre-NetWare 4.0, the responsibility could be delegated to a fixed number of user account managers, workgroup managers, and other operators; whereas in NetWare 4 there can be many levels of network administrators with varying degrees of responsibilities.

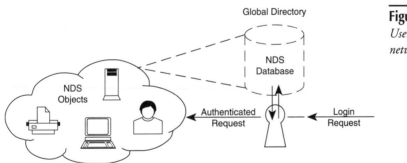

Figure 1.6

User authentication to the network.

Study Note
Because of global network management, NDS eliminates some redundant operations such as management of multiple user accounts for the same user.

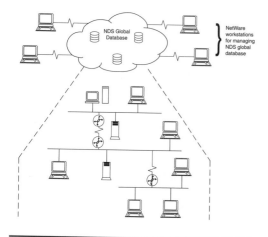

Figure 1.7
Global network management.

Independence from Physical Location of Resources

In pre-NetWare 4.0-based networks, the resources are described in a server bindery and are dependent on that server. A classic example of this is NetWare printer definitions that are tied to a specific server. If the printer has to be relocated to another server, the bindery representation of the printer has to be moved to another server (see fig. 1.8). In a large network that is in a state of flux, this can become a major task.

In NetWare 4, the resource definitions are not tied to any specific server or a physical location on the network. This means that a user can access a resource without worrying about the the server to which the resource is connected and how it can be reached. Changes to network resources are made to the NDS object that is part of a global database. The NDS object can be accessed from any station on the network, provided the user has been granted security permission for the resource.

Figure 1.8
Bindery representations of printer definitions.

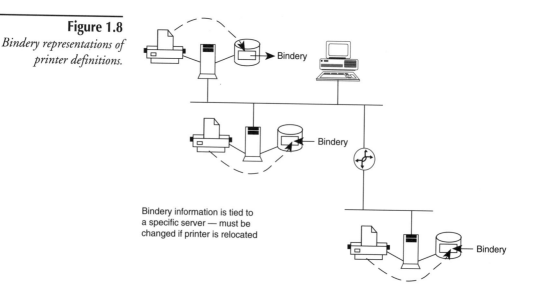

NDS is the NetWare 4 feature that allows physical resources to be relocated in a manner that is transparent to the user.

Improvements in the NetWare File System

One of NetWare's strengths has always been a fast and efficient file system. This has always been central to NetWare's popularity and capability to act as a file server. In NetWare 4, the file system has been improved. Some of these improvements are because of new features called *block suballocation,* *compression,* and *migration.*

Block Suballocation

NetWare 4 allows the disk block size to be selected at installation time to be 4 KB, 8 KB, 12 KB, 16 KB, or 64 KB (where 1 KB is 1,024 bytes). This capability also exists in NetWare 3. *x*; but in NetWare

3. *x* if a 200 byte file was created on a volume that had a disk block size of 4 KB, a 4 KB block of storage would be allocated, and the remaining 4,096 – 200 = 3,896 bytes would not be available for use. This represents a wasted space of 95 percent; and if the disk block size was 64 KB, the wasted space would be even greater. Figure 1.9 shows how block suballocation in NetWare 4 works. In NetWare 4, the unused disk block space is used in 512-byte suballocation units. This means that in the example of creating a file of 200 bytes, a 512-byte suballocation within the 4 KB disk block would be used. The remaining seven 512-byte suballocation blocks would be available for sharing by the leftover fragments of other files. If all these suballocation blocks were used, then in the NetWare 4 example there would be wasted space of only 512 – 200 = 312 bytes out of a total of 4,096 bytes; that is only eight percent wasted space. And if the disk block size was 64 KB, there would be an even smaller percentage of wasted space (about 0.5 percent). Also, if the file sizes and leftover fragments were multiples of 512-bytes, there would be no wasted space.

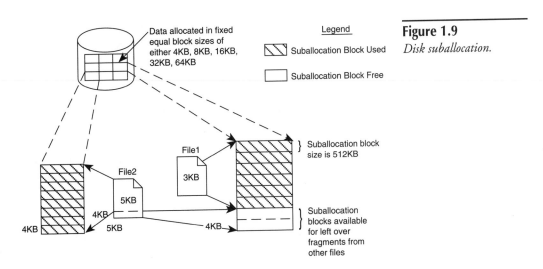

Figure 1.9
Disk suballocation.

So, block suballocation can be defined as a mechanism in NetWare 4, to allow small files and files that are not multiples of the disk block size to share space in a disk block that would otherwise have gone to waste. The improved utilization in disk space is accompanied by the extra overhead in the operating system to maintain status of disk blocks that have been suballocated, but because disk writes are done in the background, the impact of this overhead is minimal.

Another advantage of block suballocation is that you can increase the volume block size to increase disk access performance, without wasting disk space because of partially used blocks.

Disk suballocation

- Is a new feature in NetWare 4.

- Gives better utilization of disk space.

- Allows small files and files that are not multiples of the disk block size to share space in a disk block that would otherwise have gone to waste.

- Gives better utilization in disk space, but is accompanied by the extra overhead in the operating system to maintain status of disk blocks that have been suballocated.

- Minimizes overhead by performing disk writes in the background.

- Is enabled during installation of each volume.

Disk suballocation is enabled by default during a NetWare volumes installation. It can be explicitly disabled during installation. It can also be enabled

at any time after installation. Once enabled, however, it cannot be disabled without re-creating the volume.

Practical TIP Always allocate a disk block size of 64 KB for maximum gain in server disk performance, because the software and disk subsystems perform at an optimum at this block size.

NetWare File System Compression

Studies have shown that the processor utilization of many NetWare servers in many deployed networks does not often exceed 50 percent. In heavily loaded servers, it is not uncommon to see processor utilization higher than 90 percent, but such situations are relatively rare. The designers of NetWare 4 decided to put this unutilized processor *bandwidth* to use for background tasks such as file system compression. Today, many disk compression utilities are available for DOS. However, these utilities decompress disk blocks as they are read, and compress it back when they are written. This process causes the disk to appear slow because of the compression operation that accompanies each read or write operation. In NetWare 4, file compression is done in the background. Certain parameters can be set at the file server to control the frequency at which compression can be done in the background. When a file is retrieved, it is decompressed. The file blocks that are immediately decompressed are available for use, even as the rest of the file is being decompressed by special *decompression threads* (see fig. 1.10). Usually, the file remains in the decompressed state until a certain period of time that can be controlled at the server. The compression of files is always done in the background.

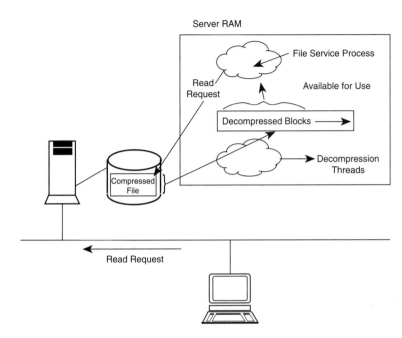

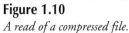

Figure 1.10
A read of a compressed file.

Using the file compression feature, the effective disk space can be increased without adding new server drives. The amount of savings in disk space depends on the nature of repeated characters or binary patterns in the file and is very high for text files. It is not uncommon to see savings of up to 63 percent or more because of file compression. This means that 500 MB of files can take up as little as 185 MB (at 63 percent compression) of disk space. With disk space being at a perennial premium on file servers, this is a great advantage.

 File compression

■ Allows increase in disk space without adding new drives.

■ Can be enabled/disabled during volume installation.

■ Can be explicitly set for files by flagging them (by using FLAG utility) so that they can be immediately compressed after use, or never compressed.

A file will not be compressed unless NetWare sees a certain gain in disk space. The network administrator can exercise explicit control by flagging files and directories for immediate compression, or never to be compressed.

The compression option can be disabled or enabled during installation of a volume on the NetWare server. By default, compression is enabled, which means that NetWare tries to compress a file if it has not been used for some time provided a minimum savings in disk space can be achieved.

Data Migration

Data migration allows infrequently used files to be moved to a *near-line* or *off-line* storage medium. Examples of near-line storage are optical disk libraries (also known as *jukeboxes*), and examples of off-line storage are tape backup devices. When data migration occurs, NetWare 4 still sees the data on the NetWare volumes because the directory entries for the migrated files are still on the NetWare volume. If a file is accessed and it has been migrated, the file is brought back in (*demigrated*) to the NetWare volume (see fig. 1.11). The net effect of data migration is that valuable disk space is freed up. When combined with compression, data migration is a very effective way of saving on disk space.

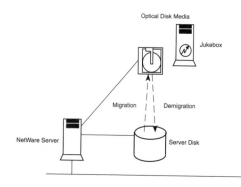

Optical Disk Media

Jukebox

Migration   Demigration

NetWare Server   Server Disk

Figure 1.11
Data migration.

Some of the earlier Control Data Corporation's super computers used data migration, but NetWare 4.0 is the first one to popularize its use amongst PC-based Network Operating Systems (NOS).

Data migration can be enabled/disabled at the time of installing the NetWare volume. The files can also be marked for migration by using the NetWare utilities.

Data migration can be implemented using *the High Capacity Storage System* (HCSS). The HCSS is a storage/retrieval system that can extend the capacity of a NetWare server by integrating optical libraries into the NetWare file system. HCSS can work in conjunction with data migration, so that migrated files can be moved from the faster but lower capacity NetWare volumes to the slower but higher capacity media that comprises the HCSS.

As far as the user is concerned, the operation of data migration and HCSS is transparent. Files that have been migrated to the HCSS are accessed with the same commands as files that reside on the NetWare volume. If a migrated file is accessed, it is automatically demigrated.

Migration is performed on an individual file basis depending on the last time the file was accessed, called the *least recently used* criteria, and the current volume usage. Least recently used criteria for files refers to files that are the least active, or that have not been accessed the longest. If the current volume usage exceeds a *capacity threshold*, data migration occurs. Capacity threshold is defined as the percentage of the server's disk that is used before data migration begins.

 Data migration

- Is a new feature of NetWare 4.

- Allows files to be migrated from server cache to server disk, and then on to other online media.

- Is performed on an individual file basis depending on the last time the file was accessed, called the *least recently used* criteria and the current volume usage.

- Occurs when the current volume usage exceeds the *capacity threshold.*

Improved File System Security and Management

Access to the NetWare 4-based network is performed when the user logs in to the NetWare directory for a network. Each organization can be expected to have its own network directory tree that reflects the usage and security needs of network users. As part of implementing network security, access to parts of the network directory tree are controlled by explicit trustee assignments. Figure 1.12 shows the different steps that must occur before a user is granted access to a file on a volume. These include logon authentication, NDS security, and NetWare file system security.

When logging in to the network, the user specifies the name of the NDS object that represents the user account. The user's login name and password are used to build a personalized key that *authenticates* a user's right to access the network. The actual algorithm used to build the personalized key is *RSA*, which stands for *Rivest, Shamir, and Adelman*, the original creators of a public encryption key algorithm. Novell licensed this technology from RSA, Inc., for use with NetWare 4.

Once the user is authenticated on the network, the user must have rights to directory objects that represent resources on the network. This is seen in figure 1.12, where a user has to pass through the NetWare Directory Services security. To access files on a volume, for example, the user must have certain rights to the volume object in the directory tree.

After the user passes through the NetWare Directory Services, the user's access to a file is controlled by the File and Directory Trustee rights. These rights are the same as those for the NetWare 3.*x* servers.

 Study Note When a user logs in to a NetWare 4 network, a personalized key is created that is then used to authenticate the user to the network.

Network management is done by the network administrator. An initial user account called ADMIN is created when a directory tree is first established. This is equivalent to the SUPERVISOR user in pre-NetWare 4.0, except that the ADMIN user has network-wide responsibility. The ADMIN user account can be deleted or renamed, and in that sense does not have any special significance as did the SUPERVISOR account in NetWare 3.*x or* 2.*x* servers that could not be renamed or deleted. Because the ADMIN account can be deleted, care should be taken to ensure that other users have the equivalent of supervisory rights to the directory tree before the ADMIN account is deleted.

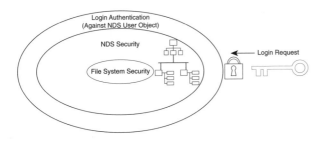

Figure 1.12
NetWare 4 security.

For secure environments, rename the ADMIN account so that an unauthorized user cannot know and use the supervisor's username and try to break system security.

The ADMIN user can create other user objects anywhere in the directory tree. This is usually done in such a manner that the users can access resources in the directory tree easily.

The network administrator can delegate to users different levels of network responsibility. For instance, a user can be delegated the authority to create other user objects but not delete them; or a user can be assigned the responsibility of managing part of a directory tree, but not access the information represented by the objects. This makes it possible to have multiple levels of network administrators in a manner that is more flexible than the NetWare 3.*x* approach of workgroup managers and user account managers.

Security in NetWare 4 can be more finely controlled by creating assistant "supervisors" who can administer network resources but who do not have access to data that needs to be protected from view such as payroll data or other financial data of an organization.

 Network users must have rights to the NDS database before they can view or make changes to it. These rights are called *object rights*.

 NetWare 4 file system security is similar to NetWare 3.*x* file system security. Trustee Assignments are the same as NetWare 3.*x*, but new file and directory attributes have been added to support new NetWare 4 features such as compression and migration.

 NetWare 4 permits the creation of supervisor accounts with varying degrees of control over the network. This is similar to the workgroup and user account manager concepts in NetWare 3.*x*, except that delegation of responsibility can be more finely controlled by assigning specific security roles to the assistant supervisors.

 The Admin supervisor user can be deleted or renamed. This prevents other users from knowing the name of the supervisor user.

Support for Network Auditing

In NetWare 4, users called *auditors* can be set up to act independently of the network administrator to audit critical activities on the network. The auditors can also audit past and present transactions on the network for any security breaches (see fig. 1.13). It is important to understand why network auditors need to be independent of the network administrator. The network administrator of the directory tree, unless specifically restricted, has unrestricted access to data and resources on the network. As a result of this, an organization has to place great trust on the network administrator. If this trust is betrayed, the network administrator can cause a great deal of damage to an organization's data and privacy of data.

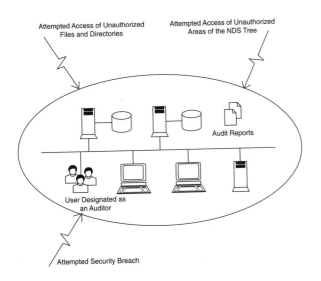

Figure 1.13
Auditing in NetWare 4.

Auditing allows auditor users to monitor actions on the network including that of the network administrator. For this reason, an auditor should not have supervisor rights or equivalence. An auditor's main function is to track events on the network; but they are unable to modify data on the network, other than the Audit Data and the Audit History files.

Auditing should not be confused with accounting features of earlier NetWare versions. Accounting allows the tracking of resource usage on the networks such as disk blocks read and written, storage charges, and service requests. This accounting capability is still available in NetWare 4.

Auditing allows the monitoring of critical events on the network such as logins and logouts, file operations, directory services object operations (creations, deletions, reads, and writes), directory object events, user events, and trustee modifications. To audit files, auditing is enabled at the volume level. For directory objects, auditing must be enabled at the container object level. Container objects are used in the NDS tree for organizational

purposes and are discussed in the next chapter. When enabled, log files are created to track audited operations.

The primary utility for implementing auditing is AUDITCON.

  The NetWare 4 auditing feature

■ Can be used to enhance NetWare 4 security and is a new feature of NetWare 4. The user assigned the job of auditing is called the *auditor*, and this user should be independent of the supervisor user.

■ Is different from the accounting feature that was available in NetWare 3.*x* and is also available in NetWare 4.*x*.

  Audited events are stored in special log files.

The types of events that can be audited are logins and logouts, file operations, directory services object operations (creations, deletions, reads, and writes), directory object events, user events, and trustee modifications.

Simplified and More Efficient Memory Management Architecture

NetWare 3.x was a great improvement over NetWare 2.2 in the way memory was managed on the server. There were, however, a few problems with memory management under NetWare 3.x as seen in figure 1.14. In NetWare 3.x, memory was managed in five pools, each serving a different purpose. The pools were for purposes such as cache movable, cache non-movable, permanent memory, and semi-permanent memory. As the names suggest, each of these memory pools was for a special purpose. To meet temporary high demands,

memory pools were permitted to borrow memory from the file cache buffer memory; but once borrowed, this memory was not returned. Under certain conditions, it was possible for this memory leakage to occur to the point that the file cache buffer memory was severely depleted, and this resulted in a severe degradation in server performance. To reset the memory pools, the server had to be restarted.

Just as NetWare 3.11 was an improvement over NetWare 2.x, NetWare 4 memory management is a considerable improvement over NetWare 3.11. For one thing, there are no separate memory pools (see fig. 1.15). There is only one main pool, and that is the file cache memory. All memory used by processes running on the server are borrowed against this pool and completely returned to it when the process terminates. The memory returned to the file cache can be reused by other processes. As a result of this, memory management is simpler because only one pool exists instead of five. And because memory management is simpler, it takes fewer processor cycles to accomplish, and memory allocation is therefore faster.

Figure 1.14

NetWare 3.x memory management.

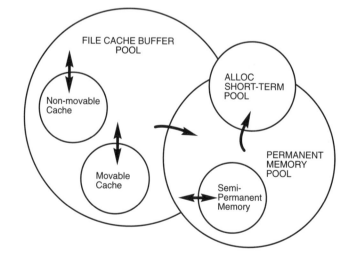

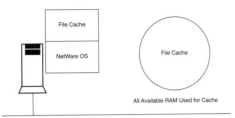

Figure 1.15
NetWare 4 memory management.

The following are some of the features of NetWare 4 memory management:

- Improved server performance because memory management is an important resource for server processes

- Integration with the paged memory architecture of the Intel processors

- Ring protection to control damage caused by misbehaved NLMs

- Easier to write applications for the NLM developer because memory management is simpler

A controversial aspect of NetWare 3.x memory usage is that all programs—the kernel and applications—run in Ring 0 of the Intel 80386 architecture. The Intel 80386 architecture defines four rings—rings 0 to 3 (see fig. 1.16). The reason behind this is to have the operating system kernel run at ring 0, and other programs at the outer rings. Programs running at ring 3, for example, can access the RAM used by programs running in ring 3, but cannot directly access RAM for programs running at rings 2, 1, and 0. So, if the operating system kernel is running in ring 0, a program at ring 3 would have to make an *inter-ring gate call* to make service requests from the operating system kernel. If the program crashes, it cannot affect the

operating system kernel. This architecture makes the system more reliable at the cost of reduced speed because of the inter-ring call overhead. An example of an operating system that uses the ring architecture is OS/2.

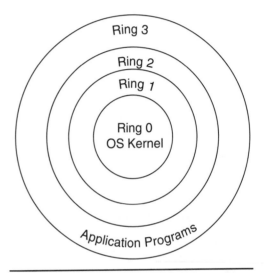

Figure 1.16
Intel 80386 processor ring architecture.

NetWare 3.x does not use the ring architecture. The NetWare 3.x operating system, NLMs, and all server processes run in ring 0. What NetWare 3.x loses in reliability, it gains in simplicity and speed.

In NetWare 4, all NLMs by default run in ring 0. The network administrator, however, can configure the server to run NLMs that are loaded in an outer ring so that offending programs cannot cause the operating system kernel that runs in ring 0 to crash. As new NLMs are added to the server, they can be loaded in an outer ring for a trial period. They will run a little slower here because they have to make an inter-ring call. If the NLMs prove to be reliable, they can be added to ring 0, where they can run faster.

NetWare 4 memory protection offers the following:

- A safe method for testing new NLMs

- The advantage of the Intel processor's ring protection scheme. The ring protection scheme controls damage caused by misbehaved NLMs.

- Simplified memory optimization for improving server performance

- Improved server performance through more efficient memory allocation

- Integration with the paged memory architecture of the Intel processors

- Increased ease in writing applications for the NLM developer because memory management is simpler

 When purchasing NLMs from third parties, check to see if they are designed to run in an outer ring of the Intel processor (80386 and higher). Not all NLMs can run in an outer ring.

Improvements in Client Networking Services

The NetWare 4 networking software for workstation operating system clients includes better support for DOS, MS Windows, and OS/2 (see fig. 1.17). DOS and MS Windows now use a DOS requester, ODI support, and packet burst protocol support.

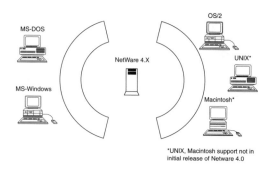

Figure 1.17
Multiple client support in NetWare 4.

The DOS requester allows the redirector capability of later releases of DOS via the interrupt mechanism INT 2F (hex) to be used. The earlier NetWare shell used the DOS INT 21 (hex) mechanism, and a software multiplexor mechanism to direct the request to appropriate system services. Because of the additional overhead of the software multiplexor mechanism, it was slightly less efficient. In NetWare 4, the DOS requester actually consists of a number of smaller components that need to be loaded only if the service is needed. These smaller components are called *Virtual Loadable Modules* (VLMs), and are loaded and managed by the VLM Manager (VLM.EXE). VLMs give you the flexibility of selectively loading only the services that are needed. VLMs are designed to understand NetWare Directory Services, and there is even a VLM component (NETX.VLM) that can be used to communicate with bindery based servers.

The ODI support is the Open Data-Link interface that provides an interface for protocol stacks to talk to network boards, which represent layer 2 (data-link layer) of the OSI model. The ODI interface was also available in earlier NetWare client software.

The *packet burst protocol* allows transmission of multiple packet requests and packet replies. It is similar to the window flow control mechanism used in other protocol suites and is an improvement over the single packet request/response behavior of the earlier NCP packet transmissions. The packet burst protocol was added to later releases of NetWare 3.*x*, and is also available for NetWare 4. The packet burst protocol is particularly useful for multiple NCP packet requests and packet replies, where a number of requests or replies can be acknowledged by a single acknowledgment packet. This eliminates some of the overhead of the round-trip delay when a sender has to wait for the last packet that was sent to be acknowledged before transmitting the next packet. It also results in fewer packets being sent, which results in reduction of network traffic and reduced time for processing packets.

Another enhancement in NetWare 4 is support for *Large Internet Packet* (LIP). Earlier NetWare routers were limited in the size of the Internet packet that could be supported. With LIP, this limit has been removed, and larger packet sizes that are common in Token Ring networks (4 KB to 16 KB) and Ethernet networks (1.5 KB) are possible.

In NetWare 4, the DOS requester

■ Replaces the NetWare shell mechanism.

■ Is implemented as VLMs.

■ Uses the ODI interface.

Packet burst can be enabled in NetWare 4 client software for efficient transfer of NCP requests and replies.

Packet burst reduces the number of packet requests/replies, which leads to a reduction in network traffic.

Integrated Storage Management Services (SMS)

Storage Management Services (SMS) in NetWare 4 provide data on the network to be backed or restored in a common data format and in a manner that is hardware and software independent. This means that backup tapes produced with an SMS format can be used by another vendor's hardware/software device that understands SMS. A *Target Service Agent* (TSA) program is run on each device that needs to be backed up, and is the target for the SBACKUP program. These targets include workstations and NetWare 3.*x* and NetWare 4 servers (see fig. 1.18).

In SMS, the SBACKUP program is responsible for backup and restore operations. SBACKUP is an NLM that runs on a NetWare server. The NBACKUP functionality of earlier NetWare releases is now consolidated in SBACKUP.

SMS consists of a number of other modules such as the *Storage Management Data Requester* (SMDR) that is used to pass commands between the SBACKUP and the TSAs, and device drivers that use the *Storage Device Interface* (SDI) to communicate between the SBACKUP program and the storage devices (see fig. 1.19).

Figure 1.18

SMS and TSAs.

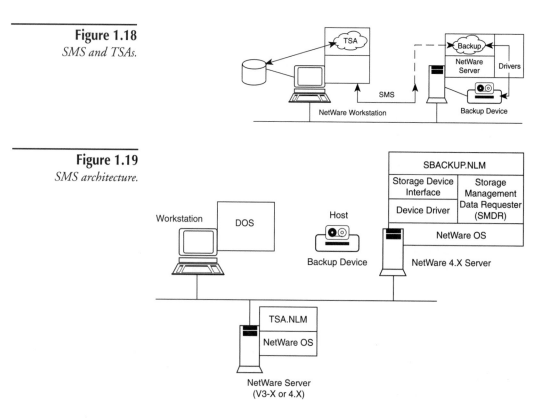

Figure 1.19

SMS architecture.

 SMS allows data on the network to be backed up or restored in a common data format that is hardware and software independent.

Backup and restoration of data in NetWare 4 is performed via SMS.

 Every device that needs to be backed up must have a TSA agent running on it.

 Besides SBACKUP, you may want to consider a number of third-party backup schemes that use SMS. These provide a simpler and streamlined user interface and many advanced backup options.

Improvements in Network Print Services Architecture

In NetWare 3.*x*, print services were defined as part of the print server definition, and the only way to do a network print job was to submit the print job to a print queue. In NetWare 4, the network print jobs can still be sent to the network print queue; but in addition, print jobs can be sent to the printer object in the NDS tree.

 NetWare 4 printing can be done by using the printer object name.

Other improvements in NetWare 4 printing include the following:

- Simpler installation in comparison to NetWare 3.*x*

- Support for a larger number of printers (up to 256) on a single print server

- Remote printers can be set up on NetWare servers

 Understand and remember the improvements in NetWare 4 covered in this section. These include the following:

- Simple installation

- Support for up to 256 printers

- Remote printer support on NetWare 4 servers

Printing issues are covered in greater detail in later chapters.

Multiple Language Support (Internationalization)

Because the character of NetWare has become international in scope, NetWare 4 has introduced support for international languages to NetWare Loadable Modules and network utilities. This means that messages and options associated with utilities can be set in the language of the user. The default language is English, but other languages can be supported during installation when running the SERVER.EXE program. After installation, the INSTALL.NLM can be used to configure date, time, and number formats.

It is even possible to have different language NLMs running on the server at the same time; or have one user using the system utility NETADMIN in French, and another user using the same utility in Italian. It is important to understand that the language support does not mean that NetWare is capable of translating messages between users using different languages. For example, if the SEND utility is used by a French language user to send a message in French to another user who is set up to use Italian, then NetWare is not smart enough to translate the message from French to Italian.

Even though the language may be the same, there may be differences in the manner in which date, time, and numbers are formatted. A classic example of this is English, which is spoken in both the United States and the United Kingdom. The default format for representing dates in the U.S. is *mm/dd/yy* (example: 10/16/93). In the U.K., the default date format would be *dd/mm/yy* (example: 16/10/93). The formatting is not just dependent on the language, but can change across different locales for the same language.

Examples of the date, time, and number formats for the U.S., U.K., France, and Germany are shown in table 1.1

The capability to support differences in language and format representations is called *internationalization*. Internationalization in NetWare is supported through *unicode* representation, which is a standard for representing data in 16 bits instead of the familiar 8-bit ASCII.

Table 1.1
Format Differences for Countries

Country	Number Format	Time Format	Date Format
U.S.A.	355,113.22	11:55:00 PM	10/16/93
U.K.	355,113.22	23:55:00	16/10/93
Germany	355.113,22	23:55:00	16.10.93
France	355 113,22	23:55:00	16.10.93

 Internationalization is a new feature available with NetWare 4.0 that

- Allows users to run utilities and read utility messages and documentation in a language supported by NetWare.

- Allows one user to use FILER in English, while another user is using FILER in French.

- Cannot translate messages broadcasted in one language to another language.

Simplified Installation and Upgrade Procedures

NetWare 4 distribution comes in CD-ROM. Distribution on high-density floppy disks is an additional cost and can be obtained by sending in a request form that accompanies the NetWare 4 distribution.

Installing NetWare 4 on CD-ROM saves time during installation, as the copying of the files from the distribution media is much faster. This leads to a simpler and faster implementation.

The CD-ROM drive can be attached to the server that is being installed, or it can be attached to a remote workstation. Figure 1.20 shows the different possibilities. In figure 1.20, the CD-ROM drive is shown as an external unit to the workstation or server. Internal CD-ROMs are also possible.

Figure 1.20
NetWare 4 installation using CD-ROM distribution.

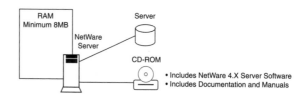

Online NetWare Manuals via DynaText

NetWare DynaText is a graphical utility that works with Windows 3.1 (or better), to give online manuals that can be accessed through a *graphical user interface* (GUI). Figure 1.21 shows a sample DynaText screen.

All the NetWare manuals are available in DynaText format. A list of these manuals and a brief description of their contents follows:

- **Master Index.** The index links to all places in the manuals. Click on a link marker to go to a place in the manual in which a term or topic can be found.

- **AppleTalk Reference.** This reference provides the information you need to understand the AppleTalk protocol stack for NetWare

servers. It describes configuration parameters for the AppleTalk protocol stack.

- **Btrieve Installation and Reference Manual.** Btrieve is a popular and efficient record manager bundled as an NLM in NetWare servers. This manual contains information on installing, configuring, executing, and monitoring the Btrieve record management system for NetWare servers.

- **Concepts.** This is a glossary of NetWare-related terms with a tutorial description of what each term means. Topics are listed alphabetically in categories ranging from AAA to ZZZ.

- **NetWare Client for DOS and MS Windows User Guide.** This manual helps you set up and install your client software. It introduces you to the client tools for managing your client on a NetWare network. The manual

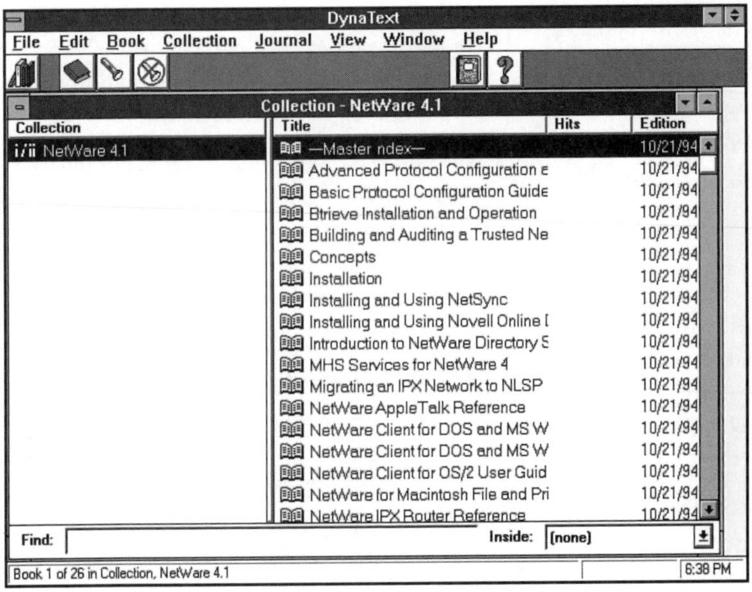

Figure 1.21

A sample DynaText screen.

covers concepts and procedures for installing and using NetWare client software on NetWare 2.x, 3.x, and 4 networks.

- **NetWare Client for DOS and MS Windows Technical Reference.** This manual describes the parameters needed to configure NetWare workstation software on NetWare 2.x, 3.x, and 4.x networks.

- **Installation.** This contains information on how to install a new NetWare 4 server.

- **NetWare IPX Router Reference.** This manual provides the information you need to understand the IPX protocol for the router. It describes the IPX configuration parameters.

- **Macintosh File and Print Services.** This manual explains how to install, configure, and maintain the NetWare for Macintosh software.

- **Using MacNDS client for NetWare 4.** This manual describes the NetWare for Macintosh MacNDS Client software. The MacNDS client software allows access to NetWare 4 NDS services from Macintosh workstations.

- **MHS Services for NetWare.** This manual explains the NetWare MHS (Message Handling Service) and how to install and manage it. The guide also describes how to use the FirstMail client software.

- **Installing and using NetSync.** This manual explains how to install and use the NetSync utility. NetSync is a management utility that enables you to manage NetWare 3.x servers from the NetWare Directory Services.

- **Introduction to NetWare Directory Services.** This manual introduces you to the

basics of NDS and helps you plan the NDS tree.

- **New Features.** This manual introduces you to features that are unique to NetWare 4.

- **NetWare client for OS/2.** This manual describes the installation and configuration of NetWare Client software for OS/2 workstations. This client software can be used for both NetWare 3.x and NetWare 4.x. The manual contains information on accessing network services form Virtual DOS machines and setting up Named Pipes and NetBIOS protocol support.

- **Print Services.** This helps you with NetWare 4 printing concepts and how you can set up, load, and use network printing utilities. It contains some troubleshooting tips and guidelines for network print services.

- **Supervising the Network.** This helps you to set up and administer the network after you complete the NetWare 4 installation. It covers issues such as managing NDS, NetWare files and directories, creating login scripts, NetWare server maintenance, network auditing, and backing up and restoring data.

- **Utilities Reference.** This contains information on how to use NetWare utilities, such as Text workstation utilities, server utilities, and GUI-based utilities. It also contains information on NDS bindery objects and their properties.

- **Upgrade and Migration.** This manual describes upgrading to NetWare 4 from other NetWare servers, such as NetWare 2.x or 3.x and IBM LAN Server.

- **TCP/IP Reference.** TCP/IP is a de facto protocol for connecting heterogeneous systems together. This manual discusses how TCP/IP can be configured and managed on the NetWare 4 server. It explains the concepts in relationship to NetWare's implementation of TCP/IP.

■ **Building and Auditing a Trusted Network Environment with NetWare 4.** This describes an overview of the security requirements for large networks and how NetWare 4 auditing can be used to meet these requirements.

■ **System Messages.** This is a list of all possible system and warning messages that you may encounter in configuring NetWare 4. It lists the messages according to the modules that generate them, and there are over 150 modules. It explains the possible cause of the error message and the action you can perform to fix it.

The command-line utilities now have a /? switch that gives additional information on how to use these utilities. This switch is very convenient, as help is available from the command line, without invoking any other on-line documentation. In reality, typing illegal command line parameters also results in help screens being displayed. For example, the NDIR help screen is displayed by typing the following command:

NDIR /?

Figure 1.22 shows the output of the NDIR /? command.

Help is also available in the menu utilities via function key F1. This help is context sensitive. The menu utilities such as FILER and PCONSOLE use the familiar C-Worthy Menu interface. Unlike previous versions of NetWare, pressing the F1 key twice does not display extended help information.

 In NetWare 4, online help is available through the following:

■ DynaText, which is a GUI application in MS Windows 3.*x* or OS/2

■ The command switch /? for command line utilities

■ The F1 function key in menu utilities

```
NDIR                    General Usage Help                        4.25
Purpose: View information about files, directories, and volumes.

For help on:                                  Type:
  Display format                              NDIR /? FOR
  Sorting features                            NDIR /? SORT
  Search filters (restrictions)               NDIR /? RES
  Attribute filters                           NDIR /? AT
  Other options                               NDIR /? OPT
  Syntax                                      NDIR /? SYN
  All help screens                            NDIR /? ALL

For example, to:                              Type:
  See all files in current directory          NDIR *.*

  See only directories on drive C:            NDIR C:\*.* /DO
```

Figure 1.22
NDIR /? help command.

NetWare 4 Utilities

A common experience many people have when upgrading from NetWare 3.x to NetWare 4.x is the discovery that some of the very familiar utilities such as SYSCON are no longer present in NetWare 4.x. SYSCON was a bindery based network administration tool and has been replaced by the more powerful NETADMIN tool that is based on NDS.

Some utilities have disappeared and been consolidated into a more functional utility. The utilities VOLINFO, SALVAGE, and PURGE, for example, have been consolidated into FILER.

Table 1.2 lists some of these changes.

Table 1.2
NetWare 4 Utility Changes

NetWare 4.0 Utility	Description
NETADMIN.EXE	Menu driven text utility used to manage NDS objects. Also can be used to assign property values and rights. Consolidates some of the features of pre-NetWare 4.0 utilities such as SYSCON, SECURITY, USERDEF, and DSPACE.
NWADMIN.EXE	MS Windows and OS/2 graphical utility to manage NDS tree and perform operations on it. Is a consolidated graphical tool for network management.
UIMPORT.EXE	Text utility for batch creation of users. Replaces the functionality of the pre-NetWare 4.0 MAKEUSER utility.
DOMAIN.NLM	Allows the creation of protected domains that allow NLMs to run in rings 1, 2, and 3 of the Intel processors. Runs as an NLM.
MONITOR.NLM	General purpose server monitor utility for monitoring the server. Runs as a server NLM and consolidates the functions of the pre-NetWare 4.0 MONITOR and FCONSOLE.
SERVMAN.NLM	Facilitates the easy viewing and changing of the many server SET parameters. Allows these changes to be stored in AUTOEXEC.NCF and STARTUP.NCF files. Runs as a server NLM.
RCONSOLE.EXE	RCONSOLE also performs the function of REMOTE.NLM ACONSOLE (asynchronous console). Used for remote management of server. Other support NLMs are RPSX.NLM and RS232.NLM.
NWSNUT.NLM	Library interface for C-worthy style graphical functions used by server based graphical tools such as MONITOR and SERVMAN.

NetWare 4.0 Utility	Description
PARTMGR.EXE	Text utility for managing partitions and their replicas.
Partition Manager	GUI equivalent of the PARTMGR utility.
DSREPAIR.NLM	Repairs inconsistencies and problems in the NDS database. Provides the functionality of the BINDFIX and BINDREST utilities used to repair the bindery.
TIMESYNC.NLM	Performs time synchronization. Is set up to load via AUTOEXEC.NCF during NetWare 4.0 server installation.
CDROM.NLM	CD-ROM support for CD drives attached to the NetWare 4.0 server.
RTDM.NLM	Real time data migration utility that runs at the server.
LIST DEVICES	Server console command. Lists device information.
SCAN FOR NEW	Server console command. Scans for any new DEVICES devices that have been added to the server.
MEDIA	Server console command. Used to confirm if requests to insert/ remove media on the server have been performed.
MAGAZINE	Server console command. Used to confirm if requests to insert/ remove magazine on the server have been performed.
MIRROR STATUS	Server console command. Used to display status of mirrored partitions.
ABORT REMIRROR	Server console command. Used to stop mirroring of partitions.
REMIRROR PARTITION	Server console command. Used to remirror partitions.
AUDITCON.EXE	Allows independent users to act as auditors. Is a superset of the pre-NetWare 4.0 ATOTAL and PAUDIT.
RIGHTS.EXE	Consolidates functions of pre-NetWare 4.0 utilities RIGHTS, GRANT, REVOKE, REMOVE, and ALLOW.
FLAG.EXE	Consolidates functions of pre-NetWare 4.0 utilities FLAG, FLAGDIR, and SMODE.
FILER	Consolidates functions of pre-NetWare 4.0 utilities FILER, SALVAGE, PURGE, DSPACE, and VOLINFO.
NPRINTER.EXE	Allows a printer attached to a workstation (DOS or OS/2), or a server to be used as a network printer.

continues

Table 1.2, Continued
NetWare 4 Utility Changes

NetWare 4.0 Utility	Description
SBACKUP.NLM	Used to perform backup across the network. Consolidates the pre-NetWare 4.0 SBACKUP and NBACKUP.
RPL.NLM	Allows remote booting for diskless workstations (PCs).
KEYB	Server console command. Allows the selection of a nationality or language for the keyboard device.
LANGUAGE	Server console command. Sets up the use of the specified language at the server.
CX.EXE	Allows users to navigate the NDS tree by changing the context. Does for NDS directory what the CD command does for file directories.
LOGIN.EXE	Used to log in or attach to a server. Uses NDS objects and consolidates pre-NetWare 4.0 utilities LOGIN and ATTACH.
NMENU.BAT	Batch utility.
MENUMAKE.EXE	Menu compiler utility.
MENUCNVT.EXE	Menu conversion utility. Menus are based on Saber menus.
NDIR.EXE	Consolidates the pre-NetWare 4.0 NDIR, LISTDIR, CHKDIR, and CHKVOL.
NETUSER.EXE	Replaces pre-NetWare 4.0 SESSION. Text graphical tool for performing drive mappings, printing, and network attachments.
SEND.EXE	Consolidates the pre-NetWare 4.0 SEND, CASTON, and CASTOFF.
NLIST.EXE	Consolidates the pre-NetWare 4.0 USERLIST and SLIST. Can be used to locate or search for objects at the DOS command line.
Tools Group for MS Windows and OS/2	Tools installed as a group in the Windows Program Manager and OS/2's desktop.

NetWare 3.11 SALVAGE and VOLINFO are options in the NetWare 4 FILER.

NetWare 3.11 ALLOW, GRANT, REVOKE, and REMOVE are consolidated as options within the NetWare 4 RIGHTS.

Study Guide for the Chapter

If preparing for the NetWare 3.11 to 4.0 Update CNE exams, review the chapter with the following goals:

- Understand and identify all the new capabilities in NetWare 4. Use the Study Tips as a quick review.

- Pay particular attention to memory protection, NDS services, and enhanced client services.

- After studying this chapter, attempt the sample test questions for this chapter. If you miss the answers to a question, review the appropriate topic until you understand the reason for the correct answer.

Chapter Summary

In this chapter, you examined the features of NetWare 4. NetWare 4 represents an exciting change in the way large enterprise wide area networks can be supported. The principal change has been the introduction of NetWare Directory Services, which enables you to superimpose a logical structure or view on a physical network, making the network easier to use and administer.

Because NDS is central to accessing resources on the network, security is integrated into NDS. When a user logs in, that user is authenticated at the NDS level. Auditing can be used to further monitor activity on the network.

Other improvements are in the areas of storage management services, enhanced client support, enhanced and integrated utilities, and better on-line documentation.

Chapter Test Questions

All test questions are multiple choice. Where a single answer is desired, it is indicated by a ○ (circle) notation that precedes the possible answers. Some questions require you to select more than one answer; these are indicated by the □ (box) preceding each answer. Certain questions will be repeated in different ways, so that you can recognize them even when the wording is different. Taking practice quizzes will not only test your knowledge but also give you confidence when you take your exam.

You will notice a large number of questions on NetWare 4 features. This is probably the most frequent type of question you will be asked on material covered in this chapter.

1. Which one of the following is a new feature in NetWare 4?

   ○ A. NetWare Drive Services

   ○ B. NetWare Directory Services

   ○ C. NetWare File Service

   ○ D. NetWare Name Service

2. Which is a new NetWare 4 feature?

   ○ A. NetWare File Service

   ○ B. NetWare Loadable Modules

   ○ C. Network auditing

   ○ D. Bindery services

3. Identify the new features of NetWare 4.

   □ A. NetWare Directory Services

   □ B. Network auditing

   □ C. Bindery services

   □ D. Authentication

   □ E. Memory management

4. Identify the new NetWare 4 features.

   □ A. Efficient memory management architecture

   □ B. Enhanced client services

   □ C. Memory reduction

   □ D. NetWare Directory Services

5. Identify the NetWare 4 features.

   □ A. Folio online help

   □ B. DynaText online help

   □ C. Simplified installation and upgrade

   □ D. Support for unlimited physical memory

6. Which of these are NetWare 4 features?

   □ A. Virtual memory support

   □ B. Ring-based memory protection

   □ C. Data translation

   □ D. Data off loading

   □ E. Data migration

7. NDS is a replacement for _____ services of NetWare 3.

   ○ A. Printer

   ○ B. Bindery

   ○ C. Directory

   ○ D. Directory sharing

8. In NetWare 4, the NDS is _____, whereas in NetWare 3, the bindery is _____.

   ○ A. flat, hierarchical

   ○ B. hierarchical, a B-tree structure

   ○ C. hierarchical, flat

   ○ D. a B-tree structure, hierarchical

9. The NDS is a _____ database of _____.

   ○ A. distributed, network services

   ○ B. hierarchical, services

   ○ C. distributed, files

   ○ D. relational, printers

10. NDS has the advantage of having _____.

    ○ A. multiple logins to the network for better security

    ○ B. a single login to the network at the cost of reduced security

    ○ C. a single login to the network

    ○ D. authenticated login to the network

11. NDS advantages are _____ and _____.

    □ A. logical organization

    □ B. relational organization

    □ C. access to resources from any location

    □ D. distributed fault redundancy

12. A primary benefit of NDS is that it makes it possible for _____.

    ○ A. users and network administrators to find the network resources without knowing the physical details of network connectivity

    ○ B. users to find physical resources if they know the location of the resource

    ○ C. users to find the phone numbers of all users on the network

    ○ D. administrators to gain access to all user objects

13. NDS controls access to _____ and _____.

    □ A. objects in the directory

    □ B. resources on the network

    □ C. physical location of servers

    □ D. duplicate login attempts

14. Advantages of NDS are that it _____ and _____.

    □ A. eliminates redundant server definitions

    □ B. eliminates redundant tasks such as adding a user account to multiple servers on the network

    □ C. reduces the risk of data loss

    □ D. provides disk fault tolerance

    □ E. simplifies access to network resources

15. Single login to a network means that _____.

    ○ A. users must login to servers one at a time

    ○ B. only a single attachment can be made to the server

    ○ C. users can gain access to network resources by logging in once

    ○ D. only users with the single attribute in their object definitions can login to the network

16. The maximum number of concurrent connections from a workstations to NetWare 4 servers is _____.

    ○ A. 8
    ○ B. 16
    ○ C. 32
    ○ D. 48
    ○ E. 50
    ○ F. 100

17. To gain access to a NetWare 4 network, the user object must be authenticated by _____.

    ○ A. the bindery
    ○ B. the registry
    ○ C. encryption
    ○ D. NDS

18. Global network management is possible in NetWare 4 because _____.

    ○ A. NDS is based on a global bindery
    ○ B. NDS is a global database
    ○ C. NDS is a secure database
    ○ D. NDS is hierarchical and relational

19. The NetWare 4 feature that can send several reply packets for a single client request is _____.

    ○ A. Internationalization protocol
    ○ B. flow control protocol
    ○ C. pipelining protocol
    ○ D. packet burst protocol

20. To execute NLMs in a separate region of memory, for NetWare 4 running on Intel procesors, the following feature/mechanism is used:

    ○ A. Virtual memory support feature
    ○ B. Ring protection mechanism
    ○ C. Memory suballocation feature
    ○ D. Tagged memory architecture of the Intel processors

21. The NetWare 4 feature that provides for restoring and backing up data on devices from different manufacturers is _____.

    ○ A. Storage Independent Data Format (SIDF)
    ○ B. Storage Independent Data Representation (SIDR)
    ○ C. Storage Management System (SMS)
    ○ D. Vendor Independent Storage System (VISS)

22. The NetWare 4 feature that allows data storage on disk to be divided into smaller units is _____.

    ○ A. disk allocation
    ○ B. garbage collection
    ○ C. fragmentation
    ○ D. suballocation

23. The NetWare 4 feature that enhances security and integrity of transactions and data is _____.

    ○ A. passwords
    ○ B. NDS
    ○ C. auditing
    ○ D. SMS

24. The NetWare 4 feature that prevents servers from crashing because of poorly written NLMs is _____.

    ○ A. NDS

    ○ B. hot fix

    ○ C. TTS

    ○ D. memory protection

25. In NetWare 4, the _____ feature enables support for documentation and utilities in several languages.

    ○ A. unicode

    ○ B. ASCII

    ○ C. internationalization

    ○ D. NDS

26. In NetWare 4, the _____ feature allows for a common data format.

    ○ A. NDS

    ○ B. XDR

    ○ C. SMS

    ○ D. ASN.1

    ○ E. ASCII

27. The _____ capability in NetWare 4 removes the limitation of _____ connections in NetWare 3.

    ○ A. NDS, 8

    ○ B. NDS, 16

    ○ C. VLM, 8

    ○ D. VLM, 16

28. The new NetWare 4 features that enhance the NetWare File System are _____.

    ☐ A. TTS

    ☐ B. suballocation

    ☐ C. network director services

    ☐ D. compression

    ☐ E. migration

    ☐ F. bindery services

    ☐ G. built-in NFS name space

29. The disk block sizes that can be set during NetWare 4 installation are _____ KB.

    ☐ A. 2

    ☐ B. 4

    ☐ C. 8

    ☐ D. 12

    ☐ E. 16

    ☐ F. 32

    ☐ G. 64

    ☐ H. 128

30. If the disk allocation block size is 4 KB, a 5 KB file will use _____ 4 KB block(s) and _____ 512-byte suballocation blocks

    ○ A. 1, 3

    ○ B. 2, 3

    ○ C. 1, 2

    ○ D. 1, 1

31. If the disk allocation block size is 32 KB, a 16 KB file will use _____.

    ○ A. one full 32 KB block

    ○ B. one partial 32 KB block and leave 32 512-byte suballocation blocks for other files

    ○ C. one full 32 KB block and 32 512-byte suballocation blocks

    ○ D. one partial 32 KB block and leave 31 512-byte suballocation blocks for other files

32. Suballocation gives _____.

    ○ A. better utilization of server memory

    ○ B. better utilization of disk space

    ○ C. improved memory management

    ○ D. improved memory management and garbage collection

33. Which of the following is true about NetWare 4 suballocation?

    ○ A. It enables small files and files that are not multiples of the disk block size to share space in a disk block that would otherwise have gone wasted.

    ○ B. All files to be stored in suballocation blocks.

    ○ C. Only files that are multiples of 1 KB to be stored in suballocation blocks.

    ○ D. Only files larger than the disk block size to take advantage of suballocation.

34. Disk suballocation is enabled _____.

    ○ A. during installation for each volume

    ○ B. using the supervisory option of the FILER utility

    ○ C. by loading the special NLM named SUBALLOC.NLM

    ○ D. only if the system determines that a minimum savings controlled by a SET parameter can be achieved

35. In NetWare 4 file compression, _____.

    ○ A. files are marked for compression at installation time

    ○ B. compression is enabled for a volume during its installation on a server

    ○ C. compression is enabled only if suballocation is enabled

    ○ D. files can be marked explicitly for compression only if their size exceeds a critical threshold set by the SET COMPRESSION THRESH-OLD parameter

36. In NetWare 4 file compression, _____.

    ○ A. files are marked for compression at installation time

    ○ B. only files for users belonging to group EVERYONE can be compressed

    ○ C. compression is enabled only if suballocation is enabled

    ○ D. files can be explicitly marked for compression

37. Data migration _____.

    ○ A. allows files to be moved from tape to disk

    ○ B. is used as a replacement for backups and restores

    ○ C. allows files to be removed from server's disk and placed onto other online media

    ○ D. allows files to be migrated from server cache to server disk, and then onto other online media

38. Data migration _____.

    ○ A. is performed on an individual file basis depending on the last time the file was accessed, called the least recently used criteria and the current volume usage

    ○ B. is performed by the file cache manager

    ○ C. is performed on an individual file basis depending on the last time the file was accessed, called the most recently used criteria and the current volume usage

    ○ D. is performed only if the MIGRATE.NLM is loaded

39. In NetWare 4, data migration _____.

    ○ A. is enabled for volume sizes that are 200 MB or more

    ○ B. occurs when the current volume usage exceeds the capacity threshold

    ○ C. is the process placing data in the RAM area reserved for this purpose

    ○ D. is the process of offloading data from server RAM to a special area on the disk reserved for that purpose

40. When a user logs in on a NetWare 4 network, a _____ is created, which is used to _____ a user's access to the network.

    ○ A. special user account, validate

    ○ B. ticket, validate

    ○ C. personalized key, authenticate

    ○ D. special password, authenticate

41. Network users must have _____ to the NDS database before they can view or make changes to it.

    ○ A. a password

    ○ B. direct access

    ○ C. rights

    ○ D. authenticated signatures

42. Which of the following statements about NetWare 4 file system security is true?

    ○ A. NetWare 4 file system security is similar to the NetWare 3 file system security.

    ○ B. NetWare 4 file system security is very different from the NetWare 3 file system security.

    ○ C. NetWare 4 file system security is similar to the NetWare 3 file system security, except in the area of trustee assignments.

    ○ D. NetWare 4 file system security is very different from the NetWare 3 file system security, except in the area of file attributes.

43. Which of the following statements about NetWare 4 network management is true?

   ○ A. NetWare 4 uses special workgroup and user accounts to delegate responsibility.

   ○ B. NetWare 4 cannot delegate responsibility to assistant supervisors as this would be a violation of good security practice.

   ○ C. NetWare 4 permits the creation of supervisor accounts with varying degrees of control over the network.

   ○ D. Network management can only be performed by the special user account ADMIN.

44. Which of the following statement about NetWare 4 is true?

   ○ A. The ADMIN user is a special account that cannot be deleted.

   ○ B. The NETADMIN user is a special account that cannot be deleted.

   ○ C. The NETADMIN user is a special account but it can be deleted.

   ○ D. The ADMIN user is a special account but it can be deleted.

45. Which of the following statements about NetWare 4 is true?

   ○ A. The ADMIN user is a special account that cannot be renamed.

   ○ B. The NETADMIN user is a special account that cannot be renamed.

   ○ C. The NETADMIN user is a special account but it can be renamed.

   ○ D. The ADMIN user is a special account but it can be renamed.

46. Which of the following statements about auditing are true?

   ☐ A. Auditing is a feature that was available in NetWare 3.

   ☐ B. Auditing is a new feature of NetWare 4.

   ☐ C. Auditing can be used to enhance NetWare 4 security.

   ☐ D. Auditing is used to track critical network events.

   ☐ E. Auditing cannot track the supervisor account activity.

   ○ F. Auditing events are stored in special log files.

47. The user who is assigned the job of auditing is called the _____.

   ○ A. workgroup manager

   ○ B. supervisor

   ○ C. network administrator

   ○ D. auditor

48. The NetWare 4 auditing feature is _____ the accounting feature that was available in _____ and is also available in _____.

   ○ A. the same as, NetWare 4, NetWare 3

   ○ B. the same as, NetWare 3, NetWare 4

   ○ C. different from, NetWare 4, NetWare 3

   ○ D. different from, NetWare 3, NetWare 4

49. Some of the advantages of NetWare 4 memory management are _____.

    ☐ A. a safe method for testing new NLMs

    ☐ B. taking advantage of the Intel processor's ring protection scheme

    ☐ C. a complex but faster memory management scheme

    ☐ D. better utilization of external cache of Intel processor

50. Some of the features of NetWare 4 memory management are _____.

    ☐ A. improved server performance through more efficient memory allocation

    ☐ B. improved server performance through a complex memory allocation scheme

    ☐ C. integration with the paged memory architecture of the Intel processors

    ☐ D. same scheme as NetWare 3 but implemented more efficiently

51. Some of the features of NetWare 4 memory management are _____.

    ☐ A. ring protection to control damage caused by misbehaved NLMs

    ☐ B. easier to write applications for the NLM developer because memory management is simpler

    ☐ C. improved server performance through an efficient memory allocation scheme

    ☐ D. improved server performance through a more complex but faster memory allocation

52. Which of the following statements about the NetWare 4 DOS requester is true?

    ○ A. The NetWare 4 DOS requester and the NetWare 3 shell are the same.

    ○ B. The NetWare 4 DOS requester can be used on a DOS workstation but must have the REQUESTR.INI properly configured for use on a Windows 3 workstation.

    ○ C. The NetWare DOS 4 requester can be used on a DOS workstation.

    ○ D. In NetWare 4 the DOS requester replaces the NetWare shell mechanism.

53. The network client is not generated in NetWare 4; instead a _____ that uses the _____ driver interface is used.

    ○ A. NetWare shell, ODI

    ○ B. DOS requester, ODI

    ○ C. NetWare shell, IPX

    ○ D. DOS requester, IPX

54. The DOS requester in NetWare 4 is implemented using _____.

    ○ A. device drivers

    ○ B. NLMs

    ○ C. VLMs

    ○ D. XLMs

55. Packet burst can be enabled in NetWare 4 client software for _____.

   ○ A. bursty network traffic

   ○ B. efficient transfer of NCP requests and replies

   ○ C. improving security on the network

   ○ D. reducing network collisions

56. Packet burst leads to which two of the following?

   ☐ A. Complex network traffic

   ☐ B. Increased response time between a workstation and a NetWare server

   ☐ C. Efficient transfer of NCP requests and replies

   ☐ D. A greater number of acknowledgment packets

   ☐ E. A reduced number of acknowledgment packets

57. Which of the following statements about Storage Management Services is true?

   ○ A. SMS allows data on the network to be backed or restored in a common data format that is hardware and software independent.

   ○ B. SMS allows data on the network to be backed or restored in a common data provided the Hardware Independent Interface (HII) is loaded on each device that is being backed up.

   ○ C. SMS is a backup and restore utility.

   ○ D. SMS is used for backing up TTS data.

58. Backup and restoration of data in NetWare 4 is performed by _____.

   ○ A. BSS (Backup Server Service)

   ○ B. BRSS (Backup and Restore Server Service)

   ○ C. SMS (Storage Management Service)

   ○ D. SBS (Storage Backup Service)

59. Which of the following statements about SMS are true ?

   ☐ A. Every device that needs to be backed up must have a TSA agent running on it.

   ☐ B. SMS is used for backing up TTS data.

   ☐ C. SMS allows data on the network to be backed up or restored in a common data format that is hardware and software independent.

   ☐ D. SMS allows data on the network to be backed up or restored in a common data provided the Hardware Independent Interface (HII) is loaded on each device that is being backed up.

60. Which of the following statements is true for NetWare 4 printing?

   ○ A. NetWare 4 printing can be done by printing to the queue name only.

   ○ B. NetWare 4 printing is the same as NetWare 3 printing.

   ○ C. NetWare 4 printing can be done by using the printer object name.

   ○ D. A NetWare 4 print server supports a maximum of 16 printers.

61. A NetWare 4 print server supports a maximum of _____ printers.

    ○ A. 16

    ○ B. 32

    ○ C. 64

    ○ D. 128

    ○ E. 256

    ○ F. 512

62. NetWare 4 printing has _____.

    ☐ A. a simple installation

    ☐ B. print servers that can each support up to 256 printers

    ☐ C. print servers that can each support up to 512 printers

    ☐ D. a limit of 512 queues per print server

    ☐ E. remote printer support on NetWare 4 servers

63. Which two of the following are true for NetWare 4?

    ☐ A. Internationalization is an enhanced implementation of the LANG.NLM extensions of NetWare 3.

    ☐ B. Internationalization allows users to run utilities, read utility messages and documentation in a language supported by NetWare.

    ☐ C. Internationalization translates user commands to machine language for processing on the NetWare 4 server.

    ☐ D. Allows one user to use FILER in English while another user is using FILER in French.

64. The NetWare 3 _____ and _____ are options in the NetWare 4 _____ utility.

    ○ A. PCONSOLE, PRINTDEF, PCONSOLE

    ○ B. VOLINFO, SALVAGE, FILER

    ○ C. SALVAGE, VOLINFO, CHKVOL

    ○ D. VOLINFO, SALVAGE, DSPACE

65. Which of the following statements about NetWare 4 is true?

    ○ A. NetWare 3 ALLOW, GRANT, REVOKE, and REMOVE are consolidated as options within the NetWare 4 RIGHTS.

    ○ B. NetWare 3 ALLOW, GRANT, REVOKE, and REMOVE are consolidated as options within the NetWare 4 TRIGHTS.

    ○ C. NetWare 3 ALLOW, GRANT, REVOKE, and REMOVE are consolidated as options within the NetWare 4 TLIST.

    ○ D. The NetWare 3 SALVAGE and VOLINFO are options in the NetWare 4 FILER utility.

    ○ E. The NetWare 3 SALVAGE and VOLINFO are options in the NetWare 4 CHKVOL utility.

NetWare Directory Services Fundamentals

In this chapter, you learn about NDS concepts and how NDS can be used to access and manage network resources. Understanding NDS services is fundamental to managing NetWare 4, because access to network resources revolves around how the NDS is represented, accessed, and managed. Many of the changes in NetWare 4 utilities have been done to facilitate an easier and more logical way of managing network resources by using an NDS representation.

Defining NDS

NetWare Directory Services (NDS) is a distributed global database of services and resources available on the network. Conceptually, this database exists when directory services are installed, and it is not tied to any physical resource such as a server. In practice, because NDS is implemented as a database, it must be stored on storage devices on the network such as physical volumes associated with physical servers. Because the size of the NDS database can become very large, and also for reliability reasons, the NDS database is not stored at any central site (except for very small networks). Portions of the NDS database are distributed on volume storage devices at strategic locations on the network. These subdivided elements of the NDS are called *partitions*.

 NetWare Directory Services

■ Is a distributed global database of network resources and services.

■ Is not confined to a central site or location.

■ Is stored on strategically located storage volumes on the network.

■ Can be subdivided into elements called partitions.

Differentiating between NDS and the NetWare Bindery

As you learned earlier, NDS treats all resources on the network as objects belonging to a global data-

base. This global database (directory) represents the network and has a structure that corresponds to a logical view of the network. The directory is not kept in a centralized location, but portions of it (partitions) are distributed across servers on the network. It is therefore a *distributed database*. This is different from the approach used in pre-NetWare 4.0-based networks, where the resources on a server were centrally located in a flat database called the *bindery*. Because the bindery served as a centralized database, it could become a single-point of failure.

 NDS provides a global directory that represents a logical view of the network.

 NetWare 4 differs from NetWare 3.*x* in the manner in which network information is stored. In a NetWare 4 network, information is stored in the NDS; in a NetWare 3.*x* network, information is stored in the bindery.

The directory database in NDS is organized in a hierarchical fashion. This hierarchical structure maps well into the organizational structure of most organizations. It can be used to represent logical relationships between network resources, such as grouping resources under a node representing a department of an organization. It is interesting to contrast the differences between the NDS and the NetWare 3.*x* bindery, because this gives an insight into the improved manner in which network resources are managed in NetWare 4.0. Table 2.1 summarizes the differences between the NDS and the NetWare bindery.

Table 2.1
NDS versus Bindery

Attribute/Feature	NDS	Bindery
Structure	Hierarchical	Flat
Users	Network-wide	Server-centric
LOGIN	Network-wide	Server-centric
Passwords	Single password	Password per server
Groups	Network-wide	Server-centric
Location	Distributed	Server-centric

 The hierarchical nature of NDS can be used to represent logical relationships between objects.

The bindery was used in earlier versions of NetWare to keep information on network resources in a flat database. This flat database did not represent the logical relationship between network resources. The bindery was server-centric and was used to store information on resources available at a NetWare server and not the entire network. As a result, tasks such as user account creation had to be performed on each server separately. User and group accounts had to be stored in the bindery of the server on which they were defined. There was no concept of a network-wide user account. (There was an attempt to provide this capability using *NNS, NetWare Name Service*, but this was not a very successful attempt and was never popular because of a number of problems dealing with the implementation of NNS.)

 Because the bindery is implemented as a flat database, it is not used to represent logical relationships between network resources.

The NDS structure is hierarchical. This enables NDS to represent relationships between network resources in a manner that is more comprehensible for the user and the network administrator. The logical representation of resources in the NDS is called *objects*. The NDS can be used to store information about objects so that this information can be queried in much the same way the white and yellow pages of a telephone directory can be used. For instance, the User object information can be used to keep information such as phone numbers, fax numbers, e-mail address, address, location, and so forth. User and group accounts in the NDS are network-wide in scope, and this eliminates the need for the network administrator to create user and group accounts on each server to which the user needs access.

Many tasks such as user and group account creation in earlier releases of NetWare, which had to be done separately on each server, are eliminated because the user/group account creation needs only to be created once in the directory. Once created, this user account can be assigned rights to any network resource represented in the NDS, such as NetWare volumes and network printers. Another benefit of the NDS is that the user needs to remember just one password to the network. Once validated, the user's trustee assignment gives the user the necessary access privileges to network resources.

The bindery is server-centric; whereas NDS is a global, distributed hierarchical database.

NDS eliminates the need for creating separate user and group accounts on each NetWare server. NDS enables user and group objects to be created that have a network-wide scope.

It is important to understand that NDS provides control of directory resources such as servers and volumes, but not over the contents of volumes such as files and directories. Access to files and directories is provided by the trustee rights mechanisms used in NetWare 3.x.

NDS provides control over directory information on network resources, but *not* over files and directories on a network volume.

Understanding the NetWare Directory Database

NDS is a global, distributed database that keeps information on network resources in a hierarchical manner. The distributed nature of NDS enables it to store information on many types of objects such as users, printers, servers, and volumes that are of interest to the network user community (see fig. 2.1). The distributed information is actually stored on NetWare servers throughout the network in a manner that is transparent to the user. A directory synchronization mechanism is used, so that directory changes on any part of the NDS database are propagated throughout the network. In other words, NDS synchronizes itself to present a consistent view of itself to the rest of the network. The directory synchronization takes place automatically without user intervention. The network administrator can set certain parameters to minimize the effect of directory synchronization on network traffic.

For security reasons, NDS is kept as a hidden data area on a storage volume. The NDS presents a hierarchical view of itself to the rest of the world. Access to any portion of the NDS is controlled by

Figure 2.1
The NDS database.

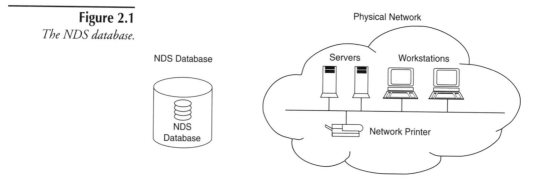

a new set of object trustee assignments made on NDS objects.

The hierarchical relationship in NDS is often described in terms of a directory tree, such as the one shown in figure 2.2.

The hierarchical relationship enables network resources to be organized in a manner that reflects how the network is used, instead of the physical topology and connectivity of the network. The directory organization can be made to more closely match the user's view of the network. For example, in figure 2.2, the engineers Tom, Mary, and Dei of the organization Network Widget, Inc., have user accounts defined under the departmental unit (called Organizational Unit, in NDS terminology) Engineers. Figure 2.3 shows that the users are not in the same physical location. In figure 2.3, engineers Tom and Mary are in Dallas, whereas user Dei is in Los Angeles; but, because they all belong to the group Engineers, they have similar needs to access network resources. Under these circumstances, it makes sense to group them in an Organizational Unit called Engineers, regardless of their physical location.

The file server for the engineers of Network Widget, Inc., is currently defined in Los Angeles. Should there be a need in the future to physically move the server to Dallas, the file server can be moved without changing the NDS view of the network. The file server EFS_1 still is under the Organizational Unit of Engineers in the NDS tree. In figure 2.2, you can see that volume EFS_1_SYS—that is physically attached to the server EFS_1—is in the Organizational Unit Engineers because it is primarily used by the engineers of the company. Another volume, called EFS_1_VOL1, is also physically attached to the server EFS_1, but its NDS representation is kept in the Organizational Unit Sales because it is primarily used by members of the sales team. One reason for the volume EFS_1_VOL1 to be kept in the Sales Organizational Unit could be that the group Sales does not as yet have its own file server. From this discussion, you can see that network resources can be placed in the NDS tree according to their use and the user's view of the network, instead of the physical location of the resource.

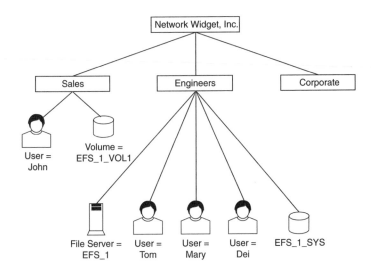

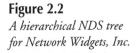

Figure 2.2
A hierarchical NDS tree for Network Widgets, Inc.

Figure 2.3

A physical network for Network Widgets, Inc.

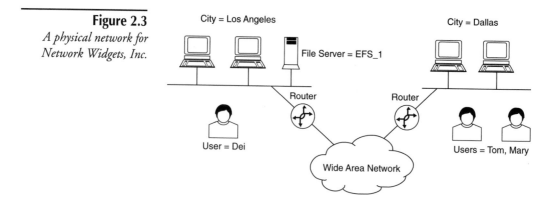

 NetWare Directory Services is

- A distributed, hierarchical database.

- A global database.

- Referred to as the directory database or directory tree.

- Represented as hidden files on servers.

- Stored on NetWare 4 servers.

- Compliant with X.500 naming rules.

- Used to store information on network resources.

- A mechanism for providing distributed information service on many types of data.

The NDS is based on the CCITT X.500 standard. *CCITT* is the *Consultative Committee for International Telephone and Telegraphy.* This is an international standard body. NDS is not in complete compliance with X.500 because it is largely based on the 1988 X.500 recommendations. The CCITT standards evolve continually, and the latest updates of these standards are published every four years. The X.500 standard has further evolved into the 1993 X.500 specification. For strategic reasons you can expect Novell's implementation of NDS to comply with the international consensus on X.500. Another area of expected change is the protocol mechanisms for keeping the NDS database updated when changes are made to it (directory synchronization). These have not been completely specified in the X.500 standards. As a result of this, Novell, like many other X.500 vendors (DEC, Retix, and so forth), had to design its own directory services synchronization protocol to deal with directory synchronization. Many X.500 vendors, including Novell, are seeking common ways to implement X.500-complaint synchronization methods and services. Novell does provide an API to exchange data between other name services. This makes it possible to build name service gateways to other name services.

NDS complies closely with the X.500 recommendations for naming objects and organizing objects in directory trees. The details of the kind of objects that make up the directory are specific to NetWare-based networks. Other general classes of objects that are not Novell-specific could be added to the NDS directory by using NDS programming APIs. This makes it possible to integrate NDS with other vendors' X.500 directory implementations.

The NDS database is called the *Directory Information Base* (*DIB*) in the X.500 specification. Novell's documentation uses the term *NDS database* or *NDS tree*, and this is the term used throughout this book.

 Study Note NetWare Directory Services provides

■ A logical view of the network that reflects the way the network is used.

■ A user's view of the network.

■ An information database that replaces the earlier NetWare bindery.

■ Access to the same information regardless of the client location.

■ A directory synchronization mechanism to keep the replicated portion of itself updated.

Defining NDS Components

NDS has a hierarchical structure, and it uses a specific terminology to describe its components.

Some terms have been derived from CCITT's X.500 recommendations, whereas others are specific to Novell. Before you can gain a working understanding of NDS, you must understand the vocabulary and terms used to describe NDS.

Tree Structure of NDS

The NDS database is organized as a hierarchical tree. A *tree* is a computer science term used to describe a way of representing data starting from a single point called the *root*. The root of this tree has branches, which can in turn branch off to other branches or leaves. Figure 2.4 illustrates this concept of tree, along with a picture of the NDS tree.

The tree has a single root (see fig. 2.4a). This is important to realize, because the NDS database also has a single root. If you have several NDS databases constructed separately from each other, they have separate roots. At the moment, you have no way of dynamically exchanging NDS information between NDS trees and their own separate roots. Tools for combining several separate NDS trees (each with its own root) into a single larger NDS tree are becoming available. An example of such a tool is DSMERGE. It allows two NDS trees to be merged.

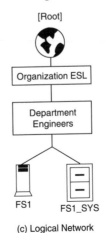

Figure 2.4
The NDS tree components.

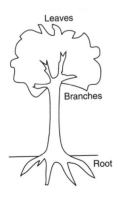

(a) Real Tree

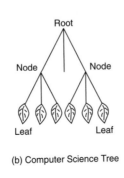

(b) Computer Science Tree

(c) Logical Network

The root of a tree describes the first level of the tree and is used to describe the entire tree.

A *branch* from the root of a tree leads to another *node* on the tree and describes a complete subtree (see fig. 2.4b). A *node* on the tree that contains other nodes is called a *container object*. (All nodes of a tree represent a logical concept of an organization or a resource and are called *objects*.) A branch of a tree can therefore be seen as a container for all the objects underneath it.

 NDS trees

■ Are used to represent the hierarchical structure of the NDS database.

■ Can have a single root that is named [Root].

■ With separate roots cannot exchange information.

 A branch of an NDS tree is a container for all the objects underneath it.

Container Objects

A *container* in NDS is an object that contains other objects such as other containers and resource and service objects. Containers provide a practical way of organizing objects by departments, geographic location, workgroups, common usage of network resources, or any other criteria that makes it easier to use the network.

The container objects provide a convenient way for organizing other nodes into groups (see fig. 2.5). This is a key advantage of NDS; that is, besides facilitating a logical organization of the NDS tree, container objects can be used as groups that can be assigned certain security rights, which then affect the security rights of all nodes in that container.

Figure 2.5

Container objects as groups.

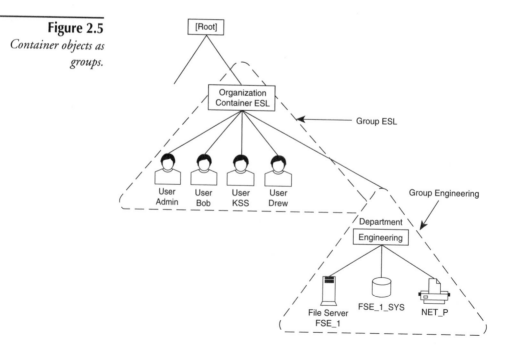

Container objects are used for

- Organizing the NDS database.

- Grouping objects in a logical way that reflects the network use.

- Assigning a common set of security rights to objects within the container.

 A leaf object

- Cannot contain other objects.

- Acts as a terminal point in the tree.

- Represents a network resource or service.

- Can exist only in a container object.

Leaf Objects

A node in the tree that does not (and cannot) contain any other nodes is called a *leaf object*. A leaf object is similar to the leaves of a real tree, which do not have any branches and other leaves coming from them. A leaf object acts as a terminal point in the tree and represents a network resource or service (see fig. 2.6). A leaf object can only exist inside a container object.

Object Class and Schema

A NetWare 4-based network can have many different types of network resources and services, and each of them is described by a special type of leaf object. In our earlier discussion, you learned about file server and Print Server objects. These are all examples of leaf objects. The object definition (also called *object type*) for an object in the NDS database is called its *object class*. In database technology

Figure 2.6
Leaf objects.

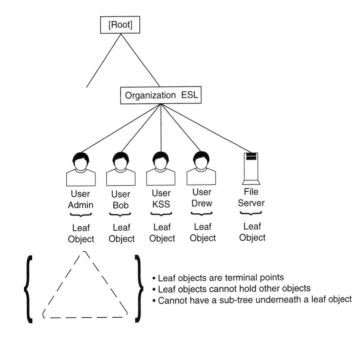

terms, the collection of the different object definitions possible in the database, and their scope and rules of existence and operation within the database is called the *schema*. Because the NDS tree is a global distributed database, database terms are sometimes used to describe the NDS tree, and you should be familiar with them. The NDS schema, is therefore a collection of object class definitions, for objects such as file servers, computers, printers, print servers, and so forth (see fig. 2.7). When an object of a type that can exist in the NDS schema is created, the object class is said to be *instantiated*. The object class implies a potential for an object of that class to exist in the database; it does not imply an existence of an object of that type. The object class must be instantiated (created) before an object belonging to that category can exist.

The different types of network resources that can exist in an NDS database is called an *object class*.

The collection of the different object definitions possible in the database, and their scope and rules of existence and operation within the database is called the *schema*.

In the example in figure 2.4c, the nodes ESL and Engineers are examples of container objects. They are container objects because they can in turn contain other objects. The leaves FS1 and FS1_SYS are examples of leaf objects. These leaves are the terminal points in the tree and cannot contain other objects.

Containers and Directories in File Systems

Containers are similar to directories in a file system. A directory in a file system can contain other subdirectories and files. Similarly, a container in NDS contains other subcontainers and leaf objects (network resources and services, see fig. 2.8). A directory in a file system can be used for organizing files. Containers in NDS are used to organize network resources.

The container typically represents an organization, department within an organization, workgroup center, responsibility center, geographical location, shared information, and network usage. The container and its relationship with other objects in the tree must be planned carefully.

Figure 2.7
NDS schema.

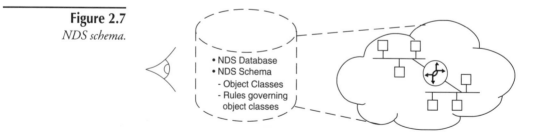

- NDS Database
- NDS Schema
  - Object Classes
  - Rules governing object classes

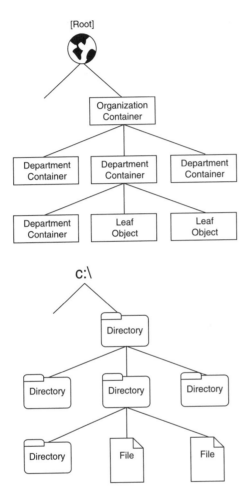

object name of [Root]. Object names are ▮ insensitive. This means that two objects with t▮ name NW4CS_SYS and nw4Cs_sYs have the same object name. Therefore, [root] and [Root] refer to the same object—the root of the directory tree.

Objects that are directly in the same container cannot have the same name. Therefore, in figure 2.9, the container ENGINEERS cannot have two Volume objects with the names NW4CS_SYS and nw4Cs_sYs. It is not even possible to have the same name for two objects that have a different object class. Therefore, container ENGINEERS cannot have both a file server object named ZAPHOD and a User object named ZAPHOD. These two objects can, however, exist in different containers, as seen in figure 2.10.

Even though object names are case-insensitive, the case of the name at the time of creating the object, is preserved for display purposes. This means that if you create an object named mY_worKstation, it appears in the case used for the object name at the time the object was created. Leaf objects can be renamed, but container objects cannot.

To make object names consistent and more readily understandable, it is important for an organization to have guidelines about object naming conventions.

Figure 2.8

Containers versus directories for a file system.

Object names

- Must be unique in the same container level regardless of the object type they represent.

- Are case-insensitive, but are displayed in the case used to create them.

- Can be renamed only if they are leaf objects.

Understanding Object Names

All nodes of the NDS tree must have a name, called the *object name*. The root of the tree has the fixed

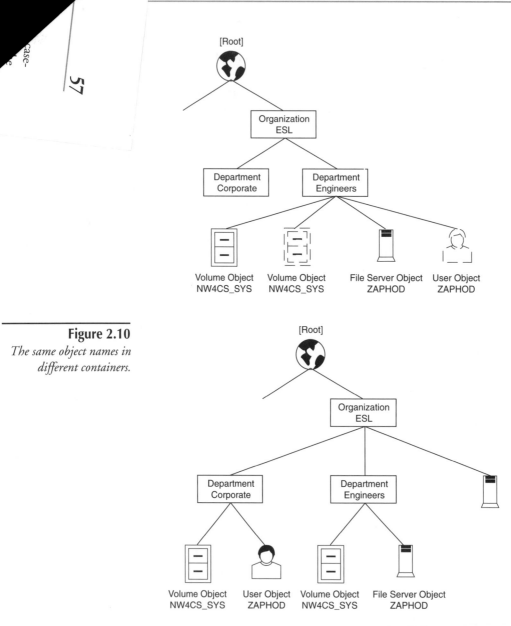

Figure 2.10

The same object names in different containers.

An object name can be up to 64 characters long and can consist of alphanumeric characters, dashes, underscores, parentheses, and even spaces. If spaces are used, you have to enclose the object name in quotation marks ("") for it to be recognized in command line utilities and LOGIN scripts. For simplicity, you might want to avoid this. It is even possible to construct a name with a single blank. Figure 2.11 shows an interesting example of an NDS tree that has two objects with a blank name. The first container object under ESL and the User object underneath it have a blank object name. Even though blank names might be permitted, it is a good idea to avoid them because the utilities that query NDS do not handle them consistently.

Brackets, periods, and percent signs are not permitted in object names. A few special characters, such as the plus sign (+) and equals sign (=), must be preceded by a backslash (\). In general, avoid using special characters in object names because the names then become confusing and difficult to use and remember.

Study Note Object names

- Have a maximum of 64 characters.
- Can have alphanumeric characters, spaces, dashes, underscores, and parentheses.
- Cannot have brackets or percent signs (unless preceded by \).

Practical TIP NDS might even allow you to use characters that are designated illegal in the documentation, for creating names of objects. They are not, however, guaranteed to work consistently in the NDS-based commands and utilities. For this reason, it is best to avoid them.

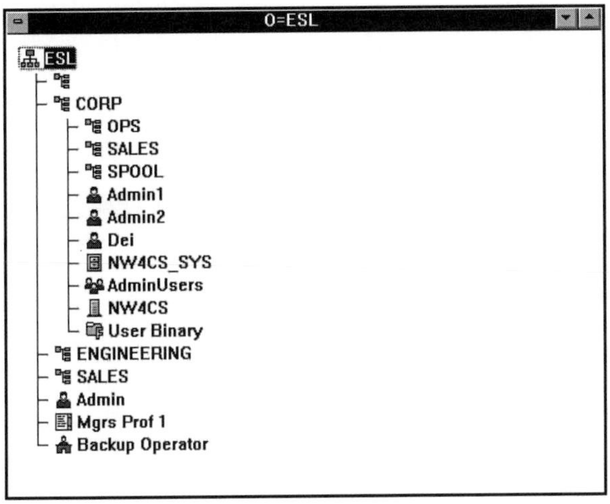
O=ESL
ESL
CORP
OPS
SALES
SPOOL
Admin1
Admin2
Dei
NW4CS_SYS
AdminUsers
NW4CS
User Binary
ENGINEERING
SALES
Admin
Mgrs Prof 1
Backup Operator

Figure 2.11
Example of a blank name object.

Defining Container Object Types

NDS supports the following container objects:

- Country object

- Organization object

- Organizational Unit object

Figure 2.12 shows the icons used to represent these different container objects. These icons are displayed when using the Windows-based network administration tools. The US container, in this figure, represents the Country object. The containers AT&T, DEC, ESL, ESL_KSS, LG, LTREE, MITEL, RSA, SCS, WELFLEET, and WIDGET all represent Organization container objects. The containers ACCOUNTING, CORP, R&D, and SALES represent Organizational Unit container objects.

The [Root] Object

The most frequently used container objects are the Organization object and the Organizational Unit

object. The Organization container object can occur under the [Root] object. The [Root] object, although not listed as a container object in Novell documentation, is a special type of container that holds all other container objects. There can be only one [Root] object per NDS tree. The [Root] object cannot be renamed or deleted. It can have rights to other objects, or other objects can have rights to it (you learn more about this in Chapter 4).

It is possible to install NetWare 4 on separate LANs, each with its own [Root] object. This could easily happen if the network was built in different segments, and final connectivity of the separate network segments was done at a later time. Under these circumstances, several [Root] objects could exist, each describing a different tree. Now, if you connect the network segments together, the networks represented by the different [Root] objects cannot communicate (see fig. 2.13) through normal NDS mechanisms. It is possible, however, to have two servers FS1 and FS2, each with its own unique tree, TREE1 and TREE2; you could do as follows:

Figure 2.12

Symbolic representations of container objects.

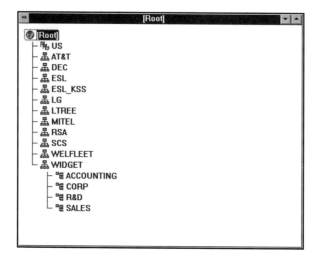

1. Log in to TREE1 as a valid NDS user.

2. MAP N FS2/SYS:

Because FS2 has a different tree, NetWare will automatically switch to bindery emulation mode and attempt to connect you in that fashion.

 When installing a NetWare 4 server that is not the first server installed, you should have physical connectivity from this NetWare 4 server to the rest of the

network, so that the server can be installed as part of the NDS tree.

 For extremely secure environments it might be desirable to have separate [Root] objects. This ensures that users in a directory tree under one [Root] cannot access or communicate with users under another [Root].

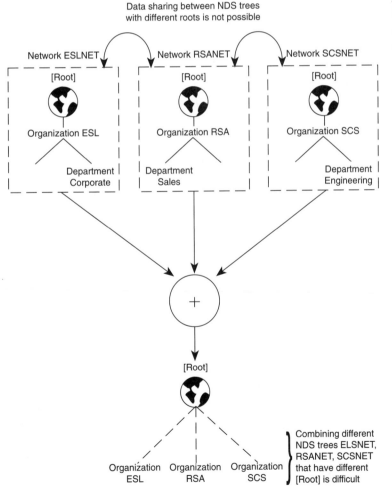

Figure 2.13
Multiple [Root] objects and the sharing of data.

The [Root] object can contain only country, organization, and alias objects. Of these, country and organization are container objects, and alias is a leaf object.

The [Root] object cannot be renamed or deleted.

 Alias is the only leaf object that can directly be under [Root].

The only container objects that can be directly under [Root] are the Country and Organization objects.

The Country Container Object

The Country object is part of the X.500 recommendations. Country object names are limited to two characters. They can be any two characters, but it is recommended that the CCITT's two-letter designations for countries be used. Figure 2.14 shows an NDS tree with the two-letter designations for several countries. From this figure, you can see that the Country object must be placed directly below the [Root] object. The Country object is optional. If used, it must occur directly under the [Root] object.

The Country object can contain only organization and alias objects.

 Alias is the only leaf object that both the [Root] and Country containers can contain.

 The only container object that the Country container can have is Organization.

 Country object names can be two characters only.

The Organization Object

The Organization object represents the name of the organization. Figure 2.15 shows an NDS tree that has the Organization objects. Notice the

Figure 2.14
Country objects in an NDS tree.

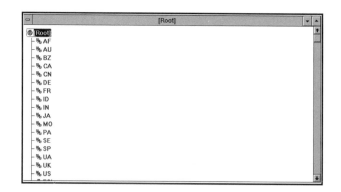

special icon used to represent the Organization object. At least one Organization object must be used in an NDS tree. It can occur directly under the [Root] object or a Country object. In figure 2.15, the Organization objects CISCO, HP, IBL, IBM, MS, and NOVELL are placed directly underneath the Country object US. Also, organizations AT&T, DEC, ESL, ESL_KSS, LG, LTREE, MITEL, RSA, SCS, WELLFLEET, and WIDGET are placed directly underneath the [Root] object. These are the only places where the NDS schema enables an Organization object to be placed.

The Organization object can contain any leaf object and Organizational Unit object, but it cannot contain another Organization object.

 The Organization object can be placed underneath the [Root] and the Country objects only.

The Organizational Unit Object

Because an organization is usually subdivided into specialized functions, such as by department, network usage, common jobs, location, workgroups, responsibility centers, and so forth, the Organizational Unit object can be used to represent the organization's subdivision. The Organizational Unit must occur under an Organization object or another Organizational Unit object. An Organizational Unit cannot occur directly under the [Root] object or Country object.

Figure 2.16 shows examples of an Organizational Unit object and the different locations in the NDS tree where it can occur. The organizations HP, MS, NOVELL in the country container object have Organizational Units such as CORP, ENGINEERING, MARKETING, and DISTRIBUTION directly underneath them. The organization ESL_KSS directly underneath the [Root] has Organizational Units CORP, ENG, and SALES underneath it. Notice that CORP is used as an Organizational Unit name in more than one organization. The object naming rules require an object name to be unique only within the same *level* of the container, and this enables the same object names to be used in different containers.

```
[Root]
 ● [Root]
 └ US
    ├ CISCO
    ├ HP
    ├ IBL
    ├ IBM
    ├ MS
    └ NOVELL
 ├ AT&T
 ├ DEC
 ├ ESL
 ├ ESL_KSS
 ├ LG
 ├ LTREE
 ├ MITEL
 ├ RSA
 ├ SCS
 ├ WELFLEET
 └ WIDGET
```

Figure 2.15
Organization objects.

Figure 2.16
Organizational Unit objects.

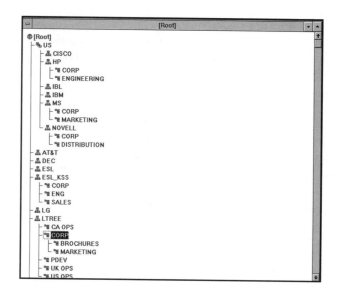

In figure 2.16, organization LTREE has an Organizational Unit CORP underneath it. And CORP has two other Organizational Units BROCHURES and MARKETING directly underneath it. This is typical of many organizations that can be expected to have subdivisions within a department of an organization.

The Organizational Unit object can contain any leaf object and Organizational Unit object.

 The Organizational Unit object

■ Can occur in an Organization or Organizational Unit object.

■ Can contain any leaf object.

Attribute Types

As part of the X.500 system of naming objects, each object type is represented by an attribute designator. For example, Country objects have the attribute type C. This means that the Country object US is represented as follows:

C=US

The other container objects, Organization and Organizational Unit, have the attribute types of O and OU, respectively. Therefore the organization IBM is represented by the following:

O=IBM

And an Organizational Unit SALES would be represented by:

OU=SALES

A leaf object that represents a resource or a service has the attribute type designator CN (Common Name). Therefore, the file server named NW4CS, would be represented as follows:

CN=NW4CS

Table 2.2 summarizes the different attribute types. All attribute types except the one for [Root] are part of the X.500 recommendations.

Table 2.2
Attribute Type Designators

Object	Container/Leaf	Attribute Type
[Root]	Container	No special attribute type. Designated by [Root] itself.
Country	Container	C
Organization	Container	O
Organizational Unit	Container	OU
Leaf object	Leaf	CN

Leaf Object Types

Leaf objects are the actual representations of network resources. The other objects such as [Root], Country, Organization, and Organizational Unit are logical in nature and are used for organizational purposes.

The NDS schema, by default permits only the following leaf objects:

■ AFP Server

■ Alias

■ Computer

■ Directory Map

■ Group

■ NetWare Server

■ Organizational Role

■ Print Server

■ Printer

■ Print Queue

■ Profile

■ User

■ Volume

■ Bindery Object

■ Bindery Queue

■ Distribution List

■ Message Routing Group

■ External Entity

■ Messaging Server

■ Unknown

 Remember the names of all the valid leaf objects for your CNE exams.

AFP Server Object

The AFP Server leaf object is currently used for informational purposes only. It represents an *AppleTalk Filing Protocol* (*AFP*) server that is on your network. This could be a Macintosh computer running the AFP protocols, or even a VAX server emulating AFP protocols. The AFP server can be used to store information such as the network address, users, and operators. One of the benefits of NDS is that it can be queried for information in a manner similar to databases. So, if for each AppleTalk server on your network you have an AFP Server object (see fig. 2.17), then you can make general queries such as: "Show me all AppleTalk servers in container O=ESL."

Alias Object

The NDS system is hierarchical, and the object naming syntax (as you learn later in this chapter) consists of enumerating the NDS objects, starting from the leaf all the way up to the top of the tree. If you try to reference an object that is not in your container, then the naming syntax becomes a little complicated, especially for end users who do not have the training to understand the NDS naming convention (see fig. 2.18).

NDS permits the definition of an object called the *alias object*. An alias object can point to a leaf or a container object. This is similar to the concept of symbolic links used in operating systems such as UNIX, except that UNIX's symbolic links apply to file systems, whereas alias objects are links to leaf objects in the NDS tree. Figure 2.19 shows the information that you need to supply at the time you create an alias object. In this dialog box, the name MyAliasName is going to be the new name of the alias object to be created under [Root] (shown highlighted in the figure). The value for the aliased object can be entered directly or by selecting the Browse icon next to this field, which shows the Select Object dialog box. Because the alias object is being created under [Root], the only possible objects that can be aliased are the Organization and Country objects. An attempt to alias another object produces an error message.

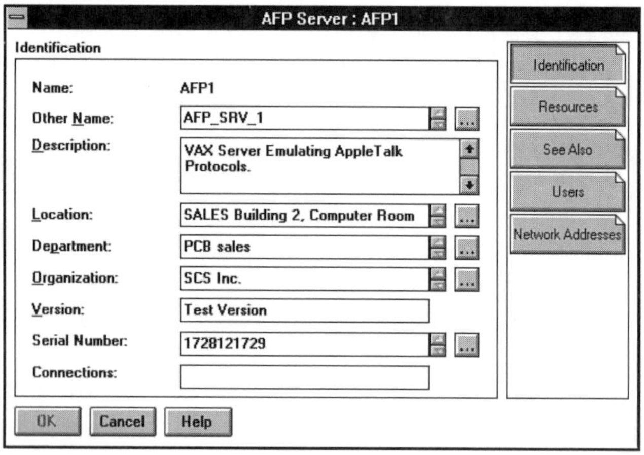

Figure 2.17

The AFP Server object.

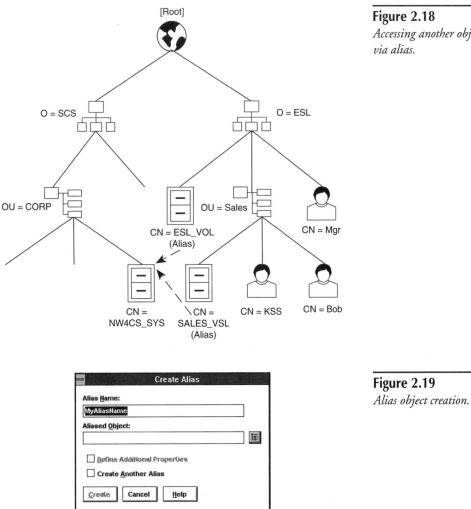

Figure 2.18
Accessing another object via alias.

Figure 2.19
Alias object creation.

Computer Object

A *Computer object* is used to represent a non-server computer such as a workstation, minicomputer, or mainframe. It can even be used to represent a router, which can be seen as a specialized computer with multiple network boards and routing logic implemented in firmware or software. A Computer object can contain information such as network address, computer serial number, computer operator, and so forth (see fig. 2.20).

Directory Map

A *Directory Map object* contains a reference or pointer to a directory on a Volume object anywhere in the NDS tree. Currently, map objects are only used in the MAP command, which enables a workstation drive letter to refer to a network directory on a server. Use of the Directory Map objects can simplify the MAP command that is used to point to Volume objects in other containers.

A very important use of the MAP command is in LOGIN scripts. LOGIN scripts are a sequence of instructions that are executed when a user logs in. They are primarily used to set up a user's network environment. Consider the situation where a LOGIN script contains the MAP command to map the drive letter G: to a directory in the Volume object named FS1_VOL in container O=ESL. If at a later point the Volume object is moved to another container, or if the directory path is changed, the mapping would be invalid and all references to the former location of the Volume object and directory would have to change. If the Directory Map object

was used to perform the mapping in the LOGIN script, only the Directory Map reference to the new volume/directory location would have to change, and the LOGIN scripts would not change. Figure 2.21 shows a Directory Map object in an NDS tree with some of its properties.

Group Object

A *Group object* refers to a collection of User objects in the NDS tree. The Group object is used as a convenience for assigning a number of users the same security rights. Figure 2.22 illustrates the concept of groups. In figure 2.22, the users belong to the same container. This is the most common use of groups. The Group object permits users from other containers to belong to the same group.

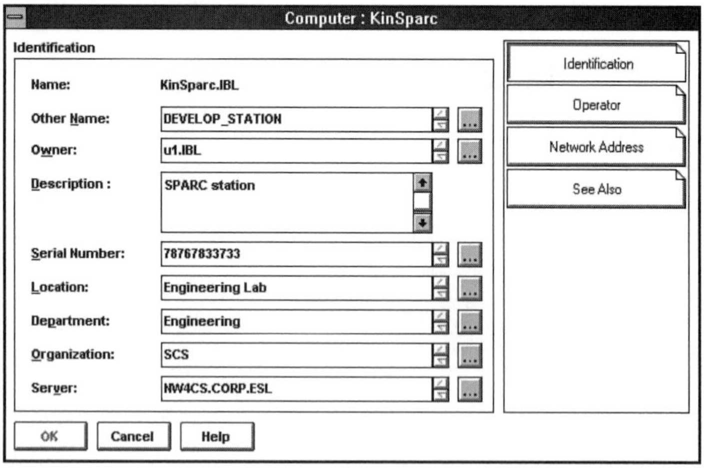

Figure 2.20

A Computer object.

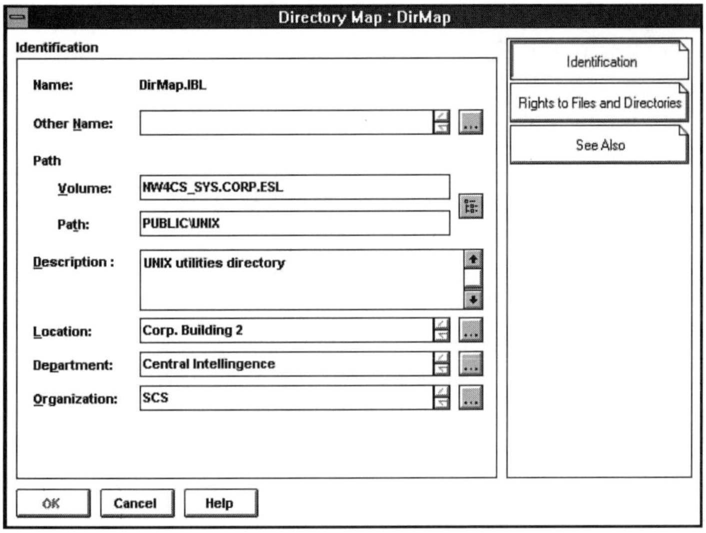

Figure 2.21

A Directory Map object.

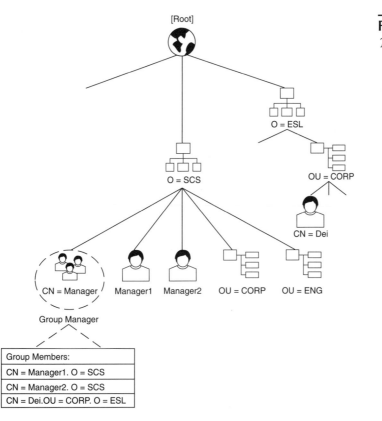

Figure 2.22

The concept of groups.

The Group object is similar to the concept of groups in NetWare 3.*x*, except that group is an NDS object rather than a bindery object. Also, no groups exist such as group EVERYONE that, by default, contain all users created on the NetWare 3.*x* server. To achieve the effect of a group such as EVERYONE, container objects can be used. All objects created in a container can be treated as a group by using the container name. A Group object has a group membership property that is a list of User objects defined anywhere in the NDS tree. Members of a Group object can be only User objects.

Container objects, on the other hand, can be used as groups; but members of a container object can be any leaf object or other container objects. Container groups can be used to provide a hierarchical relationship between groups, which is not possible with group objects or groups used in NetWare 3.*x*. For instance, in NetWare 3.*x* a group cannot contain other groups. This means that the subset relationship between groups does not exist. Using containers that have a natural hierarchical relationship between them, subset relationships between groups is possible. Figure 2.23 shows the Group object membership property.

NetWare Server Object

The *NetWare Server object* represents the physical NetWare server on a network. This is the object that provides *NCP (NetWare Core Protocol)* services. Some of the services provided by this object are represented as special objects in the NDS tree that reference the NetWare server. An example of this is the Volume object, which can be part of the physical NetWare server, but is represented as a separate Volume object.

The NetWare Server object is created during installation. One of the parameters that you specify as part of the installation is the container in which the NetWare server should be placed. The NetWare Server object contains information such as the physical location of the server object, its network address, the service it provides, and so forth.

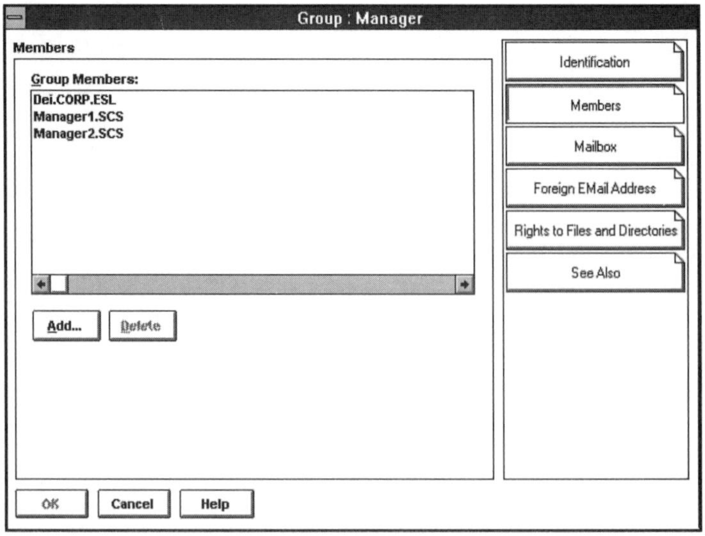

Figure 2.23

Group object membership property.

The NetWare Server object is referenced by other objects in the NDS tree. An example of this is the Volume object that references the NetWare server that acts as its host server. Without the NetWare Server object you could not reference the Volume object, and hence the files on the volume.

Figure 2.24 shows a NetWare Server object in an NDS tree and some of its properties. Notice that the status of the server is shown as being Up, and its IPX address is IPX:F0004101:000000000001: 0451. The F0004101 refers to the 8-hexadecimal-digit internal number of the NetWare server; 000000000001 refers to the 12-hexadecimal-digit node number; and 0451 refers to the 4-hexadecimal-digit socket number for receiving NCP requests. The 000000000001 is a 12-hexadecimal-digit node number and is different from the hardware address of the board, sometimes also called the *node address* or the *MAC* (*Media Access*

Control) address. The version number of the server is reported as Novell NetWare v4.10[DS]. The *DS* stands for *Directory Services.*

Organizational Role Object

The Organizational Role refers to a position or role within a department or organization. Usually a set of responsibilities and tasks are associated with that position. An example of such a role is the backup operator who needs access to certain volumes to perform the backup operation. Another example could be the print server operator. A User object can be assigned to be an occupant of the Organizational Role object. In this case, the User object inherits all the rights that have been assigned to the Organizational Role object (see fig. 2.25). If the responsibility for performing the task is passed on to another user, the user occupant of the Organizational Role object can be changed to reflect this.

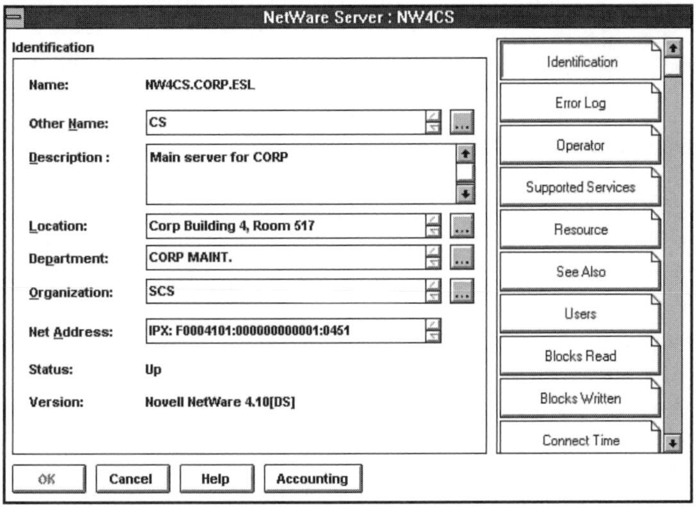

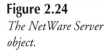

Figure 2.24
The NetWare Server object.

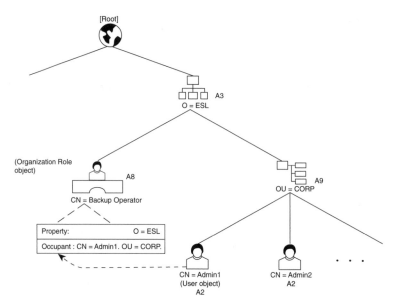

The Organizational Role object is useful in situations where the task performed by the organizational role does not change, but the person fulfilling that role changes. For example, the person assigned to perform backup tasks could change depending on the workload of individuals in an organization. Instead of changing the rights of the user for performing a certain task, these rights could be assigned just once to the Organizational Role object. The occupant of the Organizational Role object could be changed, and this would give the assigned occupant sufficient rights to perform the organizational role's task. Figure 2.26 shows the Organizational Role object and the individual occupying that role at the moment. Only User objects can be assigned to the property Occupant. Figure 2.26 indicates that the occupant of the organizational role is the User object CN=Admin1.OU=CORP.O=ESL.

Print Server Object

A *Print Server object* describes the services provided by the NetWare print server. The Print Server object is created by the utilities PCONSOLE and NWADMIN (NetWare Administrator Tool). It contains a reference to all the Printer objects that it services.

Figure 2.27 shows the Print Server object and some of its properties in the NDS tree. Notice that the print server has a property called the Advertising Name. This is the name used by the print server to advertise its services using *SAP (Service Advertising Protocol)*. The status of the print server indicates that it is down.

Print Queue Object

The *Print Queue object* is used to describe the network print queues. The print queue has a reference to the Volume object on which the actual print jobs are stored. The print queue is assigned to a Printer object. Print jobs sent to the Printer object are sent to the associated print queue. As in NetWare 3.x, print jobs can also be sent to the print queue.

Figure 2.28 shows the Print Queue object in the NDS tree. Notice that the Volume property indicates the Volume object used to support the print queue. Print queues are stored in the QUEUES directory on the specified volume.

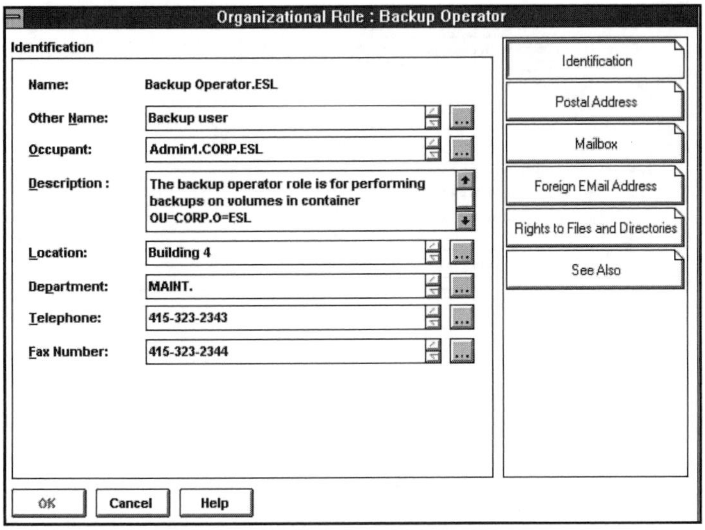

Figure 2.26

The Organizational Role object.

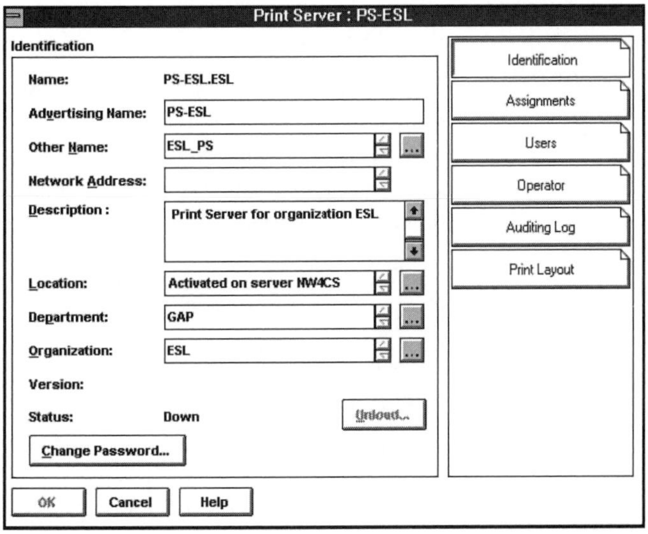

Figure 2.27

The Print Server object.

Figure 2.28

The Print Queue object.

Print Queue : Q1		

Identification

Name: Q1.ESL

Volume: NW4CS_SYS.CORP.ESL

Other Name: Queue_0

Description: Queue for postscript jobs

Location: Campus #1, Building 3, Room 689

Department: General

Organization: ESL

Operator Flags
- ☒ Allow Users To Submit Print Jobs
- ☒ Allow Service By Current Print Servers
- ☒ Allow New Print Servers To Attach

Identification

Assignments

Operator

Users

Job List

OK   Cancel   Help

Printer Object

The *Printer object* is used to describe the physical network printer device. The Print Queue object has a reference to the Volume object on which the actual print jobs are stored. The print queue in turn is assigned to one of the Printer objects. Print jobs sent to the Printer object are sent to the associated print queue. As in NetWare 3.*x*, print jobs can also be sent to the print queue.

Practical TIP

There are more restrictions when sending jobs to the printer. These include the following:

- You must be a user of all queues assigned to that printer.

- You need Browse NDS rights to the Printer object and all assigned queue objects.

- You need to designate a default queue for the printer.

Figure 2.29 shows a Printer object in the NDS tree and the properties of the print object that contain references to other printer related objects. In figure 2.29, the Print Queues property list has just one queue object assigned to it at a priority of 1 (highest). This means that print jobs sent to the Printer object are sent to the queue represented by the object: CN=Q1.O=ESL. The print server this printer services is CN=PS-ESL.O=ESL.

Profile Object

The *Profile object* represents common actions performed during the LOGIN processing. It represents a login script shared by a number of users. The User objects that share the login script can be in different containers.

The Profile object is listed as a property of a User object. It is executed when an individual uses the User object to log in to the network. Other types of LOGIN scripts such as the system LOGIN script and user LOGIN scripts exist. However, these are properties of the container object and the User object and do not exist as separate NDS objects. The Profile object is the only LOGIN script type that can exist as an independent NDS object.

Figure 2.30 shows a Profile object in an NDS tree, and the LOGIN script contained in the Profile object.

User Object

A *User object* represents the user account of the individual that logs in to the network. This is the most important object as far as the user is concerned. Changes made to this object affect the user directly. The User object must exist for every user that needs to log in to the network. The User object is defined in the NDS tree, which makes it different from NetWare 3.*x*, where User objects are defined on a server. Using this single User object, an individual can access all the servers and other network resources to which the user has been assigned rights.

Some attributes (called *properties* in NDS terms) of the User object are a home directory on a Volume object that the user has rights to, login restrictions, enabling/disabling intruder lock-out mechanisms, and so forth.

Figure 2.31 shows a User object defined in the NDS tree and some of its properties.

A User object with the special name USER_ TEMPLATE is used as a template for creating default property values for User objects within that container. You can have only one USER_ TEMPLATE object within a container (organization, Organizational Unit containers) that enables the creation of such an object.

Volume Object

The *Volume object* represents the physical volume attached to the server. It represents data storage on the network and is used to represent the file system on the network and for storing print jobs associated with a network queue.

Although the Volume object appears to be an object independent of the NetWare server, the Volume object has a logical connection to the NetWare server object to which it is attached. For this reason, Volume objects have a property called the *host server* that associates the volume with its host NetWare server (see fig. 2.32).

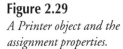

Figure 2.29
A Printer object and the assignment properties.

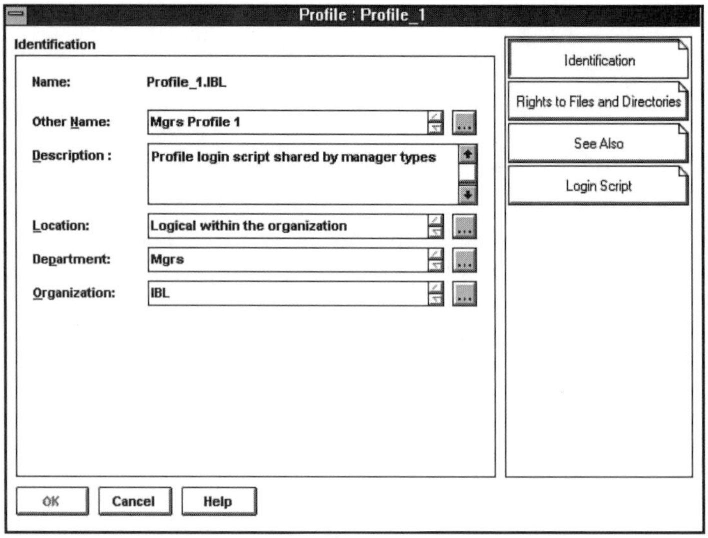

Figure 2.30
A Profile object.

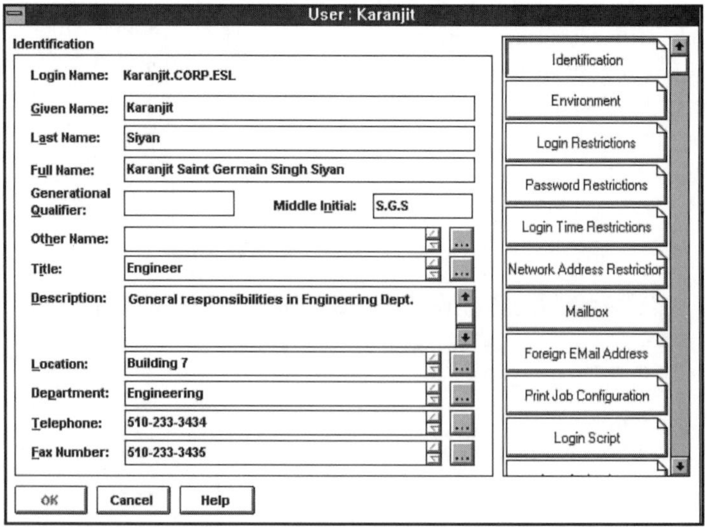

Figure 2.31
A User object.

The Volume object is created when the NetWare 4 server is first installed in a container. The volume is given a default NDS name that consists of the name of the NetWare 4 server, followed by an underscore, followed by the name of the physical volume such as SYS, VOL, and so forth. The physical name of a volume is the name given when the volume was first initialized as part of the installation process using the INSTALL *NLM* (*NetWare Loadable Module*).

```
NDS Volume object name = Object Name of
➥Server_Physical Volume Name
```

Therefore, if the NetWare server object name is NW4CS, the first physical volume on it, which has the name SYS, has an NDS name of NW4CS_SYS. If the server has a second volume named VOL1, its NDS name is NW4CS_VOL1. If you bring a server down and then up again specifying a different name, new volumes will appear, as well as the old volumes. The old volumes become known as *Unknown objects.*

The Volume object is both an NDS object and a file system object. It has characteristics of both a file system object and an NDS object. As an NDS object, the volume is managed by NDS, but its components consist of directories and files.

Bindery Object

The *Bindery object* is created when placing a NetWare 3.*x* server/service in the NDS tree as part of the upgrade or migration utility. The internals of this object cannot be managed by NDS. The Bindery object provides bindery emulation services, which allow a NetWare 4 server to be accessed by NetWare 3.*x* client software, which expects to see a bindery-based server.

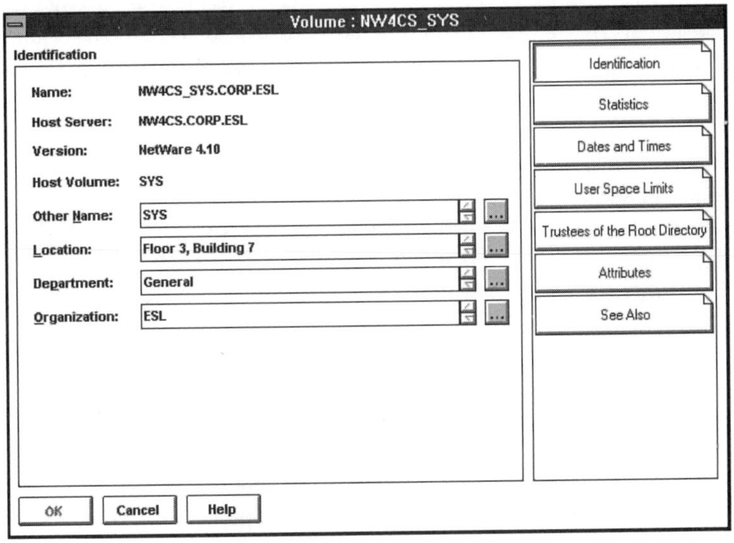

Figure 2.32
A Volume object.

Author's Note For NetWare 4 servers to be accessed by NetWare 3.*x* client software, the SET BINDERY CONTEXT parameter, which can be used to list up to 16 containers, needs to be set at the NetWare server. Certain utilities such as SBACKUP.NLM and AUDITCON.EXE use bindery emulation. These will not work correctly if BINDERY CONTEXT is not set. This parameter is set by default during the NetWare server installation. Additionally, if using Ethernet, the server must also load the driver with a frame type of ETHERNET_802.3 to support NetWare 3.*x* client software that uses this frame type. By default, NetWare 4 uses the ETHERNET_802.2 frame type. The ETHERNET 802.3 frame type, as defined by Novell, which is different from the rest of the industry's definition, does not include the *LLC* (*Logical Link Control*) layer specified by the IEEE 802.2 standard. This is the reason why Novell has begun calling the ETHERNET_802.3 frame the ETHERNET_802.3 *raw* format. The frame type ETHERNET_802.2 includes the LLC layer, which is a sublayer of the data link layer (OSI Model layer two). Use of the LLC layer in ETHERNET_802.2 identifies the upper-layer protocol that needs to handle the data portion (also called the *payload*) of the frame. In the case of NetWare 4, the default upper-layer protocol is IPX, but TCP/IP can also be used. The LLC layer enables protocol *multiplexing/ demultiplexing*. This means that support exists for delivering data to multiple protocol stacks and receiving data from multiple protocol stacks. The LLC layer also permits third-party, hardware-based routers to function properly. Without the LLC layer, hardware-based routers had to devise special techniques to discern if an ETHERNET_802.3 raw frame carried an IPX packet.

You are unlikely to be tested on the differences between the frame types ETHERNET_802.3 and ETHERNET_802.2 for the NetWare 3.*x* to 4 Update exams, but it is being included here, because the author feels that this is important for your understanding as a networking professional.

Bindery Queue Object

The *Bindery Queue object* represents a queue placed in the NDS tree as part of the upgrade or migration process. It represents a NetWare 3.*x* print queue and is used to provide compatibility with bindery-based utilities and applications.

Distribution List Object

The *Distribution List object* was defined starting with NetWare 4.1. A Distribution List object represents a collection of objects that have mailboxes. You can assign objects such as the Organizational Unit, Group or User objects to a distribution list. This enables you to send the same message to many different recipients by sending it to the Distribution List object.

Distribution lists can be nested. In other words, a distribution list can have other distribution lists as members. However, members of distribution lists do not have security equivalence to the distribution list.

Figure 2.33 shows some properties of a distribution list. The Mailbox button describes the Mailbox Location property, which is the name of the messaging server that contains the mailboxes. The Mailbox Location is a property of Organization, Organizational Role, Organizational Unit, Distribution List, Group, and User objects in NetWare Directory Services.

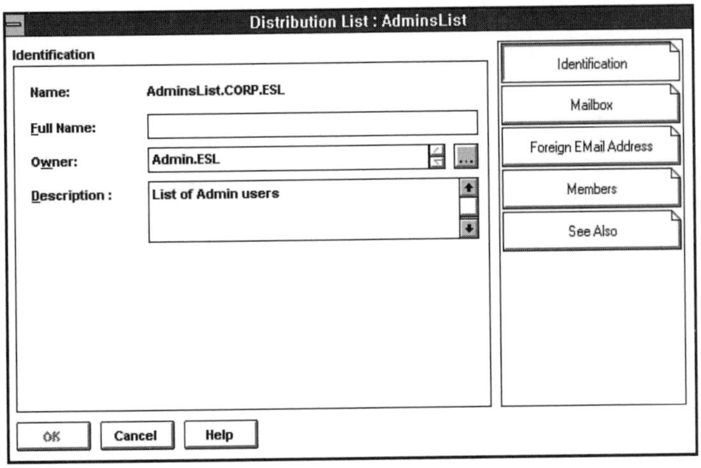

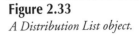

Figure 2.33
A Distribution List object.

Message Routing Group Object

The *Message Routing Group object* was defined starting with NetWare 4.1. A Message Routing Group object represents a cluster of messaging servers in the NDS tree. Because the messaging servers do frequent synchronizations among themselves, try to avoid connecting message servers in a message routing group through expensive or low-speed remote links. All messaging servers connected to the same message routing group send messages directly among themselves.

Figure 2.34 shows some message routing group properties. The Message Routing Group Name field is the name you assign to the Message Routing Group object. The Postmaster General is the User object who owns and administers the message routing group. The Postmaster General can modify the Message Routing Group object and its attributes (has Supervisor object rights to the message routing group).

Note that a user who has the following rights is called a *Postmaster*:

- Supervisor access to the *MHS* (*Message Handling System*) Messaging Server object

- Supervisor access to the Mailbox Location, Mailbox ID, and EMail Address properties of users of the MHS Messaging Server

- Read access to the message routing group that the MHS Messaging Server is in

You learn more about object and property rights later in this book.

External Entity Object

The *External Entity object* was defined starting with NetWare 4.1. An External Entity object represents a non-native NDS object or service that is imported into NDS or registered with NDS. An example of this might be a non-MHS e-mail address. By importing the non-MHS e-mail address into NDS, you can build an integrated address book for sending mail.

External entities are particularly useful if your messaging environment contains non-MHS Messaging Servers, such as *SMTP* (*Simple Mail Transfer*

Protocol) hosts, *SNADS* (*Systems Network Architecture Distribution Services*) nodes, or X.400 *MTAs* (*Message Transfer Agents*). You can then add e-mail addresses of users and distribution lists for these non-MHS servers to the NDS. These non-NDS objects are added as external entities. Having done this, the non-MHS addresses are not accessible by the native NDS messaging applications. This enables MHS users to select non-MHS users and lists from a directory list.

An External Entity object has an External Name property that specifies the NDS name of the external entity, and a Foreign E-mail Address property

that specifies the user's mailbox that is in a foreign messaging system. Figure 2.35 shows that the foreign e-mail address is an SMTP mailbox, with the address SMTP:karanjit@siyan.com. The e-mail address karanjit@siyan.com is in the format of the SMTP (Internet e-mail) address. Messages sent to this user can be delivered to an SMTP gateway.

It is important to note that an NDS object can have a Mailbox property or a foreign E-mail address property, but not both. These E-mail property values can be assigned when you create an object or at a later time.

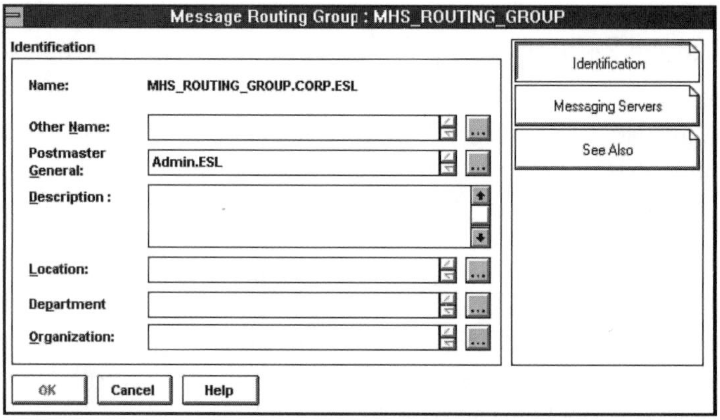

Figure 2.34

Message routing group properties.

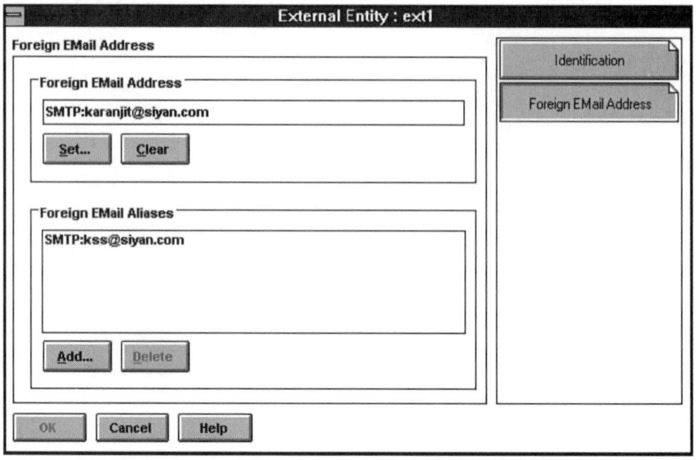

Figure 2.35

An External Entity object.

Messaging Server Object

The *Messaging Server* is a leaf object that represents a message server program, typically running on a NetWare server. The purpose of the messaging server is to route messages delivered to it. If a message recipient has a mailbox that is local to the messaging server, the message is delivered locally; otherwise, the message is transferred to other messaging servers. The messaging servers act as store-and-forward message transfer agents.

 **Author's Note** For those familar with the OSI definition of a Message Transfer Agent (MTA), the messaging server is an MTA.

The NetWare 4 servers ship with the MHS.NLM that implements the MHS messaging server. Figure 2.36 shows some properties of a messaging server.

Unknown Object

The *Unknown object* represents an NDS object whose object class cannot be determined because its NDS information has been corrupted. Figure 2.37 shows an object of unknown type under the container O=ESL. The Unknown object is the first one listed under O=ESL, and has the question mark (?) icon next to it. An Unknown object can appear if you bring a server down and then up again specifying a different name; new volumes will appear, as well as the old volumes. The old volumes become Unknown objects. Also, if the object that an alias object points to is removed, the alias object appears as an Unknown object.

 Practical TIP Too many Unknown objects in an NDS tree, can signal an NDS directory corruption problem. Running DSREPAIR utility can fix this problem.

Table 2.3 summarizes the preceding discussion of objects and gives a brief description of each type of leaf object.

Figure 2.36
Messaging server properties.

Messaging Server : NW4CS_MSG

Identification

Name:	NW4CS_MSG.CORP.ESL
NetWare Server:	NW4CS.CORP.ESL
MHS Database Location:	NW4CS_SYS.CORP.ESL.:/
Other Name:	
Description :	
Location:	
Department:	
Organization:	
Status:	Down
Version:	MHS Services 1.0

Identification
Message Routing Groups
Supported Gateways
Resource
See Also
Postmasters
Users

OK   Cancel   Help

Figure 2.37

An Unknown object.

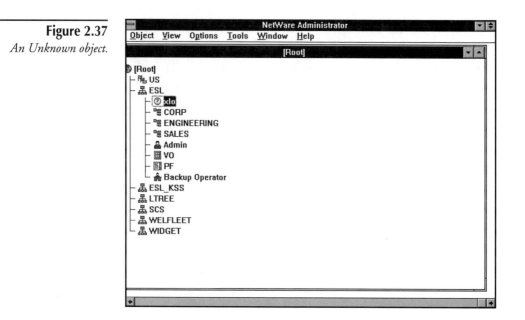

Table 2.3
Leaf Object Descriptions

Leaf Object Class	Meaning
AFP Server	An AppleTalk File Protocol server. Used for informational purposes.
Alias	A link to another object. This is a substitute name for an object that points to another object in the NDS tree.
Bindery object	The object created when placing a NetWare 3.x server/service in the NDS tree as part of the upgrade process. Internals of this object cannot be managed by NDS. It is used to provide bindery emulation services.
Bindery Queue	Created as part of the upgrade process. It represents a NetWare 3.x print queue.
Computer	Represents a computer: workstation, minicomputer, mainframe, and so forth. It is used for informational purposes.
Directory Map	Makes it possible to perform a simple drive mapping to another container. Makes it easier to maintain login scripts.
Distribution List	Represents a list of mailboxes or other distribution lists. This simplifies sending the same e-mail message to a group of users. Distribution lists can contain other distribution lists.

Leaf Object Class	Meaning
External Entity	Represents a non-native NDS object/service that is imported into NDS or registered in NDS. Example: MHS services can use External Entity objects to represent users from non-NDS directories such as SMTP, SNADS, X.400, and so on. This enables MHS to provide an integrated address book for sending mail.
Group	An object that has members that can be other objects. Similar to the concept of groups in NetWare 3.x, except that group is an NDS object, instead of a Bindery object.
Message Routing Group	Represents a group of messaging servers that can transfer messages directly amongst themselves.
Messaging Server	A Message Transfer Agent for e-mail applications.
NetWare Server	Represents a NetWare server on a network. This is the object that provides NCP (NetWare Core Protocol) services. Some of the services provided by this object are represented as special objects in the NDS tree that reference the netware server.
Organizational Role	Represents a position that has a certain set of defined tasks and responsibilities and can be performed by a user assigned that role.
Print Server	Represents the print server service.
Print Queue	Represents the network print queue that holds the print jobs before they are printed.
Printer	Represents a network printer that can accept print jobs sent to it.
Profile	Represents an object that can be used for sharing common actions that are performed during the LOGIN processing, regardless of whether they are in the same container.
Unknown	Represents an NDS object whose object class cannot be determined because its NDS information has been corrupted. Running DSREPAIR can fix this problem.
User	Represents the user account. Contains information on the users who use the network.
Volume	Represents data storage on the network. Represents the file system on the network used for storing files and print jobs associated with a network queue.

Review the key features and distinctions of each type of leaf object as summarized in table 2.3. You can expect questions on this in the CNE exams.

Object Properties

An object has attributes called properties that represent the types of information that can be stored in the object. In this sense, an NDS object is similar to a record in a database; and the properties of the object are similar to the different field types that can be in a record.

Figure 2.38 shows the file server object, which in this figure shows the properties such as Name, Network Address, and Location. The actual values

assigned for each of these properties is called the *property value.* A property value is an instance of the property type. Some properties of an object are mandatory and critical for the object to be used properly. Other properties are descriptive and used for informational and documentation purposes that enable the NDS to be used as a database of management information. The critical values are filled out by the network administrator at the time of creating the object. The values used for information and documentation can be filled out at a later time by the network supervisor who has Write access to these properties. An example of properties for the User object that are for informational purposes is the list of telephone and fax numbers for that user, the postal address, and the job title of the user. The name property for a User object is mandatory.

Figure 2.38

An NDS object and properties.

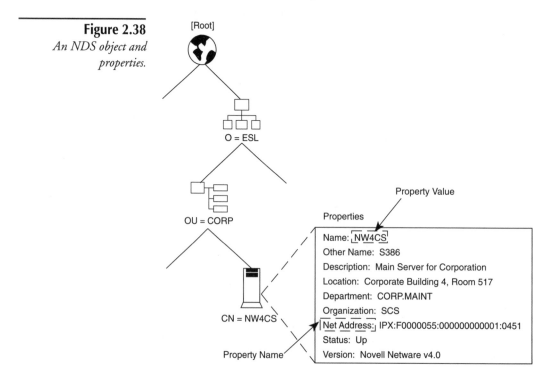

The type of information stored in an NDS object is called a *property*. The value of an information item stored in an NDS object is called a *property value*.

Some properties for an object are mandatory, and others are optional and used for descriptive purposes.

Fill out as many property values for an object as you have information for, because the NDS tree can be used as a database of information that can be queried by using tools such as NLIST.

Properties can be single-valued or multivalued. A property such as the LOGIN name of the user is single-valued, whereas the telephone number for a user is multivalued and represented as a list of values.

Properties can be single-valued or multivalued.

NDS Tree Case Study

Consider the organization MICROCON that makes advanced semiconductor devices. MICROCON's manufacturing plants and research labs are located in San Jose, but its marketing and sales departments are in New York. The San Jose facility has a VAX computer, a NetWare 4 file server used for manufacturing and testing, and another NetWare 4 server for R & D. The R & D engineers are Rick and James; the manufacturing engineers are Tom and Bill. Ed is the network administrator of the entire network.

The New York facility has two file servers, NY_FS1 and NY_FS2, that are shared by all users at that facility. Kirk is the overall network administrator.

The SALES department is a department within the MARKETING group. Currently, the sales persons are Janice, Jane, and John. Ron works in the Marketing department, which at the moment is under-staffed.

Figure 2.39 shows a diagram of the physical network for MICROCON. Figure 2.40 shows the NDS tree structure for this organization. Notice, that because users Ed and Kirk have network administrator responsibility, their User objects are defined directly under the container OU=ENGINEERING and OU=MARKETING. Shared resources that are used by all users of the San Jose and New York networks are also assigned directly within these containers. Examples of these shared resources are the printer FS1_PRT and the file servers NY_FS1 and NY_FS2. File servers FS1 and FS2 are placed in the containers OU=MANUFACTURING and OU=R&D. The SALES division is defined as a subcontainer of OU=MARKETING. The salespersons' User objects are defined in the OU=SALES container.

Using the preceding example, draw a physical network and an NDS tree for the organization Electronic Systems Lab (ESL), based in London, with facilities in Toronto, New York, and Paris. Research labs are located in Paris and Toronto, with marketing in New York and administration and sales in London. A support staff of network administrators in London manages the entire network. Network services and hardware support at other sites are performed by local contractors. Each location has its own servers and printers. London and New York both have two file servers each and three network printers, whereas other locations have a single file server and two network printers attached to the file server. As the company grows, it is expected that additional servers might be added. All locations have their own print servers.

The locations are tied together with communications links that runs at 1.544 Mps. The local networks used at each site are based on Ethernet.

Make reasonable assumptions for data not provided in this case study. For example, you might have to invent names for users at each of the locations and decide which of the users are going to be network administrators.

When you design the NDS tree for ESL, consider the following:

1. Decide on the depth of the tree. How many container levels do you need?

2. List all container objects that you need. Justify why you need each container.

3. Give appropriate names for container objects. Should they correspond to departments or geographical location?

4. Do you need one Organizational Unit, or more than one?

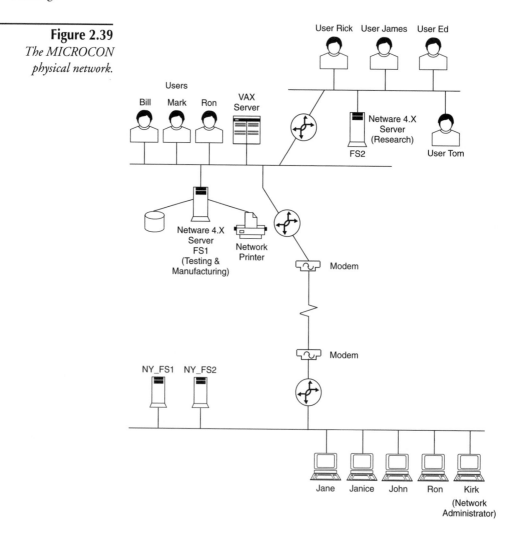

Figure 2.39
The MICROCON physical network.

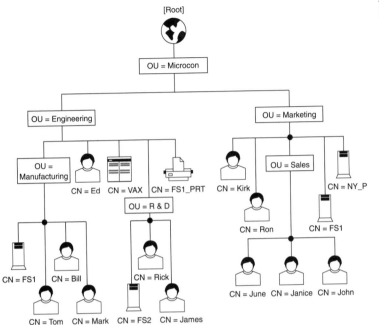

Figure 2.40
The MICROCON NDS tree.

Manipulating Objects with Tools

The two primary editing tools for creating, deleting, and moving NDS objects are as follows:

- Network Administrator Tool (NWADMIN.EXE)

- NetAdmin

Another tool for batch creation of users is UIMPORT, which is similar to the NetWare 3.*x* MAKEUSER tool. Because UIMPORT is not part of the scope of this book, it is not discussed.

The Network Administrator Tool is a Windows and OS/2 GUI tool that can be used for managing NDS objects, whereas the NetAdmin tool is a text utility for creating NDS objects using C-Worthy menus.

Setting Up the Network Administrator Tool (NWADMIN.EXE)

To set up the NWADMIN.EXE tool, you must have installed the NetWare 4 server (see Chapter 4) and the DOS/Windows client software (see Chapter 5). The following steps outline how to set up the NWADMIN tool for Microsoft Windows.

From within Windows perform the following tasks:

1. If the NetWare group does not exist, go on to step 2; otherwise, skip to step 3.

2. Create a new program group called NetWare (or any other name you prefer) by doing the following:

■ From the Program Manager, choose the **F**ile Menu.

■ Choose **F**ile, **N**ew.

■ Choose the Program **G**roup from the New Program Object dialog box and click on OK.

■ In the Program Group Properties box, enter the following information for the Description and Program Group File:

```
Description:  NetWare
Group File:   C:\WINDOWS\NWUTILS.GRP
(or whichever is the Windows direc-
tory)
```

3. If the program item for the NetWare Administrator Tool is set, you can skip this step; otherwise, perform the following to create a program item for NetWare Administrator Tool:

■ Highlight the NetWare program group.

■ From the Program Manager, choose the **F**ile Menu.

■ Choose **F**ile, **N**ew.

■ Select the Program **I**tem from the New Program Object dialog box and click on OK.

■ In the Program Item Properties box, enter the following information:

```
Description:      NetWare Adminis-
                  ↰trator Tool
Command Line:     Z:\PUBLIC\NWADMIN
Working Directory: Z:\PUBLIC
```

Choose OK to install the new program item.

4. Answer Yes to the prompt stating The specified path points to a file that may not be available during later Windows sessions. Do you want to continue?

The program item for NWADMIN should appear in the program group.

 Please note the following while performing this step.

Make sure that you are logged in to the network before performing this setup.

Your login script may map SYS:PUBLIC to a drive letter other than Z. X: is preferred because you are likely to have at least one search drive mapping that will be assigned to the letter Z. Make sure that this search drive is not "root mapped," though.

Using the NetWare Administrator Tool

This section gives you a guided tour of creating the NDS tree structure of figure 2.41 using the NetWare Administrator tool. This section assumes that you are familiar with using Microsoft Windows. The term *click* on an icon means to position the mouse pointer on the icon and to click the left key once. The term *double-click* on an icon means to position the mouse pointer on the icon and to click the left key twice in rapid succession.

The following is a guided tour of the NetWare Administrator tool.

1. Log in to the network as an Administrator account.

   When the NDS services is first installed (at the time the first NetWare 4 server is installed), a default network administrator User object Admin is created that has supervisor privileges to the entire NDS tree. You can use the Admin User object to log in to the network.

2. Activate the NetWare group and start the NetWare Administrator Tool program item. (You can do this by double-clicking on the NetWare Administrator icon.)

   You should see a screen similar to that shown in figure 2.42.

   The NDS tree in figure 2.42 shows the NDS tree starting from the current container. To see the NDS tree starting from the [Root], perform the following steps:

   ■ Choose the **V**iew menu.

   ■ Select the Set C**o**ntext option.

   ■ Set the current context to [Root]. You can do this by entering **[Root]** or by using the Browse icon to browse through the tree and select the current context.

3. Highlight the [Root] object. You can do this by clicking on it once.

   Right-click on the [Root] object to see a list of operations that can be performed under the [Root].

   Select **C**reate.

   You should see a list of objects that can be created under the [Root] object as seen in figure 2.43.

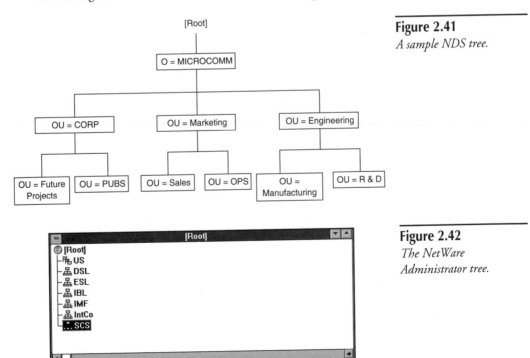

Figure 2.41
A sample NDS tree.

Figure 2.42
The NetWare Administrator tree.

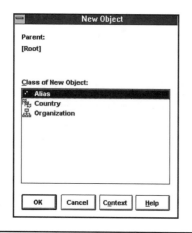

Figure 2.43
New objects under [Root] container.

4. Select the Organization object and click OK.

    You should see a dialog box for creating the Organization object (see fig. 2.44).

    Enter the name of the organization shown in figure 2.41, and select the Create button.

    You should see the name of the newly created organization MICROCOMM appear in the NDS tree.

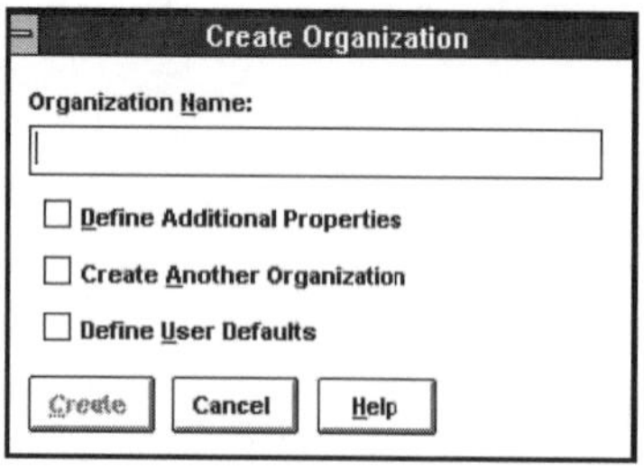

Figure 2.44
The dialog box for creating an organization container.

5. Highlight MICROCOMM and right-click.

    Select Create.

    You should see a list of objects that can be created under the Organization object (see fig. 2.45). Compare figure 2.45 with figure 2.43. Notice that the list of objects that can be created under an Organization object is much larger.

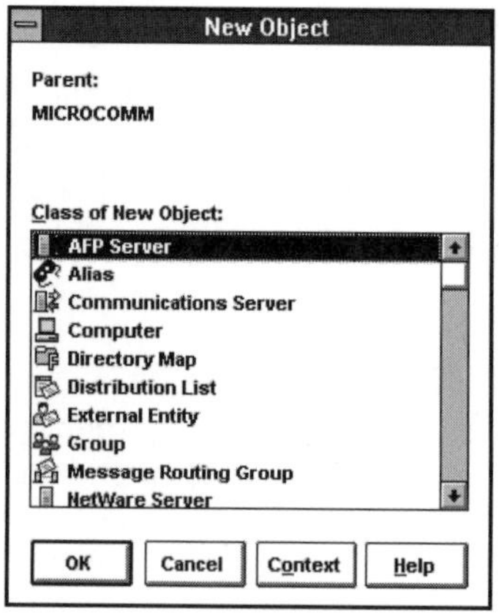

Figure 2.45
New objects under an organization container.

6. Select the Organizational Unit object and click OK.

    You should see a dialog box for creating the Organizational Unit object (see fig. 2.46).

    Enter the name of the Organizational Unit **CORP**, shown in figure 2.41, and select the Create button.

    The name of the newly created Organizational Unit CORP appears in the NDS tree, if you double-click on MICROCOMM.

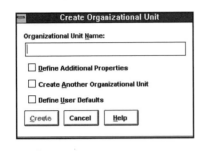

Figure 2.46

The dialog box for creating an Organizational Unit object.

7. Repeat steps 5 and 6 to create Organizational Unit container objects for MARKETING and ENGINEERING, as shown in figure 2.41. You can check the Create Another Organizational Unit check box to speed the creation of organizational units.

8. Repeat previous steps to create the rest of the organization, as shown in figure 2.41.

9. Delete the NDS tree you have just created. You cannot delete a container object that has objects defined in it. You must, therefore, start with the bottom most objects, and delete them first.

   To delete an object, right-click on the object and select the **D**elete operation. Alternatively, highlight the object; select the **O**bject menu; and select the Delete operation from the menu.

To delete a group of objects, perform the following:

1. Open up the structure to be deleted by double-clicking on the target container objects.

2. Highlight the first object to be deleted.

3. Click on the last object to be deleted while holding down the Shift key.

4. Press the Delete key and choose OK.

Using the NetAdmin Utility

This section gives you a guided tour of creating the NDS tree structure of figure 2.41 using the NetAdmin tool. NetAdmin is a text-based utility that provides a similar function as the NetWare Administrator tool. As a system administrator, it is very useful to be able to perform NDS operations using NetAdmin because you might run into situations where Microsoft Windows is not installed at a NetWare workstation. NetAdmin can work directly on top of DOS and does not require Microsoft Windows.

For this section of the guided tour, you want to accomplish the same objectives as in the preceding section, so that you can compare the differences between using the NetWare Administrator and NetAdmin tools.

1. Log in to the network as an Administrator account.

   When NDS is first installed (at the time the first NetWare 4 server is installed), a default network administrator User object Admin is created that has supervisor privileges to the entire NDS tree. You can use the Admin User object to log in to the network.

2. Invoke the program NETADMIN, by typing its name:

   `<C1>NETADMIN`

   You should see the NetAdmin screen shown in figure 2.47.

Figure 2.47

The NetAdmin options screen.

The NetAdmin utility is located in the SYS:PUBLIC directory, and you must have a search path to that directory for the NetAdmin command to work correctly.

The current context is seen on top of the screen under the label Context. If this is not set to [Root], perform the following steps to set it to [Root]:

■ Select Change context.

■ Enter [**Root**] when asked to Enter con- text:.

■ Press Enter to go back to the NetAdmin main menu, with the changed context.

3. Select Manage objects.

You should see a list of objects and their classes under the [Root] container (see fig. 2.48).

4. Press Insert.

You should see a list of objects that can be created under [Root] (see fig. 2.49).

5. Select the Organization option to create an Organization object.

You should see a box for creating the Organization object (see fig. 2.50).

Figure 2.48

Object, Class under the [Root] container.

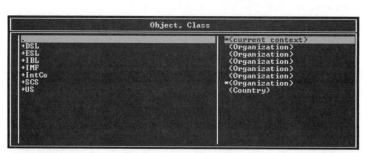

Figure 2.49

Selecting an object class under the [Root] container.

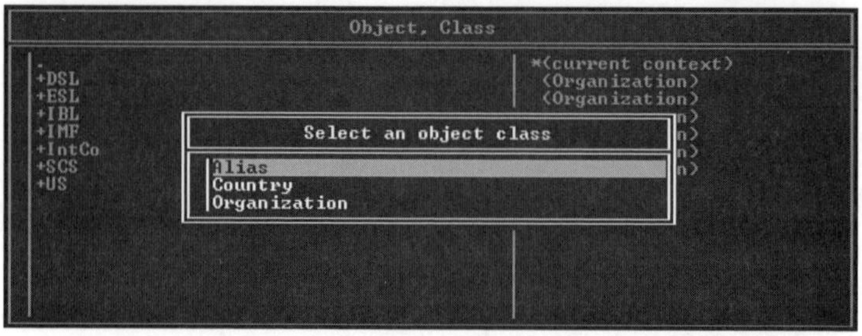

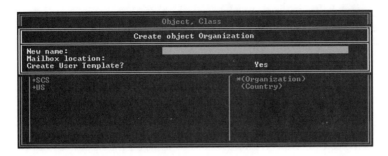

Figure 2.50

The NetAdmin dialog box for creating an organization container.

Enter the name of the organization shown in figure 2.41. You can elect to create a User Template for the Organization object at this point or defer this action until later.

6. Press F10 to save changes and perform the create operation.

   When prompted to create another Organization object, answer No.

   The name of the newly created organization MICROSYS appears in the object, class list.

7. Highlight MICROSYS and press Enter. Notice that your context has changed to O=MICROSYS.

8. Press Insert to create an object.

   You should see a list of objects that can be created under the Organization object (see fig. 2.51).

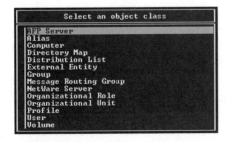

Figure 2.51

Selecting an object class under the organization container.

9. Select the Organizational Unit option to create an Organizational Unit object.

   You should see a box for creating the Organizational Unit object (see fig. 2.52).

   Enter the name of the Organizational Unit shown in figure 2.41. You can elect to create a User Template for the Organization object at this point or defer this action until later.

10. Press F10 to save changes and perform the create operation.

11. When asked to create another Organizational Unit object, answer Yes and repeat previous steps to create all the other Organizational Unit objects.

12. Review figure 2.41 and repeat previous steps to create the rest of the organization, as shown in figure 2.41.

13. Delete the NDS tree you have just created. You cannot delete a container object that has objects defined in it. You must, therefore, start with the bottommost objects, and delete them first.

    To delete an object, highlight it from the object class list and press the Delete key. You are then asked to confirm your delete operation.

Figure 2.52

The NetAdmin dialog box for creating an organizational unit.

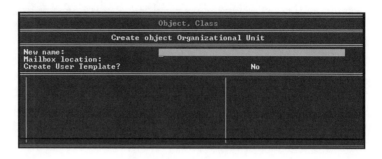

Understanding NDS Context

The NDS *context* is a term used to describe the position of an object in the NDS tree. The position is described in terms of the container that contains the object.

The context of an object is important because some NDS utilities require you to know the position (or location) of the object in the NDS tree. In general, you must know the object's position (context) in order to find it. (Commands are available, such as the NLIST command, to help you find the object's position in the NDS tree—if you know its name. These are discussed later in the chapter.)

The context can also be seen as a *pointer* that locates the object's position in the NDS tree. The context is described in terms of listing, from left to right, the NDS names of the container objects, separated by periods (.). The order of listing the container objects is to start with the immediate container and work your way up to the root.

 The position of an object in an NDS tree is called its *context*. The context indicates where an object can be found in the NDS tree.

The context of an object refers to its container.

The context can never be set to a leaf object (because leaf objects cannot contain other objects).

A special type of context called the *current context* is the current position of the attached workstation in the NDS tree. An *attached* workstation is one that is connected (logically speaking) via the network to the NDS tree.

When the network client software loads, it makes a connection to the NDS tree. If DOS is used as the workstation software, it can maintain only one current context for each DOS session. The workstation's current context can only be set to container objects, and not leaf objects, because a context is defined to be the position of the immediate container that contains the object in the NDS tree.

The current context is the default reference point used by the workstation to find other objects in the NDS tree. It is used in the same manner as the concept of the current directory in a file system. Just as the current directory cannot be set to a file name, the current context cannot be set to a leaf object.

Current context is an attached workstation's current position in the NDS tree.

The current context can be used as the reference point used to name objects.

Objects in the current context of a workstation can be referred to by their leaf object names.

It is not essential to use the full NDS name of the object, in this case. This is a great convenience to the workstation user, because the user does not have to type the full NDS name of the object. Resources not in the current context cannot be referred to by their leaf names only; you must specify the NDS path name of the object. Objects FS2 and PS2, shown in figure 2.53, must be referenced by their NDS path name.

 NDS objects in the current context of a workstation can be referred to by their leaf object names.

NDS objects not in the current context of a workstation must be referred to by their NDS path names.

 Group the resources a user accesses frequently in the user's context to simplify access to these objects.

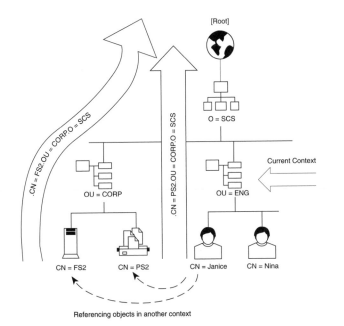

Figure 2.53
Referencing objects in another context.

Referencing objects in another context

Naming NDS Paths

In the preceding section, you observed that objects not in the current context of a workstation must be defined by their NDS path names. You have three ways of specifying the NDS path names:

- Complete name
- Typeless name
- Partial name

Complete Name

A *complete name* is the name of an NDS object that includes the leaf name and the names of the containers that contain the leaf object, starting from the leaf object and going up the tree to the [Root] object. The object names are specified with their attribute name abbreviation (attribute type). The complete name must always begin with a period (.). Periods between object names that make up the NDS name are used as separators for the object names. This is an important point to note: The leading period has a different meaning from other periods used in the NDS object name; it signifies that the name is a complete name, and the object can be referenced by *enumerating* its path all the way to the root. The path is enumerated by listing the object name and its containers all the way to the root object.

The general syntax of the complete name of an object is as follows:

```
CN=leaf_object.[OU=org_unit_name.{OU=org_unit_name}]
➥.O=org_unit.[C=country]
```

In the preceding syntax, the [] brackets and the {} braces are *meta characters* that have special mean-

ing. The [] indicate that the contents between the [] are optional. The {} indicate that there can be zero or more occurrences. The leading period is required for complete names. Without the leading period, the complete name becomes a partial name.

To summarize some of the rules of a complete name: the syntax for a complete name always begins with a period, followed by the NDS path of the object, all the way up to the [Root].

The *attribute_type_abbreviation* is CN for leaf object, OU for Organizational Units, O for Organization, and C for Country. After the name of the object, the list of containers starting with the most *immediate* container, and continuing all the way to the [Root] container is enumerated. Because only one [Root] can exist, the root object is not listed. The square brackets around the Organizational Unit list indicate that the OUs are optional. Examples of types of complete names are as follows:

```
.CN=leaf_object.O=org_unit.C=country
```

or

```
.CN=leaf_object.O=org_unit
```

The following is an example of a typeless complete name:

```
.leaf_object.org_unit.country
```

The C=*country* has been left out in the last syntax example of the complete name because the Country object is optional.

The most general case of the complete name would list the organizational units, a single organization, and a country name as shown in the following:

```
.CN=leaf_object.OU=org_unit_name.OU=org_
➥unit_name.O=org_unit.C=country
```

In the preceding syntax example, only two Organizational Unit objects are shown, but there could be any number of these objects.

In figure 2.54, the complete names of the objects FS1, PS1, PRINT_1, PRINT_2, PS2 are as follows:

```
.CN=FS1.OU=REGION_A.O=HAL
.CN=PS1.OU=REGION_A.O=HAL
.CN=PRINT_1.OU=OPS.OU=SALES.O=HAL
.CN=PRINT_2.OU=SALES.O=HAL
.CN=PS2.O=HAL
```

Partial Name

A *partial name* for an NDS object is its NDS path relative to the current context. This is in contrast to the complete name that lists the NDS path objects, relative to the root of the tree. A partial name is similar to specifying the name of a file relative to the current directory, and a complete name is similar to specifying the name of a file, using its complete path name that lists all the directories starting from the root. The partial name is also called the *Relative Distinguished Name (RDN)*.

Figure 2.54

The NDS tree for complete name examples.

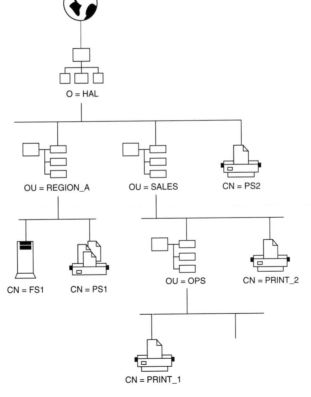

Author's Note In X.500, the object's full path name, with reference to its position in the NDS tree, is called its *Distinguished Name (DN)*; and the name relative to a context is called the *Relative Distinguished Name (RDN)*. The NDS term for this is *complete name*. The Distinguished Name of an object is formed by taking the DN of the object's parent and adding the RDN of the object to it.

The X.500-equivalent term for the NDS database is the *Directory Information Base (DIB)*, and the NDS tree is referred to as the *Directory Information Tree (DIT)* in X.500 vocabulary.

Study Note Objects in current context can be referenced by their common names.

Objects not in current context must be referenced by their partial names or complete names.

Resolving a Partial Name

The NDS must resolve the partial name to a complete name. This is done by appending the current context to the partial name and adding a period at the beginning to indicate a complete name, as follows:

```
Complete Name =   .Partial Name.Current
➥Context
```

An example might help clarify this rule:

If the current context is OU=CORP.O=ESL, the partial name for object HP_PR1 that is in the same context is CN=HP_PR1. NDS forms the complete name by appending the current context OU=CORP.O=ESL to the partial name CN=HP_PR1, and adding a period at the beginning.

```
Current Context is OU=CORP.O=ESL
Partial Name is    CN=HP_PR1
<
.  concatenated with  CN=HP_PR1  concatenated
➥with  OU=CORP.O=ESL
```

The main purpose of a partial name is to simplify the names for NDS objects that are in the current context or in the vicinity of the current context.

The examples so far have been of objects in the current context. In figure 2.55, the object FSP_1 is not in the same context as the current context that is set to O=ESL. In this case, the partial name of FSP_1 is the object name plus the list of all the containers leading up to the current context O=ESL. That is, the partial name for FSP_1 is as follows:

```
CN=FSP_1.OU=CORP
```

Similarly, the partial name of ENG_FS_VOL, if current context is O=ESL is the following:

```
CN=ENG_FS_VOL.OU=ENG
```

And the partial name of Admin, if current context is O=ESL, is as follows:

```
CN=Admin
```

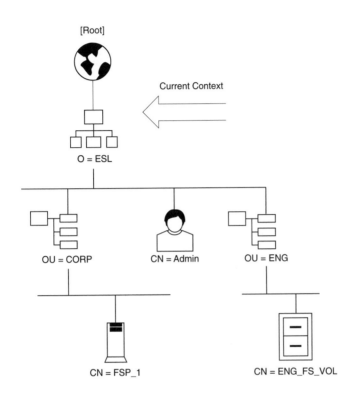

Figure 2.55
The partial name for objects not in current context, but in the same tree branch.

- Partial name of FSP_1 is CN = FSP_1. OU = CORP
- Partial name of ENG_FS_VOL is CN = ENG_FS_VOL. OU = ENG
- Partial name of Admin is CN = Admin

What if the current context is *not* set to a container that is part of the complete name leading up to the root? In this case, appending a period (.) at the end of the NDS name refers to the parent container. In figure 2.56, the current context is OU=ENG.O=ESL. If the object DEI_FS in OU=CORP is to be referenced, you can use the following partial name:

CN=DEI_FS.OU=CORP.

The trailing period (.) at the end refers to the parent container of the current context, which in this case is O=ESL. The partial name of the object DEI_FS with respect to the container O=ESL is CN=DEI_FS.OU=CORP. But because the current context is in a different tree branch (current context is OU=ENG.O=ESL and not O=ESL), a trailing period must be added at the end.

Figure 2.56

The partial name for an object when its current context is in a different branch of the NDS tree.

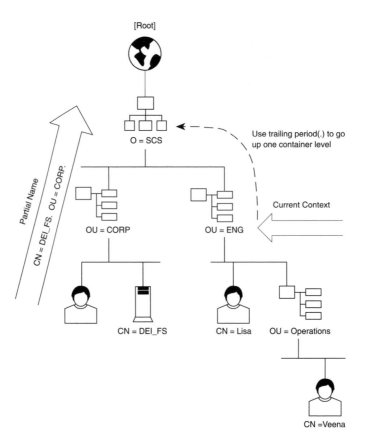

If the current context in figure 2.56 was OU=OPERATIONS.OU=ENG.O=ESL, then the same object CN=DEI_FS could be referred to by the following partial name:

`CN=DEI_FS.OU=CORP..`

Two trailing periods means two parent containers above the current context. Because the current context is OU=OPERATIONS.OU=ENG.

O=ESL, the two trailing periods refer to the container O=ESL.

Partial Name Example Exercise

The partial names for objects HP_PR1, FS1, VOL1, FS2, and BOB in figure 2.57 are listed in table 2.4 for different current context settings.

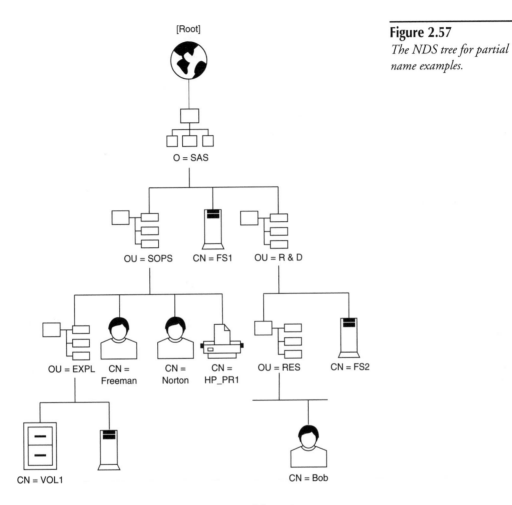

Figure 2.57
The NDS tree for partial name examples.

Table 2.4
Partial Name Examples

NDS Object	*Current Context*	*Partial Name*
HP_PR1	[Root]	CN=HP_PR1.OU=SOPS.O=SAS
HP_PR1	O=SAS	CN=HP_PR1.OU=SOPS
HP_PR1	OU=SOPS.O=SAS	CN=HP_PR1
HP_PR1	OU=R&D.O=SAS	CN=HP_PR1.OU=SOPS.

continues

Table 2.4, Continued
Partial Name Examples

NDS Object	Current Context	Partial Name
HP_PR1	OU=RES.OU=R&D.O=SAS	CN=HP_PR1.OU=SOPS..
HP_PR1	OU=EXPL.OU=SOPS.O=SAS	CN=HP_PR1.
FS1	[Root]	CN=FS1.O=SAS
FS1	O=SAS	CN=FS1
FS1	OU=SOPS.O=SAS	CN=FS1.
FS1	OU=EXPL.OU=SOPS.O=SAS	CN=FS1..
FS1	OU=R&D.O=SAS	CN=FS1.
FS1	OU=RES.OU=R&D.O=SAS	CN=FS1..
FS1_VOL1	[Root]	CN=FS1_VOL1.OU=EXPL.OU= SOPS.O=SAS
FS1_VOL1	O=SAS	CN=FS1_VOL1.OU=EXPL.OU=SOPS
FS1_VOL1	OU=SOPS.O=SAS	CN=FS1_VOL1.OU=EXPL
FS1_VOL1	OU=EXPL.OU=SOPS.O=SAS	CN=FS1_VOL1
FS1_VOL1	OU=R&D.O=SAS	CN=FS1_VOL1.OU=EXPL.OU=SOPS.
FS1_VOL1	OU=RES.OU=R&D.O=SAS	CN=FS1_VOL1.OU=EXPL.OU=SOPS..
FS2	[Root]	CN=FS2.OU=R&D.O=SAS
FS2	O=SAS	CN=FS2.OU=R&D
FS2	OU=SOPS.O=SAS	CN=FS2.OU=R&D.
FS2	OU=EXPL.OU=SOPS.O=SAS	CN=FS2.OU=R&D..
FS2	OU=R&D.O=SAS	CN=FS2
FS2	OU=RES.OU=R&D.O=SAS	CN=FS2.
BOB	[Root]	CN=BOB.OU=RES.OU=R&D.O=SAS
BOB	O=SAS	CN=BOB.OU=RES.OU=R&D
BOB	OU=SOPS.O=SAS	CN=BOB.OU=RES.OU=R&D.
BOB	OU=EXPL.OU=SOPS.O=SAS	CN=BOB.OU=RES.OU=R&D..

NDS Object	Current Context	Partial Name
BOB	OU=R&D.O=SAS	CN=BOB.OU=RES
BOB	OU=RES.OU=R&D.O=SAS	CN=BOB

Study Note Study the examples in table 2.4, so that you thoroughly understand how partial names can be formed.

Learning NDS Naming Rules

This section summarizes the naming rules discussed in many of the examples in this chapter. Next are three important concepts that deal with NDS: path, typeless naming, and period rules.

NDS Path

The NDS path name consists of a list of object names that are written left to right, beginning with the referenced object and leading up to either the [Root] object or the current context. If the object name is preceded with a period (.), the object names refer to the complete name and must lead up to the [Root]. If the NDS path name does not have a leading period, then it refers to a partial name.

Typeless Name

The complete name of the object, in addition to beginning with a period, uses the attribute type names CN, OU, O, and C to designate the type of the object as being a Common Name, Organizational Unit, Organization, and Country object, respectively.

Typeless names are NDS names that do not have the attribute type designators of CN, OU, O, or C. The following are examples of typeless names:

- Mary.CORP.IBM
- .Lisa.CORP.ESL
- OPS.ICS.US
- .Linda.SALES.LONDON.UK

When NDS encounters a typeless name, it resolves it to a complete name and supplies the appropriate attribute types.

The use of typeless names involves less typing on the part of the network administrator and can simplify the use of NDS names.

Author's Note Prior to NetWare 4.1, Novell did not recommend the use of the Country object because the NetWare 4 libraries and clients made the assumption that the top-level container was an organization container. In the NetWare 4.02 release, it was possible to use Country objects in typeless names, if the current context included a Country object and it had the same number of objects as the name being resolved. All these complex rules of resolving typeless names have been removed in NetWare 4.1 (and higher).

continues

With current releases of NetWare 4, NDS resolves the typeless name correctly regardless of whether it includes a Country object.

If your organization wants to interoperate with the *AT&T NetWare Connect Services* (*ANCS*) and other X.500 Directories that use the *North American Directory Forum* (*NADF*), you should design your directory with the Country object at the top. You should also follow the NADF naming standards for X.500 environments.

Setting Context at the Workstation

NetWare 4 client software provides the capability to set the current context before a user logs in to the workstation. This is provided by the Name Context configuration setting in the NET.CFG file. The NET.CFG file is processed at the time the NetWare client software drivers and the network requester software are started.

The format of the name context is as follows:

```
NAME CONTEXT = "NDS Complete Path of Context"
```

The NET.CFG statements are case-insensitive and can be entered in upper- or lowercase.

Suppose that it is desired to set the current context at the time of login for user Bob to the following:

```
OU=CORP.O=SCS
```

This can be done by including the following statement in the NET.CFG file:

```
Name Context = "OU=CORP.O=SCS"
```

 You cannot enter a leading period (.) in the name context parameter. For example, the following is illegal in the NET.CFG file:

```
NAME CONTEXT=".OU=CORP.O=SCS"
```

The name context can be explicitly changed by using the CX (Change Context) command, before logging in to the network. Placing the Name Context statement in NET.CFG is a convenience to the user because it can simplify access to the network resources the user most frequently uses. For this reason, it is best to place the name context in the container that contains the resources a user is most likely to use. If the name context of a user is set to the container that contains the User object, login to the network is possible by using the following command:

```
LOGIN  UserLoginName
```

For user BOB this would be as simple as the following:

```
LOGIN BOB
```

If the name context is set to a different context from the location of the User object, the user would have to use the NDS path to the User object:

```
LOGIN NDSPathToUserObject
```

For user BOB, whose User object is defined in OU=CORP.O=SCS, this would be

```
LOGIN  .CN=BOB.OU=CORP.O=SCS
```

or

```
LOGIN  .BOB.CORP.SCS
```

The second form demonstrates the use of the typeless complete name, whereas the first form shows the User object by its complete name with attribute designators (also called *typeful name* or *typed name*).

Using the Command Line for NDS Queries

The following are the two primary command line utilities for browsing the NDS tree:

■ CX (Change Context)

■ NLIST (Network List)

Used together, the CX and NLIST utilities provide a flexible and powerful mechanism for browsing and searching NDS object names and properties.

The CX Utility

The CX utility is used to change the current context. When used by itself without any parameters and options, you can employ it to find out the current context. Thus the command CX from the DOS prompt, as shown in the following example, indicates that the current context is set to O=ESL.

```
F> CX
ESL
F> CD
F:\SYSTEM
```

The command in bold is the command a user types in, and the other text is the system's response. In the preceding commands, F> is the system (DOS) prompt; and the O=ESL and the F:\SYSTEM are the results that appear after the respective execution of the CX and CD commands.

The CX command is very similar to the CD command, which enables the user to display or change the current directory for a file system. It is important to keep in mind that the CX operates on the NDS directory and not the file system directory. Changing the NDS directory context does not change the current file system directory. Therefore, in the preceding example, the CX command reveals that the current context is O=ESL, and the CD command reveals that the current directory is F:\SYSTEM. Changing the current context has no effect on the current directory setting, and changing the current directory has no effect on the current context setting.

The commands that follow refer to the NDS tree in figure 2.58.

To change the current context to OU=CORP.O=ESL, you can issue the following command:

```
F> CX  .OU=CORP.O=ESL
CORP.ESL
```

Notice that the CX command always returns the current context; this is a quick check to see if the CX command works correctly.

In the preceding command, the complete name .OU=CORP.O=ESL is used. You also can use typeless names because no Country object exists in the NDS tree. For instance, the command that follows has the same effect as the preceding command:

```
F> CX  .CORP.ESL
CORP.ESL
```

To go back one container level above, you can issue this command:

```
F> CX  .
ESL
```

The period (.) following the CX command means that you want to change your context to the parent container. You can combine periods to go up several container levels. The example that follows illustrates this:

```
F> CX
CORP.ESL
F> CX ..
[Root]
```

In the preceding example, the current container is OU=CORP.O=ESL. Using the command CX.., go two container levels up, which in this case is the [Root] container.

What would happen if you tried to go three container levels above if your current context is OU=CORP.O=ESL?

```
F> CX
CORP.ESL
```

```
F> CX ...
CX-4.20-260: An internal system error
occurred during CX's attempt to canonicalize
the context: (...)
```

If an attempt is made to change the context to a location that does not exist in the NDS tree, an error message appears.

To change the context to the [Root] you can use the /R option:

```
F> CX /R
[Root]
```

To view all container objects (tree structure) below your current context or specified context, you can use the /T option:

```
F> CX
[Root]
F> CX /T
```

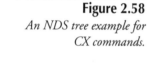

Figure 2.58

An NDS tree example for CX commands.

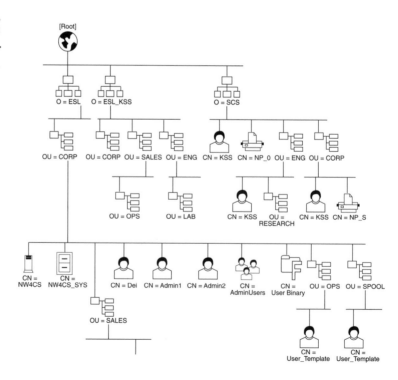

Figure 2.59 shows the output of the CX /T command issued from the [Root].

You can combine the /R with other options such as /T. If /R is combined with /T, the CX /T command is issued from the root of the tree, but the context is not changed. You can, thus, type the following commands:

```
F> CX .CORP.ESL
CORP.ESL
F> CX /T /R
F> CX
CORP.ESL
```

The command CX /T /R produces the same output as in figure 2.55, but the context before and after executing the command remains the same (OU=CORP.O=ESL).

The /A (or /ALL) option enables you to view all objects at or below the current context. It is meant to be used in conjunction with options like the /T option:

```
F> CX
CORP.ESL
F> CX /T /A
```

The command CX /T /A produces an output that is shown in figure 2.60.

You can combine the CX /T /A command with the /R option. For instance:

```
F> CX
CORP.ESL
F> CX /T /A /R
F> CX
CORP.ESL
```

The CX /T /A /R command shows all objects beginning from the [Root], but the context remains the same (OU=CORP.O=ESL) before and after executing the commands.

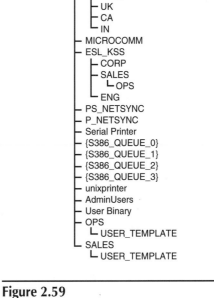

Figure 2.59

The CX /T command issued from the [Root].

To view only Container objects at a specified level, you can use the /CONT option:

```
F> CX
CORP.ESL
F> CX /CONT
```

You can combine the /CONT command with /A to see all objects within the container only:

```
F> CX
CORP.ESL
F> CX /CONT /A
```

Figure 2.61 shows the output of using the CX /CONT /A command in the current context OU=CORP.O=ESL.

What is the difference between the CX /CONT /A and the CX /T /A commands? Compare figure 2.61 with figure 2.60. The CX /CONT /A displays all objects in the current context only, whereas the CX /T /A displays all objects in the current context and in the containers below the current context.

If the CX /CONT /A is combined with the /R option, what output appears?

```
F> CX
CORP.ESL
F> CX /CONT /A /R
F> CX
CORP.ESL
```

Figure 2.61 shows the output of using the CX /CONT /A /R command in the current context OU=CORP.O=ESL. Notice that the current context before and after executing this command does not change, even though the /R option displays the tree starting from the [Root] object.

You can use the CX command with typeless and partial names. If the current context in figure 2.58 is O=ESL, for instance, the partial typeless name to change the context to OU=CORP.O=ESL is as follows:

```
F> CX
ESL
```

```
F> CX  CORP
CORP.ESL
```

If the current context is O=ESL, the following is the partial typeless name to change the context to OU=SALES.OU=CORP.O=ESL:

```
F> CX
ESL
F> CX  SALES.CORP
SALES.CORP.ESL
```

If the current context is [Root], the partial typeless name to change context to O=SCS is as follows:

```
F> CX
[Root]
F> CX SCS
SCS
```

If the current context is O=SCS, the partial typeless name to change context to O=ESL is the following:

```
F> CX
SCS
F> CX ESL.
ESL
```

The preceding example uses the trailing period rule to go one container above the current context.

If the current context is OU=CORP.O=scs, the partial typeless name to change context to OU=SALES.OU=CORP.O=ESL is this:

```
F> CX
CORP.SCS
F> CX SALES.CORP.ESL..
ESL
```

The preceding example uses the trailing period rule to go two containers above the current context.

To view additional help on using the CX command, type the following command:

```
CX /?
```

Figure 2.62 shows the two help screens that appear after you type the **CX /?** command. Table 2.6 also summarizes many common CX options.

```
CORP.ESL
  ├─ NW4CS
  ├─ NW4CS_SYS
  ├─ NW4CS_VOL1
  ├─ Dei
  ├─ Backup Operation
  ├─ Admin1
  ├─ Q_0
  ├─ PS_0
  ├─ P_0
  ├─ PF
  ├─ Anonymous
  ├─ NW4KS
  ├─ BackupOp
  ├─ Jan
  ├─ WMgr
  ├─ HACKER
  ├─ UNIXUSER
  ├─ Linksys Ps1
  ├─ QLINK1
  ├─ PLINK1
  ├─ NW4CS_VOLS
  ├─ S386+543
  ├─ Everyone
  ├─ Guest
  ├─ Karanjit
  ├─ QUEUE_0
  ├─ QUEUE_1
  ├─ QUEUE_2
  ├─ QUEUE_3
  ├─ Students
  ├─ Nobody
  ├─ Nogroup
  ├─ Nfsgroup
  ├─ User2
  ├─ Kss
  ├─ Test
  ├─ User1
  ├─ Corporate
  ├─ Engineers
  ├─ Marketing
  ├─ Newuser
  └─ Q_NETSYNC
```

Figure 2.60

The result of the CX /T /A command issued from the OU=CORP.O=ESL context.

```
CORP.ESL
  ├─ NW4CS
  ├─ NW4CS_SYS
  ├─ NW4CS_VOL1
  ├─ Dei
  ├─ Backup Operation
  ├─ Admin1
  ├─ Q_0
  ├─ PS_0
  ├─ P_0
  ├─ PF
  ├─ Anonymous
  ├─ NW4KS
  ├─ BackupOp
  ├─ Jan
  ├─ WMgr
  ├─ HACKER
  ├─ UNIXUSER
  ├─ Linksys Ps1
  ├─ QLINK1
  ├─ PLINK1
  ├─ NW4CS_VOLS
  ├─ S386+543
  ├─ Everyone
  ├─ Guest
  ├─ Karanjit
  ├─ QUEUE_0
  ├─ QUEUE_1
  ├─ QUEUE_2
  ├─ QUEUE_3
  ├─ Students
  ├─ Nobody
  ├─ Nogroup
  ├─ Nfsgroup
  ├─ User2
  ├─ Kss
  ├─ Test
  ├─ User1
  ├─ Corporate
  ├─ Engineers
  ├─ Marketing
  ├─ Newuser
  ├─ Q_NETSYNC
  ├─ PS_NETSYNC
  ├─ P_NETSYNC
  ├─ Serial Printer
  ├─ {S386_QUEUE_0}
  ├─ {S386_QUEUE_1}
  ├─ {S386_QUEUE_2}
  ├─ {S386_QUEUE_3}
  ├─ unixprinter
  ├─ AdminUsers
  ├─ User Binary
  └─ OPS
```

Figure 2.61

The CX /CONT /A command from the OU=CORP.O=ESL context.

Figure 2.62

The CX /? Help screens.

CX	Options Help	v4.00

Syntax: CX [new context] [R] [/T ∣ CONT] [/ALL]] [/C] [/?]

To:	Use:
view all container objects below the current or specified context.	/T
view container objects at the current or specified level.	/CONT
modify /T or /CONT to view ALL objects at or below the context	/ALL
change context or view objects relative to root	/R

For example, to:	Type:
view directory tree below the current context	CX /T
view containers within a specific context	CX .O=Novell /CONT

CX	General Usage Help	v4.00

Purpose: View and set current context.
Syntax: CX [new context] [/Root] [/[Tree ∣ CONT] [/All]] [/C] [/?]

New context:
    A context can be entered either relative to your current context or
    as a distinguished name relative to the directory root.
    Use trailing periods (.) to change to a context relative to a higher
    level of your current context.
    To change to a context relative to the root of the directory put a period
    at the beginning of the new context or use the /Root flag.

To view your current context type CX
Current context is OU=Engineering.O=Novell

For example, to change context:	Type:
O=Novell	CX
OU=Testing.OU=Engineering.O=Novell	CX OU=Testing
OU=Marketing.O=Novell	CX OU=Marketing.

Table 2.5
Common CX Options

Command	Description
CX .	Changes context to one container above current context
CX	Displays current context
CX /R	Changes context to root of NDS tree
CX /T	Views all container objects below current or specified context
CX /T /A	Views all objects in current context and below

Command	Description
CX /CONT	Views container objects at current or specified context only
CX /CONT /A	Views all objects at current context or specified context only
CX *new_context*	Changes context to specified context
CX /?	Obtains CX Help screens

 Use figure 2.62 and table 2.5 as a summary of the options before taking your exams.

The NLIST Command

By using the NLIST command, you can view information on different object classes. The information appears in a convenient tabular form. NLIST is the fundamental command line utility for extracting information on NDS objects. You can use NLIST to set up general-purpose queries that will search NDS objects based upon a number of search criteria, such as the following:

■ Property values

■ Existence of properties

■ A specific branch of the NDS tree

If you want to search for all the active users connected to the network, use the /A option, such as the command:

```
F> NLIST USER /A
Object Class: User
Current context: ESL
Conn          = The server connection number
*             = The asterisk means this is
               ➥your connection
User Name     = The login name of the user
Address       = The network address
```

```
Node          = The network node
Login time    = The time when the user
               ➥logged in
User Name          Address        Node
*Admin          [   E8022][    C024282D]
One User object was found in this context.
One User object was found.
```

The output of all NLIST commands produces a legend that describes the columns for the tabular information that is displayed.

An asterisk next to a connection means that the connection is your connection to the server. The output of this command is equivalent to the USERLIST /A command in NetWare 3.*x*.

To see all User objects defined in the current context and subcontainers, use the /S option:

```
F> CX
OU=CORP.O=ESL
F> NLIST USER /S
Object Class: User
Current context: CORP.ESL
User name= The name of the user
Dis           = Login disabled
Log exp       = The login expiration date, 0
➥if no expiration date
Pwd           = Yes if passwords are required
Pwd exp  = The password expiration date, 0 if
➥no expiration date
Uni   = Yes if unique passwords are required
Min   = The minimum password length, 0 if no
➥minimum
```

```
User Name    Dis  Log Exp Pwd  Pwd Exp Uni Min
-----------------------------------------------
Dei          No   0-00-00 No   0-00-00 No  0
Admin1       Yes  0-00-00 Yes  0-00-00 No  8
Admin2       No   9-01-99 No   0-00-00 No  5
A total of 3 USER objects was found in this
➥context.
Object Class: User
Current context: SPOOL.CORP.ESL
User Name    Dis  Log Exp Pwd  Pwd Exp Uni Min
-----------------------------------------------
USER_TEMPLATE No   0-00-00 No   0-00-00 No 0
One USER object was found in this context.
Object Class: User
Current context: SALES.CORP.ESL
User Name    Dis  Log Exp Pwd  Pwd Exp Uni Min
-----------------------------------------------
USER_TEMPLATE No   0-00-00 No   0-00-00 No 0
One USER object was found in this context.
Object Class: User
Current context: OPS.CORP.ESL
User Name    Dis  Log Exp Pwd  Pwd Exp Uni Min
-----------------------------------------------
USER_TEMPLATE No   0-00-00 No   0-00-00 No 0
One USER object was found in this context.
A total of 6 USER objects was found.
```

As you can see from the last two NLIST commands, the output always begins with the object class specified in the NLIST command. The current context is listed next, followed by the information returned by NLIST for the current context.

The NLIST USER /S command was issued from the context OU=CORP.O=ESL. It lists all the users found in the context OU=CORP.O=ESL and all users defined in subcontainers below this context. A total of three User objects are defined in the context OU=CORP.O=ESL. User Dei is not disabled and has no login expiration dates. User Dei also does not have unique password or minimum password length restrictions. User Admin1, on the other hand, is disabled and has required password, unique password, and eight-character

minimum password length restrictions. User Admin2 is not disabled, but the login account expires on 9-1-99; and although no password uniqueness is enforced for this user, the minimum password length is five characters. The subcontainers OU=SPOOL.OU=CORP.O=ESL, OU=SALES.OU=CORP.O=ESL, and OU=OPS. OU=CORP.O=ESL are searched next. Each reveals a User object with the name USER_TEMPLATE, which, like user Dei in the container above, has no restrictions. You learn later that you can use the user USER_TEMPLATE in a container as a model for other users created within that container.

To see property details for a specific user, such as user DEI, use the following command:

```
F> NLIST USER=DEI  /D
Object Class: User
Current context: CORP.ESL
User: Dei
     Name: Dei
     Object Trustees (ACL):
          Subject: Dei
          Property:  [All Properties
                      ➥Rights]
          Property Rights: [ R   ]
     Object Trustees (ACL):
          Subject: Dei
          Property: Login Script
          Property Rights: [ RW  ]
     Object Trustees (ACL):
          Subject: [Public]
          Property: Default Server
          Property Rights: [ R   ]
     Object Trustees (ACL):
          Subject: [Root]
          Property: Group Membership
          Property Rights: [ R   ]
     Object Trustees (ACL):
          Subject: Dei
          Property: Print Job Configuration
          Property Rights: [ RW  ]
```

```
Object Trustees (ACL):
      Subject: [Root]
      Property: Network Address
      Property Rights: [ R   ]
Full Name: Dei Siyan
Given Name: Dei
Group Membership: Manager.SCS..
Home Directory:
      Volume Name: NW4CS_SYS
      Path: USERS\Dei
      Name Space Type: DOS
Middle Initial: G
Language:
      English
Default Server: NW4CS
Object Class: User
Object Class: Organizational Person
Object Class: Person
Object Class: Top
Revision: 5
Security Equal To: Manager.SCS..
Last Name: Siyan
Title: Finance Controller
-----------------------------------------

One User object was found in this context.

One User object was found.
```

The output of the NLIST USER=Dei /D command gives detailed information on the properties for that object. Some of the properties listed for the

user are [All Properties Rights], Login Script, Default Server, Group Membership, Printer Job Configuration, Network Address, Home Directory, Language, Full Name, Given Name, Middle Initial, Group Membership, Language, Title, and Last Name.

 Notice that in the NLIST USER=Dei /D command, the following lines appear at the end:

Object Class: User

Object Class: Organizational Person

Object Class: Person

Object Class: Top

The preceding lines indicate the derivation hierarchy for User object Dei. The base class for User object Dei is User class. This is derived from the Organizational Person superclass, which is derived from the superclass Person, which is, in turn, derived from superclass Top.

The derivation principles used in NDS were discussed in an earlier Author Note in this chapter.

To search for user KSS in current container and all subcontainers, use the following command:

```
F> CX
SCS
F> NLIST USER=KSS /S
Object Class: User
Current context: SCS
User name     = The name of the user
Dis           = Login disabled
Log exp       = The login expiration date, 0 if no expiration date
Pwd           = Yes if passwords are required
Pwd exp       = The password expiration date, 0 if no expiration date
Uni           = Yes if unique passwords are required
Min           = The minimum password length, 0 if no minimum
User Name                     Dis  Log Exp Pwd  Pwd Exp Uni Min
KSS                           No   0-00-00 No   0-00-00 No   0
```

```
One USER object was found in this context.
Object Class: User
Current context: CORP.SCS
User Name                                 Dis  Log Exp Pwd  Pwd Exp Uni Min
----------------------------------------------------------------------------
KSS                                       No   0-00-00 No   0-00-00 No  0
One USER object was found in this context.
Object Class: User
Current context: ENG.SCS
User Name                                 Dis  Log Exp Pwd  Pwd Exp Uni Min
KSS                                       No   0-00-00 No   0-00-00 No   0
One USER object was found in this context.
```

The NLIST USER=KSS /S command finds all occurrences of User object KSS in the current context and all subcontainers.

To see all Printer objects within the current context and all subcontainers, issue this command:

```
F>CX
SCS
F> NLIST PRINTER /S
Current context: SCS
Partial Name                                        Object Class
----------------------------------------------------------------------
NP_0                                                Printer
One PRINTER object was found in this context.
Current context: CORP.SCS
Partial Name                                        Object Class
NP_0                                                Printer
One PRINTER object was found in this context.
A total of 2 PRINTER objects was found.
```

To search for a specific property value for an object class such as the User object class in the current context and all subcontainers, enter the following command:

```
F> CX
SCS
F> NLIST USER SHOW "Telephone Number"  /S
Object Class: User
Current context: scs
User: Manager1
     Telephone: 310-434-3344
User: Manager2
     Telephone: 310-444-4435
User: KSS
     Telephone: 415-333-4655
```

```
A total of 3 User objects was found in this context.

Object Class: User
Current context: ENG.scs
User: AMY
        Telephone: 310-444-4354
One User object was found in this context.

Object Class: User
Current context: CORP.scs
User: Linda
        Telephone: 510-233-3432
One User object was found in this context.

A total of 5 User objects was found.
```

If the /S option is left out in the preceding command (NLIST USER SHOW "Telephone Number"), only the phone numbers for users in the current context of OU=CORP.O=SCS would be displayed.

To see a specific value for a specific object, use the following:

```
F> CX
CORP.ESL
F> NLIST SERVER=NW4CS SHOW "Network Address"
Object Class: Server
Current context: CORP.ESL
Server: NW4CS
IPX/SPX Network Address
Network: F0000055
Node: 1
Socket: 451
One SERVER object was found in this context.
One SERVER object was found.
F> CX .O=SCS
SCS
F> NLIST PRINTER="NP_0" SHOW "Location" /S
Current context: SCS
Printer: NP_0
Location: Building 6, Room 404
- - - - - - - - - - - - - - - - - - - - - - - - - - - - - - - -
One PRINTER object was found in this context.
Current context: CORP.SCS
Printer: NP_0
Location: Engineering Lab Bldg, Printer Room
➥5
- - - - - - - - - - - - - - - - - - - - - - - - - - - - - - - -
One PRINTER object was found in this context.
A total of 2 PRINTER objects was found.
```

In the NLIST SERVER command, the network address of server NW4CS is queried. The network address that is reported is the internal software address of the server that consists of the internal network number, the socket number, and the node number, which is always set to 1. The internal network number is selected during installation, and the socket number identifies the file service process that handles incoming requests. The NLIST PRINTER command shows the location of the Printer object NP_0. The /S option helps find this Printer object in the current context of O=SCS and all subcontainers. Without the /S option, only the Printer object located at Building 6, Room 404 would be found, and the Printer object at location Engineering Lab Bldg, Printer Room 5 would not show up.

To search for all objects with a specific property value, use the WHERE option with the NLIST command:

```
F> CX
SCS
F> NLIST USER WHERE "Title" EQ ENGINEER
Object Class: User
Current context: SCS
User name= The name of the user
Dis          = Login disabled
Log exp   = The login expiration date, 0 if
➥no expiration date
Pwd          = Yes if passwords are required
```

```
Pwd exp  = The password expiration date, 0 if
➥no expiration date
Uni         = Yes if unique passwords are
➥required
Min         = The minimum password length, 0
➥if no minimum
User Name
Dis  Log Exp Pwd  Pwd Exp Uni Min
-------------------------------------------
KSS No  0-00-00 No  0-00-00   No  0
One USER object was found in this context.
One USER object was found.
F> NLIST USER=KSS SHOW TITLE
Object Class: User
Current context: SCS
User: KSS
Title: Engineer
One USER object was found in this context.
One USER object was found.
```

In the preceding commands, the quotes ("") are placed around property names and values that have spaces around them; otherwise, they are optional. Also the EQ operator for comparison can be replaced by the equal symbol (=). This means that each of the following commands is equivalent and produces the same results:

```
NLIST USER WHERE "Title" EQ ENGINEER
NLIST USER WHERE "Title" = ENGINEER
NLIST USER WHERE "Title" = "ENGINEER"
NLIST USER WHERE Title = "ENGINEER"
NLIST USER WHERE Title = ENGINEER
```

Table 2.6 summarizes the common NLIST options.

The help screens obtained from using the NLIST /? command are displayed in figures 2.63 to figures 2.66. Figure 2.63 is the top-level help, and the other figures are the specific help screens described in the top-level help. These help screens are shown here for your reference.

 Use figures 2.63 to 2.67 and table 2.5 as a summary for studying the NLIST command before taking the certification test.

Table 2.6
Common NDS Options

Command	Description
NLIST USER /A	Displays active users logged in to the network
NLIST VOLUME /S	Displays all volumes in the current context and subcontainers
NLIST USER=Dei /D	Shows detailed property values for a user
NLIST USER=KSS /S	Searches for a specific object in current context and all subcontainers
NLIST SERVER=FS1	Shows a specific property for a SHOW "Network Address" specific User object
NLIST PRINTER WHERE	Searches for objects that have a "LOCATION"=LAB specific property value
NLIST /?	Displays top-level help screen for NLIST

```
NLIST                   General Help Screen                  4.19

Purpose: View information about users, groups and other objects.
Syntax: NLIST class type [property search option]
                         [display option] [basic option]

For details on:                            Type:
  Property search options                  NLIST /? R
  Properties                               NLIST /? P
  Display options                          NLIST /? D
  Basic options                            NLIST /? B
  All Help Screens                         NLIST /? ALL

Class types:
  * (all class types)      User            Print Queue
  Server                   Group           Printer
  Computer                 Volume          Print Server
  Directory Map            Profile         Organization
  Organizational Unit      Alias           AFP Server

Enclose in double quotes all class types or properties containing spaces.
```

Figure 2.63

NLIST /? : Top-level help screen for NLIST.

```
NLIST                   Basic Options Help Screen            4.19

Purpose: Specify basic options for viewing objects.
Syntax: NLIST class type [= object name] [basic option]

To display:                                Use:
  Active users or servers                  /A
  Objects throughout all subordinate contexts   /S
  Objects in a specified context           /CO <context>
  Objects at [ROOT] context                /R
  Continuously without pausing             /C
  Bindery information                      /B
  Version information                      /VER
  Available Directory Services trees       /TREE

For example, to:                           Type:
  See servers in all subordinate contexts  NLIST Server /S
  See logged in users (active)             NLIST User /A
  See volumes in the context O=My Org      NLIST Volume /CO "O=My Org"
  See servers in bindery mode              NLIST Server /B
  See Directory trees in bindery mode      NLIST /Tree = *
```

Figure 2.64

NLIST /? B : Basic Options help screen for NLIST.

```
NLIST                   Property Search Help Screen          4.19

Purpose: Search for objects by property value
Syntax: NLIST object class [ = object name]
              WHERE property <operator> value

Operators:
  EQ = Equal                 LE = Less than or equal
  NE = Not Equal             GT = Greater than
  LT = Less than             GE = Greater than or equal
  EXISTS = property exists   NEXISTS = property does not exist

For example, to:               Type:
  See all users whose
    Login Grace Limit is greater   NLIST User WHERE
    than 0                               "Grace Logins Allowed" GT 0
  See all users whose
    telephone number begins      NLIST User WHERE
    with 801                           "Telephone" EQ 801*
  See all queues which have
    an operator                  NLIST Print Queue WHERE Operator EXISTS

::\>_
```

Figure 2.65

NLIST /? R : Property Search Options help screen for NLIST.

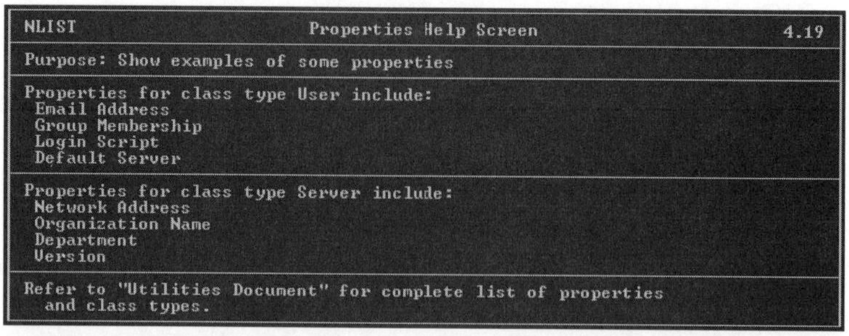

Figure 2.66
NLIST /? P : Properties help screen for NLIST.

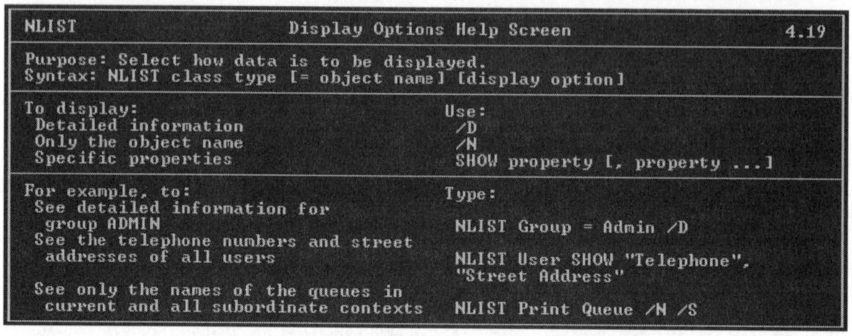

```
NLIST                    Properties Help Screen                    4.19
Purpose: Show examples of some properties

Properties for class type User include:
  Email Address
  Group Membership
  Login Script
  Default Server

Properties for class type Server include:
  Network Address
  Organization Name
  Department
  Version

Refer to "Utilities Document" for complete list of properties
  and class types.
```

Figure 2.67
NLIST /? D : Display Options help screen for NLIST.

```
NLIST                  Display Options Help Screen                  4.19
Purpose: Select how data is to be displayed.
Syntax: NLIST class type [= object name] [display option]

To display:                           Use:
  Detailed information                  /D
  Only the object name                  /N
  Specific properties                   SHOW property [, property ...]

For example, to:                      Type:
  See detailed information for
    group ADMIN                         NLIST Group = Admin /D
  See the telephone numbers and street
    addresses of all users              NLIST User SHOW "Telephone",
                                          "Street Address"
  See only the names of the queues in
    current and all subordinate contexts  NLIST Print Queue /N /S
```

Using the NetWare Administrator Tool for NDS Queries

You can generate NDS queries by using a graphical user interface tool such as the NetWare Administrator tool.

Start the Search option by performing the following steps:

1. Start NetWare Administrator tool.

2. Highlight the container object from which the search is to be carried out. If you want to search the entire NDS tree, highlight the [Root] object.

3. Select **O**bject, Sear**c**h.

After the preceding steps, you should see a screen similar to that shown in figure 2.68. The Start **F**rom text box indicates the starting point of the search, and can be set to any container object in the NDS tree. The Browse icon, next to this value can be used to browse for an appropriate container, as you can see in figure 2.69. The default is to search the entire subtree as indicated by the default check mark on the Search Entire Sub**t**ree box.

Several other object classes are listed in the **S**earch For file. In addition to the standard object classes, you can use classifications to aid in finding the objects. Table 2.7 lists these additional classifications.

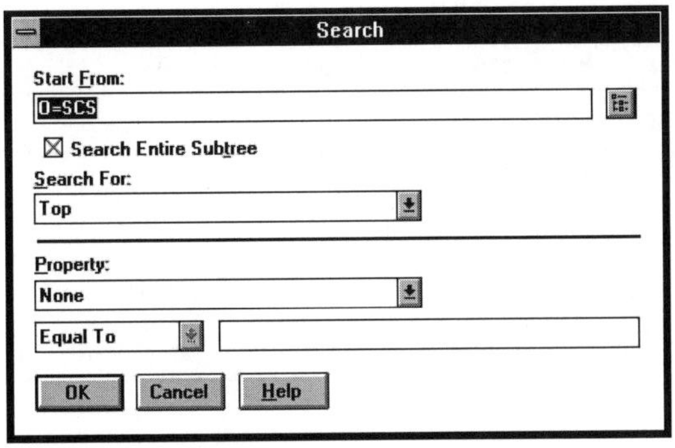

Figure 2.68
The Search option in the NetWare Administrator tool.

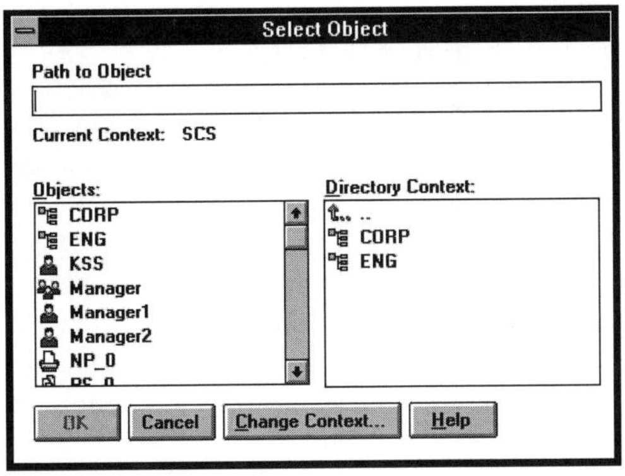

Figure 2.69
The Select Object panel used for browsing to set the value of Start From in the Search option.

Table 2.7
Additional Object Classifications for Search Options

Object Classification	Description
Device	Includes all computer and Printer objects
Locality	Not used by NDS, currently; but can be used by third-party products and tools
Organizational person	Lists all users
Partition	Used by the Partition Manager tool to indicate containers on top of a separate partition

continues

Table 2.7, Continued
Additional Object Classifications for Search Options

Object Classification	Description
Person	Includes all users
Resource	Includes printer queue and Volume objects
Server	Includes NetWare server, print server, and AFP server
Top	Includes every object in the container that is being searched

The **P**roperties list box enables you to select from the different properties that you want to search for. The comparison operators include Equal, Not Equal To, Not Present, and Present. You have a field for entering the actual property value that you want to search for.

Figure 2.70 shows the results of searching all Organizational Unit objects in the container O=SCS and its subcontainers. This figure shows that three Organizational Unit objects are found:

```
OU=CORP.O=SCS
OU=ENG.O=SCS
OU=RESEARCH.OU=ENG.O=SCS
```

Considering NDS Partitions

An NDS partition is a subset of the entire NDS database. The NDS global database must physically reside on a storage volume. Consider the following options that are available:

■ Should the entire NDS database be centralized?

■ Should you take subsets of the NDS database and distribute them? If the data base is distributed, what factors should determine how the database is to be distributed?

If the database is centralized, then a failure in the network at the central location would make the

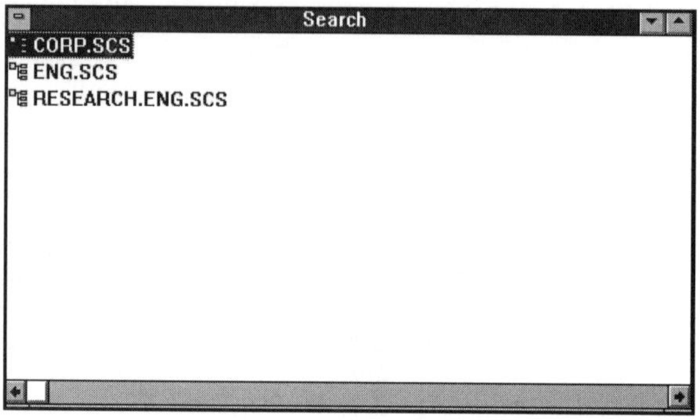

Figure 2.70

The Search results for all Organizational Unit objects in the O=SCS NDS database.

NDS database unavailable to the entire network. For small LANs, the issue of centralization is not of as much concern. But for large networks separated by wide area network links, centralization can become a reliability problem.

It is best, then, to distribute the database in such a manner so that a single failure does not disable the entire NDS service. The logical division (subset) of an NDS database is called a *partition*. The partition contains the resources (leaf objects) and also the organizational structure of a portion of the NDS tree (container objects). The partition does not contain any information on the file system structure of a network volume.

When Novell introduced NetWare 4.0, it recommended that a partition should not contain more than 500 objects. Later releases have increased this limit to 100,000 objects per partition.

Partitions can help the NDS performance in the following ways:

- Dividing NDS database so that each NDS database serves local users

- Reducing the need for NDS searches and look-ups to be performed over the slower wide area links

Figure 2.71 shows an NDS database split into two partitions, with each partition residing on a LAN segment separated by a slow wide area link of 56 Kps. In this case, most of the NDS look-ups and searches are done against the local NDS partition, without having to search over the slow wide area link.

But there is a problem with figure 2.71. What if the storage volume on which the NDS partition resides crashes? Then, the portion of the NDS that is

implemented by the NDS partition is unavailable. Users are not able to access the resources represented by the failed NDS partition. To solve this problem, a technique called replication can be used.

Replication consists of keeping a copy of an NDS partition at another location, such as on another NetWare 4 server. For example in figure 2.71, suppose that Location A kept a copy of the NDS partition for Location B on its NetWare 4 server, and Location B kept a copy of the NDS partition for Location A on its NetWare 4 server. Figure 2.72 shows this scenario in which replicas are used. If the remote server were temporarily unavailable or if the wide area link were down, the NDS queries for objects at the remote location could be serviced by the replica. Another advantage of this is that, under normal conditions, NDS queries for objects at remote locations can be satisfied by the local replica. If the NDS partition at the remote location were to change as a result of new objects being added or old objects being deleted or any other change, then the NDS partitions can synchronize themselves by sending only the new information that has changed. This is a much more efficient way of doing NDS look-ups and maintaining consistency of the NDS database.

You can have an unlimited number of replicas for each partition. The replicas for the same partition form a *replica ring*. A replica ring is a set of servers that holds a replica of a given partition. In the example in figure 2.71, the replica ring of the [Root] partition is servers FS1 and FS2.

 Limit replicas to no more than eight to ten per partition.

Replicas provide the following advantages:

- Increase NDS fault tolerance and minimize risk of any single point of failure
- Provide fast access to NDS services across slow wide area links
- Provide login access to network even when the network is down

Because a replica is a copy of the NDS partition, NDS makes the following distinctions for replicas:

- Master replica
- Read-only replica
- Read/Write replica
- Subordinate references

The *Master replica* is the original partition created for representing a subset of the NDS database. The Master replica contains the authority for the objects defined on it. All other replicas must defer to information contained in the Master replica; that is, the Master replica, by definition, contains the most recent information, and only one Master replica can exist per partition. This replica is used by the NDS synchronization mechanism to update all other replicas. The Master replica is used to create all other replicas. You need to access the server that holds the Master replica if you plan on redefining a partition boundary by performing operations such as splitting or merging. Partition operations are done by using the Partition Manager tool or utility.

Figure 2.71

NDS partitions across a wide area link.

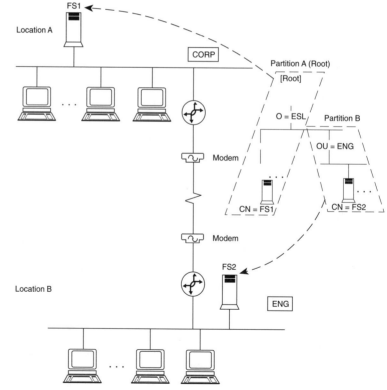

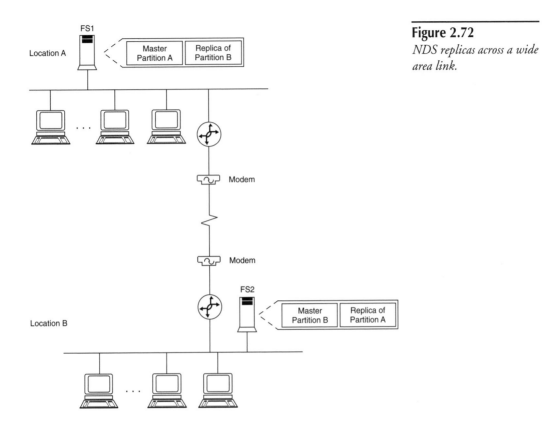

Figure 2.72

NDS replicas across a wide area link.

A *Read-only replica* contains a copy of the Master replica, but once created it cannot be modified. This is used to represent information that you can search for and view, but not change. It is similar to the concept of yellow pages on other directory systems. The Read-only replica is used as a database that can be queried, but it cannot be used for logging in to the network, because the login process modifies the NDS tree. For instance, the network address property of the User object that is logged in is altered to contain the station address of the workstation that the user is using.

A *Read/Write* replica can be used to update the NDS database and provide information to NDS queries. NDS objects in the Read/Write replica can be modified, deleted, or created; these changes are propagated to all other replicas of the partition. This replica can be used to answer NDS queries and enable users to log in to the network. To improve reliability, you can have multiple read/write replicas of a partition. You cannot use a read/write replica to redefine a partition boundary; you need a Master replica to perform this task. If the Master replica is corrupted or the server that holds the Master replica is down, you can make a read/write replica a Master replica. When the original Master replica come back online, it is deleted automatically, thus ensuring that there can be only one Master replica of a partition. Read/write replicas and Master replicas can be used for user authentication.

Subordinate reference is another partition type used by NDS for its internal operations. Subordinate references are maintained by NDS to enable *tree walking* operations. Tree walking is needed to access information on NDS objects that may be stored on another server. Tree walking refers to the process of accessing NDS objects stored in a replica that is on another server. Subordinate references do not contain NDS object data but point to the replica that does. A subordinate reference partition is automatically created on a server that holds the replica of a partition but not the child's partition. The subordinate reference points to the child's partition and acts as a pointer to the location (server) on which the child's partition exists. If you add a replica of the child partition to the server, there is no need to have a subordinate reference (pointer) to the child partition, because its replica exists on the server. In this case, the subordinate reference is automatically deleted from the server. Subordinate references are not managed or maintained by the network administrator—they are maintained by the NDS itself. You cannot use subordinate references for user authentication, viewing, searching, or managing NDS objects.

| **Author's Note** | Subordinate reference partition types existed in the earliest releases of NetWare 4. They are not a new type of partition. Their use has been documented more clearly starting with the release of NetWare 4. |

NDS partitions can be managed by the following:

■ PARTMGR.EXE, a DOS-based menu utility

■ Partition Manager option in the NetWare Administrator tool

You can use the partition manager to perform the following tasks on NDS partitions:

■ View existing NDS partitions

■ Split a partition

■ Merge partitions

Splitting a partition involves creating new partitions, and merging a partition results in deleting old partitions.

Figure 2.73 shows an NDS partition displayed using the Partition Manager GUI tool, and figure 2.74 shows the same partition using the PartMgr tool.

Cost of Synchronizing Replicas

Many NetWare 4 administration activities involve making changes to NDS objects. Changes made to NDS objects in a replica are propagated to all replicas in the replica ring. As the number of servers in a replica ring increase, the amount of time required for synchronization increases. The time cost of synchronization is further compounded when the servers in the replica ring are separated by low speed WAN links. The amount of time and network traffic needed for synchronization are the limiting factors that control the number of replicas that you can have. Novell recommends three or more replicas in a ring—the actual number depends on the cost of synchronization for the network.

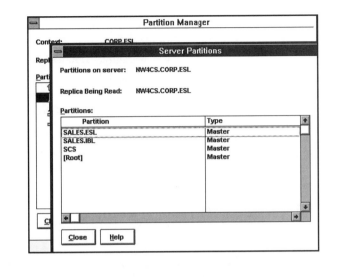

Figure 2.73

The Partition Manager used for viewing partitions.

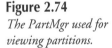

Figure 2.74

The PartMgr used for viewing partitions.

Default Partitions and Replicas

When a NetWare 4 server is installed in a container, whether a replica is created depends on how many servers already exist in the partition. The following rules summarize the creation of replicas:

■ The first partition is created on the first server that is installed in the directory. The Master replica is stored on the server on the SYS: volume. If this is the first server, a new NDS tree is created on the network, and the server will contain the Master replica of the [Root] partition.

■ If a new server is installed in an existing NDS container, the server object becomes part of the existing partition. No new partitions are created.

■ The second and third new servers receive a read/write replica of the partition; the fourth and subsequent servers do not receive any replicas.

When you merge NDS trees, servers in the source tree that contain replicas of the [Root] partition receive a read/write replica of the new [Root] of the target NDS tree. These servers also receive the subordinate reference to the [Root] partition's child partition. The servers in the target tree that contain the replica of the [Root] partition receive subordinate references for the top-level partition of the source NDS tree.

When you upgrade a NetWare 3.x server to a NetWare 4 server, the upgraded server receives a read/write replica of all partitions containing the server's bindery contexts.

Guidelines for Managing Partitions and Replicas

The following are some guidelines for managing partitions and replicas:

■ The [Root] partition is the most important of all the partitions. Consequently, you must create replicas of the [Root] partition to increase its reliability and availability. If the [Root] partition is lost, the NDS tree becomes inaccessible. You should not, however, create too many replicas of the [Root] and other high-level partitions because these partitions have multiple child partitions. Creating a replica of a [Root] partition on a server implies that the server will also receive subordinate references of all the child partitions, and this can increase the cost of synchronization.

■ Partition operations such as merging, creating, and deleting partitions affects subordinate references. You may, therefore, want to take into account the following:

    a) Do not create subordinate references linked across unreliable WAN links. If you want to make a partition change and the subordinate reference is not available, you will be unable to complete the partition operation.

    b) Reduce the number of subordinate references by observing the following:

       1. Create fewer partitions at the top of the tree, with more partitions at the lower level. This minimizes the number of subordinate references to the child partitions.

       2. Do not create unnecessary partitions. In general, create partitions that follow workgroup boundaries because workgroup boundaries generally determine how network resources are used and located in the NDS tree.

       3. Minimize the number of replicas of the [Root] and other parent partitions. This creates fewer subordinate references.

■ To meet fault tolerant needs, plan for three or more strategically placed replicas of each partition.

■ You may want to create replicas in strategically located servers to reduce login and access times for users.

■ Create partitions along workgroup boundaries. Place replicas of a partition physically close to the workgroup that needs the network resources in the partition.

■ If the network clients require bindery services, make sure that a local server contains the master, or read/write replica that contains the container specified in the bindery context. The bindery context is set by the SET BINDERY CONTEXT statement (usually placed kept in the AUTOEXEC.NCF file).

Moving Container Objects

You can move a container using the Partition Manager tool. This tool can be started from the Tools pull-down menu of the NetWare Administrator. To move a container, you must first make it the root of a partition, otherwise Partition Manager displays the message shown in fig. 2.75.

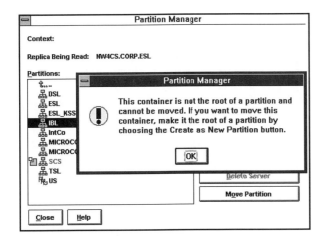

Figure 2.75
Move container warning message.

When moving containers, be aware that the complete names (distinguished names) of the NDS objects in the container being moved will change. As a result, you must perform the following:

■ Users logged in as User objects in the container being moved, must log out and log back in again with the changed NDS distinguished names.

■ Change the NAME CONTEXT= statement in the NET.CFG file for the user's workstation to the changed context of the User object.

Understanding Time Synchronization Techniques

In the preceding section, you learned that to provide fault tolerance and increase performance over slow wide area links, the NDS is partitioned and replicated. To keep the replicas properly updated, directory synchronization is used. This is done by a process called the *skulk* process that synchronizes the replicas with the updated information.

Any kind of global synchronization mechanism needs an accurate time reference that should be the same throughout the network. This ensures that the NDS operations would be timestamped accurately, regardless of where they are performed on the network. *Timestamps* are a unique code that records when the event took place, as well as the replica that originated it.

Accurate timestamps on NDS operations are essential to ensure that the NDS database is updated and synchronized correctly. A change made to a replica of a partition is propagated to all servers that are part of the replica ring. The timestamps are used for ordering the directory events that occur. For instance, the changes to NDS operations are done in the order in which their NDS modification requests are timestamped. If the timestamps on the modification requests do not have a common time reference, no guarantee can be made that the changes are made in the correct order. This could lead to all kinds of inconsistencies in the NDS database. The following is a partial list of server functions that need a consistent time standard across the network:

- Messaging applications need to timestamp messages.

- Operations performed on file systems need to apply a timestamp for changes that are made. Timestamps are recorded in the file system directory.

- NDS needs timestamps to properly collate changes to the NDS database.

It is important that all servers have the same time. Ideally, this time should match the *Universal Time Coordinated* (*UTC*) time, but this is not essential for NDS operations to be done reliably. To maintain the UTC time, an external time source is needed. The NetWare 4 time synchronization mechanism enables the use of external time sources. UTC corrects local time, and accounts for daylight savings time to give the equivalent *GMT* (*Greenwich Mean Time*). The following formula is used for calculating UTC:

```
UTC = local time ± time zone offset -
daylight savings offset
```

The time zone offset parameters are set during NetWare 4 server installation.

The type of time synchronization used on the network is identified during the NetWare 4 server installation. Because servers could reside in different time zones, the time zone must be selected accurately, and the local daylight savings time convention set correctly. For example, within the continental United States, certain areas do not use daylight savings time. The NetWare 4 server is flexible enough to use whatever method is used locally. If necessary, even the daylight savings time rules can be changed by programming them via

SET commands on the NetWare 4 server. All the time synchronization parameters can be set by the server SET command, including the rate at which the time servers synchronize.

The time synchronization choices during installation are as follows:

- Single Reference Time Servers (SRTS)

- Reference Time Servers (RTS)

- Primary Time Servers (PTS)

- Secondary Time Servers (STS)

The *Single Reference Time Server* is the default choice during a first-time installation. You can designate the first installed NetWare 4 server as the SRTS. The Single Reference Time Server is the authoritative time source on the network. All other servers synchronize their time to match the SRTS. Although the SRTS can be made to work for all kinds of networks, it is primarily recommended for small networks. For larger networks the SRTS acts as a single point of failure, and other mechanisms should be used. When SRTS is used, other types of time servers such as the Primary Time Server or the Reference Time Server cannot be used.

Practical TIP All servers on the network must be able to contact the SRTS because it is the only source of time.

Reference Time Servers are used to provide an external time source. They are designed to be accurate and usually synchronize their time from a radio clock that is slaved to the Naval Observatory or some other equally accurate time source. Another way of designing the RTS is to use a time synchronization NLM that contacts an accurate time source via modem, at regular intervals. An RTS can synchronize itself with an external time source, but it never adjusts its time from any other source on the network. For reliability, additional RTSs can be used, which should be strategically located at other points on the network. Because there could be differences in the time provided by the RTS, a voting method is used to decide the reference time that should be used on the network. All Reference Time Servers participate in this vote. If any Primary Time Servers exist, they too participate in the vote. The Primary Time Servers adjust their time to match the consensus reached as a result of the vote.

 Use an RTS when you need to have a central point to control accuracy of network time with respect to an external source.

 For large networks where synchronization with an accurate external clock is needed, a backup RTS is recommended.

Primary Time Servers synchronize their time by voting with at least one other PTS or RTS. In other words, a PTS must have another PTS or another RTS in order to synchronize its time. The network could have more than one PTS and RTS, in which case all the PTS and RTS time servers participate in the vote. Unlike an RTS, a PTS adjusts its time to match the common network time (a result of the

vote). The RTS and PTS servers poll each other to determine each other's time before casting their votes. While the PTSs are adjusting their clocks, the network time might drift slightly during the synchronization process. The other clients and servers take their time from the PTS. Having several PTSs on the network provides a measure of fault tolerance because as one PTS goes down another PTS can be used to provide an alternate time source.

 Use one PTS for every 125 to 150 Secondary Time Servers.

Secondary Time Servers synchronize their time from a PTS, RTS, or SRTS. Secondary Time Servers do not participate in the vote to obtain a common network time. If an SRTS is used, then all other servers must be Secondary Time servers and must have a path to the SRTS. If an SRTS is not used, the STS can obtain its time via PTS or RTS. To minimize network traffic and time synchronization delays, the STS should contact the nearest PTS or RTS, with a minimum of router hops and network segments between an STS and its time source.

 Secondary Time Servers do not provide time. Single Reference, Primary, and Reference Time Servers provide time and are called *time providers*.

Table 2.8 summarizes the different time server types and their chief characteristics.

Table 2.8
Time Server Types

Server Type	Time Source	Gets Time From	Adjusts Clock	Gives Time To	Description
SRTS	Yes	Hardware clock or external source	No	STS and clients	This is the default configuration. It cannot coexist with PTS and RTS. This is similar to the RTS with the difference that the SRTS claims to be always snychronized with the network time because it is the sole provider of the network time.
PTS	Yes	RTS. If there is no RTS, you must have at least one other PTS.	Yes Implements 50% correction per polling	STS and clients	PTS polls other time sources sources and votes to determine the correct network time and compensate for clock errors. The snychronization status is set based on its deviation from the calculated network time and is independent of the status of other time sources that are polled.
RTS	Yes	Hardware clock or external source	No	PTS, STS, and clients	Similar to PTS with the difference that it does not adjust its internal clock. It provides a central point of time for the entire network. RTS is assumed to be more reliable than PTS, and is therefore given a higher weight in computing common network time. You must have at leaset one PTS if you are using an RTS. Reliabilty of RTS time can be implemented

Server Type	Time Source	Gets Time From	Adjusts Clock	Gives Time To	Description
					using commerical products such as radio clocks and modems that communicate with external time sources such as atomic clocks.
STS	No	SRTS, PTS, or RTS	Yes Implements 100% correction per polling interval	Clients only	This is the default configuration if there exists an SRTS. STS does not participate in the voting process and attempts to remain synchronized with only one time source.

Methods of Time Synchronization

In NetWare 4 networks, you can use two methods for communication time synchronization information:

■ Default configuration that uses *SAP* (*Service Advertising Protocol*) to transmit and receive time

■ Custom configuration

Default Method for Time Synchronization

During NetWare 4 server installation, the installation program assumes that there are only two types of time servers: STS and SRTS. This method is simple and does not require time synchronization when new servers are added to the network.

The default method for time synchronization uses SAP to advertise time sources (PTS, RTS, SRTS).

PTS and RTS use SAP to communicate time synchronization information used for voting. Secondary time servers automatically learn where to get the network time from and require no additional configuration.

The default method is adequate for a small network with a small number of servers. Because SAP is used, the overhead introduced by it is not significant for small networks. However, as the network grows in size, and as sites are connected through relatively low-speed WAN links, the SAP overhead can become a substantial portion of the network traffic. If multiple sites separated by WAN links have a PTS or RTS at each site, SAP traffic carrying time synchronization information will have to go over the WAN links. If the WAN links are already close to the maximum capacity, the additional burden placed by time synchronization traffic could affect other network services.

The advantages of the default method for time synchronization are as follows:

■ It is easy to configure. In fact, no configuration file or configuration procedure exists. Use of SAP makes configuration automatic.

■ It is easy to understand.

■ No additional planning needs to be done.

■ The possibility of an error in synchronizing is reduced. There is no configuration error because manual configuration is not done. The time receiver, such as the STS, can only talk to other time sources such as the RTS, PTS, and SRTS. An STS will not talk to another STS.

The disadvantages of the default method for time synchronization are the following:

■ If SRTS is used, it represents a single point of failure. You can recover, by manually making an STS an SRTS by changing the TIME SERVER TYPE parameter on the server using the SET command or the SERVMAN.NLM.

■ If manual errors are made in misconfiguring a time server type—for example, accidentally creating another SRTS—then the STS can synchronize incorrectly to the wrong SRTS.

■ Use of SAP can add additional network traffic.

Custom Configuration Method for Time Synchronization

Custom configuration involves determining which servers are time sources, and deciding which servers will receive time from which time source. This means that custom configuration, unlike the default configuration is not automatic and requires some planning.

Each time server maintains a configuration file (TIMESYNC.CFG) that contains a list of authorized time sources for the server and other time related parameters. For the most part, you can copy the same configuration file to other servers and edit it to change the order in which time sources are to be contacted. The time source list should be ordered so that the closest time source appears first on the list; the least-cost (WAN speeds, communication costs) time sources should appear next in the order of increasing cost. Because the time sources that need to be contacted are listed explicitly, the custom configuration method cuts down on the amount of network traffic.

The following guidelines can be used for custom configuration:

■ STS can synchronize to the nearest PTS, RTS, or SRTS.

■ Keep the number of time sources as small as possible to reduce time synchronization traffic. Novell suggests using no more than five PTSs and RTSs.

■ Use time sources to provide local access throughout the network.

■ The time source list should be ordered so that the closest time source appears first on the list; the least-cost (WAN speeds, communication costs) time sources should appear next in the order of increasing cost.

■ If the STSs are known to be good time keepers, increase their polling interval to an hour or more. This can be done by using the SET TIMESYNC POLLING INTERVAL command. The default value of this parameter is 600 seconds (10 minutes).

The advantages of the custom method for time synchronization are as follows:

■ You have control over the time synchronization hierarchy.

■ You can reduce network traffic by judiciously distributing time sources on the network.

■ You can provide alternate time sources, in case of network failure.

The following are the disadvantages of the custom method for time synchronization:

■ Custom configuration requires a higher level of understanding and planning, especially for larger networks.

■ As new time sources are added, the configuration files on the servers need to be changed to be aware of the new time sources.

Implementing Time Synchronization

Time synchronization is implemented by the TIMESYNC.NLM. It can be configured using a number of console SET parameters or by placing configuration parameters in the TIMESYNC.CFG file kept in the SYS:SYSTEM directory. The TIMESYNC.CFG file is a text file and can be edited using any text editor. Alternatively, SERVMAN can be used to make changes in the SET parameters and save these changes in the TIMESYNC.CFG file.

It is generally better to make time synchronization changes in the TIMESYNC.CFG file rather than in the AUTOEXEC.NCF file or by using the SET commands at the server console. The

TIMESYNC.CFG file is specially designed for time synchronization, whereas the AUTOEXEC.NCF file is used for general purpose server configuration. Also, TIMESYNC.CFG is processed earlier than AUTOEXEC.NCF. TIMESYNC.CFG is processed when the server boots up and TIMESYNC.NLM loads. TIMESYNC.NLM loads before the SYS: volume is mounted after which AUTOEXEC.NCF is processed.

The following is a guideline for using SERVMAN to configure time synchronization parameters:

1. Load SERVMAN from the server console.

2. Select Server Parameters from Available Options.

   You should see the Set a parameter category menu.

3. Select Time.

   You should see the Time Parameters form (see fig. 2.76) showing the parameters that affect time synchronization. The important time parameters relevant to the scope of this book are described in detail in table 2.9.

4. After making changes in the SET parameters, press Esc until you are shown the Update Options menu (see fig. 2.77). Select Update TIMESYNC.CFG now to save parameters in the TIMESYNC.CFG file. Figure 2.78 shows the contents of the TIMESYNC.CFG file created using the Update TIMESYNC.CFG now option. Unless explicitly mentioned, the SET parameters in table 2.9 can be placed in the TIMESYNC.CFG file without the TIMESYNC keyword prefix.

Figure 2.76

Setting Time parameters in SERVMAN.

```
NetWare 4.10 Server Manager  4.14              NetWare Loadable Module
┌──────────────────────────── Time Parameters ────────────────────────────┐
│ TIMESYNC ADD Time Source                                                 │▲
│ TIMESYNC Configuration File              SYS:SYSTEM\TIMESYNC.CFG          │█
│ TIMESYNC Configured Sources              Off                             │
│ TIMESYNC Directory Tree Mode             On                              │
│ TIMESYNC Hardware Clock                  On                              │
│ TIMESYNC Polling Count                   4                               │
│ TIMESYNC Polling Interval                600                             │
│ TIMESYNC REMOVE Time Source                                              │
│ TIMESYNC RESET                           Off                             │▼
└──────────────────────────────────────────────────────────────────────────┘
        ┌──────────────────┐ Select a parameter category ─────┐
        │ Available         │   Add the name of a server to    │
        │ ┌──────────────── │  contact to the configured list. │
        │ │Server par       │           Setting:               │
        │ │Storage in       │       Maximum length: 48         │
        │ │Volume inf       │                                  │
        │ │Network in       └──────────────────────────────────┘
        │ │        ▼│Time │
        └──────────────────┘
 Enter=Edit field    Esc=Previous list    Alt+F10=Exit              F1=Help
```

To save parameter settings to a selected file (called *flushing to a file*), select Copy all parameters to a file. Figure 2.79 shows the contents of the file SETCMDS.CP that was created by selecting this option. As can be seen from this figure, not only the SET TIMESYNC parameters are changed, but all SET commands are changed.

Figure 2.77

Update options for time synchronization parameters.

```
┌───────── Update Options ─────────┐
│ Update TIMESYNC.CFG now           │
│ Copy all parameters to a file     │
│ Return to the main menu           │
└───────────────────────────────────┘
```

Figure 2.78

Sample SYS:SYSTEM\ TIMESYNC.CFG file.

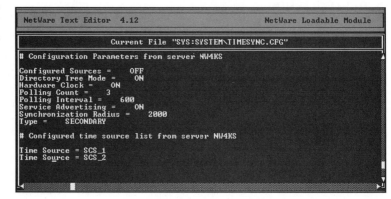

```
NetWare Text Editor  4.12                      NetWare Loadable Module
┌──────────────── Current File "SYS:SYSTEM\TIMESYNC.CFG" ──────────────┐
│ # Configuration Parameters from server NW4KS                         │▲
│                                                                      │
│ Configured Sources =    OFF                                          │
│ Directory Tree Mode =   ON                                           │
│ Hardware Clock =    ON                                               │
│ Polling Count =    3                                                 │
│ Polling Interval =    600                                            │
│ Service Advertising =    ON                                          │
│ Synchronization Radius =    2000                                     │
│ Type =    SECONDARY                                                  │
│                                                                      │
│ # Configured time source list from server NW4KS                     │
│                                                                      │
│ Time Source = SCS_1                                                  │
│ Time Source = SCS_2                                                  │▼
└──────────────────────────────────────────────────────────────────────┘
```

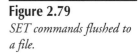

```
NetWare Text Editor  4.12                    NetWare Loadable Module

                  Current File "SYS:SYSTEM\SETCMDS.CP"

TIMESYNC ADD Time Source = SCS_1
TIMESYNC Configuration File = SYS:SYSTEM\TIMESYNC.CFG
TIMESYNC Configured Sources = Off
TIMESYNC Directory Tree Mode = On
TIMESYNC Hardware Clock = On
TIMESYNC Polling Count = 3
TIMESYNC Polling Interval = 600
TIMESYNC REMOVE Time Source =
TIMESYNC RESET = Off
TIMESYNC Restart Flag = Off
TIMESYNC Service Advertising = On
TIMESYNC Synchronization Radius = 2000
TIMESYNC Time Adjustment = None scheduled.
TIMESYNC Time Source = SCS_1
TIMESYNC Type = SECONDARY
TIMESYNC Write Parameters = Off
TIMESYNC Write Value = 3
Time Zone = MST7MDT
```

Figure 2.79

SET commands flushed to a file.

Table 2.9
SET Time Synchronization Parameters

TIMESYNC Parameter	*Description*
TIMESYNC Directory Mode=[On|Off]	When set to ON, the time servers Tree throughout the directory tree will only listen and vote with time servers in their own directory tree.
TIMESYNC Restart Flag= [ON | OFF]	This parameter is used to restart TIMESYNC.NLM with a new set of values from the TIMESYNC.CFG file without rebooting the server. After the value is changed to ON, it executes the actions described and resets to OFF. The default value is OFF.
TIMESYNC Time Source = *ts*	This adds the name of the time source, *ts*, to the configured list of servers. When used without specifying a value, it displays a list of current time servers.
TIMESYNC Type = *type*	This is used to set the *type* of time server that is active on the file server. The *type* can have any of the following values: SINGLE, REFERENCE, PRIMARY, or SECONDARY.
	SINGLE refers to Single Reference Time Servers; REFERENCE refers to Reference

continues

Table 2.9, Continued
SET Time Synchronization Parameters

TIMESYNC Parameter	Description
	Time Servers; PRIMARY refers to Primary Time Servers; SECONDARY refers to Secondary Time Servers.
	The default value is SECONDARY, except in the very first save in the tree; then the default is SINGLE.

Avoiding Time Synchronization Problems

If you are using the server hardware clock for time synchronization, make sure that the hardware clock is reliable. Novell discourages the use of the hardware clock for applications that require synchronized timestamps.

If the time server's clock is set back (as sometimes happens with bad hardware clocks and failing batteries for CMOS settings), other servers will not set their clocks back. The other servers will advance their clocks at a slower pace, and the slower server will advance its clock at a faster pace until the times converge.

If you accidentally reset server time to a future time, you risk serious corruption of the NDS database with incorrect timestamps. Try running DSREPAIR to repair the timestamps.

If the server is an SRTS or RTS, it assumes that its time is the correct time. If this time is incorrect, it can change the network time to its incorrect time value. If the server is not an SRTS or RTS, when it is started, it assumes that the network time is the correct time and adjusts its clock to the network time.

When the server is brought online, take the following steps to minimize time synchronization problems:

1. Before running SERVER.EXE, set the hardware clock (via DOS DATE and TIME commands) to the correct local time. This may mean putting the time or date commands in the AUTOEXEC.NCF file that starts the SERVER.EXE. This has the unfortunate consequence of requiring manual intervention before the SERVER.EXE can be run.

2. When the server starts, check the server's time synchronization information using the console command TIME, to make sure that the time zone and daylight savings time is correct. You can put the TIME command as the last command in the AUTOEXEC.NCF file.

3. Observe server time for a few minutes to see if there is any radical change in time. If the time changes by more than an hour, you may have incorrectly set the time parameters in the AUTOEXEC.NCF file. Take corrective actions immediately. Avoid having the server online for more than 20 minutes without fixing the server time or time synchronization parameters.

4. If you have had a history of time synchronization problems for objects in a container, avoid having network administrators for the same container in different time zones.

Study Guide for the Chapter

If preparing for the NetWare 3 to 4 Update CNE exams, review the chapter with the following goals:

- Understand and identify the NDS components and its properties. Use the Study Notes as a quick review.

- Pay particular attention to examples of current context, complete names, typeless names, partial names, differences between container and leaf objects, and use of CX and NLIST utilities.

- After studying this chapter, attempt the sample test questions for this chapter. If you miss the answer to a question, review the appropriate topic until you understand the correct answer.

Chapter Summary

In this chapter, you learned the basics of NetWare Directory Services. NDS represents an exciting way of managing the network as a logical entity. Because NDS is a key service in NetWare 4, many details of its operation were provided in this chapter. Among the concepts covered was NDS as a global database for network management. This global database is accessible from any point on the network. The nature of NDS objects was examined, and each different type of leaf and container object was described in detail. The NDS naming rules were discussed and several examples were given. The key concepts covered were current context, complete names, typeless names, partial names, and period rules.

The NDS utilities CX and NLIST, as well as their most important options, were discussed, and numerous examples of their uses were given. The chapter concluded with a discussion of partitioning, replication, and time synchronization.

Chapter Test Questions

Test questions are either single choice or multiple choice. Single answer questions are indicated by a (circle) notation that precedes the possible answers. Some questions require you to select more than one answer; these are indicated by the (box) preceding the answers. This is the convention used by the Drake Testing Exam. Not all the questions are multiple choice. Occasionally, you might get a question that asks you to type in an answer. The answer in this case is usually a one-word answer. The answer is not case-sensitive, so you can type in the answer in lower- or uppercase.

Certain questions are repeated in different ways, so that you can recognize them even when the wording is different. Taking practice quizzes not only tests your knowledge, but also gives you confidence when you take your exam.

You might notice a large number of questions on NetWare 4 container/leaf identification and NDS names. This is probably the most frequent type of question you might be asked on material covered in this chapter.

Some questions based on material coming from this chapter have a picture of an NDS tree with an associated question. Because the NDS tree and the question do not often fit on a single screen (Microsoft Windows screens are used in the CNE testing); they are often split into two screens. The first screen has the NDS tree diagram, and the second screen has the question. You can use a menu button to see each screen. Unless you have a very good memory, you should get into the habit of quickly drawing the essential details of the NDS tree (scrap paper is provided for you while taking the test), so that you can save time in answering these questions.

1. NetWare Directory Services is a _____.

   ○ A. central database of files and directories

   ○ B. distributed database of files and directories

   ○ C. distributed global database of network resources and services

   ○ D. distributed global database of files, directories, network resources and services

   ○ E. central global database of files, directories, network resources, and services

2. NDS provides a _____.

   ○ A. local directory that represents a logical and physical view of the network

   ○ B. global directory that represents a logical view of the network

   ○ C. global directory that represents a physical view of the network

   ○ D. local directory that represents a physical view of the network

   ○ E. global directory that represents a logical and physical view of the network

   ○ F. local directory that represents a logical view of the network

3. Which of the following statements about NDS and the NetWare bindery are true?

   □ A. NDS users are network-wide.

   □ B. Bindery users are network-wide.

☐ C. NDS users are server-centric.

☐ D. Bindery users are server-centric.

4. Which of the following statements about NDS are true?

    ☐ A. NDS eliminates the need for creating separate user and group accounts on each NetWare server.

    ☐ B. NDS requires separate user and group accounts to be created on each NetWare server.

    ☐ C. NDS enables User and Group objects to be created that have a network-wide scope.

    ☐ D. NDS User and Group objects have a scope that is limited to the container in which they are defined.

5. NDS information is stored on _____.

    ○ A. NetWare servers on the network in a manner that is transparent to the user

    ○ B. NetWare servers on the network but the database is not transparent to the user, and the user needs to know on which NetWare servers the NDS information is stored

    ○ C. NetWare workstations on the network in a manner that is transparent to the user

    ○ D. NetWare workstations and NetWare servers

6. The NDS database is kept consistent by _____.

    ○ A. sending alert messages whenever directory changes occur

    ○ B. sending update messages to the network administrator to run the directory synchronization services

    ○ C. running directory synchronization service at specified times such as midnight or early hours of the morning

    ○ D. directory synchronization mechanism that propagates directory changes

7. NDS is kept in _____.

    ○ A. a hidden volume on the network

    ○ B. a hidden data area on the server

    ○ C. the directory SYS:SYSTEM on the NetWare server

    ○ D. a hidden file called NDS$DB.DAT on the SYS: volume on the server

8. The NDS naming mechanism is compliant with the _____ standard.

    ○ A. X.409

    ○ B. X.400

    ○ C. X.500

    ○ D. NIS

    ○ E. NFS

9. NDS provides access to network information from _____.

   ○ A. the server console command only

   ○ B. an OS/2 workstation running NDS compliant network requester only

   ○ C. any workstation on the network

   ○ D. a Microsoft Windows workstation only

10. The topmost object in an NDS tree is called the _____.

    ○ A. root

    ○ B. \

    ○ C. [Root]

    ○ D. top

    ○ E. {root}

11. An NDS tree can have _____.

    ○ A. multiple roots

    ○ B. a single root

    ○ C. no root

    ○ D. at least one root

12. NDS trees that have different roots _____.

    ○ A. can share information between themselves using NDS

    ○ B. can share information using NDS only if the roots are made trustees of each other

    ○ C. cannot share information between themselves using NDS

    ○ D. can share information if the user is a privileged user such as the Admin user

13. Container objects are used for _____.

    ○ A. grouping multiple roots of an NDS tree

    ○ B. grouping objects in a logical way that reflects the network use

    ○ C. grouping User objects only

    ○ D. the root of the tree only

14. A leaf object _____.

    ○ A. cannot contain other objects

    ○ B. is the first-level object of an NDS tree

    ○ C. can contain other objects

    ○ D. can be used wherever a container object is normally used

15. The type of network resource that can exist in an NDS database is called _____.

    ○ A. object

    ○ B. leaf

    ○ C. object type

    ○ D. object class

    ○ E. container

16. The information contained in an object is called its _____.

    ○ A. name

    ○ B. object id

    ○ C. property

    ○ D. context

17. NDS objects in the same container level _____.

    ○ A. must have unique names

    ○ B. can have the same name

    ○ C. can have the same name only if they represent a different type of network resource or container

    ○ D. must be eight characters or less

18. A logical division of an NDS database is called a _____.

19. The container OU=CORP.O=IBL can have _____.

    ☐ A. two file server objects named CORP_FS and corp_FS

    ☐ B. a Printer object named ZEPHYR and a file server named ZEPHYR

    ☐ C. a User object named SHIVA and a file server named ZEOS

    ☐ D. a Print Server object named [PRINT]

    ☐ E. a file server named CORP FS

20. An NDS object name can be up to _____ characters.

    ○ A. 8

    ○ B. 13

    ○ C. 16

    ○ D. 21

    ○ E. 32

    ○ F. 64

    ○ G. 128

    ○ H. 256

21. An object name can be renamed _____.

    ☐ A. if the object is a container

    ☐ B. if the object is [Root]

    ☐ C. if the object is a leaf

    ☐ D. if this is the bottom most container in the NDS tree

22. Which of these are container objects?

    ☐ A. Organizational Unit

    ☐ B. File Server

    ☐ C. Organization

    ☐ D. Print Server

23. Which of the following are true for the [Root] object?

    ☐ A. There can be only one root per NDS tree.

    ☐ B. An NDS tree can have multiple shared roots.

    ☐ C. The root object can be deleted. This is a quick way of deleting the entire NDS tree.

    ☐ D. The root object cannot be deleted.

    ☐ E. The root object can be renamed.

24. Which of the following leaf objects can be under the [Root] container?

    ○ A. Country

    ○ B. Organization

    ○ C. Server

    ○ D. Alias

    ○ E. Organizational Unit

25. Which of the following container objects can be under the [Root] container?

    ☐ A. Country

    ☐ B. Organization

    ☐ C. Server

    ☐ D. Alias

    ☐ E. Organizational Unit

    ☐ F. [Root]

26. Country object names are limited to _____ characters.

    ○ A. 1

    ○ B. 3

    ○ C. 2

    ○ D. 8

    ○ E. 64

    ○ F. 128

27. The Country object can contain the following container object(s):

    ○ A. [Root]

    ○ B. Country

    ○ C. Organization

    ○ D. Server

    ○ E. Alias

    ○ F. Organizational Unit

28. Which of the following leaf objects can be under the country container?

    ○ A. Country

    ○ B. Organization

    ○ C. Server

    ○ D. Alias

    ○ E. Organizational Unit

29. Which of the following statements about Country objects are true?

    ☐ A. A Country object can exist under the [Root] object only.

    ☐ B. A Country object can exist under an Organization object.

    ☐ C. A Country object name can be two characters or less.

    ☐ D. A Country object name must be two characters exactly.

    ☐ E. A Country object can exist inside another Country object, so smaller countries inside larger countries can be defined.

30. Which of the following objects cannot be underneath the Organization object?

    ☐ A. Country

    ☐ B. Organization

    ☐ C. Server

    ☐ D. Alias

    ☐ E. Organizational Unit

    ☐ F. [Root]

31. Under which of the following objects can the Organization object be placed?

    ☐ A. Country

    ☐ B. Organization

    ☐ C. Server

☐ D. Alias

☐ E. Organizational Unit

☐ F. [Root]

32. Under which of the following container objects can the Organizational Unit object be placed?

   ☐ A. Country

   ☐ B. Organization

   ☐ C. Server

   ☐ D. Alias

   ☐ E. Organizational Unit

   ☐ F. [Root]

33. Which container object(s) can be placed under the Organizational Unit object?

   ○ A. Country

   ○ B. Organization

   ○ C. Server

   ○ D. Alias

   ○ E. Organizational Unit

   ○ F. [Root]

34. The attribute type abbreviation for the Country object is _____.

   ○ A. CN

   ○ B. C

   ○ C. CX

   ○ D. O

   ○ E. OU

   ○ F. CO

35. The attribute type abbreviation for the Organizational Unit object is _____.

   ○ A. CN

   ○ B. C

   ○ C. CX

   ○ D. O

   ○ E. OU

   ○ F. OG

36. Which of these are valid leaf objects?

   ☐ A. Alias

   ☐ B. Organization

   ☐ C. Directory Map

   ☐ D. Map

   ☐ E. User

   ☐ F. Print Server

37. Which of these are valid leaf objects?

   ☐ A. Computer

   ☐ B. NetWare server

   ☐ C. Main Frame

   ☐ D. AFP server

   ☐ E. Comm server

38. Which of the following leaf objects are used for informational purposes only?

   ☐ A. NetWare server

   ☐ B. AFP server

   ☐ C. Volume

   ☐ D. Computer

   ☐ E. Directory Map

39. Which of the following leaf objects can be used to refer to an object in a different location?

  ○ A. Computer

  ○ B. Link

  ○ C. Print Queue

  ○ D. Alias

  ○ E. Symbolic Link

40. Which of the following leaf objects can be used to simplify creation of login scripts?

  ○ A. Map

  ○ B. Link

  ○ C. Directory Map

  ○ D. Alias

  ○ E. Map Directory

41. Which of the following leaf objects can be used for grouping only users?

  ☐ A. Group

  ☐ B. Organizational Role

  ☐ C. Organizational Unit

  ☐ D. Profile

  ☐ E. User

42. Which of the following objects can be used to create groups of users and other NDS objects?

  ○ A. Group

  ○ B. Organizational Role

  ○ C. Organizational Unit

  ○ D. Profile

  ○ E. User

43. Which of the following objects represents a login script?

  ○ A. Group

  ○ B. Organizational Role

  ○ C. Organizational Unit

  ○ D. Profile

  ○ E. Directory Map

44. Which of the following objects represents a queue for network printing?

  ○ A. Queue

  ○ B. Printer

  ○ C. Print Server

  ○ D. Print Queue

  ○ E. Profile

45. Which of the following objects relate to network printing?

  ☐ A. Queue

  ☐ B. Printer

  ☐ C. Print Server

  ☐ D. Print Queue

  ☐ E. Profile

46. Files and directories are stored on which of the following NDS objects?

  ○ A. Queue

  ○ B. Volume

  ○ C. NetWare Server

  ○ D. Partition

  ○ E. Computer

47. Which of the following objects indicates a corruption in the NDS?

    ○ A. Queue

    ○ B. Unknown

    ○ C. Strange

    ○ D. Invalid

    ○ E. Profile

48. Which of the following objects represents a print queue that came from a NetWare 3.*x* server?

    ○ A. Bindery Queue

    ○ B. Emulator

    ○ C. Bindery object

    ○ D. AFP Server

    ○ E. NetWare Server

49. Which tool should you use if you see too many occurrences of the leaf object Unknown?

    ○ A. VREPAIR

    ○ B. BINDFIX

    ○ C. DSFIX

    ○ D. DSREPAIR

50. Which of the following are true for properties?

    ☐ A. All property values are mandatory.

    ☐ B. All property values are optional.

    ☐ C. Some property values are mandatory, whereas others are optional.

    ☐ D. All property values are single-valued.

    ☐ E. All property values are multi-valued.

    ☐ F. Property values can be single-valued or multi-valued.

51. Which of the following are tools for creating and managing NDS objects?

    ☐ A. SYSCON

    ☐ B. NetAdmin

    ☐ C. NET ADMIN

    ☐ D. NetWare Administrator (NWADMIN)

    ☐ E. FILER

52. Which of the following is a tool for creating a batch of User objects?

    ○ A. SYSCON

    ○ B. NetAdmin

    ○ C. UIMPORT

    ○ D. NetWare Administrator (NWADMIN)

    ○ E. FILER

53. The context is _____.

    ○ A. the position of an object in an NDS tree

    ○ B. a pointer to a leaf object

    ○ C. a pointer to a container object

    ○ D. the position of a file in a directory on a specified Volume object

54. The context is used to _____.

    ○ A. locate a file in a directory

    ○ B. locate a file in a Volume object

○ C. locate where an object can be found in the NDS tree

○ D. locate the NDS tree in which the object can be found

55. Which of the following statements about context are true?

☐ A. The context of an object refers to its container object.

☐ B. Context can never be set to the [Root] object.

☐ C. Context can never be set to a leaf object.

☐ D. Setting a context correctly can simplify referencing NDS objects.

56. Current context _____.

○ A. is an attached workstation's current position in the NDS tree

○ B. can never be set to [Root]

○ C. can never be changed once it is set

○ D. can only be changed by the Admin user

57. Given the NDS tree shown above, what is the partial name of object George_Patton if the current context is set to OU=SOPS.O=SAL?

○ A. CN=George_Patton.OU=SOPS.O= SAL

○ B. CN=George_Patton.OU=SOPS.O= SAL

○ C. CN=George_Patton

○ D. CN=George_Patton.OU=SOPS

○ E. CN=George_Patton.OU=R&D.O= SOPS

58. Which of the following names are complete typeless names?

☐ A. .CN=Veena

☐ B. Veena

☐ C. .Veena.CORP.SCS

☐ D. .CN=Veena.OU=CORP.O=SCS

☐ E. .FS1.SALES.ESL

☐ F. FS1.SALES.ESL

59. Which of the following names are partial typeless names?

☐ A. .CN=Veena

☐ B. Veena

☐ C. Veena.CORP.SCS

☐ D. CN=Veena.OU=CORP.O=SCS

60. The default name context can be set for a workstation by setting the _____.

○ A. SET CONTEXT parameter in the NET.CFG file

○ B. NAME CONTEXT parameter in the NET.CFG file

○ C. SET CONTEXT parameter in the SHELL.CFG file

○ D. NAME CONTEXT parameter in the SHELL.CFG file

61. To set the default context to OU= CORP.O=SCS, use the following statement in the NET.CFG file:

○ A. NAME CONTEXT O=CORP.O=SCS

○ B. "NAME CONTEXT" = O=CORP.O=SCS

○ C. NAME CONTEXT =
     "O=CORP.O=SCS"

○ D. NAME CONTEXT
     "O=CORP.O=SCS"

62. To change context to the root of the tree, use the command _____.

   ○ A. CX

   ○ B. CX /R

   ○ C. CX .

   ○ D. CX /T

   ○ E. CX /T /A

   ○ F. CX /CONT

63. To view all objects in current context and below, use the command _____.

   ○ A. CX

   ○ B. CX /R

   ○ C. CX .

   ○ D. CX /T

   ○ E. CX /T /A

   ○ F. CX /CONT

64. To view container objects at current context only, you can use which of the following commands?

   ○ A. CX

   ○ B. CX /R

   ○ C. CX .

   ○ D. CX /T

○ E. CX /T /A

○ F. CX /CONT

65. To view all objects at current context, which of the following commands can you use?

   ○ A. CX /CONT /A

   ○ B. CX /R

   ○ C. CX .

   ○ D. CX /T

   ○ E. CX /T /A

   ○ F. CX /CONT

66. The command

   `NLIST SERVER=FS1 SHOW "Network Address"`

   performs the following task:

   ○ A. Displays active users logged in to the network

   ○ B. Displays all volumes in the current context and subcontainers

   ○ C. Shows detail property values for a user

   ○ D. Searches for a specific object in current context and all subcontainers

   ○ E. Shows a specific property for a specific server object

   ○ F. Searches for objects that have a specific property value

   ○ G. Displays top-level help screen for NLIST

67. The command

    `NLIST PRINTER WHERE "LOCATION"=LAB`

    performs the following task:

    ○ A. Displays active users logged in to the network

    ○ B. Displays all volumes in the current context and subcontainers

    ○ C. Shows detail property values for a user

    ○ D. Searches for a specific object in current context and all subcontainers

    ○ E. Shows a specific property for a specific User object

    ○ F. Searches for objects that have a specific property value

    ○ G. Displays top-level help screen for NLIST

68. Which of the following tools can be used to manage NDS partitions?

    ☐ A. PartMgr

    ☐ B. NetAdmin

    ☐ C. FILER

    ☐ D. Partition Manager

    ☐ E. SYSCON

69. Time synchronization is important in NDS because _____.

    ○ A. it ensures that clocks are accurate

    ○ B. it ensures that NDS changes are done in the correct order

    ○ C. it is generally a good practice to keep clock accurate

    ○ D. backups need to be performed at the correct time

70. Which of these are valid time servers used by NDS?

    ☐ A. Radio Clock Time server

    ☐ B. Single Reference Time server

    ☐ C. Reference Time server

    ☐ D. UTC Time server

    ☐ E. Primary Time server

    ☐ F. Master Time server

    ☐ G. Secondary Time server

71. The Partition Manager can be used to _____.

    ☐ A. split partitions

    ☐ B. merge partitions

    ☐ C. view partitions

    ☐ D. mirror partitions

    ☐ E. create partitions

72. What is the position of an object in the NDS tree called?

73. What is a copy of a partition called?

Implementing NetWare Security

In this chapter you will learn about NetWare 4 security and how it differs from NetWare 3 security. You will also learn how NetWare 3 and NetWare 4 security are similar. A major difference between NetWare 3 and NetWare 4 security lies in the area of NDS security. This chapter will therefore focus mainly on NDS security issues.

Overview of Network Security

NetWare 3 security is illustrated in figure 3.1. The two main components of NetWare 3 security are

- Login security

- File system security

In NetWare 4, another element to network security has been added, NDS security. The three elements of NetWare 4 security are

- Login security

- NDS security

- File system security

Figure 3.2 illustrates this concept. At each level (or element) of security, a number of tools and options exist. To implement security effectively on a network, you need to understand how to implement the different options at each level, and what tools NetWare 4 provides to implement network security.

 The three components of NetWare 4 security are

- Login security

- NDS security

- File system security

Figure 3.1

NetWare 3 network security.

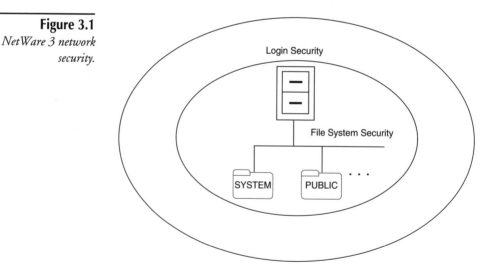

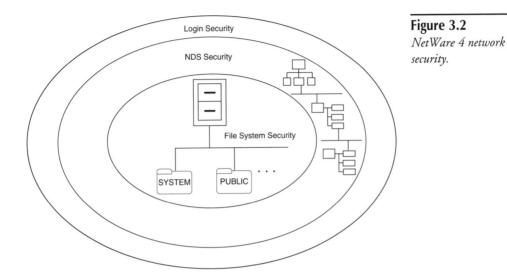

Figure 3.2
NetWare 4 network security.

Login Security

Login security, shown in figures 3.1 and 3.2, includes a number of components. Login security controls who can gain initial entry into the network. Unlike NetWare 3, where a login is authenticated against the definition of the user in a server's bindery, the NetWare 4 login of a user must be authenticated against a global NDS database. For instance, a user logging in as object CN=KARANJIT in container O=ESL must, after initial attachment to the network, enter the following command:

```
LOGIN .CN=KARANJIT.O=ESL
```

or

```
LOGIN .KARANJIT.ESL
```

The first login command specifies the complete name of the User object. The second form uses the typeless complete name. This assures that the user can log in from any context in the NDS tree. The context (as you recall from Chapter 2, "NetWare

Directory Services Fundamentals") is the location (pointer) in the NDS tree. The user can also use partial names to log in to the network. For example, if the current context is [Root], the following commands could be used:

```
LOGIN CN=KARANJIT.O=ESL
```

or

```
LOGIN KARANJIT.ESL
```

If the current context is O=ESL, the container that holds the User object being logged in to, the following commands could be used:

```
LOGIN CN=KARANJIT
```

or

```
LOGIN KARANJIT
```

Before a user can successfully log in, the user has to pass through several login restriction checks (see fig. 3.3). These login restrictions are

Figure 3.3
Login restrictions.

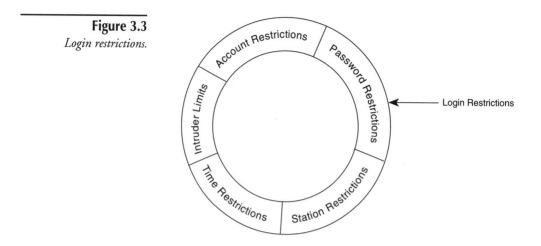

- Account restrictions
- Password restrictions
- Station restrictions
- Time restrictions
- Intruder limits

The login restrictions shown in figure 3.3 are similar to those used in NetWare 3, except that the restrictions are applied to NDS objects, and they are implemented using the NetWare administrator and the NETADMIN tool.

NDS Security Concepts

Once the user is validated for network services, NDS security determines what network resources (NDS objects) the user can access. The kinds of operations a user is permitted to perform on NDS objects, and on files and directories in volumes on the network, are called *rights*. The operations permissible on NDS objects are called *NDS object rights*, and the operations permissible on a NetWare file system are called *file system rights*. These two are quite different. The discussion in this section focusses on NDS object rights.

An NDS object right has many uses. Suppose a user wants to view the structure of a tree. Should the user be allowed to view the directory structure? Viewing the structure of (also called *browsing*) a tree would be very valuable for a user if the user needs to find out what network resources are available on the network. One object right, called Browse, allows the user to view the directory structure. Other useful rights are the Create, Delete, and Rename objects rights. You would not want an ordinary user to have these rights. An administrator should have a special right, called the Supervisor right, which grants the administrator all privileges to a directory object.

When a right is assigned to a container directory object, should all objects in that container have those rights? Objects in a container that receive rights from a *parent* (a superior object) container are said to *inherit* rights. Inheritance is a very important property and is used in object rights to simplify the assignment of rights. Consider the situation of an Organizational Unit container that has 1,000 objects underneath it (see fig. 3.4). For the most part, a user or group needs the same right to all the objects in that container. If objects could not inherit rights from their parent container, each of the 1,000 objects would have to be granted a right individually!

Most administrators would not appreciate performing such a task. On the other hand, because objects can inherit rights, the desired object right can be granted just once for the Organizational Unit container (see fig. 3.5). What if some objects

in the container need a different set of rights? In this case, there needs to be a mechanism to block the flow of rights below a certain container (see fig 3.6). This mechanism is called the Inheritance Rights Filter (IRF) and will be discussed in greater depth in the section, "The Inherited Rights Filter," later in this chapter.

Another important question is: Do you want any network administrator to have complete control over the NDS tree for the entire organization? Such control would give this user access to all network resources. Many large organizations are reluctant to do this. NDS object rights include the ability to restrict access to portions of the NDS tree, even to administrator users. Take care to prevent a situation where *no one* has administrative rights to a portion of the NDS tree.

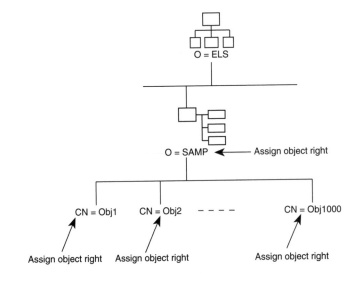

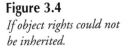

Figure 3.4
If object rights could not be inherited.

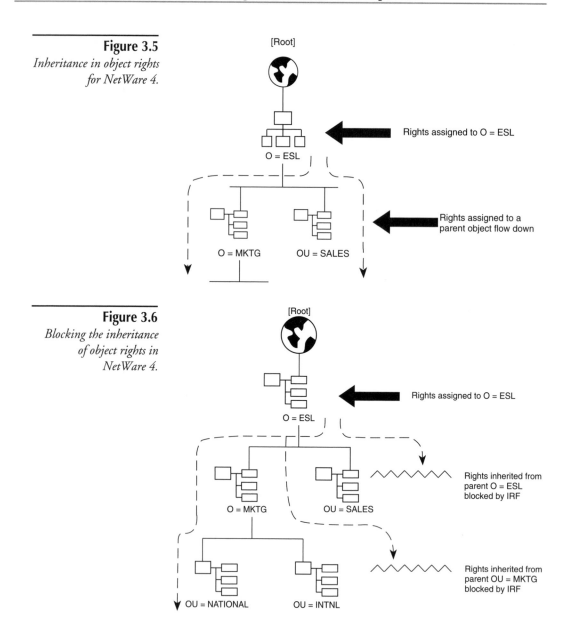

Figure 3.5
Inheritance in object rights for NetWare 4.

[Root]

Rights assigned to O = ESL

O = ESL

Rights assigned to a parent object flow down

O = MKTG

OU = SALES

Figure 3.6
Blocking the inheritance of object rights in NetWare 4.

[Root]

Rights assigned to O = ESL

O = ESL

Rights inherited from parent O = ESL blocked by IRF

O = MKTG

OU = SALES

Rights inherited from parent OU = MKTG blocked by IRF

OU = NATIONAL

OU = INTNL

NDS Rights

NDS provides for two types of rights: the rights to perform operations on the NDS tree structure, and the rights to perform operations on properties of an object (see fig. 3.7). These two rights are quite different.

For instance, when working with the NDS structure, you may want to browse the tree or rename an object. When you are examining the properties of an object, the Browse right is not meaningful. You would typically want to be able to read the value of a property or write to it. For example, you may want users to have Read access to their e-mail address property, but you may not want users to change their e-mail addresses. You may, on the other hand, allow users to modify their login scripts. In this case, they need to have Write access to the login script property for the User object.

NDS rights that deal with the structure of objects in the NDS tree are called *object rights.* These are used to view and manage objects in the NDS tree.

NDS rights that deal with accessing the values stored in the properties of an object are called *property rights.* Property rights determine what a user can do with the values of a property.

An NDS object granted a specific right is called the *trustee* of the object (see fig. 3.8). The trustee can be any object in the NDS tree. It is easy to understand that User objects and Group objects can be trustees because they all deal with users. But it may seem strange at first to think of a container object as a trustee to another object. In Chapter 2 you learned that container objects are a convenient way of grouping NDS objects into a logical structure that reflects the organization of an enterprise. Container objects can be considered as groups, where the members of the container are the NDS objects in the container. Making a container a trustee to another object gives all objects in that container rights to the designated object. Moreover, these rights *flow down* to other containers and objects, unless explicitly blocked at the tree level.

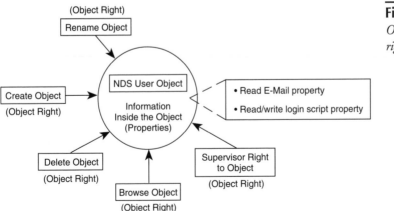

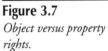

Figure 3.7

Object versus property rights.

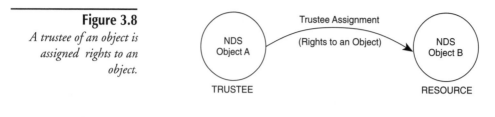

Figure 3.8

A trustee of an object is assigned rights to an object.

In summary, there are two types of NDS rights:

■ Object rights

■ Property rights

The next few sections discuss object rights. This will be followed by a discussion of property rights.

 An NDS object that is granted a specific right is called the *trustee* of the object.

The two types of NDS rights are object rights and property rights.

The specific right that is granted to an NDS object is called a trustee assignment. There are two types of trustee assignments:

■ Object trustee assignments

■ Property trustee assignments

Clarifying Terminology

When a right is assigned to an object *A*, for another object *B*, the object *A* is called a *trustee* of object *B*. The process of granting this right is called a *trustee assignment*. Often, the object that has been granted the right, and the right that has been granted, are called a *trustee assignment*. A trustee can be any other object. In NetWare 3, a trustee could be a user account or a group account. In NetWare 4, other leaf objects and container objects can also be made trustees.

When a User object is a trustee, the user who is logged in as the User object can perform the operations allowed by the trustee assignment. When a container is made a trustee of an object, all objects in that container can perform the operations allowed by the trustee assignment. Similarly, when a Group object is made a trustee for an object, all User objects that are listed in the Group object's Group Membership property can perform the operations allowed by the trustee assignment.

Object Rights

Object rights are assigned to an object in the NDS tree and control the operations that can be performed on the object as a whole. They do not control access to information within the object, with one important exception. This occurs when a Supervisor object right has been granted to an NDS object. Granting the Supervisor object right enables full control over the information inside the object.

Control of information kept inside the object (property) is accomplished by property rights. Table 3.1 shows the different object rights that are possible.

 Remember the five object trustee rights, their codes, and their functions.

Table 3.1
Object Rights

Object Right	Abbreviation	Description
Supervisor	S	Grants all rights. Assigning this right automatically gives Supervisor rights to the object's All Properties (discussed in a later section).
Browse	B	Grants the right to see an object in the NDS tree. When a request is made to search for an object, its name is returned.
Create	C	Applies to container objects only. Gives the right to create a new directory object within the container. Cannot be given to leaf objects, because they cannot contain subordinate objects.
Delete	D	Grants the right to delete an NDS object. Only leaf objects and empty container objects can be deleted.
Rename	R	Grants the right to rename an object. Applies to leaf and container objects.

Supervisor Object Right

The Supervisor right grants all possible rights to the User object. An object with Supervisor rights has full access to the information inside the object. This is an exception. Normally, the object rights do not affect access to the contents of the object.

A special right, called the All Properties property, is used to describe all the properties. When a Supervisor right is assigned, a Supervisor property right is also assigned to All Properties. For this reason, an object can access all the information inside the object if the object has the Supervisor right. Needless to say, you must assign this right with care. If necessary, you can block the Supervisor right to branches of an NDS tree by removing this right from the Inheritance Rights filter for the top-level container of a tree branch.

Browse Object Right

The Browse object right is perhaps the most common right assigned. If you are familiar with NetWare file system security, the Browse object right is similar to the File Scan right for file systems. A browse right for an object gives the trustee the ability to see the object's name in the NDS tree. Without this right (if a Supervisor right is not given), the object is hidden from the user's view.

If the Browse right is not granted to a trustee for a container, the trustee is denied access to all containers and objects within that tree branch. The default is to give everyone the Browse right to the [Root] object. Because all objects in a directory tree are under the [Root] object, the Browse right is inherited by (in other words, it *flows down to*) all objects in the NDS tree.

If, for security reasons, you want to deny access to users in a specific part of the NDS tree, you can do this by blocking the Browse right (using the IRF) for the container that represents the tree branch.

Create Object Right

The Create object right gives the trustee the ability to create subordinate objects underneath the container. Because leaf objects cannot have subordinate objects beneath them, you cannot assign the Create right to leaf objects. Figure 3.9 shows an attempt to assign an object right to the leaf object User1.CORP.ESL_XXX. Notice that the object right Create is not shown as an option for this user.

In addition to Create rights, you must also have Browse rights to a container before you can create an object underneath it using a tool such as the NetWare Administrator.

Delete Object Right

This grants the trustee the right to delete an object. A container object can only be deleted if it has no other objects underneath it. You must delete the leaf and subcontainer objects before you can delete a container. As you can see, this rule exists primarily to prevent inadvertent damage to the NDS tree.

If a file server is active, its object cannot be deleted. Again, this is for security reasons, so that access to the file server is not lost while users are connected to it.

 You can, however, delete a file server's volume object, even while users are logged in to it. This can have disastrous consequences, as users cannot access the volume using NDS. Don't try this on a production system!

Rename Object Right

The Rename object right enables the trustee to change the Name property for the object. Both leaf and container objects names can be changed. In releases prior to NetWare 4.02, only the leaf object names could be changed.

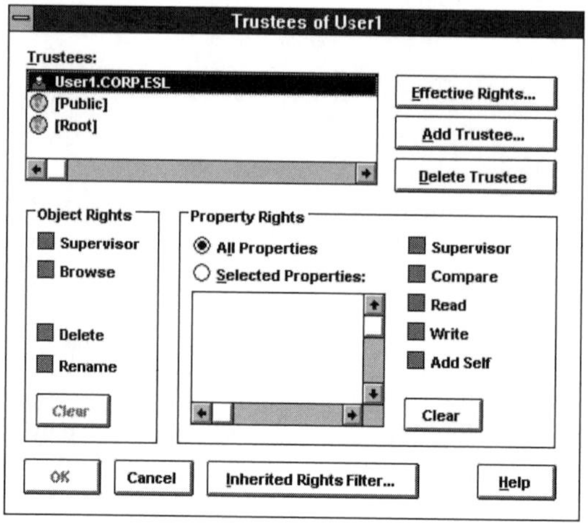

Figure 3.9
You cannot assign the Create right to leaf objects.

Carefully consider the names you assign to container objects. Take into account how easily recognizable the container name is to users of the network, its length (it shouldn't be too long), and how it will appear in the NDS tree (lowercase, uppercase, or mixed case).

The [Public] Trustee

Earlier I mentioned that everyone is given the Browse right. If you are familiar with NetWare 3, you may recall that almost everyone was given the Read and File Scan (RF) rights to SYS:PUBLIC. This was done using the group called EVERY-ONE. There are no default groups called EVERY-ONE (or anything similar) in NetWare 4. So how do you assign to everyone the Browse right?

The problem is further compounded by the fact that the Browse right would be nice to have for users who are not logged in to the network, but merely *attached.*

The difference is that users who are logged in to the network have been *authenticated* by NDS. Users who are attached have a connection to the SYS:LOGIN directory of a NetWare file server, so that they can access LOGIN.EXE, CX.EXE, NLIST.EXE, and other programs that they can use to log in to the network, or so they can search the NDS tree for the name of a resource. Network security, in most cases, is not threatened if a user can see the names of network resources. In extremely secure environments, the Browse right can be revoked from any part of the NDS tree. Another useful aspect of the Browse right that is available for attached users or workstations is that it permits the NDS to interface with third-party tools or other X.500 implementations that may wish to search Novell's implementation of NDS (DIB—Directory Information Base, in X.500 terms) for resource descriptions.

To solve this problem, the designers of NDS created an *implicit* group called [Public]. An *implicit* group has an implied membership that is based upon how the network or a resource in it is accessed. In the case of the group [Public], all workstations that are *attached* (connected to but not yet logged in) to a NetWare 4 network are automatically members of the group [Public]. This makes it possible to assign rights to workstations that are not authenticated by NetWare 4.

[Public] is a special trustee that includes all users who have a network connection, even though they may not be authenticated by the network.

When the system is first installed, the group [Public] is made a trustee of [Root] and given the Browse object right to the root object [Root]. Figure 3.10 illustrates this trustee assignment, and figure 3.11 shows the NetWare Administrator dialog box in which you assign these rights. The Browse object right is inherited by all containers and their subcontainers, down to the individual leaf objects. This allows a user to browse the directory tree.

Figure 3.10

Browse right to trustee [Public] on [Root] object.

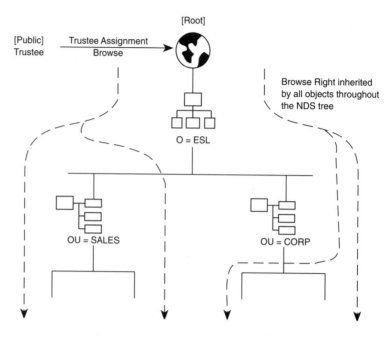

Figure 3.11

The NetWare Administrator dialog box showing default trustee assignments to [Root] object.

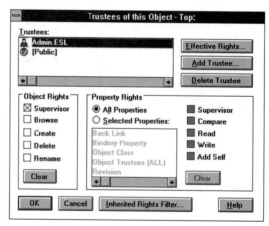

There may be situations where you want users to browse only portions of the NDS tree. In this case, the default trustee assignment of Browse for [Public] to [Root] object can be removed, and this right assigned to the root container (the top of the tree branch) for which the user needs to see directory resources. See figures 3.12 and 3.13, which illustrate this concept. These figures show that the Browse right can be granted to all connected users to a specific tree branch. In figures 3.12 and 3.13, the root of this tree branch is at the Organization

object level O=ESL; it could also be at a lower level in the tree, such as an Organizational Unit level.

[Public] is similar to the NetWare 3 group EVERYONE, except for these differences:

- [Public] does not have an explicit membership; that is, users cannot be added or deleted.

- Membership to [Public] is based on being connected to the network.

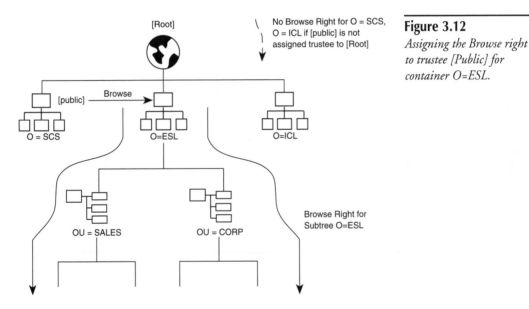

Figure 3.12

Assigning the Browse right to trustee [Public] for container O=ESL.

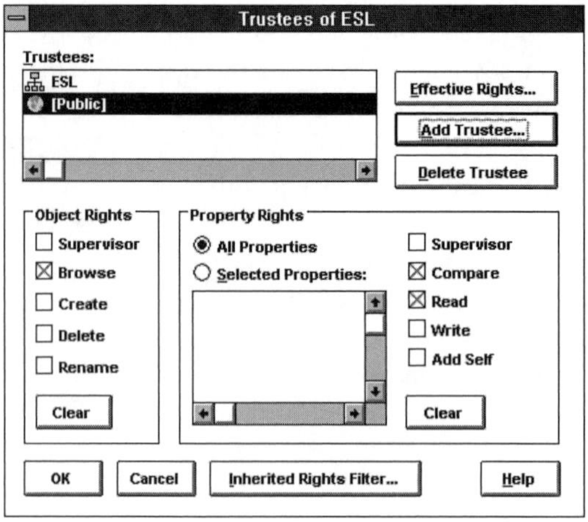

Figure 3.13
*The NetWare
Administrator dialog box
showing the Browse right
to [Public] for container
O=ESL.*

Default Object Rights

NetWare 4 sets certain default system rights to simplify the number of administration tasks you would otherwise have to perform. One of these default rights is the Browse right that the [Public] trustee gives to the [Root] object. Some of the other default rights are discussed in this section.

The container object that contains the SYS volume object is given the Read and File scan (RF) rights to the SYS:PUBLIC directory of the volume object. Figure 3.14 shows that the CORP.ESL container, which is the parent container of the server volume object, is given the Access Rights Read and File Scan. This allows all objects, such as User and Group objects, defined in that container to inherit these rights. In essence, this is equivalent to assigning Read and File Scan rights to group EVERY-ONE in NetWare 4. If you have upgraded your server from NetWare 3 to NetWare 4, and if the group EVERYONE had Read and File Scan rights to SYS:PUBLIC, you will also see the Group object Everyone in the container where the upgraded NetWare 4 server and volume objects are installed. You should also see the Group object Everyone as

a trustee to SYS:PUBLIC with Read and File Scan rights.

The initial user Admin is by default given the Supervisor object right to [Root]. This means that the Admin user inherits Supervisor object rights to all objects and their contents in the NDS tree. For this reason you must carefully guard the password to the initial Admin user. The Admin user by default is placed in the Organization object container and is named Admin. For security reasons, it may be advisable to rename this User object and move it to another context.

The User object, by default, has the following object trustees assigned to it:

- The [Root] object is made a trustee to the User object and given the Browse object right (see fig. 3.15). This means that any NDS object can browse the User object.

- If the creator of the User object is not the Admin user, who has Supervisor rights, the creator is made a trustee with Supervisor object rights to the newly created object.

- The creator of the Server object is given the Supervisor object right to the Server object.

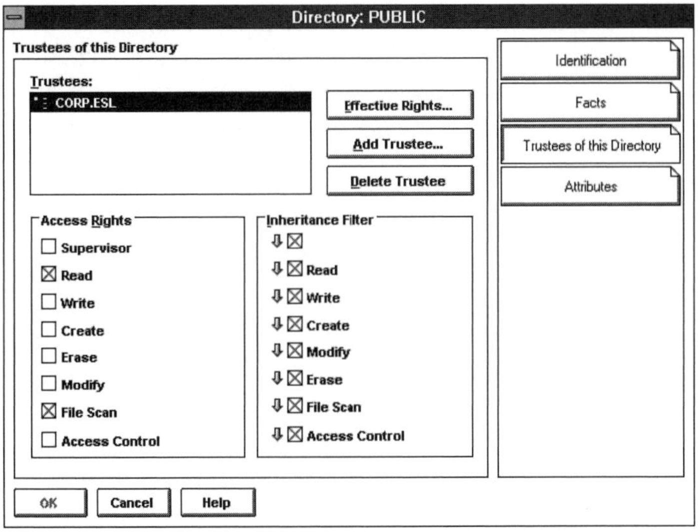

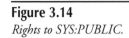

Figure 3.14
Rights to SYS:PUBLIC.

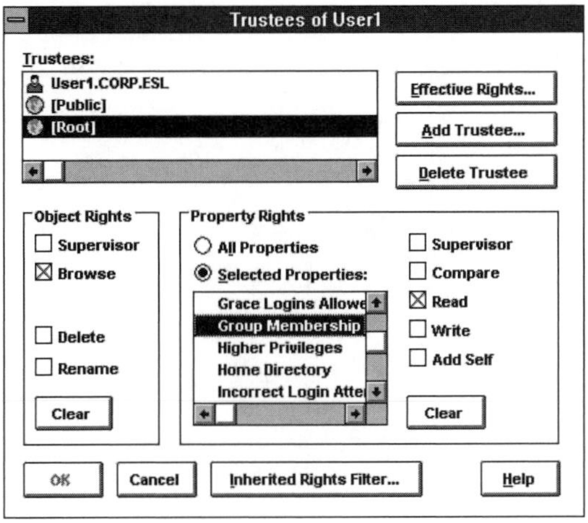

Figure 3.15
The default [Root] trustee assignment for the User object.

Inheritance of Object Rights

When you make an object trustee assignment, all objects that are subordinate to the trustee inherit the right granted to it. In the case of container objects, this means that all leaf objects in the container, and all subcontainers, inherit this right. This inheritance of rights is sometimes called the *flowing down* of rights. If an object is given an explicit trustee assignment at a lower level in the tree, any object rights that were inherited from above are overwritten.

Figure 3.16 shows an example of an NDS tree, where User object KSS is made a trustee of the organization container O=ESL.

The trustee assignment that has been given is the [B C D] rights. This is the right to Browse, Create, and Delete objects. The container O=ESL has two subcontainers: the Organizational Units OU=CORP and OU=ENG. The rights assigned to KSS for O=ESL flow to these subcontainers. It is important to realize that the [B C D] right is only for a specific trustee; in this case, the trustee is the User object. The user rights to Organizational Unit container OU=ENG flow to its two subcontainers OU=OPS and OU=LAB.

The rights inherited by the OU=LAB container flow further down the tree, but the OU=R&D subcontainer has an explicit trustee assignment of [B] for User object KSS. This explicit trustee assignment overrides the trustee assignment user KSS inherits for OU=R&D from the parent container OU=LAB. The trustee assignment for User object KSS then becomes the new right [B]. This new right flows down to subordinate containers below OU=R&D. In figure 3.16 these subordinate containers are OU=LASER and OU=NNET. User object KSS inherits the right [B] to these containers.

It is also interesting to see that in OU=OPS, underneath the OU=ENG container, no explicit trustee assignment is given to user KSS. In this case, the trustee assignment [B C D] flows down and is inherited by the OU=MAINT container that is subordinate to OU=OPS.

Figure 3.16

Inheriting object rights.

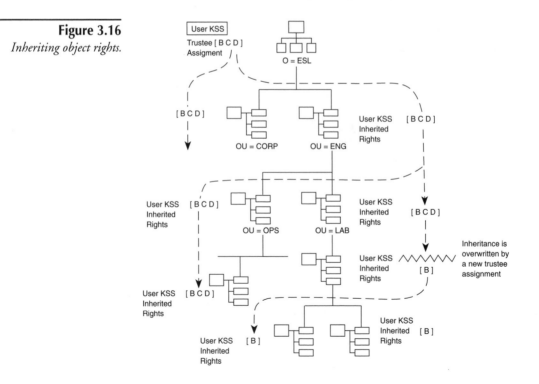

Besides an explicit trustee assignment that over-rides any inherited rights, inheritance can also be controlled by the use of the Inherited Rights Filter. This topic is discussed next.

 The NDS rights that are inherited are different from the NetWare File System Rights. Object rights granted to a volume object are not inherited by the file directories in that volume object.

You must be careful about assigning rights to top-level containers. Assigning rights to the [Root] container will give User objects that right to the entire tree, unless this right is explicitly removed using IRF.

The Inherited Rights Filter

The Inherited Rights Filter is a part of the ACL property of the object called the *Object Trustees* property. It can be used to control which inherited rights are allowed to be received from above.

Every NDS object has an Inherited Rights Filter (IRF). The default value of the IRF is all object rights [S B C D R]. This means that an NDS object has the potential to inherit all rights. The IRF is often confused with the actual object right. The sole purpose of the IRF is to block a right from flowing further down. The IRF cannot be used to block an explicit trustee assignment. The explicit trustee assignment overrides any inherited rights received from above, and causes the IRF to be ignored.

The IRF functions in a manner similar to the Inherited Rights Filter for the NetWare 4 file system (which is the same as NetWare 3's Inherited Rights Mask, except for the name change). The important difference is that the Supervisor right can be removed for IRF for NDS. In the NetWare file system, the supervisor right cannot be removed from the IRF for a file or directory.

When the Supervisor right is removed from the IRF for an NDS object, the Supervisor right is essentially blocked from that tree branch. Before removing a Supervisor right from the IRF of an NDS object, you must make another object a trustee with Supervisor rights for that object.

In the NetWare 4.0, you receive a warning message when you attempt to remove the Supervisor object right from an IRF. You can, however, override this warning and remove the Supervisor right from the IRF anyway. This essentially produces a *black hole* in the tree that no one can access. Starting with NetWare 4.01, the warning has been changed to an error message. If you attempt to remove the Supervisor right from an IRF, an error message is produced instead. This error message informs you that

```
You cannot filter the Supervisor object right
because no object has explicit Supervisor
object right to this object
```

Figure 3.17 shows an attempt to remove the Supervisor right from an NDS object. The trustee CORP.ESL is highlighted in the Trustees box, which means that the operations are performed relative to this trustee object. The error message you see in the figure was produced when an unsuccessful attempt was made to remove the Supervisor right from the IRF.

If you are interested in experimenting with this, try the following:

1. Log in as an Admin user and start the NetWare Administrator.

2. Right-click on a container and select Trustees of this Object.

3. Highlight the container in the Trustee List box and select the Inherited Rights Filter button. You should see the Inherited Rights Filter screen (see fig. 3.18).

4. Click on any of the object rights in the Filter panel. You should be able to view the rights.

5. Try to remove the Supervisor object right by clicking on the check box. You should see the error message in figure 3.17.

If at least one Supervisor trustee assignment to an object exists, the Supervisor object right can be removed from the IRF. In this case, though the Supervisor right is blocked, there is at least one object that can manage the object and its subordinate objects.

Figure 3.17

An attempt to remove Supervisor right from an IRF for a container object.

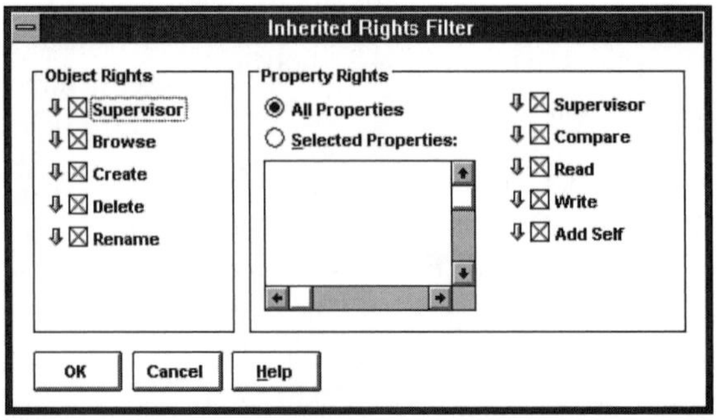

Figure 3.18

The Inherited Rights Filter screen.

Security Equivalence

You can grant a User object all the security rights of another NDS object. This is called *security equivalence,* and is a property of the User object. Figure 3.19 shows that user Dei is made security equivalent to the users Jan.CORP.ESL and Lisa.ESL, the Organization Role BackupOp.CORP.ESL, the group Mgrs.ESL and the Organizational Unit SALES.ESL. This example indicates that Dei inherits, by the definition of security equivalence, whatever rights the previosuly mentioned objects have. These rights are in addition to the rights that user Dei already has.

 Security equivalence is a property of the User object.

Because security equivalence is a property of the User object, take care that the user does not have the right to make changes to this property. If a user does have the right to change the Security Equivalence property and the Write property to the ACL property of an Admin User object, the user could assign an Admin User object as one of the values for the security equivalence property. This would give the user all the rights the Admin user has. The default for a newly created user is that users can read their security equivalence property, and you should not normally have to change this value.

One situation where security equivalence may be particularly useful is when a user in an organization needs access to files and directories of another user. This user could be made security equivalent to the user whose files and directories need to be accessed. To perform this task, you need to have the Write property right for the User object (property rights are discussed later in this chapter).

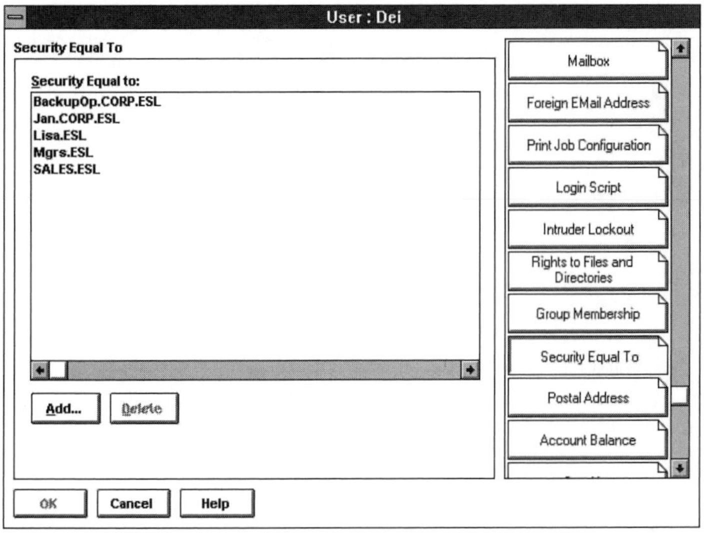

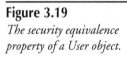

Figure 3.19

The security equivalence property of a User object.

Object Effective Rights

An object's effective rights are the rights that a user actually has to the object. The effective right is not the same as the rights inherited from a parent container, because these can be blocked by the IRF. Also, a user may have a right blocked for it, but may inherit a right because a group that the user belongs to has an explicit or inherited trustee assignment for the object. By the same token, an effective right is not the same as an explicit trustee assignment; a user can inherit other rights because a group that the user belongs to has an explicit or inherited trustee assignment for the object.

The effective rights need to be determined for each situation. Because of the hierarchical structure of the NDS tree, a right may be inherited from a number of sources. This makes the determination of NDS rights an interesting and challenging task. Consider the example shown in figure 3.20.

To determine the effective rights of user KSS to the printer object HP_PRINTER, you must consider the effective rights that come from any of the following sources.

- **Explicitly assigned as a trustee.** This includes the trustee assignment on HP_PRINTER that lists user KSS as a trustee (see fig. 3.21).

- **Inherited from a trustee's parent container.** This includes the trustee assignment on HP_PRINTER that lists OU=CORP as a trustee. This also includes trustee assignment on HP_PRINTER that lists other parent containers such as O=ESL and [Root] as trustees, since the user KSS is in the tree branch with these objects as roots of the tree branch (see fig. 3.22).

Figure 3.20

Sources for determining effective rights.

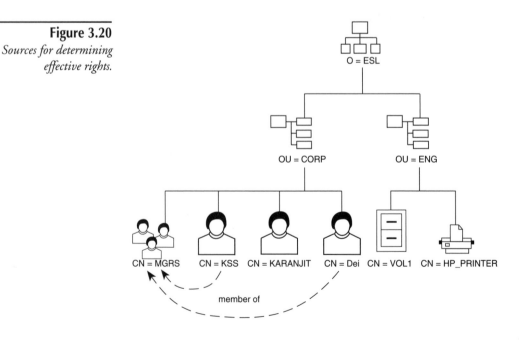

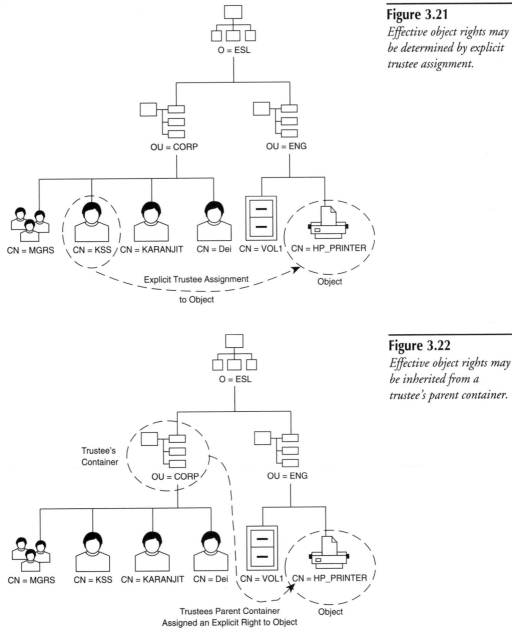

Figure 3.21

Effective object rights may be determined by explicit trustee assignment.

Figure 3.22

Effective object rights may be inherited from a trustee's parent container.

- **Inherited from direct assignment to an object's container.** This includes the trustee assignment on the container OU=ENG that lists user KSS as a trustee (see fig. 3.23). The rights so assigned must pass through the object HP_PRINTER's IRF.

- **Inherited by assigning the trustee's container to the object's container.** Trustee assignment on the container OU=ENG that lists User object KSS's parent containers such as OU=CORP, O=ESL and [Root] as a trustee (see fig. 3.24). The rights so assigned must pass through the object HP_PRINTER's IRF.

- **Inherited by trustee assignment to a Group object.** Any trustee assignment made to the Group object MGRS in which the user KSS is a member of (see fig. 3.25).

- **Inherited by trustee assignment to a security equivalent object.** If user KSS is made a security equivalent to object KARANJIT, any right that the user KARANJIT has to HP_PRINTER is automatically inherited by user KSS (see fig. 3.26).

 Study the different ways listed in this section that an object can derive its effective rights.

As you can see from the preceding discussion, to determine effective rights you must consider the following:

- The rights explicitly granted to a User object.

- The rights inherited from above.

Figure 3.23

Effective object rights may be inherited from direct assignment to object's container.

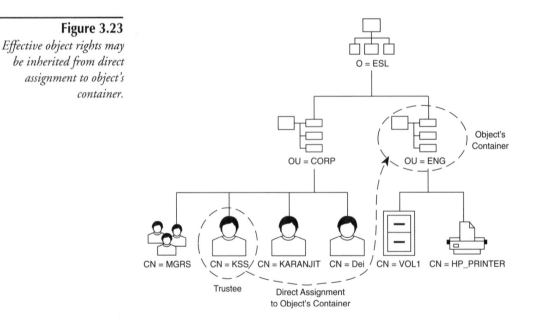

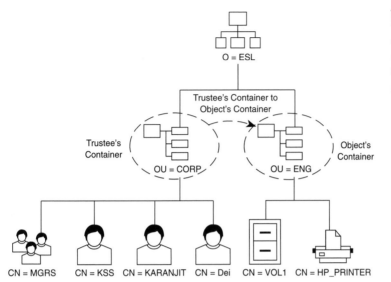

Figure 3.24
Effective object rights may be inherited by assigning the trustee's container to the object's container.

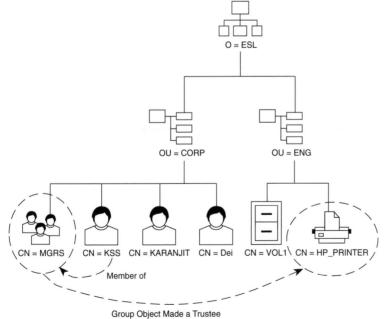

Figure 3.25
Effective object rights may be inherited by trustee assignment to a Group object.

Figure 3.26

Effective object rights may be inherited by trustee assignment to a security equivalent object.

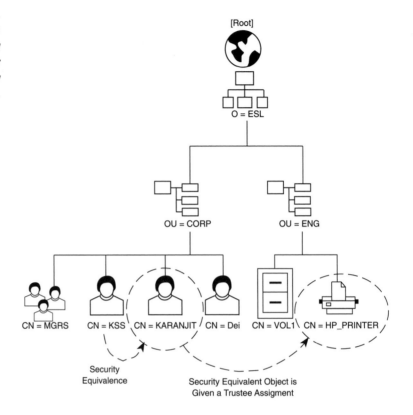

- The rights granted to container objects between the object and [Root]. This applies to container objects that are between the object and [Root] and the trustee and [Root].

- The rights granted through security equivalence.

The next section presents case studies that will give you practice in determining effective rights.

Calculating Object Effective Rights

Understanding how to determine effective rights for an object in the NDS tree is extremely important for NetWare 4 administration. For this reason a number of case studies will be presented that will help you understand how effective rights work in NetWare 4.

Figure 3.27 shows a worksheet you can use for determining effective rights. This figure also shows a partial directory tree with the containers O=ESL, OU=CORP, and OU=ACCTG. The worksheet for computing effective rights shows the entries for each of these containers. For each container, there are entries for the following:

- Inherited Rights Filter (IRF)

- Inherited Rights

- Trustee Assignment

- Effective Rights

When you practice determining effective rights, you'll find the worksheet is an invaluable aid, because it systematically shows the rights at each level. With more experience and practice in determining effective rights, you may be able to dispense with the use of a worksheet and determine effective rights more directly.

Three case studies are presented, each with a discussion of solutions. The case studies range from simple to complex. The more practice you have the more confident you will feel—not just for passing the exams, but also for the real-life task of designing security on a NetWare 4 network.

Case Study 1

Figure 3.28 shows a directory tree for organization IBL. Drew is made a trustee of Organization O=IBL and given the rights of Browse, Create, and Rename. The IRFs for the containers are shown as follows:

IRF for O=IBL	[S B C D R]
IRF for OU=CORP	[B C D]
IRF for OU=MKTG	[S D R]

List Drew's effective rights in containers O=IBL, OU=CORP, and OU=MKTG. Assume that Drew does not inherit rights from any sources other than the ones listed in the case study.

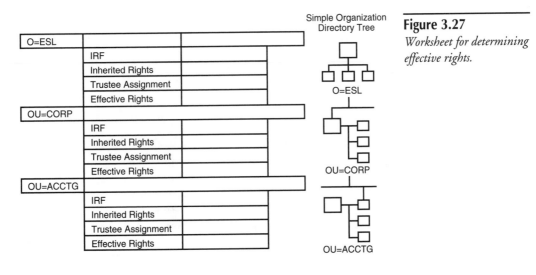

Simple Organization
Directory Tree

Figure 3.27

Worksheet for determining effective rights.

Figure 3.28

The NDS tree for case study 1.

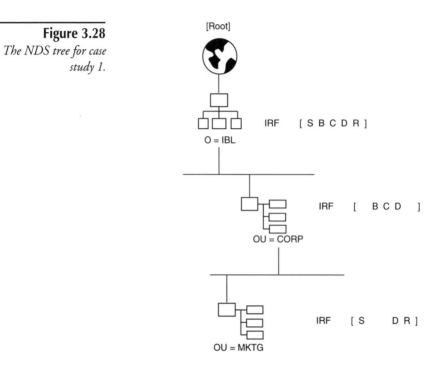

Figure 3.29 shows the completed worksheet. The explanations for entries in the worksheet are presented next.

Figure 3.29

The completed worksheet for case study 1.

O=IBL			
	IRF	S B C D R	
	Inherited Rights	None	
	Trustee Assignment	B C R	Drew
	Effective Rights	B C R	

OU=CORP			
	IRF	B C D	
	Inherited Rights	B C	
	Trustee Assignment	None	
	Effective Rights	B C	Drew

OU=MKTG			
	IRF	S D R	
	Inherited Rights	No Rights	
	Trustee Assignment	None	
	Effective Rights	No Rights	Drew

Entries for O=IBL

The IRF, according to the case study, is [S B C D R]. There are no rights inherited from above; therefore, the entry for inherited rights is *None*. An explicit trustee assignment of [B C R] has been given to the user. The explicit trustee assignment overrides any other inherited rights, so the effective rights for the user in container O=IBL are the same as the explicit trustee assignment. That is, the effective rights of the user for O=IBL are [B C R]

Entries for OU=CORP

The IRF, according to the case study, is [B C D]. The rights inherited from above are the effective rights of the parent container *masked* with the IRF for this container:

IRF	[B C D]
Effective rights of parent	[B C R]
Inherited rights	[B C]

The masking operation is a *logical AND* operation, which means that an entry needs to be in both sets of rights for it to be in the final result.

The inherited rights for OU=CORP are [B C]. Since no trustee assignment is made in OU=CORP, the effective rights are the same as the inherited rights. That is, effective rights for OU=CORP are [B C].

Entries for OU=MKTG

The IRF, according to the case study, is [S D R]. The rights inherited from above are the effective rights of the parent container *masked* with the IRF for this container:

RF	[S D R]
Effective rights of parent	[B C]
Inherited rights	[ ]

The inherited rights for OU=MKTG are [ ], or *No Rights*. Since no trustee assignment is made in OU=MKTG, the effective rights are the same as the inherited rights. That is, effective rights for OU=MKTG are *No Rights*.

Case Study 2

Case study 2 involves a directory tree for organization SCS. Karanjit is made a trustee of Organization O=SCS and given the rights of Supervisor. Karanjit is also given a trustee assignment of Browse, Create, Delete, and Rename to OU=ENG. The IRFs for the containers are shown as follows:

IRF for O=SCS	[S B C D R]
IRF for OU=ENG	[S B C]
IRF for OU=LAB	[B R]

Calculate Karanjit's effective rights in containers O=SCS, OU=ENG, and OU=LAB. Assume that Karanjit does not inherit rights from any source other than the ones listed in the case study.

Figure 3.30 shows the completed worksheet. The explanations for entries in the worksheet are presented next.

Entries for O=SCS

The IRF, according to the case study, is [S B C D R]. There are no rights inherited from above; therefore, the entry for inherited rights is *None*. An explicit trustee assignment of [S] has been given to the user. The explicit trustee assignment overrides

Figure 3.30

The completed worksheet for case study 2.

O=SCS		
IRF	S B C D R	
Inherited Rights		
Trustee Assignment	S	Karanjit
Effective Rights	S (B C D R)	
OU=ENG		
IRF	S B C	
Inherited Rights	S (B C D R)	
Trustee Assignment	B C D R	Karanjit
Effective Rights	B C D R	
OU=LAB		
IRF	B R	
Inherited Rights	B R	
Trustee Assignment	None	
Effective Rights	B R	Karanjit

any other inherited rights, so the effective rights for the user in container O=SCS are the same as the explicit trustee assignment. That is, effective rights of the user for O=SCS are [S (B C D R)]. The rights in parenthesis, (B C D R), are implied rights. If the trustee has Supervisor rights, the trustee automatically has the other rights.

Entries for OU=ENG

The IRF, according to the case study, is [S B C]. The rights inherited from above are the effective rights of the parent container *masked* with the IRF for this container:

IRF	[S B C]
Effective rights of parent	[S (B C D R)]
Inherited Rights	[S (B C D R)]

The masking operation is a *logical AND* operation, which means that an entry needs to be in both sets of rights for it to be in the final result.

The inherited rights for OU=CORP are [S (B C D R)]. Because a trustee assignment of [B C D R] is made in OU=ENG, the effective rights are the same as the explicit trustee assignment, and override any inherited rights. That is, effective rights for

OU=ENG are [B C D R]. What is interesting about this case study is that the inherited rights to OU=ENG were all object rights. But by explicitly assigning a lesser right, this lesser right overrides the greater rights inherited from above.

Entries for OU=LAB

The IRF, according to the case study, is [B R]. The rights inherited from above are the effective rights of the parent container *masked* with the IRF for this container:

IRF	[B R]
Effective rights of parent	[B C D R]
Inherited Rights	[B R]

The inherited rights for OU=LAB are [B R]. Because no explicit trustee assignment to OU=LAB, the effective rights are the same as the inherited rights. That is, effective rights for OU=LAB are [B R].

Case Study 3

Figure 3.31 shows a directory tree for organization SCS.

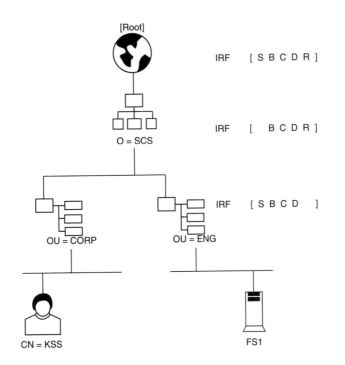

Figure 3.31
The NDS tree for case study 3.

[Public] is given the Browse right to the [Root] object. The Organizational Unit container OU=CORP is given the Rename right to OU=ENG and the Supervisor right to O=SCS. User KSS is given a trustee assignment of Browse, Create, Delete, and Rename to O=SCS.

The IRFs for the containers are shown as follows:

IRF for [Root]	[S B C D R]
IRF for O=SCS	[B C D R]
IRF for OU=ENG	[S B C D]

Determine KSS's effective rights in containers [Root], O=SCS, and OU=ENG. Assume that KSS does not inherit rights from any source other than the ones listed in the case study.

Figure 3.32 shows the completed worksheet. The explanations for entries in the worksheet are presented next.

Entries for [Root]

The IRF, according to the case study, is [S B C D R]. There are no rights inherited from above; therefore, the entry for inherited rights is *None.* An explicit trustee assignment of [B] has been given through [Public], of which KSS is automatically a member. The explicit trustee assignment overrides any other inherited rights for [Public] (of which there are none). So, the effective rights for the user KSS in container [Root] are the same as the explicit rights through [Public].

Figure 3.32

The completed worksheet for case study 3.

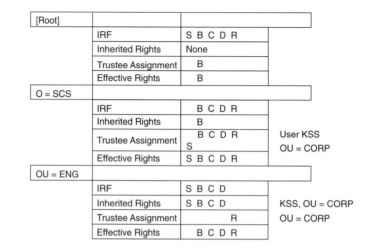

[Root]		
	IRF	S B C D R
	Inherited Rights	None
	Trustee Assignment	B
	Effective Rights	B
O = SCS		
	IRF	B C D R
	Inherited Rights	B
	Trustee Assignment	B C D R / S
	Effective Rights	S B C D R
OU = ENG		
	IRF	S B C D
	Inherited Rights	S B C D
	Trustee Assignment	R
	Effective Rights	B C D R

User KSS
OU = CORP

KSS, OU = CORP
OU = CORP

Entries for O=SCS

The IRF, according to the case study, is [S B C D R]. The rights inherited from above are the effective rights of the parent container masked with the IRF for this container:

IRF   [S B C D R]

Effective rights of parent   [B   ]
_____

Inherited Rights   [B   ]

The masking operation is a *logical AND* operation, which means that an entry needs to be in both sets of rights for it to be in the final result.

The inherited right for O=SCS is [B], and its source is [Public].

An explicit trustee assignment of [B C D R] is made to O=SCS for user KSS. The explicit trustee assignment overrides any other inherited rights *for user KSS only.* There is also an explicit trustee assignment of [S] for group OU=CORP. This would override any inherited rights for OU=CORP, if there were any. The effective rights are the sum of

the inherited rights for [Public], and explicit trustee assignments for user KSS and OU=CORP.

Inherited Rights for [Public]   [B   ]

Trustee Assignment
for user KSS   [B C D R]

Trustee Assignment
for OU=CORP   [S   ]
_____

Effective Rights for KSS   [S B C D R]

The Effective rights are through [Public] and trustee assignment to KSS and OU=CORP.

Entries for OU=ENG

The IRF, according to the case study, is [S B C D]. The rights inherited from above are the effective rights of the parent container *masked* with the IRF for this container:

IRF   [S B C D   ]

Effective rights of parent   [S B C D R]
_____

Inherited Rights   [S B C D   ]

The inherited rights for OU=ENG are [S B C D], and the source of these rights is [Public], user KSS, and OU=CORP. KSS's contribution to this right is [B C D R], [Public]'s contribution is [B], and OU=CORP's contribution is [S]. An explicit trustee assignment of [R] has been given to container OU=CORP, of which user KSS is a member object. This explicit trustee assignment overrides any other inherited rights for user container OU=CORP only. OU=CORP has an inherited rights value of [S], and this is overridden by the new trustee assignment of [R]. What remains of the inherited rights is just the [B C D].

Inherited Rights for KSS, [Public]	[B C D]
Trustee Assignment for container OU=CORP	[R]
Effective Rights for KSS	[B C D R]

Property Rights

Property rights are used to control access to information inside an NDS object. All objects have properties, since all objects are used to store information. An object can have many properties. And different objects can be expected to have different properties. For example, a volume object has a *host server* property whose value is the name of the NetWare server the volume is associated with. But this property does not exist for a User object.

Similarly, a user has a *group membership* property that does not exist for a volume object. The group membership is an example of a *multi-valued* property. Another example is the telephone number property. A user can have several phone numbers, so the telephone property for the user can accommodate multiple values. The location property of an object is single valued, since an object can have only one location.

Table 3.2 lists the property rights defined for an NDS object.

The Supervisor property right grants all rights to a property. If you want, you can block this property with the Inherited Rights Filter.

The Compare property right grants the right to compare the value of a property. The Compare property right allows a trustee to compare the property value to any value. The result of this comparison is a logical True if there is a match or a logical False if there is no match. This property right is useful for NDS tools that need to check for the existence of a specific value. The Compare right does not give you the right to read a property value. This right is granted by a special property value.

The Read property right grants the right to read a value for a property. This property right is useful for NDS tools that need to display selected property values of an NDS object. If a trustee can read the value, it follows that the trustee should be able to compare the property value against another value. For this reason, a Read property right includes the Compare property right.

The Write property right allows the property value to be changed. Some property values are multi-valued. In this case, the Write property allows the trustee to remove or add values to the property.

Table 3.2
Property Rights Summary

Property Right	Abbreviation	Description
Supervisor	S	Grants all rights to all properties.
Compare	C	Grants the right to compare the value to a property. Does not allow you to see the value.
Read	R	Grants right to read the value of a property. Read includes the Compare right, even if the Compare right is not explicitly given.
Write	W	Grants the right to add to, remove from, or change any values of the property.
Add or Delete Self	A	Applies to list property values such as group membership. Grants the trustee the right to add or remove itself from the property value. The trustee cannot add or delete other values of the property. This is useful for mailing lists and group lists.

The Add or Delete Self property right allows the addition of a new property value or the removal of an existing property value. This right applies to multi-valued properties such as group memberships, mailing lists, or the Access Control List (ACL). The Add or Delete Self property right cannot be used to change the value of a property other than itself.

The Write property right includes the Add or Delete Self property.

All Properties Right Versus the Selected Property Right

Property rights can be assigned selectively to specific properties, or they can be applied to all the properties of an object. When a property right is assigned to all the properties of an object, it is called the *All Properties Right*. When a property right refers to an individual or selected property, it is called *Selected Property Right*. An example of property right assignment is when a User object is created in a container. The User object is given the Read property right to all of its properties (All Properties). It is also given a Read/Write property right to its login script property and the Print Job Configuration property. This allows users to modify their user login script and print job configuration. Should you wish to prevent a user from performing these activities, you will have to restrict these property rights.

The All Properties Right is a convenient way of assigning default property rights to all properties. If there are some exceptions to this default, the Selected Property Right can be used to individually set the property right of any property. The Selected Property Right overrides the property right set by the All Properties Right.

The Access Control List Property

Every object has an Access Control List (ACL) property, also called the Object Trustees property. This property contains a list of all trustees that have a trustee assignment to the object or its property. It does not list other objects that this object may have a right to. Because of this, to grant a right, you must go to the object and then assign a trustee. You cannot go to the trustee and add objects that this trustee may have rights to.

The ACL property value can be used to specify any of the following:

- An object right, such as the [S B C D R] rights

- A right to all properties of the object, called the *All Properties Right*

- A right to a specific property

Since an ACL is a property of the object that describes the trustee assignments to the object, it can include a trustee assignment to itself. This trustee assignment to the ACL property would describe which of the operations described by the property rights [S C R W A] a trustee could perform.

Consider what would happen if a trustee had a Write property right to the ACL. Such a trustee could then modify the ACL, and grant and revoke privileges by changing the ACL value. Specifically, it could grant itself Supervisor right to the object; this would give the trustee complete control over the object and its subordinates (unless blocked by an IRF or explicit assignment).

In actual practice, it is unlikely that you would want to give an Admin user just the Write right to the ACL property. You would probably want to give the Admin user Supervisor object right. This would give complete control over the object and its subordinates, unless as noted earlier, you block the Supervisor right.

Normally, you would probably not single out the ACL property (which appears as *Object Trustee property* in the NetWare Administrator Tool) to give property rights to. But you could inadvertently grant the Write right to All Properties. This in turn would grant the Write right to the ACL property, and then the problem described earlier would exist.

Do not assign users the Write property right to the ACL property or the All Properties.

NDS Rights and the File System

A trustee who has the Write property right to the NetWare server's ACL property is granted the Supervisor file system right to the root of each of the server's volumes. It is therefore important that you do not inadvertently give the Write right to the server's ACL property, or the Write right to the Server object (All Properties of the Server object).

Normally, the NDS rights are independent from the file system rights. The only exception is the one pointed out in the previous example. Actually, the exception is necessary to provide an easy way for a trustee with Supervisor rights to access files and directories in volume objects.

A trustee who has the Write property right to the NetWare server's ACL property is granted the Supervisor file system right to the root of each of the server's volumes.

Consider the Admin user, who is normally given the Supervisor object right to the root container of the tree branch that user is expected to manage. This user would then have Supervisor rights to all objects in the tree branch, unless the Supervisor right is explicitly blocked. The Supervisor object right would grant to the user the Supervisor property right to All Properties for all objects, including the Server object. If the user has the Write property right to the Server object, the user then inherits the Supervisor NetWare File System right to the root of all volumes for which the server is a host.

To make a user an administrator of a tree branch, grant the user supervisor privileges to the root of the tree branch.

The Admin user could be explicitly granted the Supervisor NetWare File System right to a volume object also. In general, any NDS object can be granted an explicit NetWare File System right to a

file or directory in any volume object, even though an NDS object is usually granted NDS security rights. Figure 3.33 shows a situation where the user Admin1.CORP.ESL has been granted Supervisor, Read, and File Scan rights to the SYSTEM directory of a volume, and figure 3.34 shows that the NDS Group object Nfsgroup.CORP.ESL has been granted Read and File Scan rights.

Exercise care when assigning a container object a right to another NDS object or a NetWare file system. A right assigned to a container object is inherited by all objects within that container, because a container acts as a *logical group* of NDS objects.

For instance, if a Supervisor NetWare file system right is assigned to the [Root] object, all objects in the [Root] directory will be assigned the Supervisor NetWare file system right. And since [Root] is the highest container of an NDS tree, this would include all objects in the NDS tree.

Figure 3.33

Assigning NetWare file system rights to a user NDS object.

Directory: SYSTEM

Trustees of this Directory

Trustees:
- Admin1.CORP.ESL
- Nfsgroup.CORP.ESL

Effective Rights...

Add Trustee...

Delete Trustee

Identification

Facts

Trustees of this Directory

Attributes

Access Rights
- ☒ Supervisor
- ☒ Read
- ☐ Write
- ☐ Create
- ☐ Erase
- ☐ Modify
- ☒ File Scan
- ☐ Access Control

Inheritance Filter
- ⬇ ☒
- ☐ Read
- ☐ Write
- ☐ Create
- ☐ Modify
- ☐ Erase
- ☐ File Scan
- ☐ Access Control

OK   Cancel   Help

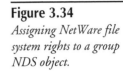

Figure 3.34
Assigning NetWare file system rights to a group NDS object.

Determining Property Effective Rights

Determining property effective rights is similar to calculating object effective rights. The same rules of inheritance apply.

You can deal with objects' property rights in terms of their All Property rights or Selected Property rights. Only All Property rights can be inherited. Selected Property rights *cannot be inherited.* Consider what would happen if a Selected Property were allowed to be inherited. A Selected Property may have no meaning for objects further down in the tree. For instance, intruder detection is a property of a container object, and if this property were inherited by an object that does not have an intruder detection property, such as a User object, it would not make sense. On the other hand, it may be convenient to assign rights to information inside objects, regardless of the different types of

properties NDS objects can have. This can be done by allowing the All Properties right to be inherited.

The All Properties right and Selected Properties right each have a separate inherited rights filter, so a right can be blocked at any level. Also, a right assigned to a Selected Property overrides the rights that may be inherited through the All Properties Rights.

Case Study 1

Figure 3.35 shows a directory tree for organization IBL. Drew is made a trustee of Organization O=IBL and given the All Properties rights of Create, Read, and Add/Delete Self. The All Properties IRFs for the containers are shown as follows:

IRF for O=IBL	[S C R W A]
IRF for OU=CORP	[C R W]
IRF for OU=MKTG	[S W A]

Figure 3.35
The NDS tree for case study 1.

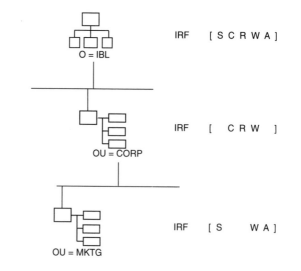

IRF   [S C R W A]

IRF   [C R W   ]

IRF   [S   W A]

Calculate Drew's property effective rights in containers O=IBL, OU=CORP, and OU=MKTG. Assume that Drew does not inherit rights from any source other than the ones listed in the case study.

Figure 3.36 shows the completed worksheet. The explanations for entries in the worksheet are presented next.

Entries for O=IBL

The IRF, according to the case study, is [S C R W A]. There are no rights inherited from above; therefore, the entry for Inherited Rights is *None*. An explicit trustee assignment of [C R A] has been given to the user. The explicit trustee assignment overrides any other inherited rights; so the effective rights for the user in container O=IBL are the same as the explicit trustee assignment. That is, the property effective rights of the user for O=IBL are [C R A].

Entries for OU=CORP

The IRF, according to the case study, is [C R W]. The rights inherited from above are the effective rights of the parent container *masked* with the IRF for this container:

IRF	[C R W]
Effective rights of parent	[C R A]
Inherited rights	[C R]

The masking operation is a *logical AND* operation, which means that an entry needs to be in both the rights for it to be in the final result.

The inherited rights for OU=CORP are [C R]. Because no trustee assignment is made in OU=CORP, the effective rights are the same as the Inherited Rights. That is, property effective rights for OU=CORP are [C R].

O = IBL		
IRF	S C R W A	
Inherited Rights	None	
Trustee Assignment	C R A	
Effective Rights	C R A	

OU = CORP		
IRF	C R W	
Inherited Rights	C R	
Trustee Assignment	None	
Effective Rights	C R	

OU = MKTG		
IRF	S W A	
Inherited Rights	No Rights	
Trustee Assignment	None	
Effective Rights	No Rights	

Figure 3.36

The completed worksheet for case study 1.

Entries for OU=MKTG

The IRF, according to the case study, is [S W A]. The rights inherited from above are the effective rights of the parent container *masked* with the IRF for this container:

IRF	[S W A]
Effective rights of parent	[C R]
Inherited Rights	[ ]

The inherited rights for OU=MKTG are [ ], or *No Rights*. Since no trustee assignment is made in OU=MKTG, the effective rights are the same as the inherited rights. That is, property effective rights for OU=MKTG are *No Rights*.

Case Study 2

Figure 3.37 shows a directory tree for organization IBL. James is made a trustee of Organization O=IBL and is given the All Properties right of Create, Read, and Write. The All Properties IRFs for the containers are shown as follows:

IRF for O=IBL	[S C R W A]
IRF for OU=CORP	[S C R W A]
IRF for OU=MKTG	[S R]

Calculate James's property effective rights in containers O=IBL, OU=CORP, and OU=MKTG. Assume that James does not inherit rights from any source other than the ones listed in the case study.

Figure 3.38 shows the completed worksheet. The explanations for entries in the worksheet are presented next.

Entries for O=IBL

The IRF, according to the case study, is [S C R W A]. There are no rights inherited from above; therefore the entry for inherited rights is *None*. An explicit trustee assignment of [C R W] has been given to the user. The explicit trustee assignment overrides any other inherited rights; so the effective rights for the user in container O=IBL are the same as the explicit trustee assignment. That is, the property effective rights of the user for O=IBL are [C R W (A)]. The [(A)] right is implied from the Write right.

Figure 3.37

The NDS tree for case study 2.

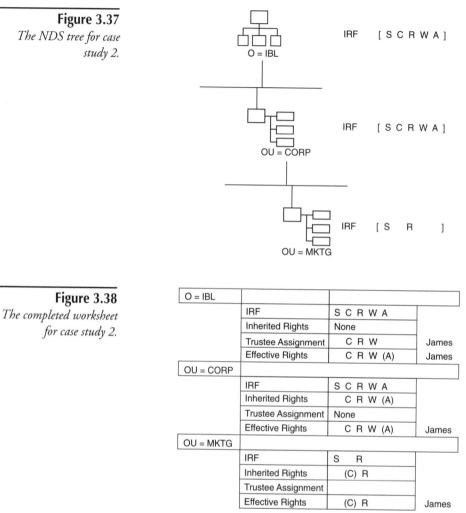

IRF   [S C R W A]

IRF   [S C R W A]

IRF   [S   R   ]

Figure 3.38

The completed worksheet for case study 2.

O = IBL			
IRF	S C R W A		
Inherited Rights	None		
Trustee Assignment	C R W		James
Effective Rights	C R W (A)		James

OU = CORP			
IRF	S C R W A		
Inherited Rights	C R W (A)		
Trustee Assignment	None		
Effective Rights	C R W (A)		James

OU = MKTG			
IRF	S R		
Inherited Rights	(C) R		
Trustee Assignment			
Effective Rights	(C) R		James

Entries for OU=CORP

The IRF, according to the case study, is [S C R W A]. The rights inherited from above are the effective rights of the parent container *masked* with the IRF for this container:

IRF   [S C R W   A]

Effective rights of parent   [C R W   (A)]

Inherited Rights   [C R W   (A)]

The masking operation is a *logical AND* operation, which means that an entry needs to be in both sets of rights for it to be in the final result.

The inherited rights for OU=CORP are [C R W (A)]. Because no trustee assignment is made in OU=CORP, the effective rights are the same as the inherited rights. That is, property effective rights for OU=CORP are [C R W (A)].

Entries for OU=MKTG

The IRF, according to the case study, is [S R]. The rights inherited from above are the effective rights of the parent container *masked* with the IRF for this container:

IRF	[S C R W A]
IRF	[S R]
Effective rights of parent	[C R W (A)]
───────────────────	
Inherited Rights	[(C) R]

The inherited rights for OU=MKTG are [(C) R]. The [(C)] inherited right is implied because of the presence of the Read right in the inherited rights. Because no trustee assignment is made in OU=MKTG, the effective rights are the same as the inherited rights. That is, property effective rights for OU=MKTG are [(C) R].

Case Study 3

Figure 3.39 shows a directory tree for organization DCS. James is made a trustee of Organization DCS and is given the All Properties right of Create, Read, and Write. James is a member of the group ATEAM. ATEAM is given the All Properties right Write and Add/Delete Self to OU=SALES. James is also made a trustee of Organizational Unit OU=MKTG, and given the All Properties right of Write. The All Properties IRFs for the containers are shown as follows:

IRF for O=DCS	[S C R W A]
IRF for OU=SALES	[S C R W A]
IRF for OU=MKTG	[S R]

Calculate James's property effective rights in containers O=DCS, OU=SALES, and OU=MKTG. Assume that James does not inherit rights from any source other than the ones listed in the case study.

Figure 3.40 shows the completed worksheet containing the answers. The explanations for entries in the worksheet are presented next.

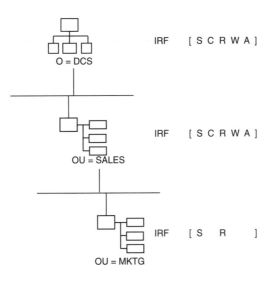

IRF   [S C R W A]

IRF   [S C R W A]

IRF   [S   R   ]

O = DCS

OU = SALES

OU = MKTG

Figure 3.39
The NDS tree for case study 3.

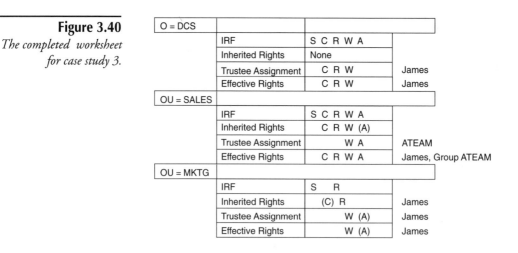

Figure 3.40

The completed worksheet for case study 3.

Entries for O=DCS

The IRF, according to the case study, is [S C R W A]. There are no rights inherited from above; therefore, the entry for inherited rights is *None*. An explicit trustee assignment of [C R W] has been given to the user. The explicit trustee assignment overrides any other inherited rights, so the effective rights for the user in container O=DCS are the same as the explicit trustee assignment. That is, the property effective rights of the user for O=DCS are [C R W (A)]. The [(A)] right is implied from the Write right.

Entries for OU=SALES

The IRF, according to the case study, is [S C R W A]. The rights inherited from above are the effective rights of the parent container *masked* with the IRF for this container:

IRF	[S C R W A]
Effective rights of parent	[C R W (A)]
Inherited Rights	[C R W (A)]

The masking operation is a logical AND operation, which means that an entry needs to be in both sets of rights for it to be in the final result.

The inherited rights for OU=SALES are [C R W (A)]. A trustee assignment is made to Group object SALES of Write and Add/Delete Self. This would override any inherited trustee assignments for Group object ATEAM. But since no trustee assignments are inherited for Group object ATEAM, there are no rights to override. You cannot override the inherited rights of [C R W (A)], because these rights are for User object James and not Group object ATEAM.

Because James is a member of group ATEAM, his rights to OU=SALES are the sum of the inherited and effective rights.

Inherited Rights for user James	[C R W (A)]
Trustee Assignment for ATEAM	[W A]
Effective Rights for James	[C R W A]

That is, property effective rights of User object James for OU=SALES are [C R W A]. Notice that the Add/Delete to Self right is no longer an implied right because it was explicitly assigned to group ATEAM. Also, the Write right is derived from both the Inherited Rights and trustee assignment to Group object ATEAM. If this right were removed from the Trustee Assignment, the Write right would still exist in the Effective rights because it would then be derived from the Inherited Rights.

Entries for OU=MKTG

The IRF, according to the case study, is [S R]. The rights inherited from above are the effective rights of the parent container masked with the IRF for this container:

IRF	[S	R		]
Effective rights of parent	[	C R W	A]
Inherited Rights	[(C) R		]

The inherited rights for OU=MKTG are [(C) R]. The actual right inherited is [R], but the [(C)] inherited right is implied because of the presence of the Read right in the Inherited Rights. Both of these rights are due to rights assigned to user James. Because an explicit trustee assignment is made in OU=MKTG to user James, the explicit trustee assignmnet of [W] overrides the inherited rights. That is, property effective rights for OU=MKTG are [W (A)].

IRF	[S C R W	A]
Inherited Rights for James	[(C) R]
Trustee Assignment for James	[	W (A)]
Effective Rights for James	[	W (A)]

Examining Default Object Rights

NetWare 4 sets certain default system rights to simplify the number of administrative tasks you would otherwise have to perform. One of these default rights is the Browse right that the [Public] trustee gives to the [Root] object. Other default rights are discussed in the following paragraphs.

The Container object that contains the SYS: volume object receives the Read and File Scan (RF) rights to the SYS:PUBLIC directory of the volume object. These rights are indicated in figure 3.41, which shows that the CORP.ESL container that is the Parent container of the server volume object is given the Access Rights of Read and File Scan. This allows all objects, such as user and Group objects, defined in that container to inherit these rights.

In essence, this is equivalent to assigning Read and File Scan rights to group EVERYONE in NetWare 3. If you have upgraded your server from NetWare 3 to NetWare 4, and if the group EVERYONE had Read and File Scan rights to SYS:PUBLIC, you will also see the Group object EVERYONE in the container where the upgraded NetWare 4 server and volume objects are installed. You should also see the Group object EVERYONE as a trustee to SYS:PUBLIC with Read and File Scan rights.

The initial user Admin is by default given the Supervisor object right to [Root]. This means that the Admin user inherits Supervisor object rights to all objects and their contents in the NDS tree. For this reason the password to the initial Admin user must be guarded with care. The Admin user by default is placed in the Organization object container and is named Admin. For security reasons, it may be advisable to rename this User object first and then move it to another context.

The User object, by default, has the following object trustees assigned to it:

- The [Root] object is made a trustee to the User object and is given the Browse object right (see fig. 4.42), which means that any NDS object can browse the User object.

- If the creator of the User object is not the Admin user, who has Supervisor rights, the creator is made a trustee with Supervisor rights to the newly created object.

Another default right is that the creator (Admin) of the Server object is given the Supervisor object right to the Server object. Assigning Supervisor rights to Server objects also gives Supervisor rights to All Properties. Supervisor All Properties right also implies Write property right to the ACL property of the Server object. Anyone who has the Write property right to the ACL property of the Server object is given Supervisor right to the root of the server's volumes. It is implied that assigning the Supervisor right to a Server object gives all file system rights to volumes attached to that server.

The default rights assigned during NDS installation, file Server object installation, and User object creation are summarized in tables 3.3, 3.4 and 3.5.

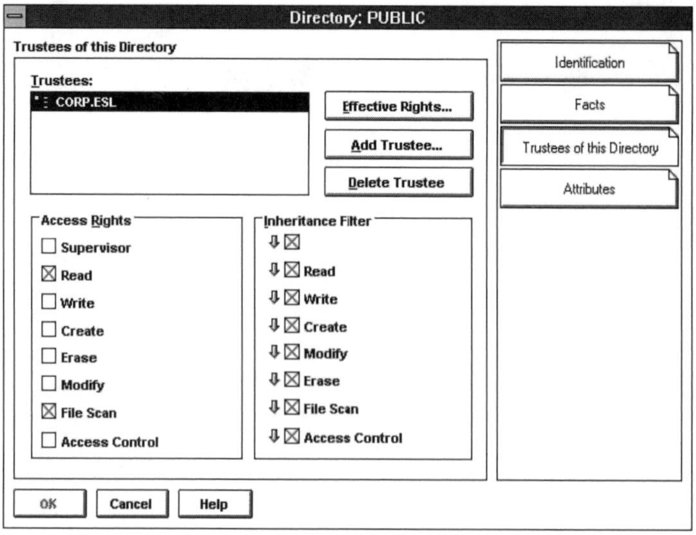

Figure 3.41

The rights to SYS:PUBLIC.

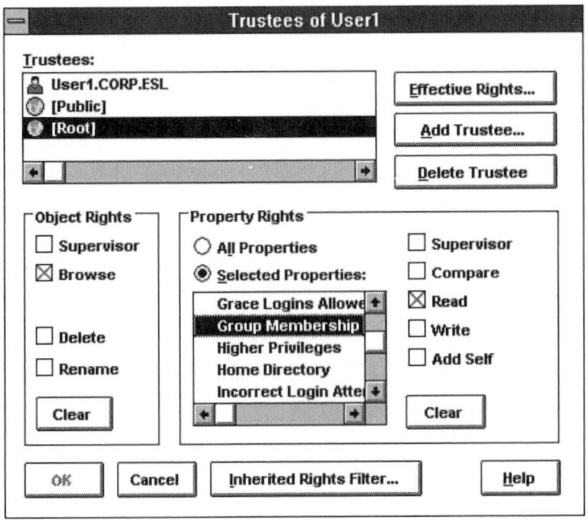

Figure 3.42

The default [Root] trustee assignment for User object.

Table 3.3
Default NDS Rights During NDS Installation

Trustee	NDS Right	Comments
Admin	[S] object right to [Root]	Allows Admin user to administer the entire NDS tree
[Public]	[B] object right to [Root]	Allows users to view the NDS tree using CX and NLIST in the SYS:LOGIN directory without first being authenticated by the NDS tree

Table 3.4
Default NDS Rights During Server Installation

Trustee	NDS Right	Comments
Server object creator	[S] object right to Server object	Allows the creator (usually the administrator of container) to administer the Server object
[Public]	[R] (Read) property right Messaging Server property	Allows network messaging clients to identify the to messaging server assigned to the server
Server	[S] object right to server object	Allows priveleged processes running on the server to modify parameters in the Server object

Table 3.5
Default NDS Rights for User Object

Trustee	NDS Right	Comments
[Public]	[R] (Read) property right to Default Server property of User object	Allows network clients to identify the default server for the user
[Root]	[R] (Read) property right to Network Address and Group membership property of user object	Allows authenticated network clients of the NDS tree to identify the login network addressand the group memberships of the user
User	[R] (Read) property right to All Properties of User object	Allows user to read the values of any property stored in the User object
	[RW] (Read, Write) property rights to the Login Script property for the User object	Allows users to change their login scripts
	[RW] (Read, Write) property rights to the Print Job Configuration property for the User object	Allows users to change their print job configurations

Network Administration Strategies

The NDS tree can potentially be very big because it is used to represent network resources in an organization. For a small organization, the NDS tree can be managed by a single administrator user. For larger organizations, it is more practical for the functions of network administration to be carried out by a number of users. In this case, the network administration tasks need to be divided among several network administrators. One way of doing this is to assign an administrator to each tree branch.

Figure 3.43 shows the NDS tree for organization O=ESL with several administrators for the department tree branches. Each of the tree branches with

the organization units OU=CORP, OU=ENG, and OU=MKTG have administrators CN=Admin. OU=CORP.O=ESL, CN=Admin.OU=ENG.O= ESL and CN=Admin.OU=MKTG.O=ESL, respectively. Typically, these Administrators have complete responsibility for managing their NDS tree branch, but no rights to manage another tree branch. The department Administrators do not have rights to manage objects in the context O=ESL. Resources in context O=ESL are managed by user CN=Admin.O=ESL that is defined in the O=ESL context. The CN=Admin.O=ESL Administrator can create new organization containers and manage rights to the [Root] object, but typically does not have rights to manage the tree branches for the individual departments.

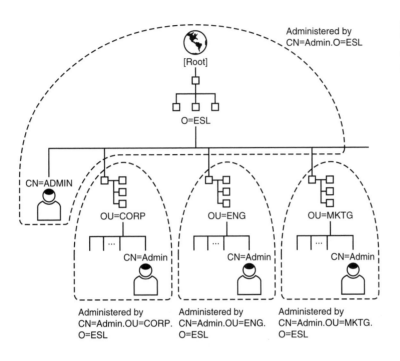

Figure 3.43

Administrators per NDS tree branch

A second way to manage the NDS tree is to have one administrator account that manages the entire NDS tree (this is called centralized administration), or additionally assign assistant network administrators who help the main network administrator. This is similar to the workgroup manager concept used in NetWare 3.

In general, centralized administration is appropriate for small networks that want to have a single administrator. There are, however, some tasks that should be centrally administered; these include the following:

- Naming the directory tree

- Installing the first NetWare server in the directory tree

- Creating the top levels of a directory tree

- Managing partitioning, replication, and time synchronization

- Assigning container administrators (administrator of subtrees)

Distributed management is generally preferred for larger networks that can have a large NDS tree. The following tasks can generally be distributed:

- Creating user accounts

- Defining and configuring print services

- Assigning file system trustees

- Creating workgroup managers

- Installing additional servers in the NDS tree

- Performing file system backups

Considerations for Setting Up a Container Administrator and Assigning Rights

If only one person is expected to be the administrator of a container, you can create the appropriate trustee assignments for the user.

If you need to assign more than one person as an administrator for the container, you can make use of the Organizational Role object. If you decide to use Organizational Role objects, you should, as a precaution, give another user Supervisor object trustee assignments to the container, in case the Organizational Role object is accidentally (or deliberately) deleted. The Organizational Role is particularly useful when the users who are assigned administrative responsibilities are changed often, but the administrator's responsibility does not change. When a user is made an occupant of an Organizational Role, the Organizational Role object is listed in the User object's Security Equal To property.

The following are guidelines for setting up container administrators using Organizational Role objects:

1. Create an Organizational Role object in the container to be managed.

2. Make the Organizational Role object a trustee to the container with appropriate trustee rights.

   The choice of trustee rights will depend on the extent of control to be given to the container administrator versus the control to be retained by the original network administrator.

3. Assign any necessary rights to the file system for the container administrator.

4. Make administrator users occupants of the Organizational Role object.

Although you could use the Security Equal To property of User objects to create multiple container administrators, this approach is not recommended. If the User object that has the explicit administrator rights is deleted, all User objects that had derived administrator rights because of security equivalence will lose the administrator rights. In certain situations, such as the exclusive container administrator, this could result in loss of administrative control over the container and the corresponding tree branch.

Only administrator users who need to manage NDS objects on a regular basis need additional NDS rights. Most ordinary users do not need to create and delete objects or to modify their property values. Novell offers the following NDS security guidelines.

1. Start with the default assignments.

   The default assignments are adequate for most users and most circumstances. The defaults are designed to give users access to information they need without giving them excessive rights.

2. Avoid assigning rights through All Properties of an object.

   All Property rights may give users access to private information about users and other objects. In some cases, excessive rights may accrue to users, because they have rights to critical properties such as the Object Trustee (ACL) property of an object.

3. Use Selected Property rights to assign or restrict properties. Remember that Selected Property rights override All Property rights.

4. Be careful how you assign Write property right to the Object Trustees (ACL) property of an object.

The Write property right to the ACL of an object enables users to add themselves as trustees to the object and give themselves Supervisor rights. Remember that if you have All Properties Supervisor or Write property right to an object, you will automatically have Write property to the ACL of the object, unless you use the Selected property IRF for the ACL property to block the Write right.

5. Assigning Supervisor object right grants to the trustee the All Properties Supervisor property right to the object.

Because of the all inclusive privileges that are implied by Supervisor object rights, you may want to assign to the container administrator a more limited set of rights. For example, you may assign the [B C D R] object rights to the container, and selected property rights to specific properties. If you decide to use the All Property rights, ensure that the user does not derive the Write property right to the Object Trustees (ACL) property. You can prevent inheritance of rights by using explicit trustee assignment to a property or using the selected property IRF.

6. Use caution in assigning Supervisor object right to the Server object.

Assigning a trustee Supervisor object right to the Server object gives to the trustee the All Properties right to the Server object. The All Properties Supervisor property right to the Server object, gives to the user the Write property right to the ACL of the Server object. The Write Property right to the ACL of the Server object gives to the user, the Supervisor file system right to the root of all volumes attached to the server.

7. Be careful about filtering the Supervisor object right and deleting the only user who has rights to a subtree.

In decentralized administration, it is common for the container administrator to be the only user to have Supervisor object right to the container. Others are prevented from having Supervisor object right, by the use of the IRF. If the only user that has Supervisor object right (the container administrator, in this case) is deleted, that particular branch of the NDS tree can no longer be managed.

The following are additional considerations for assigning rights:

1. When assigning rights to a container administrator, it is preferable to assign all rights explicitly, rather than just assign the [S] object right. This ensures that the container administrator can still manage the branch if the [S] object right is blocked by an IRF setting at a lower level.

2. Because the IRF can be used to restrict the rights of an Admin user, consider adding the Admin user as an occupant of the administrator Organizational Role (if one is used) for each container. This will enable the Admin user to perform container administration, even if the IRF is used to block the Admin users rights.

3. Decide whether the container administrator will manage the file systems for that container.

If the administrator is to manage the file system, give the administrator effective Supervisor object right to the Server object. If the administrator has Supervisor object right to the conatiner, this right will flow down to the Server objects in the container (unless blocked by and IRF setting on the Server object).

If the administrator is *not* to manage the file system, revoke from the user the Supervisor object right to the Server object. This can be done by removing the Supervisor right from IRF of the Server object. Before doing this, give another user Supervisor object right to the Server object and hence to the file system.

4. If the tree branch is not yet created, give the container administrator only the Create object right. The Container administrator will be given the Supervisor object right to every object he or she creates.

5. Use groups to simplify assignment of rights.

   Assign rights to containers that use the natural grouping property of containers in order to assign rights to users in the container.

   Use NDS Group object to assign rights to users. Give the NDS Group object appropriate rights, and make users who need these specific rights members of the group.

   The members of an NDS Group object, can be from different containers. Such groups objects are sometimes referred to as *global groups*. If the users are separated from the resources they need by WAN links, consider the implication of accessing the resource over the WAN link.

The Exclusive Container Administrator

An exclusive container administrator has Supervisor rights over a specific container only. All rights for other network administrators outside the container are blocked. This approach allows administration functions to be compartmentalized on a container basis, and is useful in organizations that need to have strict security.

As figure 3.43 indicates, in this approach, you must block the rights of the original Administrator account CN=Admin.O=ESL. The general procedure for creating a separate Admin account for a department is shown below. The description will be given in terms of creating a separate Administrator for OU=CORP.O=ESL (see fig. 3.44). The administrator account for the OU=CORP.O=ESL tree branch will be referred to by the name CN=Admin.OU=CORP.O=ESL. If you need to perform this procedure on your NDS tree, you will probably have different names for the root of the tree branch and the Admin user accounts, and you will have to make appropriate substitutions for these names.

1. Create an Admin account in the Department container. In the case of figure 3.44, this is the user CN=Admin.OU=CORP.O=ESL.

2. Assign to the newly created Admin account the following rights:

   Assign the object rights [S B C D R] to OU=CORP.O=ESL.

   Assign the All Property rights [S C R W A] to OU=CORP.O=ESL.

3. Revoke rights from the IRF for OU=CORP.O=ESL to block access rights for other network administrators outside the tree branch. This prevents CN=Admin.O=ESL from inheriting access rights to OU=CORP. You should set the following rights:

   Set the IRF for object rights to [B].

   Set the IRF for All Properties for OU=CORP to [R].

   Keeping the Browse right in the IRF for object rights allows users to see the objects in the CORP tree branch. The All Properties Read right will allow other network administrators to read the properties of NDS objects in the tree branch, unless an object has a selected property right to override this.

4. Remove any trustee assignments to OU=CORP and any of its subcontainers for the original administrator (CN=Admin.O=ESL).

5. Make sure that the new container administrator, CN=Admin.OU=CORP.O=ESL, has Supervisor object rights to himself or herself. Also ensure that no other user such as CN=Admin.O=ESL has rights to CN=Admin.OU=CORP.O=ESL. If another user has access rights to CN=Admin.OU=CORP.O=ESL, he or she can restrict the right to this user.

6. Make sure that no other user is a security equivalent to the newly created Administrator and that there are no aliases to this User object.

Before revoking the Supervisor object right from the IRF for a container, you must have a user who has Supervisor object right to that container. Otherwise, the system will prevent you from revoking the Supervisor IRF right, and you will get an error message that says, "You cannot filter the Supervisor object right because no object has explicit Supervisor object right to this object."

The NetWare utilities do not prevent you from deleting the only User object that has Supervisor object rights to the tree branch. You can, therefore, lose control of an NDS tree branch if you inadvertently (or by design) delete the User object that has Supervisor object rights to the NDS tree branch. If you delete the only User object that has Supervisor object rights to the NDS tree branch, you have created a black hole in the NDS tree.

If you use an Organization Role object to create exclusive container administrators, create an explicit trustee assignment for at least one of the container administrators User objects. This prevents loss of administrative control over a container in case the Organizational Role object is deleted.

Setting Up Central Administration of Containers (Non-Exclusive Container Administrator)

Because of the risk of losing control over a tree branch by either delegating responsibility to a department administrator or through inadvertent creation of a "black hole" in the NDS tree, you may want to use a central network administration with work group managers that act as assistant administrators. You must implement security in such a manner so that you can prevent loss of control over a tree branch. You can use the following procedure as a guideline. The description will be given in terms of creating an assistant Administrator for OU=CORP.O=ESL (see fig. 3.45). The administrator account for the OU=CORP.O=ESL tree branch will be referred to by the name CN=WMgr.OU=CORP.O=ESL. If you need to perform this procedure on your NDS tree, you will probably have different names for the root of the tree branch and the Admin user accounts, and you will have to make appropriate substitutions for these names.

1. Create a Workgroup Manager account, CN=WMgr, in the Department container. In the case of figure 3.44, this is the user CN=WMgr.OU=CORP.O=ESL.

2. Assign to the newly created Workgroup Manager account the following rights:

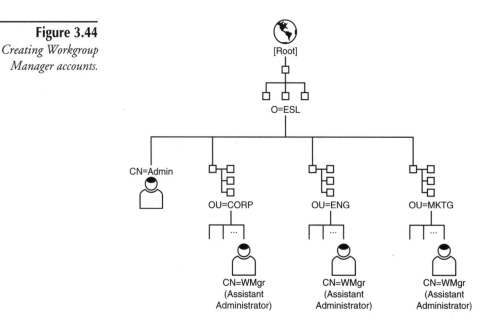

Figure 3.44

Creating Workgroup Manager accounts.

Assign the object rights [B C D R] to OU=CORP.O=ESL.

Assign the All Property rights [C R W A] to OU=CORP.O=ESL.

Assign the Selected Property rights [C R] to Object Trustees (ACL). This is important; otherwise the Workgroup Manager can inherit the Write property right for the ACL property through the All Properties rights, and this gives the Workgroup Manager the ability to modify the trustees for the CORP container, and even give himself or herself the Supervisor object right to the CORP container.

3. Make sure that CN=Admin.O=ESL has an explicit Supervisor trustee assignment to manage OU=CORP. You can do this by assigning the following rights to CN=Admin.O=ESL:

Assign the Object rights [S B C D R] to OU=CORP.O=ESL.

Assign the All Property rights [S C R W A] to OU=CORP.O=ESL.

4. Make sure that CN=Admin.O=ESL has an explicit Supervisor trustee assignment to CN=WMgr.OU=CORP.O=ESL. This can be done by assigning the following rights for CN=Admin.O=ESL:

Assign the Object rights [S B C D R] to CN=WMgr.OU=CORP.O=ESL.

Assign the All Property rights [S C R W A] to CN=WMgr.OU=CORP.O=ESL.

5. Remove rights from the IRF for CN=WMgr.OU=CORP.O=ESL. This prevents the Workgroup Manager from inheriting excessive management rights. Set the IRF as follows:

Set the IRF for Object rights for CN=WMgr.OU=CORP.O=ESL to [B].

Set the IRF for All Properties rights for CN=WMgr.OU=CORP.O=ESL to [C R].

6. Restrict Workgroup Manager CN=WMgr. OU=CORP.O=ESL rights as follows:

Set the Object rights for CN=WMgr.OU= CORP.O=ESL to [B].

Selected Property right for CN=WMgr.OU= CORP.O=ESL set to [C R] for ACL property.

Set the Selected Property right for CN=WMgr.OU=CORP.O=ESL to [R W] for Login Script property.

Set the Selected Property right for CN=WMgr.OU=CORP.O=ESL to [R W] for Print Job Configuration property.

The Danger of Giving a Workgroup Manager Write Property Rights to the ACL of a Container

A common problem in setting up a workgroup manager who acts as an assistant administrator is the failure to revoke Write property rights from the ACL property of the container.

Consider a workgroup manager CN=WMgr.OU= CORP.O=ESL who has been given the following rights to manage the OU=CORP.O=ESL tree branch.

■ Object rights of [B C D R] to OU=CORP.O=ESL

■ All Property rights of [C R W A] to OU=CORP.O=ESL

Figure 3.45 shows the [B C D R] object rights and [C R W A] All Properties rights assigned for WMgr.CORP.ESL. Because the [C R W A] All Properties implies that the user WMgr.CORP.ESL has Write property right to the OU=CORP.O=ESL container's ACL property, the user WMgr. CORP.ESL can modify this ACL property.

Figure 3.46 shows that a possible scenario is that the WMgr.CORP.ESL has acquired Supervisor object rights, by selecting Trustees of this Object for the CORP container, using the NetWare Administrator, and adding explicit rights to himself or herself.

To prevent this scenario from occurring, you should explicitly assign to the workgroup manager the Selected Property right of [C R] to the ACL property for the container.

Types of Administrative Accounts

The Admin account created for the Directory tree should be retained, even if you decide not to use central administration. This account is needed for centralized operations such as partition management, NDS backups, and restructuring of the top level of the NDS tree. You need not name the administrator account for the NDS tree Admin; it can be renamed to any other valid user name.

Because users can be assigned different rights at each level of the NDS tree, NetWare 4 administration gives you extreme flexibility in setting up an administrative structure to suit your organization. Table 3.6 shows some example network administrative roles, recommended by Novell, that you may find useful. This table also shows the rights assignments required for the administrative role.

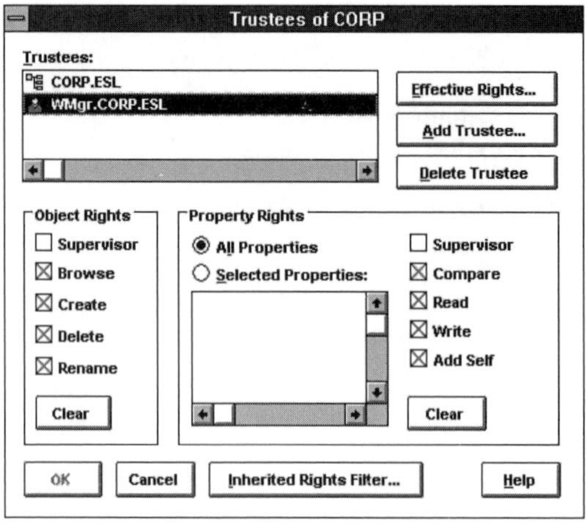

Figure 3.45

The workgroup manager rights to Container object.

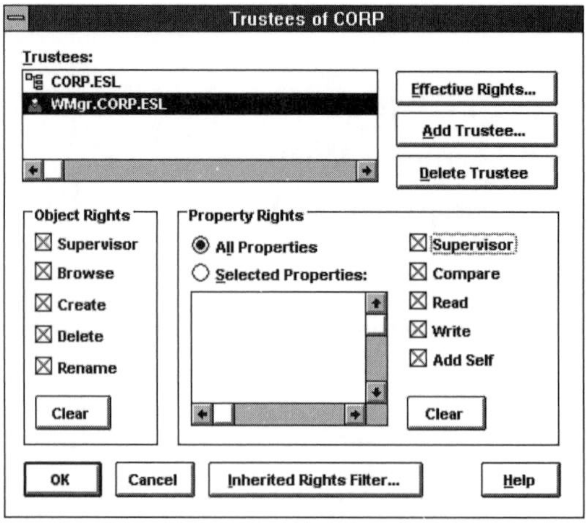

Figure 3.46

The workgroup manager acquires Supervisor object right because of Write property right to container.

Table 3.6
Example Administrative Roles

Role Performed by Administrator	Recommended Account	Rights	Functions
Enterprise NDS	Admin User object such as the default Admin object	[S] object right to [Root] during initial installation	Install the first server and name the NDS tree. Create top-level of the NDS tree. Manage partitioning, replication and time synchronization. Assign container administrators. Upgrade servers, clients, and applications. Enable auditing and issuing initial auditor password.
Container Administrator	User object assigned rights to container or occupant of an Organizational Role object	[SBCDR] object rights to appropriate container	Perform backup and restore operations. Create and configure print services for the container. Upgrade server, client, and application software for users in containers. Monitor file system performance. Install NDS objects in container. Monitor server performance. Write and maintain login scripts. Monitor disk space usage; assign file system trustees. Track errors.

Table 3.6, Continued
Example Administrative Roles

Role Performed by Administrator	Recommended Account	Rights	Functions
Print Server Operator	PS operator user	Organizational Role whose occupants are users who are print server operators	Add to Print Server Operator property of print server Load and bring down the print server.
Print Queue Operator	PQ operator user	Organizational Role whose occupants are users who are print queue operators	Add to Print Queue Operator property of print queue Manage print jobs in queue (delete, change order, hold/resume print jobs). Change queue status.

Objects with Special Rights Assignments

The following objects may require additional rights because of their need to access specific network resources:

■ Profile login script

■ Directory map

■ Alias of User object

■ Mailing list administrator

Special Rights for the Profile Login Script Object

The Profile object contains the profile login script. User objects have a property called Profile that can be set to point to a Profile object. The profile login script is a way of implementing a common login script that is shared by any user that has his or her Profile property pointing to the same Profile object. The profile login script is executed after the system login script (if one exists) but before the user's login script (if one exists). The system login script is the login script for the user's container. If the user's login script does not exist, and the NO_DEFAULT directive has not been specified in the system or profile login script, the default login script is run.

The following simple exercise will demonstrate the rights needed to run a profile login script:

1. Create a container O=IBL, and a User object James in that container.

2. Create the Profile object CProf in O=IBL and examine its default trustees.

   Notice that the Profile object CN=CProf. O=IBL does not have any default trustees.

3. In the Profile Login script for the Profile object CN=CProf.O=IBL, place the following login script statement:

   ```
   WRITE "Profile login script for CProf is
   ➡executed"
   ```

4. Set the Profile property for the user to point to the CN=CProf.O=IBL object.

   Beginning with NetWare 4.1, if you have not assigned to the user the Read property right to the profile objects login script property, you will see a message informing you of this. Save the assignment to the profile object, but for the time being do not assign any additional trustees to the profile object.

5. Login as the user CN=James.O=IBL.

   Notice that the profile login script for the user James is not executed. The reason for this is that user James does not have [R] property right to the Profile object's Login Script property.

6. Log on as Admin. Make user CN=James.O =IBL a trustee of CN=CProf.O=IBL with the [R] Selected Property rights to the Login Script property.

7. Log on as the user CN=James.O=IBL.

   Notice that the profile login script for the user James is executed. The reason for this is that user James now has [R] property right to the Profile object's Login Script property.

When a Profile object is created, it does not have any default trustees. A user whose Profile property is set to a Profile object must be able to read the profile login script in order to execute it. This means that the user must have the Read property right to the Profile object's Login Script property.

 The Novell documentation says that if the User and the Profile object are in the same container, no additional rights to the Profile object are needed. If the container in which the profile login script was created was made a trustee of the Profile object and given the Read property right to its Login Script, this would be true. As the previous exercise indicates, this is not true for NetWare 4, and a user must have the Read property right to the profile login script, even if the user and the Profile object are in the same container.

When a Profile object is created, it does not have any default trustees. To execute the Profile Login Script, you must have the [R] property right to the Profile object's Login Script property.

Follow these steps to set up profile login script for a user.

1. Create the Profile object and set its profile login script.

2. Set the Profile property of a user to point to the Profile object.

3. Assign to the user the [R] property right to the Profile object's Login Script property.

If all users are in the same container, you can assign the container a trustee of the Profile object and give it the [R] property right to the Profile object's Login Script property.

Typically, users who share a profile login script are in different containers. If they are in the same container, using the system login script for that container is usually sufficient. If the users are members of a Group object or an Organizational

Role object, you can make the Group object or Organizational Role object a trustee of the Profile object. Alternatively, you may want to individually assign users trustees of the Profile object.

Special Rights for the Directory Map Object

The Directory Map object simplifies the use of the MAP command and makes the MAP command independent of changes to the location of the directory being mapped to. In order to use the Directory Map object, you must have the Read All Properties right to the Directory Map object. When a Directory Map object is first created it does not have any default trustee assignment. You must explicitly assign the [R] All Properties right to the Directory Map object.

The following shows an attempt to map to a Directory Map object (CN=DirMap.O=ESL) by a user who does not have the Read All Properties right to the Directory Map object:

```
F:\>MAP G: = .CN=DirMap.O=ESL
MAP-4.12-195: Directory [CN=DIRMAP.O=ESL]
cannot be located.
```

If the user is assigned the [R] All Properties right to the CN=DirMap.O=ESL, the above command works correctly as shown:

```
F:\>MAP G: = .CN=DirMap.O=ESL
Drive G: = NW4KS_SYS.CORP: \DOC
```

In the previous example, the Directory Map object, CN=DirMap.O=ESL, was set to point to the NW4KS_SYS:DOC directory. The user should have at least [R F] file system right to the directory being pointed to for the MAP command to work.

 Study Note

When a Directory Map object is first created, it does not have any default trustee assignment. Before you can use the Directory Map object, you must assign the [R] All Properties right to the Directory Map object. Note that the [R] property right also implies the [C] property right.

You may want to make the container in which the Directory Map object is defined a trustee to the Directory Map object and give to the container the [R] All Properties right. This will give all users in the container the [R] All Properties right to the Directory Map object and allow them to use it.

The Directory Map object has a property called Rights to Files and Directories. Assigning rights to a file system via this property does not cause these rights to be inherited by the users mapping to the Directory Map object.

Special Rights for Alias User Objects

To understand the rights needed by alias users to execute their login scripts, consider the situation in figure 3.47, which shows an NDS tree for organizations IBL and UNE.

Organization IBL has a user James defined in the container O=IBL, and organization UNE has an Alias object Bond that is an alias to CN=James.O=IBL. The user CN=Bond.O=UNE is the *alias user,* and the user CN=James.O=IBL is called the *aliased user.* The O=IBL has a system login script set that has the following login script statement:

```
WRITE "Executing login script for container
➡IBL"
```

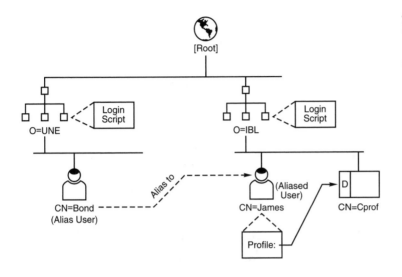

Figure 3.47
The Alias User object and login scripts.

User CN=James.O=IBL has his Profile property set to the Profile object CN=CProf.O=IBL. The profile login script has the following login statement:

```
WRITE "Executing profile login script CProf"
```

User CN=James.O=IBL has the following statements in his user login script:

```
WRITE "Executing login script for user James"
```

Additionally, user CN=James.O=IBL is a trustee of the Profile object CN=CProf.O=IBL and has the [R] property right to the Profile object's Login Script property. Because Bond is an alias to user James, Bond is automatically a trustee of CN=CProf.O=IBL with the same rights. The NetWare Administrator does not allow you to add the alias and the aliased user as trustees of the same object (try it, to verify this for your NetWare 4 server).

If you log on as user CN=James.O=IBL, you will see messages similar to the following:

```
Executing login script for container IBL
```

```
Executing profile login script CProf
Executing login script for user James
```

If you log in as the alias user CN=Bond.O=UNE, you will see messages similar to the following:

```
Executing profile login script CProf
Executing login script for user James
```

Notice that the login script for the O=IBL container is not executed for the user CN=Bond.O=UNE. When an alias user logs in, it runs the container login script for the container the alias user is in, and not the container login script for the aliased user.

If you were to create a system login script for container O=UNE, and place in it the statement:

```
WRITE "Executing login script for container
↪UNE"
```

and then log in as the alias user CN=Bond.O=UNE, you will see messages similar to the following:

```
Executing profile login script CProf
Executing login script for user James
```

Notice that the login script for O=UNE container is not executed for the user CN=Bond.O=UNE, even though it has been set. In order for an alias user to execute the login script of the container it is defined in, the alias user must be granted the [R] property right to the Login Script property of its container. If this is done, logging on as alias user CN=Bond.O=UNE will produce messages similar to the following, showing that the alias user's container login script is executed.

```
Executing login script for container UNE
Executing profile login script CProf
Executing login script for user James
```

Author's Note It may seem a little strange that the alias user needs to be granted an explicit trustee assignment to the Login Script property of the container, especially because the container is made a trustee of itself and given the [R] Selected Property right to its Login Script property.

The reason for assigning the alias user an explicit trustee assignment to the Login Script property of the container is because the alias user is really a "phantom" user whose true existence is in the container that holds the aliased user, even though the alias user does not execute the system login script of the aliased user. The aliased user needs to have [R] property right to the alias container's Login Script property.

If you assign the alias user the [R] property right to its container and then go back to reexamine the trustee assignments of the alias's container,

you will see that the aliased user is listed as a trustee, even though you initially made the alias user a trustee of the container.

The alias user does not execute the system login script of the aliased user. It executes the login script of the container in which it is defined.

For the alias user to execute the login script of the container it is defined in, the alias user must be granted the [R] property right to the Login Script property of its container.

Special Rights for the Mailing List Administrator

One of the properties of User objects, Organizational Role objects, Organizational Unit objects and Organization objects is the e-mail Address property. This property can be used to enter the electronic mail address for the object. The actual value of the e-mail address will depend on the type of e-mail system that is being used.

Some organizations prefer to delegate the responsibility of maintaining properties such as e-mail address, telephone number, fax number, and postal address to a special user called the Mailing List Administrator. The Mailing List Administrator should be able to modify these properties and should therefore have Read and Write property rights to the properties they will manage. The Mailing List Administrator account can be implemented as a User object. If a more formal designation is needed for the Mailing List Administrator, it can also be implemented as an Organizational Role object.

The Mailing List Administrator should have the [R W] property rights for the following properties that the Mailing List Administrator will manage:

- E-mail address

- Telephone number

- Fax number

- Postal address:

    Street
    City
    State or Province
    Postal (ZIP) code
    Post Office Box properties

The trustee rights assigned to the Mailing List Administrator must be assigned for each NDS object the Mailing List Administrator will manage. For a large organization, this can become a very laborious process. You might be tempted to give to the Mailing List Administrator rights for the users he or she will manage through a Group object or a Container object, but you will end up giving the Mailing Administrator more rights than he or she should have. Also, assigning the All Properties rights to the Mailing List Administrator would give the Write property right for the ACL property. If the Mailing List Administrator has the Write property to the ACL of an object, the Mailing List Administrator can modify the trustee assignments to the object.

Rights for Traveling Users

As traveling users try to use their time more efficiently by accessing their organizations network from remote locations, special considerations for NDS rights need to be given to such users. The following discussion is based on Novell's classifications of traveling users:

- Users who divide their work time between home and office

- Users who need access from a temporary location while they are working on special projects

- Users who spend a considerable amount of their work time traveling and need access to the network regularly from remote locations

For each type of user you should consider the following issues:

- Access to files on server volumes

- Access to applications

- Access to files from several remote locations

- Access to resources such as printers and e-mail accounts

- Authenticating to NDS and NDS objects

- Number of traveling users

- Type of computer used by traveling users (portable versus desktop)

Users Traveling between Two Offices

The users who divide their time between two work locations need access to similar resources in both locations. This is especially true if they do the same type of work at each location. Novell reccommends the following as one of the ways of handling this situation:

- Create two User objects, one in each location

- Give required rights to each user for the resources needed at each location

- Give necessary rights to Profile Login Script and Directory Map objects

Users Traveling to Locations Temporarily or User Traveling to Many Remote Locations

Users who are at a location temporarily or those that travel on a regular basis to many remote locations need access to appropriate files, directories, printers, and applications. Novell recommends the following as one way to handle this situation:

- Create an alias User object, or assign the user to a Group or Organizational Role object.

- Give required rights to Alias, Group, or Organizational Role objects for network directories and resources.

- Give necessary rights to Alias, Group, or Organizational Role objects to read any Profile Login Script and Directory Map objects.

- When creating aliases, make the original User object a trustee to the alias's container and grant the user Read property rights to the containers login script property.

Guidelines for Determining Excessive Rights

Occasionally you may discover that a user or group of users has excessive rights. Excessive rights are any

rights that are above and beyond those required by users to complete their tasks. Excessive rights can also give users the ability to acquire additional rights or restrict rights of other users. To correct the problem of excessive rights, you must be able to trace the origin of these rights. In a NetWare 4 environment, this can be particularly challenging because of the many levels of NetWare security and the large number of sources from which rights can be acquired. The following is a guideline for determining excessive rights:

1. Determine the explicit rights granted to the following objects:

   User objects

   Group and Organizational Role objects

   Containers between the user and the [Root]

   Security equivalencies

   Rights granted to the [Public] and the [Root] trustee

2. Determine the rights inherited through explicit trustee assignments to any of the objects listed in the previous item. Also, determine if a user inherits rights through group membership, container membership, or security equivalence.

3. Use the NetWare tools to determine trustee assignments and effective rights.

For NDS rights, you can use NETADMIN or NWADMIN:

Use the following as an outline to determine the NDS Effective Rights using NWADMIN:

1. Right-click on resource you want to check.

2. Select Trustees of this Object.

3. Click on the Effective Rights button.

4. Click on the Browse button, locate the User object, and click on OK. You should see the Effective Rights for the user.

For File System rights, you can use NWADMIN, NETADMIN, FILER, or the RIGHTS command.

Use the following as an outline to determine the file system Effective Rights using NWADMIN:

1. Double-click on the volume object to see the directory tree structure underneath it.

2. Right-click on directory you want to check.

3. Select Trustees of this Object.

4. Click on the Effective Rights button.

5. Click on the Browse button, locate the User object, and click on OK. You should see the Effective Rights for the user.

Guidelines for Determining the Cause of Insufficient Rights

This is the opposite of the problem discussed in the previous section. Occasionally you may run into a situation where a user does not have sufficient rights to perform a task or has just lost those rights because of changes made to the NDS. In this case, you must consider the following:

1. Check to see whether any explicit rights the user is supposed to have have been granted. Check to see if any IRFs are blocking the user's rights. If they are, you can set the IRF to pass

the desired rights or make an explicit trustee assignment.

2. Check to see whether the user is a member of the Group or Organizational Role objects that have been assigned the rights needed by the user.

3. If the user was given rights through security equivalence, check the user's security equivalence property to see if the security equivalencies exist. Also, check to see whether the user still exists. This is the risk when making one user a security equivalent to another user.

4. Check the rights of the container through which the user inherits the rights. If a reorganization of the NDS tree has taken place, certain rights may not have been properly assigned to Container objects.

NetWare File System Security

The NetWare file system security works the same as in NetWare 3. Because this is a book about upgrading from NetWare 3 to NetWare 4, a detailed discussion is beyond the scope of this book. This section will point out the major differences between NetWare 3 and NetWare 4. For further details, refer to the companion training guide, *NetWare 4 System Administration.* For details about NetWare 3 File System Rights, refer to *NetWare: The Professional Reference.* Both titles are from New Riders Publishing; see the back of this book for more information.

When a User object is created, no automatic file system rights are created, except to the user's home directory if one was specified at the time of creation. Figure 3.48 shows the rights to newly created user CN=KSS.O=IMF to the home directory USERS\KSS in volume CN=FS1_SYS.OU=SALES.O=ESL. Notice that the user has [S R W C E M F A] rights to his home directory; that is, the user has all rights to his home directory.

In NetWare 3, the term *Inherited Rights Mask* (IRM) was used to describe the mechanism to block the flow of NetWare file system rights. In NetWare 4, the term *Inherited Rights Filter* (IRF) is used for both file system rights and NDS object rights.

> **Author's Note** Another minor distinction, though not documented in the Novell manuals, is that in NetWare 3 the Supervisor file system rights were called *Supervisory*. They are now called *Supervisor* in NetWare 4.

As in NetWare 3, the file system Supervisor right granted to a directory also grants Supervisor rights to files and directories below the directory.

One major conceptual difference between the NetWare 3 and NetWare 4 file system is the scope of the trustee. In NetWare 3, the trustee could only be a user account or a group account defined in the server's bindery. In NetWare 4, User objects and Group objects in containers other than where the volume is installed can be assigned trustees. The trustee is not limited to the user and Group objects—it can be any NDS object, such as another container object. If a container object is made a trustee of a file or directory, all objects within it (including, of course, user and Group objects) inherit the trustee rights to the file or directory.

Any NDS object that has a Write right to the ACL property (Object Trustee property) of the NetWare Server object is also granted the Supervisor right to the root of each of the volumes hosted by the

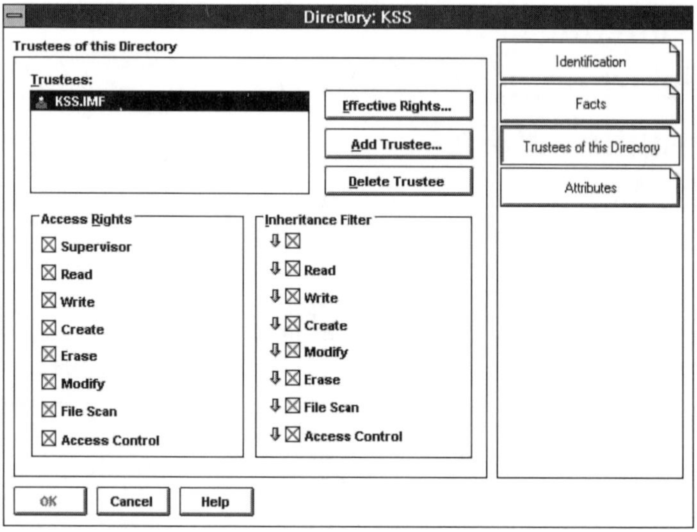

Figure 3.48

The rights of user KSS in home directory.

NetWare server. Because a Supervisor file/directory right cannot be blocked by an IRF, this should be a consideration in setting up security rights.

The Write property right can be granted through any of the following:

■ Write right to All Properties of the NetWare Server object.

■ Write right to the Selected Property ACL (Object Trustee) for the NetWare Server object.

■ Supervisor right to the All Properties right or ACL property (Selected Property) for the NetWare Server object.

■ Supervisor object right to the NetWare Server object. This causes the object to have

Supervisor right to the All Properties of the NetWare Server object.

■ Security equivalence to an object that has any of the rights listed above.

Directory and File Attribute in NetWare 4 are a *superset* of the rights for NetWare 3. That is, NetWare 4 directory and file attributes include all those for NetWare 3, and additionally, the rights listed in table 3.7.

The attributes Migrate (M), Compress (Co), and Can't Compress (Cc) are status attributes and indicate the status of individual files only. The other attributes—Don't Migrate (Dm), Don't Compress (Dc), and Immediate Compress (Ic)— apply to both files and directories and specify actions that are to be performed or prevented from occurring.

Table 3.7
Additional NetWare 4 Attributes

Attribute	File/Directory	Abbreviation	Description
Migrate	File	M	Indicates that the file has migrated to near-line storage
Don't Migrate	File/ Directory	Dm	Prevents a file or the files in a directory frommigrating
Compress	File	Co	Indicates if a file has been compressed
Don't Compress	File/ Directory	Dc	Prevents a file or the files in a directory from being compressed
Immediate Compress	File/ Directory	Ic	Specified file or files in a directory are marked for compression as soon as the OD can perform compression
Can't Compress	File	Cc	Indicates that a file cannot be compressed because of limited space saving benefit

The attributes Migrate (M), Compress (Co), and Can't Compress (Cc) are status attributes and indicate the status of individual files only; the attributes Don't Migrate (Dm), Don't Compress (Dc), and Immediate Compress (Ic) apply to both files and directories.

The Data Migration feature is installed using INSTALL.NLM and requires a near-line-storage medium that acts as a secondary to the primary hard disk storage area.

The compression feature is enabled or disabled on a volume-by-volume basis during installation. It can be further controlled by a variety of SET parameters.

 The Data Migration feature is installed using INSTALL.NLM, and the compression feature is installed on a per-volume basis.

Study Guide for the Chapter

If you are preparing for the NetWare 3.11 to 4.0 Update CNE exams, review the chapter with the following goals:

- Review the different types of login restrictions that can be performed in NetWare 4. Understand the basics of NetWare login authentication. Understand how NDS security is implemented. Use the Study Notes for quick review.

- Pay particular attention to the topics of NDS trustee assignments for objects and properties.

Understand how inheritance and security equivalence can be used in computing effective rights. Go through the case studies, and understand the reasoning behind the solutions to these case studies.

- After studying this chapter, attempt the sample test questions for this chapter. If you miss the answer or answers to a question, review the appropriate topic until you understand the reason for the correct answer.

Next to Chapter 2, "NetWare Directory Services Fundamentals," this is the most important chapter because it deals with issues of NDS security, which is important to understand in order to implement NDS effectively.

Chapter Summary

In this chapter, you have learned the basics of NetWare 4 security. NetWare security is layered. The first layer you must pass through is Login Authentication and Login Restriction. The second layer is NDS security. The last (third) layer is the NetWare File System security.

You were presented with a detailed explanation of how Login Authentication is done. Certain mathematical equations were presented to show you how authentication works. You can use this as a reference, and to further your understanding. You will not be tested on the details of the authentication process, however, as shown by these mathematical equations.

Most of the chapter was spent on NDS security issues, as this is a new area for NetWare 3 administrators. A number of case studies were presented to help you understand how NDS security works.

Chapter Test Questions

Test questions can have a single correct answer or multiple correct answers. Where a single answer is desired, they are indicated by a ○ (circle) notation that precedes the possible answers. Where more than one answer is required, these are indicated by the □ (box) preceding each answer. Not all the questions are multiple choice. Occasionally, you will be asked for a short (usually one-word) answer. The answer in this case is usually a one-word answer. Answers are not case sensitive.

Certain questions will be repeated in different ways, so that you can recognize them even when the wording is different. Taking practice quizzes will not only test your knowledge but also will give you confidence when you take your exam.

For questions dealing with calculating effective rights, the answers should include any implied rights. For example, if the computed effective property right is [R], your answer should also include the Compare (C) right, as the Read right also includes the Compare right. Therefore, the correct answer would be [C R] and not just [R]. In the case studies, the notation [(C) R] was used to indicate that the Compare right was an implied right. Unless the test question asks you to make the distinction between actual effective right and implied right, you should include both in your answer.

1. Which of these are components of NetWare 4 security?

   □ A. Login Security

   □ B. Auditing Security

   □ C. NDS Security

   □ D. Directory Security

   □ E. File System Security

   □ F. File Security

   □ G. Management Security

2. The command to log in as a user Tom in the organization ICL, regardless of the current context, is _____.

   ○ A. LOGIN TOM

   ○ B. LOGIN TOM.ICL

   ○ C. LOGIN .TOM.ICL

   ○ D. LOGIN TOM.ICL

3. The command to log in as a user Mona defined in the Organizational Unit ART, in the organization RAL, given that the current context is O=RAL, is _____.

   ○ A. LOGIN Mona.ART

   ○ B. LOGIN Mona.ART.RAL

   ○ C. LOGIN Mona.RAL.ART

   ○ D. LOGIN Mona

4. Which of these is a valid NetWare 4 login restriction?

   ○ A. Login authentication

   ○ B. Password encryption

   ○ C. Account restrictions

   ○ D. Container restriction

5. Which of these is a valid NetWare 4 login restriction?

   ○ A. Password authentication

   ○ B. Login authentication

   ○ C. Password encryption

   ○ D. Password restriction

6. Which of these are valid login restrictions for NetWare 4?

   ☐ A. Account restrictions

   ☐ B. Password authentication

   ☐ C. Network address restrictions

   ☐ D. Password synchronization and timeout

   ☐ E. Time restrictions

7. Password restrictions in NetWare 4 _____.

   ○ A. can be set to allow a user to change passwords

   ○ B. allow a user to encrypt the user password

   ○ C. require that only the Admin user can change the user's password

   ○ D. require that only a user with Supervisor object rights to the User object can change the user password

8. Which of these are normally associated with NDS security?

   ☐ A. Object rights

   ☐ B. File rights

   ☐ C. Property rights

   ☐ D. File and directory rights

   ☐ E. Inherited Rights Mask

9. Which one of these is an object trustee right?

   ○ A. Read

   ○ B. Write

   ○ C. Browse

   ○ D. File Scan

10. Which one of these is an object trustee right?

    ○ A. Read

    ○ B. Compare

    ○ C. Add/Delete

    ○ D. Rename

11. Which of these grants all rights to the object?

    ○ A. Administrator rights

    ○ B. Container rights to [Root]

    ○ C. Add/Delete Self rights

    ○ D. Supervisor rights

12. Which right allows you to see an object in the NDS tree?

    ☐ A. Create

    ☐ B. Supervisor

    ☐ C. Browse

    ☐ D. Scan

    ☐ E. View

13. Which is the minimal object right that allows you to see an object in the NDS tree?

    ○ A. Create

    ○ B. Supervisor

    ○ C. Browse

    ○ D. Scan

    ○ E. View

14. The Rename trustee assignment can be used to rename a(n) _____ object.

    ☐ A. Root

    ☐ B. Country

☐ C. Leaf

☐ D. Organization

☐ E. Organizational Unit

15. Which one of these NDS objects cannot have Create rights?

   ○ A. Root

   ○ B. Container

   ○ C. Leaf

   ○ D. Organization

   ○ E. Organizational Unit

16. Which of the following statements about [Public] is true?

   ○ A. [Public] is a special trustee that includes all users in a container object.

   ○ B. [Public] is a special trustee that includes all users in an Organization object.

   ○ C. [Public] is a special trustee that includes all users in an Organizational Unit object.

   ○ D. [Public] is a special trustee that includes all users connected to the network.

17. Which of the following statements about [Public] is true?

   ○ A. [Public] is a special trustee that includes all users in a container object.

   ○ B. [Public] is a special trustee that includes all users in an Organization object.

   ○ C. [Public] is a special trustee that includes all users connected to the network but who are not necessarily logged in to the network.

   ○ D. [Public] is a special trustee that includes all users in a [root] object.

18. The Create object right applies to _____ objects only.

   ○ A. Root

   ○ B. Container

   ○ C. Leaf

   ○ D. Organization

   ○ E. Organizational Unit

19. Which of the following statements about [Public] is true?

   ○ A. [Public] is similar to other Group objects whose members can be added or deleted.

   ○ B. [Public] members can be added but are automatically deleted when a user breaks a network connection.

   ○ C. [Public] members initially include all possible User objects, but membership is removed if the workstation a user is logged out of does not respond within a programmable time interval.

   ○ D. [Public] members cannot be added or deleted explicitly.

20. A newly created User object by default is given the following right:

    ○ A. The [Root] object is made a trustee of the container object the user is installed in.

    ○ B. The [Root] object is made a trustee of the User object and given Rename rights.

    ○ C. The [Root] object is made a trustee of the User object and given Supervisor rights.

    ○ D. The [Root] object is made a trustee of the User object and given Browse rights.

    ○ E. The [Root] object is made a trustee of the User object and given Delete rights.

21. When an NDS tree is newly created, the [Public] trustee is given _____.

    ○ A. Read object rights to [Root]

    ○ B. Read object rights to every container object immediately under [Root]

    ○ C. Create object rights to every container object immediately under [Root]

    ○ D. Browse object rights to [Root]

    ○ E. Browse object rights to every container object immediately under [Root]

22. The Admin user account for a newly created NDS tree is given _____.

    ○ A. Write rights to the ACL property of every Server object

    ○ B. Supervisor object rights to all container objects

    ○ C. Supervisor object rights to all leaf objects

    ○ D. Supervisor object rights to [Root]

23. Object rights granted to a volume are generally _____.

    ○ A. inherited by the file system

    ○ B. not inherited by the file system

    ○ C. inherited by the file system if the user is an Admin user

    ○ D. not inherited by the file system unless the user is an Admin user

24. Assigning a user rights to the [Root] container will give _____.

    ○ A. container objects the right to all leaf objects in their container

    ○ B. the User objects rights to the entire tree

    ○ C. that user the right to the entire tree unless this right is explicitly removed using IRF

    ○ D. leaf objects the right to all container objects

25. Which of the following statements about IRF is true?

    ○ A. The IRF is the same as the inherited rights.

    ○ B. The IRF is the same as the effective rights.

○ C. The IRF can be used to block any object right.

○ D. The IRF is set only for container objects.

26. Which of the following statements about IRF is true?

   ○ A. The IRF is the same as the inherited rights.

   ○ B. The IRF is the same as the effective rights.

   ○ C. The IRF is set only for leaf objects.

   ○ D. The Supervisor right can be removed from the IRF.

27. Which of the following statements about IRF is true?

   ○ A. The IRF is used to determine the inherited rights.

   ○ B. The IRF is the same as the effective rights.

   ○ C. The IRF is set only for leaf objects.

   ○ D. The Supervisor right cannot be removed from the IRF.

28. Security equivalence is a property of the _____.

   ○ A. Leaf object

   ○ B. container object

   ○ C. Root object

   ○ D. User object

   ○ E. Group object

29. If a user has the Write property right to the Security equivalence property and Write property to ACL property of an Admin User object, _____.

   ○ A. the user can read other users' security equivalence

   ○ B. the user can modify other users' security equivalence

   ○ C. the user can become security equivalent to another user, but not the Admin user

   ○ D. the user can become security equivalent to the Admin user

30. An effective right can originate from any of the following sources:

   ☐ A. Explicit trustee assignment

   ☐ B. Inherited from trustee's parent container

   ☐ C. Inherited from direct assignment to object's container

   ☐ D. Inherited from the leaf object

   ☐ E. Inherited from assignment of trustee's container to object's container

31. An effective right can originate from any of the following sources:

   ☐ A. Trustee assignment to a Group object

   ☐ B. Trustee assignment to a security equivalent object

   ☐ C. Inherited from the container's Inherited Rights Filter

☐ D. Inherited from the leaf object

☐ E. Inherited from assignment of trustee's container to object's container

32. Which of the following is not a consideration in determining effective rights for an object in a given tree branch?

☐ A. The rights not granted to a container object

☐ B. The rights explicitly granted to a User object

☐ C. The rights inherited from above

☐ D. The rights granted to container objects in another tree branch

33. Which of the following is a consideration in computing effective rights for an object in a given tree branch?

☐ A. The rights granted to container objects in another tree branch

☐ B. The rights granted to an NDS tree with a different root

☐ C. The rights granted to container objects between the object and the [Root]

☐ D. The rights granted through security equivalence

34. To determine the effective rights, which of the following can be used?

☐ A. Inherited Rights Mask

☐ B. Inherited Rights Filter

☐ C. inherited rights

☐ D. explicit trustee assignment

☐ E. induced rights

35. The Supervisor object right _____.

○ A. grants Read rights to all properties

○ B. grants Write rights to all properties

○ C. grants Compare rights to all properties

○ D. grants Add/self rights to all properties

○ E. grants all rights to all properties for an object

36. The Write property right grants you _____.

○ A. the right to change any values to the property

○ B. the right to remove and change any values to the property

○ C. the right to add, remove, and change any values to the property

○ D. the right to read, add, remove, and change any values to the property

37. The Add/Delete Self property _____.

○ A. grants the trustee the right to add/remove itself from the property value

○ B. grants the trustee the right to read and add/remove itself from the property value

○ C. grants the trustee the right to read/write and add/remove itself from the property value

○ D. grants the trustee the right to compare, read/write, and add/remove itself from the property value

38. When a property right is assigned to all the properties of an object, it is called the _____.

    ○ A. All Properties right

    ○ B. Universal Properties right

    ○ C. Read All Properties right

    ○ D. Write All Properties right

39. The Selected Property Right overrides the property right set by the _____.

    ○ A. object trustee rights

    ○ B. Selected Property Rights of parent

    ○ C. All Properties right

    ○ D. Inherited Rights Filter

    ○ E. inherited rights

40. The ACL Property contains _____.

    ○ A. a list of trustees of the parent container

    ○ B. a list of trustees of the leaf object

    ○ C. a list of all trustees that have a trustee assignment to the object or its property

    ○ D. object trustee and file security rights

41. If a user was given a Write right to the ACL property of an object, the user _____.

    ○ A. could only assign himself the right of the parent container

    ○ B. could become a Supervisor of the object by changing the ACL

    ○ C. could become the Admin user of the container object only

    ○ D. cannot acquire Admin privileges

42. A trustee who has the Write property right to a NetWare server's ACL _____.

    ○ A. is assigned the Write file system privileges to the root of the volumes attached to the server

    ○ B. is assigned the Read/Write file system privileges to the root of the volumes attached to the server

    ○ C. is assigned the Read/File Scan/Write file system privileges to the root of the volumes attached to the server

    ○ D. is assigned the Supervisor file system privileges to the root of the volumes attached to the server

43. The Add/Remove Itself is a right that _____.

    ○ A. is granted in an object trustee assignment

    ○ B. allows a trustee to add/delete itself from any property value

    ○ C. allows a trustee to add/delete itself from a list property value

    ○ D. applies to the NetWare file system only

44. To make a user an administrator of a tree branch, _____.

    ○ A. grant the user Supervisor privileges to the root of the tree branch

    ○ B. grant the user Supervisor privileges to the root of the NDS tree

    ○ C. grant the user Write privileges to the All Properties of the root of the tree branch

    ○ D. grant the user Supervisor privileges to the All Properties of the root of the tree branch

45. The NetWare File System right can be assigned to _____.

    ○ A. only User objects

    ○ B. only user and Group objects

    ○ C. any NDS object

    ○ D. only user/Group objects and container objects

46. When a User object is created with a home directory, _____.

    ○ A. the user is given Read and Write rights [R W] to his or her home directory

    ○ B. the user is given all rights [S R W C E M F A] to his or her home directory

    ○ C. the user is given all rights [S R W C E M F A] to his or her home directory and Read and File Scan [R F] to the SYS:PUBLIC directory

    ○ D. the user is given all rights [S R W C E M F A] to his or her home directory, and Read and File Scan [R F] to the SYS:PUBLIC and SYS: directory

47. Which of the following attributes apply to files only?

    ☐ A. Don't Migrate (Dm)

    ☐ B. Migrate (M)

    ☐ C. Don't Compress (Dc)

    ☐ D. Immediate Compress (Ic)

    ☐ E. Compress (Co)

    ☐ F. Can't Compress (Cc)

48. Which of the following attributes apply to both files and directories?

    ☐ A. Don't Migrate (Dm)

    ☐ B. Migrate (M)

    ☐ C. Don't Compress (Dc)

    ☐ D. Immediate Compress (Ic)

    ☐ E. Compress (Co)

    ☐ F. Can't Compress (Cc)

49. The Data Migration feature is installed using _____.

    ○ A. INSTALL.NLM

    ○ B. MONITOR.NLM

    ○ C. MIGRATE.NLM

    ○ D. EDIT.NLM

50. The NetWare 4 compression is installed on a _____.

    ○ A. directory basis

    ○ B. file basis

    ○ C. volume basis

    ○ D. file server

51. The Migrate (M) attribute _____.

    ○ A. indicates that the file has migrated to near-line storage

    ○ B. prevents a file or the files in a directory from migrating

    ○ C. indicates whether a file has been compressed

    ○ D. prevents a file or the files in a directory from being compressed

○ E. specifies that a file or files in a directory are marked for compression as soon as the server can perform compression

○ F. indicates that a file cannot be compressed because of limited space saving benefit

52. The Don't Migrate (Dm) attribute _____.

○ A. indicates that the file has migrated to near-line storage

○ B. prevents a file or the files in a directory from migrating

○ C. indicates if a file has been compressed

○ D. prevents a file or the files in a directory from being compressed

○ E. specifies that a file or the files in a directory are marked for migration as soon as the server can perform compression

○ F. indicates that a file cannot be migrated because of limited space saving benefit

53. The Compress (Co) attribute _____.

○ A. indicates that the file has migrated to near-line storage

○ B. prevents a file or the files in a directory from migrating

○ C. indicates whether a file has been compressed

○ D. prevents a file or the files in a directory from being compressed

○ E. specifies that a file or the files in a directory are marked for compression as soon as the server can perform compression

○ F. indicates that a file cannot be compressed because of limited space-saving benefit

54. The Don't Compress (Dc) attribute _____.

○ A. indicates that the file has migrated to near-line storage

○ B. prevents a file or the files in a directory from migrating

○ C. indicates whether a file has been compressed

○ D. prevents a file or the files in a directory from being compressed

○ E. specifies that a file or the files in a directory are marked for compression as soon as the server can perform compression

○ F. indicates that a file cannot be compressed because of limited space-saving benefit

55. The Immediate Compress (Ic) attribute _____.

○ A. indicates that the file has migrated to near-line storage

○ B. prevents a file or the files in a directory from migrating

○ C. indicates if a file has been compressed

○ D. prevents a file or the files in a directory from being compressed

  E. specifies that a file or the files in a directory are marked for compression as soon as the server can perform compression

  F. indicates that a file cannot be compressed because of limited space-saving benefit

56. The Can't Compress (Cc) attribute _____.

  A. indicates that the file has migrated to near-line storage

  B. prevents a file or the files in a directory from migrating

  C. indicates whether a file has been compressed

  D. prevents a file or the files in a directory from being compressed

  E. specifies that a file or the files in a directory are marked for compression as soon as the server can perform compression

  F. indicates that a file cannot be compressed because of limited space-saving benefit

57. The figure that follows shows a directory tree for organization IBL. BJoy is made a trustee of Organization O=IBL and is given the rights of Browse and Create. The IRF for the containers are shown as follows:

IRF for O=IBL   [S B C D R]

IRF for OU=CORP [S B   ]

IRF for OU=MKTG [B   ]

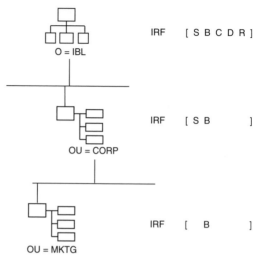

What are BJoy's effective rights in container OU=MKTG? Assume that BJoy does not inherit rights from any source other than the ones listed in the case study.

  A. Browse, Create

  B. Browse

  C. Browse, Create, Delete

  D. Supervisor

  E. No Rights

58. The figure that follows shows a directory tree for organization IBL. BJoy is made a trustee of Organization O=IBL and given the rights of Supervisor, Browse, and Create. BJoy is also given a trustee assignment of Browse in OU=MKTG. The IRFs for the containers are shown as follows:

IRF for O=IBL   [S B C D R]

IRF for OU=CORP [S B C   ]

IRF for OU=MKTG [D R]

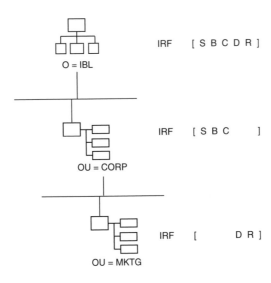

IRF for O=IBL   [S   C   R   W   A]

IRF for OU=CORP   [C   R   W   ]

IRF for OU=MKTG   [S   W   A]

The [Public] group has been given Browse right to [Root].

What are BJoy's effective rights in container OU=MKTG? Assume that BJoy does not inherit rights from any source other than the ones listed in the case study.

○ A. Supervisor, Browse, Create

○ B. Browse

○ C. Browse, Create, Delete

○ D. Delete, Rename

○ E. Create, Delete

○ F. No Rights

59. The following figure shows a directory tree for organization IBL. BJoy is made a trustee of Organization O=IBL and given the All Properties rights of Supervisor, Compare, Read. The IRFs for the containers are shown as follows:

What are BJoy's effective rights in container OU=MKTG? Assume that BJoy does not inherit rights from any source other than the ones listed in the case study.

○ A. Supervisor, Compare, Write, Read

○ B. Supervisor

○ C. Supervisor, Write, Add/Delete Self

○ D. Compare, Read, Write

○ E. No Rights

60. The figure that follows shows a directory tree for organization IBL. BJoy is made a trustee of Organization O=IBL and is given the rights of Supervisor, Read. BJoy is also given a trustee assignment of Write in OU=MKTG. The IRFs for the containers are shown as follows:

IRF for O=IBL   [S   C   R   W   A]

IRF for OU=CORP   [S   C   R   ]

IRF for OU=MKTG [R   W   A]

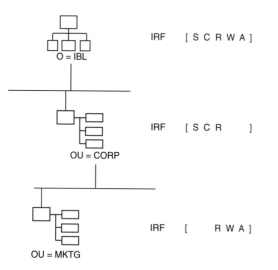

IRF   [S C R W A]

IRF   [S C R]

IRF   [R W A]

What are BJoy's effective rights in container OU=MKTG? Assume that BJoy does not inherit rights from any source other than the ones listed in the case study.

○ A. Supervisor, Compare, Write, Read, Add/Delete Self

○ B. Write, Add/Delete Self

○ C. Supervisor, Write, Add/Delete Self

○ D. Compare, Read, Write, Add/Delete Self

○ E. No Rights

NetWare 4 Client Support

This chapter introduces you to the concepts behind NetWare 4 client software support. NetWare client software is used to provide connection to the network. Login authentication and access to NDS are provided by components in the network client software. This chapter examines the network client software components and explains how you can configure them.

Examining NetWare Workstation Architecture and Components

The NetWare 4 client software is modular, and its components are diagrammed in figure 4.1. From an architectural point of view, the workstation consists of the following:

1. DOS Requester

2. Communication Protocol

3. Link Support Layer

4. LAN Driver

The DOS Requester

When an application makes a request for services, DOS examines this request. If the request is for local resources, the request is handled by DOS. If the request is for network resources, the request is sent to the DOS requester. Starting with DOS 3.1, DOS has provided redirection services. The

NetWare DOS requester shares system tables, such as the drive table, with DOS (see fig. 4.2). DOS keeps track of which drive letter entries in the table are for DOS and the DOS requester. When an application makes a request for a file on a particular drive letter, DOS is able, after consulting the shared drive table, to direct the request to the DOS requester or local DOS system services.

 In NetWare 4, DOS and the NetWare DOS requester share a common drive table.

The DOS requester takes the application request and translates it into an equivalent *NetWare Core Protocol* (NCP) request. NCP is the protocol used to carry requests for services to a NetWare file server. The NetWare file servers have an NCP server process that can handle multiple requests for network services and then send the result of processing the NCP requests back to the sender. The NCP requests are carried across the network by a transport communication protocol. The default communication protocol for a NetWare client is Inter-network Packet eXchange (IPX) protocol.

Figure 4.1

NetWare 4 client components.

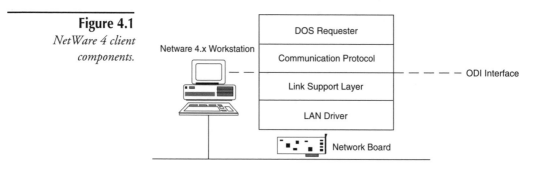

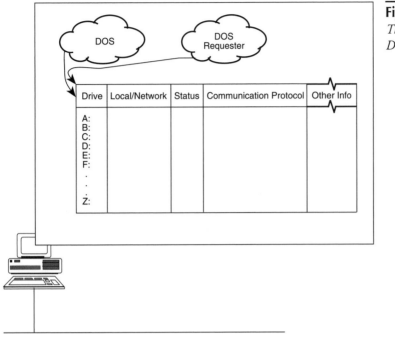

Figure 4.2
The DOS requester and DOS drive tables.

 In NetWare 4, the request for a network service is first seen by DOS.

 Application requests for network services are translated into NCP requests for services.

The default communication protocol used for sending NCP requests is IPX.

The Communication Protocol

The communication protocol uses the network board to send the packets across the network. Between the communication protocol and the network board is the Open Datalink Interface (ODI). Many choices of communication protocols exist, such as SPX/IPX, TCP/IP, AppleTalk, OSI, and so on.

You have many choices of communication protocols when using an ODI interface.

The Link Support Layer and MLID Drivers

The link support layer provides an ODI interface to the communication protocol. This interface enables multiple protocol stacks to coexist in harmony and even share the same network board driver. The ODI driver is also called the Multiple Link Interface Driver (MLID) because it can support multiple interfaces to communication protocols by way of the link support layer. The communication protocols are written to the DDI interface, and so is the MLID driver.

Implementing the NetWare Client Architecture Components

The software components that correspond to the architectural components (DOS requester, communication protocol, link support layer, and network driver) are shown in figure 4.3.

The DOS requester is implemented by Virtual Loadable Modules (VLMs). VLM break up the monolithic NetWare shell (NETX.COM or NETX.EXE) in earlier versions of NetWare (pre-NetWare 3.12) and divide it into smaller components, each of which you can selectively load.

The communication protocol is implemented by terminate-and-stay-resident (TSR) programs. The default IPX protocol is implemented by the

IPXODI.COM program. Although the name of the file makes no mention of Sequenced Packet Exchange (SPX) protocol, IPXODI.COM includes the SPX protocol. The SPX protocol is not normally used by NetWare 4 but is used in applications such as Remote Console (RCONSOLE) and for establishing connections between print servers and remote printers. These applications require a reliable virtual-circuit connection, which is implemented with the SPX protocol. The IPXODI technology has not changed from NetWare 3. The same IPXODI switches and options that were used in NetWare 3 are also used in NetWare 4.

The link support layer is implemented by LSL-.COM for DOS. Like IPXODI.COM, the LSL.COM program is also a TSR. You must load LSL.COM before loading the ODI driver.

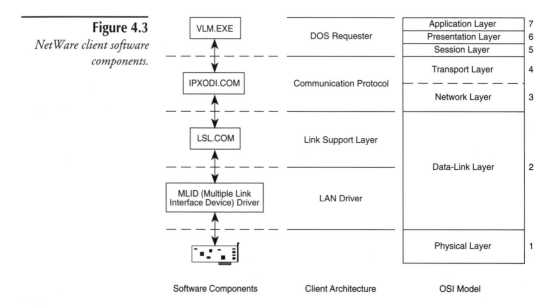

Figure 4.3

NetWare client software components.

Comparing the NetWare DOS Requester with the NetWare Shell

The NetWare shell was used in pre-NetWare 4 versions such as NetWare 3. Figure 4.4 shows the architectural overview of the NetWare 3 shell components and the NetWare 4 client architecture.

The NetWare 3 shell is the front end to DOS and can be seen as a component that provides the interface between an application and DOS. Application requests for system services are intercepted by the shell. Most system services use the INT 21 (hexadecimal) software interrupt. The NetWare shell takes over this interrupt (see fig. 4.5), and

when a system request arrives, the shell determines whether the request should be passed to DOS or sent as an NCP request to the communication protocol. Besides intercepting system calls through INT 21 (hexadecimal)—called by programmers hooking to an interrupt vector—the shell intercepts other system calls through software interrupts 24 (hexadecimal) and 17 (hexadecimal). The shell keeps a different drive table than DOS and does not share data structures with DOS. The shell also keeps track of a Drive Connection ID table, Drive Handle table, Drive Flag table, and File Server Name table. When used to log in to the server, the shell initializes its tables with information on that connection. The drive mappings for a particular session, for example, are stored in the Drive Connection ID table.

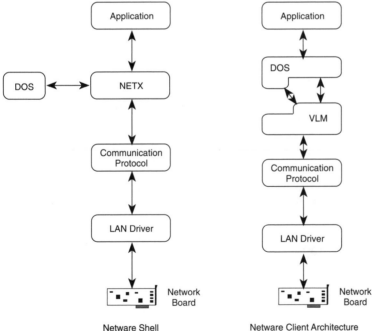

Figure 4.4

NetWare shell and NetWare 4 client architecture.

Figure 4.5

The NetWare shell and INT 21 (hex).

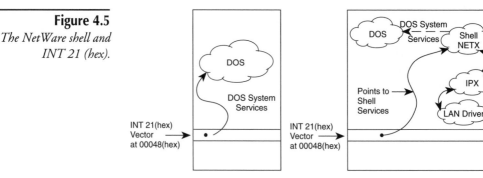

Map of DOS memory before loading shell   Map of DOS memory after loading shell

 The NetWare 3 shell

■ Acts as a front end to DOS.

■ Intercepts application requests for system services.

■ Intercepts system calls made to INT 21 (hex).

■ Does not share drive tables or data structures with DOS.

A limitation of the NetWare 3 shell is that it has a maximum of eight connection slots in the table and a 64 KB size. The eight-connection table size means that the shell can be used to make connections to no more than eight servers at a time. For large networks consisting of many servers, this restriction can turn out to be a true limitation. The 64 KB size comes from the fact that the shell is implemented as a .COM file (NETX.COM). A .COM file cannot be larger than 64 KB. Later versions of the shell have been implemented as .EXE files that can have more than 64 KB. You want the shell to be as small as possible, but increased functionality and capability require larger sized shells.

 The NetWare shell has a limit of eight connections and a maximum size of 64 KB.

The NetWare 3 shell supports DOS 3 and higher, and the NetWare 4 DOS requester requires DOS 3.1 and higher. The reason that the DOS requester requires at least DOS 3.1 is because DOS 3.1 is the first version of DOS that includes a redirector capability.

 The NetWare 4 requester requires DOS 3.1 or higher.

The DOS requester shares tables with DOS, which reduces memory used for system tables. Network file and print services are sent by DOS to the NetWare DOS requester. The NetWare DOS requester is a collection of software modules, each implementing a specialized function of the NetWare requester. Some of these functions are equivalent to those that were implemented in NetWare 3, and others are new to NetWare 4. An example of one function that is new to NetWare 4 is NetWare Directory Services; another is the authentication module that implements the RSA encryption used as part of the login authentication.

The DOS requester approach provides support for 2 to 50 connections and uses the DOS software interrupt INT 2F (hexadecimal) to provide the DOS redirection capability. The requester requires more memory than the NetWare 3 shell for background authentication and added functionality. But the requester is broken into smaller software modules (called VLMs), which can be managed more easily by memory managers that can place them in expanded memory or high memory. The NetWare DOS requester includes support for multiple languages including English, French, Spanish, German, and Italian.

Table 4.1 summarizes the differences between the DOS requester and the NetWare shell.

 Study the differences between the DOS requester and the NetWare shell outlined in table 4.1.

Table 4.1
Comparing the DOS Requester with the NetWare Shell

NetWare DOS Requester	*NetWare 3 Shell*
Uses DOS redirector by way of INT 2F hex.	Intercepts system services by way of INT 21 hex.
Requires DOS 3.1 or higher.	Supports DOS 3 and higher.
Can have 2 to 50 simultaneous connections.	Can have up to 8 simultaneous connections.
Memory requirements are larger because of background authentication and added functionality.	Memory requirements are limited to 64 KB.
Shares drive and status tables with DOS, reducing system table memory requirements.	Keeps its own set of drive tables that are independent DOS. Intercepted call for network services makes use of the separate system tables.
Multiple language support.	Lack of multiple language support.

Examining NetWare DOS Requester Components

The NetWare DOS requester consists of a Manager program called VLM.EXE. When you load VLM.EXE, it in turn loads the VLMs. Program files that provide specific functions, are readily identified by a VLM extension.

 The NetWare DOS requester consists of two major components:

■ Virtual Loadable Modules (VLMs)

■ The VLM Manager

Comparing VLMs with NLMs

With the introduction of VLMs at the workstation, Novell hopes to add the same flexibility that exists when you use NetWare Loadable Modules (NLMs) at the server. Figure 4.6 shows a comparison of these approaches. Novell has specified how NLMs can be written, and many third-party vendors provide management capabilities and applications that let you connect directly to

internal NetWare resources, with the NLM acting as an extension of the operating system itself. As the use of VLMs becomes more popular, third-party products that extend the workstation's network capability will increase. As new VLMs become available, they can connect to the VLM bus shown in figure 4.6 and provide a clean way of extending the capability of the network client software.

Examining the VLM Manager

The VLM Manager, implemented by VLM.EXE, is a TSR, and it can manage any VLM program file written to the VLM specification.

 The VLM Manager is a TSR and is implemented by VLM.EXE.

The data flow and communications between VLMs are managed by the VLM Manager. The VLM Manager is also responsible for handling application requests and forwarding them to the appropriate VLM that can process the request. It also manages memory services, such as the need for memory allocation and deallocation, on behalf of the VLMs.

Figure 4.6

The VLM bus and the NLM bus.

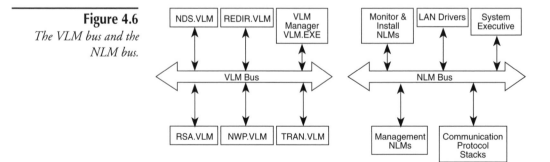

999999999999999999999999999999

The VLM Manager is responsible for the following:

- Managing data flow and communications between VLMs

- Forwarding application requests to the appropriate VLM for processing

- Controlling VLMs' access to memory at the workstation

The VLM Manager loads the VLM program files in a default order if you have specified the USE DEFAULT=ON option in the NetWare DOS Requester section of the NET.CFG file. If the USE DEFAULT=ON option is not specified, the VLMs must be loaded in another order, which you must specify in the NET.CFG file. If you are not using all of the default VLMs, you might want to explicitly specify which VLMs you are loading.

To load VLMs in the default order, specify the DEFAULT=ON option under the NetWare DOS Requester section of the NET.CFG file.

Loading VLMs in the Default Order

If you specify the USE DEFAULT=ON option in the NetWare DOS Requester section of the NET.CFG file, the VLM Manager loads 12 VLMs. The order in which they are loaded reflects the order in which they are used for a NetWare 4 client that has been enabled for directory services.

The default load order is as follows:

1. CONN.VLM

2. IPXNCP.VLM

3. TRAN.VLM

4. SECURITY.VLM

5. NDS.VLM

6. BIND.VLM

7. NWP.VLM

8. FIO.VLM

9. GENERAL.VLM

10. REDIR.VLM

11. PRINT.VLM

12. NETX.VLM

Understanding the Types of VLMs

VLMs can be classified into two types: those that are responsible for controlling the interactions between VLMs, and those that perform specific functions.

The VLMs that perform specific functions are called child VLMs. A *child VLM* is able to perform a designated task but does not have complete knowledge of how to obtain requests for processing from other VLMs. This job is the responsibility of the multiplexor VLMs. *A multiplexor VLM* is able to direct specific tasks, such as an application request, to the appropriate child VLM (see fig. 4.7).

VLMs can be classified as child VLMs and multiplexor VLMs.

Figures 4.8 and 4.9 show examples of the relationship between multiplexor VLMs and child VLMs. The multiplexor VLMs include NWP.VLM and TRAN.VLM.

Figure 4.7
Multiplexor and child VLMs.

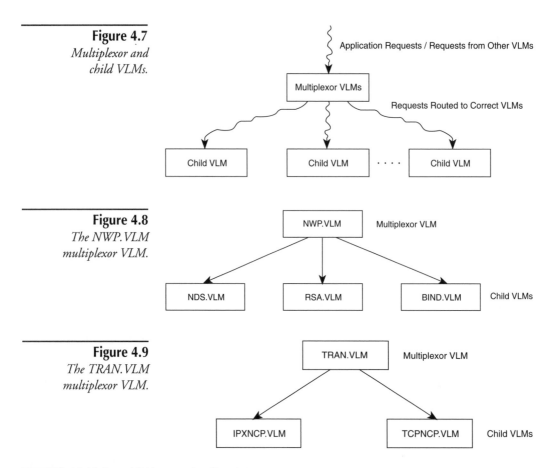

Figure 4.8
The NWP.VLM multiplexor VLM.

Figure 4.9
The TRAN.VLM multiplexor VLM.

Multiplexor VLMs route (or direct) specific tasks to the appropriate child VLM.

NWP.VLM is the NetWare protocol multiplexor VLM whose child VLMs are those that deal with NetWare Directory Services: NDS.VLM, RSA.VLM, and BIND.VLM. NDS.VLM implements the client portion of the NetWare Directory service that is capable of making requests for NDS services against the NDS database. RSA.VLM implements the Rivest, Shamir, Adleman public key encryption that is used in the login and back-ground authentication of NetWare client services. BIND.VLM enables a NetWare 4 server's resources to be viewed as part of a fictitious bindery. In other words, BIND.VLM provides a virtual bindery view of a NetWare 4 server. This feature is called bindery emulation. For bindery emulation to work, you must load another VLM called NETX.VLM to provide the equivalent of the NetWare 3 NETX.EXE (or NETX.COM) functionality.

NWP.VLM is a protocol multiplexor VLM whose child VLMs are NDS.VLM, RSA.VLM, and BIND.VLM.

NDS.VLM implements the client portion of the NetWare Directory Service that is capable of making requests for NDS services against the NDS database.

RSA.VLM implements the Rivest, Shamir, Adleman public key encryption that is used in the login and background authentication of NetWare client services.

BIND.VLM provides bindery emulation services.

TRAN.VLM is the transport multiplexor VLM whose children are IPXNCP.VLM and TCPNCP.VLM. This multiplexor VLM is responsible for sending the data from an application process to the correct network service protocol for processing. An example of the network service protocol is the NetWare Core Protocol (NCP).

The names of the children IPXNCP.VLM and TCPNCP.VLM are misleading. You might think of IPXNCP.VLM, for instance, as a replacement for IPXODI.COM, which implements the SPX/IPX protocol for ODI drivers. On the contrary, IPXNCP.VLM implements the proper formatting of a network service request into an NCP request packet. This request is sent through the appropriate ODI communication protocol stack. In the case of IPXNCP.VLM, this protocol is the IPX protocol implemented by IPXODI.COM. Novell or third-party solution providers can add additional protocol stacks.

TCPNCP.VLM is used by NetWare/IP. This product enables NCP calls to be transported across an IP internet. You have to load NLMs on a NetWare server to turn it into a NetWare/IP Server. On the workstation, you would load the following files:

LSL.COM

NE2000.COM (or a suitable MLID)

TCPIP.EXE (same as is used in the LAN Workplace for DOS product)

NWIP.EXE (NetWare/IP client module)

VLM.EXE

 TRAN.VLM is a protocol multiplexor VLM whose child VLMs are IPXNCP.VLM and TCPNCP.VLM.

IPXNCP.VLM implements the proper formatting of a network service request into an NCP request packet.

You must load child VLMs before you load their multiplexor VLM. Thus, you must load NDS.VLM, BIND.VLM, or RSA.VLM before loading the multiplexor VLM NWP.VLM. The first child VLM to be loaded becomes the default VLM for that multiplexor. This means that this VLM is checked first to see if it needs to handle the data. If NDS.VLM is loaded before BIND.VLM, for example, the default VLM for NWP.VLM is NDS.VLM.

You must load child VLMs before loading their multiplexor VLMs. The first child VLM to be loaded becomes the default VLM for that multiplexor.

Working with Virtual Loadable Modules

VLMs implement specific functions of the DOS requester. The redirector function is provided by REDIR.VLM, for example, and the printing function is provided by PRINT.VLM. Isolating the functionality of the requester into separate modules called VLMs gives you the flexibility of loading only the service that you need. Also, because the

VLMs are smaller program files, they can be better managed by the different extended and expanded memory managers.

Figure 4.10 shows the VLMs and the interrelationships between them.

The VLMs shown in figure 4.10 can be grouped into three service categories:

■ DOS Redirection

■ Service Protocol

■ Transport Protocol

These three categories are also sometimes called the DOS Redirection Layer, the Service Protocol Layer, and the Transport Protocol Layer, with the DOS Redirection Layer being at the top and the Transport Protocol Layer being at the bottom (see fig. 4.11).

The DOS Redirection Layer is implemented by REDIR.VLM, which provides a client application with access to remote network file and print services.

The Service Protocol Layer handles specific functions such as connection management, network file input/output, network printing, and other miscellaneous services such as message broadcast. Most of these services are used by REDIR.VLM to implement its job. Examples of modules that are in this layer are NWP.VLM (NetWare protocol multiplexor) and its child VLMs (NDS.VLM, RSA.VLM, BIND.VLM, and PNW.VLM), FIO.VLM (file input/output VLM), and PRINT.VLM (network print redirector). PNW=VLM is the Personal NetWare VLM used to support the peer-to-peer capabilities of the Personal NetWare product.

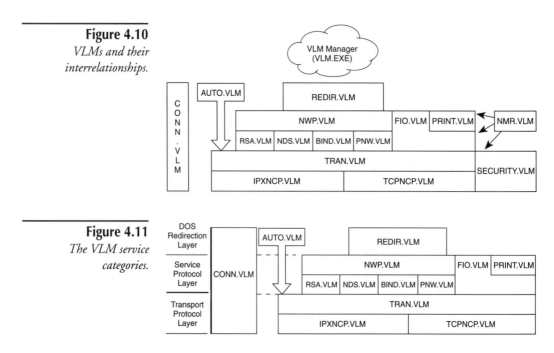

Figure 4.10
VLMs and their interrelationships.

Figure 4.11
The VLM service categories.

The Transport Protocol Layer is responsible for converting the service requests generated by the Service Protocol Layer VLMs into appropriate network requests for services. The network requests are formatted into the proper NetWare Core Protocol (NCP) packets by VLMs such as IPXNCP.VLM and TCPNCP.VLM. The transport VLMs (IPXNCP.VLM and TCPNCP.VLM) provided at this layer are managed by the TRAN.VLM multiplexor VLM.

 The VLMs can be grouped into three service categories:

■ **DOS Redirection.** The DOS Redirection Layer is implemented by REDIR.VLM, which provides a client application with access to remote network file and print services.

■ **Service Protocol.** The Service Protocol Layer handles specific functions such as connection management, network file input/output, network printing, and other miscellaneous services such as message broadcast.

■ **Transport Protocol.** The Transport Protocol Layer is responsible for converting the service requests generated by the Service Protocol Layer VLMs into appropriate network requests for services.

Summarizing VLM Functions

Table 4.2 provides a summary of the names of the major VLMs and their functions. The list is not exhaustive. It includes only the important VLMs that are within the scope of this book.

Table 4.2
A Summary of the Major VLMs

VLM Name	Brief Description
BIND.VLM	Bindery emulation; child of NWP.VLM
CONN.VLM	Connection table manager
FIO.VLM	File input/output for network requests
GENERAL.VLM	Miscellaneous functions for other VLMs such as NETX.VLM and REDIR.VLM
IPXNCP.VLM	Transport protocol processing using IPX; child of TRAN.VLM
NDS.VLM	NetWare Directory Services; child of NWP.VLM
NETX.VLM	Shell compatibility
NWP.VLM	NetWare protocol multiplexor
PRINT.VLM	Print redirector
REDIR.VLM	Redirector
RSA.VLM	Background authentication service
TRAN.VLM	Transport protocol multiplexor

Use table 4.2 as a quick summary for reviewing the functions of a VLM.

Understanding DOS Client Installation

In earlier NetWare versions, you had to use a program such as WSGEN or SHGEN to provide a communication protocol module IPX.COM, which implemented the SPX/IPX stack and was linked to the appropriate network driver. The ODI drivers eliminated the need for static linking by providing a flexible way of binding the protocol stack (such as IPXODI.COM) to the driver.

NetWare 4 provides an install program file (INSTALL.EXE) that you can run to set up the client software in the language of your choice. The language support includes English, French, German, Spanish, and Italian. As you learned in the preceding sections, the NETX shell has been replaced by the Virtual Memory Manager (VLM.EXE), which loads a number of VLMs. The installation program installs the VLMs in the appropriate workstation directories and creates the necessary batch files to load the ODI drivers and protocol stacks and run the VLM.EXE program.

You can install the NetWare DOS requester from either the CD-ROM or floppy disk distribution. If you are installing from the CD-ROM distribution, you need to go to the \CLIENT\DOSWIN directory on the CD-ROM distribution and type **install**. If installing from a floppy disk, you need the disks labeled WSDOS-1, WSWIN-1, and WSDRV-2.

The following steps describe the procedure for installing NetWare from floppy disks. Unless a CD-ROM drive is attached to a workstation, this method is perhaps the most common one used for a first-time installation. You also can copy the NetWare workstation client software to a network drive and run the installation program from that drive. The directory structure on the network drive is the same as that on the CD-ROM. You must make the directory (in which the client INSTALL program is located) your current drive, and then run the INSTALL command.

Follow these steps to install NetWare from floppy disks:

1. Insert the disk labeled NetWare Client DOS/ Windows (WSDOS-1) in a floppy drive. Change your current directory to this drive. Sample contents of this directory are shown here. Notice that the directory contains an executable file called INSTALL.EXE.

```
Volume in drive A is WSDOS_1
  Directory of A:\

_RUN      OVL    2,815 02-01-94    8:33a
WSDOS_1         18,716 11-08-94    8:07p
CMPQ_RUN  OVL    2,815 02-01-94    8:33a
IBM_RUN   OVL    2,815 02-01-94    8:33a
INSTALL   CFG    6,564 10-21-94   11:36a
INSTALL   EXE  105,522 10-21-94    9:00a
NWUNPACK  EXE   38,818 06-15-94    8:34a
TEXTUTIL  IDX    9,170 12-10-90    1:37p
NLS       <DIR>        11-09-94   12:33a
DOS       <DIR>        11-09-94   12:34a
   10 file(s)      187,235 bytes
            528,896 bytes free
```

2. Run the INSTALL.EXE program to start the NetWare client software installation. You then should see a screen on NetWare client installation.

   In Step 1, you can change the destination where the client software is installed or select the default destination directory of C:\NWCLIENT. Unless you have a strong preference or reason, using the default name is best, especially if you are installing a number of VLM client installations and want to use a standard convention.

In Step 2, you can allow the installation program to make changes to your CONFIG.SYS and AUTOEXEC.BAT files. If you allow the installation program to make the changes, it adds a LASTDRIVE=Z statement to the CONFIG.SYS file. Ordinarily, you should allow the installation program to make these changes; otherwise, you will have to make these changes manually. You cannot then use this file for the NetWare shell (NETX.EXE or NETX.COM) for normal operation. With LASTDRIVE=Z, the NetWare shells assign the next available "drive," which is "[:" as a network drive. In the AUTOEXEC.BAT file, the program adds the following statement:

```
@CALL C:\NWCLIENT\STARTNET
```

(If you use a directory other than NWCLIENT for the client installation, the NWCLIENT in the CALL statement is replaced with the appropriate directory name.)

When you use LASTDRIVE=Z:, the NETX shells take the next available drive, which is "[:". This causes problems and causes the login script to not work properly. When you do not use Z: as the LASTDRIVE, the VLM shells will still load, but full NETX.VLM capability is not realized. With LASTDRIVE=X in the CONFIG.SYS file, the following message comes up:

```
VLM.EXE      -NetWare virtual loadable
➥module manager v1.20 (941108)
(C) Copyright 1994 Novell, Inc.  All
➥Rights Reserved.
Patent pending.
```

```
The VLM.EXE file is pre-initializing the
➥VLMs............
The VLM.EXE file is using extended
➥memory (XMS).
DOS is only configured for 24 drives,
➥NETX.VLM requires 26 drives
➥for full functionality.  The NETX.VLM
➥file will load with partial support.
Add LASTDRIVE=Z to the CONFIG.SYS file,
➥reboot the workstation; then load the
➥NETX.VLM file.
You are attached to server FS1
```

In Step 3, you can choose to install MS Windows support for your workstation. The default directory for MS Windows support is C:\WINDOWS. If your Windows installation is another directory, you have to edit this field and enter the Windows directory.

> **Note** If you want to use the workstation for network administration, you should have MS Windows installed and select the option to install MS Windows support for your workstation. The Network Administrator is better for performing many network administration tasks relating to management of the NDS directory.

In Step 4, you can configure your workstation for backup by a NetWare server running backup software such as SBACKUP. If you configure this option, the TSA_SMS program for backing up your workstation will be installed and configured on your workstation.

3. When you are done making changes in Steps 1, 2, 3, and 4, press Enter in Step 5 to install the LAN driver for your workstation network board. You should see a message that prompts you to Insert the Driver Disk.

4. Insert the driver disk labeled NetWare Client DOS/Windows, and press Enter. You then should see a list of drivers supported on the network.

   If you already have the driver loaded (from a previous installation), the installation program recognizes it and gives you the choice of loading this LAN driver.

5. Select from the list of drivers the driver that matches the NIC in your workstation. You then should see a list of NIC parameters for the board that you have selected.

6. To change a value of a parameter, highlight it and press Enter. If you do not know the parameter settings for your board, you might have to abort the installation and restart it after you determine the network board settings. You can determine the network board settings by examining the jumper and switch settings (sometimes in consultation with the network board manual) or if your network board ships with a software setup utility, you can use this. If you have an IPX.COM and IPXODI.COM installed for your board, you can use IPX I or IPXODI. (Alternatively, examine the NET.CFG file.)

 Avoid using IO Base Port address 378 hex, which is used by the parallel printer port LPT1. Also avoid using IRQ 3, which is used by COM2, unless you have the COM2 port disabled.

Device	Port Address
LPT1	0378h
LPT2	03BCh
COM1	03F8h
COM2	02F8h

You should select the correct frame type for the board.

Note If you are using the NetWare 4 client software to access a NetWare 3 server using an Ethernet board, select the frame type of ETHERNET_802.3 in addition to the default ETHERNET_802.2 frame type. For Token Ring, select the frame type of TOKEN-RING. If you are running AppleTalk client software programs, they require a frame type of ETHERNET_SNAP and TOKEN-RING_SNAP for Ethernet and Token Ring, respectively.

The default order of Token Ring frame transmission is that the Most Significant Bit (MSB) is transmitted first. Normally, you should not have to change this setting, unless the board vendor recommends this change.

7. After making parameter changes, press Esc to continue. You should be back to the NetWare Client Install screen with the driver selected.

   In Step 6, press Enter to continue with installation.

   You next see a status message that the selected driver is being installed, and you are asked to insert the WSDOS-1 disk.

8. Insert the WSDOS-1 disk in the floppy drive, and press Enter. You should see a status display of files being copied to the workstation and then a completion message that informs you of the changes that have been made.

   The changes made to the AUTOEXEC.BAT and CONFIG.SYS files are stored in the AUTOEXEC.NEW and CONFIG.NEW files in the client directory.

9. Edit the files AUTOEXEC.NEW and CONFIG.NEW in the client directory, and reboot the workstation. Samples of AUTOEXEC.NEW and CONFIG.NEW are shown here. Notice that CONFIG.NEW has LASTDRIVE set to Z. The client software is started by the following statement in the AUTOEXEC.NEW file:

```
@CALL C:\NWCLIENT\STARTNET
```

AUTOEXEC.NEW:

```
@CALL C:\NWCLIENT\STARNET
@ECHO OFF
PROMPT $P$G
C:\WIN\SMARTDRV.EXE
PATHC:\HJWIN;c:\hj2;c:\bin;c:\windows;c:\scsi
➥doskey
set FTP_ETC=c:\pctcp\etc
set NSE_DOWNLOAD=D:\DOWNLOAD
SET TEMP=C:\WINDOWS\TEMP
```

CONFIG.NEW:

```
DEVICE=C:\DOS\SETVER.exe
DEVICE=C:\scsi\ASPI4DOS.SYS
DEVICE=C:\scsi\ASWCDSNY.SYS /D:ASPICDO
files=50
buffers=50
DEVICE=C:\WINDOWS\HIMEM.SYS
shell=command.com /p /e:800
DEVICE=C:\WINDOWS\SMARTDRV.EXE
➥/DOUBLE_BUFFER
STACKS=9,256
LASTDRIVE=Z
```

The client installation program places the @CALL C:\NWCLIENT\STARTNET at the beginning of the AUTOEXEC.BAT file. If you want your PATH and PROMPT statements in the AUTO-EXEC.BAT file to be processed before the client software is loaded, edit your AUTOEXEC.BAT file to relocate the @CALL C:\NWCLIENT \STARTNET statement.

Optimizing Workstation Memory

You might want to use the LOADHIGH commands to load some of the TSRs high. For instance, you might try the following sequence in the STARTNET.BAT file:

```
@ECHO OFF
C:
CD \NWCLIENT
SET NWLANGUAGE=ENGLISH    (Replace ENGLISH
➥with the language of choice)
LOADHIGH LSL
LOADHIGH SMC8000      (Replace with name of
➥your ODI driver)
LOADHIGH IPXODI
VLM
CD \
```

You might also try running MEMAKER for MS-DOS 6.*x* and higher to see how memory optimization can be done.

Using VLM Options

You can load the VLM Manager with a number of interesting options. These options are reminiscent of the options that are used in the NETX shell program, but additional options have been added.

You can conveniently display the list of available options by typing this command:

```
VLM /?
```

The following listing shows the help messages displayed when you execute the VLM /? command:

```
VLM.EXE     - NetWare virtual loadable
➥module manager  v1.20 (941108)
(C) Copyright 1994 Novell, Inc.  All Rights
➥Reserved.
Patent pending.
```

```
Available command line options:
/?      Display this help screen.
/U      Unload the VLM.EXE file from memory
/C=[path\]filename.ext
        Specify a configuration file to use
➥(Default is NET.CFG).
/Mx     The memory type the VLM.EXE file uses
➥where x is one of the following:
        C = Conventional memory.
        X = Extended memory (XMS).
        E = Expanded memory (EMS).
/D      Display the VLM.EXE file diagnostics.
/PS=<server name>
        Preferred server name to attach to
➥during load.
/PT=<tree name>
        Preferred tree name to attach to
➥during load.
/Vx     The detail level of message display
➥where x is one of the following:
        0 = Display copyright and critical
➥errors only.
        1 = Also display warning messages.
        2 = Also display VLM module names.
        3 = Also display configuration file
➥parameters.
        4 = Also display diagnostics messages.
```

Unloading VLM.EXE

If you do not have TSRs loaded after loading VLM.EXE, you can unload VLM.EXE by typing this command:

```
VLM /U
```

If the VLM Manager thinks that it is unsafe to unload itself, it does not unload and displays a warning message instead.

Specifying the Configuration File

When VLM.EXE loads, it looks for configuration information in the NET.CFG file. Specifically it

looks for the NetWare DOS Requester section of the NET.CFG file and processes configuration statements in that section. Earlier, you saw examples of the statements USE DEFAULTS=ON and USE DEFAULTS=OFF, which you can use to enable or disable the default load order.

You can use the /C option to specify another configuration file besides the default NET.CFG. If you want to specify the configuration file C:\CONFIG\STAND.CFG file, for example, use the command:

```
VLM  /C=C:\CONFIG\STAND.CFG
```

Specifying the Memory Type

You can load the VLMs in conventional, extended, or expanded memory. To load in extended and expanded memory, you should have the appropriate extended and expanded memory drivers loaded.

To load in extended memory, use the command

```
VLM /MX
```

To load in expanded memory, use the command

```
VLM /ME
```

To load in conventional memory (default), use the command

```
VLM /MC
```

Indicating the First Network Drive

When the VLM loads, it attaches to the nearest server. It does this by issuing a GetNearestServer Service Advertising Protocol (SAP) request, and waiting for all NetWare servers to respond. The VLM then connects to the server that was returned in the first GiveNearestServer SAP response. Next, the VLM attaches the next available drive in the workstation's drive table to the SYS:LOGIN volume of this server (see fig. 4.12).

The SYS:LOGIN directory contains a number of programs that can be used to access the network. Some of the main programs are LOGIN.EXE, CX.EXE, and NLIST.EXE. Also, OS/2 workstations can use a subdirectory called OS2 in SYS:LOGIN to connect to the network. To maintain compatibility with the NETX behavior, you can specify the first network drive to be used in the NetWare DOS Requester section by adding this statement under the NetWare DOS Requester section.

```
FIRST NETWORK DRIVE=F
```

Without this statement, the next available drive D is mapped to SYS:LOGIN. If the FIRST NETWORK DRIVE parameter is not specified, for instance, the next available drive depends on what devices are in use. If you have a hard drive set up as C: and a CD ROM unit set up as D:, you would get E: as the first network drive.

After the network drive attaches to SYS:LOGIN, you must change the current drive to the attached network drive and type the LOGIN command. Thus, the typical login sequence is

```
F:
LOGIN SpecifyLoginName
```

You can place all these commands in a batch file for automation.

Specifying the Initial Server

If you want to specify the server that you want to log in to initially, you must use the preferred server (/PS) option. If you want to log in to the server FS1, for instance, you must use the following command:

```
VLM /PS=FS1
```

The /PS option works in a similar manner to the preferred option for the NETX shell. You also can use the PREFERRED SERVER parameter in the NET.CFG file. This parameter is primarily meant for clients who use BIND.VLM rather than NDS.VLM. For a NetWare 4 client, an initial connection is made to the preferred server. If this server happens to be a NetWare 4 server, an attachment to the preferred tree is made.

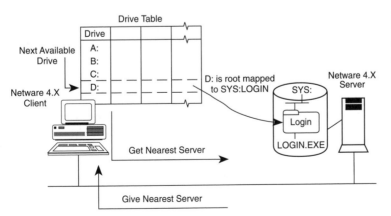

Figure 4.12

Attaching the network drive to SYS:LOGIN.

Specifying a Preferred Tree

In a NetWare 4 network, multiple NetWare Directory Service trees are possible. Most organizations prefer having a single tree because of the difficulty in restructuring and merging trees; and also because a single tree meets the needs of complex organizational structures. In some situations, however, multiple NDS trees might be useful, perhaps for security reasons so that you can prohibit information exchange between two NDS trees. Another reason could be the establishment of an experimental NDS tree on a production network that already has an NDS tree in use. Many system administrators might want to work with an experimental network to learn about structuring an NDS tree before making these changes on a production network.

Using the preferred tree (/PT) option gives you a choice of connecting to a particular tree. If you want to connect to an experimental NDS tree called EXPNET, for instance, use the following command:

```
VLM /PT=EXPNET
```

To connect to a production network called CNET, you might want to unload the VLM and reconnect. You thus would use these commands, the first to unload, and the second to connect to the CNET tree:

```
VLM   /U
VLM   /PT=CNET
```

You also can use the PREFERREDTREE=*treeName* option in the NET.CFG file to specify a preferred tree option.

Requesting Messages

During the loading of the VLM you can obtain important messages relating to warning, error, and diagnostic information. These messages can provide a valuable diagnostic aid when you are trying to figure out the load order of the VLMs.

The general command for loading VLMs with different verbosity levels for messages is the following, where *x* is a number from 0 to 4:

```
VLM /Vx
```

If you want to display copyright and critical error messages only, use the following command to load the VLMs:

```
VLM /V0
```

If, in addition to copyright and critical error messages, you want to display warning messages, use the following command to load the VLMs:

```
VLM /V1
```

If, in addition to copyright, critical error messages, and warning messages, you want to display the names of the VLM modules as they load, use the following command to load the VLMs:

```
VLM /V2
```

If you also want to display configuration file parameters, use the following command to load the VLMs:

```
VLM /V3
```

The following sample listing shows the messages produced when you load the VLM with a /V3 option:

```
C:\NWCLIENT> VLM /V3
VLM.EXE      - NetWare virtual loadable
➥module manager  v1.20 (941108)
(C) Copyright 1994 Novell, Inc.  All Rights
➥Reserved.
Patent pending.
SET STATION TIME OFF
USE DEFAULTS OFF
VLM CONN.VLM
VLM IPXNCP.VLM
VLM TRAN.VLM
VLM SECURITY.VLM
VLM NDS.VLM
VLM BIND.VLM
VLM RSA.VLM
VLM NWP.VLM
VLM FIO.VLM
VLM GENERAL.VLM
VLM REDIR.VLM
VLM PRINT.VLM
VLM NETX.VLM
VLM AUTO.VLM


The VLM.EXE file is pre-initializing the
➥VLMs..............
The VLM.EXE file is using extended memory
➥(XMS).
CONN.VLM      - NetWare connection table
➥manager  v1.20 (941108)
AVERAGE NAME LENGTH 15
CONNECTIONS 5
IPXNCP.VLM    - NetWare IPX transport module
➥v1.20 (941108)
PB BUFFERS 4
TRAN.VLM      - NetWare transport multiplexor
➥module  v1.20 (941108)
SECURITY.VLM - NetWare security enhancement
➥module  v1.20 (941108)
CONNECTIONS 5
NAME CONTEXT "OU=CORP.O=ESL"
CONNECTIONS 5
NDS.VLM       - NetWare directory services
➥protocol module  v1.20 (941108)
BIND.VLM      - NetWare bindery protocol
➥module  v1.20 (941108)
PREFERRED SERVER NW4CS
RSA.VLM       - NetWare RSA authentication
➥module  v1.20 (941108)
```

```
NWP.VLM       - NetWare protocol multiplexor
➥module  v1.20 (941108)
MESSAGE TIMEOUT 180
FIO.VLM       - NetWare file input-output
➥module  v1.20 (941108)
PB BUFFERS 4
CONNECTIONS 5
GENERAL.VLM   - NetWare general purpose
➥function module  v1.20 (941108)
FIRST NETWORK DRIVE F
REDIR.VLM     - NetWare DOS redirector module
➥v1.20 (941108)
FIRST NETWORK DRIVE F
SHOW DOTS OFF
PRINT.VLM     - NetWare printer redirection
➥module  v1.20 (941108)
NETX.VLM      - NetWare workstation shell
➥module  v4.20 (941108)
FIRST NETWORK DRIVE F
CONNECTIONS 5
AUTO.VLM      - NetWare auto-reconnect module
➥v1.20 (941108)
You are attached to server NW4CS
```

If, in addition to copyright, critical error messages, warning messages, names of the VLMs as they load, and configuration file parameters, you want to display diagnostic information, use the following command to load the VLMs:

```
VLM /V4
```

The following sample listing shows the messages produced when you load the VLM with a /V4 option:

```
C:\NWCLIENT> VLM /V4
VLM.EXE      - NetWare virtual loadable
➥module manager  v1.20 (941108)
(C) Copyright 1994 Novell, Inc.  All Rights
➥Reserved.
Patent pending.
SET STATION TIME OFF
USE DEFAULTS OFF
VLM CONN.VLM
VLM IPXNCP.VLM
VLM TRAN.VLM
```

```
VLM SECURITY.VLM
VLM NDS.VLM
VLM BIND.VLM
VLM RSA.VLM
VLM NWP.VLM
VLM FIO.VLM
VLM GENERAL.VLM
VLM REDIR.VLM
VLM PRINT.VLM
VLM NETX.VLM
VLM AUTO.VLM


The VLM.EXE file is pre-initializing the
➥VLMs..............
The VLM.EXE file is using extended memory
➥(XMS).
CONN.VLM     - NetWare connection table
➥manager  v1.20 (941108)
AVERAGE NAME LENGTH 15
CONNECTIONS 5
IPXNCP.VLM   - NetWare IPX transport module
➥v1.20 (941108)
PB BUFFERS 4
TRAN.VLM     - NetWare transport multiplexor
➥module  v1.20 (941108)
SECURITY.VLM - NetWare security enhancement
➥module  v1.20 (941108)
CONNECTIONS 5
NAME CONTEXT "OU=CORP.O=ESL"
CONNECTIONS 5
NDS.VLM      - NetWare directory services
➥protocol module  v1.20 (941108)
BIND.VLM     - NetWare bindery protocol
➥module  v1.20 (941108)
PREFERRED SERVER NW4CS
RSA.VLM      - NetWare RSA authentication
➥module  v1.20 (941108)
NWP.VLM      - NetWare protocol multiplexor
➥module  v1.20 (941108)
MESSAGE TIMEOUT 180
FIO.VLM      - NetWare file input-output
➥module  v1.20 (941108)
PB BUFFERS 4
CONNECTIONS 5
GENERAL.VLM  - NetWare general purpose
➥function module v1.20 (941108)
FIRST NETWORK DRIVE F
```

```
REDIR.VLM    - NetWare DOS redirector module
➥v1.20 (941108)
FIRST NETWORK DRIVE F
SHOW DOTS OFF
PRINT.VLM    - NetWare printer redirection
➥module  v1.20 (941108)
NETX.VLM     - NetWare workstation shell
➥module  v4.20 (941108)
FIRST NETWORK DRIVE F
CONNECTIONS 5
AUTO.VLM     - NetWare auto-reconnect module
➥v1.20 (941108)
You are attached to server NW4CS
```

Notice that the preceding output contains the statements in the NET.CFG file that are displayed when they are processed.

Be familar with the different VLM options. Use the VLM /? listing as a quick review.

Obtaining VLM Diagnostic Information

After you have loaded the VLM Manager, you can obtain diagnostic information on it by running VLM with the diagnose option (/D). Many of the numbers displayed (especially those in columns) are expressed as hexadecimal numbers, as you can see in the following example:

```
F:\> VLM  /D
VLM.EXE      - NetWare virtual loadable
➥module manager  v1.20 (941108)
C) Copyright 1994 Novell, Inc.  All Rights
➥Reserved.
Patent pending.
The VLM.EXE file v1.2  is currently loaded
VLM transient switch count  : 0
VLM call count              : 192
VLM current ID              : 0000h
VLM memory type             : CON
VLM modules loaded count    : 12
```

```
VLM block ID (0 if CON)     : 0000h
VLM transient block         :1EC3h
VLM global seg (0 if CON)   : 0000h
VLM async queue (h, t, s)   : 0000:0000,
➥1DDE:0030, 0
VLM busy queue (h, t, s)    : 0000:0000,
➥1DDE:003C, 0
VLM re-entrance level       : 1
VLM full map count          : 0
VLM Control Block information      Address
➥TMemSize  GMemSize  SMemSize
ID   Flag Func Maps Call TSeg GSeg Low  High
➥Para K    Para K    Para K
- - - - - - - - - - - - - - - - - - - - - - - - - - - - - -
001 A000 0005 0000 0052 1DDE 1354 FFFF FFFF
➥00F4 0003 0000 0000 0000 0000
010 A000 0011 0000 0012 1EC3 1F7B FFFF FFFF
➥00B8 0002 0018 0000 0194 0006
021 A000 000B 0000 0005 1F93 2079 FFFF FFFF
➥00E6 0003 00A2 0002 0066 0001
020 E000 000B 0000 0009 1F93 2079 FFFF FFFF
➥00E6 0003 00A2 0002 0066 0001
061 A000 0005 0000 0005 211B 2221 FFFF FFFF
➥0106 0004 0000 0000 00CD 0003
032 A000 0010 0000 0007 2221 2392 FFFF FFFF
➥0171 0005 00B9 0002 003E 0000
031 A000 0010 0000 0006 244B 2503 FFFF FFFF
➥00B8 0002 001C 0000 002D 0000
030 A000 0011 0000 0007 251F 25D0 FFFF FFFF
➥00B1 0002 0071 0001 004A 0001
041 A000 000B 0000 0005 2641 27E3 FFFF FFFF
➥01A2 0006 0283 0010 0021 0000
043 A000 000A 0000 0006 2A66 2AD2 FFFF FFFF
➥006C 0001 001E 0000 0050 0001
040 A000 0009 0000 001E 2AF0 2D2B FFFF FFFF
➥023B 0008 005F 0001 004B 0001
042 A000 000E 0000 0006 2D8A 2E64 FFFF FFFF
➥00DA 0003 00AC 0002 0059 0001
050 A000 0007 0000 0007 2F10 3125 FFFF FFFF
➥0215 0008 00F2 0003 007D 0001
Total    0DAA      069E
Maximum 023B      0283          0194
```

Explanations of the diagnostic information are beyond the scope of this book.

Exploring New NET.CFG Options

NET.CFG is a text file that contains configuration statements dealing with configuring the ODI driver, providing the binding among the communication protocol and the ODI driver and the NetWare requester. A new section called the NetWare DOS Requester has been defined for the NetWare 4 clients. You need to indent the configuration statements under the NetWare DOS Requester heading at least two spaces. The more important of these statements are discussed next.

In this section, you learn only about the NET.CFG parameters that are different from NetWare 3. Even after the scope is limited in this fashion, many details can be presented on NetWare 4-specific parameters. Instead, only the details that you need to know for the NetWare 3 to 4 Update exams are presented here. For further details, refer to the companion volume *NetWare 4 Training Guide: NetWare 4 Administration,* by New Riders Publishing.

Using NAME CONTEXT

You use the NAME CONTEXT statement to establish the context of the workstation on attachment to the NDS tree. The statement's syntax is as follows:

```
NAME CONTEXT = "complete name path"
```

Replace *complete name path* with the complete name of the context to be set initially. You should set the initial name context for users to the container that contains most of the resources they are likely to use. You must include the complete name in the quotation marks.

An example of the use of NAME CONTEXT is

```
NetWare DOS Requester
NAME CONTEXT = "OU=CORP.O=ESL"
```

 Review the syntax for NAME CON-
TEXT and how you can use it.

Using PREFERRED TREE

Use the PREFERRED TREE option to specify the NDS tree to which the VLMs are to attach initially when they are loaded. The PREFERRED TREE option has meaning when the NDS.VLM is loaded because the option refers to an NDS tree. The syntax for using the PREFERRED TREE option is the following:

```
PREFERRED TREE = tree name
```

Replace *tree name* with the name of the NDS tree.

The following is an example of the use of PRE-FERRED TREE:

```
NetWare DOS Requester
PREFERRED TREE = CNET
```

 Review the syntax for PREFERRED
TREE and how you can use it.

Using FIRST NETWORK DRIVE

In the NetWare 4 client, the DOS drive table is shared between DOS and the DOS requester. When the VLMs load, the redirector assigns the first available DOS drive letter to the network drive. If the workstation has a single hard disk partition (drive C), drive D becomes the first network drive. To maintain compatibility with

applications and batch/script files that might require the first network drive to be F (the default with the NETX shell programs), a new statement called FIRST NETWORK DRIVE has been provided.

The following is the syntax for using the FIRST NETWORK DRIVE option:

```
FIRST NETWORK DRIVE = drive letter
```

Replace *drive letter* with a drive letter that is not in local use.

An example of the use of FIRST NETWORK DRIVE is the following:

```
NetWare DOS Requester
FIRST NETWORK DRIVE = F
```

 Review the syntax for FIRST NET-
WORK DRIVE and how you can use it.

Using PB BUFFERS

The packet burst capability can be configured with the PB BUFFERS statement in the NetWare DOS Requester section. The default value is PB BUFF-ERS = 3. This capability also exists with NetWare 3. In NetWare 4, however, a formalized requirement insists that you place this statement in the NetWare DOS Requester section.

The syntax for using the PB BUFFERS option is the following:

```
PB BUFFERS = n
```

Replace *n* with a number from 0 to 10. A value of 0 disables the packet burst option. Any other value from 1 to 10 enables the packet burst and also specifies the number of buffers for the packet burst.

This sample command enables the PB BUFFERS option and specifies 3 buffers for the burst mode:

```
NetWare DOS Requester
PB BUFFERS = 3
```

 Review the syntax for PB BUFFERS and how you can use it.

Using USE DEFAULTS and the VLM Statement

The VLMs are loaded by default in the load sequence described previously in this chapter (see "Loading VLMs in the Default Order"). To disable the default load sequence, you must use this command:

```
USE DEFAULTS=OFF
```

If the default load sequence is disabled, you must specify the VLMs to load, using the VLM statement:

```
VLM=nameOfVLM
```

Replace *nameOfVLM* with the name of the VLM to load.

An example of the use of these statements is

```
NetWare DOS Requester
        USE DEFAULTS=OFF
        VLM=CONN.VLM
        VLM=IPXNCP.VLM
              :
              :
        (and other VLMs)
```

You also can use the VLM statement with the default load order to specify optional VLMs to be loaded. To load the AUTO.VLM after the default

load sequence, for example, use these commands:

```
NetWare DOS Requester
USE DEFAULTS=ON
VLM=AUTO.VLM
```

 Review the syntax for USE DEFAULTS and how you can use it.

Specifying Frame Types

The default frame type for NetWare 4 has been changed to ETHERNET_802.2. You need to specify this frame type in the Link Driver section. If you have NetWare 3 servers on the network that use their default frame type of ETHERNET_802.3, you must additionally specify the ETHERNET_802.3 frame type. If you are using TCP/IP protocol stack software such as LAN WorkPlace or FTP Software's PC/TCP (running on top of ODI drivers), you must additionally specify the ETHERNET_II frame type.

The following lines show an example of the frame type for SMC8000 boards for NetWare 3 server compatibility:

```
Link Driver SMC8000
        int         3
        port        280
        mem         D0000
        frame       ETHERNET_802.2
        frame       ETHERNET_802.3
```

The following lines show an example of the frame type for SMC8000 boards for NetWare 3 server and TCP/IP compatibility:

```
Link Driver SMC8000
        int         3
        port        280
        mem         D0000
```

```
frame    ETHERNET_802.2
frame    ETHERNET_802.3
frame    ETHERNET_II
```

The default Ethernet frame type for NetWare 4 is ETHERNET_802.2.

Understanding Requirements for Windows Workstations

For MS Windows workstations, you should set the SHOW DOTS=ON parameter in the NET.CFG file.

If you allow the client INSTALL program to install Windows support, the PROGRAM.INI and SYSTEM.INI files are modified, with the originals kept in PROGRAM.BNW and SYSTEM.BNW.

The .BNW extension indicates Before NetWare.

In the PROGRAM.INI file, a new group file NWUTILS.GRP is added under the section [Groups]. The SYSTEM.INI file is modified to contain the line "NETWORK.DRV=Novell NetWare (4.0)" in the [Boot.Description] section. The [386enh] section is also modified to load the virtual drivers VNETBIOS, VNETWARE.386, VIPX.386, and VCLIENT.386, and statements for enhanced support are added.

Specify the SHOW DOTS=ON statement in the NET.CFG for MS Windows stations.

Support for Non-DOS Clients

NetWare 4 includes support for a number of non-DOS clients such as OS/2, Macintosh, Unix, Windows 95, and Windows NT. To all of these different clients, NetWare 4 can provide communication, file, and print services. This section will discuss NetWare 4 support for Macintosh and OS/2 clients. Discussion of support for other types of clients is beyond the scope of this book.

Configuring NetWare 4 Server for Macintosh Clients

NetWare 4 comes bundled with a copy of the NetWare for Macintosh product. This product contains a number of NLMs that support the Macintosh file sharing and communication protocols. For example, the NLMs support the Apple Filing Protocol (AFP), which enables the NetWare 4 server to emulate an Apple Share server for Macintosh clients. Other protocols such as the Printer Access Protocol (PAP), Apple Transaction Protocol (ATP), Apple Data Stream Protocol (ADSP), Datagram Delivery Protocol (DDP) are also supported.

To configure the NetWare 4 server for Macintosh the following tasks need to be performed:

- ■ Install NetWare for Macintosh on the server
- ■ Configure NetWare for Macintosh services
- ■ Install Macintosh client software

Installing NetWare for Macintosh on the Server

The following steps are a guided tour for installing NetWare for Macintosh services on a NetWare 4 server.

1. Load the INSTALL NLM on the server

    LOAD INSTALL

2. Select Product Options.

3. Select Choose an item or product listed above.

4. Select Install NetWare for Macintosh client (see fig. 4.13).

    You should see the source from which the files will be installed (see fig. 4.14). Verify that the source path is correct. Change the source path if necessary, and press Enter.

If you are connected to a remote NetWare server, you will be asked to authenticate using a valid user name and password.

5. You will see a status of files being copied, and then the menu shown in figure 4.15.

6. Select Install NW-MAC option.

    You will see a status window indicating the files that are being copied.

    The installation will create the directory NW-MAC in SYS:SYSTEM. Below the NE-MAC directory, the subdirectories FONTS, PSUTILS, PPDS, ATPSCON and SETUP will be created. Files will then be copied from the source path to these directories.

7. Once all the files are copied, you will see a form for the Final Installation Options (see fig. 4.16).

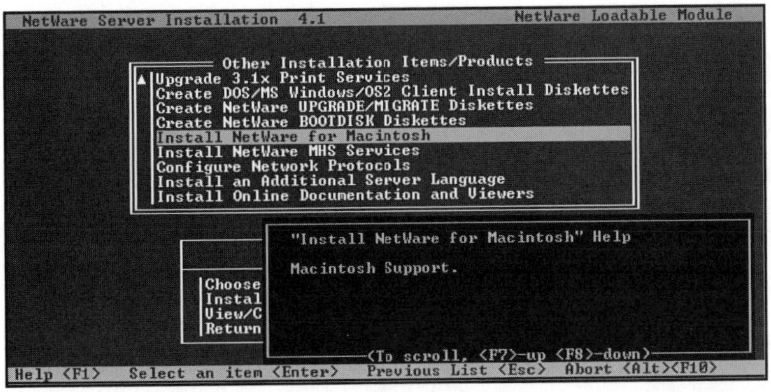

Figure 4.13

Selecting the Install NetWare for Macintosh client option.

Figure 4.14

CD-ROM Source from which the files are installed.

Figure 4.15

Install NetWare for Macintosh menu option.

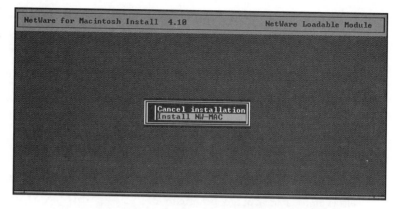

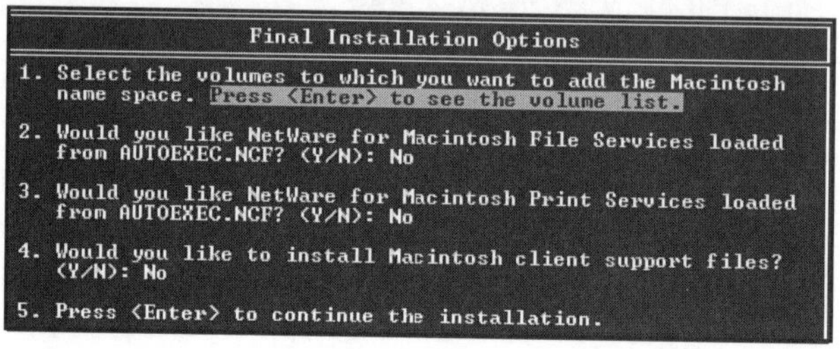

Figure 4.16

Final Installation Options form.

8. Press Enter with Option 1 highlighted to specify the names of the volumes to which the Macintosh name space will be added. To mark a volume, highlight it and press Enter (see fig. 4.17).

    Press Esc, and select Yes, save changes and continue.

9. Option 2 is used to specify if the NetWare for Macintosh file services are to be loaded from the AUTOEXEC.NCF file. Select Yes.

10. Option 3 is used to specify if the NetWare for Macintosh print services are to be loaded from the AUTOEXEC.NCF file. Select Yes.

11. Option 4 is used to install the Macintosh client support files. This allows the Macintosh users to install the Macintosh client software on their workstations. Select Yes.

12. Press Enter with option 5 highlighted to continue with the installation.

    Answer Yes, when asked to confirm the installation options.

13. You will see a message about the Macintosh name space being added to the selected volumes.

    The Macintosh files are installed. You are now ready to configure the Macintosh name services. This is described in the next section.

Figure 4.17

Selecting volumes to which name space is to be added.

Configuring NetWare for Macintosh Services

After the NetWare for Macintosh files are installed, the NetWare for Macintosh services must be configured. You must perform the following configuration tasks:

- Configure AppleTalk stack

- Configure file services

- Configure print services

These tasks can be configured from the NetWare for Macintosh Configuration menu (see fig. 4.18) that is displayed at the end of the procedure for the NetWare for Macintosh installation.

When you make a selection from figure 4.18, an NLM is loaded to perform the task. Table 4.4

shows the NLMs that are loaded for the options in the NetWare for Macintosh Configuration menu. These NLMs can be loaded directly from the server console or from the NetWare for Macintosh Configuration menu. After the initial installation of NetWare for Macintosh, you can access the NetWare for Macintosh Configuration menu by performing the following:

1. At the server console where you have installed the NetWare for Macintosh product, type the following:

   LOAD INSTALL

2. Select Product Options.

3. Select View/Configure/Remove Installed Products.

4. Select the NW-MAC entry.

Table 4.4
NetWare for Macintosh Configuration NLMs

Option	NLM
Configure AppleTalk stack	INETCFG.NLM
Configure File Services	AFPCON.NLM
Configure Print Services	ATPSCON.NLM
Configure CD-ROM services	HFSCDCON.NLM

Figure 4.18
*NetWare for Macintosh
Configuration menu.*

To configure the AppleTalk stack, you must run the INETCFG.NLM (or select the Configure AppleTalk Stack option). Configuring the AppleTalk stack involves the following tasks:

■ Identify the network board

■ Enable AppleTalk routing

■ Bind the AppleTalk protocol to the network driver

After the AppleTalk protocol stack is configured, you must configure AppleTalk File Services. You can use AFPCON to configure AppleTalk File services. The following is a partial list of file services that can be configured using AFPCON:

■ Allow Guest Logins

■ Allow users to save passwords for autologins

■ Set maximum number of AFP connections

■ Shutdown AFP server

■ Restart AFP server

■ View volume information

During installation all the necessary files needed for NetWare for Macintosh services are copied.

NetWare for Macintosh print services are bi-directional. To use these print services, you must configure them first. The following is a partial list of configuration options that can be performed using ATPSCON:

■ Quick Configuration

■ Configure Print Servers

■ Configure Spoolers

■ Define Printer Models

■ Log Options

■ Management Options

■ Change Context

Installing Macintosh Client Software

With the NetWare for Macintosh product installed and configured on the NetWare server, you can log on to the NetWare server from a Macintosh workstation using AppleShare because the NetWare server emulates an AppleTalk File server. However, to take full advantage of the NetWare 4 network, you must install the MacNDS client on the Macintosh workstations. The MacNDS client software provides access to the NDS for Macintosh workstations running under the System 7 operating system.

The following is a guided tour on installing the MacNDS client software:

1. Ensure that bindery services are enabled on the NetWare 4 server. This is usually done by default during server installation when the SET BINDERY CONTEXT statement is placed in the AUTOEXEC.NCF file.

2. Connect the Macintosh workstation to the NetWare 4 network and select the Chooser option from the Apple menu.

3. Make sure that the AppleTalk button is active; if necessary, click on the active button to activate AppleTalk.

4. Click on the AppleShare button. You should see the NetWare 4 server name on which NetWare for Macintosh is running in the Select a file server panel.

5. Highlight the file server name and click on OK.

6. When the logon console panel appears, select the Registered User button and log in as with the bindery emulated user Supervisor.

7. Once you are logged in successfully, you will see the Macintosh volume icon. Click on this to open it, and open the PUBLIC\MAC folder.

   Next, open the proper language folder, and locate the MacNDS.SEA file in the language folder.

8. Double-click on the MacNDS.SEA folder.

9. In the dialog box that appears, identify the location where the decompressed files should be installed. Typically, this should be on the local Macintosh volume. If you use the default setting, the MacNDS folder will be created in the language folder on the network volume.

10. Locate the installation script in the MacNDS folder and run this script.

11. Run the MacNCP program and set the default values for the NetWare 4 NDS tree, the context, and the name of the user (you can also use complete names). Click on the Verify button to see that you have entered the information correctly.

12. Activate the Chooser program again, and use the preceding steps to log on to the network. You will see a new option added enabling you to log in as an NDS user.

Configuring OS/2 Clients

Configuring OS/2 clients involves preparing the server to optionally provide OS/2 long file-name support and installing the OS/2 client software.

Configuring the NetWare Server for OS/2 Clients

OS/2 clients use the same IPX/SPX protocol for communicating with the NetWare 4 server as do the DOS clients. So no additional communication settings need to be done at the NetWare server for OS/2 clients. OS/2 clients can make use of the file and prints services used by DOS clients.

However, OS/2 clients have the option of using the High Performance File System (HPFS) which supports long names and extended attributes. OS/2 long file names can be up to 255 characters. Extended attributes are additional names and values describing the file name that can be attached to the long file names.

To add support for HPFS to the NetWare file system, you need to add this name space support using explicit commands. You need to first load the OS/2 name space on the NetWare file server. This is done using the following server console command, which can be placed in the STARTUP.NCF file:

```
LOAD OS2
```

The LOAD OS2 command identifies the name space and loads the protocols and algorithms needed to understand the HPFS file system structure.

Next, you need to add the OS/2 name space to the NetWare volume that will support HPFS. You can do this using the following command:

```
ADD NAME SPACE OS2 TO volumename
```

Replace *volumename* with the physical volume name such as SYS or VOL1. The ADD NAME SPACE command creates additional directory entries in the directory entry table (DET) for the volume. These additional directory entries contain the long file names for the OS/2 volume and other OS/2 file name related information.

Because the OS/2 directory entries need to be created only once for a given volume, you need to execute the ADD NAME SPACE command only once during the initial OS/2 configuration for that volume. After the OS/2 name space has been added to the volume, you need to only load the OS2.NAM module. The OS2.NAM module is loaded from the STARTUP.NCF file and the OS2.NAM file is kept in the server boot directory (C:\NWSERVER). Actually, once you add the name space to a volume, the name space module will be autoloaded before the volume is mounted, even if the LOAD namespace statement is missing from the STARTUP-.NCF file. If the namespace file cannot be found in the server boot directory, the corresponding NetWare volume to which the namespace is added will not mount.

Installing OS/2 Client Software

The NetWare Client for OS/2 can be found on the NetWare 4 installation CD-ROM, in the SYS:PUBLIC\CLIENT\OS2 directory. You can create OS/2 client installation disks by running the MAKEDISK batch file that can be found in the OS2 client subdirectory on the CD-ROM or the SYS:PUBLIC\CLIENT.

After you create these OS/2 client installation disks, you run the INSTALL program in the first installation disk from an OS/2 workstation connected to a NetWare 4 network.

Study Guide for the Chapter

If you're preparing for the NetWare 3 to 4 Update CNE exams, review this chapter with the following goals:

■ Understand and identify the differences between the NetWare shell and the NetWare DOS requester. Use the STUDY TIPS as a quick review.

■ Pay particular attention to the different VLM components and their functions.

■ After studying this chapter, attempt the sample test questions for this chapter. If you miss the answer to a question, review the appropriate topic until you understand the reason for the correct answer.

Chapter Summary

In this chapter, you have learned about the components of NetWare 4 client software support. The architecture of the VLM requester and the individual VLM components were examined. The ODI interface was discussed briefly, and the differences between the DOS NETX shell and the DOS requester were examined. You also learned about the different types of VLMs such as multiplexor and child VLMs.

The DOS client installation steps were shown in detail, and each of the installation choices were discussed. The different VLM options were covered, and the diagnostic option for VLM was presented in detail. Toward the end of the chapter, you were introduced to some of the major NetWare 4 NET.CFG parameters.

Chapter Test Questions

Test questions either have a single correct answer or multiple answers. Where a single answer is requested, a ○ (circle) notation precedes the possible answers. Some questions require you to select more than one answer; these questions are indicated by the □ (box) preceding each answer. Not all the questions are multiple choice. Occasionally, you will get a question that asks you to type in an answer. The answer in this case is usually a one-word answer. The answer is not case sensitive, so you can type the answer in lower- or uppercase.

Certain questions are repeated in different ways so that you can recognize them even when the wording is different. Taking practice quizzes not only tests your knowledge but also gives you confidence when you take your exam.

1. Which of the following is a NetWare 4 client component?

    ○ A. The DOS requester

    ○ B. DOS

    ○ C. TCPIP.EXE

    ○ D. NETX.COM

2. Which of the following are NetWare 4 client components?

    □ A. MLID Driver

    □ B. LSL.COM

    □ C. WSGEN.EXE

    □ D. NETX.COM

3. Which of the following are not NetWare 4 client components?

    □ A. ODI Driver

    □ B. LSL.COM

    □ C. IPXODI.COM

    □ D. Windows

    □ E. VLM.EXE

    □ F. NETX.COM

4. Which of the following are not NetWare 4 client components?

    □ A. LSL.COM

    □ B. IPXODI.COM

    □ C. DOS

    □ D. VLM.COM

    □ E. ODI Network Driver

    □ F. NETX.COM

5. In NetWare 4, the request for a network service is first seen by _____.

    ○ A. NETX.COM

    ○ B. NETX.EXE

    ○ C. VLM.EXE

    ○ D. DOS

6. In NetWare 4 client architecture, _____.

    ○ A. DOS and the NetWare DOS requester share a common drive table

    ○ B. DOS and the NetWare DOS requester have separate drive tables

   ○ C. DOS and the NetWare DOS requester have separate drive tables for all but the network drives

   ○ D. DOS and the NetWare DOS requester share a common drive table only if the DOS requester is loaded with an appropriate share drive table option

7. Application requests for network services are translated into _____.

   ○ A. DOS requests for services

   ○ B. NCP requests for services

   ○ C. NETBIOS requests

   ○ D. Shell requests

8. The default communication protocol used for sending NCP requests is _____.

   ○ A. TCP

   ○ B. SPX

   ○ C. IPX

   ○ D. NCP

9. When using the ODI interface, there _____.

   ○ A. is only one choice of communication protocol

   ○ B. are many choices of communication protocols

   ○ C. are many choices of communication protocols if the driver is loaded with a PROTOCOL=MANY option in NET.CFG

   ○ D. is only one choice of communication protocol if the driver is loaded with a PROTOCOL=SINGLE option in NET.CFG

10. The NetWare 3.*x* shell (NETX.EXE) acts as _____.

   ○ A. a back end to DOS

   ○ B. a front end to DOS

   ○ C. a multiplexor for DOS

   ○ D. a demultiplexor for DOS

11. The NetWare shell (NETX.EXE) _____.

   ○ A. receives requests for system services from DOS

   ○ B. receives requests for system services from the DOS redirector

   ○ C. intercepts application requests for system services

   ○ D. does not intercept application requests for system services

12. The NetWare shell (NETX.EXE) intercepts _____.

   ○ A. system calls made to INT 21 (hex)

   ○ B. only BIOS calls made to INT 21 (hex)

   ○ C. system calls made to INT 31 (hex)

   ○ D. only BIOS calls made to INT 31 (hex)

13. The NetWare shell (NETX.EXE) has a limit of _____ connections and a size of _____ KB.

    ○ A. 16, 64

    ○ B. 8, 64

    ○ C. 16, 128

    ○ D. 8, 128

14. The NetWare 4 requester requires _____.

    ○ A. DOS 2.0 or higher

    ○ B. DOS 3.0 or higher

    ○ C. DOS 3.1 or higher

    ○ D. DOS 3.3 or higher

    ○ E. DOS 4.0 or higher

    ○ F. DOS 5.0 or higher

15. The NetWare DOS requester uses the _____.

    ○ A. DOS system services via INT 2F (hex)

    ○ B. DOS system services via INT 21 (hex)

    ○ C. DOS redirector via INT 21 (hex)

    ○ D. DOS redirector via INT 2F (hex)

16. The NetWare DOS requester can have _____ simultaneous connections.

    ○ A. 2 to 8

    ○ B. 2 to 16

    ○ C. 2 to 32

    ○ D. 2 to 50

    ○ E. 2 to 100

17. The NetWare DOS requester _____.

    ○ A. shares drive and status tables with DOS

    ○ B. shares drive and status tables with DOS, which results in reduced system table memory requirements

    ○ C. does not share drive and status tables with DOS

    ○ D. does not share drive and status tables with DOS and needs more memory than the NetWare shell

18. The NetWare DOS requester Virtual Memory Manager is implemented by _____.

    ○ A. VLM.COM

    ○ B. VLM.EXE

    ○ C. VLMGR.COM

    ○ D. VLMGR.EXE

19. The NetWare DOS requester consists of which of the following?

    □ A. The DOS shell

    □ B. The Interrupt 2F multiplexor

    □ C. The Virtual Loadable Modules (VLMs)

    □ D. VLM Manager

    □ E. VLMs and VLM tables

20. The VLM Manager is responsible for which of the following?

    □ A. Controlling VLMs' access to memory at the server

    □ B. Controlling VLMs' access to memory at the workstation

☐ C. Managing data flow and communications between VLMs

☐ D. Managing data flow and communications between VLMs and DOS

☐ E. Forwarding application requests to NETBIOS for processing

☐ F. Forwarding application requests to the appropriate VLM for processing

21. To load VLMs in the default order, specify _____.

  ○ A. the USE DEFAULT=ON option in the NetWare DOS Requester heading in the NET.CFG file

  ○ B. the USE DEFAULT=OFF option in the NetWare DOS Requester heading in the NET.CFG file

  ○ C. the USE ORDER=DEFAULT option in the NetWare DOS Requester heading in the NET.CFG file

  ○ D. the ORDER=DEFAULT option in the NetWare DOS Requester heading in the NET.CFG file

22. VLMs can be classified as which of the following?

  ☐ A. Child VLMs

  ☐ B. Parent VLMs

  ☐ C. Multiplexor VLMs

  ☐ D. Ancestor VLMs

  ☐ E. Root VLMs

23. Multiplexor VLMs _____.

  ○ A. route specific tasks to DOS

  ○ B. route specific tasks to the appropriate parent VLM

  ○ C. route specific tasks to the appropriate shell VLMs

  ○ D. route specific tasks to the appropriate child VLM

24. Which of the following are features of the NetWare 4 DOS Requestor?

  ☐ A. Multiple language support

  ☐ B. Support for 2 to 50 simultaneous connections

  ☐ C. Shared drive and status tables that reduce system table memory requirements

  ☐ D. DOS redirector support via INT 21 (hex)

  ☐ E. Background authentication

  ☐ F. Separate drive and status table from DOS

25. Which VLM provides support for viewing bindery information on NetWare 3.x servers?

  ○ A. CONN.VLM

  ○ B. NETX.VLM

  ○ C. RSA.VLM

  ○ D. NDS.VLM

  ○ E. TRAN.VLM

  ○ F. NWP.VLM

  ○ G. BIND.VLM

26. Which VLM provides support for compatibility with the NetWare 3.x shell?

    ○ A. CONN.VLM

    ○ B. NETX.VLM

    ○ C. RSA.VLM

    ○ D. NDS.VLM

    ○ E. TRAN.VLM

    ○ F. NWP.VLM

    ○ G. BIND.VLM

27. Which VLM provides support for keeping track of connection status?

    ○ A. CONN.VLM

    ○ B. NETX.VLM

    ○ C. RSA.VLM

    ○ D. NDS.VLM

    ○ E. TRAN.VLM

    ○ F. NWP.VLM

    ○ G. BIND.VLM

28. Which VLM provides support for background authentication?

    ○ A. CONN.VLM

    ○ B. SECURITY.VLM

    ○ C. RSA.VLM

    ○ D. NDS.VLM

    ○ E. TRAN.VLM

    ○ F. NWP.VLM

    ○ G. BIND.VLM

29. Which VLM provides support for NetWare Directory Services?

    ○ A. CONN.VLM

    ○ B. NETX.VLM

    ○ C. RSA.VLM

    ○ D. NDS.VLM

    ○ E. TRAN.VLM

    ○ F. NWP.VLM

    ○ G. BIND.VLM

30. Which VLM provides support for multiple transport protocols?

    ○ A. CONN.VLM

    ○ B. NETX.VLM

    ○ C. RSA.VLM

    ○ D. NDS.VLM

    ○ E. TRAN.VLM

    ○ F. NWP.VLM

    ○ G. BIND.VLM

31. Which VLM provides support for network file input and output?

    ○ A. CONN.VLM

    ○ B. FIO.VLM

    ○ C. GENERAL.VLM

    ○ D. PRINT.VLM

    ○ E. REDIR.VLM

    ○ F. IPXNCP.VLM

32. Which VLM provides support for miscellaneous functions to other VLMs?

    ○ A. CONN.VLM

    ○ B. FIO.VLM

    ○ C. GENERAL.VLM

    ○ D. MISC.VLM

    ○ E. REDIR.VLM

    ○ F. IPXNCP.VLM

33. Which VLM provides support for network print redirection?

    ○ A. CONN.VLM

    ○ B. FIO.VLM

    ○ C. GENERAL.VLM

    ○ D. PRINT.VLM

    ○ E. REDIR.VLM

    ○ F. PREDIR.VLM

34. Which VLM provides support for DOS redirection?

    ○ A. CONN.VLM

    ○ B. FIO.VLM

    ○ C. GENERAL.VLM

    ○ D. REDIRECT.VLM

    ○ E. REDIR.VLM

    ○ F. IPXNCP.VLM

35. Which VLM provides support for IPX transport protocol processing?

    ○ A. CONN.VLM

    ○ B. IPXTRAN.VLM

    ○ C. GENERAL.VLM

    ○ D. PRINT.VLM

    ○ E. REDIR.VLM

    ○ F. IPXNCP.VLM

36. The command for help on VLM options is which of the following?

    ☐ A. VLM ?

    ☐ B. VLM help

    ☐ C. VLM I

    ☐ D. VLM /?

37. To unload the VLMs, use the following commands:

    ☐ A. VLM U

    ☐ B. VLM UNLOAD

    ☐ C. VLM /U

    ☐ D. VLM /?

38. To specify an alternate configuration file of ALTERN.CFG for a VLM, the command is

    _____.

    ○ A. VLM ALTERN.CFG

    ○ B. VLM /F ALTERN.CFG

    ○ C. VLM /A=ALTERN.CFG

    ○ D. VLM /C=ALTERN.CFG

39. The command to load VLMs in conventional memory is _____.

    ○ A. VLM /MC

    ○ B. VLM /ME

    ○ C. VLM /MX

○ D. VLM /M=C

○ E. VLM /M=E

○ F. VLM /M=X

40. The command to load VLMs in expanded memory is _____.

○ A. VLM /MC

○ B. VLM /ME

○ C. VLM /MX

○ D. VLM /M=C

○ E. VLM /M=E

○ F. VLM /M=X

41. The commands to display VLM diagnostics for an already loaded VLM are:

☐ A. VLM /DIAG

☐ B. VLM DIAGNOSTICS

☐ C. VLM /D

☐ D. VLM D

42. Which VLM commands enable you to attach to a server named ENG_FS3 during the VLM load?

☐ A. VLM /PSERV=ENG_FS3

☐ B. VLM PS=ENG_PS3

☐ C. VLM PSERV=ENG_FS3

☐ D. VLM /PS=ENG_PS3

43. To display only the VLM copyright message and critical errors during loading, the command is _____.

○ A. VLM /V4

○ B. VLM /V3

○ C. VLM /V2

○ D. VLM /V1

○ E. VLM /V0

44. To attach to a tree named CSNET during VLM load, the command is _____.

○ A. VLM /PTREE=CSNET

○ B. VLM PTREE=CSNET

○ C. VLM PTREE=CSNET

○ D. VLM /PT=CSNET

45. To specify a tree of ANSNET to attach to, using the NET.CFG file, you must specify _____ in the NET.CFG file:

○ A. PREFERRED TREE = "ANSNET"

○ B. PREFERRED TREE = ANSNET

○ C. ATTACHED NET = ANSNET

○ D. ATTACHED NET = "ANSNET"

46. To specify the container OU=LAB.OU-=ENG.O=ESL as an initial context, you can specify _____ in the NET.CFG file.

○ A. NAME CONTEXT = OU=LAB.OU=ENG.O=ESL

○ B. NAME CONTEXT = "OU=LAB.OU=ENG.O=ESL"

○ C. NAME CONTEXT = ".OU=LAB.OU=ENG.O=ESL"

○ D. NAME CONTEXT = ".OU=LAB.OU=ENG.O=ESL."

47. To enable the packet burst capability with 3 buffers, use the _____ command in the NET.CFG file.

    ○ A. PB BUFFERS=3

    ○ B. PBURST BUFFERS=3

    ○ C. PACKET BURST=3

    ○ D. PACKET BUFFERS=3

    ○ E. PACKET BURST BUFFERS=3

48. The default Ethernet frame type for NetWare 4 is _____.

    ○ A. ETHERNET_802.1

    ○ B. ETHERNET_802.2

    ○ C. ETHERNET_802.3

    ○ D. ETHERNET_II

    ○ E. ETHERNET_SNAP

49. For MS Windows NetWare 4 clients, specify _____ in the NET.CFG file.

    ○ A. SHOW DOUBLE DOTS=ON

    ○ B. SHOW DOTS=OFF

    ○ C. SHOW DOTS=ON

    ○ D. SHOW DOUBLE DOTS=OFF

50. Which of the following are multiplexor VLMs?

    ☐ A. REDIR.VLM

    ☐ B. NWP.VLM

    ☐ C. NDS.VLM

    ☐ D. BIND.VLM

    ☐ E. PRINT.VLM

    ☐ F. TRAN.VLM

    ☐ G. IPXNCP.VLM

51. Which of the following are child VLMs?

    ☐ A. REDIR.VLM

    ☐ B. NWP.VLM

    ☐ C. NDS.VLM

    ☐ D. BIND.VLM

    ☐ E. PRINT.VLM

    ☐ F. TRAN.VLM

    ☐ G. IPXNCP.VLM

52. Which VLM implements a public key encryption that is used for background authentication of NetWare client services?

    ○ A. PUBLIC.VLM

    ○ B. ENCRYPT.VLM

    ○ C. SECURITY.VLM

    ○ D. RSA.VLM

53. Which VLM implements the proper formatting of a network service request into an NCP request packet?

    ○ A. REDIR.VLM

    ○ B. BIND.VLM

    ○ C. NETX.VLM

    ○ D. IPXNCP.VLM

54. The VLMs can be grouped into the following service categories:

    ☐ A. DOS Redirection

    ☐ B. Application Protocol

    ☐ C. Service Protocol

    ☐ D. Network Protocol

    ☐ E. Transport Protocol

55. The DOS Redirection Service is implemented by _____, which provides a client application with access to remote network file and print services.

   ○ A. NETX.VLM

   ○ B. BIND.VLM

   ○ C. REDIR.VLM

   ○ D. NWP.VLM

56. The Service Protocol Layer handles specific functions such as _____.

   ○ A. connection management, network file input/output, network printing, and other miscellaneous services such as message broadcast

   ○ B. session management for the OSI model

   ○ C. services for the multiplexor VLMs

   ○ D. services for the child VLMs

57. The CONN.VLM implements the connection table manager and provides support for _____.

   ○ A. the DOS redirection layer

   ○ B. the Service protocol layer

   ○ C. the Transport protocol layer

   ○ D. all the service layers

58. After loading the ODI LAN Driver, which component needs to be loaded next for a NetWare 4 client?

   ○ A. LSL

   ○ B. IPXODI

   ○ C. VLM

   ○ D. NETX

59. Which of the following are, by default, necessary to load VLMs?

   ☐ A. IPXODI

   ☐ B. NETX

   ☐ C. LSL

   ☐ D. VLM

60. Which of the following are correct for IPXODI?

   ☐ A. IPXODI is generated by a special program.

   ☐ B. IPXODI is not generated.

   ☐ C. IPXODI reads configuration information in the NET.CFG file.

   ☐ D. IPXODI reads configuration information in the CONFIG.SYS file.

61. Which of these statements are needed in NET.CFG for a NetWare 4 client to connect to a NetWare 4-based network with FIRST NETWORK DRIVE set to E?

   ☐ A. FRAME ETHERNET_802.3

   ☐ B. FRAME ETHERNET_802.2

   ☐ C. FIRST NETWORK DRIVE=F

   ☐ D. FIRST NETWORK DRIVE=E

62. Which of the following configuration statements are placed under the NetWare DOS Requester heading in the NET.CFG file?

   ☐ A. FRAME ETHERNET_802.3

   ☐ B. FIRST NETWORK DRIVE=F

   ☐ C. FRAME ETHERNET_802.2

   ☐ D. PB BUFFERS=3

   ☐ E. PREFERRED TREE=SCSNET

NetWare 4 Utilities

In this chapter you will learn about NetWare 4 client utility changes and differences in the login script processing mechanisms. This chapter also discusses command-line utility changes. Some of the NetWare 3 utilities have been consolidated into a single utility in many cases. In other cases, the older bindery-based utilities have disappeared and are replaced by newer utilities that are NDS aware. Many of the utilities have a bindery emulation mode, and can be used to work with NetWare 3 servers.

Another major change in the NetWare 4 utilities is that they support multiple languages. This support was not available in NetWare v3.11, though it is available in NetWare v3.12 (and future NetWare 3 versions).

The Menu utility for creating a menu-driven interface in NetWare 4 is different from that available in NetWare 3.11; it is the same as that in NetWare 3.12 (and higher). It has been improved vastly, and is based on the popular Saber menus.

Other major changes are in the area of login script processing. The login script processing is really not a utility function in NetWare. Because the login script processing is done by the LOGIN.EXE program in SYS:LOGIN, however, the discussion here refers to the different forms of inputs (login scripts) accepted by the newer LOGIN.EXE for NetWare 4.

Overview of Utility Changes

NetWare 4 utilities can be classified into the following broad categories:

1. Command line

2. Menu driven (Character based)

3. Graphical User Interface (Pixel based)

Some command-line utilities have been consolidated into a single utility with options for different modes of operations. Others have been entirely replaced by newer utilities that deal with NDS services. An important example of the latter is the NetWare 3 SYSCON utility. This has been replaced by NETADMIN. There is a SYSCON.BAT file in SYS:PUBLIC that contains a statement to print a message that you should use the NETADMIN utility instead.

 NetWare 4 utilities can be divided into three categories: command line, menu driven, and GUI based.

Many of the utilities such as NETADMIN, NETUSER, and the familiar PCONSOLE are menu driven. The menus are produced by using the extended ASCII character set that contains the line drawing characters. These menus are based on the popular C-Worthy interface.

A new set of utilities that provides a Graphical User Interface (GUI) for MS Windows and OS/2's Presentation Manager has been introduced. The most important of these is the NetWare Administrator Tool that is implemented by a program named NWADMIN.EXE. This provides an easy way to depict the NDS tree structure graphically and carry out directory operations on the tree. Most network management tasks can be performed by the NetWare Administrator Tool. Another GUI utility of interest to NetWare 4 users is the NetWare User implemented by NWUSER.EXE. This provides a graphical interface to provide drive mapping, message sending, and other functions. The hot key for this program is F6.

The utility changes are reviewed in greater detail next.

 NETADMIN and NETUSER are examples of new menu-based utilities.

NWADMIN.EXE and NWUSER.EXE are examples of GUI-based utilities.

NWADMIN.EXE can be used to show the NDS tree graphically, and to carry out most NDS operations.

The default hot key to invoke NWUSER.EXE is F6.

MAP Utility Changes

One of the most useful utilities in NetWare is the MAP command utility. It is used to provide a network drive or search drive mapping to a remote file system.

The MAP command syntax is essentially the same as in NetWare 3. Users of NetWare 3 should feel at home using NetWare 4's MAP command. Additional capabilities and functions have been added, however.

With NetWare 4, you can create a mapping by using the NDS name of the Volume object. If you wanted to create a drive mapping H: to the PUBLIC/BIN directory in the Volume object CN=FS1_VOL.OU=SALES.O=SCS, for example, you would use the following MAP command:

```
MAP H: = .CN=FS1_VOL.OU=SALES.O=SCS:PUBLIC
➡/BIN
```

The above MAP command shows that the complete name for the Volume object FS1_VOL is used. A typeless complete name also can be used, as shown following, provided the Country container object is not part of the NDS path name:

```
MAP H: = .FS1_VOL.SALES.SCS:PUBLIC/BIN
```

The previous examples use the complete name of the Volume object. You also can use partial names. The examples shown next use partial typeless names for providing the same drive mapping from different contexts.

If the current context is OU=SALES.O=SCS, you can use the following MAP command:

```
MAP H: = FS1_VOL:PUBLIC/BIN
```

If the current context is O=SCS, you can use the following MAP command:

```
MAP H: = FS1_VOL.SALES:PUBLIC/BIN
```

If the current context is OU=LAB.OU =ENG.O=SCS, you can use the following MAP command:

```
MAP H: = FS1_VOL.SALES..:PUBLIC/BIN
```

 Understand the use of NDS names in MAP commands. Practice using the syntax of the MAP command with NDS object names.

If you want to make the drive H a search drive, issue the following command:

```
MAP CHANGE H:
```

or

```
MAP C H:
```

Note that the "C" option is an abbreviation for the "Change" option.

The C option is called the Change option and makes the drive letter the last search drive. The same effect can be achieved by using the following command:

```
MAP INS S16: =
➡.CN=FS1_VOL.OU=SALES.O=SCS:PUBLIC/BIN
```

Using the C option saves some typing if you already have a drive mapping to a NetWare directory.

 Understand how the Change (C) option is used in the MAP command. The Change (C) option in the MAP command can be used to convert a network drive into a search drive and vice versa.

If the default server that you are logged in to is FS1, you can access the PUBLIC/BIN directory on the Volume object CN=VOL.OU=SALES.O=SCS using the NetWare 3 syntax

```
MAP H: = VOL:PUBLIC/BIN
```

or

```
MAP H: = FS1/VOL:PUBLIC\BIN
```

These forms of mapping enable compatibility with NetWare 3 mappings. This is particularly useful when login scripts are being upgraded from NetWare 3 to NetWare 4. Using the Volume object names gives you flexibility in mapping to volumes that are in different contexts.

Figure 5.1 shows the help obtained using the MAP /? command.

FLAG Utility Changes

The NetWare 4 FLAG utility consolidates the functions of the NetWare 3 FLAG, FLAGDIR, and SMODE commands. A single FLAG utility can be used to change both the file and directory attributes, and also the search mode for executable files. The FLAG utility also enables you to change the owner of a directory or a file, and can be used on local drives.

The functions of the FLAG utility also can be performed by the FILER menu utility.

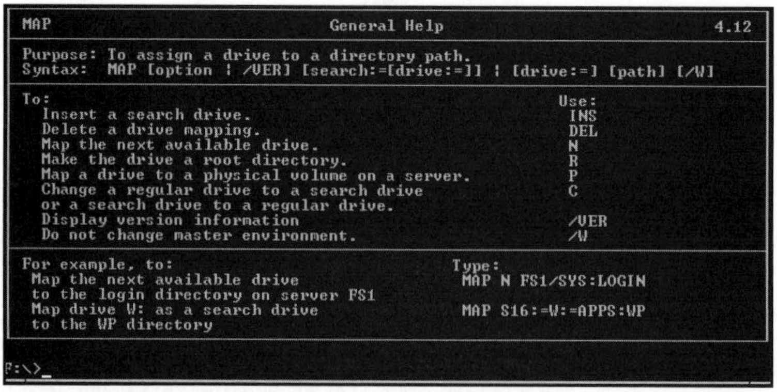

Figure 5.1

The MAP /? Help summary.

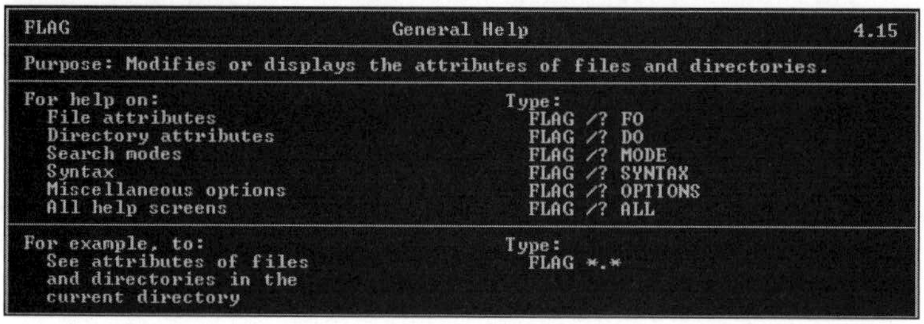

```
MAP                              General Help                         4.12
Purpose: To assign a drive to a directory path.
Syntax:  MAP [option | /VER] [search:=[drive:=]] | [drive:=] [path] [/W]

To:                                                          Use:
  Insert a search drive.                                     INS
  Delete a drive mapping.                                    DEL
  Map the next available drive.                              N
  Make the drive a root directory.                           R
  Map a drive to a physical volume on a server.              P
  Change a regular drive to a search drive                   C
  or a search drive to a regular drive.
  Display version information                                /VER
  Do not change master environment.                          /W

For example, to:                              Type:
  Map the next available drive                MAP N FS1/SYS:LOGIN
  to the login directory on server FS1
  Map drive W: as a search drive              MAP S16:=W:=APPS:WP
  to the WP directory

F:\>_
```

Figure 5.2

A summary of FLAG command usage on-screen.

```
FLAG                             General Help                         4.15
Purpose: Modifies or displays the attributes of files and directories.

For help on:                                  Type:
  File attributes                             FLAG /? FO
  Directory attributes                        FLAG /? DO
  Search modes                                FLAG /? MODE
  Syntax                                      FLAG /? SYNTAX
  Miscellaneous options                       FLAG /? OPTIONS
  All help screens                            FLAG /? ALL

For example, to:                              Type:
  See attributes of files                     FLAG *.*
  and directories in the
  current directory
```

Figure 5.2 shows a summary of the FLAG command usage.

 The NetWare 4 FLAG utility consolidates the functions of the NetWare 3 FLAG, FLAGDIR, and SMODE commands.

The FLAG utility operations also can be performed by the FILER utility.

NDIR Utility Changes

The NetWare 4 NDIR utility consolidates the functions of the NetWare 3 NDIR, LISTDIR, and VOLINFO commands. You can use a single NDIR utility to view file, directory, and volume information. To display volume information you must use the /VOL option.

 The NDIR command can be used to view file, directory, and volume information.

Example:

```
F:\> NDIR /VOL

Statistics for fixed volume NW4CS/SYS:
Space statistics are in KB (1024 bytes).

Total volume space:                    1,296,384  100.00%
    Space used by 4,004 entries:         109,632    8.46%
    Deleted space not yet purgeable:           0    0.00%
                                       ------ ----
    Space remaining on volume:         1,186,752   91.54%
    Space available to CN=Admin.O=ESL: 1,186,752   91.54%

    Maximum directory entries:             9,728
    Available directory entries:           5,441   55.93%

    Space used if files were not compressed:  1,136
    Space used by compressed files:             421
                                            ------ ----
    Space saved by compressing files:           715   62.94%

    Uncompressed space used:              109,659
```

 The NDIR command can be used to find information on space saved using the file compression feature.

You can view subdirectories by using the /S option. In NetWare 3, the /SUB option had to be used with NDIR to view subdirectories. This led to inconsistencies with the DOS XCOPY command, which also uses /S option. Use of a common /S option removes some of these inconsistencies. Also, the /S is used in NLIST to view subcontainers, and this usage is compatible with the /S option in NDIR that is used to view subdirectories.

 The /S option of NDIR enables you to view information on subdirectories.

The NetWare 4 NDIR utility consolidates the functions of NetWare 3 NDIR, LISTDIR, and VOLINFO commands.

To search for files that can be found on the search drives, use the /FI option. The following list shows an example of this usage:

```
F:\> NDIR P*.EXE  /FI
Searching for P*.EXE

F:\PUBLIC
    partmgr.exe     400841   5-19-93   9:53:16
    pconsole.exe    796026   5-19-93  18:02:18
    printcon.exe    452401   5-26-93  10:32:24
    printdef.exe    492880   6-01-93  10:55:18
    psc.exe         289146   5-19-93  11:17:00
    purge.exe       204727   5-19-93   9:45:25
Z:\PUBLIC
    partmgr.exe     400841   5-19-93   9:53:16
    pconsole.exe    796026   5-19-93  18:02:18
    printcon.exe    452401   5-26-93  10:32:24
    printdef.exe    492880   6-01-93  10:55:18
    psc.exe         289146   5-19-93  11:17:00
    purge.exe       204727   5-19-93   9:45:25
C:\WINDOWS
    packager.exe     76480   3-10-92   3:10:00
    pbrush.exe      183376   3-10-92   3:10:00
    printman.exe     43248   3-10-92   3:10:00
    progman.exe     115312   3-10-92   3:10:00
    pifedit.exe      55168   3-10-92   3:10:00
C:\PCTCP
    ping.exe         22045   6-16-92   2:35:07
    passwd.exe        8653   6-16-92   2:36:01
    pop3.exe         31293   6-16-92   2:36:14
C:\BIN
    pe.exe           45241   7-04-92  15:21:12
    pkcfg.exe        28570   2-01-93   2:04:08
    pkzip.exe        42552  10-24-92   0:51:13
    pkzipfix.exe      7687   2-01-93   2:04:08
    prune.exe         6309   7-04-92  15:21:14
    pkunzip.exe      28959   2-01-93   2:04:08
C:\DOS
    print.exe        15656   4-09-91   5:00:00

NDIR found 27 matching files.
```

Notice that all files in search drives beginning with a "P" are displayed.

You can use the /FI option in NDIR to search for file names on the search drives.

The NDIR /FI command is equivalent to the *which* command found on many Unix systems.

Another improvement is that NDIR also works with local drives. The NetWare 3.11 NDIR did not work with local drives. The following example shows the output of using NDIR on a local drive:

```
F:\> NDIR C:\
NDIR is searching the directory.  Please wait...
Files                  = Files contained in this path
Size                   = Number of bytes in the file
Last Update            = Date file was last updated
DOS Attr               = DOS file attributes

C:\BIN*.*
Files           Size    Last Update DOS Attr
---------------------------------------------------
AUTOEXEC.000     134    9-21-93     1:05p  [Rw-A]
AUTOEXEC.01      125    9-20-93     8:14p  [Rw-A]
AUTOEXEC.BAT     198    9-21-93     9:01p  [Rw-A]
AUTOEXEC.BNW     170    9-21-93     8:39p  [Rw-A]
AUTOEXEC.OLD     134    9-21-93     1:05p  [Rw-A]
COMMAND.COM   47,845    4-09-91     5:00a  [Rw-A]
CONFIG.000       103    9-20-93     9:08p  [Rw-A]
CONFIG.BNW       146    9-21-93     8:39p  [Rw-A]
CONFIG.OLD       103    9-20-93     9:08p  [Rw-A]
CONFIG.SYS       161    9-21-93     9:01p  [Rw-A]
IO.SYS        33,430    4-09-91     5:00a  [RoSyHA]
MSDOS.SYS     37,394    4-09-91     5:00a  [RoSyHA]
ZIP.BAT          107    9-21-93    12:58p  [Rw-A]

Directories            = Directories contained in this path
Created                = Date directory was created
```

```
C:\BIN*.*
Directories      Created
- - - - - - - - - - - - - - - - - - - - - - - - - - -
BIN              9-20-93  6:21p
CONFIG           9-20-93  9:34p
DIAGNOSE         9-20-93  9:34p
DOS              9-20-93  9:34p
LANWATCH         9-20-93  9:34p
LDE              9-20-93  9:34p
LL5              9-20-93  9:34p
LLINS            9-20-93  9:34p
NW               9-20-93  6:26p
NWCLIENT         9-21-93  8:56p
PCTCP            9-20-93  9:34p
SOSS             9-20-93  9:34p
WINDOWS          9-21-93  8:37p

     120,050  bytes
          13  Files
          13  Directories
```

Figures 5.3 to 5.9 show a summary of the NDIR
command usage.

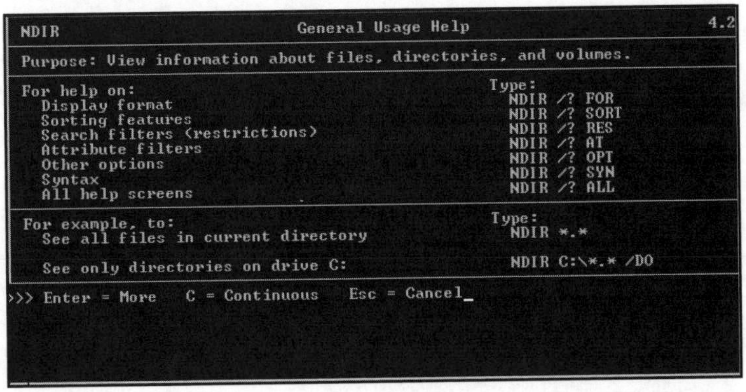

Figure 5.3
*The NDIR /? Help
summary.*

Figure 5.4
The NDIR /? FOR Help.

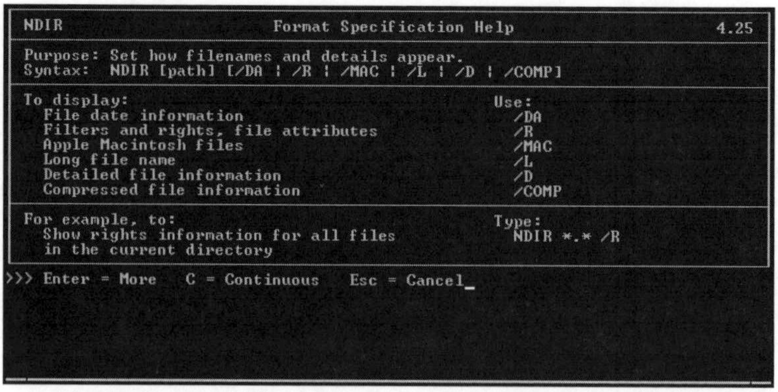

```
NDIR                       Format Specification Help                    4.25

 Purpose: Set how filenames and details appear.
 Syntax:  NDIR [path] [/DA | /R | /MAC | /L | /D | /COMP]

 To display:                                        Use:
   File date information                              /DA
   Filters and rights, file attributes                /R
   Apple Macintosh files                              /MAC
   Long file name                                     /L
   Detailed file information                          /D
   Compressed file information                        /COMP

 For example, to:                                   Type:
   Show rights information for all files              NDIR *.* /R
   in the current directory

>>> Enter = More    C = Continuous    Esc = Cancel_
```

Figure 5.5
*The NDIR /? AT Help
menu.*

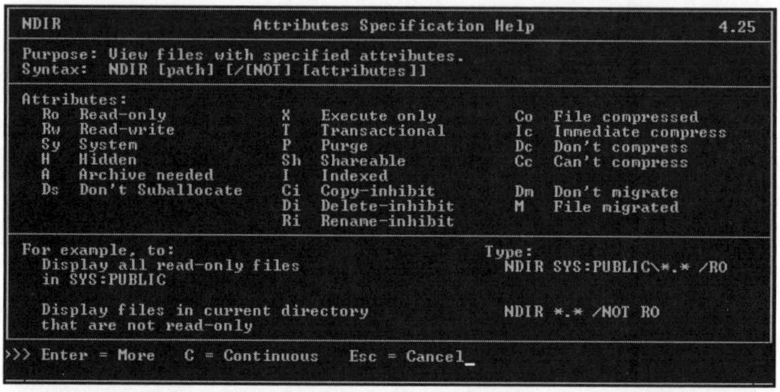

```
NDIR                     Attributes Specification Help                  4.25

 Purpose: View files with specified attributes.
 Syntax:  NDIR [path] [/[NOT] [attributes]]

 Attributes:
   Ro  Read-only          X   Execute only      Co  File compressed
   Rw  Read-write         T   Transactional     Ic  Immediate compress
   Sy  System             P   Purge             Dc  Don't compress
   H   Hidden             Sh  Shareable         Cc  Can't compress
   A   Archive needed     I   Indexed
   Ds  Don't Suballocate  Ci  Copy-inhibit      Dm  Don't migrate
                          Di  Delete-inhibit    M   File migrated
                          Ri  Rename-inhibit

 For example, to:                                   Type:
   Display all read-only files                        NDIR SYS:PUBLIC\*.* /RO
   in SYS:PUBLIC

   Display files in current directory                 NDIR *.* /NOT RO
   that are not read-only

>>> Enter = More    C = Continuous    Esc = Cancel_
```

Figure 5.6
*The NDIR /? SORT Help
menu.*

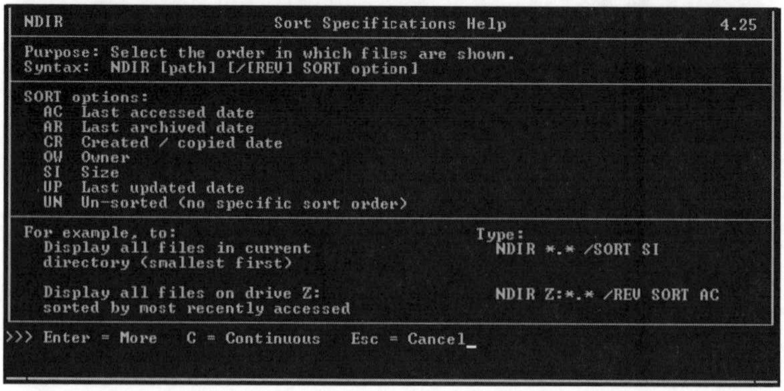

```
NDIR                      Sort Specifications Help                      4.25

 Purpose: Select the order in which files are shown.
 Syntax:  NDIR [path] [/[REV] SORT option]

 SORT options:
   AC  Last accessed date
   AR  Last archived date
   CR  Created / copied date
   OW  Owner
   SI  Size
   UP  Last updated date
   UN  Un-sorted (no specific sort order)

 For example, to:                                   Type:
   Display all files in current                       NDIR *.* /SORT SI
   directory (smallest first)

   Display all files on drive Z:                      NDIR Z:*.* /REV SORT AC
   sorted by most recently accessed

>>> Enter = More    C = Continuous    Esc = Cancel_
```

```
NDIR                    Restrictions Specification Help              4.25

Purpose: Restrict which files are shown.
Syntax:  NDIR [path] [/options [NOT] operator value]

Options:                              Operators:
  AC  Last accessed date                LE  Less than
  AR  Last archived date                GR  Greater than
  CR  Created/copied date               EQ  Equal to
  OW  Owner                             BEF Before
  SI  Size                              AFT After
  UP  Last updated date
  NAM Name space

Date formats must be mm-dd-yy or mm/dd/yy.

For example, to:                       Type:
  Display all files updated              NDIR *.* /UP BEF 6-05-91
  before June 5, 1991

  Display files not owned by the         NDIR *.* /OW NOT EQ ADMIN
  user ADMIN

>>> Enter = More    C = Continuous    Esc = Cancel_
```

Figure 5.7

The NDIR /? RES Help menu.

```
NDIR                         Options Help                           4.25

Syntax:  NDIR [path] [/FO : /DO] [/S] : [/VOL : /VER : /V : /SPA : /FI] [/C]

To:                                        Use:
  View files only                            /FO
  View directories only                      /DO
  List information in all sub-directories    /S
  Continuously through the information       /C
  View volume information                    /VOL
  View directory space information           /SPA
  View where a file is found in search drives /FI
  Display version information                /VER or /V

For example, to:                       Type:
  Search for all *.bat files on          NDIR C:\*.BAT /S
  drive C:

  Find where command.com is located      NDIR command.com /FI
  in your search drives

>>> Enter = More    C = Continuous    Esc = Cancel_
```

Figure 5.8

The NDIR /? OPT Help menu.

```
NDIR                         Syntax Help                            4.25

NDIR [path] [ [/<Formats>]    [/[NOT]<Attributes>]
              [/[REV] SORT <Restrictions> : UNsorted]
              [/<Restrictions> [NOT] <Operator> value] ]
              [/<Options>]

Formats:      DA  Dates          D   Detail      L    Long
              R   Rights         MAC Macintosh   COMP Compressed

Attributes:   RO,RW,Sy,H,A,X,T,P,Sh,Ds,I,Ci,Di,Ri,Co,Ic,Dc,Cc,Dm,M

Restrictions: OW  Owner     SI  Size     UP  Update   NAM Name space
              AC  Access    AR  Archive  CR  Create

Operators:    LE  Less than          GR  Greater than
              EQ  Equal to           BEF Before        AFT After

Options:      FO  Files only         VOL Volume        VER Version
              DO  Directories only                     SPA Space
              SUB Sub-directories     C   Continuous    FI  Find
```

Figure 5.9

The NDIR /? SYN Help menu.

RIGHTS Utility Changes

The NetWare 4 RIGHTS utility consolidates the functions of the NetWare 3 RIGHTS, GRANT, REVOKE, REMOVE, and ALLOW commands. The RIGHTS utility includes a number of options to implement the functionality of the different NetWare 3 commands.

Figures 5.10 to 5.15 show a summary of the RIGHTS command usage.

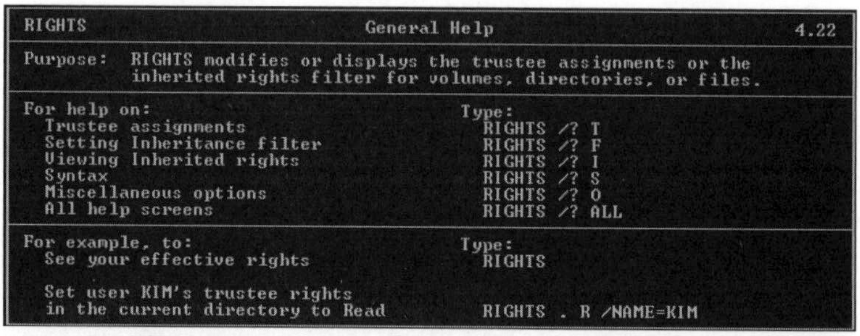

Figure 5.10

The RIGHTS /? Help summary.

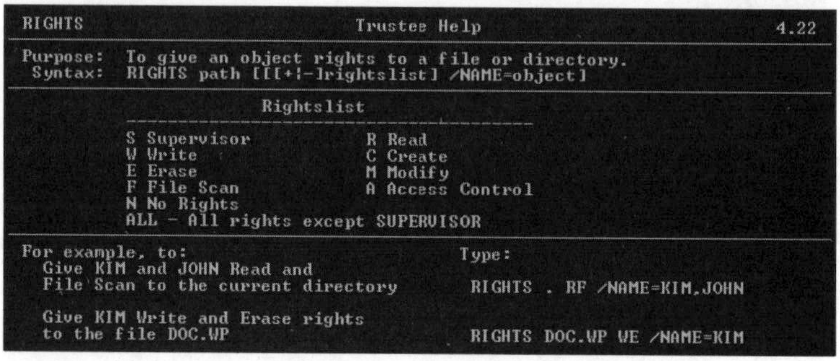

```
RIGHTS                          General Help                        4.22

Purpose:   RIGHTS modifies or displays the trustee assignments or the
           inherited rights filter for volumes, directories, or files.

For help on:                        Type:
  Trustee assignments               RIGHTS /? T
  Setting Inheritance filter        RIGHTS /? F
  Viewing Inherited rights          RIGHTS /? I
  Syntax                            RIGHTS /? S
  Miscellaneous options             RIGHTS /? O
  All help screens                  RIGHTS /? ALL

For example, to:                    Type:
  See your effective rights          RIGHTS

  Set user KIM's trustee rights
  in the current directory to Read   RIGHTS . R /NAME=KIM
```

Figure 5.11

The RIGHTS /? T summary.

```
RIGHTS                          Trustee Help                        4.22

Purpose:   To give an object rights to a file or directory.
Syntax:    RIGHTS path [[[+!-]rightslist] /NAME=object]

                    Rightslist
              ────────────────────────────────
              S Supervisor      R Read
              W Write           C Create
              E Erase           M Modify
              F File Scan       A Access Control
              N No Rights
              ALL - All rights except SUPERVISOR

For example, to:                    Type:
  Give KIM and JOHN Read and
  File Scan to the current directory  RIGHTS . RF /NAME=KIM.JOHN

  Give KIM Write and Erase rights
  to the file DOC.WP                  RIGHTS DOC.WP WE /NAME=KIM
```

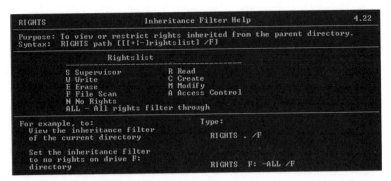

```
RIGHTS                 Inheritance Filter Help                    4.22

Purpose: To view or restrict rights inherited from the parent directory.
Syntax:  RIGHTS path [[[+!-]rightslist] /F]

                        Rightslist

        S Supervisor              R Read
        W Write                   C Create
        E Erase                   M Modify
        F File Scan               A Access Control
        N No Rights
        ALL - All rights filter through

For example, to:                 Type:
  View the inheritance filter
  of the current directory              RIGHTS . /F

  Set the inheritance filter
  to no rights on drive F:
  directory                            RIGHTS  F: -ALL /F
```

Figure 5.12

The RIGHTS /? F summary.

```
RIGHTS                  Derived Rights Help                       4.22

Purpose:  To view or remove file or directory trustees, or to see where an
          object's rights came from.
Syntax:   RIGHTS [path] [[REM] /NAME=object [/I] ! [/T]]

To:                              Use:
  View trustees                    /T
  Remove a trustee                 REM
  View where the rights were       /I
  assigned and inherited

For example, to:                 Type:
  View trustees of SYS:PUBLIC           RIGHTS SYS:PUBLIC /T

  Remove trustee KIM from
  drive F:                              RIGHTS F: REM /NAME=KIM

  Display where user KIM's rights came
  from for the current directory        RIGHTS . /NAME=KIM /I
```

Figure 5.13

The RIGHTS /? I summary.

```
RIGHTS                      Syntax Help                           4.22

Syntax:  RIGHTS [/VER] ! [/? [T!F!I!S!O!A]] !
         [<path [[+!-]rightslist </NAME=object!/F>] ! [/T] ! [/I]> [/S] [/C]]

To:                                            Use:
  Set the owner                                  /NAME=
  View the trustees                              /T
  View/modify the inheritance filter             /F
  View/modify the inherited rights               /I
  Search subdirectories                          /S
  Scroll continuously                            /C
  Display version information                    /VER
  Access on-line help                            /?

                        Rightslist

  S Supervisor     R Read       W Write      C Create
  E Erase          M Modify     F File Scan  A Access Control
  N No Rights      All - All rights except SUPERVISOR
  REM - Remove trustee
```

Figure 5.14

The RIGHTS /? S summary.

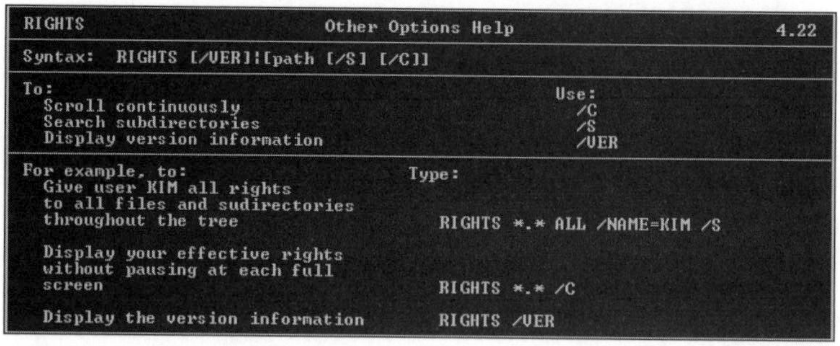

Figure 5.15

The RIGHTS /? O summary.

```
RIGHTS                    Other Options Help                        4.22
Syntax:  RIGHTS [/VER]:[path [/S] [/C]]

To:                                                    Use:
   Scroll continuously                                  /C
   Search subdirectories                                /S
   Display version information                          /VER

For example, to:                        Type:
   Give user KIM all rights
   to all files and sudirectories
   throughout the tree              RIGHTS *.* ALL /NAME=KIM /S

   Display your effective rights
   without pausing at each full
   screen                           RIGHTS *.* /C

   Display the version information  RIGHTS /VER
```

To view the rights for user KSS in the SYS:USERS/KSS directory, use the following command:

```
F:\>RIGHTS SYS:USERS/KSS

   NW4CS\SYS:USERS\KSS
   Your rights for this directory are:  [ RWCE F ]
      Read from a file in a directory.              (R)
      Write to a file in a directory.               (W)
      Create subdirectories and files.              (C)
      Erase directory and files.                    (E)
      Scan for files and directories.               (F)
```

The preceding command is the same as the NetWare 3 RIGHTS command, and will work only if you are logged in as user KSS.

To set the rights for user KSS in the SYS:USERS/KSS directory so that the user has all rights except Supervisor rights, use the following command:

```
F:\> RIGHTS SYS:USERS/KSS   CRWEMFA /NAME=.KSS.CORP.SCS

NW4CS\SYS:USERS
Directories                                     Rights
-----------------------------------------------------------------
KSS                                             [ RWCEMFA]
```

Rights for one directory were changed for .KSS.CORP.SCS.

To assign all rights (SRWCEMFA) to SYS:USERS for user .KSS.CORP.SCS, you can use the command:

```
RIGHTS SYS:USERS/KSS ALL /NAME=.KSS.CORP.SCS
```

The preceding command is equivalent to the NetWare 3 GRANT command.

To view the trustee assignments for a specified directory, such as SYS:USERS/KSS, use the command:

```
F:\> RIGHTS SYS:PUBLIC  /T
NW4CS\SYS:\PUBLIC
```

User trustees:

```
CN=KSS.OU=CORP.O=SCS                        [ R    F ]
- - - - - - - - -
```

Group trustees:

```
CN=Everyone.OU=CORP.O=ESL                   [ R    F ]
- - - - - - - - -
```

Other trustees:

```
OU=CORP.O=ESL                               [ R    F ]
```

The preceding command is equivalent to the NetWare 3 TLIST command. Please note that group Everyone is not a predefined group under NetWare. It appears in this example because the server was upgraded from NetWare 3 to NetWare 4.

To see your rights that have been inherited for SYS:PUBLIC for the user KSS defined in container OU=CORP.O=SCS, use the command:

```
F:\>RIGHTS SYS:PUBLIC   /NAME=.KSS.CORP.SCS   /I

Name= .KSS.CORP.SCS
Path                                             Rights
- - - - - - - - - - - - - - - - - - - - - - - - - - - - - - - - - - - - - - - -
NW4CS\SYS:

Inherited Rights Filter:                      [          ]
Inherits from above:                          [          ]
                                              - - - - - - - - - - - - - - - -
Effective Rights =                            [          ]
- - - - - - - - - - - - - - - - - - - - - - - - - - - - - - - - - - - - - - - -
NW4CS\SYS:\PUBLIC

Inherited Rights Filter:                       [SRWCEMFA]

Inherits from above:                          [          ]
KSS.CORP.SCS                                  [ R  F  ]
                                              - - - - - - - - - - - - - -
Effective Rights =                            [ R  F  ]
- - - - - - - - - - - - - - - - - - - - - - - - - - - - - - - - - - - - - - - -
```

The /I option allows you to see inherited rights. It shows you the sequence of steps as to how rights are computed.

The NetWare 4 RIGHTS utility consolidates the functions of the NetWare 3 RIGHTS, GRANT, REVOKE, REMOVE, and ALLOW commands.

The RIGHTS utility allows you to do the following:

- View/set the rights of a directory or file

- View trustee assignments to a specified directory

- See inherited rights

- View and set the inherited rights filter

The /NAME option is used to specify the User object in the RIGHTS command.

SEND Utility Changes

The NetWare 4 SEND utility consolidates the functions of the NetWare 3 SEND, CASTON, and CASTOFF commands. The SEND utility includes a number of options to implement the functionality of the different NetWare 3 commands.

Figures 5.16 and 5.17 show a summary of the SEND command usage.

The NetWare 3 CASTOFF command has been replaced with the following command:

SEND /A=N

This command is equivalent to the NetWare 3 CASTOFF ALL command. This will prevent messages from all users, including the server console, from being displayed on your screen.

Figure 5.16
The SEND /? Help summary.

```
SEND                          General Help Screen                        4.11
Purpose: Send messages or set how messages are received.
Directory Services syntax:
    SEND "message" [TO] <user, group or server object> |
    SEND /A=[A] | /A=N | /A=C | /A=P       |
    SEND /S
    SEND /P

Bindery syntax:
    SEND "message" [TO] [server/]<user | group | CONSOLE |
         EVERYBODY | station number> /B

For example to:                              Type:
   Send message to .cn=Pat.o=novell             SEND "Hi" .cn=Pat.o=novell
   Send message to Lynn
     on server BOO                              SEND "Hi" boo/Lynn /B
   Castoff all incoming
     messages                                   SEND /A=N
>>> Enter = More    C = Continuous    Esc = Cancel_
```

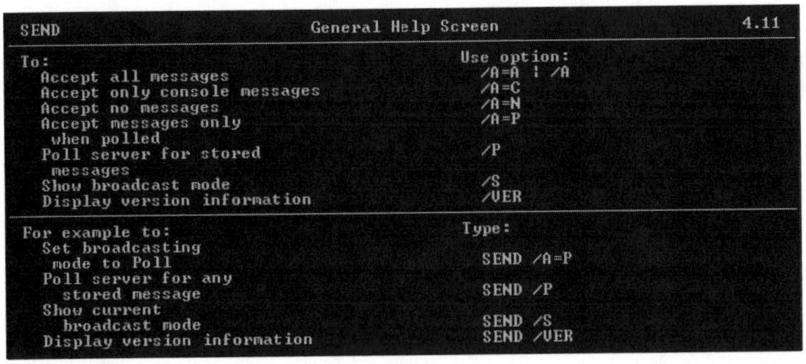

Figure 5.17

The second screen of the SEND /? Help summary.

The SEND /A=N command is equivalent to the NetWare 3 CASTOFF ALL command, and prevents users from receiving network messages on the screen.

To disable receipt of messages from all users, except the server console (that is, allow messages from the server console only), use the command:

SEND /A=C

This command is equivalent to the NetWare 3 CASTOFF command, which allows only messages from the server console to be received.

The SEND /A=C command is equivalent to the NetWare 3 CASTOFF command, and prevents users from receiving network messages. Messages sent from the server console are still received.

To set the send mode to a poll mode you can use the command:

SEND /A=P

With this command set, the user can poll the server at a later time to see if any messages are waiting for him or her. To poll the server for broadcast messages, you can use the command:

SEND /P

Another change from NetWare 2.*x* and 3 is that the SEND messages appear at the top of the screen instead of the bottom.

The NetWare 4 SEND utility consolidates the functions of the NetWare 3 SEND, CASTON, and CASTOFF commands.

NetWare Menu Utilities

The NetWare 4 menu utilities are based on C-Worthy libraries and menu interface. They have the same look and feel as the NetWare 3 menu utilities. One of the improvements that has been made is that context-sensitive help has been added. Whenever you highlight a new option, a *comment line* at the bottom of the screen changes to provide a brief explanation of what the option does. You can always press the F1 key to obtain more detailed help on the option.

Some of the menu utilities provide a bindery emulation mode. You can use the function key F4 to toggle between bindery emulation and NDS mode.

Table 5.1 summarizes the fundamental changes you need to know in preparing for your exams.

Table 5.1
Menu Utility Changes

NetWare 4 Utility	NetWare 3 Utilities That Are Replaced
NETADMIN	SYSCON
NETUSER	SESSION
FILER	FILER, SALVAGE, VOLINFO, DSPACE

> **Study Note**
> You should know the NetWare 3 utilities that a NetWare 4 utility replaces, as shown in table 5.1.

Use the F4 function key in some menu utilities to toggle from NDS mode to bindery emulation mode.

The NETADMIN Utility

The NETADMIN utility was discussed in Chapter 3, "Implementing NetWare Security." It can be used for managing NDS objects. Figure 5.18 shows the NETADMIN main menu that appears when the NETADMIN utility is invoked. NETADMIN's main menu offers the following options:

1. Manage objects

2. Manage according to search pattern

3. Change context

If Manage objects is selected, a list of objects and their class appears as shown in figure 5.19. Highlighting a container object and pressing Enter changes your context to that container, and a list of objects and their classes is displayed. Press Ins to view a list of objects that you can create in a context (see fig. 5.20). Press Del on a highlighted object to delete that object.

Selecting Manage according to search pattern from the NETADMIN main menu enables you to enter a search pattern for an object (see fig. 5.21). The Change context option enables you to change your current context. The current context is shown at the top of the screen. You can press Ins to navigate the NDS tree. Figure 5.22 shows the choice of container objects that can be navigated when Ins is pressed.

Figure 5.18
The NETADMIN main menu.

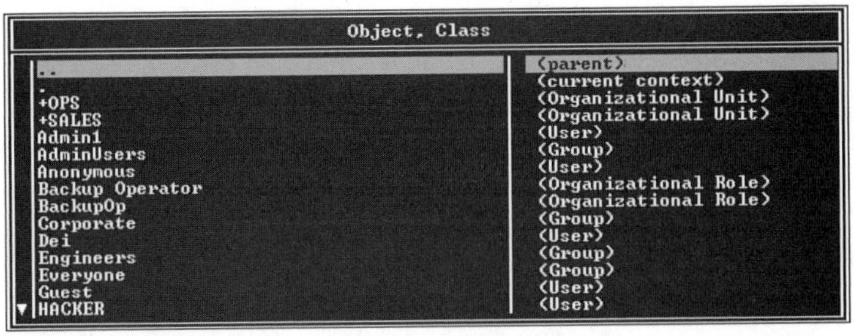

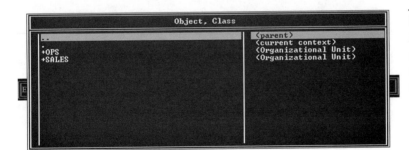

Figure 5.19
The NETADMIN Manage objects selection.

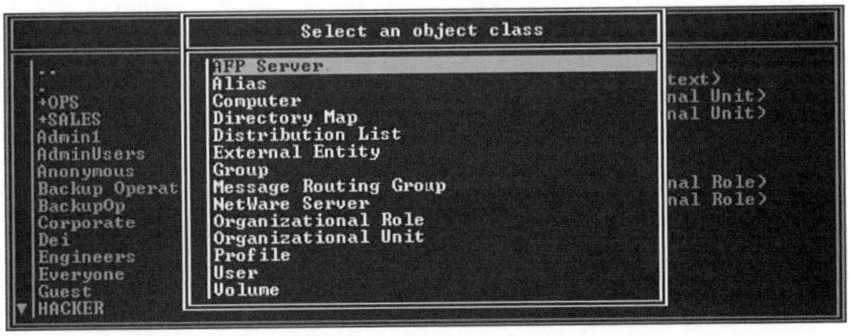

Figure 5.20
The NETADMIN choice of objects to create.

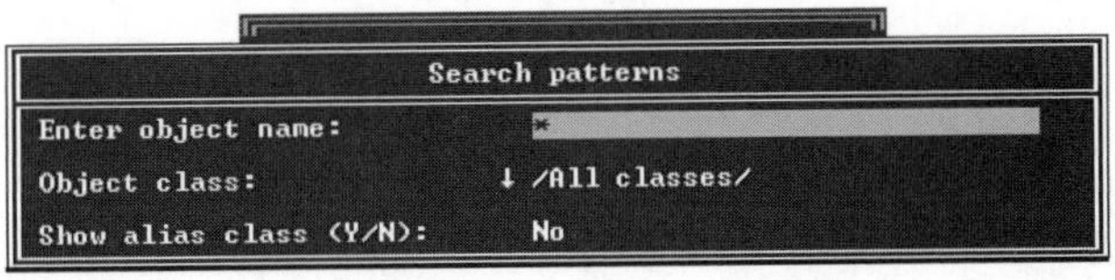

Figure 5.21
Managing NETADMIN according to search patterns.

Figure 5.22
NETADMIN choice of container objects to navigate for changing context.

The NETUSER Utility

NETUSER can be used to perform many of the command-line utility functions using a menu-driven utility. For users who are not accustomed to using the command line, this can be the most practical way of accomplishing network-related tasks on their own.

The following are some of the tasks that can be performed using NETUSER:

■ Selecting network drive mappings

■ Mapping search drives

■ Selecting a printer

■ Attaching to a server

■ Sending messages on a network

Figure 5.23 shows the main menu for NETUSER when the command NETUSER is run at a work-station.

If the Printing option is selected, a list of available ports that can be used to redirect the print job is displayed. Highlighting a printer port and pressing Enter gives you a choice of sending a print job or changing printers. The printers must be mapped (redirected) to a network printer before you can send a print job.

 Practical TIP If you change printers to an NDS Print object, the name of the default Queue object, not the name of the Printer object, appears in the NETUSER (grayed out) status box at the top of the screen.

Choosing the Messages option from the NETUSER main menu enables you to send messages to users and groups (see fig. 5.24). You also can set Receive Messages to ON or OFF. The current Receive Message status is displayed on the top half of the screen, and the option to set this value to is shown on the Messages options screen.

Figure 5.23

The NETUSER main menu.

```
NetUser  4.03
Context: OU=CORP.O=ESL                    Friday  April  21, 1995  12:15pm

          You are CN=Admin..CORP.ESL
          LPT1: Local Printer
          LPT2: Local Printer
          LPT3: Local Printer
          Receive message: ON


                        Available Options
                        Printing
                        Messages
                        Drives
                        Attachments
                        Change Context



Press <Enter> to redirect ports to network printers or print queues and create,
modify or delete print jobs.
Enter=Select    Esc=Escape                                        F1=Help
```

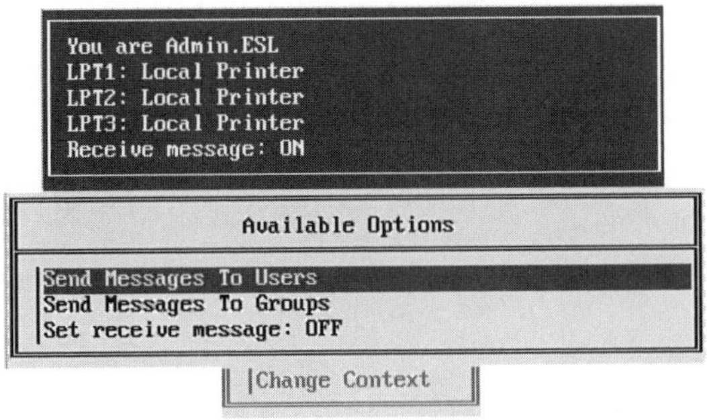

```
You are Admin.ESL
LPT1: Local Printer
LPT2: Local Printer
LPT3: Local Printer
Receive message: ON
```

```
              Available Options
Send Messages To Users
Send Messages To Groups
Set receive message: OFF
```
```
    |Change Context
```

Figure 5.24

The NETUSER Messages options.

Choosing the Drives option from the main menu enables you to perform network drive and search drive mappings. When you try to map a drive, you also are given the option to map root the drive (see fig. 5.25).

Choosing the Attachments option from the main menu enables you to attach to other servers (see fig. 5.26). You can attach to up to 50 servers. Press Ins to see a list of any other NCP servers that you can connect to. The Change Context option enables

you to select a new context. The current context is displayed at the top of the screen.

 The NETUSER utility, which replaces the NetWare 3 SESSION utility, can be used for selecting network drive mappings, mapping search drives, selecting a printer, attaching to a server, and sending messages on a network.

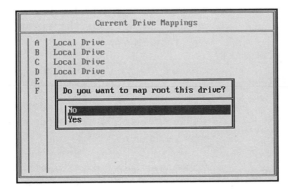

```
              Current Drive Mappings
A | Local Drive
B | Local Drive
C | Local Drive
D | Local Drive
E |
F | Do you want to map root this drive?
  |
  | No
  | Yes
```

Figure 5.25

The NETUSER option to map root a drive.

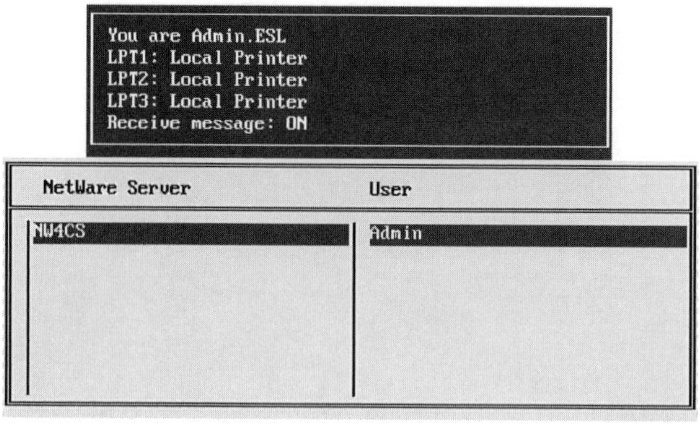

Figure 5.26
*The NETUSER
Attachments options.*

```
You are Admin.ESL
LPT1: Local Printer
LPT2: Local Printer
LPT3: Local Printer
Receive message: ON
```

```
NetWare Server                    User

NW4CS                            Admin
```

The FILER Utility

The FILER utility combines the functions of the NetWare 3 FILER, SALVAGE, DSPACE, and VOLINFO commands.

FILER can be used to perform many file-, directory-, and volume-related tasks.

The following are some of the tasks that can be performed using FILER:

- Viewing file contents and directories

- Viewing/setting directory and file rights

- Viewing/setting directory and file attributes

- Copying, moving, and deleting files

- Deleting the entire subdirectory structure (including non-empty subdirectories)

- Limiting disk space on a volume and directory

- Purging and salvaging files and directories

Figure 5.27 shows the main menu for FILER when the command FILER is run at a workstation.

The Manage files and directories option in the main menu shows you a list of directories and files in the current directory (see fig. 5.28).

Choosing the Manage according to search pattern option from the FILER main menu enables you to set search patterns for the files and directories you want to to view (see fig. 5.29).

Choosing the Select current directory option from the main menu enables you to set the current directory (see fig. 5.30). The current path is displayed at the top of the screen.

Choosing the View volume information option from the main menu enables you to view statistics, features, and date and time information for a volume (see fig. 5.31). The volume information is shown in figures 5.32, 5.33, and 5.34.

Choosing the Salvage deleted files option from the main menu enables you to view and recover deleted files, salvage from deleted directories, and set salvage options (see fig. 5.35). Choosing the Purge deleted files option from the main menu enables you to set a file pattern for all files to be purged (see fig. 5.36).

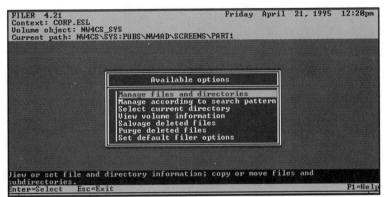

Figure 5.27
The FILER main menu.

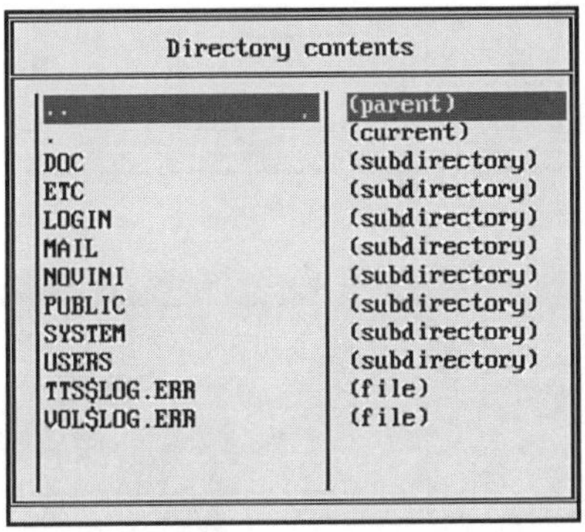

```
Directory contents
..                        (parent)
.                         (current)
DOC                       (subdirectory)
ETC                       (subdirectory)
LOGIN                     (subdirectory)
MAIL                      (subdirectory)
NOVINI                    (subdirectory)
PUBLIC                    (subdirectory)
SYSTEM                    (subdirectory)
USERS                     (subdirectory)
TTS$LOG.ERR               (file)
VOL$LOG.ERR               (file)
```

Figure 5.28
The FILER Directory contents box.

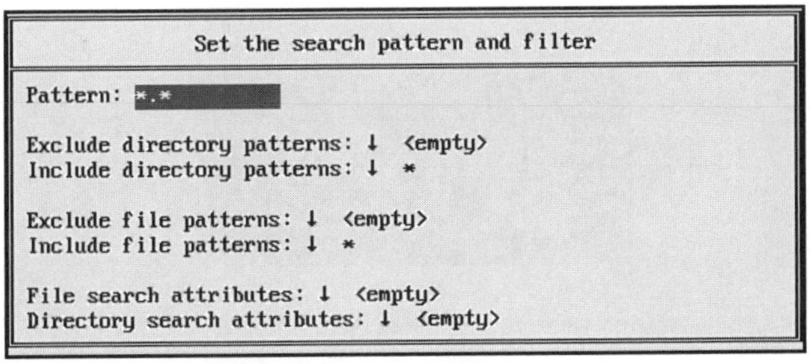

```
Set the search pattern and filter

Pattern: *.*

Exclude directory patterns: ↓  <empty>
Include directory patterns: ↓  *

Exclude file patterns: ↓  <empty>
Include file patterns: ↓  *

File search attributes: ↓  <empty>
Directory search attributes: ↓  <empty>
```

Figure 5.29
Setting search patterns in FILER.

Figure 5.30

Setting the current directory in FILER.

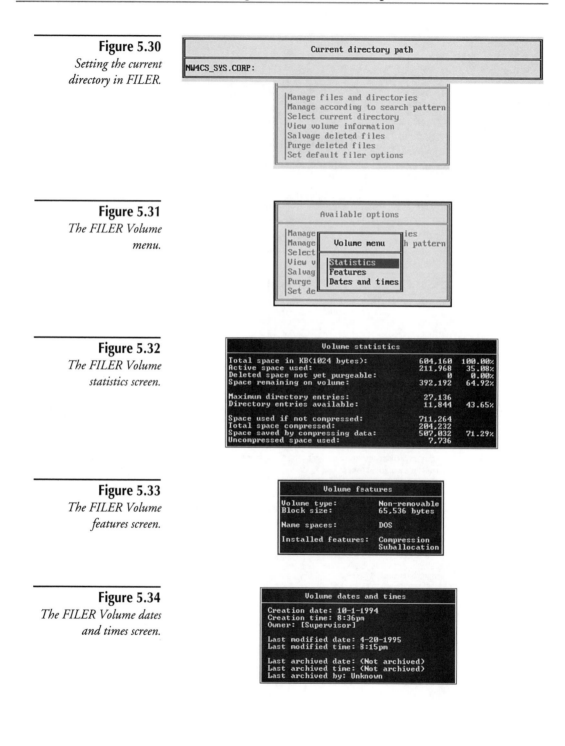

```
                    Current directory path
NW4CS_SYS.CORP:
```

```
Manage files and directories
Manage according to search pattern
Select current directory
View volume information
Salvage deleted files
Purge deleted files
Set default filer options
```

Figure 5.31

The FILER Volume menu.

```
              Available options
Manage                              ies
Manage      Volume menu          h pattern
Select
View v   Statistics
Salvag   Features
Purge    Dates and times
Set de
```

Figure 5.32

The FILER Volume statistics screen.

```
                   Volume statistics
Total space in KB(1024 bytes):        604,160   100.00%
Active space used:                    211,968    35.08%
Deleted space not yet purgeable:            0     0.00%
Space remaining on volume:            392,192    64.92%

Maximum directory entries:             27,136
Directory entries available:           11,844    43.65%

Space used if not compressed:         711,264
Total space compressed:               204,232
Space saved by compressing data:      507,032    71.29%
Uncompressed space used:                7,736
```

Figure 5.33

The FILER Volume features screen.

```
              Volume features
Volume type:          Non-removable
Block size:           65,536 bytes

Name spaces:          DOS

Installed features:   Compression
                      Suballocation
```

Figure 5.34

The FILER Volume dates and times screen.

```
            Volume dates and times
Creation date: 10-1-1994
Creation time: 8:36pm
Owner: [Supervisor]

Last modified date: 4-20-1995
Last modified time: 8:15pm

Last archived date: <Not archived>
Last archived time: <Not archived>
Last archived by: Unknown
```

The "Set default filer options" option in the main menu gives you the ability to confirm deletions, confirm copy operations, and confirm overwrites (see fig. 5.37). It also allows you to specify if file attributes should be preserved, and if you should be notified if you are going to lose file attribute information when copying from one name space to another. NetWare 4 allows the implementation of sparse files. *Sparse files* are common in database applications when a file may currently contain only a few of the total records that the file can contain. Because the valuable data is a small portion of the overall file size, a sparse representation of a file that occupies much less space can be designed. You can specify if the files should be copied in their sparse format or not. You can also specify if the compressed files should be copied in the compressed state or not.

 The NetWare 4 FILER utility combines the functions of the NetWare 3 FILER, SALVAGE, DSPACE, and VOLINFO commands.

You can use FILER to perform the following functions:

■ View file contents and directories

■ View/set directory and file rights

■ View/set directory and file attributes

■ Copy, move, and delete files

■ Delete entire subdirectory structures (including non-empty subdirectories)

■ Limit disk space on a volume and directory

■ Purge and salvage files and directories

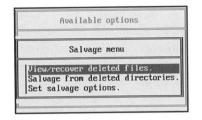

Figure 5.35
The FILER Salvage menu.

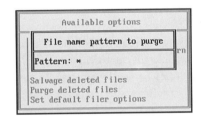

Figure 5.36
Deleting a file name pattern in FILER.

Figure 5.37
The FILER settings screen.

The UIMPORT Utility

When you create User objects in the NDS tree, you must use a standard convention to create User object names. One way of doing this is through creating User objects en masse by using the UIMPORT (User Import) utility. UIMPORT creates User objects based on the contents of two files: a data file and a control file. Both of these are text (ASCII) files. The UIMPORT data file contains the values of properties of User objects such as user name, last name, telephone number, and so on, and the control file contains a description of the fields in the data file.

Because the user property values of a number of users can be placed in a single data file, a uniform naming convention can be more easily enforced. The data in the text file is in the Comma Separated Value (CSV) format. The CSV format is a popular way of exporting/importing database records between two different database systems. It consists of values that are separated by commas. An example of a CSV format follows:

Karanjit, Siyan, Engineer, 709-1234, KARANJIT@SCS, M/S 505, SCS Engineering, Eng, Dev

The data items are separated by the comma delimiter. Values that have a space character are enclosed in quotes. The different data items can be considered as fields of a record.

Using a text editor, you can maintain information on users in the form of a data file that has text records in CSV format. It may, however, be more convenient to maintain the database of users using a commercial database such as dBASE, XQL/SQL/Btrieve, MS Access, Paradox, or Ingres. You can then export the information in this database in the CSV format to the UIMPORT data file. This can

Figure 5.38
Using UIMPORT.

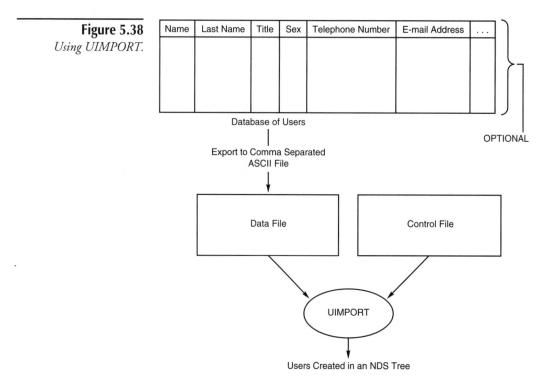

then be used with the UIMPORT command, whose general syntax follows:

```
UIMPORT    controlfile    datafile
```

The *controlfile* contains import control information and a description of the order of the fields in the *datafile*. Figure 5.38 illustrates the process of using UIMPORT.

The following is an example of a data file and the corresponding control file in the following command:

```
UIMPORT USERS.CTL USERS.DAT
```

UIMPORT data file USERS.DAT:

Karanjit, Siyan, Engineer, 709-1234, KARANJIT@SCS, "M/S 505", "SCS Engineering"

Michael, Singh, Accountant, 709-7884, Michael@SCS, "M/S 506", "SCS Accounting"

Amar, Sigal, Manager, "", Amar@SCS, "M/S 508", "SCS Corp"

"Rama", "Sinha", "Manager", "709-2344", "Rama@SCS", "M/S 608", "SCS Corp"

Notice that each record contains the user's object name, last name, telephone number, e-mail address, postal address, department, and groups. Property values that are missing are represented as "". This is seen in the third record, which does not have the telephone number property value set. Values that have a space as part of their value are placed in quotes (M/S 505, SCS Accounting), but you also can place quotes around all values. You can see this in the fourth record, in which all values, regardless of whether they have a space or not, have quotes around them.

The following is an example of the content of the UIMPORT control file USERS.CTL:

IMPORT CONTROL

```
User Template = Y
Create Home Directory = Y
Home Directory Path = "USERS"
Home Directory Volume =
➥".CN=NW4CS_SYS.OU=CORP.O=ESL"
```

FIELDS

```
Name
Last Name
Title
Telephone Number
Email Address
Postal Address
Department
```

The statements in the Import Control section contain information such as whether to use the settings in the USER_TEMPLATE User object (for values of User object properties that are not specified in the data file), whether to create a home directory, the home directory path to use, the volume on which the home directory should be placed, and so on.

 Study Note To use UIMPORT, you must first export the user information into a delimited ASCII file.

The sections IMPORT CONTROL and FIELDS begin on the first column of the control file. The parameters under each section must be indented by one or more spaces or a tab.

Figure 5.39 shows the results of running the UIMPORT command with the data and control files listed previously. The first command that is shown on the screen is the CX command to change to the context where the User objects are created.

Figure 5.39
Running UIMPORT.

```
F:\USERS\KSS>CX .O=SCS
O=SCS

F:\USERS\KSS>UIMPORT USERS.CTL USERS.DAT
Import context: O=SCS
Creating user Karanjit, Copying Template User, Generating key pair, Adding to gr
oup everyone,+ Done.
Creating user Michael, Copying Template User, Generating key pair, Adding to gro
up everyone,+ Done.
Creating user Amar, Copying Template User, Generating key pair, Adding to group
everyone,- Done.
Creating user Rama, Copying Template User, Generating key pair, Adding to group
everyone,! Done.

F:\USERS\KSS>
```

You can use the IMPORT command NAME CONTEXT to specify the context in which to create the User objects. The following example uses the same fields as the previous example using the USERS.CTL control file. You can change the control file as indicated to avoid.

IMPORT CONTROL

```
User Template = Y
Create Home Directory = Y
Home Directory Path = "USERS"
Home Directory Volume =
➡".CN=NW4CS_SYS.OU=CORP.O=ESL"
Name Context = O=SCS
```

FIELDS

```
Name
Last Name
Title
Telephone Number
Email Address
Postal Address
Department
```

The user database can be more general than the properties needed for the NDS User object. It may have fields such as social security number, employee identification number, sex of the user, and

so on. Ideally, the UIMPORT data file should be created so that it does not contain fields that are needed in the User object. Even if the user data file contains unwanted fields, however, you can use the SKIP keyword in the control file to cause UIMPORT to skip the corresponding data field in the data file. Consider the following data file that has two additional fields for employee identification and sex of the user:

Karanjit, Siyan, Engineer, E1830, M, 709-1234, KARANJIT@SCS, "M/S 505", "SCS Engineering"

Michael, Singh, Accountant, E8833, M, 709-7884, Michael@SCS, "M/S 506", "SCS Accounting"

Amar, Sigal, Manager, "", E8323, M, Amar@SCS, "M/S 508", "SCS Corp"

"Rama", "Sinha", "Manager", E3433, M, "709-2344", "Rama@SCS", "M/S 608", "SCS Corp"

To ignore these additional fields, you can use SKIP in the control file as shown in the following example:

IMPORT CONTROL

```
User Template = Y
Create Home Directory = Y
Home Directory Path = "USERS"
Home Directory Volume =
➥".CN=NW4CS_SYS.OU=CORP.O=ESL"
Name Context = O=SCS
```

FIELDS

```
Name
Last Name
Title
Skip
Skip
Telephone Number
Email Address
Postal Address
Department
```

If the data fields have a comma or quotation marks as part of the data value, you can inform UIMPORT to use an alternate character as a separator or as a quotation character. To use the percent character as a separator and the circumflex (^) character rather than quotes, the data file and control files can look similar to the following:

Karanjit% Siyan% Engineer% 709-1234% KARANJIT@SCS% ^M/S 505^% ^SCS Engineer^

Michael% Sigal% Accountant% 709-7884% Michael@SCS% ^M/S 506^% ^SCS Accounting^

Amar% Anand% Manager% ^^% Amar@SCS% "M/S 508^% ^Special Hush Projects^

^Rama^% ^Kumar^% ^Manager^% ^709-2344^% ^Rama@SCS^% ^M/S, 608^% ^Accounting ^

The following is an example of a UIMPORT control file USERS.DAT showing alternate separator and quote characters:

IMPORT CONTROL

```
User Template = Y
Create Home Directory = Y
Home Directory Path = "USERS"
Home Directory Volume =
➥".CN=NW4CS_SYS.OU=CORP.O=ESL"
separator=%
quote=^
```

FIELDS

```
Name
Last Name
Title
Telephone Number
Email Address
Postal Address
Department
```

Each user record in the UIMPORT data file usually takes up a single line. A single UIMPORT data file line can be 8 KB characters. If the record size exceeds this value, you can continue to the next line. To continue a user record on a new line, the previous line must end in the separator character (usually ",").

 You can use UIMPORT to create new user objects or update existing ones.

UIMPORT can be used to perform the following functions:

■ Load new User objects in the NDS tree

■ Update User object properties

■ Delete User objects

■ Delete property values of User objects

User objects are by default updated in the current context, unless the Name Context statement is specified in the UIMPORT control file. The following describes the syntax of the Name Context statement:

```
Name Context = context
```

context should be replaced by the complete name of the container (but without a leading period) in which the user objects will be placed.

NetWare Graphical User Interface Utilities

NetWare GUI utilities are designed to run with Microsoft Windows and OS/2's Presentation Manager. They can be used to provide a graphical way for managing network resources. Because the NDS is organized as a directory information tree, a graphical representation can capture the geometry

of the tree more easily than command-line or menu-driven utilities. The most important graphical tool is NetWare Administrator, which is described in Chapters 2 and 4. The NetWare Administrator can be used for managing NetWare resources that are represented as NDS objects in a directory information tree. The NetWare Administrator tool also can be used to manage files and directories in a volume (see fig. 5.40).

The NetWare User Tool, implemented by the NWUSER.EXE program, performs the following functions, many of which are similar to those provided by the menu utility NETUSER:

- **NetWare Drive Connections.** This allows you to view, modify, and create network and search drives.

- **NetWare Send Messages.** This can be used to send messages on the network, including individual messages as well as broadcast messages.

Figure 5.40

Accessing the NetWare file system with the NetWare Administrator.

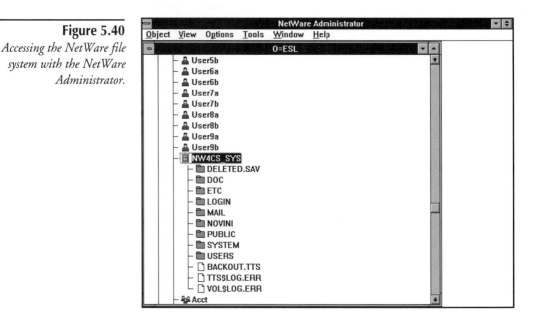

- **NetWare Server Connections.** This can be used to attach to other NetWare servers.

- **NetWare Printer Connections.** This can be used to redirect printer requests to local ports to network printers.

- **NetWare Settings.** This contains many of the network configuration options for the NetWare User Tool. It is also used to enable the hot key (function key F6) for invoking the NetWare User Tool.

 The NetWare User Tool can be used for sending messages, establishing NetWare settings, and making drive connections, server connections, and printer connections.

NetWare Language Support for Commands and Utilities

NetWare 4 includes support for international languages such as English, French, German, Spanish, and Italian. This means that help messages, utility menus, and help screens can be presented in the language of choice. The language help files for each of the utilities are placed in the directory SYS:PUBLIC\NLS. The default language for NetWare 4 is English. For MS Windows support, a directory called \WINDOWS\NLS is created (if \WINDOWS is the installation directory for MS Windows). This directory contains the language support files.

 The language help files for the NetWare utilities are placed in SYS:PUBLIC\NLS.

If a language other than English is to be specified, you must set the environment variable NWLANGUAGE. This is done by using the following command at the command prompt or by placing the command in a batch file such as the AUTOEXEC.BAT file:

```
SET NWLANGUAGE=language1, language2, ...
```

where *language1* is replaced by the first language, and *language2* is replaced by the second language and will be used if support for the first language is not found.

 The NWLANGUAGE environment variable is set to specify languages other than English.

The User object has a Language property. A user's preference for a language also can be supplied by setting the value of this property.

NetWare 4 contains provisions for using alternate character sets for display purposes. These alternate character sets are supplied through *code page* definitions. Code page tables are represented using the *unicode* translation table. A unicode representation of a character is a 16-bit representation (defined by the Unicode Consortium) and allows for the use of 65,536 symbols, which can accommodate the most complex natural language that is in use today.

 A user's preference for a language can be specified by setting the language property for the user.

Care must be taken in creating NetWare file names and directories using alternate code page tables. You might be unable to access these files from workstations that use a different code page table. If different code page tables are in use, you must use a character set that is common to all the code page tables.

Novell Menu Changes

Novell menus allow you to create a menu-driven user interface, where you have the choice of selecting the menu titles and the options in a specific menu. You can associate a number of commands with each option or specify that another submenu be invoked when an option is selected.

In NetWare 3.11 this was provided by Novell menus. The NetWare 3.11 Novell menus were adequate in simple situations, but many network administrators preferred the use of more robust third-party tools. An example of such a tool is the Saber menus. In NetWare 4, Novell has licensed the Saber menu technology and used it to build the Novell menus that are used with NetWare 4. Currently, the NetWare 4 menus do not have the full functionality of the commercial Saber menu system package, but they are a vast improvement over the NetWare 3 Novell menus. The NetWare 3.12 (and higher versions) Novell menus also use the NMENU utility, and are the same as the NetWare 4 Novell menus. NMENU is a batch program that invokes other utilities such as MENUEXE.EXE and MENURSET.EXE.

One of the improvements to the NetWare 4 menu utility is the requirement for less memory, which enables programs that need more memory to be run from the NMENU utility.

A scripting language is used to create the source file for the NMENU utility. The source (SRC extension) file is then compiled to produce a data file (DAT extension). The data file is then used with an NMENU.BAT utility that interprets and executes the DAT file. The steps to perform these operations are depicted in figure 5.41.

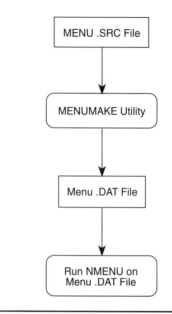

Figure 5.41
The Novell menu compilation steps.

Older menu script files (MNU extension) that were used with the scripting language of the NetWare 3.11 Novell Menu utility can be converted to the NetWare 4 menu script language by using a conversion tool called MENUCNVT.EXE. The conversion process is shown in figure 5.42.

 Older menu scripts can be converted to NetWare menu scripts by using MENUCNVT.EXE.

If the older Novell menu script file is named MAIN.MNU, then to convert, compile, and run the menu using the NetWare 4 menu system, you can perform the following steps:

1. Execute MENUCNVT MAIN.MNU (Produces a MAIN.SRC file).

2. Examine the MAIN.SRC file and edit it as necessary.

3. Execute MENUMAKE MAIN.SRC (Produces a MAIN.DAT file).

4. Execute MENU MAIN.DAT.

 The MENUMAKE utility is used to compile the menu script (SRC) file to the menu object file (DAT).

 The utility used to run a NetWare 4 menu is NMENU.

Menu Parts

A NetWare menu can consist of four components (see fig. 5.43). The components are specified in the menu source file and are listed as follows:

- A main menu that has a title and at least one option

- Commands to be executed when an option is selected

- Submenus that are displayed when an option is selected

- Prompts for user input

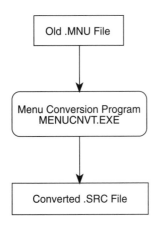

Figure 5.42
The Novell menu conversion process.

Figure 5.43
The parts of a menu.

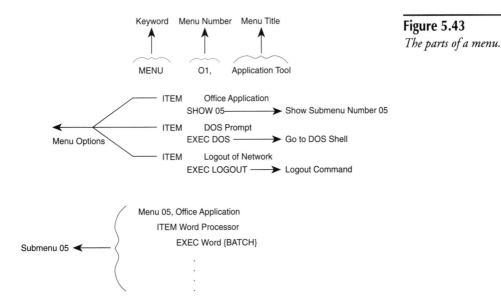

The first two parts listed are necessary. The remaining parts, such as the submenus and prompted user input, are optional.

Menu Commands

The principal menu commands are MENU, ITEM, and EXEC. The MENU and ITEM commands are used for organizing the structure and appearance of the menu. The EXEC command is used for controlling the execution of commands when a particular item is selected. In general, menu commands can be divided into two categories:

■ Organizational commands

■ Control commands

These two categories of commands are discussed in greater detail in the following sections.

 Menu commands can be divided into the categories of organizational commands and control commands.

Organizational Commands

Organizational commands are responsible for the overall organization and contents of the menu. They also determine the appearance of the menu on-screen. Currently, only two commands are defined for this category:

■ MENU

■ ITEM

Every menu and submenu is defined by a MENU command. The parameters for the MENU command are a menu number and the title of the menu. Its general syntax follows:

```
MENU menuNumber,menuTitle
```

The *menuNumber* is unique per menu and it can be any number between 1 and 255. There is no special ordering relationship between the menu numbers and the menus that are displayed. The only requirement is that they be unique. There should not be any spaces between the *menuNumber*, the comma, and the *menuTitle*. The *menuTitle* is a string of characters that should not exceed 40 characters, and is displayed at the top of the menu. It is used to identify the title of the menu.

 Novell menus have two organizational commands: MENU and ITEM.

If a menu is given a number of 5 and a title of "Available Options," for example, its menu command should appear as follows:

```
MENU 5,Available Options
```

The preceding command would define the start of the menu Available Options that is identified by the menu number 5.

The ITEM organizational command is used to define the option that is displayed for a menu. The items are listed in the order in which you want them to appear in the menu. An option consists of a text string parameter to the ITEM command. The general syntax of the ITEM command is as follows:

```
ITEM  itemText { itemOption itemOption ... }
```

or

```
ITEM  ^tagchar itemText { itemOption
➥ itemOption ... }
```

In the first format for the ITEM command, every *itemText* is preceded by a letter that is automatically assigned by the Menu utility. The letters are from A to Z, with the first ITEM command being assigned A, the next B, and so on. These letters or *item tags* serve as a shortcut to selecting the option. Pressing the letter key corresponding to an option causes that menu item to be selected. The item tags do not determine the order in which the menu is displayed. The display order is determined by the order in which the items are listed. The *itemText* is the text string that you want displayed for the menu option. The *itemOptions* are placed within { } braces, and consist of zero or more item options that further qualify the menu option. The *itemOptions* are discussed in greater detail in the following section. An example of the syntax for the first format follows:

```
ITEM    NetAdmin Tool { }
```

The *itemText* is "NetAdmin Tool." No *itemOptions* are specified, and therefore the braces are empty, in which case they can be left out. For example:

```
ITEM Display Context EXEC CX
```

If this were the first ITEM listed under a MENU command, it would have a tag character of A; if this were the second item, its tag character would be B, and so on.

The second format for the command is similar to the first format. The difference is that ^*tagchar* can precede *itemText*. The caret (^) character followed by a single character, the *tagchar*, allows this character to override the default letter assignment for that item. If you wanted to use digits 1 to 6 to designate the menu options, for example, you would use the following statements:

```
ITEM  ^1First Option { }
ITEM  ^2Second Option { }
ITEM  ^3Third Option { }
ITEM  ^4Fourth Option { }
ITEM  ^5Fifth Option { }
ITEM  ^6Sixth Option { }
```

The item options are displayed in the order in which they are listed. The Menu utility makes no attempt to sort them based on any tag characters you specify.

 You should be familiar with the syntax of the MENU and ITEM commands as discussed in this section.

ITEM Options

The *itemOptions* that are placed in the brackets in the ITEM command further qualify how the commands associated with the ITEM are executed. The listing that follows shows the ITEM command and the commands that are executed when an item is selected:

```
ITEM Menu Option Text { }
command 1
command 2
    :
command N
```

The commands that are executed when the ITEM is selected are listed immediately following the ITEM. These commands are preceded by one of the following key words: EXEC, LOAD, SHOW, GETO, GETR, and GETP, and are discussed in greater detail in the next section.

 The commands for an ITEM follow immediately after the ITEM statement. The command can be EXEC, LOAD, SHOW, GETO, GETR, or GETP.

The following commands can be substituted for *itemOption* in brackets:

■ BATCH

■ CHDIR

■ SHOW

■ PAUSE

Valid item options in the ITEM command are BATCH, CHDIR, SHOW, and PAUSE.

The BATCH item option is used to free up additional memory when running an application. The Novell NetWare 4 Menu utility by itself takes up 32 KB of RAM. For applications that take up a large amount of memory, it is desirable to use as much RAM as possible. By using the BATCH option, the commands associated with the menu are written in a temporary batch file. The Menu utility is removed from memory, and the batch file is run. The last command in the batch file reinvokes the Menu utility. To run the NETADMIN utility using a batch file, you would use the following command:

```
ITEM NetAdmin Utility {BATCH}
EXEC NETADMIN
```

 The BATCH item option is used to free up memory taken by the Novell Menu utility when running an application.

 The Novell NetWare 4 menu utility uses about 32 KB of RAM.

The CHDIR item option is used to restore the default directory to the one that existed prior to executing the command. Some programs give you the option of changing the default directory when they are run. After exiting these programs, you may be placed in a default directory that is different from the one that was in use prior to executing the program. It is often desirable to have the same default directory when programs are excepted from the menu utility. To keep the same default directory throughout the execution of a program called TELNET, you could use the following statement:

```
ITEM Telnet Application{CHDIR}
EXEC TELNET
```

 The CHDIR item option is used to restore the default directory to the one that existed prior to executing the command.

The different item options can be combined. To execute FILER as a batch file and to retain the same default directory, for example, you could use the following statements:

```
ITEM Filer Utility {BATCH CHDIR}
EXEC FILER
```

 To free up memory taken up by the Menu utility and restore the default directory to the one that existed prior to executing an application, you can combine the BATCH and CHDIR item options.

The order in which the item options are placed inside the brackets is not significant. Therefore, the above statements are equivalent to these :

```
ITEM Filer Utility {CHDIR BATCH}
EXEC FILER
```

The SHOW item option is used to display in the upper-left hand corner of the screen the name of the DOS command executed from the Menu utility as it executes. This is particularly useful if the DOS command that is executing is passed a parameter, which is also displayed as the command executes. The following is an example of this usage:

```
ITEM Directory Contents Listing {SHOW}
EXEC DIR
```

 The SHOW item option is used to display on the upper-left corner of the screen the name of the DOS command executed from the Menu utility as it executes.

The PAUSE option causes the message Press any key to continue to appear after the execution of a command(s). This gives the user an opportunity to read the screen before proceeding to the next step. The Menu utility will not proceed to the next step unless the user presses a key. The following is an example of using the PAUSE option:

```
ITEM Search for files that have "SCS
➥(C)opyright"  {PAUSE}
EXEC GREP  "SCS (C)opyright"  *.*
```

 The PAUSE option causes the message Press any key to continue to appear after a command is executed.

Table 5.2 summarizes the different ITEM options that were discussed previously.

 Be familiar with the syntax and meaning of the item options summarized in table 5.2.

Menu Control Commands

The MENU and ITEM commands that were discussed in the previous section are used to determine the contents of a menu or submenu and the manner in which options should be displayed or run. The actual commands that are processed occur after the ITEM command. These commands are called *control commands*, and they are used to execute applications from within the menu utility (NMENU), load menu definitions kept in separate files, show submenus, and obtain user input. There are six control commands that begin with key words listed as follows:

■ EXEC

■ LOAD

■ SHOW

■ GETO

■ GETR

■ GETP

Table 5.2
ITEM Options

Item Option	Description	Example
BATCH	Frees up RAM occupied by the Menu utility (32 KB) when a program runs.	ITEM Application X {BATCH}
CHDIR	Restores the default directory to that which existed prior to running the commands associated with the menu item.	ITEM Application X {CHDIR}
SHOW	Shows DOS commands on the upper-left corner of the screen as they execute.	ITEM Application X {SHOW}
PAUSE	Pauses the display, and waits for the user to press a key, at the end of executing a command.	ITEM Application X {PAUSE}

The first three of the control commands listed here (EXEC, LOAD, SHOW) deal with executing programs, and loading and displaying submenus. The last three of these commands (GETO, GETR, GETP) solicit input from the user, which can then be used as parameters for commands and programs that are executed.

 The EXEC (or EXECUTE) menu command is used to run an application.

The EXEC Control Command

The EXEC (or EXECUTE) command is used to run an application. The command that is run can be an EXE, COM, or BAT, an internal DOS command, or any of the following:

- DOS
- EXIT
- LOGOUT

An example of using the EXEC command for a DOS internal command is shown as follows:

```
ITEM  ^DShow Directory listing {SHOW}
EXEC DIR
```

An example of using the EXEC command for a NetWare EXE program file is shown as follows:

```
ITEM  ^UNetwork User {BATCH}
EXEC NETUSER
```

The EXEC DOS command runs a second copy of the command shell. For DOS, this is the COMMAND.COM command processor. When a second copy of the command shell runs, you are presented with a command prompt and can type in any DOS or application command. The NMENU utility and the previous copy of the command shell

are still loaded, so you are limited by the remaining memory available for your DOS application. An example of the use of the EXEC DOS command is shown as follows:

```
ITEM  Exit to DOS { }
EXEC DOS
```

To return to the Novell Menu utility, you must type the EXIT command at the command prompt. This terminates the second shell and returns you to the Menu utility.

 The EXEC DOS command runs a second copy of the command shell, and enables users to run DOS commands from the second command interpreter.

For secure environments, you might want to control the applications a user can run on the network. In this case, you might want to restrict the user's access to the command prompt, and not use the EXEC DOS command.

 To make the Novell menus secure, you should not use the EXEC DOS command in an item option.

If you want to give users the option of exiting the menu program completely and going to the DOS prompt, you can use the EXEC EXIT command. This command terminates the Menu utility program, which causes the system to remove the program from memory. Control is returned to the command shell and the command prompt. If, for security reasons, you want to control a user's access to the command, you should not use the EXEC EXIT command. An example of the use of the EXEC EXIT command is shown below:

```
ITEM  Exit NMENU { }
EXEC EXIT
```

In many environments it is desirable to control a user's access to the command prompt. None of the options, EXEC DOS or EXEC EXIT, are suitable for this purpose because they give a user access to the command prompt. Yet it is necessary for a user to terminate the use of the network and the Novell menus. To accomplish this, a special EXEC LOGOUT command has been defined. The EXEC LOGOUT option logs the user out of the network and simultaneously terminates the Novell Menu utility.

The following is an example of the use of the EXEC LOGOUT command:

```
ITEM  Exit Novell Menus and logout { }
EXEC LOGOUT
```

 To make a menu secure, you can exit the Novell menus using the EXEC LOGOUT control command.

Table 5.3 summarizes the different EXEC commands:

The SHOW Control Command

A menu is defined using the MENU command in which you must define the menu number and the menu title. There can be many such menu commands in a single file. The first menu command in a compiled file that is passed as a parameter to the NMENU command becomes the first menu that is displayed. This is the main menu. All other menus in the file are displayed by using the SHOW command. The syntax of the SHOW command is

```
SHOW menuNumber
```

where *menuNumber* is replaced with a number that represents the menu number defined in the MENU statement for the submenu that should be displayed. There can be up to 255 submenus or menu commands (menu definitions) in a single menu file.

The submenu that is displayed is *cascaded* in relationship to the previous menu. Its position on the screen is determined automatically by the Novell Menu utility. Currently there is no way of changing the position at which the menu is displayed.

Table 5.3
EXEC Command Summary

EXEC Type	Description
EXEC *command*	Replaces *command* with a DOS internal/external command, an EXE or COM program file, or a DOS batch file.
EXEC DOS	Starts a secondary shell and gives the user access to the command prompt via the secondary shell.
EXEC EXIT	Terminates the Novell Menu (NMENU) utility, and returns control to the command shell and the command prompt.
EXEC LOGOUT	Terminates the Novell Menu (NMENU) utility, and logs the user out of the network. Provides a secure option to exit the Novell Menus.

The SHOW control command is used to display a menu by its menu number.

 The Menu GET commands obtain input from the user through the Novell menus.

The LOAD Control Command

A menu is defined using the MENU command, in which you must define the menu number and the menu title. There is a limit of up to 255 submenus or menu commands (menu definitions) in a single menu file. For large menu systems, it is necessary to place the menu definitions in separate files. You might decide to use separate files for menu systems that are not large to help you organize and manage the menu definitions. To load a menu that is in a separate file, you must use the LOAD command.

The syntax of the LOAD command is

```
LOAD menuName
```

where *menuName* is replaced by the file name of the compiled menu file. When the LOAD command is executed, the original menu system is left running, but a second menu is added to the screen.

 The LOAD command is used to load menus compiled in a separate file.

The GETx Commands

There are three forms of the GETx commands: GETO, GETR, and GETP. Like the other control commands, GETx commands are listed after an ITEM command and are executed when the menu item is selected. The following is an example of some of the GETx commands:

```
ITEM   ^LDirectory Listing
GETO   Enter directory name: {} 45,, {}
EXEC DIR %
```

The GETO Command

The GETO command is used for obtaining an optional input from the user. The O in GETO is for the word "optional." When the GETO command is executed, as shown in the previous example, a dialog box is displayed. The message in the dialog box, the width of the user input, the initial value of the user input, and so on are passed as parameters to the GETO command.

 The GETO command is used for obtaining optional input from the user.

When using the GETO, GETR, and GETP commands, pressing Enter signals that you have completed the information, and pressing F10 signals that you want to continue the menu execution.

The user has a choice of making or not making an entry (optional GET). In either case, when the user presses F10, execution continues. If the user makes an entry, the entered value is passed as a parameter to the command that follows. In the preceding example, the command that follows is the EXEC DIR command. In this example, if a user had made the entry F:\SYSTEM, the following EXEC command would be executed:

```
EXEC DIR F:\SYSTEM
```

This command would display the contents of the directory F:\SYSTEM. If the user had not made any entry, but just typed F10, the following EXEC command would be executed:

```
EXEC DIR
```

This command would display the contents of the current directory.

The % character can be used as a placeholder for a single instance of user input. The above example of the use of the GETO command can be alternatively expressed using the % placeholder:

```
ITEM ^LDirectory Listing
GETO Enter directory name: {} 45,, {}
EXEC DIR %
```

The GETR Command

The GETR command works in a manner similar to the GETO command. The big difference is that the GETR command requires users to enter information. Just pressing F10 only (or Enter if GETR is in its own dialog box) will not cause the GETR command to continue execution. The menu display will pause, and will not continue until a valid input has been entered.

 The GETR command requires input from the user.

An example of the use of GETR is shown as follows:

```
ITEM User Command
GETR Enter a user command: {}80,,{}
EXEC %
```

This command passes the user typed string as a command to be executed by the EXEC command.

The GETP Command

The GETP command works in a manner similar to the other GETx commands described in this chapter. A special feature of GETP is that it assigns a variable to the user input. This variable can then be used in other commands. The following is an example of the use of the GETP command:

```
ITEM  Network Copy {PAUSE SHOW}
GETP  Source: {} 60,, {}
GETP  Destination: {} 60,,{}
EXEC  NCOPY  %1 %2
```

The first GETP parameter assigns the user input to the variable %1, and the second GETP command assigns its user input to %2. These parameters are used in the EXEC NCOPY command as the source and destination, respectively.

 The GETP command can be used to assign parameters to the user input.

Table 5.4 summarizes the different GETx commands.

Table 5.4
GETx Commands

GETx Command	Description
GETO	Obtains optional user input from the user
GETR	Obtains required user input from the user
GETP	Obtains user input that is assigned to variables %1, %2, and so on

 Study table 5.4 and understand the different types of GETx commands.

GETx Parameter Options

In the examples of the use of the GETx commands in the previous section, you noticed the use of brackets and commas as part of the syntax of the GET*x* command. This syntax is part of a general syntax that gives you options to control the width of the user input and the initial value that is displayed for the user. You also can modify the user input by prepending or appending special text string values to the user input. The syntax of these parameters is shown as follows:

```
GETx  promptString, {prependString}
➤ length,prefillString,{appendString}
```

or

```
GETx  promptString, {prependString}
➤ length,prefillString,SECURE {appendString}
```

The *x* in GET*x* is replaced by O, R, or P, according to the GET command being used. The *promptString* is the text that is displayed for the GET command, and is meant as an aid to the user to enter the appropriate value. The *prependString* placed inside the brackets is a string attached to the beginning of the data the user enters. If there is no value that you want to prepend to the entered data, you must enter nothing inside the brackets. The following is an example of the use of the prepend string:

```
ITEM  ZIP code for Montana Residents
GETR  {MT }5,,{}
EXEC  RecZip %
```

In this example the prepend string MT will be prepended to the supplied user input. The RecZip represents a custom application that processes user-supplied data.

The *length* specifies the size of the user input field. It is the number of characters the user can enter for the GET command. The *length* field is mandatory and can have a maximum value of 80 characters.

The example that follows shows a maximum length field of 80 being used:

```
ITEM  Address Information
GETR  Enter your street address {}80,,{}
EXEC  RecData %
```

RecData in the EXEC command in this example is meant as an example of a custom application (RecData) that can process the user-supplied information.

The *prefillString* is the initial value placed in the user's response field. It is used as the default value that the user can accept, if the user chooses not to enter a different value. The *prefillString* is optional. The *prefillString* is separated from the *length* field by a comma and no spaces. If no prefill string is used, it can be omitted, as shown in the following example:

```
ITEM  Get user information
GETO  Enter your company name:{}50,,{}
EXEC  RecData  %
```

The following example shows a prefill string being used:

```
ITEM  Get user information
GETO  Enter your company name:{}50,IBM,{}
EXEC  RecData  %
```

Here, the Enter your company name: field in the dialog box for the GETO command will have an initial value of IBM. The user can accept this value or override it with a different value. The user-supplied value is used as a parameter to a custom application called RecData.

The SECURE keyword is optional. If present, it must occur between the *prefillString* parameter and the {*appendString*} parameter. If the SECURE keyword exists as part of the GET command syntax, it means that the typed-in user data will not be displayed (hidden). This is useful if the user wants to enter a password, security code, or some other confidential data. An example of the use of the SECURE keyword is shown as follows:

```
ITEM  Security Information
GETR  Enter Personal Identification
➥ Number(PIN): {}4,,SECURE{}
EXEC  ValidPIN %
```

ValidPIN in the EXEC command is meant to signify a custom application—one that, perhaps, validates the user-supplied PIN data.

The *appendString* placed inside the brackets is a string attached to the end (appended) of the data the user enters. If there is no value that you want to append to the entered data, you must enter nothing inside the brackets. An example of the use of the append string is shown here:

```
ITEM  Security Information
GETR  Enter Personal Identification
Number(PIN): {}4,,SECURE{KXVZ}
EXEC  ProcPIN
```

In this example, the append string KXVZ is appended to the supplied user input. The ProcPIN represents a custom application that processes the user-supplied data. In this example, the append string is used as a special security code that is sent in conjunction with the user-supplied data to the processing program ProcPIN.

If several GET commands are listed under an ITEM command, the GET fields are grouped in the order of occurrence with 10 GETs per dialog box. In other words, there can be a maximum of 10 GET command prompts per dialog box. If you want to override this default behavior and have a GET command appear in its own dialog box, you must use the caret (^) at the beginning of the prompt text for the GET command. The following example shows how each of the GET commands can appear in their own dialog box:

```
ITEM  Enter User Information
GETP  ^User Name:{}50,,{}
GETP  ^Address:{}80,,{}
GETP  ^Password:{}30,,SECURE{}
EXEC  ProcUser %1 %2 %3
```

ProcUser represents a custom application that processes the user-supplied input.

There can be no more than 100 GET commands per ITEM command. Also, the GETO and GETR commands must be entered between the ITEM and the EXEC line that is associated with them. The general syntax of the GET*x* command is shown as follows:

```
GETx  promptString, {prependString}
length,prefillString,[SECURE]{appendString}
```

The brackets around SECURE imply that SECURE is optional; it is not part of the syntax for GET*x*.

Table 5.5 summarizes the different GET parameters that have been discussed.

 Use table 5.5 to review the GET parameters. Also study the examples on the use of the GET parameters in this section.

Table 5.5
GET Parameters

GETx Parameter	Description
promptString	The message that must be displayed to the user.
prependString	The user-entered data is prepended with the prependString placed in the first set of brackets.
length	The maximum number of characters for the user field. Its maximum value is 80 characters.
prefillString	Used as the default response, in case the user does not enter a value.
SECURE	The information typed in by the user is not displayed. Used for secure data such as passwords and codes.
appendString	The user-entered data is appended with the appendString placed in the first set of brackets.

Login Scripts

Many of the NetWare 3 login script commands can be used with NetWare 4. NetWare 4 includes a few additional login script commands, but the greatest difference is in the area of login script organization. NetWare 3 uses three types of login scripts: system, user, and default login scripts. NetWare 4 has an additional login script type called the *profile* login script. The scope of the system login script has changed also. In NetWare 3, the system login script applies to all user accounts defined on the file server. In NetWare 4, the system login script applies to user accounts for the container on which it is defined.

Because of the limited scope of this book, this section focuses on the differences between NetWare 3 and NetWare 4 login scripts. For more information on the login script statements, refer to the companion volume, *NetWare Training Guide: NetWare 4 Administration*, by New Riders Publishing.

Login Script Types

NetWare 4 supports four types of login scripts:

- System login script
- Profile login script
- User login script
- Default login script

The *system* login script is a property of the Organization and Organizational Unit container objects. The *profile* login script is a property of the Profile leaf object. The *user* login script is a property of the User object. The *default* login script does not exist as an object or a property; it is contained in the LOGIN.EXE utility that is used for logging on to the network. Because login scripts are properties of objects, NDS tools such as NETADMIN or the NetWare Administrator can be used for creating and modifying login scripts.

Each of these different login script types are discussed in the following sections.

System Login Script

The system login script is a property of the Organization and Organizational Unit container objects, and its scope is the user objects defined in that container. This means that system login scripts are a convenient way of specifying the commands that should be executed for all users belonging to an organization or department (organizational unit) within the organization.

 The NDS objects that can contain the system login script are Organization and Organizational Unit objects.

The system login script is executed for only the immediate users in that container. In figure 5.44, the system login script for organization O=SCS applies only to users Admin, KSS, and Dei, which are defined in that container. They do not apply to users Lisa, Janice, nor Bill in container OU=ENG.O=SCS. The container OU=ENG has its own system login script, and this applies to users Lisa, Janice, and Bill. The container OU =SALES.O=SCS does not have a system login script. This means that for users Nina, John, and Dorsch there is no system login script. If a container does not have a system login script, it does not inherit the system login script from a parent container.

The system login script is the first type of login script that is executed and it can be used to set up the general environment for all users in a container.

To create a system login script, you must highlight the container object using NETADMIN or the NetWare Administration tool, and select the container's Login Script property for modification.

Figure 5.44

The scope of the system login script.

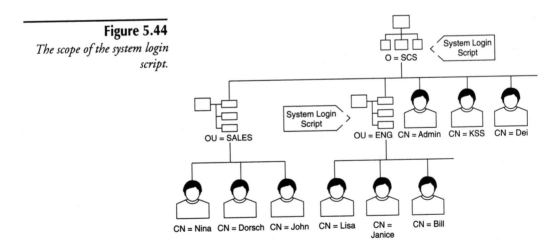

Profile Login Script

The profile login script is a property of the Profile object. The Profile object is a leaf object whose sole purpose is to contain the profile login script (see fig. 5.45). If a group of users has common needs, they fit a certain *profile*. In this case a Profile object can be assigned to each of the users.

Every User object has a profile login script property (as well as a user login script property). The profile login script property for a user can contain the name of a Profile object. A User object can have only one profile login script. If the profile login property for a User object is set to a Profile object, the profile login script (property of the Profile object) is executed every time that user logs in. If the profile login property for a User object is not set, no profile login script is executed when that User object is logged in.

 The profile login script is set by assigning a Profile object to the User object's profile login property.

The profile login script is executed after the system login script.

The profile login script seems to be similar to the system login script. What, then, is its purpose? The system login script applies only to user objects that are in the immediate container. There might be situations when users belonging to different containers have a common need for setting up their user environment. The profile login script property for users can be set to the same Profile object, even if the user objects are defined in different containers. This makes it possible for users in different containers to have a common login script.

 The profile login script is executed after the system login script but before the user login script.

The User object can have only one profile login script.

Figure 5.45
The profile login script.

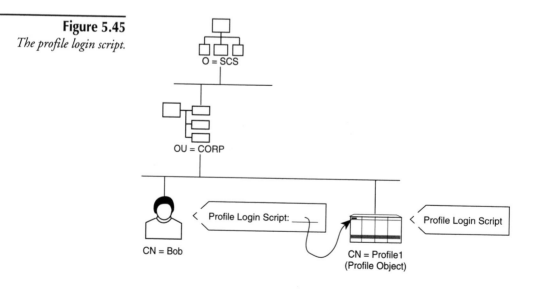

User Login Script

Every User object has a login script property (see fig. 5.46). The value for the login script property can be a sequence of login script commands. The same type of login script commands that are used for the system and profile login script can be used for user login scripts.

The user login script is set by entering login script commands for the User object's user login property.

The user login script is executed after the profile login script (if any).

The user login script can be used to customize a user's login environment. The other login scripts (system and profile) are used to share common login script commands with other users. A user might have special needs that are not addressed by these "group" login scripts. In that case, use the user login script to further customize the user's environment.

Default Login Script

The default login script is unlike all other login scripts in that, whereas the other login scripts can be modified, the default login script cannot be modified. The default login script is fixed, and can be considered to be "contained" in the login program, LOGIN.EXE. It is meant to provide a minimum user environment in case a user logs in and does not have a user login script. This is certainly true the first time the user Admin logs into a newly installed network, which does not have any system, profile, or user login script set up. The Admin user can at least perform some basic administration without having to create drive mappings.

Figure 5.46

The user login script.

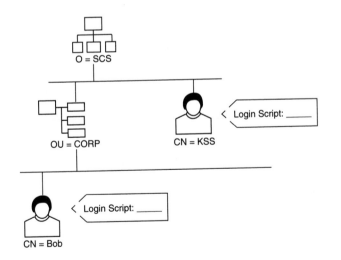

After a user login script is created for a user, the default login script will not execute for that user. In some situations, all the login script needs of a user can be met by the system login script or the profile login script. In such a case, there is no need to have a user login script. However, because the user login script has not been set, the default login script will execute, in addition to any system and profile login scripts. One of the default actions the default login script performs is to set up a search drive mapping to SYS:PUBLIC. If the system or profile login script already maps a search drive to SYS:PUBLIC, a second search drive mapping to SYS:PUBLIC will be created unless the user login script property is set, or the NO_DEFAULT login directive exists in the system or profile login script.

The default login script, which is contained in the LOGIN.EXE file, is executed if the user login script is not set.

The NO_DEFAULT Directive

The NO_DEFAULT directive in the system or profile login script can explicitly disable the execution of the default login script (see fig. 5.47). This is useful if you want to override the default mappings that are created when the user login script property is not set, but do not want to set the user login property because the login scripts of the system or profile login script are sufficient to set up the required user environment.

The NO_DEFAULT directive is used to prevent the default login script from executing and is set in the system or profile login script.

Figure 5.47

Using the NO_DEFAULT login script command.

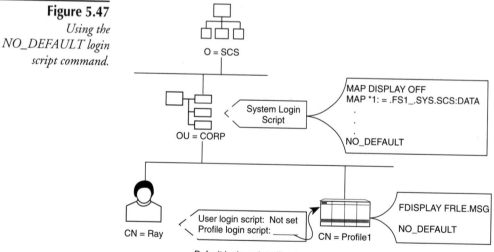

Login Script Execution Order

The order of execution for the login script types is illustrated in figure 5.48 and also listed here. The following steps are executed when the user logs in to a NetWare 4 network:

1. If a user's container has the system login script property set, the system login script is executed for that user.

2. If a user's profile login script property is set to a Profile object, the profile login script for that Profile object is executed for that user.

3. If a user's user login script property is set, the user login script for that User object is executed.

4. If a user's user login script property is not set, the default is executed unless the NO_DEFAULT login script command has been included in the system or profile login script.

Some examples might help illustrate the preceding steps. Figure 5.49 shows an example of the NDS tree for organization O=TEC that has a system login script.

Under O=TEC are two organizational unit objects. One of the organizational unit objects (OU=ENG) has a system login script, while the other (OU=EXP) does not have a system login script. The users Admin, KSS, and Bill have a user login script, but user Charles does not have a login script. The user

Figure 5.48

The order of execution of the login scripts.

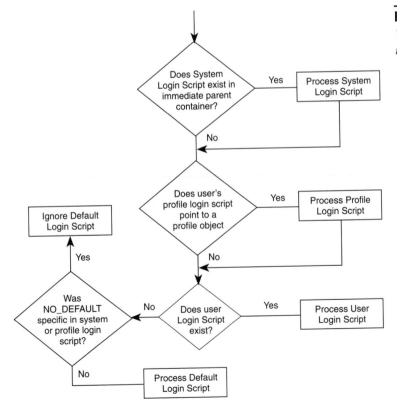

KSS also has a profile login script property set to the Profile object CN=Profile1.OU=ENG.O=TEC. The order of execution of login scripts for the different users is explained next.

User KSS:

User KSS's container has a system login script. Therefore the system login script for OU=ENG is executed first. User KSS also has a profile login script. This is executed next. Finally, a check is made to see if user KSS has a user login script. Because user KSS has a user login script, this is executed next. The order of login script executions for user KSS follows:

1. System login script for OU=ENG

2. Profile login script for Profile object PROFILE1.ENG.TEC

3. User login script for KSS

User Bill:

User Bill's container has a system login script. Therefore the system login script for OU=ENG is executed first. User Bill does not have a profile login script. A check is made to see if user Bill has a user login script. Because user Bill has a user login script, this is executed next. The order of login script executions for user KSS follows:

1. System login script for OU=ENG

2. User login script for Bill

User Admin:

User Admin's container has a system login script. Therefore the system login script for O=TEC is executed first. User Admin does not have a profile login script. A check is made to see if user Admin has a user login script. Because user Admin has a user login script, this is executed next. The order of login script executions for user Admin follows:

1. System login script for O=TEC

2. User login script for Admin

User Charles:

User Charles's container OU=EXP does not have a system login script. Therefore no system login

Figure 5.49

An example of login script execution.

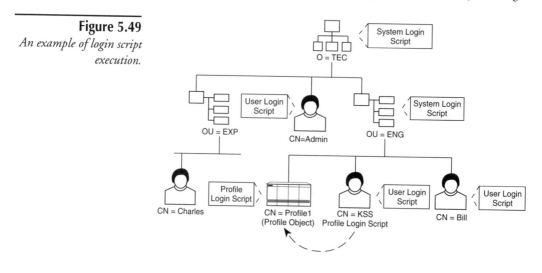

script is executed. User Charles does not have a profile login script. A check is made to see if user Charles has a user login script. Because user Charles does not have a user login script, the default login script is executed next.

 The following list contains the login script execution order:

1. System login script

2. Profile login script

3. User login script, *or* default login script if user login script property is not set

Upgrade Considerations for Login Scripts

When upgrading from an earlier NetWare version to NetWare 4, the first system login script encountered for a file server that is placed in a container object becomes the system login script property of that container object. Any subsequent system login scripts from file servers that are placed in the same container are ignored. Therefore it is important to upgrade the server that contains the most up-to-date version of the system login script first.

 The first system login script encountered for a file server that is placed in a container object becomes the system login script property of that container object.

Even though the earlier NetWare login scripts are compatible with NetWare 4, you should review the upgraded login scripts to see if you can take advantage of the new NetWare 4 features. If the directories on which you want to map network drives are on Volume objects that are in a different context to

that where the users are defined, you will have to modify the login script MAP commands to refer to the NDS name of Volume objects.

Rights to Execute Login Script Property Value

The login script is a property of the NDS object—the system login script is a property of the Organization or Organizational Unit container, the profile login script is a property of the Profile object, and the user login script is a property of the User object. For a User object to execute the login scripts when the User object is logged in, that User object must have certain rights to that login script property.

Containers are granted the Read property right to their login script. The User object in the container must have the Browse right to the container object and the Read property right to the login script in order to execute the system login script. The Browse right to the container is usually granted by inheritance. It is typical in most NDS trees, for example, to make [public] a trustee of [Root] with the Browse right. Users in a container, then, inherit the Browse right.

 The User object in the container must have the Browse right to the container object and the Read property right to the login script in order to execute the system login script.

 Containers are granted the Read property right to their login script (system login script).

Profile login scripts are assigned by setting a user's profile login script property to the name of the Profile object. The user needs to be made a trustee of the Profile object. When a user is made a trustee of the Profile object, the following rights are by default assigned to the user:

■ The Browse object right to the Profile object

■ Read and Compare property rights to the All Properties of the Profile object

Because of the All Properties Read and Compare rights, the user inherits these rights for the profile login script property, also.

 When a user is made a trustee of the Profile object, the user is given the Browse object right to the Profile object, and Read and Compare property rights to the All Properties of the Profile object.

Users are by default assigned Read and Write property rights to their user login script property. The Write property right allows users to modify their own login scripts. In some network environments, it might not be desirable for users to modify their login scripts. In such a case, the Write property right to the login script must be removed.

 Users are by default assigned Read and Write property rights to their user login script property.

Most NetWare 4 commands are the same as those for NetWare 3. The new login script commands are listed in table 5.6.

 Study the login commands listed in table 5.6.

Table 5.6
New Login Script Commands

Login Command	Description
ATTACH	Attaches to bindery-based servers. Also can attach to NetWare 4 servers in bindery emulation mode.
CLS	Clears screen. This had to be done by the #COMMAND /C CLS in earlier NetWare versions.
CONTEXT *newcontext*	Changes the user's context from login script.
INCLUDE *NDSObjectName*	Invokes login scripts that are properties of other NDS objects. The traditional INCLUDE *filename* used in NetWare 3 also works in NetWare 4.
LASTLOGINTIME	Displays the last time the user logged in. Used for informational purpose.
MAP CHANGE *or* MAP C	Changes drive from ordinary network drive to search drive and vice versa.
MAP NP	No Prompt. Overrides existing mapping without prompting user to verify the operation.

Login Command	Description
MAP P	Maps drive pointer to physical volume rather than the Volume object.
NO_SWAP	Prevents LOGIN.EXE from being swapped out to high memory.
SWAP	Can result in LOGIN.EXE being swapped out if there is insufficient memory to run LOGIN.EXE, especially when executing # commands.
PROFILE *profobject*	Overrides the profile script assigned to a user or specified at the command line, and causes the user to execute a PROFILE script *profobject*.
SET_TIME [ON|OFF]	SET_TIME ON synchronizes workstation time to server that it is first attached to. This is the default behavior. SET_TIME OFF disables this default behavior.
NO_DEFAULT	When used in system login script or profile login script, it disables the default login script from running.

Study Guide for the Chapter

If preparing for the NetWare 3.11 to 4 Update CNE exams, review the chapter with the following goals:

■ Understand and identify the differences between the NetWare 3 and NetWare 4 command-line utility changes. Know, for instance, which NetWare 4 utility replaces SYSCON, DSPACE, SALVAGE, and so on. Use the Study Notes as a quick review.

■ Pay particular attention to the different types of login scripts and their order of execution. Practice determining the order of execution for users in an NDS tree when the system login script, profile login script, and user login script are present or absent. Also pay attention to the differences between the different GET commands.

■ After studying this chapter, attempt the sample test questions. If you miss the answer to a question, review the appropriate topic until you understand the reason for the correct answer.

Chapter Summary

In this chapter you learned about NetWare 4 client utility changes and differences between NetWare 3 and NetWare 4 login script processing mechanisms. You also learned about the command-line utility changes. Some of the NetWare 3 utilities have been consolidated into a single utility in many cases, and in other cases the older bindery-based utilities have disappeared and are replaced by newer utilities that are NDS aware. Many of the utilities have a bindery emulation mode, and can be used to work with NetWare 3 servers.

This chapter examined the new Novell Menu utility (NMENU) for creating a menu-driven interface. This utility has been improved over the NetWare 3.11 MENU.EXE utility, and is based on the popular Saber menus.

Other major changes are in the area of login script processing. NetWare 4 defines a system login script, profile login script, user login script, and the default login script.

Chapter Test Questions

Some questions have a single correct answer, whereas others have multiple correct answers. The questions that require a single answer are indicated by a ○ (circle) notation that precedes the possible answers. The questions that require you to select more than one answer are indicated by the □ (box) preceding each answer. Not all the questions are multiple choice. Occasionally, you might encounter a question that asks you to type in an answer. The answer in this case is usually a one-word answer. The answer is not case sensitive; you can type it in lower- or uppercase.

Certain questions are repeated in different ways so that you can recognize them even when the wording is different. Taking practice quizzes not only tests your knowledge but also gives you confidence when you take your exam.

1. NetWare 4 utilities can be divided into which three categories?

   □ A. Command-line

   □ B. Batch mode

   □ C. Menu-driven (text-based)

   □ D. GUI-based

   □ E. Run-time

2. Which of the following are examples of menu-based text utilities?

   □ A. NETADMIN

   □ B. NETUSER

   □ C. NWADMIN

   □ D. NWUSER

   □ E. FILER

3. Which NetWare tool can be used to show the NDS tree graphically and perform NDS operations?

   ○ A. NETADMIN

   ○ B. NDSTREE

   ○ C. WINTREE

   ○ D. NWADMIN

   ○ E. NWUSER

   ○ F. NWSYSCON

4. The command to map drive G to the APPS directory on Volume object NW4CS_SYS that is in the context OU=ENG.O=SCS is _____.

   ○ A. MAP G:=
      NW4CS_SYS:APPS

   ○ B. MAP INS G:=
      NW4CS_SYS:APPS

   ○ C. MAP G:=.CN=NW4CS_SYS.OU=
      SCS.O=ENG:APPS

   ○ D. MAP G:=.CN=NW4CS_SYS.OU=
      ENG.O=SCS:SYS/APPS

   ○ E. MAP G:=.CN=NW4CS_SYS.OU=
      ENG.O=SCS:APPS

5. If current context is OU=LAB.OU=ENG.O=SCS, which of the following MAP commands could be used to map drive H to the PUBLIC/BIN on volume FS1_VOL in the context OU=SALES.O=SCS?

   ○ A. MAP H: =
      FS1_VOL.SALES..:PUBLIC/BIN

   ○ B. MAP H: =
      FS1_VOL.SALES.:PUBLIC/BIN

○ C. MAP H: =
FS1_VOL.SALES.SCS:PUBLIC/
BIN

○ D. MAP H: =
CN=FS1_VOL.OU=SALES.O=
SCS:PUBLIC/BIN

6. The CHANGE (C) option in the MAP command can be used to _____.

○ A. alter the search mode

○ B. convert a network drive into a search drive

○ C. convert a search drive into a network drive

○ D. convert a network drive into a search drive and vice versa

7. The NetWare 4 FLAG utility consolidates the functions of the NetWare 3 _____.

○ A. FLAG, FLAGDIR

○ B. FLAG, SMODE

○ C. FLAGDIR, SMODE, FILER

○ D. FLAGDIR, SMODE, FLAG

8. The NDIR command can be used to find information on _____.

○ A. network users

○ B. network users and objects

○ C. NetWare Directory Service objects

○ D. space saved using the file compression feature

9. The NetWare 4 NDIR utility consolidates the functions of NetWare 3 _____.

○ A. NDIR, LISTDIR

○ B. LISTDIR, VOLINFO

○ C. NDIR, LISTDIR, VOLINFO

○ D. NDIR, VOLINFO

○ E. NDIR, LISTDIR, VOLINFO, FLAG

10. The /FI option in NDIR can be used to _____.

○ A. display attributes for a file

○ B. display and set attributes for a file

○ C. search for file names on all network drives

○ D. search for file names on the search drives

11. The RIGHTS command enables you to _____.

☐ A. view/set the rights of a directory or file

☐ B. remove a directory

☐ C. view trustee assignments to a specified directory

☐ D. see how rights are inherited for a specific directory

☐ E. view/set the Inherited Rights for NDS objects

☐ F. view/set the Inherited Rights Filter for files and directories

12. The option used to specify the User object in the RIGHTS command is _____.

    ○ A. /USER

    ○ B. /NAME

    ○ C. /USR

    ○ D. /N

    ○ E. /US

    ○ F. /NAM

13. The NetWare 4 RIGHTS utility consolidates the functions of the following NetWare 3 utilities:

    ○ A. RIGHTS, GRANT, REVOKE

    ○ B. RIGHTS, GRANT, ALLOW

    ○ C. RIGHTS, GRANT, REVOKE, REMOVE

    ○ D. RIGHTS, GRANT, REVOKE, REMOVE, ALLOW

    ○ E. RIGHTS, ALLOW, GRANT, REVOKE

    ○ F. RIGHTS, GRANT, REVOKE, REMOVE, ALLOW, SMODE

14. The command that prevents users from receiving all network messages on the screen is _____.

    ○ A. SEND /A=N

    ○ B. SEND /A=C

    ○ C. SEND /A=Y

    ○ D. CASTOFF

    ○ E. CASTOFF ALL

    ○ F. CASTOFF /ALL

15. The SEND /A=C is equivalent to the NetWare 3 _____

    ○ A. CASTOFF

    ○ B. CASTOFF ALL

    ○ C. IGNORE MSG

    ○ D. IGNORE ALL

16. The NetWare 4 SEND utility consolidates the functions of the NetWare 3 _____.

    ○ A. SEND, CASTON

    ○ B. SEND, CASTOFF

    ○ C. CASTON, CASTOFF

    ○ D. SEND, CASTON, CASTOFF

17. NETUSER can be used for _____.

    ☐ A. assigning network drive mappings

    ☐ B. creating NDS objects

    ☐ C. creating user objects

    ☐ D. selecting a printer

    ☐ E. creating form definitions

    ☐ F. changing file attributes

18. The FILER utility combines the functions of which NetWare 3 menu-based utility?

    ○ A. SESSION, FILER, SALVAGE, LISTDIR, VOLINFO, DSPACE

    ○ B. FILER, SALVAGE, LISTDIR, VOLINFO

    ○ C. FILER, SALVAGE, DSPACE, VOLINFO

    ○ D. SESSION, SALVAGE, LISTDIR, VOLINFO, DSPACE

    ○ E. FILER, SALVAGE, DSPACE, RIGHTS

19. The NetWare 4 FILER can be used to _____.

    ☐ A. view file contents and directories

    ☐ B. create Volume objects

    ☐ C. view/set directory and file rights

    ☐ D. create file container objects

    ☐ E. delete entire subdirectories, includ-
           ing files in them

20. Which environment variable is set to specify
    languages other than English?

    ○ A. LANGUAGE

    ○ B. NWLANGUAGE

    ○ C. NWCLANGUAGE

    ○ D. NLS

    ○ E. NLSLANGUAGE

    ○ F. NLSLANG

21. A user's preference for a language can be
    specified by _____.

    ○ A. setting the language environment
           variable for the user

    ○ B. setting the language property for the
           user

    ○ C. loading the language driver in
           CONFIG.SYS

    ○ D. setting the language property in the
           user's container object

22. Older menu scripts can be converted to
    NetWare menu scripts by using _____.

    ○ A. CNVTMENU

    ○ B. MENUCNVT

    ○ C. OLDMENU

    ○ D. OLDMENUC

    ○ E. MENUCONV

23. The utility to compile the menu script (SRC)
    file to the menu object file (DAT) is _____.

    ○ A. MAKEMENU

    ○ B. MENUMAKE

    ○ C. MENUCOMP

    ○ D. COMPMENU

    ○ E. MNUMAKE

    ○ F. MAKEMNU

24. The utility used to run a NetWare 4 menu is
    _____.

    ○ A. MENU

    ○ B. NOVMENU

    ○ C. NMENU

    ○ D. MENUN

    ○ E. MENU4

25. Novell Menus have the following organiza-
    tional commands:

    ☐ A. MENU

    ☐ B. EXEC

    ☐ C. GETR

    ☐ D. ITEM

    ☐ E. GETP

26. The commands following an ITEM statement
    can be _____.

    ○ A. EXEC, LOAD, SHOW

    ○ B. GETO, GETR, GETP

○ C. LOAD, SHOW, GETO

○ D. EXEC, LOAD, SHOW, GETO, GETR, GETP

○ E. EXEC, LOAD, SHOW, GETO, GETR, GETP, ITEM

27. Valid item options in the ITEM command are _____.

○ A. BATCH, CHDIR

○ B. CHDIR, SHOW

○ C. BATCH, CHDIR, SHOW, PAUSE

○ D. SHOW, PAUSE, BATCH, SECURE

○ E. CHDIR, SHOW, PAUSE, SECURE, BATCH

28. To free up memory taken up by the Menu Utility and restore the default directory to the one that existed prior to executing an application, you can combine the _____ and _____ item options.

○ A. PAUSE, CHDIR

○ B. SHOW, PAUSE

○ C. CHDIR, SHOW

○ D. BATCH, CHDIR

29. To make the Novell menus secure, you should _____.

○ A. use the EXEC DOS command in an item option

○ B. not use the EXEC DOS command in an item option

○ C. use the EXEC SECURE command in an item option

○ D. use the EXEC SHELL command in an item option

30. To make a menu secure, you can exit the Novell menus using the _____ command.

○ A. EXEC DOS

○ B. EXEC EXIT

○ C. EXEC LOGOUT

○ D. EXEC SECURE

31. The menu command used to display a menu by its menu number is _____.

○ A. LOAD

○ B. SHOW

○ C. EXEC

○ D. DISPLAY

32. Which menu commands obtain input from the user through the Novell menus?

○ A. LOAD

○ B. SHOW

○ C. PUT

○ D. GET

○ E. READ

○ F. INPUT

33. Which command is used for obtaining optional input from the user?

○ A. GET

○ B. GETR

○ C. GETO

○ D. GETP

34. The NDS objects that can contain the system login script are _____.

    ☐ A. Organization

    ☐ B. Organizational Unit

    ☐ C. Root

    ☐ D. User

    ☐ E. Group

35. How is the profile login script set for a user?

    ○ A. By assigning a profile login script to the User object's profile property

    ○ B. By assigning a profile login script to the user's container profile login property

    ○ C. By assigning a Profile object to the User object's profile login property

    ○ D. By assigning a Profile object to the user's container profile login property

36. The profile login script is executed _____.

    ○ A. before the system login script, but after the user script

    ○ B. after the system login script, but before the user script

    ○ C. after the system login script, but before the container's script

    ○ D. before the system login script, but after the container's script

37. A User object can have _____ profile login script(s).

    ○ A. 1

    ○ B. 2

    ○ C. up to 8

    ○ D. any number of

38. The user login script is set by _____.

    ○ A. entering login script commands in the User object's user login property using SYSCON

    ○ B. entering login script commands in a text file using any text editor and assigning the file name to the User object's login property

    ○ C. entering login script commands in the User object's user login property using FILER

    ○ D. entering login script commands for the User object's user login property

40. The default login script is executed if _____.

    ○ A. the system login script is not set

    ○ B. the profile login script is not set

    ○ C. the system and profile login scripts are not set

    ○ D. the user login script is not set

41. The default login script is contained in the _____.

    ○ A. LOGIN.EXE file

    ○ B. user's default login script property

    ○ C. user container's default login script property

    ○ D. Organization object's default login script property list

42. Which command is used to prevent the default login script from executing and is set in the system or profile login scripts?

  ○ A. EXIT_DEFAULT_LOGIN

  ○ B. NO_DEFAULT_LOGIN

  ○ C. SKIP_DEFAULT

  ○ D. QUIT_DEFAULT

  ○ E. ABANDON_DEFAULT

  ○ F. NO_DEFAULT

43. The login script execution order is _____.

  ○ A. profile login script, system login script, user login script

  ○ B. user login script, profile login script, system login script

  ○ C. system login script, user login script, profile login script

  ○ D. system login script, profile login script, user login script

44. Which of the following statements about system login script files during the upgrade process is true?

  ○ A. The first system login script encountered for a file server that is placed in a container object becomes the profile login script property of that container object.

  ○ B. The last system login script encountered for a file server that is placed in a container object becomes the system login script property of that container object.

  ○ C. The first system login script encountered for a file server that is placed in a container object becomes the system login script property of that container object, provided that there are no profile login scripts defined for the container object.

  ○ D. The first system login script encountered for a file server that is placed in a container object becomes the system login script property of that container object.

45. The User object in the container must have the _____.

  ○ A. Browse right to the container object and the Read property right to the login script in order to execute the system login script

  ○ B. Read right to the container object and the Read property right to the login script in order to execute the system login script

  ○ C. Create right to the container object and the Read and Write property right to the login script in order to execute the system login script

  ○ D. Write right to the container object and the Read and Compare property right to the login script in order to execute the system login script

46. Containers are granted _____.

  ○ A. the Read and Write property right to their system login script

  ○ B. the Read property right to their system login script

C. the Read, Compare, and Write property rights to their system login script

D. the Write property right to their system login script

47. If a user is made a trustee of the Profile object, the default rights are assigned in what manner?

  A. The user is given the Create object right to the Profile object, and Read and Compare property rights to the All Properties of the Profile object.

  B. The user is given the Create and Delete object right to the Profile object, and Read and Compare property rights to the All Properties of the Profile object.

  C. The user is given the Browse object right to the Profile object, and Read and Compare property rights to the All Properties of the Profile object.

  D. The user is given the Browse object right to the Profile object, and Read and Write property rights to the All Properties of the Profile object.

48. Users are by default assigned _____.

  A. Read and Write property rights to their user login script property

  B. Read and Compare property rights to their user login script property

  C. Read property rights to their user login script property

  D. Supervisor property rights to their user login script property

49. The login script command to clear the screen is _____.

  A. CLEAR

  B. CLS

  C. CLEAR DISPLAY

  D. CLEAR SCREEN

50. The login script command to change a user's context is _____.

  A. LCX

  B. CONTEXT

  C. CX

  D. CHANGE CONTEXT

51. The login script command to execute other login script commands as if they were a subroutine is _____.

  A. CALL

  B. SUBROUTINE

  C. INCLUDE

  D. PROC

  E. PROCEDURE

52. The login script command to display the last time a user logged in is _____.

  A. LOGINDATE

  B. LOGINTIME

  C. LAST_LOGINDATE

  D. LAST_LOGINTIME

  E. LASTLOGINTIME

53. The login script command to change drives from an ordinary network drive to a search drive and vice versa is _____.

   ○ A. MAP CHANGE

   ○ B. MAP INS

   ○ C. MAP CH

   ○ D. MAP TOGGLE

54. The login script command NO_DEFAULT _____.

   ○ A. prevents the user login script command from executing if placed in the system or profile login script

   ○ B. prevents the system login script command from executing if placed in the system login script

   ○ C. prevents the profile login script command from executing if placed in the profile login script

   ○ D. prevents the default login script command from executing if placed in the system or profile login script

55. Given that G is mapped to SYS:PUBLIC/BIN, the command MAP C G: _____.

   ○ A. deletes the search drive mapping G

   ○ B. is illegal

   ○ C. makes C a search drive that points to G

   ○ D. assigns a search drive to SYS:PUBLIC/BIN

   ○ E. creates a search drive to C

NetWare 4 Auditing

With NetWare 4, the NetWare operating system includes a powerful feature called auditing that can be used to augment NetWare security. In large systems such as the operating systems that run on mainframes and mini-computers, it is common to have an auditing capability that allows selected events, such as access to a specified file or directory, to be monitored. Moreover, the person performing the auditing is independent of the system administrator, which avoids the concentration of power within a single individual.

In this chapter you will learn about the auditing features and capabilities of NetWare 4. In particular, you will learn about the following:

- The role differences between the network administrator and the auditor

- The AUDITCON tool for auditing

- How events in the file system and the NDS can be audited

- How reports can be prepared from the audit log

Examining the Need for Auditing

In NetWare 3 (and earlier versions) there was a feature called accounting that could be activated on a newly installed server using the SYSCON utility. Once the accounting feature was activated, the system administrator could track the number of blocks read and written, the services requested from the NetWare server, and the number of blocks of storage utilized by a user over a period of time. Although these statistics were interesting, their value was somewhat limited. Most NetWare 3 system managers did not make use of these accounting functions in any serious way. What was more often needed was a way to track the usage of individual files and directories.

Knowing the number of times an application was accessed over a particular period, for example, enables the network administrator to determine if the number of licenses for a particular application is adequate. If an organization has purchased a 50-user license for an application when there are at most 20 users who use the application, then it is better to use a 20- or 25-user version.

Another example would be to find out who is accessing system administrator tools such as NETADMIN.EXE or RCONSOLE.EXE. This could help in discovering a breach in security.

The NetWare 3 accounting feature is also available in NetWare 4. NetWare accounting is quite different from the NetWare 4 auditing. Although accounting provides interesting information on the number of blocks read and written, it cannot tell you how or when a specific file or directory was accessed. Auditing, on the other hand, can be used to obtain information on individual files and directories, and how they are accessed over a period of time. It also can be used to audit changes in the NDS tree, server events, or creation/deletion of queues.

 The NetWare accounting feature is different from the NetWare auditing feature.

 NetWare auditing can be used to enhance NetWare security.

Understanding the Function and Role of a Network Auditor

On most networks, the administrator is all-powerful, in the sense that he or she can access all resources on the network without any restrictions. Such unrestricted power is necessary if the network supervisor is to be able to support the users effectively. It also means that the network supervisor can access sensitive and classified data on the network without any checks, other than the trust that he or she will not abuse this trust. From a practical and political viewpoint, it might be desirable to have a deterrence against a dishonest network supervisor. This deterrence can be implemented using auditing.

Sensitive files can be audited for events that perform an operation on the files such as a read and write. Any time a user, including the network supervisor, accesses the audited file, that action is recorded in an *audit log*, which can be used to discover the users who accessed the audited file. The network supervisor is unlikely to surreptitiously access classified files if he or she knows that the file is audited. Auditing cannot prevent a network supervisor from accessing a file, but should such an access be performed, the event will be stored in the audit log and will be discovered by the auditor.

For this reason, the network supervisor and the auditor should not be the same person. The auditor could be any user on the network. What makes the auditor special is that the auditor user has knowledge about the audit password, which is needed to access the auditing functions of an audit tool called AUDITCON. Because the only distinction between an ordinary user and an auditor is knowledge of the password, the audit password must be guarded from non-auditing users, including the network supervisor. Typically, the network supervisor enables auditing and creates a password for the auditor. Once this password is given to the auditor, the auditor should immediately change the password without telling the network supervisor what it is.

 The auditor should be independent of the network supervisor.

The auditor should change the initial audit password assigned by the supervisor as soon as possible. The network supervisor should not have knowledge of the changed audit password.

Reviewing Auditing Features in NetWare 4

NetWare 4 auditing enables the auditor to act independently of the network supervisor to perform the following functions:

- Keep track of file system events such as changes and access to files and directories

- Track events such as changes and access to NDS objects

The auditor does not have to be a specially created user. Any existing user can be set up to perform the role of an auditor.

The network supervisor must designate a network user to be an auditor, and only the network supervisor can do this. The network supervisor designates an auditor by performing the following:

1. Enabling auditing on volumes or containers. For file system events, auditing is enabled at the volume level. For NDS events, auditing is enabled at the container level.

2. Creating an auditor password and notifying a designated user (the auditor) of the password.

3. Training the auditor on the use of the AUDITCON utility and how it can be used to change the password.

Only the network supervisor can designate a network user to be an auditor.

To assign an auditor, the network supervisor must enable auditing on volumes, containers, or both, create an audit password, and notify a designated user about the password.

The auditor performs auditing functions using the AUDITCON utility that can be found in SYS:PUBLIC. Because most users have Read and File Scan trustee rights to this directory, no special trustee rights assignment has to be made for the auditor to access these files. The auditor should not have access to the SYS:SYSTEM directory; the network supervisor and auditor tasks need to be kept separate. Even though the auditor does not have full access to a directory or a file, the auditor can audit file/directory events.

 Auditing functions are performed using AUDITCON. The AUDITCON.EXE is kept in the SYS:PUBLIC directory.

The auditor should not have access rights to the SYS:SYSTEM directory.

The first function the auditor must perform is to assign a new auditor password of which the network supervisor shall not have knowledge. This is a very crucial step in maintaining the independence between the auditor and the network supervisor. If the network supervisor knows the audit password, he or she can perform auditing functions.

 On being assigned a password by the network supervisor, the auditor must change the audit password.

It is important for the auditor to select the right types of events to track. A common mistake is to flag too many events that are not of consequence to network security. This causes the generation of voluminous audit reports, which often go unread and are therefore ignored. The auditor should be trained in the use of the AUDITCON features and functions.

After the audit events have been identified, the auditor can generate audit reports and view the audit report on-screen, or print the audit report. These steps are described in detail in the sections that follow. The steps needed for auditing are shown in figure 6.1.

 The auditor can

■ Keep track of file system events.

■ Track events such as changes and access to NDS objects and trustee rights.

The Admin user (or user with Supervisor object rights) can enable auditing on a volume or a container basis.

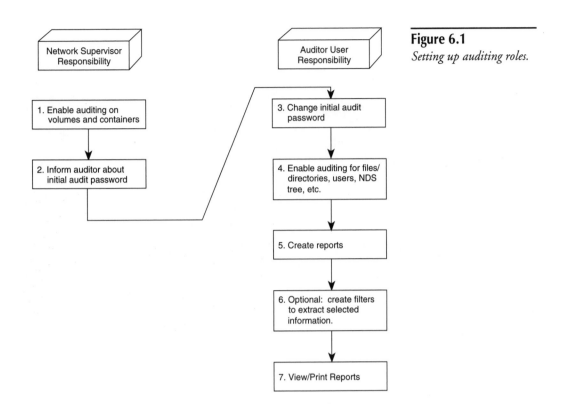

Figure 6.1
Setting up auditing roles.

Using the AUDITCON Tool

The AUDITCON.EXE is the primary tool for performing network auditing. Figure 6.2 shows the main menu for the AUDITCON tool; it shows that one of the options is Enable volume auditing. Presence of this option in the main AUDITCON screen indicates that auditing has not been enabled for this volume. Select this option to enable auditing for that volume.

 If the AUDITCON main menu includes the option Enable volume auditing, then volume auditing has not been enabled.

When the Audit directory services option is selected (see fig. 6.3), you have a choice of selecting the NDS sub-tree starting from a particular container that should be audited (option Audit directory tree). There also is an option to change the context for the session (option Change session context). The session context is displayed at the top of the screen. In the example in figure 6.3, the session context is CORP.ESL.

Figure 6.2
*The AUDITCON Main
Screen when auditing has
not been enabled.*

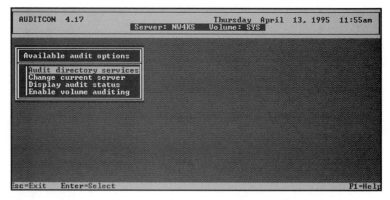

Figure 6.3
The Audit Directory Services Screen.

The option Change current server (refer to fig. 6.2) enables you to log on to other servers for the purpose of auditing volumes on other servers.

The option Display audit status shows the status of audit files on the current volume. For the example

under discussion where auditing has not been enabled, selection of this option should indicate an Auditing status of Off (see fig. 6.4).

The Display audit status option shows the status of the audit files on the current volume.

The Enable volume auditing option allows you to enable auditing for a specific volume.

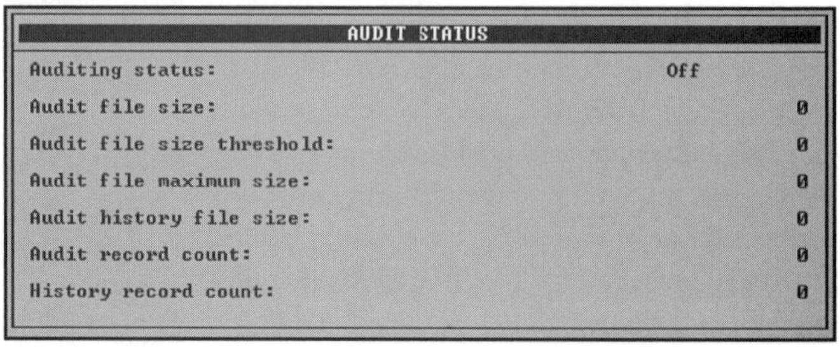

Figure 6.4
*Display Audit Status
when auditing is disabled.*

AUDIT STATUS	
Auditing status:	Off
Audit file size:	0
Audit file size threshold:	0
Audit file maximum size:	0
Audit history file size:	0
Audit record count:	0
History record count:	0

Using the Audit Files

When an audit event occurs, it is logged in a file named NET$AUDT.DAT that is kept at the root of each volume and is flagged "open." Flagging this file open ensures that non-auditors on the network cannot access this file. The NET$AUDT.DAT file only contains auditing information for volume auditing for this volume. NDS auditing data is stored in the NDS DATABASE.

 The audit log file is NET$AUDT.DAT.

The NET$AUDT.DAT file is flagged open to prevent non-auditors from accessing the file.

It might be desirable on some networks to keep track of the auditor's activities. The purpose of this is to have a deterrence against the power that an auditor has. It would, for example, be useful to know which auditor accessed the audit log file NET$AUDT.DAT. NetWare 4 solves this problem by keeping an audit history file called AUD$HIST.DAT that is also kept in the root of a volume and is flagged "open." This audit history file keeps track of the auditor's access to the audit log file NET$AUDT.DAT and records the date, time, and the auditor who accessed this file. Any enabling or disabling of monitor functions on the volume is also kept in the audit history file. If the auditor clears the history file to "hide" a questionable event, the first entry in the new history file will record the fact that the history file was cleared.

 The AUD$HIST.DAT file is the audit history file and is used to keep track of the auditor's access to the NET$AUDT.DAT file.

A record of the enabling or disabling of monitor functions on the volume is kept in the audit history file AUD$HIST.DAT.

 If there is more than one auditor on the network, they should be given separate user accounts. This is so that their auditing activities are recorded under their respective user names.

The audit log file (NET$AUDT.DAT) and the audit history file (AUD$HIST.DAT) are kept in the root of a volume and are flagged open.

The information in the NET$AUDT.DAT file is kept in a binary form. The auditor uses the binary audit files to generate an audit report. The audit report is a text file and is stored on the network. Because a text report file can be read by anyone, it must be guarded to ensure that no ordinary user has access to it. Otherwise, any user who has Read access rights to this file will become privy to its contents. The audit report can also be viewed on-screen. This process creates a temporary file that is deleted upon exiting the view.

Enabling Auditing

The first steps in figure 6.1 were for the network supervisor to enable auditing for a volume or container and select an audit password. These steps are described in this section.

1. You must determine the volume to be audited. This decision is based on which volume is used for keeping sensitive data to be tracked, or the volume that contains program files whose usage needs to be monitored.

2. Log in to the network as an Admin user and run AUDITCON.

3. From the main menu option, select Enable volume auditing.

4. Enter the volume password (see fig. 6.5). You are asked to retype the password for verification purposes. If there is an audit data file on the volume, it is moved to an old audit data file. If there already is an old data file, it is deleted.

Study Note
You must have supervisor equivalent file system rights to enable auditing on the volume.

After enabling the volume auditing, the main screen of the AUDITCON will change (see fig. 6.6). The Enable audit status option will be missing from the Available Audit Options menu.

If you select the Display audit status option, you will see that the volume auditing has been enabled (see fig. 6.7).

5. Exit AUDITCON.

6. Give the audit password to the auditor and instruct the auditor to change the password immediately.

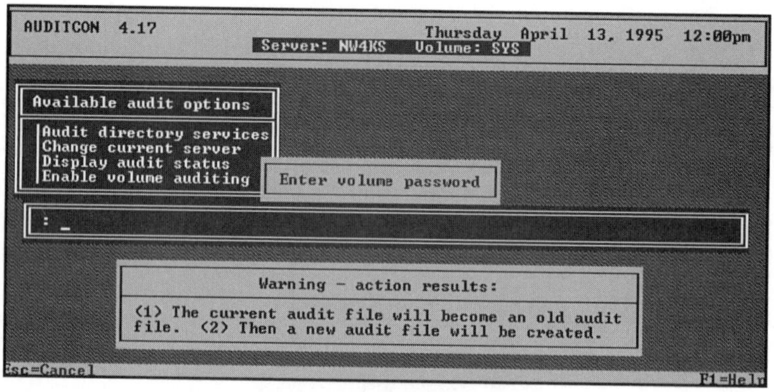

Figure 6.5
The Enable Volume Auditing screen.

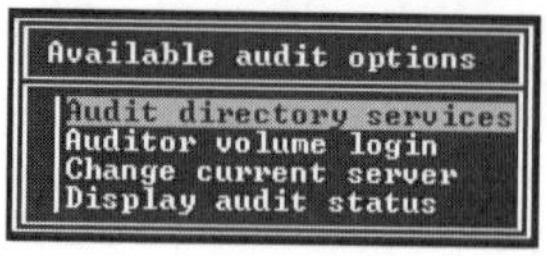

Figure 6.6
The AUDITCON main screen with volume auditing enabled.

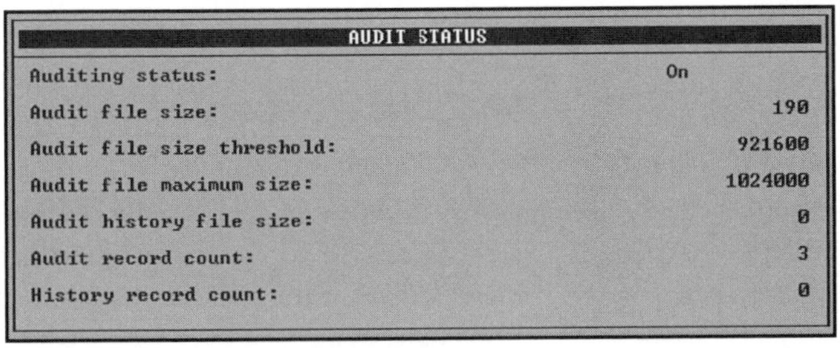

```
                    AUDIT STATUS
  Auditing status:                          On
  Audit file size:                              190
  Audit file size threshold:                 921600
  Audit file maximum size:                  1024000
  Audit history file size:                        0
  Audit record count:                             3
  History record count:                           0
```

Figure 6.7

Display Audit Status when auditing is enabled.

Changing the Audit Password

The network supervisor empowers a user to be an auditor by informing the user about the volume password. The auditor must change the password at the earliest opportunity to maintain independence from the network supervisor. The auditor password must be guarded with care to maintain the independence of the auditor. If the auditor password is forgotten, it cannot be recovered. Disabling of auditing requires knowledge of the auditor password and can only be done using AUDITCON. If this password is forgotten, the only way to disable auditing would be to delete the volume and re-create it.

If the audit password is forgotten, the only way to disable auditing is to delete the volume and re-create it.

The following steps guide you through the process of changing the auditor password:

1. Log in to the network as an auditor user and run AUDITCON.

2. From the main menu of the AUDITCON utility, select Auditor volume login. You are prompted for a password (see fig. 6.8).

3. Enter the password that was initially defined by the network supervisor. This password is needed to gain access to the AUDITCON functions. You should see that the main AUDITCON screen changes (see fig. 6.9) with the following new options:

Figure 6.8

The AUDITCON Auditor Volume Login.

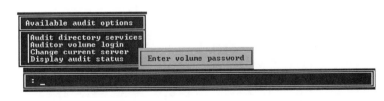

- Audit files maintenance
- Auditing configuration
- Auditing reports

Figure 6.9

The AUDITCON Main Screen after volume login.

Practical TIP After AUDITCON validates the volume login password, the additional options that are available on the AUDITCON main screen are Audit files maintenance, Auditing configuration, Auditing reports, Reports from old offline file, Changing current server, and Displaying audit status.

4. Select Audit configuration from the Available audit options menu. You should see a list of Auditing configuration options (see fig. 6.10).

5. Select Change audit password from the Auditing configuration options menu.

6. You are presented with a screen to enter the current volume password (see fig. 6.11). This is to validate the auditor.

7. You are then asked to enter a new audit password. AUDITCON does not check to see if the password you entered is different from the initial password given to you by the network supervisor.

8. Exit AUDITCON.

Use the new password with AUDITCON.

Figure 6.10

The AUDITCON Auditing configuration options menu.

After the auditor password has been changed, the auditing function can be performed. Some of the common auditing functions are outlined in the following sections.

Figure 6.11
The AUDITCON Change Audit Password option.

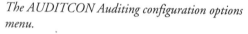

Auditing Configuration Options

The screen for Auditing configuration options is presented to an auditor when the auditor is authenticated by supplying the correct Audit Volume Login password. This menu option presents a number of interesting choices which follow:

■ Audit by event

■ Audit by file/directory

■ Audit by user

■ Audit options configuration

■ Change audit password

■ Disable volume auditing

■ Display audit status

The most important of these configuration options are explained in the following sections.

Audit by Event

The *Audit by event* option enables you to select among four different types of events to be audited (see fig. 6.12). These events are as follows:

■ File events

■ QMS events

■ Server events

■ User events

 The Audit by event option enables you to monitor file events, QMS events, server events, and user events.

Figure 6.12
The Audit by event option.

Audit by File Event

The *File events* option audits file and directory operations such as open/read/write file, create file/directory, and delete file/directory. These events can be monitored on a global basis, by *user or file*, and by *user and file*. *Global* auditing means that the operations will cause the event to be logged, regardless of the user, file, or directory name on the audited volume. Auditing on a *user or file* basis means that the event will be recorded if it applies to an audited user or an audited file. Auditing on a *user and file* basis means that the event will be recorded if it applies to an audited user and an audited file or directory.

The "or" and "and" in these options act as the Boolean logical "or" and "and" operators. These options act as filters and control the amount of audited data that goes into the audit files.

 The File events option audits file and directory operations such as open/read/write file, create file/directory, and delete file/directory.

Selecting an audit event option in the global mode indicates that all occurrences of the event, throughout the volume and regardless of the user who performs them, are recorded.

Auditing on a *user or file* basis means that the event will be recorded regardless of the user who performs them for an audited file, or regardless of the directory where the event occurred for an audited user.

Auditing on a *user and file* basis means that you are recording all occurrences of the event that apply for a specific user and a specific file or directory.

Audit by QMS Events

The *QMS events* option enables auditing of operations that affect the printer queue, such as the creation and deletion of print queues.

 "QMS events" refers to operations such as the creation and deletion of printer queues.

Audit by Server Events

Server events enables you to monitor events such as bringing down the server, restarting the server, or mounting a volume attached to the server. All server events are recorded globally.

 Server events monitor events such as bringing down the server, restarting the server, or mounting a volume attached to the server.

Audit by User Events

User events refers to the creation/deletion of user objects, and user logins and logouts. Trustee assignment changes affecting users are also audited by this event type.

 User events refers to the creation/deletion of user objects, user logins and logouts, and changes in trustee assignments.

Table 6.1 summarizes the Audit by event types.

Audit by File/Directory

When the Audit by file/directory option is selected, you are presented with a list of files and directories in the current directory that can be audited (see fig. 6.13). You can select to audit any of the files and directories in the list. A column next to the file or directory contains the audit status (off or audited). If a file or directory is selected for auditing, an audit record is entered in the NET$AUDT.DAT file whenever an operation is performed on the selected file or directory.

 The Audit by file/directory allows you to select the file or directory to be audited.

The F10 function key can be used to switch the audit status on and off. A dot-dot (..) symbol indicates the parent directory and can be used to "move up" one directory level. In general, pressing Enter when any directory is highlighted allows you to examine the contents of that directory.

 To enable the audit status for a file or directory, you must use the F10 key.

Table 6.1
Audit by Event Types

Event Type	Description
File events	Audits file and directory operations such as open/read/write file, create file/directory, delete file/directory
QMS events	Audits operations such as creating and deleting print queues
Server events	Audits events such as bringing down the server, restarting the server, or mounting a volume
User events	Audits creation/deletion of user objects, and user logins and logouts, trustee assignment changes

```
                            Audit by file/directory
 Ava        ..              (parent)              off
 A          CDROM$$.ROM     (subdirectory)        off
 A     A    CSERVE          (subdirectory)        off
 A     A    DELETED.SAV     (subdirectory)        off
 A     A    DOC             (subdirectory)        off
 A     A    DOCVIEW         (subdirectory)        off
 R     A    ETC             (subdirectory)        off
 C     A    HOME            (subdirectory)        off
 D     C    LANALYZR        (subdirectory)        off
       D    LANSKOOL        (subdirectory)        off
       D    LICENSE         (subdirectory)        off
            LOGIN           (subdirectory)        off
            MAIL            (subdirectory)        off
            MHS             (subdirectory)        off
            MIGRATE         (subdirectory)        off
   ▼        NCDTREE         (subdirectory)        off
```

Figure 6.13
The Audit by file/directory option.

Audit by User

Audit by user gives you a list of users who can be audited (see fig. 6.14). You can select any of the users whom you wish to audit. A column next to the user name contains the audit status (off or audited) for that user. If a user is selected for auditing, an audit record is entered in the NET$AUDT.DAT file whenever that user performs an audited operation. The users in the list in figure 6.14 are bindery emulation users. To audit other users outside the file server's bindery context, you will have to use NDS Auditing. When you do volume auditing by user, it offsets only bindery-emulated users, and the events are stored in the

NET$AUDT.DAT file. When you select NDS Auditing, any users can be audited regardless of the context in which they are defined.

The Audit by user option enables you to select the users to be audited.

The F10 function key is used to switch the audit status for the user on and off.

To enable the audit status for a user, you must use the F10 key.

Figure 6.14

The Audit by user option.

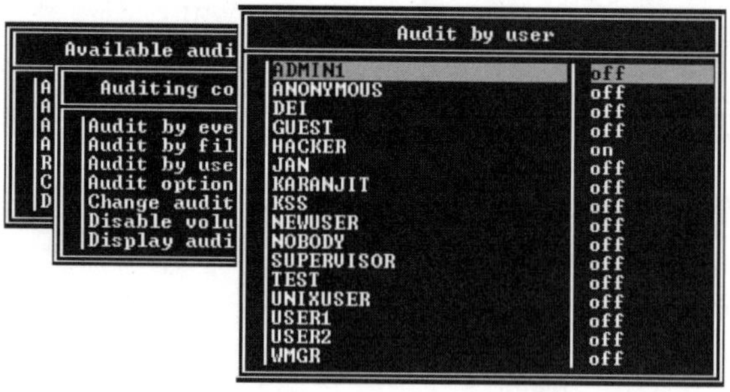

Audit Configuration

The Audit configuration options can be selected from the Available configuration options (see fig. 6.15), and allows the auditor to configure auditing parameters. The auditing parameters are kept in the NET$AUDT.CFG file on the root of the audited volume.

The following parameters can be changed:

- Audit file maximum size

- Audit file threshold size

- Allow concurrent auditor logins

- Broadcast errors to all users

- Force dual-level audit passwords

- Recovery options when audit file is full or unrecoverable write error occurs:

  Dismount volume

  Disable event recording

  Minutes between warning messages

Audit File Maximum Size

The *Audit file maximum size* parameter enables you to enter the NET$AUDT.DAT audit log file size in bytes. The default file size is 1,024,000 bytes.

When the file size is full, it must be reset or deleted. Certain recovery options such as dismounting a volume or disabling event recording can also be triggered when the audit log file gets full. If you want to increase the audit log file size, you should consult with the network administrator; this affects available disk space on a volume.

 The *Audit file maximum size* parameter enables you to control the size of the NET$AUDT.DAT audit log file size in bytes.

Audit File Threshold Size

The *Audit file threshold size* parameter is used to specify the size of the audit log file, which, upon reaching, the system should start sending warning messages. The warning messages are sent at a default interval of three minutes, but can be changed by the *Minutes between warning messages* field. The default value is set to about 90 percent of the *Audit file maximum size*.

 The *Audit file threshold size* is used to specify the size of the audit log file, which, upon reaching, the system should start sending warning messages to the server console.

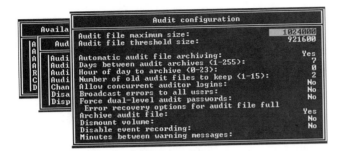

Figure 6.15

The Audit Configuration option.

Allow Concurrent Auditor Logins

The *Allow concurrent auditor logins* parameter, when set to Yes, can be used to allow more than one auditor access to a volume or container. Because audit access is allowed by password, auditors must share the same password. If this value is set to its default value of No, any attempt by a second auditor to log in to a volume or container that is already in use will produce the error in figure 6.16.

 The *Allow concurrent auditor logins* parameter can be used to allow more than one auditor access to a volume or container.

Broadcast Errors to All Users

The *Broadcast errors to all users* parameter sends a message to all attached workstations when the NET$AUDT.DAT file reaches its threshold value defined in *Audit file threshold size*.

Force Dual-Level Audit Passwords

The *Force dual-level audit passwords* parameter implements a second password that must be entered to save configuration or change settings. This second password is in addition to entering the first password for volume or container login for auditing purposes. By default, the *Force dual-level audit passwords* field is set to No.

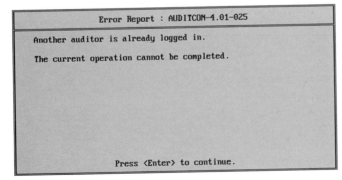

Figure 6.16

Audit error disallowing concurrent usage when Allow concurrent auditor logins is set to No.

When the audit log is full, certain recovery options, such as dismounting a volume or disabling event recording, can be triggered. If the *Dismount volume* field is set to Yes, the volume is automatically dismounted when the audit file is full. The network supervisor will have to remount the volume, at which point you can take actions such as deleting or saving the audit log file and resetting it. Before setting this option to Yes, the auditor should consult the network supervisor because it can cause a serious disruption to users on the network. Unless applications running at the client workstations are written in a robust manner, they can get locked if the volume is dismounted. This option must be selected only if the security requirements of maintaining a complete audit log are more important than the disruption of network applications. By default, the value of the *Dismount volume* field is set to No.

Alternatively, if the audit log file is full, you can set the *Disable event recording* to Yes to stop the recording of any additional audit events. By default, the value of this parameter is set to Yes.

 The *Force dual-level audit passwords* parameter implements a second password that must be entered to save configuration or change settings.

An even better option is the *Archive audit file* option. With this option enabled (set to Yes), if the audit log file is full, the audit file is closed, archived, and replaced by a new audit file. The *Number of old audit files to keep* can be set to control the number of archived audit files to keep. This parameter's value can range from 1 to 15 and has a default value of 2.

The *Minutes before warning messages* is the time in minutes a warning message is sent to the server console (and also attached workstations if

Broadcast errors to all users is set to Yes) when the audit file size reaches the *Audit file threshold size*.

 The *Dismount volume* field allows the dismounting of a volume when the audit log file is full. The *Disable event recording* parameter can be used to stop the recording of any additional audit events when the audit log file is full.

The auditing parameters are kept in the NET$AUDT.CFG file on the root of the audited volume.

Auditing a Network User for a Specific Directory

It is sometimes useful to audit the actions a user can perform. Examples of these operations can be file creation/deletion/read or directory creation and deletion. The following steps outline how a network user can be audited for file read operations in a specific directory called SYS:PAYROLL.

1. Log in to the network as an auditor user and run AUDITCON.

2. From the main menu of the AUDITCON utility, select Auditor volume login.

3. From the main menu select Auditing configuration.

4. From the Auditing configuration, select Audit by event.

5. From the Audit by event menu, select Audit by file events. You should see a screen similar to that in figure 6.17.

   The screen does not show all the operations that can be audited for files and directories. You can use the cursor keys or the PgDn or

```
                    Audit by file events
┌─────────────────────────────────────────────┬──────┐
│ Create directory - global                     │ off  │
│ Create directory - user and directory         │ off  │
│ Create directory - user or directory          │ off  │
│ Delete directory - global                     │ off  │
│ Delete directory - user and directory         │ off  │
│ Delete directory - user or directory          │ off  │
│ File close - global                           │ off  │
│ File close - user and file                    │ off  │
│ File close - user or file                     │ off  │
│ File create - global                          │ off  │
│ File create - user and file                   │ off  │
│ File create - user or file                    │ off  │
│ File delete - global                          │ off  │
│ File delete - user and file                   │ off  │
│ File delete - user or file                    │ off  │
│ File open - global                            │ off  │
└─────────────────────────────────────────────┴──────┘
```

Figure 6.17

The Audit by file events screen.

PgUp keys to examine other entries. Using the PgDn key, you can see the other entries for operations that can be audited (see fig. 6.18). The second screen shows an entry for File read - user and file. This is the entry you must select for auditing a specified user for reading a file in a specified directory. It means that the system will track events that apply to an audited user and an audited file/directory.

6. Selecting File read - user and file can be done by using the F10 key (see fig. 6.19). Answer Yes to save changes.

   Up to this point, you have only turned on auditing for a file event of the type File read - user and file. You must next specify the directory and the user to be audited.

7. Press Esc a few times to go back to the Auditing configuration menu.

8. From the Auditing configuration menu, select Audit by file/directory. You should see a screen similar to that in figure 6.20.

9. Use the cursor keys and the Enter key to select the directory to be audited. Use the F10 key to switch the audit on and off. Figure 6.21 shows the screen after selecting SYS:PAYROLL directory to be audited.

   Press Esc and answer Yes to save changes.

10. Press Esc to go back to the Auditing configuration menu.

11. From the Auditing configuration menu, select Audit by user. You should see a screen similar to that in figure 6.22.

12. Use the F10 key to mark a user for auditing and answer Yes to save changes. Figure 6.23 shows the screen after selecting user HACKER to be audited.

 Study figures 6.17 and 6.18 to see the different types of file events that can be audited.

```
                    Audit by file events
┌─────────────────────────────────────────────┬──────┐
│ File delete - user and file                   │ off  │
│ File delete - user or file                    │ off  │
│ File open - global                            │ off  │
│ File open - user and file                     │ off  │
│ File open - user or file                      │ off  │
│ File read - user and file                     │ off  │
│ File read - user or file                      │ off  │
│ File rename/move - global                     │ off  │
│ File rename/move - user and file              │ off  │
│ File rename/move - user or file               │ off  │
│ File salvage                                  │ off  │
│ File write - user and file                    │ off  │
│ File write - user or file                     │ off  │
│ Modify directory entry - global               │ off  │
│ Modify directory entry - user and file        │ off  │
│ Modify directory entry - user or file         │ off  │
└─────────────────────────────────────────────┴──────┘
```

Figure 6.18

The Audit by file events screen—second screen.

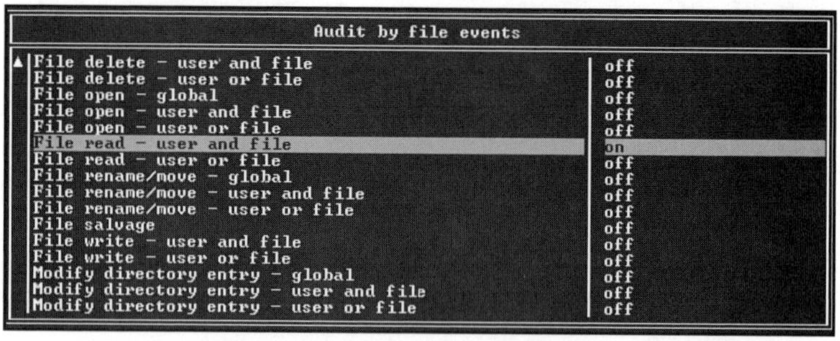

Figure 6.19

Auditing File read - user and file.

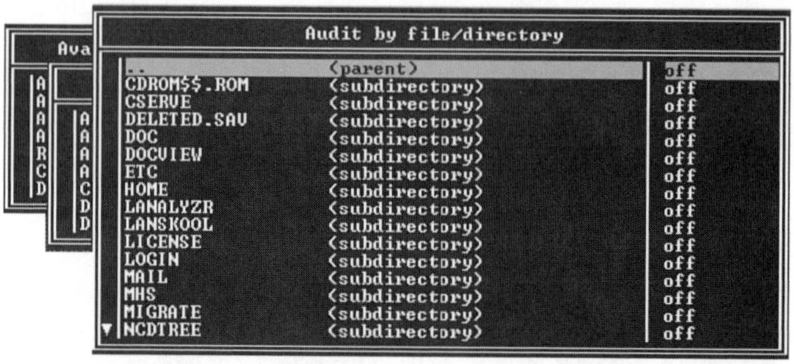

Figure 6.20

The Audit by file/directory for directory selection.

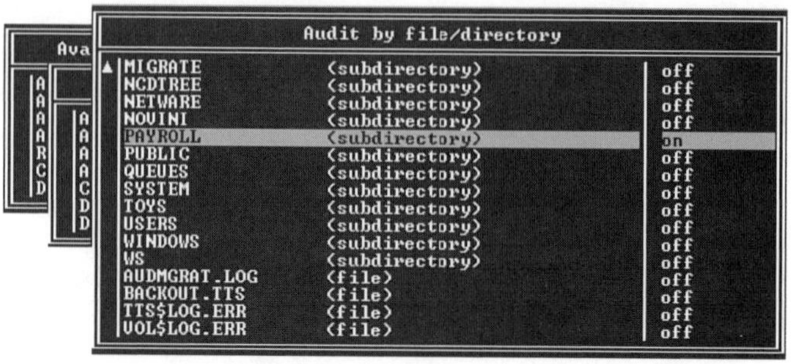

Figure 6.21

An audited directory.

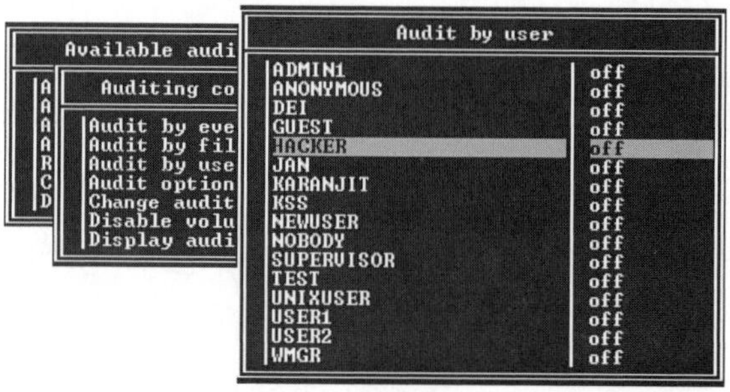

Figure 6.22

A user selection in the Audit by user screen.

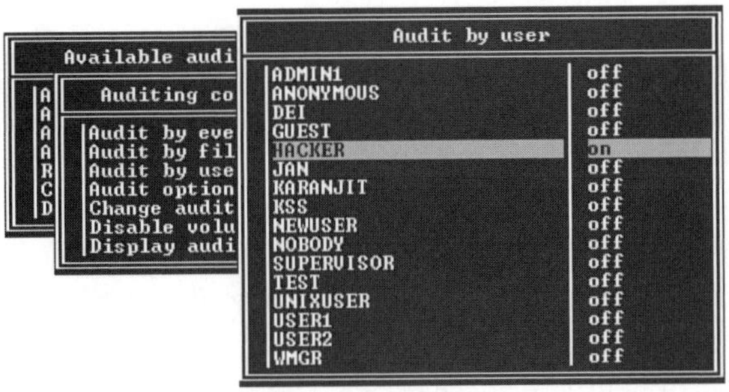

Figure 6.23
An audited user.

Auditing a Specific File

The auditor can flag files and directories to be audited, which is done by performing the steps that follow. The steps show how a particular file can be audited. An example of auditing a file could be to audit all attempts to access an application program executable file, such as NETADMIN.EXE, to find out the frequency of access to this file. This knowledge could be used to determine all users who attempted to access this program file.

1. Log in to the network as an auditor user and run AUDITCON.

2. From the main menu of the AUDITCON utility, select Auditor volume login.

3. You must specify the password for the volume. Select Audit configuration from the main menu.

4. From the Audit configuration menu, select Audit by event.

5. You can audit a specific file by selecting the

File open - user or file option from the Audit by file events menu.

Specifying File open - user or file means that you will track all occurrences of an event when it applies to an audited user or an audited file. In this case, you are interested in an audited file.

Press Esc and answer Yes to save changes.

6. Press Esc a few times to go back to the Auditing configuration menu.

7. From the Auditing configuration menu, select Audit by file/directory. You should see a screen similar to that in figure 6.20.

8. Use the cursor keys and the Enter key to select the directory to be audited. Use the F10 key to switch audit on and off. Figure 6.24 shows the screen after selecting SYS:PUBLIC\NETADMIN.EXE file to be audited.

Press Esc and answer Yes to save changes.

9. Exit AUDITCON.

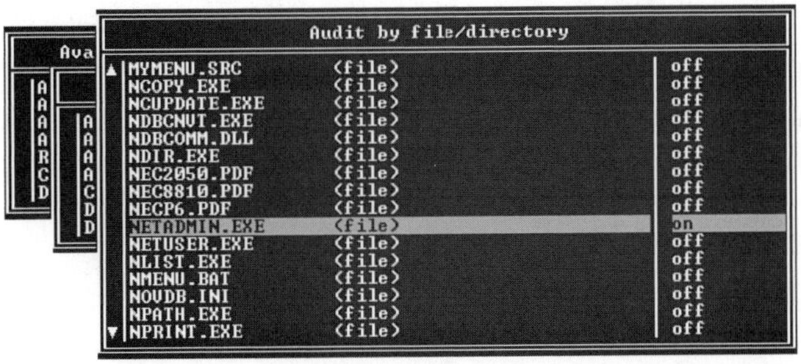

Figure 6.24
The audited file NETADMIN.EXE.

Auditing a Volume for Directory Creations and Deletions

Situations arise where it is useful to audit operations such as the creation and deletion of directories and subdirectories. It might also be useful to audit these events throughout the volume, regardless of the user performing the event. The following steps outline how this can be done.

1. Log in to the network as an auditor user and run AUDITCON.

2. From the main menu of the AUDITCON utility, select Auditor volume login.

3. You must specify the password for the volume. Select Audit configuration from the main menu.

4. From the Audit Configuration menu, select Audit by event, and then Audit by file events. You should see the screen shown in figure 6.17.

5. You can audit creation or deletion of any directory by selecting from the Audit by file events menu the options Create directory - global and Delete directory - global.

   Specifying "global" mode means that you will track all occurrences of an event throughout the volume, regardless of the user.

   Use the F10 key to switch the audit status on and off. Press Esc and answer Yes to save changes.

   Figure 6.25 shows the screen after making the previous selections.

6. Exit AUDITCON.

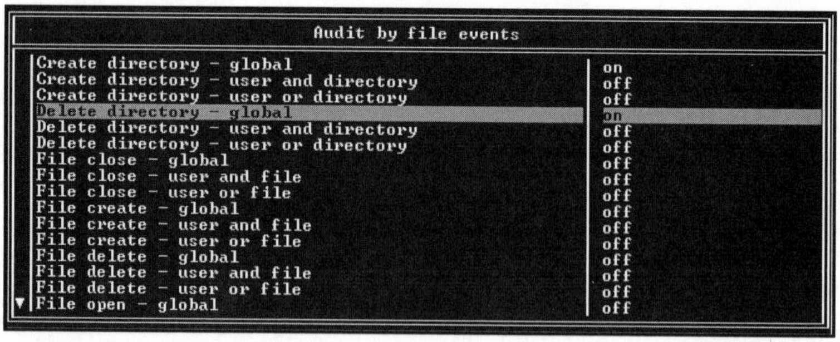

Figure 6.25
Audited create/delete directories.

```
                          Audit by file events
 Create directory - global                        on
 Create directory - user and directory            off
 Create directory - user or directory             off
 Delete directory - global                        on
 Delete directory - user and directory            off
 Delete directory - user or directory             off
 File close - global                              off
 File close - user and file                       off
 File close - user or file                        off
 File create - global                             off
 File create - user and file                      off
 File create - user or file                       off
 File delete - global                             off
 File delete - user and file                      off
 File delete - user or file                       off
 File open - global                               off
```

Auditing the NDS

AUDITCON can be used to keep track of NDS object creation/deletion. The auditor must have Browse object rights to the container that is audited. The following steps outline how the audit password can be changed for a container, and also how a user object can be audited.

1. Log in to the network as an auditor user and run AUDITCON.

2. From the main menu of the AUDITCON utility, select Audit directory services.

3. From the Audit directory service menu, select Audit directory tree. You should see a screen similar to figure 6.26, if your context is set to [Root].

```
                  Audit directory tree
 ..[Root]                        Top
   DSL                           Organization
   ESL                           Organization
   ESL_KSS                       Organization
   IBL                           Organization
   IntCo                         Organization
   MICROCOMM                     Organization
   MICROCONN                     Organization
   SCS                           Organization
   TSL                           Organization
   US                            Country
```

Figure 6.26
The Audit directory tree.

4. Highlight the container that should be audited. In this example, the O=ESL container is selected. Use the F10 key to switch the audit status. You should see a screen similar to figure 6.27 showing the Available audit options.

The *Display audit status* option shows the audit status of the container object. If auditing has not been enabled for this container, you should see the screen in figure 6.28. If the auditing is enabled, you should see a screen similar to figure 6.29.

```
                  Audit directory tree
 ..[Root]                        Top
   DSL                           Organization
   ESL                                       ation
   ESL_KSS    ┌─────────────────────────┐    ation
   IBL        │ Available audit options │    ation
   IntCo      ├─────────────────────────┤    ation
   MICROCOMM  │ Display audit status    │    ation
   MICROCONN  │ Enable container auditing│   ation
   SCS        └─────────────────────────┘ Organization
   TSL                            Organization
   US                             Country
```

Figure 6.27
Available audit options for a container when auditing is disabled.

```
╔══════════════ AUDIT STATUS ══════════════╗
 Auditing status:                    Off
 Audit file size:                            0
 Audit file size threshold:                  0
 Audit file maximum size:                    0
 Audit record count:                         0
```

Figure 6.28
The Audit Status for a container when auditing is disabled.

```
╔══════════════ AUDIT STATUS ══════════════╗
 Auditing status:                    On
 Audit file size:                          792
 Audit file size threshold:              921600
 Audit file maximum size:               1024000
 Audit record count:                        16
```

Figure 6.29
The Audit Status for a container when auditing is enabled.

The Admin user, or a user with Supervisor file system rights, must select the *Enable Container Auditing* option to enable auditing.

5. You are prompted to enter the container password.

6. The Available audit options changes for the audited container (see fig. 6.30).

7. From Available audit options, select Auditor container login.

8. Select Auditing configuration. You should see the Auditing configuration options menu (see fig. 6.31).

9. To change the password, select Change audit password. You are asked to enter the current password. After this, you are asked to enter a new password, and then asked to retype it. The retyping of the password is for verification purposes.

10. From the Auditing configuration menu, select Audit by DS events. You should see the different types of events that can be audited (see fig. 6.32). You might have to use the cursor keys or

the PgDn and PgUp keys to see all of the directory service events that can be audited. Figure 6.33 shows the other DS events.

 Study figures 6.32 and 6.33 to see the different types of DS events that can be audited.

11. To audit the following events, highlight each event and use the F10 key to switch them to the AUDITED status. Figure 6.34 shows that these events have been enabled.

- Change ACL
- Log in user
- Log out user
- Change password

Press Esc and answer Yes to save changes.

12. Exit AUDITCON.

 The auditor must have Browse object rights to the container that is audited.

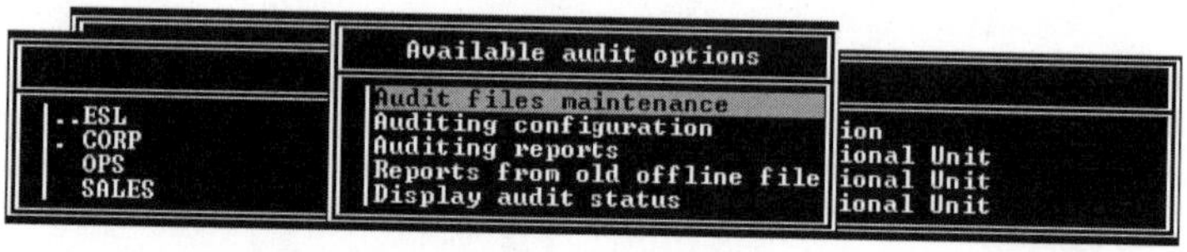

Figure 6.30
Available audit options for a container when auditing is enabled.

Figure 6.31
Auditing Configuration for containers.

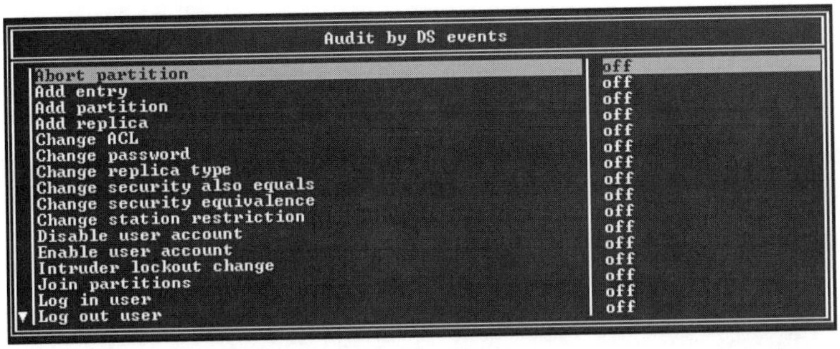

Figure 6.32
Auditing by DS events.

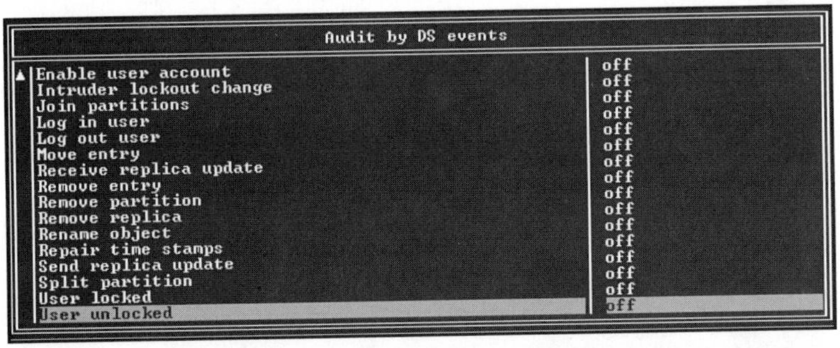

Figure 6.33
Auditing by DS events—second screen.

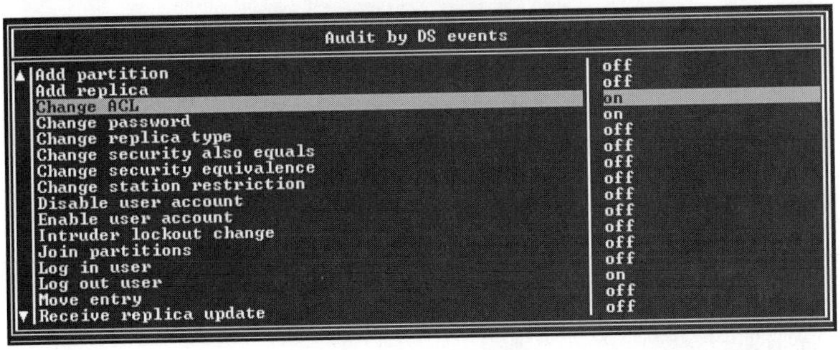

Figure 6.34
Auditing by DS events showing events that are audited.

Generating Audit Reports

The AUDITCON tool has the capability to view the contents of the NET$AUDT.DAT and the AUD$HIST.DAT file through a simple report generation option. The reports are written to a text file and can be printed or stored for safe keeping. Because the report is a text file, you should exercise caution to make sure that ordinary users do not have access to this text file. It is not a good idea, for example, to keep the report in the SYS:PUBLIC directory where users typically have Read and File Scan access rights. It is best to print the file and delete and purge it from the network.

The report option also allows the setting of filters to view selected data. This is useful in situations where large amounts of audit data are generated.

The following steps guide you in generating an audit report.

1. Log in to the network as an auditor user and run AUDITCON. Next log on to Volume Auditing or Directory Services Auditing.

2. From the main menu of the AUDITCON utility, select Auditing reports. You should see a screen similar to that in figure 6.35.

3. You can create new filters by selecting Edit report filters or view the audit log and audit history files. You also can view a filter that you have created previously.

   A later section in this chapter will guide you in creating a filter.

4. To view the Audit file, select Report audit file from the Auditing reports menu.

5. You are asked to enter the file name for the report. You can accept the default name of AUDITDAT.TXT or choose another (see fig. 6.36). The auditor must have [RWCEM] rights to the current directory. These rights are needed because the auditor creates temporary files.

6. You are asked to select a filter. If a filter has not been defined, only the default filter, _no_filter_, will be displayed (see fig. 6.37).

7. To view a report, you can select View audit file from Auditing reports. Figure 6.38 shows an example report.

8. To view the history file, you can select View audit history from Auditing Reports. Figure 6.39 shows an example history report.

9. Exit AUDITCON.

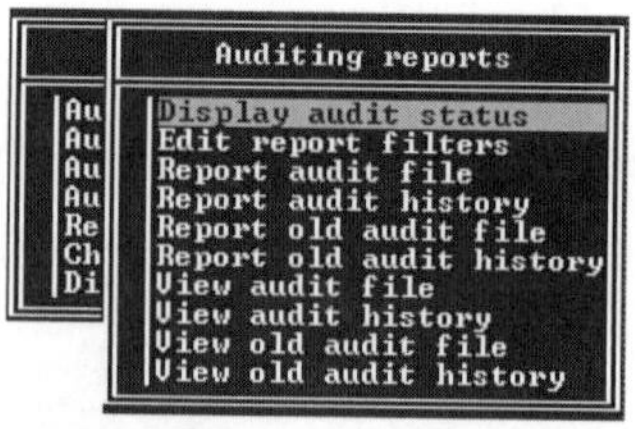

Figure 6.35

Auditing reports.

Figure 6.36

Auditing reports—enter a file name.

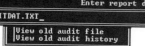

Figure 6.37

The default filter for Auditing reports is _no_filter_.

```
AUDITCON  4.17                        Saturday  April  15, 1995  10:22am
  Server: NW4KS    Volume: SYS                      --- END ---

--- 4-13-1995 ---
12:01:52 Start volume audit file, event 78, NW4KS\SYS
12:01:52 Active connection, event 58, address 000E8022:0080C7D66F0F, status 0,
         user Admin.ESL, connection 3
--- 4-14-1995 ---
00:32:56 Volume dismount, event 56, status 0, user server, connection 0
--- 4-15-1995 ---
09:34:46 Volume mount, event 55, status 0, user server, connection 0
10:16:38 Active connection, event 58, address 000E8022:0080C7D66F0F, status 0,
         user Admin.ESL, connection 4
10:21:36 Create directory, event 75, PAYROLL, access mask 1FF, status 255,
         user Admin.ESL, connection 4
10:21:36 Create directory, event 75, PAYROLL\HIDE, access mask 1FF, status 0,
         user Admin.ESL, connection 4
```

Figure 6.38

Audit reports—viewing audit report.

```
AUDITCON  4.17                        Saturday  April  15, 1995  10:24am
  Server: NW4KS    Volume: SYS                      --- HOME ---

--- 4-13-1995 ---
12:01:52 Start volume audit file, event 78, NW4KS\SYS
12:01:52 Active connection, event 58, address 000E8022:0080C7D66F0F, status 0,
         user Admin.ESL, connection 3
12:01:52 Enable volume auditing, event 65, status 0,
         user Admin.ESL, connection 3
12:05:12 Auditor login, event 59, address 000E8022:0080C7D66F0F, status 0,
         user Admin.ESL, connection 3
12:05:18 Auditor logout, event 66, status 0,
         user Admin.ESL, connection 3
12:06:34 Auditor login, event 59, address 000E8022:0080C7D66F0F, status 0,
         user Admin.ESL, connection 3
12:23:18 Write audit bit map, event 70, status 0,
         user Admin.ESL, connection 3
12:31:46 Write audit bit map, event 70, status 0,
         user Admin.ESL, connection 3
12:38:18 Write audit bit map, event 70, status 0,
         user Admin.ESL, connection 3
12:51:46 Auditor logout, event 66, status 0,
         user Admin.ESL, connection 3
--- 4-15-1995 ---
```

Figure 6.39

Audit history reports—viewing audit history report.

Creating a Report Filter

Because of the large amounts of audit data that can be generated, it is useful to know how filters can be created to select only the audit data of interest. The following steps guide you through creating a simple filter.

1. Log in to the network as an auditor user and run AUDITCON.

2. From the main menu, select Auditor volume login and supply the audit password.

3. From the main menu of the AUDITCON utility, select Auditing reports. You should see a screen similar to that in figure 6.35.

4. You can create new filters by selecting Edit report filters. When a list of filters appears, press Ins. You should see the Edit report filter menu (see fig. 6.40).

You can set a filter using any of the following criteria:

■ Date/time

■ Event

■ Exclude/include paths and files

■ Exclude/include users

5. To select a report by its date and time, select Report by date/time and press Ins (see fig.

6.41). This enables you to select the start date and time and the end date and time for the audit events that are of interest. After you make your changes, press Esc.

Figure 6.42 shows a date and time filter set up from October 1, 1993, 12:00:00 p.m. to October 31, 1997, 11:59:59 p.m.

Press Esc to go back to the Edit report filter menu.

6. To select a report by file events select Report by event (see fig. 6.43). You should be able to set up a filter by file events, QMS events, server events, or user events.

    Figure 6.44 shows the Report by file events. There are two columns against file events. These show the audit status and the report status. By default, an audited event is also reported. In figure 6.44 the File open - user or file and File read - user or file events are audited, and also reported. To switch the report status on or off, use the F10 key.

7. The Report exclude paths/files option and the Report include paths/files option in the Edit report filter menu can be selected to exclude or include information on specific files or directories.

8. The Report exclude users option and the Report include users option can be selected to exclude or include information on specific users. The Report exclude users list is by

default empty, and the Report include users option contains the asterisk (*) entry indicating all users are included. You can use the Ins and Del keys to insert and delete user names from this list.

Figure 6.45 shows that auditing information for only the user HACKER will be presented.

9. After making the filter edits, press Esc a few times. You are presented with an option of saving the filter under a name (see fig. 6.46). Enter a suitable filter name and press Enter.

10. You can test your filter by selecting View audit file from Auditing reports and selecting the newly defined filter.

Figure 6.47 shows an example of a report that uses a filter for looking at information for the user HACKER. Notice that the information is on user HACKER only. Also, in this filter, the File open - user or file event has been filtered out, but the File read - user or file file event has been retained in the filter.

 You can set a report filter using any of the following criteria:

■ Date/time

■ Event

■ Exclude/include paths and files

■ Exclude/include users

Figure 6.40

The Edit report filter menu.

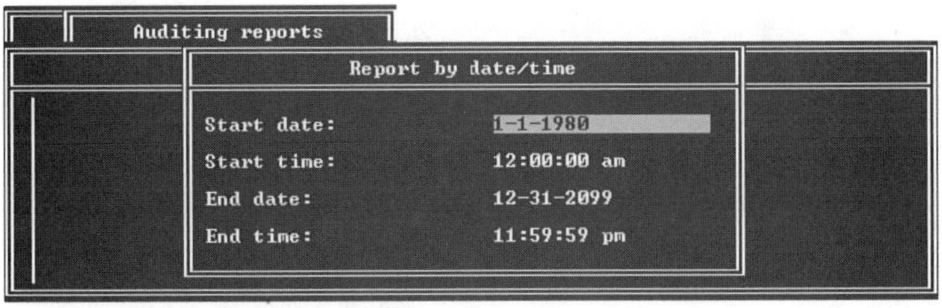

Figure 6.41
Edit report filter—the date and time form.

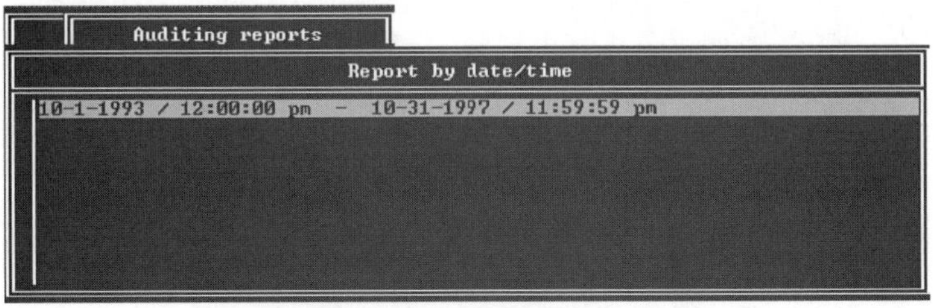

Figure 6.42
Edit report filter—the date and time filter.

Figure 6.43
Edit Report Filter—Report By Event.

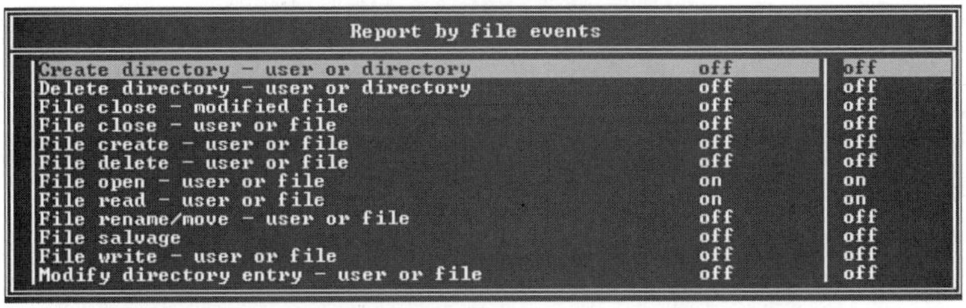

Figure 6.44
Edit report filter—report by file events.

Figure 6.45
Edit report filter—report include users.

Figure 6.46

Edit report filter—saving filter name.

Figure 6.47

Edit report filter—using a filter on a report.

```
AUDITCON  4.17                          Saturday  April  15, 1995  10:46am
 Server: NW4KS    Volume: SYS                               -- PAUSE --
-- 4-15-1995 --
10:44:34 Active connection, event 58, address 000E8022:0080C7D66F0F, status 0,
         user HACKER, connection 4
10:44:34 Create directory, event 75, PAYROLL\STUFF, access mask 1FF, status 0,
         user HACKER, connection 4
10:44:50 Create file, event 12, PAYROLL\STUFF\SECRET, rights RWE, status 0,
         user HACKER, connection 4
10:46:08 Create file, event 12, PAYROLL\STUFF\NO_NAME.ARF, rights RWE, status 0,
         user HACKER, connection 4
10:46:10 Open file, event 27, PAYROLL\STUFF\NO_NAME.ARF, rights RE, status 0,
         user HACKER, connection 4
10:46:10 Read file, event 42, PAYROLL\STUFF\NO_NAME.ARF, length 25, offset 0,
         status 0, user HACKER, connection 4
10:46:12 Create file, event 12, PAYROLL\STUFF\2, rights RWE, status 0,
         user HACKER, connection 4
10:46:12 Create file, event 12, PAYROLL\STUFF\3, rights RWE, status 0,
         user HACKER, connection 4
10:46:16 Open file, event 27, PAYROLL\STUFF\NO_NAME.ARF, rights RE, status 0,
         user HACKER, connection 4
10:46:16 Read file, event 42, PAYROLL\STUFF\NO_NAME.ARF, length 25, offset 0,
         status 0, user HACKER, connection 4
```

Managing Audit Reports

The audit reports are generated as text files. Although the original audit files NET$AUDT.DAT and AUD$HIST.DAT are flagged open and not accessible to non-auditors, the text files can be read by any user who has Read rights to them. For this reason, it is best to print the audit report and delete and purge the original. If an electronic text file of the report is desired, it can be off-loaded onto a floppy disk.

Study Note The audit reports are stored in ASCII text files.

As a security consideration, the audit report text files must not be accessible to non-auditor users.

After printing an audit report, the report text file should be stored offline or deleted and purged from the network.

The following steps outline the procedure to print an audit report:

1. Log in to the network as an auditor user and run AUDITCON. Next, log in to Volume or Directory Services auditing.

2. From the main menu of the AUDITCON utility, select Auditing reports.

3. Select Report audit File or Report audit history from the Auditing reports menu.

4. You are asked to enter the file name for the report. Enter the full path name for the report.

5. Exit AUDITCON.

6. Print the Audit report text file. You can use NPRINT, NETUSER, PCONSOLE, or CAPTURE commands for printing. Alternatively, you can import the text file into a word

processor and use the print function within the word processor.

7. Optionally, you can copy the report file onto a floppy and delete and purge the report file on the network.

Maintaining Audit Files

AUDITCON has options to manage existing audit log files. These options are typically used when the audit log files get full. Using these options, the auditor can move existing audit log files to old audit log files, and reset audit log files.

The following steps outline how this is accomplished:

1. Log in to the network as an auditor user and run AUDITCON.

2. From the main menu of the AUDITCON utility, select Auditor volume login.

3. You must specify the password for the volume.

4. From the Available audit options menu, select Audit files maintenance. You should see the Audit files maintenance menu (see fig. 6.48).

Figure 6.48
The Audit files maintenance menu.

The *Close old audit file* option is used for closing an old audit file so that it can be accessed outside AUDITCON. This option closes the file so that it can be accessed. A user must have appropriate trustee rights to access the closed file.

The *Copy old audit file* option enables you to copy an old audit file. This file is copied as a compressed non-readable file. You can specify the name and the destination of the file. The default name is AUDITOLD.DAT. If you want to copy this file in a readable report format, you can do this by activating the Auditing reports menu and selecting Report audit file.

The *Delete old audit file* option enables you to delete an old audit file. The current audit file is not affected.

The *Display audit status* option enables you to view the audit status on files such as audit file size, audit file threshold, the maximum audit file size, the history file size, the audit record count, and the history record count.

The *Reset audit data file* option moves current data in audit file to the old audit data file. Any data that exists in the old audit data file is overwritten. For this reason, you might want to use the *Copy old audit file* to save the data in the old audit file, before using the *Reset audit data file* option. The Audit data file is reset to zero records and will continue gathering audit events based on the current configuration settings.

 The *Audit files maintenance* option can be used to close and copy old audit files, delete old audit files, display audit status, and reset audit data.

Study Guide for the Chapter

If preparing for the NetWare 3 to 4 Update CNE exams, review this chapter with the following goals:

- Understand and identify the differences between the roles of a network supervisor and the auditor. Understand how the network supervisor enables a user to act as an auditor and the independence between the network supervisor and the auditor. Use the Study Tips for quick review.

- Pay particular attention to details such as the name of the auditing tool, its location, and the names and locations of audit log files. Also, understand the security issues related to the creation of the report text file.

- After studying this chapter, attempt the sample test questions. If you miss the answers to a question, review the appropriate topic until you understand the reason for the correct answer.

Chapter Summary

In this chapter you learned about the auditing capabilities of NetWare 4. The principal tool for auditing is AUDITCON. The AUDITCON can be used for monitoring file system events, QMS events, server events, user events, and NDS events. The differences between these different types of events were described in this chapter. You also learned about the different parameters for audit configuration, such as setting audit file maximum size and specifying which recovery options to select in case the audit file is full.

This chapter also presented an outline of steps to be performed for setting up different auditing scenarios. Toward the end of the chapter you learned about report generation and filter creation for generating reports on selected events.

Chapter Test Questions

Test questions can have a single correct answer or multiple correct answers. Where a single answer is desired, they are indicated by a ○ (circle) notation that precedes the possible answers. Some questions require you to select more than one answer; these are indicated by a □ (box) preceding each answer. Occasionally, you might get a question that asks you to type in an answer. The answer in this case is usually a one word answer. The answer is not case sensitive; you can type in lower- or uppercase.

Certain questions are repeated in different ways so that you can recognize them even when the wording is different. Taking practice quizzes not only tests your knowledge but gives you confidence when you take your exam.

1. The NetWare auditing feature _____.

   ○ A. is the new name for the NetWare accounting feature

   ○ B. exists in NetWare 3 and NetWare 4

   ○ C. is a feature of NetWare 4

   ○ D. is used for login authentication

2. NetWare auditing can be used to _____.

   ○ A. enhance NetWare security

   ○ B. authenticate network users

   ○ C. replace NetWare accounting

   ○ D. validate service passwords

3. Earlier versions of NetWare, such as NetWare 3, _____.

   ○ A. provided the capability to keep track of file/directory access, or changes to the network made by a user

   ○ B. did not provide the capability to keep track of file/directory access, or changes to the network made by a user

   ○ C. provided the capability to keep track of file/directory access, or changes to the network made by a user if the Read Audit flag was set

   ○ D. provided the capability to keep track of file/directory access, or changes to the network made by a user if the Read Audit and Write Audit flag was set

4. The auditor should be _____.

   ○ A. the same as the network supervisor

   ○ B. the same as the console operator

   ○ C. independent of the network supervisor

   ○ D. independent of the network supervisor only if the independent auditor property is set for the NDS volume

5. The auditor should _____.

   ○ A. change the initial audit password assigned by the supervisor but let the supervisor know of the password

   ○ B. not change the initial audit password assigned by the supervisor

   ○ C. change the initial audit password assigned by the supervisor, but the supervisor can then use the NetWare Administrator to discover the changed password

   D. change the initial audit password assigned by the supervisor as soon as possible

6. The network supervisor should _____.

   A. have knowledge of the changed audit password

   B. have knowledge of the changed audit password since it is preferred that the network supervisor should be able to perform auditing functions

   C. not have knowledge of the changed audit password

   D. have knowledge of the changed audit password because the network supervisor can then make backup copies of the audit log file

7. Which of the following is true about network auditing?

   A. Only the network supervisor can enable auditing and set the initial auditing password.

   B. Any user can designate another network user to be an auditor.

   C. Only a user who has Supervisor trustee right to the root of the volume can designate another user as a network auditor.

   D. Only a user who has Supervisor trustee right to the root of the volume, and the Supervisor All Properties right, can designate another user as a network auditor.

8. To assign an auditor, _____.

   A. the network supervisor must use the AUDITUSR tool

   B. the network supervisor must enable auditing on volumes and/or containers

   C. the network supervisor must set the Audit Volume property to Yes using NETADMIN or the NetWare Administrator tool

   D. the network supervisor must set the Audit Volume property list to the users who are assigned as auditors

9. Auditing functions are performed using _____.

   A. AUDITCON

   B. SYSCON

   C. NETADMIN

   D. AUDITUSR

   E. AUDITOOL

10. The AUDITCON.EXE is kept in the _____ directory.

   A. SYS:LOGIN

   B. SYS:ETC

   C. SYS:PUBLIC

   D. SYS:SYSTEM

11. The auditor should have _____.

   A. Read and File Scan access rights to the SYS:SYSTEM directory

   B. Supervisor access rights to the SYS:SYSTEM directory

C. Supervisor access rights to the SYS:PUBLIC directory

D. No access rights to the SYS:SYSTEM directory

12. The auditor can perform which of the following:

☐ A. Assign trustee rights to volumes.

☐ B. Keep track of file system events.

☐ C. Track events such as changes and access to NDS objects and trustee rights.

☐ D. Perform supervisory tasks on the audited volume.

☐ E. Change the audit password.

13. The Display Audit Status option shows _____.

○ A. the status of the audit log file only

○ B. the status of the audit history file only

○ C. the status of the audit files on all volumes

○ D. the status of the audit files on the current volume

14. The option Enable Volume Auditing enables you to _____.

○ A. enable auditing for a specific volume and container

○ B. disable auditing for a specific volume or container

○ C. enable auditing for a specific volume

○ D. disable auditing for a specific volume

15. The audit log file is _____.

○ A. NET$AUDT.DAT

○ B. AUDT$NET.DAT

○ C. LOG$AUDT.DAT

○ D. AUDT$LOG.DAT

16. The NET$AUDT.DAT file is _____.

○ A. flagged open to prevent auditors from accessing the file

○ B. flagged open to prevent non-auditors from accessing the file

○ C. flagged with Rename Inhibit and Delete Inhibit flag to prevent non-auditors from modifying the file

○ D. flagged as Read-Only to prevent non-auditors from writing to the file

17. The AUD$HIST.DAT file is the _____.

○ A. Audit Log file

○ B. Audit Log file and is used to keep track of the history of audited events

○ C. Audit History file and is used to keep track of the auditor's access to the AUDT$NET.DAT file

○ D. Audit History file and is used to keep track of the auditor's access to the NET$AUDT.DAT file

18. The audit log file and the audit history file are kept _____.

○ A. in the SYS:SYSTEM\AUDITLOG directory

○ B. in the SYS:SYSTEM\AUDIT directory

C. on the root of a volume

D. in the SYS:SYSTEM directory

19. What rights must you have to enable auditing on the volume?

A. Supervisor rights to the root of the volume

B. Supervisor equivalent rights

C. Supervisor rights to the volumes All Properties

D. Audit Rights to the volume

20. If the audit password is forgotten, you can disable auditing _____.

A. by disabling it through AUDITCON after you get the password using a tool called AUDTPASS that is available to network supervisors only

B. by disabling it through AUDITCON after you get the password using NETADMIN

C. by deleting the volume and re-creating it

D. by disabling it through AUDITCON

21. The Audit by event option enables you to monitor which of the following?

A. Network events

B. File events

C. Network alerts

D. QMS events

E. Server events

F. User events

22. The File events option audits which of the following?

A. File and directory operations such as open/read/write file

B. Queue creation/deletion

C. Create file/directory

D. User object creation

E. Delete file/directory

23. Selecting an audit event option in the global mode _____.

A. indicates that all occurrences of the event throughout the volume and regardless of the user who performs them will be recorded

B. indicates that all occurrences of the event throughout the volume for a specific user will be recorded

C. means that the event will be recorded regardless of the user who performs it for an audited file, or regardless of the directory where the event occurred for an audited user

D. means that you are recording all occurrences of the event that apply for a specific user and a specific file or directory

24. Selecting an audit event option on a user or file basis _____.

A. indicates that all occurrences of the event throughout the volume and regardless of the user who performs them will be recorded

B. indicates that all occurrences of the event throughout the volume for a specific user will be recorded

C. means that the event will be recorded regardless of the user who performs it for an audited file, or regardless of the directory where the event occurred for an audited user

D. means that you are recording all occurrences of the event that apply for a specific user and a specific file or directory

25. QMS Events auditing refers to operations such as _____.

   A. user object changes

   B. creating and deleting of printer queues

   C. user login and logouts

   D. downing and restarting the server

26. Server events auditing refers to operations such as _____.

   A. user object changes

   B. creating and deleting of printer queues

   C. user login and logouts

   D. downing and restarting the server

27. User events auditing refers to operations such as _____.

   A. user object changes

   B. creating and deleting of printer queues

   C. user login and logouts

   D. downing and restarting the server

28. The Audit by file/directory enables you to _____.

   A. select the directory to be audited

   B. select the file or directory to be audited

   C. select the file to be audited

   D. select the file, directory, or container to be audited

29. To enable the audit status for a file or directory, you must use the _____ key.

   A. F3

   B. Alt+F1

   C. F10

   D. F5

30. The Audit by user option enables you to select the _____.

   A. users whose Audit Property Flag is set to be audited

   B. users to be audited in the server's bindery context

   C. users and group objects to be audited

   D. users, group, or users within a container to be audited

31. To enable the audit status for a user, you must use the _____ key.

   A. F3

   B. Alt+F1

   C. F2

   D. F10

   E. F5

32. The Audit file maximum size parameter enables you to _____.

    ○ A. control the size of the NET$AUDT.DAT audit log file size in bytes

    ○ B. control the size of the AUDT$NET.DAT audit log file size in bytes

    ○ C. specify a size of the audit log file, when the system should start sending warning messages to the server console

    ○ D. specify a size of the audit history file, when the system should start sending warning messages to the server console

33. The Audit file threshold size parameter enables you to _____.

    ○ A. control the size of the NET$AUDT.DAT audit log file size in bytes

    ○ B. control the size of the AUDT$NET.DAT audit log file size in bytes

    ○ C. specify a size of the audit log file, when the system should start sending warning messages to the server console

    ○ D. specify a size of the audit history file, when the system should start sending warning messages to the server console

34. The Allow concurrent auditor logins can be used to enable _____.

    ○ A. any user audit access to a volume or container

    ○ B. no more than three auditors access to a volume or container if the audit files are flagged with the Sharable attribute

    ○ C. more than one auditor access to a volume or container if the audit files are flagged with the Sharable attribute

    ○ D. more than one auditor access to a volume or container

35. The Broadcast errors parameter in the Audit Configuration sends a message _____.

    ○ A. to server consoles only when the AUDT$NET.DAT file reaches its threshold value

    ○ B. to server consoles only when the NET$AUDT.DAT file reaches its threshold value

    ○ C. to all attached workstations when the NET$AUDT.DAT file reaches its threshold value

    ○ D. to all attached workstations when the AUDT$NET.DAT file reaches its threshold value

36. The Force dual-level audit password implements _____.

    ○ A. an alternate password that must be entered to log in to AUDITCON

    ○ B. a second password that must be entered to save configuration or change settings

○ C. a second password that must be entered to log in to AUDITCON

○ D. a second password that must be entered if there is more than one auditor for a volume or container

37. The Dismount volume parameter for audit configuration allows the _____.

   ○ A. stopping of recording audit events when the audit log file reaches a threshold size

   ○ B. stopping of recording audit events when the audit log file is full

   ○ C. dismounting of volume when the audit log file is full

   ○ D. dismounting of volume when the audit log file reaches a threshold size

38. The Disable event recording parameter for audit configuration allows the _____.

   ○ A. stopping of recording audit events when the audit log file reaches a threshold size

   ○ B. stopping of recording audit events when the audit log file is full

   ○ C. dismounting of volume when the audit log file is full

   ○ D. dismounting of volume when the audit log file reaches a threshold size

39. You can set a report filter in AUDITCON using any of the following criteria:

   ☐ A. Date/Time

   ☐ B. Event

   ☐ C. Container

   ☐ D. Exclude/Include Paths and Files

   ☐ E. Directory Tree

40. You can set a report filter in AUDITCON using any of the following criteria:

   ☐ A. Exclude/Include Users

   ☐ B. Event

   ☐ C. Container

   ☐ D. Directory Tree

41. The audit reports are stored in _____ files.

   ○ A. binary

   ○ B. ASCII text

   ○ C. binary compressed

   ○ D. ASCII hidden text

42. The audit report files _____.

   ○ A. can be generated on local drives only

   ○ B. should be accessible to auditor users and network supervisor

   ○ C. must not be accessible to non-auditor users

   ○ D. must not be accessible to auditor users

43. After printing an audit report, _____.

   ○ A. the report text file should be stored offline or deleted and purged from the network

   ○ B. the report text file should always remain on the network

○ C. the report text file should be flagged with the Rename Inhibit attribute flag

○ D. the report text file should be flagged with the Rename Inhibit and Delete Inhibit attribute flags

44. The Audit Files Maintenance option can be used to do which of the following:

☐ A. Close and copy old audit files

☐ B. Close and copy current audit files

☐ C. Delete old audit files

☐ D. Delete current audit files

☐ E. Reset audit data file

☐ F. Display audit status

☐ G. Change audit options

45. Disabling and Enabling of volume auditing is stored in the _____ file.

○ A. NET$AUDT.DAT

○ B. AUDT$NET.DAT

○ C. AUD$HIST.DAT

○ D. HIST$AUD.DAT

46. The auditor must have a minimum of _____ rights to the container being audited.

○ A. Supervisor

○ B. Create

○ C. Create and Delete

○ D. Rename

○ E. Browse

○ F. Browse and Rename

47. The audit configuration changes are kept in the _____ file on the root of the volume being audited.

○ A. NET$AUDT.DAT

○ B. AUDT$NET.CFG

○ C. AUD$HIST.DAT

○ D. HIST$AUD.CFG

○ E. NET$AUDT.CFG

NetWare 4 Printing

NetWare enables you to share printers among a number of users. The printer sharing must be done in a serial fashion. The nature of the print operation is such that an entire print job must be completed before allowing another to start; otherwise, you get an unrecognizable printer output consisting of a mixture of characters from different print jobs. To print jobs in a serial fashion, the jobs might have to wait in a queue.

This chapter describes the printing concepts used in NetWare 4. The properties of print objects, such as Print Queue, Printer, and Print Server, are described in detail. The critical properties needed to configure these objects to provide network printing and the tools used to accomplish these goals are discussed. In addition, the different methods used to print jobs to a network printer are presented.

Network Printing Concepts

In earlier versions of NetWare, the only way a printer could be shared was to attach it to a server. Up to five printers could be attached in this fashion. This type of configuration was called *core print services*. Core print services are still available in NetWare 2.2, but were removed from NetWare 3.*x*. In NetWare 4, there are no core (built-in) print services.

You have to add print services to NetWare 4 before you can enable network printing. The primary tools to add print services are:

- NetWare Administrator Tool
- PCONSOLE

Other support utilities, such as PRINTDEF, PRINTCON, and PSC, still exist in NetWare 4. Because the scope of this book is to describe only the differences between NetWare 3.*x* and NetWare 4, these tools are not described.

 The primary tools used for network print configuration are the NetWare Administrator and PCONSOLE.

To enable printing in NetWare 4, you need the following:

- Printers
- Print queues
- Print servers

Administrators of NetWare 3.*x* networks will recognize that these are the same concepts that were used with NetWare 3.*x*. The big difference here is that these components are objects in the NDS tree.

The objects model physical and logical concepts. Thus the Printer object corresponds to the printer device attached to the network (directly or through a server or workstation). In NetWare 4, you can submit a job to the Printer object. This is done by specifying the NDS name of the Printer object when printing a job. The Printer object contains a logical association with the Print Queue and Print Server object so that the job is processed by the appropriate print server and ends up in the correct network queue.

 The components needed to configure NetWare 4 printing are defined as NDS objects.

 The NDS object classes needed to configure network printing are Print Queue, Printer, and Print Server.

 In NetWare 4, a print job can be sent to the Printer object.

Figure 7.1 shows the physical components of network printing, and figure 7.2 shows the logical components as part of the NDS tree. As displayed in figure 7.1, print jobs submitted by the workstation are processed by the print server, stored in a queue on some storage volume, and then printed to a network printer. These physical print components are represented as objects in the NDS tree in figure 7.2. The print jobs are submitted by the User objects User A and User B, to the Printer object, HP_PRINTER. Printer jobs also can be submitted to the Print Queue object HP_QUEUE, which is the traditional method for printing in NetWare 3.*x*.

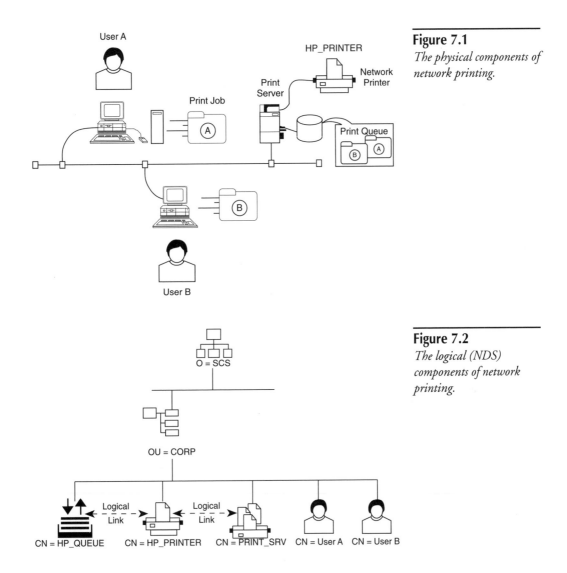

Figure 7.1
The physical components of network printing.

Figure 7.2
The logical (NDS) components of network printing.

If an application does not understand the network Printer objects or Print Queue objects, the CAPTURE command can be used to redirect a local printer to a Printer object or Print Queue object. The CAPTURE command for NetWare 4 contains appropriate options to support this mode of operation.

Print Queue Object

The Print Queue object is a logical representation of the physical print queue. The physical print queue is a directory on a storage volume where the print jobs are kept while they are waiting to be printed. The Print Queue object can be created using the NetWare Administrator or the PCONSOLE utility. The Print Queue object should be placed in the context it is most likely to be used. Figure 7.3 shows the NDS tree where the Print Queue object is placed in the O=SCS container. It is expected that users throughout the SCS organization will have access to the Print Queue object. This includes users in the departments CORP, ENG, and SALES represented by the organizational unit containers. Figure 7.4 shows a Print Queue object in the OU=CORP.O=SCS container. The Print Queue object in this container is expected to be used by users of OU=CORP in the organization O=SCS.

The Print Queue object is a logical representation of the physical print queue.

One of the properties of a Print Queue object is the physical location of the queue. This queue is always located on a storage volume that must be specified at the time of creating the Print Queue object. The print queue is placed in a subdirectory of the QUEUES directory (see fig. 7.5). If the QUEUES

directory does not exist when the queue is created, the QUEUES directory is automatically created.

The Volume property for a Print Queue object is mandatory. It describes the volume that will be used to hold print jobs waiting to be printed.

The print queue is placed as a subdirectory of the QUEUES directory. The QUEUES directory can be on any volume.

Figure 7.6 shows the properties of the Print Queue object. Notice that the Volume property is set to CN=NW4CS_SYS.OU=CORP.O=ESL. The properties, such as Other Names, Description, Location, Department and Organization, are not set when the queue is initially created through PCONSOLE. It is a good practice to set these values to a meaningful description of the Queue object. Figure 7.7 shows that Queue_0 has the authorized print server CN=PS-CORP. OU=CORP.O=SCS and the printer that services

Figure 7.3

The Print Queue object in an organization container.

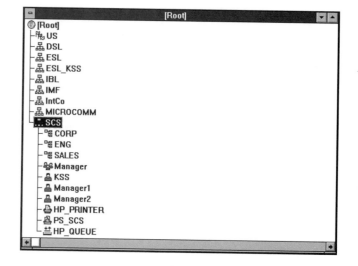

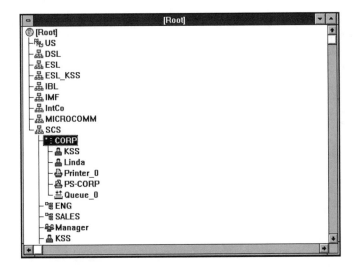

Figure 7.4

The Print Queue object in an organizational unit container.

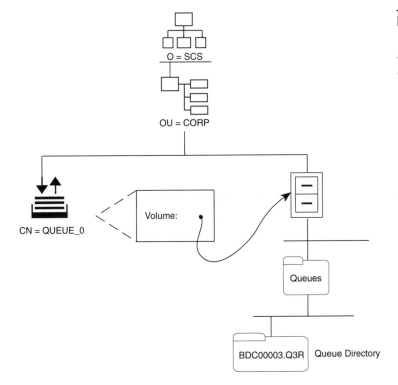

Figure 7.5

The Print Queue object and the QUEUES directory.

Figure 7.6

The Print Queue object properties.

```
┌─────────────────────────────────────────────────────────────────┐
│ ▭                        Print Queue : Queue_0                    │
│ Identification                                                    │
│   ┌───────────────────────────────────────┐  ┌─────────────────┐ │
│   Name:        Queue_0.CORP.SCS           │  │  Identification │ │
│                                            │  └─────────────────┘ │
│   Volume:      NW4CS_SYS.CORP.ESL         │  ┌─────────────────┐ │
│                                            │  │   Assignments   │ │
│   Other Name:  [                    ] ▢▢  │  └─────────────────┘ │
│   Description: [                    ] ▲    │  ┌─────────────────┐ │
│                [                    ]      │  │    Operator     │ │
│                [                    ] ▼    │  └─────────────────┘ │
│                                            │  ┌─────────────────┐ │
│   Location:    [                    ] ▢▢  │  │     Users       │ │
│   Department:  [                    ] ▢▢  │  └─────────────────┘ │
│   Organization:[                    ] ▢▢  │  ┌─────────────────┐ │
│  ┌Operator Flags────────────────────────┐ │  │    Job List     │ │
│  │ ☒ Allow Users To Submit Print Jobs   │ │  └─────────────────┘ │
│  │ ☒ Allow Service By Current Print Servers                      │
│  │ ☒ Allow New Print Servers To Attach  │ │                     │
│  └──────────────────────────────────────┘ │                     │
│   [ OK ]   [ Cancel ]   [ Help ]                                 │
└─────────────────────────────────────────────────────────────────┘
```

this queue is CN=Printer_0.OU=CORP.O=SCS. This shows you how the logical association to the Printer object and Print Server object is made. The Operators property of the Print Queue object is a list of users who can perform administrative tasks on the queue.

Figure 7.8 shows that there is only one operator for the queue named CN=Admin.O=ESL. The Users property of the queue is those users who can send print jobs to this queue. Figure 7.9 shows that these are the users CN=Admin.O=ESL and the container OU=CORP.O=SCS. Assigning a container to the Users property of the print queue means that all users within that container can send print jobs to the queue. This is because of the grouping nature of container objects.

Figure 7.10 shows the queue directories that were created for the Queue objects CN=HP_QUEUE. O=SCS and CN=Queue_0.OU=CORP.O=SCS.

 Study Note Assigning a container object to the Users property of the print queue means that all users within that container can send print jobs to the queue.

In figures 7.7 through 7.10, you can see that the Print Queue object has the following important properties:

- **Volume property.** Used to describe the location of the physical print queue directory.

- **Authorized Print Servers property.** List of print servers that are authorized to use the print queue.

- **Printers Servicing Print Queue property.** List of printers that service the print queue.

- **Operators property.** List of users assigned to manage the queue.

- **Users property.** List of users who can print jobs to the queue.

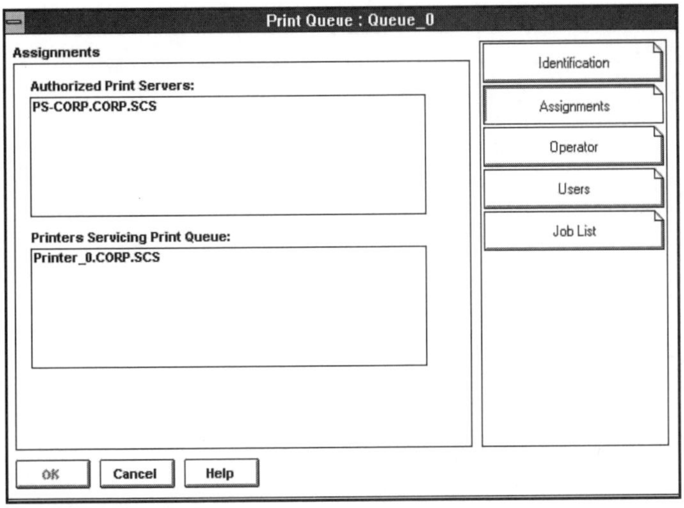

Figure 7.7
The Print Queue object assignments.

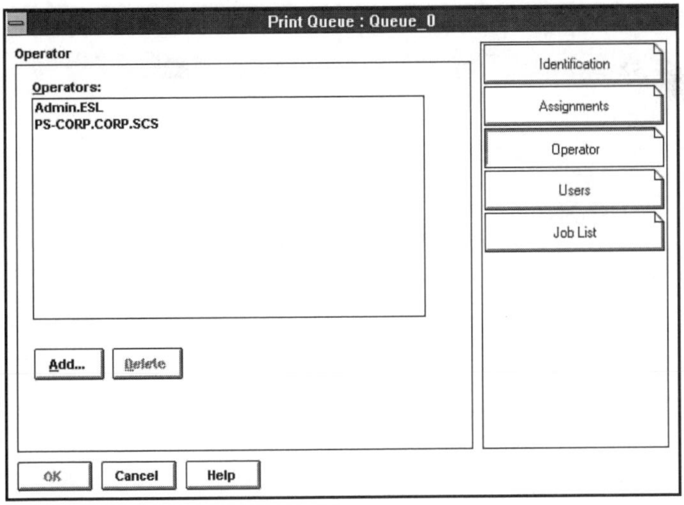

Figure 7.8
The print queue operator.

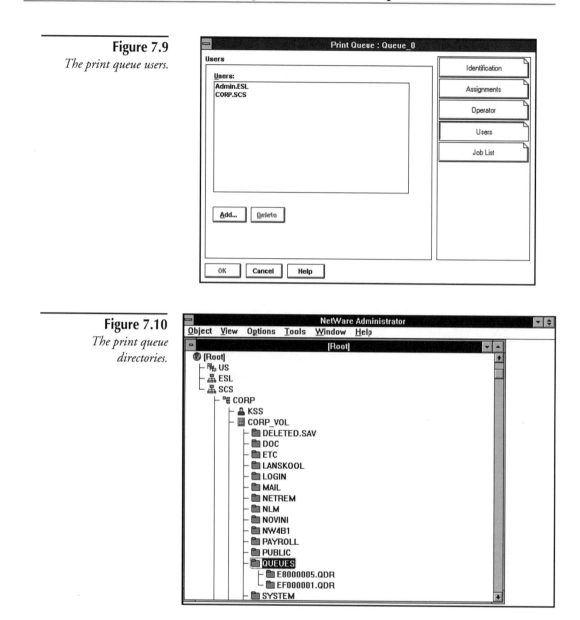

Figure 7.9

The print queue users.

Figure 7.10

The print queue directories.

The Print Job List property of the Queue object can be used to view the print queue jobs (see fig. 7.11). You can see that print jobs are assigned sequence numbers and a Job ID. The print job status, the name of the file being printed, and the form number used are also displayed.

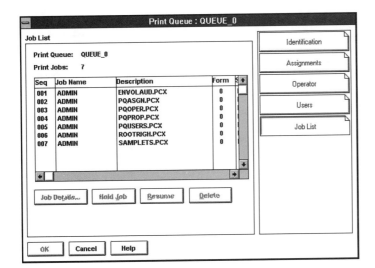

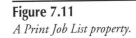

Figure 7.11
A Print Job List property.

Study Note

The Print Job List property of the Print Queue object can be used to view the print jobs in the queue.

Printer Object

The *Printer object* is a logical representation of the physical printer. The physical printer can be directly connected to the network (if it has a network interface), or to a workstation or a file server. The Printer object can be created by using the NetWare Administrator or the PCONSOLE utility. The Printer object should be placed in the context it is most likely to be used.

Figure 7.3 showed the NDS tree where the Printer object is placed in the O=SCS container. It is expected that users throughout the SCS organization will have access to the Printer. This includes

users in the departments CORP, ENG, and SALES represented by the organizational unit containers. Figure 7.4 showed a Printer object in the OU=CORP.O=SCS container. The Printer object in this container is expected to be used by users of OU=CORP in the organization O=SCS.

Figure 7.12 shows the properties of the Printer object. The Name property (Common Name) is the only property that is set on this screen. The other properties, such as Other Names, Description, Location, Department, and Organization, are not set when the queue is initially created through PCONSOLE. It is a good practice to set these values to a meaningful description of the Queue object.

The Printer Features property can be seen by selecting the Printer Features button (see fig. 7.12). Figure 7.13 shows the Printer Features property of CN=Printer_0.OU=CORP.O=SCS.

Figure 7.12

The Printer object properties.

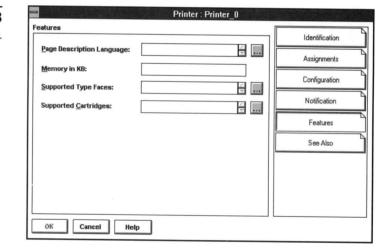

Figure 7.13

The Printer Features.

Figure 7.14 shows the assignments for the Printer_0. The printer is assigned to the print server CN=PS-CORP.OU=CORP.O=SCS (see property Print Server), and the queue CN=Queue_0.OU=CORP.O=SCS is assigned to the Printer object (see property Print Queues). This shows you how the logical association to the Print Server object and Print Queue object is made. There could be several Print Queue objects assigned to the Printer object. One of the Print Queue objects is the default object. If no specific Queue object is specified, the default print queue is used (see property Default Print Queue).

Figure 7.15 shows some of the configuration properties for the Printer object. This shows the Printer Type (LPT1, Serial, AppleTalk, UNIX, AIO, XNP). The Banner Type can be Text or PostScript. The Service Interval shows how often the print server checks the print queue for print jobs assigned to this printer. This can be a value from 1 second to 15 seconds (default). The Buffer Size in K represents how large each segment of print data sent to the printer can be. The buffer size can range from 3 KB to 255 KB and has a default value of 3 KB. The Network Address Restriction shows the network address the printer can use. It can only be used if the printer location is set to Manual mode. The Service Mode for Forms property is used to change forms.

Figure 7.16 shows the notification form for printers. The print job owner is notified of printer status changes.

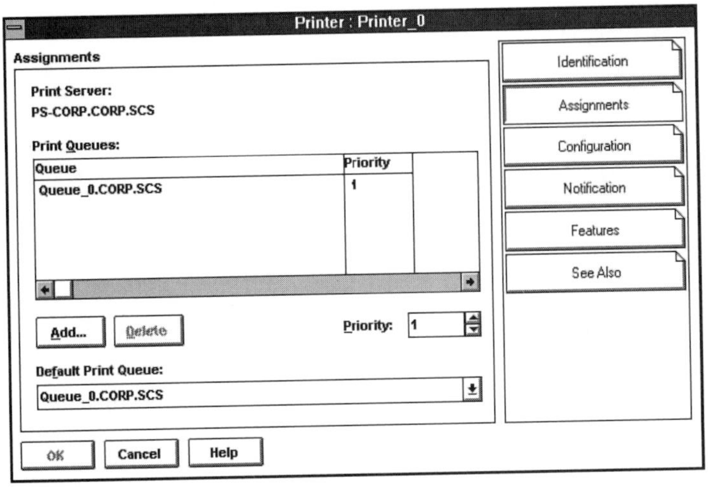

Figure 7.14
The printer assignments.

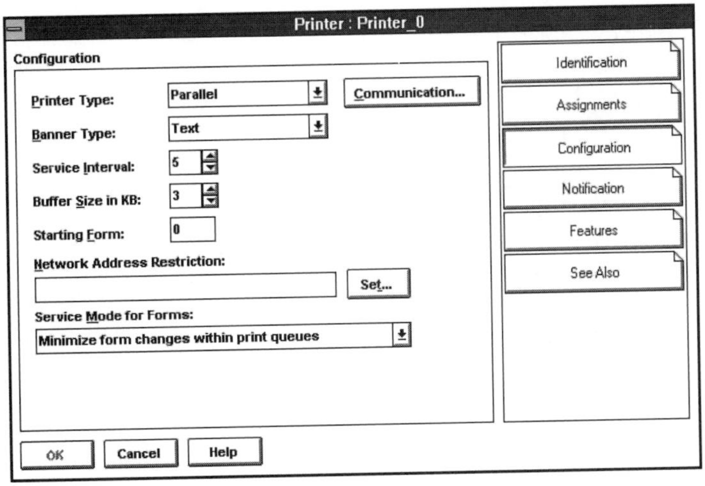

Figure 7.15
Some of the configuration properties for Printer object.

Figure 7.16

The notification properties for Printer object.

```
┌──────────────────────────────────────────────────────────────────────┐
│ ▬                           Printer : Printer_0                        │
│ Notification                                                          │
│ ┌──────────────────────────────────┐        ┌─────────────────────┐  │
│   Notification:                              │    Identification    │  │
│   ┌─────────────────────────┬──────┬──────┐  ├─────────────────────┤  │
│   │ Notify                  │ First│ Next │  │     Assignments     │  │
│   │ (Print job owner)       │  1   │  1   │  ├─────────────────────┤  │
│   │                         │      │      │  │    Configuration    │  │
│   │                         │      │      │  ├─────────────────────┤  │
│   │                         │      │      │  │    Notification     │  │
│   │                         │      │      │  ├─────────────────────┤  │
│   │                         │      │      │  │      Features       │  │
│   │ ←                    →  │      │      │  ├─────────────────────┤  │
│   └─────────────────────────┴──────┴──────┘  │      See Also       │  │
│                                              └─────────────────────┘  │
│   ┌───────┐ ┌────────┐  ┌─Notification Settings─┐                     │
│   │ Add...│ │ Delete │  │ First [in Minutes]:  □│                     │
│   └───────┘ └────────┘  │                       │                     │
│   ⊠ Notify Print Job Owner  Next [in Minutes]:  □│                    │
│                         └───────────────────────┘                     │
│                                                                       │
│   ┌──────┐  ┌────────┐  ┌──────┐                                      │
│   │  OK  │  │ Cancel │  │ Help │                                      │
│   └──────┘  └────────┘  └──────┘                                      │
└──────────────────────────────────────────────────────────────────────┘
```

In figures 7.12 to 7.16, the Printer object has the following important properties:

- **Name property.** The NDS name of the Printer object. It can be used to send print jobs to the printer.

- **Print Server property.** Name of the print server to which the printer is assigned.

- **Print Queues property.** List of print queues that are assigned to Printer object.

- **Configuration property.** Used to match the physical configuration parameters of the printer specification.

- **Notification property.** List of users to be notified about printer problems.

Before describing the last printing object, the Print Server object, you need to understand how this object is used by the print server and the PSERVER.NLM.

 Study Note The Print Server property for a Printer object is set to the print server to which the printer is assigned.

The Print Queues property for a Printer object lists the print queues that are assigned to a Printer object.

The Configuration property of the Printer object must match the physical configuration parameters of the printer.

The Notification property of the Printer object lists the users to be notified about printer problems.

The Print Server and PSERVER.NLM

The Print Server object describes the print server. It is activated by the PSERVER.NLM, and can therefore run on NetWare servers only. This program takes the Print Server object name as a parameter when it is loaded.

```
LOAD PSERVER PrintServerObjectName
```

This command can be run on any NetWare server that is in the NDS tree. The *PrintServerObjectName* is replaced by the complete name of the Print Server object. Thus, to activate the Print Server object CN=PS-CORP.OU=CORP.O=SCS, run the following at one of the NetWare servers, the PSERVER.NLM as shown:

```
LOAD PSERVER .CN=PS-CORP.OU=CORP.O=SCS
```

The PSERVER.NLM is the only type of print server program available from Novell. The PSERVER.EXE of NetWare 3.*x* is no longer supported in NetWare 4.

The PSERVER.NLM can support up to 256 printers. Up to 5 of the 256 printers can be attached to

the server where PSERVER.NLM is run (local printers). The remaining 251 printers can be attached anywhere else on the network (remote printer). These remote printers can be on other NetWare servers, workstations, or directly attached to the network.

 The PSERVER.NLM can support 256 printers: 5 local printers and 251 remote printers.

Figure 7.17 shows the types of printers used with a print server, and figure 7.18 shows the operation of the PSERVER.NLM. The PSERVER.NLM monitors the queue and the printer and directs print jobs in the network print queue to the appropriate network printer.

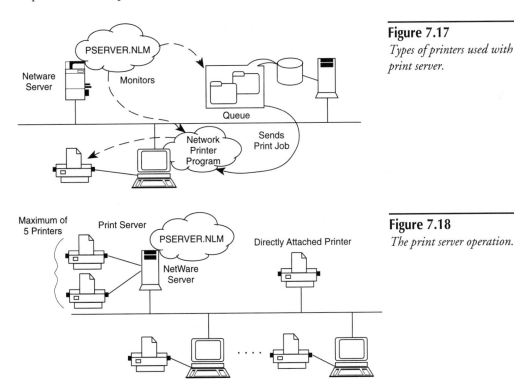

Figure 7.17
Types of printers used with print server.

Figure 7.18
The print server operation.

Earlier versions of NetWare (3.*x*) supported only 16 printers; 5 of the printers could be local and the remaining 11 could be remote.

With this background, you now are ready to understand the properties of the Print Server object.

Print Server Object

The *Print Server object* is a logical representation of the print server program (PSERVER.NLM) running at a server. The Print Server object can be created using the NetWare Administrator or the PCONSOLE utility. The Printer object should be placed in the context it is most likely to be used. Figure 7.3 shows the NDS tree where the Printer object is placed in the O=SCS container. It is expected that users throughout the SCS organization will have access to this Print Server object. This includes users in the departments CORP, ENG, and SALES represented by the organizational unit containers. Figure 7.4 shows a Print Server object in the OU=CORP.O=SCS container. The Print Server object in this container is expected to be used by users of OU=CORP in the organization O=SCS.

Figure 7.19 shows the properties of the Printer object. Besides the Name property (common name), the only property that is set on this screen is the Advertising Name. Server programs in the NetWare environment, such as the PSERVER.NLM that activates a print server from the description in the Print Server object, advertise their existence using the Service Advertising Protocol (SAP). Figure 7.20 shows a packet trace captured using LANalyzer.

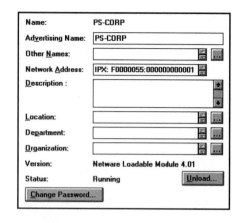

Figure 7.19
The Print Server object properties.

 It is interesting to note that the PS-CORP has a service type of 71. All SAP services are identified by their SAP type value. A well-known service such as the print server has a published value of 71. The NetWare 4 server, on the other hand, has a service type of 263. This is the same type used for NetWare 3.*x* servers. The directory tree name CNET is advertised by server type 632. For more information on how the SAP protocol works, see *NetWare: The Professional Reference* from New Riders Publishing.

 The Advertising Name property of the Print Server object is the name used by the PSERVER.NLM to advertise its existence using the Service Advertising Protocol (SAP).

```
10/12/93                 LANalyzer Network Analyzer            02:52
Press ALT-T to toggle between summary modes           Trace Summary
                       ━━━━━ Trace Buffer ━━━━━
Created On 10/12/93 02:47:53   Elapsed Time 00:00:48   Total Packets     35

   Pkt# Source        Destination  Layer  Highest Layer
↓    1 wstdig034529 wstdig24282D bcast: signature char=bcast message waiting ◄
     2 wstdigDD145C Broadcast      sap: Resp General Service server=PS-CORP
     3 wstdigDD145C Broadcast      sap: Resp General Service server=PS-CORP
     4 wstdig034529 wstdig24282D bcast: signature char=bcast message waiting
     5 wstdig034529 wstdig24282D bcast: signature char=bcast message waiting
     6 wstdig034529 wstdig24282D bcast: signature char=bcast message waiting
     7 wstdig034529 wstdig24282D bcast: signature char=bcast message waiting
     8 wstdig034529 wstdigDD145C  ser: Novell Serialization (Copy Protection)
     9 wstdig034529 wstdig24282D bcast: signature char=bcast message waiting
    10 wstdig034529 wstdig24282D bcast: signature char=bcast message waiting
    11 wstdig034529 wstdig24282D bcast: signature char=bcast message waiting
    12 wstdig034529 wstdig24282D bcast: signature char=bcast message waiting
    13 wstdig034529 wstdig24282D bcast: signature char=bcast message waiting
    14 wstdig034529 wstdig24282D bcast: signature char=bcast message waiting
    15 wstdig034529 wstdig24282D bcast: signature char=bcast message waiting
    16 wstdig034529 Broadcast      sap: Resp General Service server=CNET

F1      F2      F3      F4      F5      F6      F7      F8      F9      F10
Help    Load    Print   Options Save    Decode  Compare Find    Go To   Back
```

Figure 7.20

The print server SAP protocol trace.

The other properties, such as Other Names, Description, Location, Department, and Organization, are not set when the queue is initially created through PCONSOLE. It is good practice to set these values to a meaningful description of the Queue object. The Network Address property is only set when the print server is running. The print server in figure 7.19 is running. This is shown by the Status field and the Version property that reports the version number of the PSERVER.NLM that is running. The Network Address property shows that the print server is at F0000055:000000000001. The F0000055 is the internal network number of the NetWare server on which the PSERVER is running, and 000000000001 is its node address.

The node address for the server on the internal network is always 1.

The Network Address property of the Print Server object is set only when the print server is running and refers to the internal network number and logical network node address of the NetWare servers on which the PSERVER is running.

You can unload the print server by selecting the Unload button (see fig. 7.19). The print server also can be unloaded directly from the NetWare console on which it was loaded or through the PCONSOLE program. The print server password is used to secure access to the Print Server object and can be changed through the Change Password option.

You can unload a running print server by using NetWare Administrator or PCONSOLE, or from the PSERVER.NLM.

The print server assignments are shown in figure 7.21. The Printers property is a list of printers assigned to print servers. The figure shows that there are two printers assigned to the Print Server object PS-CORP. These printers are CN= HP_PRINTER.O=SCS and CN=Printer_ 0.OU=CORP.O=SCS.

Figure 7.22 shows that the Operators property for PS-CORP is set to CN=Admin.O=ESL. This property describes the list of users who can perform administration tasks on the print server. Figure 7.23 shows the Users property for PS-CORP, which is set to OU=CORP.O=SCS. This means that all users in the OU=CORP.O=SCS container can use the print server.

Figure 7.21

The Print Server object assignments.

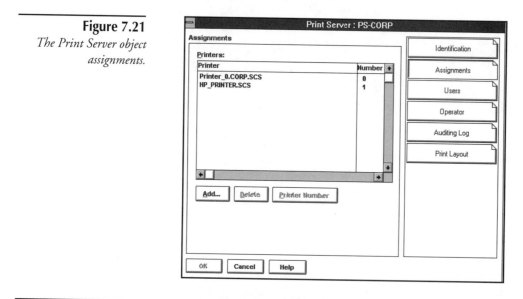

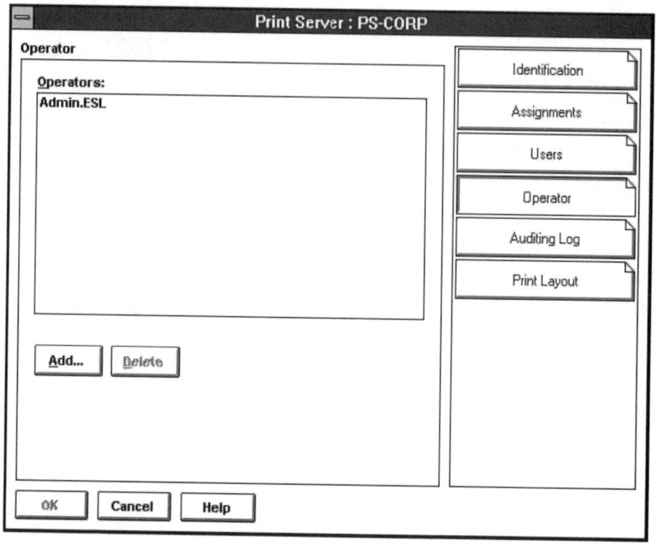

Figure 7.22

The print server operators.

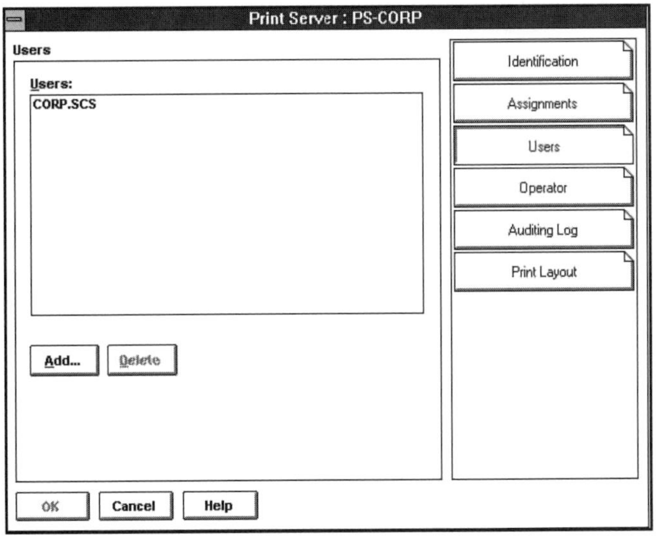

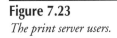

Figure 7.23
The print server users.

From figures 7.19 and 7.21 through 7.23, the Print Server object has the following important properties:

■ **Operators property.** A list of users assigned to manage the print server.

■ **Users property.** A list of users who can use the print server.

■ **Printers property.** A list of printers assigned to the print server.

■ **Password property.** This is used to secure the print server. You need this to manage the PSERVER.NLM running at a NetWare server.

Note that the Print Server object properties are read into the server memory when PSERVER.NLM loads. Any changes made to the Print Server object are not registered with the print server, unless you bring the print server down (unload PSERVER.NLM) and bring it up again (load PSERVER.NLM).

 The Password property of the Print Server object is used to secure the print server.

 Changes made to the Print Server object properties are not registered with the print server, unless you bring the print server down and up again. You can, however, create a print queue and assign it to a Printer object which has already been assigned to an active print server, and print a job through the newly created queue. However, if you assign a new Printer object to the printer's property of a print server, it will not be registered unless you bring the print server down and up again.

Loading of Printer Definition

When the PSERVER.NLM loads, it activates the Printer objects defined in the specified Print Server object's printers property list. If the printer is defined local to the PSERVER.NLM, a program called NPRINTER.NLM is autoloaded to activate any attached local printers (see fig. 7.24). For this reason, printers attached locally to the NetWare Server on which PSERVER.NLM is run are called *autoload printers*. In figure 7.24, you can see that the Printer_0 was loaded successfully, but the second printer failed to load because it also was trying to use interrupt line 7, which was already in use by the first printer. If the second printer was defined on a different port from LPT1, this problem would not exist.

 Study Note Printer definitions that are local to the print server are autoloaded by the NPRINTER.NLM when PSERVER.NLM is run.

Printers that are attached to other NetWare servers or workstations are called *remote printers*. Remote printers must have the NPRINTER program manually loaded on them. For NetWare servers, the NPRINTER program is NPRINTER.NLM, and for workstations, the NPRINTER program is NPRINTER.EXE. Because the NPRINTER program must be manually loaded with remote printers, they are referred to as *manual load* printers.

 Study Note Printer definitions that are remote from the print server must be manually loaded by the NPRINTER.NLM.

NPRINTER.EXE is available for both DOS and OS/2 printers.

Figure 7.24

Load PSERVER.NLM console messages.

```
Loading module PSERVER.NLM
  NetWare 386 Print Server
  Version 4.01    June 14, 1993
  Copyright (c) 1992-1993 Novell, Inc. All rights reserved.
      Loading module NPRINTER.NLM
  NetWare Network Printer Driver v4.01
  Version 4.01    June 30, 1993
  Copyright (c) 1992-1993 Novell, Inc. All rights reserved.
  90 program messages in ENGLISH (language #4) were loaded.
Loading module NPRINTER.NLM
  NetWare Network Printer Driver v4.01
  Version 4.01    June 30, 1993
  Copyright (c) 1992-1993 Novell, Inc. All rights reserved.
  90 program messages in ENGLISH (language #4) were loaded.

Network printer Printer_0 (number 0) loaded
and attached to print server PS-CORP.

NPRINTER-NLM-4.1-10: Interrupt number 7 or the printer port requested
by printer 1 on print server PS-CORP is not available.
(Error code 3)

Network printer not loaded.
NW4KS:
```

The NPRINTER Program

The syntax for loading the NPRINTER program is either of the following statements:

```
NPRINTER [PrintServerObjectName]
➥[PrinterObjectName]
LOAD NPRINTER [PrintServerObjectName]
➥[PrinterObjectName]
```

The first form is used for DOS and OS/2 workstations and the second form is used for loading the printer definition on a NetWare server. Multiple printers can be serviced at the NetWare server by running the LOAD NPRINTER command several times and specifying a different printer number each time.

 The NPRINTER.EXE is used to load remote printers at a workstation.

The NPRINTER.NLM is autoloaded for local printers attached to the print server and must be manually loaded for printers attached to remote NetWare servers.

The *PrintServerObjectName* refers to the Print Server object to which the printer is assigned. Because a Print Server object could have more than one Printer object assigned to it, the second parameter, *PrinterObjectName,* further qualifies the statement by specifying the actual Printer object name. You also can load the printer definition directly by leaving out the Print Server object name. Thus, to

load Printer object CN=HP_PRINTER.O=SCS at a workstation as a remote printer, you can use:

```
NPRINTER  .CN=HP_PRINTER.O=SCS
```

When the print server loads, it assigns printer numbers to all of the Printer object definitions activated by it. Figure 7.25 shows the printer numbers assigned to the Printer objects CN=Printer_0.OU=CORP.O=SCS and CN=HP_PRINTER.O=SCS when the CN=PS-CORP.OU=CORP.O=SCS printer loads. NPRINTER supports an alternative syntax, where the printer number can be used instead of the Printer object name. That is,

```
NPRINTER PrintServerObjectName PrinterNumber
```

 If the NPRINTER command does not work, try using a complete name for the Print Server object name.

The second NPRINTER syntax allows it to be compatible with the NetWare 3.*x* RPRINTER syntax. RPRINTER.EXE that was used in NetWare 3.*x* to set up remote printing is no longer used. Its functionality has been replaced by the NPRINTER.EXE program. You need to load NPRINTER at a workstation or server to set up a remote printer. A *remote printer* is a network printer that is not attached to the NetWare server where the PSERVER.NLM program runs.

Figure 7.25
The Printer List on the print server.

An example of the second type of NPRINTER syntax is

```
NPRINTER .CN=PSERV.OU=CORP.O=ESL 1
```

where the printer number is used instead of the Printer object name. Figure 7.26 shows the effect of executing the preceding command. Notice that the status message says that the HP_PRINTER (printer 1) is installed. The NPRINTER.EXE runs as a TSR.

If NPRINTER is used without any options, it runs as a menu utility.

To unload the NPRINTER.EXE, use the following command:

```
NPRINTER /U
```

To see the status of a printer, use the following command:

```
NPRINTER /S
```

The following list shows the output produced by running NPRINTER /S on a workstation that had NPRINTER loaded in a prior step:

```
NetWare Network Printer Driver v4.01.
(c) Copyright 1988 - 1993, Novell, Inc. All
Rights Reserved.
Print server:      PS-CORP
Printer name:      HP_PRINTER
Printer number:    1
Printer port:      Unknown
Using IRQ:         None (Polled Mode)
TSR status:        Shared Mode
NPRINTER status:   Waiting for Print Job
Printer status:    Out of Paper
```

Figure 7.27 shows a summary of the different types of NPRINTER programs that are possible.

If NPRINTER is used without any options, it runs as a menu utility.

Figure 7.26

Activating a printer with the NPRINTER command.

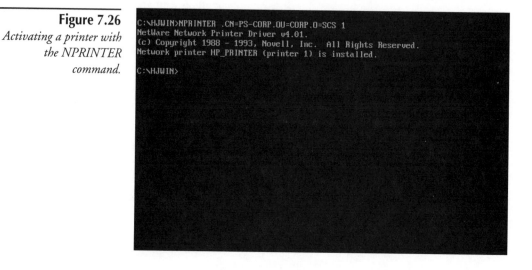

```
C:\HJWIN>NPRINTER .CN=PS-CORP.OU=CORP.O=SCS 1
NetWare Network Printer Driver v4.01.
(c) Copyright 1988 - 1993, Novell, Inc.  All Rights Reserved.
Network printer HP_PRINTER (printer 1) is installed.

C:\HJWIN>
```

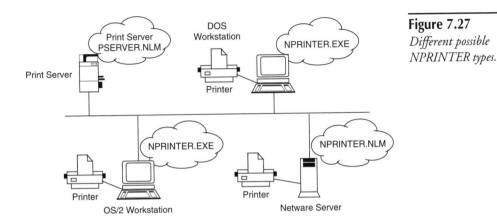

Figure 7.27

Different possible NPRINTER types.

Interactions between Print Queue, Print Server, and Printer Objects

When configuring network printing objects, certain critical properties for each of these objects need to be set up. You saw the use of some of these critical properties in the earlier discussion on Print Queue, Printer, and Print Server objects.

Figure 7.28 shows the important or critical properties for the Print Queue, Printer, and Print Server objects. The print queue is assigned to the Print Queues property of the Printer object, and the Printer object is assigned to the Printers property of the Print Server object. This assignment allows a link to be made between the different printing objects, regardless of their context. That is, the network print configuration objects (Printer Queue, Print, and Print Server objects) can be placed in the same context or a different context. You should, however, try to create them in contexts in which they are most likely to be used.

The diagram in figure 7.28 shows a one-to-one correspondence between the Print Queue, Printer, and Print Server object. This is the simplest and most often used setup. More complex, many-to-one assignments can be made. Figure 7.29 shows that multiple queues can be assigned to a single Printer object, and multiple Printer objects can be assigned to a single Print Server object.

To create the Print configuration objects, you should minimally have the Create object right to the container where these objects will be placed. The quickest way to create these objects is to use the Quick Setup option under PCONSOLE. If you do not have the Create object right (or the Supervisor object right), this option will not be shown on the PCONSOLE menu.

 Study Note To create the Print configuration objects, you should have the Create object right to the container where these objects will be placed.

The quickest way to configure network Printing is to use the Quick Setup option under PCONSOLE.

continues

Figure 7.28
*Setting of Critical
Properties for print objects.*

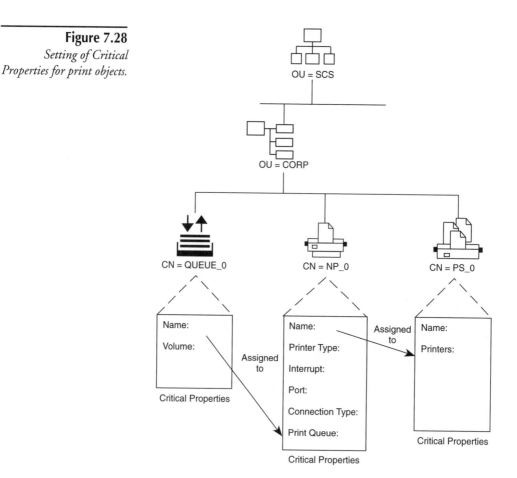

If you do not have the Create object right, the Quick Setup option will not be shown on the PCONSOLE menu.

By default, the creator of the Print objects is made a trustee and given all object rights and property rights to that object. Figure 7.30 shows the trustee rights to object PS-CORP. The creator of the object is Admin.ESL. This user has all rights to Object Rights (Supervisor, Browse, Delete, and Rename) and the All Properties rights (Supervisor, Compare, Read, Write, and Add Self).

 By default, the creator of the Print objects is made a trustee and given all object and property rights to that object.

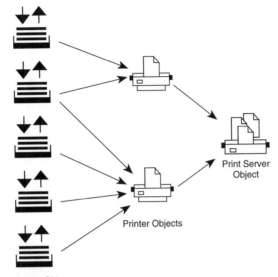

Print Server
Object

Printer Objects

Print Queue Objects

Figure 7.29
Many-to-one relationship between print objects.

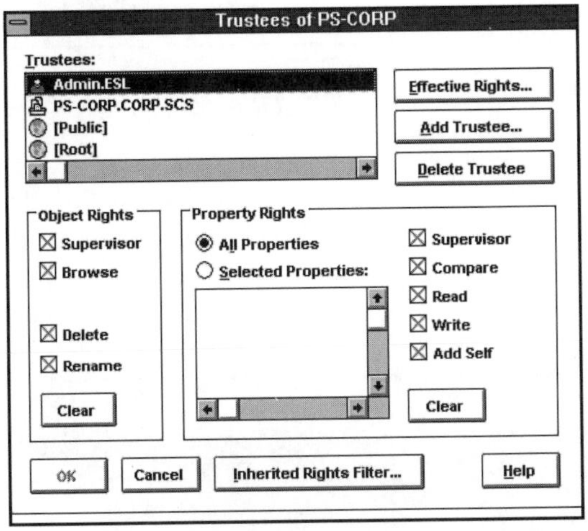

Figure 7.30
Trustee right of owner to Print Server object.

Configuring Network Print Services

As mentioned earlier, the primary tools for configuring network services are PCONSOLE and Network Administrator. But only PCONSOLE has the Quick Setup option. The other options in PCONSOLE are the same as in the PCONSOLE for NetWare 3.*x*, only they have been modified to work with NDS objects.

If you use the NetWare Administrator tool to create Print objects, you have to make sure that their critical properties are defined, and also the logical links between them are properly defined.

The NETADMIN.EXE program cannot be used to create Print objects. You also cannot use this tool to view or edit properties of Print objects. Figure 7.31 shows that the Queue object Queue_0 cannot be edited or viewed using NETADMIN.

The PCONSOLE Utility

Now you will be given a guided tour on implementing network Printing using the PCONSOLE

utility. You will create print queues, Printer objects, and Print Server objects, and configure them.

1. Log in as an Admin user, and run PCONSOLE. You can log in as another user as long as you have Create, Delete, and Browse privileges to the container where you are creating the print objects. Should you want to rename any print objects you create, you also might want to have Rename object rights to leaf objects in the container.

   When you run PCONSOLE, the screen shown in figure 7.32 appears.

Figure 7.32
The PCONSOLE main menu.

2. Select Change Context from PCONSOLE, and change your context to the container where you want to place the print objects. In this guided tour, the container name is

Figure 7.31
Attempt to view/edit Queue object from NETADMIN.

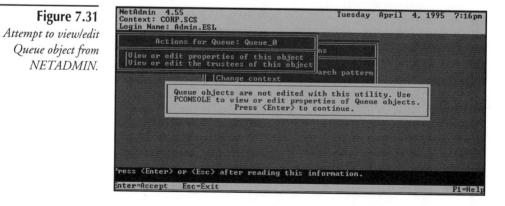

OU=CORP.O=ESL_*XXX*. If you are practicing using PCONSOLE, you might want to create an organization with a similar name. Substitute any characters for *XXX* so that you can experiment with different organization trees. You can always delete these trees later.

You can see your context reported on the top half of the PCONSOLE screen.

3. Select Print Queues from Available Options. You should see a list of Print Queue objects defined in the OU=CORP.O=ESL_*XXX* context. The list initially should be empty, unless you have already created Print Queue objects in this container (see fig. 7.33).

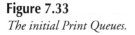
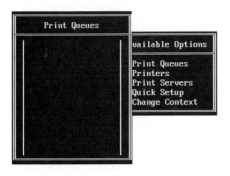

Figure 7.33
The initial Print Queues.

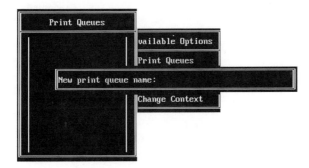

4. Press Ins to create a Queue object. A screen appears asking you to enter the new queue name (see fig. 7.34).

5. Enter the name of the Print Queue object as QUEUE_1. (You can choose any other name, but for the purpose of this exercise it is referred to as QUEUE_1.) A screen appears asking you to enter the queue's volume (see fig. 7.35). The queue has to be placed on a volume object. It is created as a subdirectory (with the name of the *Print Queue ID*) under the QUEUES directory.

6. Enter the name of a volume object. (For the purpose of this exercise, the volume name is referred to as CORP_VOL.) You can use the volume object name on your NetWare 4 server, or create an alias in your current context to the server volume, name it CORP_VOL and use this name. If you use an alias name for the volume object, PCONSOLE replaces it with the name of the aliased volume object.

You also can press Ins and browse through the NDS directory tree, searching for the volume to place the queue on.

After you enter the volume name to use with the Print Queue object, the newly created Print Queue object appears in the Print Queues list (see fig. 7.36).

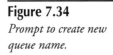

Figure 7.34
Prompt to create new queue name.

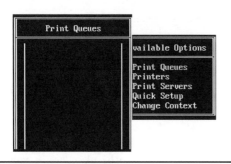

Figure 7.35
Entering a queue's Volume name.

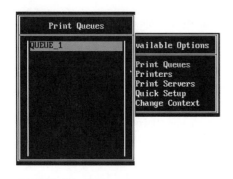

Figure 7.36
A newly created queue in the Print Queue list.

7. Create a Printer object. Press Esc to return to the main PCONSOLE menu.

   Select Printers from Available Options. You should see a list of Printer objects defined in the OU=CORP.O=ESL_*XXX* context. The list initially should be empty (see fig. 7.37).

8. Press Ins to create a Printer object. A screen appears asking you to enter the new printer name (see fig. 7.38).

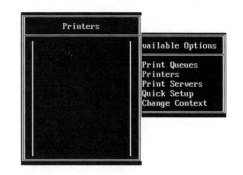

Figure 7.37
The initial Printer list.

9. Enter the name of the Printer object as PRINTER_1. (You can chose any other name, but for the purpose of this exercise, it is referred to as PRINTER_1.) The newly created Printer object appears in the Printers list (see fig. 7.39).

10. Select the Printer object that you created from the Printers list. A Printer Configuration screen appears (see fig. 7.40).

11. Assuming that you have a parallel printer, configure the printer as follows. If you have a serial printer, use one of the COM*x* ports.

Printer Type:	Parallel
Configuration:	Port: LPT1
Location:	Manual Load or Autoload
Interrupt:	7
Address restriction:	No
Print Queues Assigned:	Assign QUEUE_1 to this printer

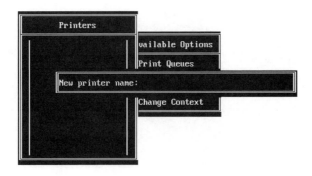

Figure 7.38
Prompt to create new printer.

You should use F10 to save your configuration information. When you assign the Queue object that you created earlier, you will select the print queues assigned: (See list) field from the Printer Configuration screen. This list can be viewed by pressing Enter. You will see a Print Queue list. Press Ins and select the name of the Queue object. You also can browse the directory tree to look for Queue objects by selecting the .. (parent) entry. After you select the entry, a screen similar to figure 7.41 appears.

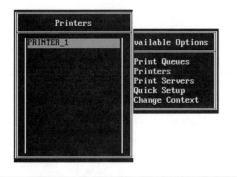

Figure 7.39
Newly created printer in the Printers list.

The priority column displays the priority for jobs in queue. You can select the queue name entry to change its priority from 1 (highest) to 10 (lowest).

The state column displays codes that have the following meaning:

A = Printer is actively servicing the queue

C = Printer is configured to service this queue

D = This is the default print queue

Press Esc to return to the configuration screen. In the print configuration screen, you can also select the Notification field to select the users/ groups that should be notified when there is a printer problem. The default Notification list contains the Print job owner value.

12. Save printer configuration changes by using F10.

    Return to the main Available Options menu.

13. The last step is to create a Print Server object.

    Select the Print Servers option from the Available Options menu.

Printer PRINTER_1 Configuration
Print server: (None)
Printer number: (None)
Printer status:
Printer type: Parallel
Configuration: (See form)
Starting form: 0
Buffer size in KB: 3
Banner type: Text
Service mode for forms: Minimize form changes within print queues
Sampling frequency: 15
Print queues assigned: (See list)
Notification: (See list)

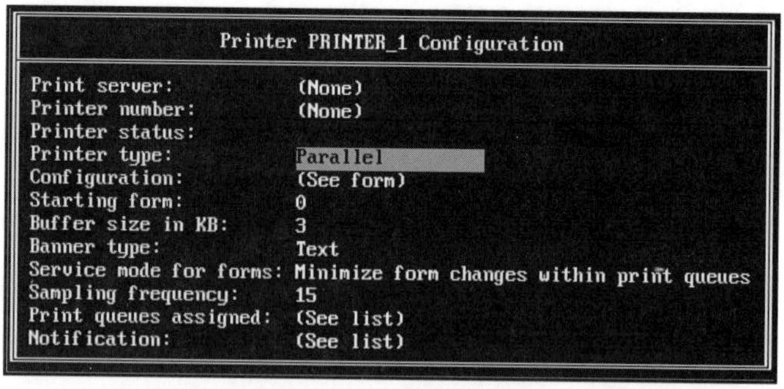

Figure 7.40
The Printer Configuration screen.

Print Queue
Priority State
QUEUE_1
1 [C][D]

Figure 7.41
Print Queue Priority and State.

You should see a list of Print Server objects defined in the OU=CORP.O=ESL_*XXX* context. The list should initially be empty (see fig. 7.42).

Print Servers
vailable Options
Print Queues
Printers
Print Servers
Quick Setup
Change Context

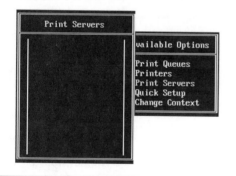

Figure 7.42
The initial Print Servers list.

14. Press Ins to create a Printer object. You should see a screen asking you to enter the new print server name (see fig. 7.43).

15. Enter the name of the print server as PSRV_1 (or any other print server name). You will see a message that you should wait while the Print Server object is being created, after which you should see the newly created Printer object in the Print Servers list (see fig. 7.44).

16. Your next step is to configure the Print Server object. Select the Print Server object you have created from the Print Servers list. You should see a list of Print Server Information options (see fig. 7.45).

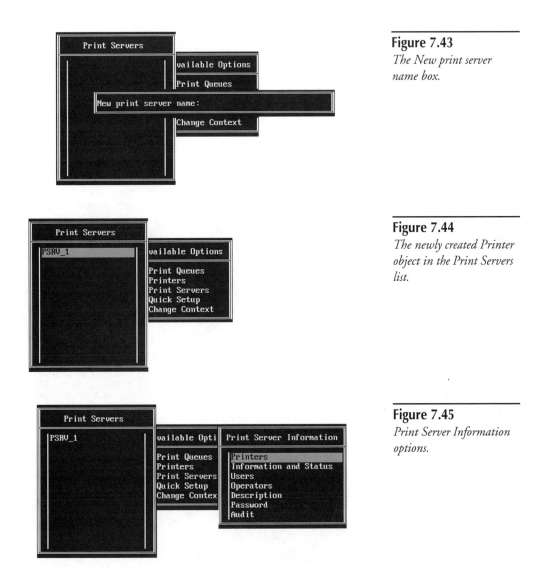

Figure 7.43
The New print server name box.

Figure 7.44
The newly created Printer object in the Print Servers list.

Figure 7.45
Print Server Information options.

17. Select the Printers option from the Print Server Information list. You should see a list of Serviced Printers. Initially the list should be empty.

    Press Ins. You should see a list of Printer objects that can be assigned to the print server (see fig. 7.46). You also can browse through the NDS structure to locate the desired Printer object.

18. Select the Printer object you created earlier (PRINTER_1) and assign it to the print server. You should see a list of serviced Printer objects that are assigned to the print server (see fig. 7.47).

You can assign up to 256 Printer objects to a Print Server object. If you need to assign more than 256 printers, define another Print Server object.

19. Return to the main Available Options menu by pressing Esc a few times. You have created a Print Queue, Printer, and Print Server object and configured them properly.

The next step is to load the print server (PSERVER.NLM) on a server.

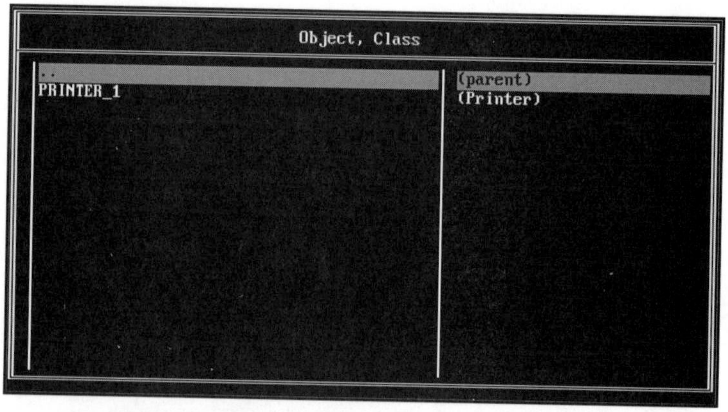

Figure 7.46
Printer objects list.

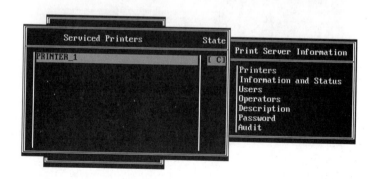

Figure 7.47
Printers assigned to print server.

The LOAD PSERVER Command

The syntax for the PSERVER command is as follows:

```
LOAD PSERVER PrintServerObject
```

To load the PSERVER.NLM for the Print Server object CN=PSRV_1.OU=CORP.O=ESL_XXX that you created in the previous section, use the command:

```
LOAD PSERVER .CN=PSRV_1.OU=CORP.O=ESL_XXX
```

When the PSERVER.NLM loads, you should see a list of Available Options for the PSERVER.NLM (see fig. 7.48). Selecting Printer Status should show the list of printers that are defined for the Print Server object (see fig. 7.49). Selecting any of the printers listed shows the printer status (see fig. 7.50). Selecting Print Server Information from Available Options shows the print server information and status (see fig. 7.51).

Figure 7.48
The PSERVER main screen.

Figure 7.49
The PSERVER Printer List.

```
Printer:    CN=Printer_0.OU=CORP.O=SCS
Type:       Automatic load (Local), LPT1
                                              Printer control

Current status:  Waiting for job

Queues serviced:  (See list)
Service mode:     Minimize form changes within print queues
Mounted form:     0

NetWare server:
Print queue:
Print job ID:
Description:
Print job form:

Copies requested:              Finished:
Size of 1 copy:                Finished:
Percent complete:
```

Figure 7.50
PSERVER Printer Status.

```
         Print Server Information and Status
Version:           4.10.c
Type:              Netware Loadable Module
Advertising name:  PS_0
Number of printers: 2
Queue service modes: 4
Current status:    Running
```

Figure 7.51
Changing printer server status.

You can change the Current Status field in the Print Server Information (see fig. 7.51) from Running to Unload to unload the print server immediately. If you want to wait until all print jobs are finished before unloading the print server, you can set Current status field to Unload after active print jobs.

 To activate the print server you must run the PSERVER.NLM at a NetWare 4 server and give it the name of the print server as a parameter.

Examining Print Server Status Using PCONSOLE

The PCONSOLE can be used to monitor print server status, also. The steps to perform this are outlined as follows:

1. Start PCONSOLE and change context to where the print server is defined.

2. Select Print Servers from Available Options.

3. Select a print server to examine from the list of print servers.

4. Select Information and Status from the Print Server Information menu.

You should see a screen showing Print Server Information and Status (see fig. 7.52). Comparing figure 7.52 with 7.51, you can see that they present the same type of information.

Quick Setup Configuration

The Quick Setup information option in PCONSOLE can be used to create in a single step a Print Queue, Printer, and Print Server object that have all of their critical properties defined. The print objects are created to have the proper logical links between themselves. This means that the Print Queue object is assigned to the Printer object's Print Queues list property, and the Printer object is assigned to the Print Server object's Printers list property.

 The Quick Setup option in PCONSOLE can be used to create in a single step a Print Queue, Printer, and Print Server object that have all of their critical properties defined.

The print objects that are created have default names of Q1 for Print Queue objects, P1 for Printer objects, and PS-*container* for the Print Server object. The *container* in the print server name PS-*container* is the name of the container in which the print server is defined. At the time of

Figure 7.52

The PCONSOLE Print Server Information and Status screen.

```
             Print Server Information and Status
 ┌──────────────────────────────────────────────────────────┐
 │ Print server type:    386 Loadable Module                │
 │ Print server version: 4.0.1                              │
 │ Number of printers:   2                                  │
 │ Current server status: Running                           │
 │ Advertising name:     PS-CORP                            │
 └──────────────────────────────────────────────────────────┘
```

creation of these objects, you can change the default names to any other names (as long as they do not conflict with leaf names of other objects in the container).

Quick Setup will also make assumptions about the printer properties. For the Printer object it defines the following property values.

Banner type: Text

Printer type: Parallel

Location: Auto Load (Local)

Interrupt: None (polled mode)

Port: LPT1

The Banner type can be Text or PostScript. The Text setting is used to print NetWare's standard print banner. If your printer uses the PostScript language and you want your printer to print a PostScript banner, you can use the PostScript setting.

These values can be modified during Quick Setup, but they should match your physical printer configuration.

 Any of the default parameters of Quick Setup can be modified at the time of creating print objects using Quick Setup.

 If you want to set up a remote printer, use the Manual Load value for the Location.

You will now be presented with a guided tour on using the Quick Setup Option of PCONSOLE.

1. Log in as an Admin user and run PCONSOLE.

2. If your context is not OU=CORP.O =ESL_*XXX* where *XXX* is replaced by your group identity, select Change Context and change your context to where you want to create the print objects.

3. Select Quick Setup from Available Options.

If your context is a container, such as [Root], where print objects cannot be created, you will not see the Quick Setup option in the Available Options menu.

After selecting the Quick Setup option, you should see the Print Services Quick Setup screen (see fig. 7.53).

4. Change the names of these objects to whatever names you want to use.

5. Change printer configuration to match your needs.

The printer location at Auto Load (Local) means local printer, and at Manual Load means remote printer.

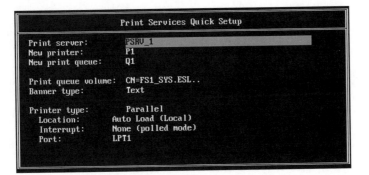

Figure 7.53
The Print Services Quick Setup screen.

Sending a Print Job

After the network printing is set up, you can submit print jobs using the following tools:

- NETUSER
- CAPTURE
- NPRINT
- PCONSOLE
- NWUSER

NETUSER is a menu-driven tool that can be used to perform common network-related tasks such as network printing, messaging, drive mappings, and attaching to other servers. This is a new tool that was first introduced with NetWare 4.

NPRINT and CAPTURE are commands that take a number of options and can be used for sending a print job to a network printer or queue.

NWUSER is the Windows-based graphical user tool. It can be used for sending print jobs as well as network-related tasks such as messaging, drive mapping, and attaching to servers.

 If you redirect your job to the printer, the name of the default queue for the printer appears in the NETUSER screen and not the name of the printer.

 Network print jobs can be sent using

- NETUSER
- CAPTURE
- NPRINT

- PCONSOLE
- NWUSER

These printing tools will be briefly examined next.

Printing Using NETUSER

Figure 7.54 shows that one of the options available to NETUSER is Printing. Selecting the Printing option shows you a list of available printer ports local to your workstation. You can select any of these ports for network redirection. After selecting a port, you are given a choice of examining Print Jobs or redirecting the selected port by using Change Printers (see fig. 7.55). You cannot examine print jobs on a printer port that has not been captured (redirected to a network printer).

Figure 7.54
NETUSER options.

After selecting Change Printers, you are given a list of printers and queues in the current context. If no printers or queues are shown, you can use Ins to browse the NDS tree. Figure 7.56 shows that a queue, Queue_0, and a printer, Printer_0 NDS, objects were found in the context OU=CORP.O=SCS. You can select either the Printer_0 or the Queue_0 object to direct the network print jobs.

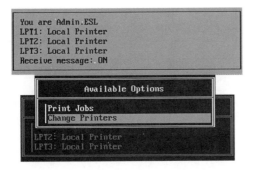

Figure 7.55
Changing printers with NETUSER.

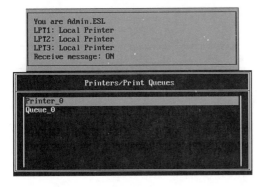

Figure 7.56
The Printers/Print Queues list.

After redirecting a local printer, the Available Ports menu in NETUSER will show the queue name the port is redirected to (see 7.57). You can now select the Print Jobs option to send a print job to the network queue. From this point on the procedure for sending print jobs is similar to that for PCONSOLE. That is, you can press Ins and browse directories for files to print.

NETUSER can be used to redirect a local printer port to a network queue or network printer, and send print jobs.

Figure 7.57
Available Ports showing printer redirection.

Printing Using CAPTURE

The CAPTURE command is used to redirect a local printer port to a network queue or network printer. Table 7.1 shows the CAPTURE options. Option abbreviations are shown in bold. Therefore, the option **EndCap** can be abbreviated as **EC**.

The **P**rinter=*name* option can be used to specify the network Printer object name to send print jobs to.

The ENDCAP command is no longer used with NetWare 4. Instead CAPTURE has a new **EndCap** option to stop printer redirection. To stop the capture of local printport LPT1:, you can use:

```
CAPTURE EndCap
```

or

```
CAPTURE EC
```

To stop printer redirection for all local printers, you can use the **EndCap ALL** option:

```
CAPTURE EndCap ALL
```

or

```
CAPTURE EC ALL
```

Table 7.1
CAPTURE Options

Option	Description
SHow	Shows current status of local printer ports. Used as an option by itself.
Printer=*name*	Specifies network printer to which redirected print jobs should be sent to. If *name* is a complete NDS name with embedded blanks, quotes can be used.
Local=*n*	Redirects local LPT port *n*. This option cannot be used on the NPRINT command.
Queue=*name*	Indicates Queue object to which print job should be sent.
End**C**ap	Ends redirection to local ports.
End**C**ap **ALL**	Ends redirection of all local printer ports.
CReate=*path*	Sends print job to file *path*.
Keep	Retains print job in queue, if workstation fails.
Job=*jc*	Specifies print job configuration to use. No need to specify other options.
NoBanner	Suppresses printing of banner page.
Banner=*name*	Prints banner page. Limit is 12 characters for banner *name*. Appears in lower half of page.
NAMe=*name*	Default is name of file being printed. Indicates text in upper part of banner page. Limit is a 12-character name.
Form=*n*	Specifies form number or name that is to be used for print job.
Copies=*n*	Specifies number of copies for print job (1 - 255).
Tabs=*n*	Number of spaces to use for a tab character.
No **T**abs	Suppresses tab expansion to space characters.
TImeout=*n*	Number of seconds to wait before closing job.
Form **F**eed	Generates a form feed character at end of print job.
No **F**orm **F**eed	Suppresses form feed character at end of job.
AUtoendcap	Captured data should be closed and sent to printer on exiting application.
NoAutoendcap	Captured data should *not* be closed and sent to printer on exiting application.
NOTIfy	Specifies that user receive notification of print job completion.

Option	Description
No**NOTI**fy	Specifies that user not receive notification of print job completion.
/?	Help.
/? ALL	Displays all help screens.
Verbose	Provides detailed information on command as it is executed.

The CAPTURE command is used to redirect a local printer port to a network queue or network printer.

The ENDCAP command is no longer used with NetWare 4. Instead CAP-TURE has a new **E**nd**C**ap option to stop printer redirection.

Printing Using NPRINT

To print a job using NPRINT, use the following syntax:

```
NPRINT     filename [option]
```

The *option* can be replaced by any of the options in table 7.2.

Table 7.2
NPRINT Options

Option	Description
Server=*name*	Specifies a non-NDS server (bindery server) whose bindery contains the print queue definition.
Printer=*name*	Specifies network printer to which redirected print jobs should be sent. If *name* is a complete NDS name with embedded blanks, quotes can be used.
Local=*n*	Redirects local LPT port *n*.
Queue=*name*	Indicates Queue object to which print job should be sent.
Job=*jc*	Specifies print job configuration to use. No need to specify other options.
No**B**anner	Suppresses printing of banner page.
Banner=*name*	Prints banner page. Limit is 12-characters for banner *name*. Appears in lower half of page.
NAMe=*name*	Default is name of file being printed. Indicates text in upper part of banner page. Limit is a 12-character name.

continues

Table 7.2, Continued
NPRINT Options

Option	Description
Form=*n*	Specifies form number or name that is to be used for print job.
Copies=*n*	Specifies number of copies for print job (1-6500).
Tabs=*n*	Number of spaces to use for a tab character, or can be from 1 to 18.
No **T**abs	Suppresses tab expansion to space characters.
Form **F**eed	Generates a form feed character at end of print job.
No **F**orm **F**eed	Suppresses a form feed character at end of job.
NOTIfy	Specifies that user receive notification of print job completion.
No**NOTI**fy	Specifies that user not receive notification of print job completion.
/?	Help.
/? ALL	Displays all help screens.
Verbose	Provides detailed information on command as it is executed.

Printing Using PCONSOLE

To print using PCONSOLE, select the Print Queues option from Available Options in PCONSOLE. If the print queue you want to print to is not displayed, use Change Context to change context to the container that has the Queue object.

After selecting the Queue name from the Print Queues list you will see a menu on Print Queue Information. Select Print Jobs option. You should see the jobs in the current queue. Press Ins, type a directory name to print from and press Enter. You should see a list of files in the current directory that you can select for printing (see. fig. 7.58). Select the files that you want to print. You will be given a choice of Print Job Configurations to use for printing. If no print job configurations have been defined for the current container, you can select the (Defaults) print job configuration. Figure 7.59 shows a default configuration for printing a file. You can modify any of the default values, and press F10 to save your changes and send print job to the selected queue.

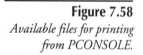

Figure 7.58

Available files for printing from PCONSOLE.

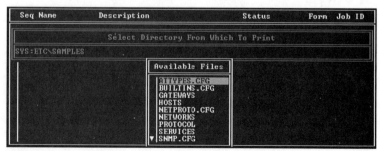

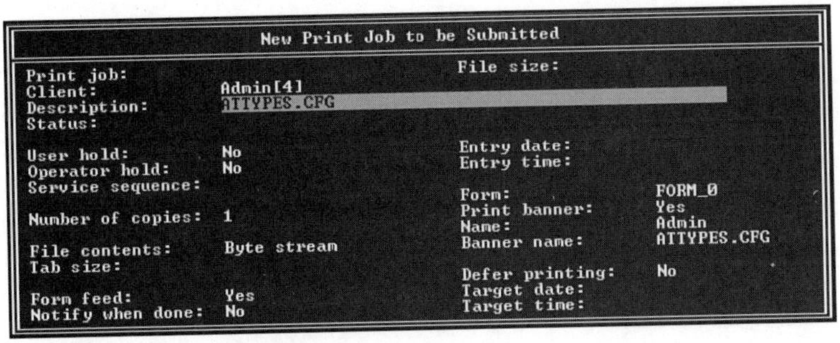

Figure 7.59
A default print job.

Network Printing Tools

Table 7.3 shows the list of network printing tools that are available for NetWare 4. The PCONSOLE, PSERVER, NPRINTER, and NWADMIN

(Network Administrator) have been discussed so far. The PRINTCON and PRINTDEF tools will be discussed briefly.

Table 7.3
Network Printing Tools

Program	*Extension*	*Executed On*	*Used For*
PCONSOLE	.EXE	Workstation	Creating and configuring print servers, print queues, and Printer objects
PRINTCON	.EXE	Workstation	Creating and configuring print job configurations
PRINTDEF	.EXE	Workstation	Defining print forms, importing and exporting print device definitions
PSERVER	.NLM	Server	Activates the Print server object
NPRINTER	.EXE	Workstation	Allows network printer attached to a station to be shared
NPRINTER	.NLM	Server	Allows network printer attached to a server not running PSERVER.NLM to be shared

continues

Table 7.3, Continued
Network Printing Tools

Program	Extension	Executed On	Used For
NWADMIN	.EXE	Workstation	GUI utility to perform printer management functions
PSC	.EXE	Workstation	Command-line utility to control and see status of printers and print servers
PUPGRADE	.NLM	Server	Used to upgrade NetWare 3.1x print environment to NetWare 4

 Be familiar with the functions of each of the print utilities described in table 7.3.

NetWare 4 offers PRINTCON and PRINTDEF for print job configuration. The print job configuration can be used as the Job Configuration parameter in CAPTURE and NPRINT to simplify the options by aggregating them under a print job configuration template. It is also used when submitting jobs to a queue using the Print Job option in NETUSER and PCONSOLE.

The PRINTCON Utility

Figure 7.60 shows the main menu for PRINTCON. Edit Print Job Configurations is used to create new print job configurations. Select Default Print Job Configuration allows you to select the print job configuration that will be used as a default. Change Current Object allows you to change the container object or User object for which the print job configuration will be defined.

Print job configurations are stored as the Print Job Configuration property of an Organization, Organizational Unit, or User object. If stored in a container, all users within the container can use the print job configuration. If the print job configuration is stored as a property of a User object, only that user can make use of the print job configuration.

 Print job configurations are stored as the Print Job Configuration property of an Organization, Organizational Unit, or User object.

PRINTCON can operate in the directory mode (default) or the bindery mode. F4 can be used to toggle between these two modes. This allows the NetWare 4 PRINTCON to be used with the NetWare 3.x bindery. In NetWare 3.x print job configurations are stored in the bindery.

Details of the PRINTCON operation are not presented, as they are similar to NetWare 3.x's PRINTCON and are beyond the scope of this book.

Figure 7.60
The PRINTCON main menu.

The PRINTDEF Utility

Figure 7.61 shows the main menu for PRINTDEF. The Print Devices option is used to modify printer definitions for print devices. The Print Forms option allows you to create and modify printer form definitions. The Change Current Context option allows you to change the container object for which the form definition will be defined.

Figure 7.61
The PRINTDEF main menu.

Print device definitions and forms are stored in the Print Devices and Print Forms property of the container object. If stored in a container, all users and print job configurations within the container can use the print device definition.

PRINTDEF can operate in the directory mode (default) or the bindery mode. F4 can be used to toggle between these two modes. This allows the NetWare 4 PRINTDEF to be used with the NetWare 3.*x* bindery. In NetWare 3.*x* print device definitions are stored in the bindery.

 Print device definitions and forms are stored in the Print Devices and Print Forms property of the container object.

Details of the PRINTDEF operation are not presented, as they are similar to NetWare 3.*x*'s PRINTDEF and are beyond the scope of this book.

 F4 can be used to toggle between directory and bindery modes for PRINTCON and PRINTDEF.

The PUPGRADE Utility

The PUPGRADE NLM is run at the server and upgrades the NetWare 3.1*x* print environment to NetWare 4. The following is a brief outline on using PUPGRADE.

1. From the server console, type the following command:

   LOAD PUPGRADE

   You will be prompted to enter the Admin name and password.

2. After being authenticated, you will see the main PUPGRADE menu (see fig. 7.62).

Figure 7.63
The PUPGRADE main menu.

The Upgrade PRINTCON Databases option is used to upgrade NetWare 3 print job configurations to the NetWare 4 directory services environment.

The Upgrade PRINTDEF Database option is used to upgrade NetWare 3 print device definitions and forms to the NetWare 4 directory services environment.

The Upgrade Print Servers and Printers option is used to upgrade NetWare 3 print servers and printers to the NetWare 4 directory services environment.

3. Select the Upgrade Print Servers and Printers option.

4. Select the bindery print server to upgrade.

5. Exit PUPGRADE (Alt+F10).

Study Guide for the Chapter

If preparing for exams, review the chapter with the following goals:

■ Remember the names and understand what each printing utility covered in this chapter does. Use the Study Notes as a quick review.

■ Pay particular attention to PCONSOLE and Quick Setup.

■ After studying this chapter, attempt the sample test questions. If you miss the answers to a question, review the appropriate topic until you understand the reason for the correct answer.

Chapter Summary

This chapter described the basic printing concepts used in NetWare 4. The properties of print objects, such as Print Queue, Printer, and Print Server objects, were covered in detail. To configure network printing, the critical properties of these objects must be set correctly. Network print configuration can be done by using either PCONSOLE or the NetWare Administrator. Use of the PCONSOLE tool to configure printing using the Quick Setup and the step-by-step approach were presented in detail.

Sending print jobs on the network can be done by using NETUSER, CAPTURE, NPRINT, PCONSOLE and NWUSER. These methods and the options available within them were discussed.

Chapter Test Questions

Most of the test questions are multiple choice. When a single answer is desired, that is indicated by a ○ (circle) notation that precedes the possible answers. Some questions require that you select more than one answer; these are indicated by a ☐ (box) preceding each answer. Occasionally, you might get a question that asks you to type in an answer. In this case, the answer usually is a one word answer. The answer is not case-sensitive; you can type the answer in lower- or uppercase.

Certain questions are repeated in different ways so that you can recognize them even when the wording is different. Taking practice quizzes will not only test your knowledge, but will give you confidence when you take your exam.

1. The primary tools used for network print configuration are _____.

   ☐ A. NetWare Administrator Tool

   ☐ B. NetWare User Tool

   ☐ C. NETADMIN

   ☐ D. PRNADMIN

   ☐ E. PCONSOLE

2. The NDS objects needed to configure network printing are _____.

   ☐ A. Alias objects

   ☐ B. Country objects

   ☐ C. Print Queue objects

   ☐ D. Print Job Configuration objects

   ☐ E. Printer objects

   ☐ F. Print Server objects

3. In NetWare 4 a print job can be captured to a _____.

   ☐ A. Print Server object

   ☐ B. Printer object

   ☐ C. container object that has the Print Queue object

   ☐ D. Print Queue object

4. The Print Queue object represents the _____.

   ○ A. queue directory on a volume

   ○ B. queue in server RAM

   ○ C. global network queue for printing and communications

   ○ D. network printer directly attached to the network

5. Which of the following properties of the Print Queue object should always have their value set?

   ☐ A. Common Name

   ☐ B. Description

   ☐ C. Volume

   ☐ D. Department

   ☐ E. Organization

6. The print queue is implemented by _____.

   ○ A. the QUEUES directory

   ○ B. the subdirectory of the QUEUES directory

   ○ C. the SYS:QUEUES directory

   ○ D. the subdirectory of the SYSTEM directory

7. The Operators property of the Print Queue object is _____.

   ○ A. a list of users who can use the queue

   ○ B. a list of users who can perform administrative tasks on the queue

   ○ C. a list of users with Supervisor All Properties right to the Print Queue object

   ○ D. container objects whose users can perform administrative tasks on the queue

8. Assigning a container object to the Users property of the print queue means _____.

   ○ A. that all users within that container are denied access to the queue

   ○ B. that all users within that container and its parent container are denied access to the Queue

   ○ C. that all users within that container can send print jobs to the queue

   ○ D. that all users within that container can perform administration tasks on the queue

9. The Authorized print servers property for the Print Queue object is a list of _____.

   ○ A. printers and print servers that are authorized to use the print queue

   ○ B. printers that are authorized to use the print queue

   ○ C. printers that are not authorized to use the print queue

   ○ D. print servers that are authorized to use the print queue

   ○ E. printers that service the print queue

10. The Printers Servicing Print Queue property for Print Queue objects is a list of _____.

   ○ A. print servers that are authorized to use the print queue

   ○ B. queues that service the print queue

   ○ C. printers that service the print queue

   ○ D. printers and print servers that are authorized to use the print queue

11. The Job List property of the Print Queue object can be used to _____.

   ○ A. display the printers and print servers associated with the print queue

   ○ B. view the printers associated with the print queue and view print queue jobs

   ○ C. view the printers associated with the print queue

   ○ D. view the print queue job

12. The Print Server property for a Printer object is set to the _____.

   ○ A. print server to which the printer is assigned

   ○ B. print servers to which the printer is assigned

   ○ C. print servers assigned to the Printer object

   ○ D. print server assigned to the Printer object

13. The Print Queues property for a Printer object lists the _____.

   ○ A. print queue that is assigned to a Printer object

   ○ B. print queues that are assigned to a Printer object

   ○ C. print queue to which the Printer object is assigned

   ○ D. print queues to which the Printer object is assigned

14. The Configuration property of the Printer object _____.

   ○ A. contains a list of users who are allowed to configure the printer

   ○ B. contains a list of print queues that are assigned to the printer

   ○ C. can be set to match the physical configuration parameters of the printer

   ○ D. is optional

15. The Notification property of the Printer object _____.

   ○ A. contains the network address of the server to which console messages should be sent concerning printer problems

   ○ B. lists the vendor contact to be notified about printer problems

   ○ C. lists the supervisor-equivalent users to be notified about printer problems

   ○ D. lists the users to be notified about printer problems

16. The PSERVER.NLM used to load a Print Server object can support _____ printers.

   ○ A. 16

   ○ B. 32

   ○ C. 64

   ○ D. 100

   ○ E. 128

   ○ F. 256

   ○ G. 1,024

17. The Advertising Name property of the Print Server object is the name used by the _____ to advertise its existence using the _____.

   ○ A. PRINTCON, NetWare Core Protocol

   ○ B. PSERVER, NetWare Core Protocol

   ○ C. PRINTCON, Service Advertising Protocol

   ○ D. PSERVER, Service Advertising Protocol

18. The Network Address property of the Print Server object _____.

   ○ A. must be assigned during print configuration and refers to the internal network number and node address of the NetWare server on which the PSERVER is running

   ○ B. is set only when the print server is running and refers to the internal network number and node address of the NetWare server on which the PSERVER is running

C. must be assigned during print configuration and refers to the network number and node address of the NetWare server on which the PSERVER is running

D. is set only when the print server is running and refers to the network number and node address of the NetWare server on which the PSERVER is running

19. You can unload a running print server using _____.

☐ A. NetWare Administrator

☐ B. PRINTCON

☐ C. PCONSOLE

☐ D. PSERVER running on the server

☐ E. NETUSER

☐ F. NETADMIN

20. The Operators property of the Print Server object is _____.

○ A. a list of users who can use the print server

○ B. a list of users who can perform administrative tasks on the print server

○ C. a list of users with Supervisor All Properties right to the Print Server object

○ D. container objects whose users can perform administrative tasks on the print server

21. The Printers property of the Print Server object lists the _____.

○ A. printers that are assigned to a Print Server object

○ B. printer that is assigned to a Print Server object

○ C. printers to which the Print Server object is assigned

○ D. printer to which the Print Server object is assigned

22. The Password property of the Print Server object _____.

○ A. is used to secure access to the print server

○ B. must be supplied whenever a user submits a print job

○ C. is used to set up a password for printer and Print Server objects

○ D. is mandatory and is used to secure access to the printer

23. Changes made to the Print Server object properties of a running print server _____.

○ A. are not registered with the print server, unless you select the Update Configuration option from the PSERVER menu option

○ B. are not registered with the print server, unless you bring the print server down and up again

○ C. are registered with the print server immediately

○ D. are registered with the print server within the Poll Interval Time property value of the print server

24. Printer definitions that are local to the print server are _____.

    ○ A. autoloaded

    ○ B. manually loaded

    ○ C. autoloaded only if the Auto Load property of the Print Server object is set

    ○ D. loaded when the PSERVER.EXE loads

25. Printer definitions that are remote from the print server are _____.

    ○ A. autoloaded

    ○ B. manually loaded

    ○ C. autoloaded only if the Auto Load property of the Print Server object is set

    ○ D. loaded when the PSERVER.EXE loads

26. Remote printers, in NetWare 4 can be loaded using _____.

    ☐ A. PCONSOLE.EXE

    ☐ B. NPRINTER.EXE

    ☐ C. RPRINTER.EXE

    ☐ D. PSERVER.EXE

    ☐ E. NPRINTER.NLM

    ☐ F. PRINTCON.EXE

27. In NetWare 4, remote printers at workstations can be loaded using _____.

    ○ A. PCONSOLE.EXE

    ○ B. NPRINTER.EXE

    ○ C. RPRINTER.EXE

    ○ D. PSERVER.EXE

    ○ E. NPRINTER.NLM

    ○ F. PRINTCON.EX

28. In NetWare 4, remote printers at NetWare servers can be loaded using _____.

    ○ A. PCONSOLE.NLM

    ○ B. NPRINTER.EXE

    ○ C. RPRINTER.NLM

    ○ D. PSERVER.NLM

    ○ E. NPRINTER.NLM

    ○ F. PRINTCON.NLM

29. If NPRINTER is used without any options, _____.

    ○ A. it displays a summary help screen

    ○ B. it displays an error message

    ○ C. it runs as a menu utility

    ○ D. it can be used to send print jobs through a menu interface

30. To create the print related NDS objects, you should have a minimum of _____.

    ○ A. the supervisor object rights to the container where these objects will be placed

    ○ B. the Create and Rename object rights to the container where these objects will be placed

    ○ C. the Create and Delete object rights to the container where these objects will be placed

    ○ D. the Create object right to the container where these objects will be placed

31. The quickest way to configure network printing is to use the _____.

    ○ A. Quick Setup option under NetWare Administrator

    ○ B. Fast Setup option under NPRINTER

    ○ C. Quick Setup option under PCONSOLE

    ○ D. Fast Setup option under PCONSOLE

32. If you do not have the Create object right to a container where you are using the Quick Setup option _____.

    ○ A. the Quick Setup option will produce an error message on the screen

    ○ B. the Quick Setup option will not be shown on the PCONSOLE menu

    ○ C. the Quick Setup option will log an error message on the server log

    ○ D. the Quick Setup option will log an error message on the server log and console

33. Which rights are by default assigned to the creator of print objects?

    ○ A. Create, Delete, Browse, and Rename object rights and property rights to the created object

    ○ B. Supervisor and Browse object rights to the created object

    ○ C. All object rights and property rights to the created object

    ○ D. All object rights to the created object

34. To activate the print server you must run the _____ at a NetWare 4 server and give it the name of the _____ as a parameter.

    ○ A. NPRINTER.NLM, Print Server object

    ○ B. NPRINTER.NLM, Printer object

    ○ C. PSERVER.NLM, Print Server object

    ○ D. PSERVER.NLM, Printer object

35. The Quick Setup option in PCONSOLE can be used to _____.

    ○ A. create in a single step a Print Queue, Printer, and Print Server object, but the critical properties defined have to be defined separately

    ○ B. create in a single step a Print Queue, Printer, and Print Server object that have all of their critical properties defined.

    ○ C. create the Print Queue and Print Server object, but the Print Server object has to be defined separately

    ○ D. print network jobs quickly

36. Which of the following tools can be used in printing network print jobs?

    ☐ A. NETUSER

    ☐ B. CAPTURE

    ☐ C. PRINTCON

    ☐ D. PRINTDEF

37. Which of the following tools can be used in printing network print jobs?

    ☐ A. PRINTCON

    ☐ B. NPRINT

    ☐ C. NETUSER

    ☐ D. PCONSOLE

    ☐ E. NETADMIN

38. NETUSER can be used to _____.

    ☐ A. print jobs to a network queue

    ☐ B. redirect a local printer port to a network queue only

    ☐ C. redirect a local printer port to a network queue or network printer

    ☐ D. redirect a remote printer port to a network queue or network printer

39. The CAPTURE command is used to _____.

    ○ A. redirect a local printer port to a network printer only

    ○ B. redirect a local printer port to a network queue or network printer

    ○ C. redirect a local printer port to a network queue only

    ○ D. redirect a remote printer port to a network queue or network printer

40. The NetWare 4 command to end capture of local port LPT1: is _____.

    ○ A. ENDCAP

    ○ B. CAPTURE EC

    ○ C. CAPTURE

    ○ D. CAPTURE STOP

41. Which command-line utility can be used to control and see status of printers and print servers?

    ○ A. PRINTCON

    ○ B. NETUSER

    ○ C. NPRINTER

    ○ D. PCONSOLE

    ○ E. PSC

    ○ F. PSERVER

42. Print job configurations can be stored as _____.

    ☐ A. the Print Job Configuration property of an Organization object

    ☐ B. the Print Job Configuration property of a Country object

    ☐ C. the Print Job Configuration property of a User object

    ☐ D. the Print Job Configuration property of an Organizational Unit object

    ☐ E. the Print Job Configuration property of a Print Server object

43. Print device definitions are stored in the _____.

    ○ A. Print Devices property of the Printer object

    ○ B. Devices property of the User object

    ○ C. Print Devices property of the container object

    ○ D. Print Devices property of the container or User object

44. Print form definitions are stored in the _____.

   ○ A. Print Forms property of the
       container object

   ○ B. Print Forms property of the
       container or User object

   ○ C. Forms property of the User object

   ○ D. Print Forms property of the Printer
       object

45. The _____ function key can be used to
   toggle between directory and bindery modes
   for PRINTCON and PRINTDEF.

   ○ A. F1

   ○ B. F2

   ○ C. F4

   ○ D. F5

   ○ E. F6

46. Which of the following statements for NetWare
   4 printing are true?

   ☐ A. Printer, Print Queue, and Print
       Server objects can be created using
       NETADMIN.

   ☐ B. To setup a remote printer you can
       use the NPRINTER.EXE program.

   ☐ C. Printer, Print Queue, and Print
       Server objects can be created using
       PCONSOLE.

   ☐ D. The password property can be set
       for Print Queue objects.

NetWare 4 Server Management

This chapter describes the changes that have taken place for managing the NetWare 4 server. The focus is on issues such as new and enhanced console utilities. The console commands that are new to NetWare 4 are also discussed in this chapter.

NetWare 4 includes support for the protected operating system domain feature, which allows NLMs to run in an area of memory separate from the kernel. In addition, issues concerning the protected domain feature are discussed.

An Overview of Server Management Changes

Many of the commands in NetWare 4 have been enhanced while others have remained the same from a user interface perspective. NetWare 4 has a completely redesigned memory architecture that allows it to manage memory from a global pool rather than the separate memory pools of the NetWare 3 architecture. Because of this, some of the problems of memory depletion from dedicated memory pools that could occur while running NetWare 3 console commands and utilities have been eliminated.

A console HELP command is available that enables you to quickly obtain help on the syntax and provides a brief overview of what the command does. Figure 8.1 shows the output from typing the HELP command. To obtain more detailed help on the command LANGUAGE, enter the following command:

HELP LANGUAGE

Figure 8.2 shows help on the LANGUAGE command. Thus, typing the LANGUAGE command displays the current language (see fig. 8.3).

 Study Note

The new console command for obtaining help on console commands is HELP.

Figure 8.1

The Console HELP command.

```
ABORT REMIRROR          ADD NAME SPACE          BIND
BROADCAST               CLEAR STATION           CLS
CONFIG                  DISABLE LOGIN           DISABLE TTS
DISMOUNT                DISPLAY NETWORKS        DISPLAY SERVERS
DOWN                    ECHO OFF                ECHO ON
ENABLE LOGIN            ENABLE TTS              EXIT
FILE SERVER NAME        IPX INTERNAL NET        LANGUAGE
LIST DEVICES            LOAD                    MAGAZINE INSERTED
MAGAZINE NOT INSERTED   MAGAZINE NOT REMOVED    MAGAZINE REMOVED
MEDIA INSERTED          MEDIA NOT INSERTED      MEDIA NOT REMOVED
MEDIA REMOVED           MEMORY MAP              MEMORY
MIRROR STATUS           MODULES                 MOUNT
NAME                    OFF                     PAUSE
#                       PROTOCOL                REGISTER MEMORY
REMOVE DOS              REMIRROR PARTITION      REM
RESET ROUTER            RESTART SERVER          SCAN FOR NEW DEVICES
SEARCH                  SECURE CONSOLE          ;
SEND                    SET TIME ZONE           SET TIME
SET                     SPEED                   SPOOL
TIME                    TRACK OFF               TRACK ON
UNBIND                  UNLOAD                  VERSION
VOLUME                  HELP

Type HELP [command] to display specific command help
NW4CS:
```

Figure 8.2

The HELP LANGUAGE command.

```
NW4CS:HELP LANGUAGE
LANGUAGE                         Display current NLM language.
LANGUAGE list                    Display list of available languages.
LANGUAGE name|number             Set preferred NLM language by name or number.
LANGUAGE add number name         Add a new language name and number.
LANGUAGE ren number new_name     Rename the language specified by number.
  Example:  language spanish

NW4CS:
```

```
NW4CS:HELP LANGUAGE
LANGUAGE                    Display current NLM language.
LANGUAGE list               Display list of available languages.
LANGUAGE name:number        Set preferred NLM language by name or number.
LANGUAGE add number name    Add a new language name and number.
LANGUAGE ren number new_name Rename the language specified by number.
 Example:  language spanish

NW4CS:LANGUAGE
  Current NLM language is (4) ENGLISH.

NW4CS:
```

Figure 8.3

The LANGUAGE command.

Table 8.1 shows the new console commands and provides a brief description of each.

The LANGUAGE command is used to specify the language to be used for the message files. This allows the NLMs that are written to support internationalization to display their options and help files in different languages. The general syntax for LANGUAGE is

```
LANGUAGE [language] [option]
```

The brackets ([ ]) around the parameters indicate that they are optional.

The *language* parameter can be the name of the language or a language identification number. The language and assigned codes are shown in table 8.2. Check the version of NetWare 4 that you have for

Table 8.1
New Console Commands

Command	Description
ABORT REMIRROR	Terminates remirroring of the specified logical partition
REMIRROR PARTITION	Attempts to start the remirroring of the specified partition
MIRROR STATUS	Displays a list of the mirrored logical partitions and its status
LIST DEVICES	Displays a list of storage devices
SCAN FOR NEW DEVICES	Registers any devices that have been added since the server was started
MAGAZINE	Used to respond to console alert messages to perform the indicated action, such as magazine insertion and removal
MEDIA	Used to respond to console alert messages to perform the indicated action, such as media insertion and removal
RESTART SERVER	Restarts a downed server
LANGUAGE	Allows the NLMs to use specific language files

the languages that are available. To select the SPANISH language, you can execute the following:

```
LANGUAGE SPANISH
```

or

```
LANGUAGE 14
```

Similarly, you can use the language name or language identification number for any of the other languages listed in table 8.2, provided that this support has been installed at the server.

Figure 8.4 shows the server console screen that has these commands issued. Figure 8.5 shows the MONITOR NLM running after the LANGUAGE command was set to use Spanish language message files. This assumes that support for the language has been installed on the server. Figure 8.5 also shows that the Esc command was typed. You can see the prompt in Spanish for exiting the MONITOR NLM. Figure 8.6 shows the top level help for the MONITOR NLM.

The Language Message files can be installed using the INSTALL NLM.

Table 8.2
Language Parameter Values for the LANGUAGE Command

Identification Number	Name
0	Canadian French
1	Chinese
2	Danish
3	Dutch
4	English
5	Finnish
6	French
7	German
8	Italian
9	Japanese
10	Korean
11	Norwegian
12	Portuguese
13	Russian
14	Spanish
15	Swedish

Figure 8.4

The LANGUAGE command for Spanish.

```
NW4CS:LANGUAGE SPANISH
   Current NLM language changed to (14) SPANISH.
NW4CS:
```

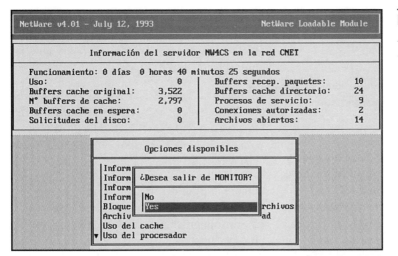

Figure 8.5
MONITOR NLM in Spanish.

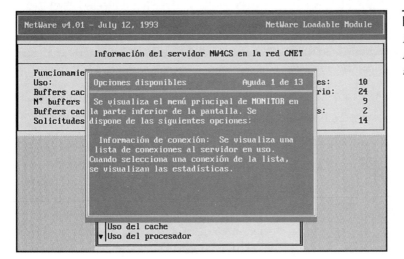

Figure 8.6
Help screen for MONITOR NLM in Spanish.

Remote Console Changes

The Remote Console utility is a very useful utility for managing the server. It is run at the workstation as the RCONSOLE.EXE. REMOTE.NLM and RSPX.NLM need to be loaded at the server. First load the REMOTE.NLM and then the RSPX.NLM. When REMOTE.NLM loads, you can specify a password as an argument to the LOAD REMOTE command. If you do not specify a password the REMOTE NLM prompts you for one. The commands to run Remote Console are shown here.

Use the following commands at the server:

```
LOAD REMOTE password
LOAD RSPX
```

Use the following command (located in the SYS:SYSTEM directory) at the workstation:

```
RCONSOLE
```

Figure 8.7 shows the Remote Console components. In this figure, it is clear that RSPX is lower in the functional hierarchy than REMOTE.NLM, because RSPX implements the communication protocol stack and REMOTE.NLM implements the Remote Console Facility. For this reason, you might think that RSPX.NLM should be loaded first. When RSPX.NLM loads, it expects to bind logically to entry points in the LAN driver and the application it connects to. The LAN drivers already are loaded when the server is activated. So RSPX can bind to the LAN driver without any problem.

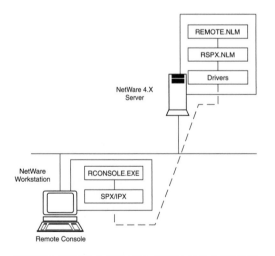

Figure 8.7
Remote Console components.

If the REMOTE.NLM is not already loaded, RSPX.NLM will not be able to connect logically to it. For this reason, REMOTE.NLM should be loaded before RSPX.NLM.

A major difference between RCONSOLE in NetWare 4 and prior NetWare versions is that the functions of ACONSOLE, used for asynchronous communications I/O, are now integrated in the NetWare 4 RCONSOLE.

Figure 8.8 shows the opening screen when RCONSOLE is run at a workstation. Notice that the two options shown are Asynchronous and SPX. If Asynchronous is selected, you are given a list of Asynchronous Options (see fig. 8.9). The Connect To Remote Location option enables you to view a list of remote locations accessible through RCONSOLE. Before you can use this option, you must use the Configure option to configure asynchronous operations.

Selecting the Asynchronous Configuration option (see fig. 8.10) enables you to select the device and modem configuration parameters. You can select the baud rate (bits per second), the modem initialization and reset command, the modem reconnect command, modem dial command, and modem hang-up command. You can supply a user identification by which the connecting station will be known to the remote server. You also can enter a call back number. The modem type can be Hayes-compatible or a null modem. The choice of null modem cable is useful, especially when used with serial line boosters (amplifiers). You then can manage the server from fairly long distances within a local building without using the LAN. This is particularly useful if there is a problem with the network cabling.

When the SPX option is selected, as shown in figure 8.8, you are given a list of available servers to

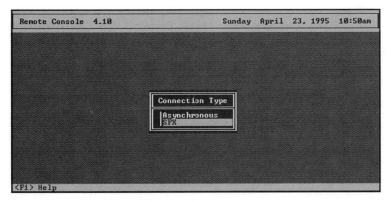

Figure 8.8

The Remote Console main screen.

Figure 8.9

The Asynchronous Options screen.

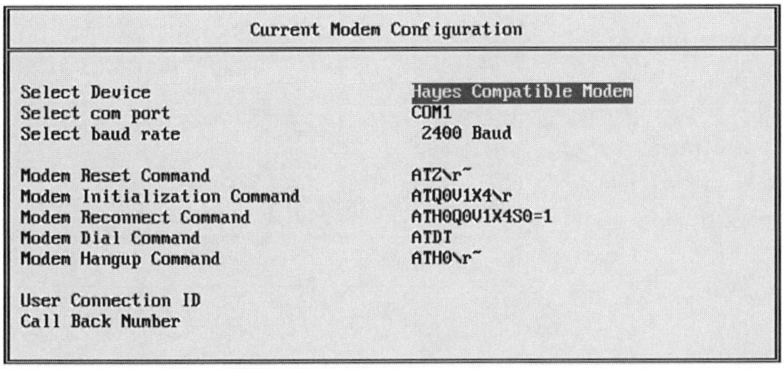

Figure 8.10

The Asynchronous Configuration option.

connect to (see fig. 8.11). When you select a server, you are prompted for a password. After typing the password used with the REMOTE (or the first Admin password), you are given a connection to the server console (see fig. 8.12). The connection message on the screen lists the date and time the connection took place, and the network number and node address of the station that was granted the connection. In figure 8.12, you can see that the network number is 000E8022 and the node address is 0080C7D66F0F.

Figure 8.11

The RCONSOLE Available Servers list.

Figure 8.12

Connection granted to remote console.

```
4-23-95  10:54:04 am:     RSPX-4.10-28
          Remote console connection granted for 000E8022:0080C7D66F0F
NW4KS:
NW4KS:
NW4KS:
NW4KS:
NW4KS:
NW4KS:
NW4KS:
NW4KS:
NW4KS:
NW4KS:
NW4KS:
NW4KS:
NW4KS:
NW4KS:
NW4KS:
NW4KS:
NW4KS:
NW4KS: _
```

In earlier NetWare versions, you could invoke the RCONSOLE menu by using the + key on the numeric keypad. The control keys for NetWare 4 RCONSOLE are different. To see the RCONSOLE menu, you must press Alt+F1 (at the same time). Figure 8.13 shows the RCONSOLE menu when the Alt+F1 key is pressed. The two new options are Invoke Operating System Shell that exits to the workstation command shell, and Workstation Address. You must enter **EXIT** to return to the RCONSOLE menu. The new Workstation Address enables you to see the workstation's node address (see fig. 8.14). In figure 8.14, the workstation address is shown in the box on the top left corner.

Other shortcut keys also are available. The Alt+F2 key combination enables you to quit RCONSOLE. The Alt+F3 and Alt+F4 key combinations enable you to scroll through screen consoles. The Alt+F5 key combination enables you to view the workstation address. The RCONSOLE control keys are summarized in table 8.3.

Study Note

The two new RCONSOLE options are Invoke Operating System Shell, which exits to the workstation command shell, and Workstation Address.

The RCONSOLE Workstation Address option enables you to see the workstation's node address.

Table 8.3
RCONSOLE Control Keys

Control Key	Action
Alt+F1	Invokes RCONSOLE menu
Alt+F2	Exits RCONSOLE
Alt+F3 and Alt+F4	Scrolls forward and backward through console screens
Alt+F5	Views workstation node (network) address

Study Note

Remember the RCONSOLE control keys shown in table 8.4 when preparing for your exams.

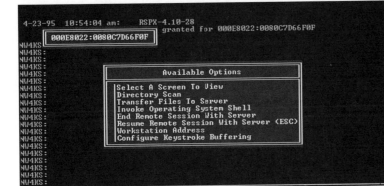

Figure 8.13
*RCONSOLE Available
Options.*

Figure 8.14
*RCONSOLE Workstation
Address option.*

Memory Allocation

NetWare 4 allocates memory in 4 KB units called
pages. This enables server memory to be allocated in
discontiguous pages, and still be viewed as logically
contiguous memory, thus resulting in efficient
memory management.

NetWare 4 gives to each process (NLM) a certain
amount of memory called its *memory allocation
pool.* Each process requests additional memory for
its use from its own allocation pool and returns
memory to this pool when it no longer needs the
memory. Memory that is assigned to the process

allocation pools is mapped to a global pool of
memory pages.

In any memory management system, reclaiming
unused memory is important for efficient memory
utilization and maintaining system performance.
In NetWare 4, memory deallocation and garbage
collection is used to reclaim unused memory.
Memory can be explicitly deallocated by processes
using the system API called *Free( ).* This system call
marks the memory as being deallocated. The next
step is to recover the memory marked for
deallocation. This step is performed by a procedure

called *garbage collection.* The following server console SET parameters can be used to optimize garbage collection:

- SET GARBAGE COLLECTION INTERVAL = *minutes.* This is used to control the time interval in minutes at which the garbage collection process runs. The parameter value ranges from 1 to 60 minutes and has a default value of 15.

- SET NUMBER OF FREES FOR GARBAGE COLLECTION = *number.* This sets the threshold number for the number of calls to the system API *Free()* that triggers the start of garbage collection. Remember that the call to *Free()* marks the memory as deallocated, but the actual deallocation must be performed by garbage collection. The parameter value ranges from 100 to 100,000 and has a default value of 5,000.

- SET MINIMUM FREE MEMORY FOR GARBAGE COLLECTION = *bytes.* This sets the minimum number of bytes that must be available to be freed up before garbage collection can occur. The parameter value ranges from 1,000 to 1,000,000 bytes and has a default value of 8,000 bytes.

NetWare 4 NLMs

A number of new NLMs are supported (see table 8.4). Some of these NLMS, such as NWSNUT and CDROM, are now also supported by NetWare 3.12. These are described for the sake of completeness, because they were first introduced in NetWare 4.0. The sections that follow discuss their function and capabilities.

Table 8.4
New NetWare 4 NLMs

NLM Name	Description
DOMAIN	Creates a protected domain for running NLMs
DSREPAIR	Allows repair of problems with the NDS database
RTDM	Supports the Real Time Data Migration feature
NWSNUT	NLM Utility User Interface library
TIMESYNC	Time Synchronization NLM to ensure that server times are synchronized across the network
DSMERGE	Used to merge roots of separate directory services tree
CDROM	Allows a CD-ROM attached to the server to be shared
KEYB	Allows keyboards for different languages to be used at the server console
SERVMAN	Allows the configuration of SET, SPX/IPX, and other server parameters

The DOMAIN NLM

The DOMAIN NLM uses the ring protection architecture of the Intel 80×86 processor family to create memory domains. Figure 8.15 shows the Intel Ring architecture and how it is used by

NetWare 4 OS. The NetWare OS kernel runs in Ring 0, the most privileged mode of the processor. Running an untested or malfunctioning NLM in this ring could crash the server. Using the ring architecture of the Intel 80×386 processors, the untested NLMs can be run in an outer ring, such as Ring 3. NLMs in this ring obtain services from the kernel through a protected inter-ring gate call mechanism that prevents direct access to the Ring 0 memory. There is a small overhead associated with the intergate calls, so NLMs running in a protected domain will run slower than if they ran in Ring 0 (kernel or unprotected domain). On the other hand, misbehaved NLMs running in a protected domain are prevented from altering the operating system environment.

To enable the protected OS domain capability, you must run the DOMAIN.NLM. The syntax for running the DOMAIN NLM, assuming it is on the NLM search path, is as follows:

```
LOAD DOMAIN [/R 1 ¦ 2 ¦ 3]
```

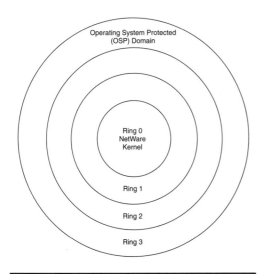

Figure 8.15
Intel Ring Architecture and NetWare 4.

When you run the command LOAD DOMAIN, the protected domain is set up in the default ring of 3. You can use the /R *n* option to load the domain in ring number *n*, where *n* is 1, 2, or 3. Thus, to set up a protected domain using ring 2, use the command

```
LOAD DOMAIN /R 2
```

Check your version of NetWare 4 to see whether other domain support is available.

The DOMAIN.NLM must be loaded before loading any other NLM, such as MONITOR, INSTALL, and so on. After the DOMAIN loads, other domain-specific commands become available (see table 8.5).

Table 8.5
Domain Commands

Domain Command	Description
DOMAIN	This displays the current domain and the modules in the current domain. Modules in other domains are also listed.
DOMAIN HELP	Displays help information on DOMAIN.
DOMAIN RING=*n*	Changes the OSP domain to Ring *n*.
DOMAIN= *domain_name*	Changes the current domain. *domain_name* can be OS (Ring 0) or OS_PROTECTED (the ring where OSP is established). Use this command preceding any NLMs that you want to load.

Remember the DOMAIN commands listed in table 8.5 when preparing for your exams.

When the DOMAIN NLM is loaded, you can use the command DOMAIN=OS or DOMAIN= OS_PROTECTED to change current domain to the OS domain (Ring 0) or the protected domain. NLMs loaded from the LOAD command are loaded in the current domain, so you can use this DOMAIN command to load the NLMs in the OS or OS_PROTECTED domain.

The key word OS_PROTECTED can be abbreviated as OSP. This allows you to type the shorter DOMAIN=OSP instead of DOMAIN= OS_PROTECTED.

Figure 8.16 shows the effect of running the DOMAIN command on the top part of the screen. When the DOMAIN command is run, a list of NLMs in the domains are reported (see fig. 8.17). Figure 8.17 reports that the current domain is "OS" and this is ring 0. The OS_PROTECTED domain is ring 3. All NLMs are loaded in ring 0. These include the REMOTE.NLM and the RSPX.NLM that were loaded after the LOAD DOMAIN command.

To load the EDIT.NLM in the protected domain, issue this command:

```
DOMAIN=OS_PROTECTED
```

Figure 8.18 shows the effect of executing the preceding command. Notice that the status

Figure 8.16

The LOAD DOMAIN command.

```
NW4CS:LOAD DOMAIN
Loading module DOMAIN.NLM
   NetWare Domain Protection
   Version 4.01     June 14, 1993
   Copyright 1993 Novell, Inc.  All rights reserved.
   1348 RPC descriptions loaded from DOMAIN.NLM.
NW4CS:LOAD REMOTE XYZZY
Loading module REMOTE.NLM
   NetWare Remote Console
   Version 4.01     June 21, 1993
   Copyright 1993 Novell, Inc.  All rights reserved.
NW4CS:LOAD RSPX
Loading module RSPX.NLM
   NetWare Remote Console SPX Driver
   Version 4.01     June 21, 1993
   Copyright 1993 Novell, Inc.  All rights reserved.

10-10-93   2:07:06 pm:     RSPX-4.1-28
      Remote console connection granted for 000E8022:0000C0664E19

NW4CS:
```

Figure 8.17

The DOMAIN command.

```
NW4CS:DOMAIN
   Domain "OS" in ring 0 is the current domain.
            NetWare Remote Console SPX Driver
            NetWare Remote Console
            NetWare OS Loader
            Protected Alloc Memory
            NetWare ISA Device Driver
            NetWare Directory Services (290)
            Time Synchronization Services
            Novell Generic Media Support Module
            Novell Ethernet Topology Support Module
            SMC EtherCard PLUS Server Driver v4.16 (930503)
            NetWare Domain Protection
            NetWare Server Operating System
   Domain "OS_PROTECTED" in ring 3.
NW4CS:
```

message shows that the current domain is OS_PROTECTED. Next, issue this command to load the EDIT NLM:

`LOAD EDIT`

Figure 8.19 shows that the EDIT NLM was loaded successfully, and figure 8.20 shows a list of NLMs in the different domains obtained using the DOMAIN command. Notice that the current domain (OS_PROTECTED in this case) is listed first and reports that it contains the NetWare Text Editor NLM (EDIT.NLM).

 Memory protection in NetWare 4 has the following benefits:

■ Secures NetWare services and the operating system environment

■ Tests new services and NLMs and protects against loss of data in case of failure of NLMs

■ Permits graceful termination of NLMs that fail

■ Protects operating system and services running in ring 0 from failure in NLMs running in an outer ring

```
NW4CS:DOMAIN
  Domain "OS" in ring 0 is the current domain.
          NetWare NLM Utility User Interface
          NetWare Remote Console SPX Driver
          NetWare Remote Console
          NetWare OS Loader
          Protected Alloc Memory
          NetWare ISA Device Driver
          NetWare Directory Services (290)
          Time Synchronization Services
          Novell Generic Media Support Module
          Novell Ethernet Topology Support Module
          SMC EtherCard PLUS Server Driver v4.16 (930503)
          NetWare Domain Protection
          NetWare Server Operating System
  Domain "OS_PROTECTED" in ring 3.
NW4CS:DOMAIN=OS_PROTECTED
Current Loader Domain is OS_PROTECTED
NW4CS:
```

Figure 8.18
The DOMAIN= OS_PROTECTED command.

```
NW4CS:DOMAIN
  Domain "OS" in ring 0 is the current domain.
          NetWare NLM Utility User Interface
          NetWare Remote Console SPX Driver
          NetWare Remote Console
          NetWare OS Loader
          Protected Alloc Memory
          NetWare ISA Device Driver
          NetWare Directory Services (290)
          Time Synchronization Services
          Novell Generic Media Support Module
          Novell Ethernet Topology Support Module
          SMC EtherCard PLUS Server Driver v4.16 (930503)
          NetWare Domain Protection
          NetWare Server Operating System
  Domain "OS_PROTECTED" in ring 3.
NW4CS:DOMAIN=OS_PROTECTED
Current Loader Domain is OS_PROTECTED
NW4CS:LOAD EDIT
Loading module EDIT.NLM
  NetWare Text Editor
  Version 4.00c   May 6, 1993
  Copyright 1993 Novell, Inc.  All rights reserved.
NW4CS:
```

Figure 8.19
Successful loading EDIT in OS_PROTECTED command.

Figure 8.20
EDIT NLM in OS_PROTECTED domain.

```
NW4CS:DOMAIN=OS_PROTECTED
Current Loader Domain is OS_PROTECTED
NW4CS:LOAD EDIT
Loading module EDIT.NLM
  NetWare Text Editor
  Version 4.00c  May 6, 1993
  Copyright 1993 Novell, Inc.  All rights reserved.
NW4CS:DOMAIN
 Domain "OS_PROTECTED" in ring 3 is the current domain.
        NetWare Text Editor
 Domain "OS" in ring 0.
        NetWare NLM Utility User Interface
        NetWare Remote Console SPX Driver
        NetWare Remote Console
        NetWare OS Loader
        Protected Alloc Memory
        NetWare ISA Device Driver
        NetWare Directory Services (290)
        Time Synchronization Services
        Novell Generic Media Support Module
        Novell Ethernet Topology Support Module
        SMC EtherCard PLUS Server Driver v4.16 (930503)
        NetWare Domain Protection
        NetWare Server Operating System
NW4CS:
```

Understanding the DSREPAIR NLM

The DSREPAIR utility is used to correct problems with the NetWare Directory Service Database, such as unknown object type objects or corrupted NDS objects. It also repairs NDS records, schema, bindery object representations in the NDS, and external references to other X.500 directories. The syntax of using DSREPAIR is

```
LOAD DSREPAIR [=U] [-L logfilename]
```

The =U and -L options are optional. The =U option specifies that the DSREPAIR should be run

in the unattended mode, without any user intervention. The -L option can be used to specify a file name *logfilename* where errors are to be logged. The default error log file is SYS:SYSTEM\ DSREPAIR.LOG.

The default error log file used by DSREPAIR is SYS:SYSTEM\ DSREPAIR.LOG.

Figure 8.21 shows the options when DSREPAIR is loaded. You can run the DSREPAIR.NLM in the unattended full repair mode by selecting the Unattended full repair option. This is the simplest mode

Figure 8.21
The DSREPAIR main screen.

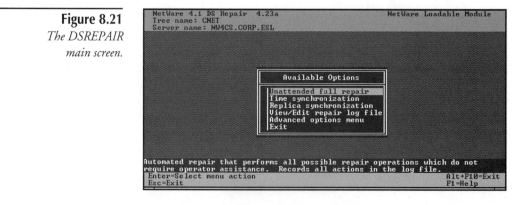

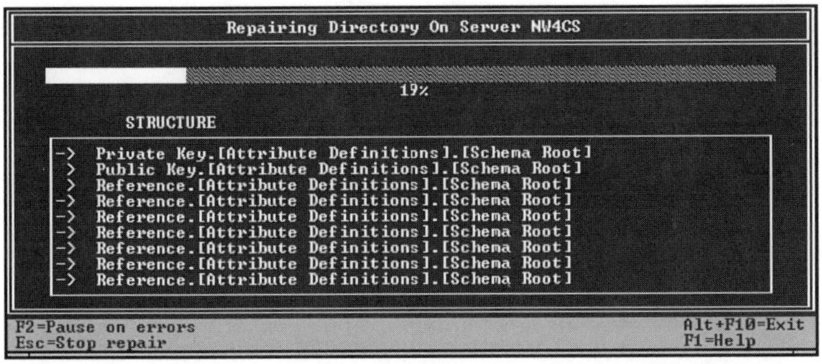

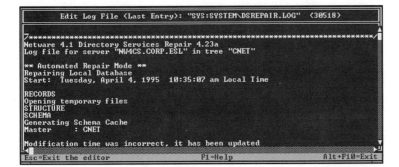

Figure 8.22
The status messages generated when you run DSREPAIR.

Figure 8.23
The DSREPAIR repair log.

for running DSREPAIR. Figure 8.22 shows the status messages being generated for the Unattended full repair option. At the end of the DSREPAIR session the repair log is displayed (see fig. 8.23). You can select the Time synchronization and Replica synchronization options to perform the indicated tasks.

If you select the Advanced Options menu, you will see a list of advanced configuration choices (see fig 8.24). A useful option is the Create a database dump file option, which copies the NDS database in a compressed form into the DSREPAIR.DIB file that you can use for off-line repairs (see fig. 8.25).

 The DSREPAIR log messages are logged in the SYS:SYSTEM\DSREPAIR.LOG file.

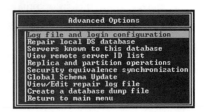

Figure 8.24
DSREPAIR advanced options.

Figure 8.25
DSREPAIR's Create a database dump file option.

RTDM Support

The RTDM NLM is used to enable support for data migration. The syntax for loading the RTDM is as follows:

```
LOAD RTDM
```

RTDM is an enabling module that manages the movement of data from one media type to another in a user-transparent fashion. You still need the near-line storage hardware and the drivers from the manufacturer to implement data migration. *Data migration* is a feature of NetWare 4 that allows data that has not been used in a defined period of time to be migrated to secondary storage devices.

Data migration is implemented by using the High Capacity Storage System (HCSS). HCSS is a storage/retrieval system that can extend the capacity of a NetWare server by integrating optical libraries into the NetWare file system. HCSS can work in conjunction with data migration so that migrated files can be moved from the faster but lower-capacity NetWare volumes to the slower but higher-capacity media that comprise the HCSS.

As far as the user is concerned, the operation of data migration and HCSS is transparent. Files that have been migrated to the HCSS are accessed with the same commands as files that reside on the NetWare volume. If a migrated file is accessed, it is automatically de-migrated.

Migration is performed on an individual file basis depending on the last time the file was accessed, called the *least recently used criteria* and the *current volume usage*. *Least recently used criteria* for files refers to files that are the least active, or have not been accessed for the longest period of time. If the current volume usage exceeds the capacity threshold, data migration occurs. The capacity threshold

is defined as the percentage of the server's disk that is used before data migration begins.

Migration allows high-capacity secondary devices to be treated as a logical extension of the server's disk storage. A volume's effective storage appears to be much larger than it really is. When data stored on near-line storage devices is needed, it is brought back in (*de-migrated*). If the data is not in use for a predefined interval of time, it is migrated back to near-line storage.

NWSNUT NLM

The NWSNUT NLM provides the NLM Utility User Interface. It is a library NLM that exports its functions to other NLMs. It implements the server console display routines that have the look and feel of the C-Worthy libraries used for the workstation utilities. Management utilities, such as MONITOR and INSTALL, make use of this library to provide a consistent, menu-driven user interface. The syntax for loading NWSNUT is as follows:

```
LOAD NWSNUT
```

NWSNUT is autoloaded by many of the modules that need its services.

For compatibility with NetWare 3.11 NLMs, the NUT.NLM is provided. Normally, you do not need to worry about this NLM, as it is autoloaded by the NetWare 3 NLMs.

TIMESYNC NLM

The TIMESYNC NLM is used to monitor the internal network time on the server and use information on time obtained from other time servers to synchronize the server time. This NLM is autoloaded whenever the NetWare server is started.

When TIMESYNC loads, it reads a file called SYS:SYSTEM\TIMESYNC.CFG that contains the time configuration parameters. These parameters also can be set by the SET commands or the SERVMAN utility. The time parameter also can be specified as an argument to TIMESYNC NLM. The general syntax for activating TIMESYNC NLM is as follows:

```
LOAD TIMESYNC [timeParameters]
```

where *timeParameters* are the time parameters for the TIMESYNC NLM.

DSMERGE NLM

The DSMERGE NLM is used to merge the roots of two separate NDS trees into one single tree. Remember that information between separate NDS trees (trees that have separate roots) cannot be directly shared. It might be desirable to merge the trees to share this information. Normally, the network NDS tree should be designed beforehand so that the use of DSMERGE is minimized. But in the case of unforeseen events, such as corporate mergers, it might be desirable to have a single NDS tree.

Use a tool such as SBACKUP to back up the NDS database on the two trees before attempting the directory merge. The general syntax for loading DSMERGE is as follows:

```
LOAD DSMERGE
```

This command should be run on the server that has the source tree that you will be merging with the target tree. The objects in the source tree become part of the target tree. As a result of the DSMERGE operations, only the root objects are merged. Container objects and leaf objects maintain their identity under the newly merged root. This means that complete names of objects in the source and target

trees should not change in the merged tree. You must make sure that containers at the top level in the source and target trees have unique names.

 Study Note In the DSMERGE utility

■ The objects in the source tree become part of the target tree.

■ Only the root objects are merged.

Another issue concerning merging of NDS trees is that the time source for the two NDS trees must be coordinated. If an external time source is being used, both trees must have access to the external time source. Additionally, make sure that all servers (repositories of NDS replicas) in the NDS trees are up and running before attempting DSMERGE.

CD-ROM Support

CD-ROM support is enabled by loading CDROM. Before doing this, you must ensure that the appropriate device drivers for your CD-ROM are running. For SCSI devices, you can load either ASPICD.DSK or CDNASPI.DSK. Because these drivers are normally placed in the C:\NWSERVER directory, make sure you specify the correct path name. Alternatively, you can use the SEARCH ADD command as shown in the following:

```
SEARCH ADD C:\NWSERVER
LOAD CDNASPI
```

Figure 8.26 shows the result of loading the CDNASPI driver. The CD-ROM unit is the SONY CDU-541 and has the SCSI ID of 01. The disk drive is set to a SCSI ID of 0, and the tape drive (HP 35470A) has a SCSI ID of 1. The host bus adapter SCSI ID is 7. This is typical for CDs.

Figure 8.26

The LOAD CDNASPI command.

```
NW4KS:LOAD CDNASPI
Loading module CDNASPI.DSK
   Meridian Data NetWare 386 CDROM/ASPI Device Driver
   Version 2.00     June 16, 1993
   Copyright 1992 by Meridian Data, Inc. All rights reserved.
SERVER-4.00-1587:   This module is using 1 outdated API call
   You should upgrade to a newer module when it becomes available.

Meridian Data CDROM/ASPI Device Driver for NetWare 3.1x or Above, Version 2.00
Copyright 1992 by Meridian Data, Inc. All rights reserved.
Number of SCSI adapters installed: 1
Host adapter 0 is SCSI ID 7
SCSI ID: 00 is logical device 00 MICROP    1528-15MD1076301
SCSI ID: 01 is logical device 00 SONY      CD-ROM CDU-541
SCSI ID: 02 is logical device 01 HP        HP35470A
NW4KS:
```

Next you must load the CDROM NLM. Figure 8.27 shows the effect of loading the CD-ROM driver. Notice that the CD-ROM supports the ISO 9660 and the High Sierra format. The device is identified as device 1.

After the CD-ROM loads, a number of CD commands become available. For a listing of these commands, enter the command

CD HELP

Figure 8.28 shows the help screen for CD commands. The CD DEVICE LIST or CD VOLUME LIST commands can be used to obtain the volume name or volume number. You need the volume name or number to mount the CD. Figure 8.29 and figure 8.30 show the effect of executing the CD DEVICE LIST and the CD VOLUME LIST commands.

The next step is to mount the CD. This can be done by using the following:

CD MOUNT *volumename*

or

CD MOUNT *volumenumber*

where *volumename* and *volumenumber* were obtained from the CD DEVICE LIST or the CD VOLUME LIST command. Figure 8.31 shows the

Figure 8.27

The LOAD CDROM command.

```
   Meridian Data NetWare 386 CDROM/ASPI Device Driver
   Version 2.00     June 16, 1993
   Copyright 1992 by Meridian Data, Inc. All rights reserved.
SERVER-4.00-1587:   This module is using 1 outdated API call
   You should upgrade to a newer module when it becomes available.

Meridian Data CDROM/ASPI Device Driver for NetWare 3.1x or Above, Version 2.00
Copyright 1992 by Meridian Data, Inc. All rights reserved.
Number of SCSI adapters installed: 1
Host adapter 0 is SCSI ID 7
SCSI ID: 00 is logical device 00 MICROP    1528-15MD1076301
SCSI ID: 01 is logical device 00 SONY      CD-ROM CDU-541
SCSI ID: 02 is logical device 01 HP        HP35470A
NW4KS:LOAD CDROM
Loading module CDROM.NLM
   Netware 4.xx ISO-9660 and High Sierra CD-Rom Support Module
   Version 4.02    June 28, 1993
   Copyright 1993 Novell, Inc. All rights reserved.

10-10-93   6:37:31 pm:    SERVER-4.0-1355
   Device # 1 CDNET_DRIVE00 (A7000000) deactivated due to media dismount


For CD-ROM Support HELP enter 'cd help' on the command line.
NW4KS:
```

```
CD-ROM NLM Command Line Options:
  CD DEVICE LIST
  CD VOLUME LIST
  CD MOUNT [No.] [volume name] ('/mac' or '/nfs', '/G=x' or '/R')
  CD DISMOUNT [No.] [volume name]
  CD CHANGE [No.] [volume name] ('/mac' or '/nfs', '/G=x' or '/R')
  CD DIR [No.] [volume name]
  CD GROUP ([group name] and [group num])
  CD HELP

The [volume name] can be obtained from the first 2 options.
The [No.] can be obtained from the first 2 options.
The '/mac' is used to add Macintosh Name Space Support.
The '/nfs' is used to add NFS Name Space Support.
The '/G=x' is used to set the default volume group access rights.
The 'x' is the number listed from the GROUP Command.
The [group name] is to add a group name ('del' as name will remove group name).
The [group num] is used to add a new group name to the group access list (1-9).
The '/R' is used to reuse the created data file on the 'SYS' Volume.
The '/Z' is used to remove any file with a file length of zero.

When mounting or changing a CD-ROM disc a deactivation of the selected device
will occur.  Do not be alarmed.
NW4KS:
```

Figure 8.28
The CD HELP command.

```
NW4KS:CD DEVICE LIST

*** CD ROM Device List
No. Act. Device Name                              Volume Name    Mounted
 1   Y   Device # 1 CDNET_DRIVE00 (A7000000)      NETWARE_40        N

NW4KS:
NW4KS:
```

Figure 8.29
The CD DEVICE LIST command.

```
NW4KS:cd volume list

*** CD ROM Volume List
No. Volume Name      Mounted Device Name
 1  NETWARE_40          N    Device # 1 CDNET_DRIVE00 (A7000000)

NW4KS:
```

Figure 8.30
The CD VOLUME LIST command.

effect of executing the CD MOUNT command. If error messages are generated (see fig. 8.31), it is because the CD-ROM is a read-only volume. You can safely ignore these error messages. The mounting process will appear to be slow, so be patient. At the end of the mounting process, a message appears telling you if the mounted volume is ready.

Author's Note

Hopefully, by the time you read this, the problem with error messages appearing will be eliminated. The CD MOUNT command should know that it cannot write to a read-only volume. Also, the CD mount time can be made much faster.

Figure 8.31

The CD MOUNT command messages.

```
10-10-93   7:47:26 pm:     SERVER-4.0-2330
           Error writing to the directory on NW4KS/NETWARE_40.

10-10-93   7:47:26 pm:     SERVER-4.0-2330
           Error writing to the directory on NW4KS/NETWARE_40.

10-10-93   7:47:26 pm:     SERVER-4.0-2330
           Error writing to the directory on NW4KS/NETWARE_40.

10-10-93   7:47:26 pm:     SERVER-4.0-2330
           Error writing to the directory on NW4KS/NETWARE_40.

10-10-93   7:47:26 pm:     SERVER-4.0-2330
           Error writing to the directory on NW4KS/NETWARE_40.

10-10-93   7:47:26 pm:     SERVER-4.0-2330
           Error writing to the directory on NW4KS/NETWARE_40.

Volume NETWARE_40 is read only
NW4KS:
```

The CD-ROM is now available for use. Figure 8.32 shows the INSTALL screen with the mounted CD-ROM volume. Its default block size is 4 KB, and File Compression, Block Suballocation, and Data Migration are turned off because they do not apply to a read-only volume. The CD-ROM volume name is NETWARE_40, so to map drive H to this volume, use the following command:

```
MAP H:=NETWARE_40:
```

```
            Volume Information

Volume Name:            NETWARE_40

Volume Block Size:      4 KB Blocks

Status:                 Mounted

File Compression:       Off

Block Suballocation:    Off

Data Migration:         Off
```

Figure 8.32

The INSTALL screen, showing the mounted CD-ROM volume.

KEYB NLM and International Language Support

The KEYB NLM is used to change the keyboard type for a specific language for the server console. The general syntax of the command is as follows:

```
LOAD KEYB [parameter]
```

where *parameter* is a country (United States, France, Germany, Italian, Spain, and so on).

Figure 8.33 shows the effect of loading the KEYB without a parameter. Help on the different keyboard types that are supported is presented. Figure 8.34 shows the effect of loading the keyboard of the country France. The keyboard support for France, implemented by code page 437, is loaded. This code page provides the translation to the characters used by keyboards for France. An example of the effect produced by this command on United States keyboards is that the keys Q and A are exchanged. That is, using an American keyboard, if you press the Q key the letter *A* is displayed, and if you press the A key, the letter *Q* is displayed.

```
LOAD KEYB FRANCE
```

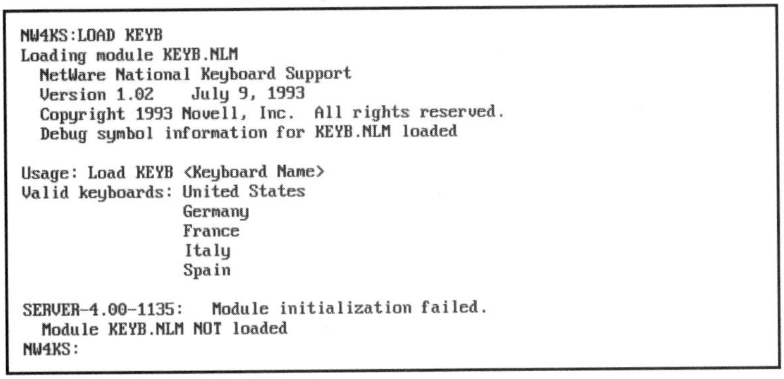

```
NW4KS:LOAD KEYB
Loading module KEYB.NLM
   NetWare National Keyboard Support
   Version 1.02    July 9, 1993
   Copyright 1993 Novell, Inc.  All rights reserved.
   Debug symbol information for KEYB.NLM loaded

Usage: Load KEYB <Keyboard Name>
Valid keyboards: United States
                 Germany
                 France
                 Italy
                 Spain

SERVER-4.00-1135:  Module initialization failed.
   Module KEYB.NLM NOT loaded
NW4KS:
```

Figure 8.33
The LOAD KEYB command.

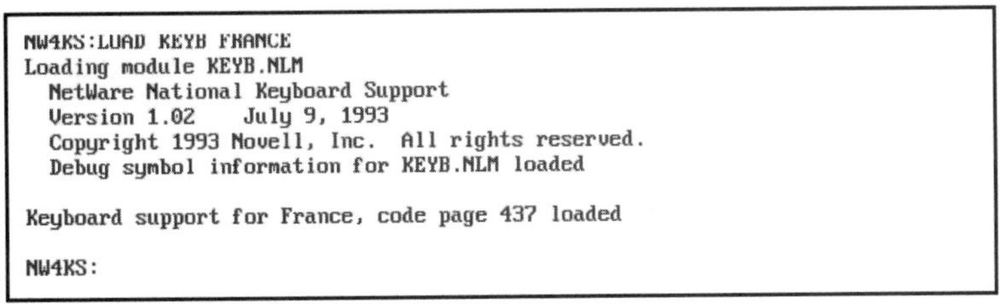

```
NW4KS:LOAD KEYB FRANCE
Loading module KEYB.NLM
   NetWare National Keyboard Support
   Version 1.02    July 9, 1993
   Copyright 1993 Novell, Inc.  All rights reserved.
   Debug symbol information for KEYB.NLM loaded

Keyboard support for France, code page 437 loaded

NW4KS:
```

Figure 8.34
The LOAD KEYB FRANCE command.

SCHDELAY NLM

The SCHDELAY NLM is used to prioritize server processes. Its primary purpose is to increase the scheduling delay for processes. This can reduce server CPU utilization if it is too high.

The general syntax for this NLM is as follows:

```
LOAD SCHDELAY [processName = number]
```

where *processName* is the name of the process and *number* is the amount of delay.

Loading SCHDELAY without any parameters shows the list of processes that are running and their current delay values (see fig. 8.35), which are 0 in this case. To increase the delay of the Media Manager process to 5, use the following command:

```
LOAD SCHDELAY MEDIA MANAGER=5
```

Figure 8.36 shows the effect of executing the preceding command. To change the delay for a particular process to 0 (no delay), use the following command:

```
LOAD SCHDELAY processName = 0
```

To change the delay for all processes to 0 (no delay), use the following command:

```
LOAD SCHDELAY ALL PROCESSES = 0
```

You also can control the scheduling delay by using MONITOR. Figure 8.37 shows the screen displayed when you select Scheduling Information from the Available Options in MONITOR. Notice from the command executed in figure 8.36 that the scheduling delay for Media Manager is 5. You can increase or decrease the scheduling delay by highlighting the process name and using the + or – keys.

Figure 8.35
The LOAD SCHDELAY
command.

```
NW4KS:LOAD SCHDELAY
Loading module SCHDELAY.NLM
  NetWare 386 Scheduling Delay Control
  Version 1.02      February 1, 1993
  Copyright 1993 Novell, Inc.  All rights reserved.
  Debug symbol information for SCHDELAY.NLM loaded

  Process Name           Sch Delay
  ------------           ---------

  RSPX                       0
  Remote                     0
  Console Command            0
  TimeSyncMain               0
  Directory Service          0
  Remirror                   0
  Media Manager              0
  Sync Clock Event           0
  MakeThread                 0
NW4KS:
```

Figure 8.36
The LOAD SCHDELAY
MEDIA MANAGER
command

```
NW4KS:LOAD SCHDELAY MEDIA MANAGER=5
Loading module SCHDELAY.NLM
  NetWare 386 Scheduling Delay Control
  Version 1.02      February 1, 1993
  Copyright 1993 Novell, Inc.  All rights reserved.
  Debug symbol information for SCHDELAY.NLM loaded

  Setting "Media Manager" Scheduling Delay to 5.
NW4KS:
```

Figure 8.37
Scheduling information in
MONITOR.

```
   Name                  Sch Delay      Time      Count     Load
  ┌─────────────────────────────────────────────────────────────┐
   Console Command Process     0         0          0      0.00 %
   Directory Service Process   0         0          0      0.00 %
   MakeThread Process          0         0          0      0.00 %
   Media Manager Process       5         0          0      0.00 %
   Monitor Main Process        0         0          0      0.00 %
   Remirror Process            0         0          0      0.00 %
   Remote Process              0       77,783      134      3.22 %
   RSPX Process                0         0          0      0.00 %
   Sync Clock Event Process    0         0          0      0.00 %
   TimeSyncMain Process        0        44          2      0.00 %

   Interrupts                           2,858       41      0.11 %
   Idle Loop                        2,328,923       38     96.52 %
   Work                                 3,258      137      0.13 %

   Total Sample Time:               2,424,791
   Histogram Overhead Time:            11,991    ( 0.49 %)
   Adjusted Sample Time:            2,412,800
```

The SERVMAN Tool

The SERVMAN tool is a new server manager NLM that enables you to change and view the SET parameters, configure SPX/IPX, and view network information.

The SET commands are used to control the server performance and configuration parameters. The syntax for loading SERVMAN is as follows:

LOAD SERVMAN

Figure 8.38 shows the SERVMAN main screen. The Server parameters option enables you to view or change the SET parameters. Changes made here are used to update the STARTUP.NCF or AUTOEXEC.NCF files. The SERVMAN is also an excellent tool for obtaining quick, online help concerning the meaning of each of the SET parameters. The SET parameters are organized in categories for easy reference. Figure 8.39 shows these categories when you select the Server Parameter option from the list of Available Options. To view any of the SET parameters in a particular category, simply select that category. Figure 8.40 shows the SET TIME parameters in the Time category. As each parameter is highlighted, a brief description is displayed.

Another interesting category is the File system category. Some of the newer parameters here deal with file compression. (File compression is discussed in Chapter 1.) Figures 8.41 and 8.42 together show all the compression-related SET parameters.

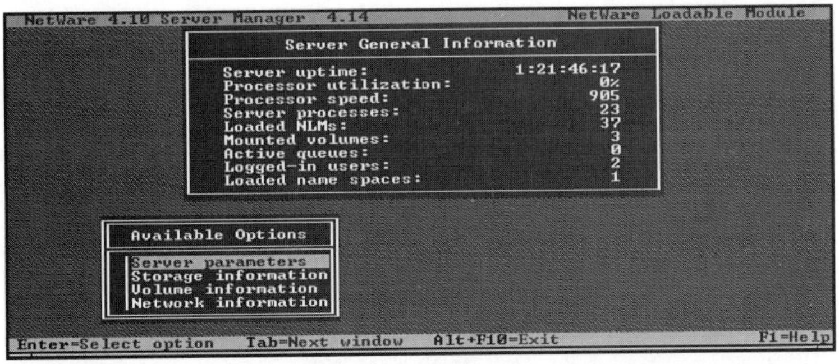

Figure 8.38
The SERVMAN main menu.

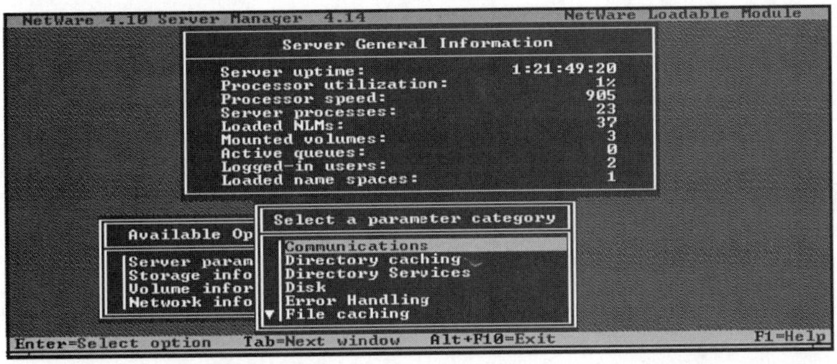

Figure 8.39
SERVMAN server parameter categories.

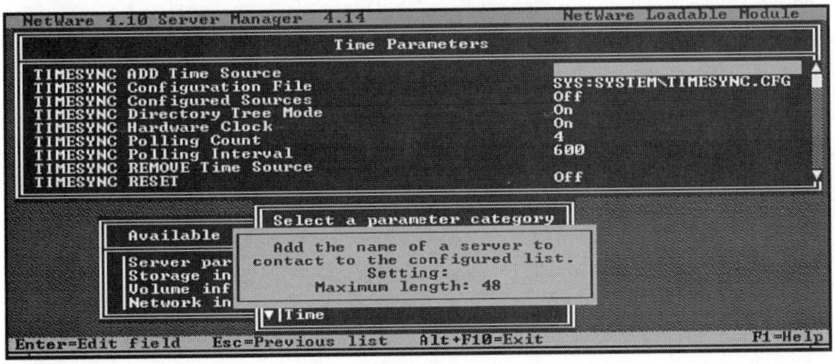

Figure 8.40
The Time category.

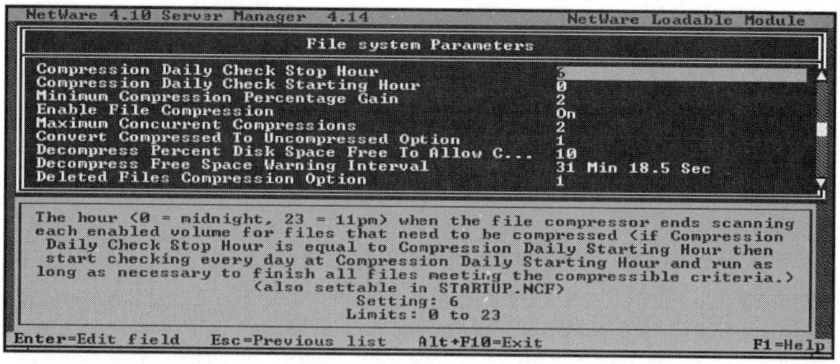

Figure 8.41

The File system compression parameters, screen 1.

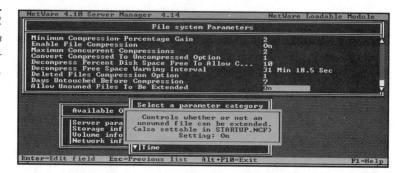

Figure 8.42

The File system compression parameters, screen 2.

You can use these parameters to control the start time (Compression Daily Check Starting Hour) and the stop time (Compression Daily Check Stop Hour) for the file compressor.

You can set the Minimum Compression Percentage Gain parameter to determine whether a file should be compressed. The default value for this parameter is 2, which means that unless there is at least a two percent reduction of the compressed file, the system does not keep the file in the compressed state.

The Days Untouched Before Compression parameter determines how long (in days) the system waits after the file was last accessed before compressing it. The Decompress Percent Disk Space

Free To Allow Commit parameter is used to determine the free disk space required before compression can begin. Its default value is 10 percent.

The Maximum Concurrent Compressions parameter can be used to limit the number of compressions occurring. Compression is a low-priority task and should not normally have an impact on the server performance. If you reduce this parameter, your server performance is affected.

The Storage Information option can be used to display information on the storage objects (see fig. 8.43). Adapters displayed are not indented. Devices, Magazines, and Changers are indented once. Partitions are indented twice.

The Volume Information option can be used to display information on the mounted volumes (see fig. 8.44). Information on the highlighted volume is displayed on the top part of the screen.

The Network Information option can be used to display information on the network. Besides monitoring the network traffic, such as the number of packets transmitted and received, you can use this screen for troubleshooting.

 If the number of unclaimed packets is high, an attempt is being made by network users to obtain a service that is not supported on the server. This parameter represents the number of packets for which there is no protocol stack to process it.

If the value for Packets Waiting to Be Sent or Get ECB Requests Failed is high, there are insufficient communication buffers to handle the network traffic.

```
          Server General Information
      Server uptime:             1:22:16:20
      Processor utilization:             0%
      Processor speed:                  905
      Server processes:                  23
      Loaded NLMs:                       37
      Mounted volumes:                    3
      Active queues:                      0
      Logged-in users:                    2
      Loaded name spaces:                 1
```

```
          Storage Objects
   1.  ISADISK.DSK Adapter      1
   2.     Device # 0 ISA Type 001 <20000000>
   3.        DOS Partition <16-bit FAT> #    0 on Device #  0
   4.        NetWare Partition #    1 on Device #  0
   5.  AHA1540.DSK Adapter      2
   6.     Device # 1 HP        C3323-300       4269 <5D000000>
```

Figure 8.43

The Storage Information option.

```
          SYS: Volume Information
   File system name:            NetWare 4.0 File System
   Loaded name spaces:                            DOS
   Read only:                                     Off
   Compression:                                    On
   Sub allocation:                                 On
   Sub allocation unit size:                      512
   Migration:                                     Off
   Migrated files:                                  0
   Block size:                                  64 KB
   Sectors per block:                             128
   Total blocks:                                9,440
   Free blocks:                                 4,491
   FAT blocks:                                      4
   Freeable limbo blocks:                       2,108
   Non-freeable limbo blocks:                       0
   Directory size <blocks>:                        98
   Directory entries:                          25,088
   Used directory entries:                     13,816
   Extended directory space:                        0
```

Figure 8.44

The Volume Information option.

The MONITOR NLM

The main MONITOR screen (see fig. 8.45) and the main SERVMAN screen (see fig. 8.46) show a number of general statistics for the server and the network. The parameters that are displayed on the screen give an overview of the network and server

status. Figure 8.45 shows the expanded view of the parameters. To toggle between the expanded and summary view of the parameters, use the Tab key.

The top part of the screen in figure 8.45 displays the NetWare 4 version and release date. The Information for Server field shows the name of the server being monitored and the name of the NDS tree on which the server is located. Figure 8.45 shows that the name of the server is NW4KS and the NDS tree name is CNET.

The Server Up Time field on the MONITOR (see fig. 8.45) and the SERVMAN screen (see fig. 8.46) shows how long the server has been up since the last time it was started. The Utilization field in MONITOR and Processor Utilization field in SERVMAN show the CPU utilization of the server. This is expressed as the percentage of time the server is busy.

The Original Cache Buffers field in the MONITOR screen shows the total number of cache buffers that were available when the server was first started. Use the following formula to calculate the original cache buffers:

Figure 8.45

General MONITOR statistics.

Original Cache Buffers = $(M - N - D)/B$

where:

M	=	Total server memory
N	=	Memory used by the NetWare 4 kernel
D	=	Memory used by DOS on server
B	=	Block size

The original cache buffers as reported by the screen in figure 8.45 are 3,532. Assuming a block size of 4 KB (4096 bytes), the initial memory allocated for cache buffers is 3543×4096, or 14,512,128 bytes. The server in figure 8.45 had a total memory of 16 MB (16,777,216 bytes). This means that the memory used by the NetWare OS kernel and DOS is 16 MB – 14,512,128 bytes, which equals 2,265,088 bytes, or 2.2 MB.

The Total Cache Buffers in the MONITOR screen is the number of buffers currently available. As NLMs are loaded, this number decreases. The number in figure 8.45 is 870 buffers. This means that *Original Cache Buffers – Total Cache Buffers =* 3,532 – 870 = 2,662 cache buffers that are used by additional NLMs. On the server in figure 8.45, the additional NLMs were MONITOR, SERVMAN, and TCPIP NLMs. The total number of NLMs

Figure 8.46

General SERVMAN statistics.

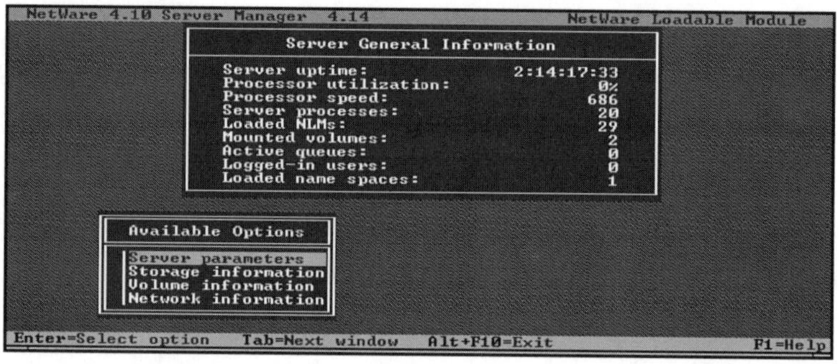

that are loaded can be seen in the NLMs Loaded field in the SERVMAN screen (see fig. 8.46).

The Dirty Cache Buffers in the MONITOR screen is the number of buffers that contain file data that is yet to be written to the disk. These buffers are called *dirty* because the information in them is not synchronized to the disk. The SET Dirty Disk Cache Delay Time parameter can be used to control the minimum amount of time the server waits before synchronizing a dirty disk cache buffer to disk. It has a default value of 3.3 seconds and can range from 0 to 10 seconds. For applications where data integrity is very important, you can set this parameter to 0 to avoid having dirty disk blocks not synchronized to disk. If Dirty Cache Buffers is consistently high, it indicates a high level of write I/O activity where the background process that writes file cache buffers to disk is unable to keep up with the I/O activity.

The Current Disk Requests in the MONITOR screen indicates the number of disk I/O requests that are in queue waiting to be serviced. If Current Disk Requests is consistently high, it indicates a high level of I/O activity. Using a faster disk controller/disk combination, or splitting the I/O activity across several volumes or servers, will generally improve I/O response times.

The Packet Receive Buffers in the MONITOR screen is the number of communication buffers at the server that can process workstation requests. This parameter is in the range controlled by the SET Minimum Packet Receive Buffers and the SET Maximum Packet Receive Buffers parameters.

The Directory Cache Buffers in the MONITOR screen is the number of buffers reserved for directory caching. In NetWare 4, portions of the directory entry tables are cached to improve directory search response times.

The Current Service Processes in the MONITOR and SERVMAN screen is the number of processes dedicated by the NetWare 4 OS to handle station requests. During peak server activity, when workstation requests exceed the number of service processes that have been assigned, additional service processes are assigned. Once assigned, the memory allocated to the service processes is not reduced unless the server is restarted. You can control the rate at which new service processes are allocated by the SET New Process Service Wait Time that delays the request for a new service process. This parameter can range from 0.3 to 20 seconds and has a default value of 2.2 seconds. The SET Maximum Service Processes parameter limits the growth of the number of processes that handle packets, and can be set to a value between 5 and 100. It has a default value of 40. This value is reported by the Maximum Service Processes.

The Current Licensed Connections on the MONITOR screen and the Users Logged In on the SERVMAN screen are the number of licensed connections to the server. This number reflects the number of users that are using resources on this server. This value is different from the Active Connections that can be displayed by selecting the Connection Information option on the MONITOR screen. Active Connections includes the licensed connections and any other network devices (usually workstations) that are attached to the server but are not making use of server resources. The Maximum Licensed Connections shows the maximum number of licenses for the server.

The Open Files in the MONITOR screen is the number of files that are currently open at the server. NetWare 4 can support 100,000 open files. To view file names that are opened by a particular user, you must select the Connection Information, highlight the user name, and press Enter.

The SERVMAN General Information reports other information (see fig. 8.46) such as Processor Speed, which indicates how fast the processor is. For details on how the processor speed is calculated, refer to the author's *NetWare: The Professional Reference* from New Riders Publishing. Mounted Volumes indicates the number of server volumes that are mounted, including any CD-ROM volumes that may be mounted. Active Queues refers to the number of print queues that are active on the server. Logged-In Users is the same as Current Licensed Connections in MONITOR. Name Spaces Loaded shows the number of name spaces that are supported. This value should be at least 1, because the DOS name space is always supported.

Review and understand the functions of each of the parameters in the main screens for MONITOR and SERVMAN.

Learn to identify unusually large or small values of MONITOR parameters. You may get questions asking you what is unusual or normal about a particular parameter value.

Examining Memory Utilization

As discussed earlier in this chapter, NetWare 4 manages memory in 4 KB page sizes. The memory for NLMs is allocated from a common file cache pool and released to this common pool when the NLM is unloaded.

The memory needed by an NLM is the memory for itself plus any other NLMs it depends on. Because common NLMs such as CLIB, STREAMS, and TLI can be shared by a number of NLMs, the overall system memory requirements are reduced. The memory used by an NLM is approximately the same as the size of the NLM file. Certain NLMs allocate additional memory when they are running, and this must be factored into the estimated memory usage for that NLM.

The memory used by an NLM is approximately the same as the size of the NLM file. You can get an estimate of the memory used by an NLM by using the System Module Information and Memory Utilization options within MONITOR.

Viewing System Module Information

Figure 8.47 shows the System Module Information for the NetWare Directory Services. To see this figure, select System Module Information from Available Options in MONITOR. Highlight Netware 4.1 Directory Services, and press Enter. From figure 8.47, you can see that the name of the NetWare Directory Services is DS.NLM and it uses 590,039 bytes. You can also see a list of *resource tags* used by the NLM. When an NLM makes use of resources, it can register the name of the resource and other information on the resource as a set of resource tags. This allows the server to monitor and track how these resources are used. Figure 8.48 shows that the Alloc memory for NDS Alloc memory tag uses 49,216 bytes of memory. To view the memory used by a resource tag, highlight the resource and press Enter.

```
                    General Information
     Serve                                      :43:19
     Utili                                           3%
     Origi     Module size:      590,039 bytes   3,532
     Total     Load file name:  DS.NLM           1,099
     Dirty                                            0
     Curre                                            0

          System Modules              Resource Tags
▲ NetWare 3.11 Compatible NLM Support Module │ ATB/BSAFE Secure Memory
  NetWare 4.01/4.02/4.10 ISADISK Device Driv │ ATB/BSAFE Semaphores
  NetWare 4.1 Bindery Synchronizer           │ Debug Command
  NetWare 4.1 Directory Services             │ DS AES Process
  NetWare 4.1 Directory Services Loader      │ DS Alloc Memory
  NetWare 4.1 Remote Console                 │ DS Events
▼ NetWare 4.10 C NLM Runtime Library         │▼ DS Name Service
```

Figure 8.47
System Module information for DS.NLM.

```
                    General Information
     Serve                                      :43:19
     Utili                                           3%
     Origi     Module size:      590,039 bytes   3,532
     Total     Load file name:  DS.NLM           1,099
     Dirty                                            0
     Curre                                            0

                   Resource Information
    Tag:        DS Alloc Memory
    Module:     NetWare 4.1 Directory Services
    Resource:   Alloc Memory (Bytes)
    In use:     49,360
```

Figure 8.48
Memory used by a resource tag in MONITOR.

Viewing Memory Utilization

When you select Memory Utilization from Available Options in MONITOR, the top part of the screen will change to show allocated memory information for all modules (see fig. 8.49).

■ 4 KB cache pages is the number of cache pages in the memory allocation pool. This pool is the set of pages from which memory is allocated.

■ Cache page blocks is the memory that has already been allocated and is in the allocated memory pool.

■ Percent in use is the percentage of memory in the allocated memory pool (Cache page blocks) that is in use, and the Percent Free is 100 minus the Percent in use.

■ Memory blocks in use is the number of pieces of memory that have been allocated and are currently in use.

■ Memory bytes in use is the number of bytes of memory that have been allocated and are currently in use.

■ Memory blocks free is the number of pieces of memory that have been freed and are available for reuse.

■ Memory bytes free is the number of bytes of memory that have been freed and are available for reuse.

To see memory allocation for an individual system module, highlight the module and press Enter. The lower part of the screen will display the memory allocated for that module. Figure 8.50 shows the memory utilization for the NetWare Directory Services. The description of these parameters is the same as that discussed for all the system modules, except that the values refer to the individual system module rather than all the system modules.

Figure 8.49

Allocated memory information for all modules using MONITOR.

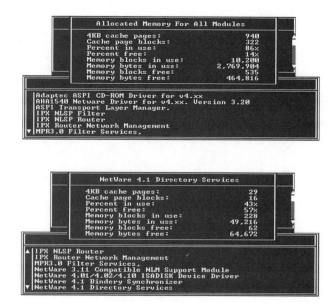

Figure 8.50

Allocated memory information for NetWare Directory Services using MONITOR.

You can perform garbage collection from the screen in figure 8.50. *Garbage collection* looks for whole pages in the free area of the allocated memory pool and returns them to the system. To perform garbage collection for the selected module, press the F3 key. To perform garbage collection for the entire system, press the F5 key.

 Garbage collection (freeing up memory) can be performed from the Memory Utilization option of MONITOR. The F3 key is used to perform garbage collection of a selected module, and the F5 key is used to perform garbage collection for all modules.

 Memory for an NLM is approximately the size of the NLM file, plus any prerequsite NLMs. Some NLMs may require additional memory as they run.

Examining Cache Utilization

NetWare improves the performance of disk reads and writes by allocating an area of server RAM called the *file cache* and reading disk blocks into the file cache area. Subsequent reads of the same disk block can be satisfied from the file cache. Reads from the file cache are much faster than reading directly from the disk. Similarly, writes are done to the cache and returned as being completed even if the actual write to the disk is not immediately done. A background process called the *lazy cache write process* flushes the written blocks in the cache to server disk. When a read request is satisfied from the file cache, it is called a *cache hit*. Cache utilization can be defined as the percentage of cache hits.

 A cache hit means that the server found the data in the file cache kept in the server memory, rather than having to obtain the data from the disk.

Managing Cache Utilization

To observe cache utilization, select Cache Utilization from Available Options in MONITOR. The parameters for cache utilization are described in table 8.6.

Table 8.6
Cache Utilization Parameters

Cache Parameter	Description
Allocate Block Count	The number of disk cache block requests that have been made since the server was started.
Allocated From AVAIL	The number of disk cache blocks that were satisfied from the AVAIL list that consists of blocks that are not currently used.
Allocated from LRU	The number of disk cache blocks that were satisfied from the LRU list that consists of blocks that are Least Recently Used (oldest blocks not referenced).
Allocate Wait	The number of times a cache block request had to wait because there were no available cache blocks.
Allocate Still Waiting	The number of times a cache block request had to wait behind another cache block request in the queue that was still waiting because there were no available cache blocks.
	The number of times the queue size for memory allocation requests was more than 1.
LRU Sitting Time	The time since the oldest block in the LRU list was last referenced.
Short Term Cache Hits	The percentage of disk cache requests that were satisfied with cache blocks that were already in the file cache *over the last one second.*
Short Term Cache Dirty Hits	The percentage of disk cache requests that were satisfied with cache blocks that were already in the file cache, but the disk block was *dirty* (not yet flushed to disk), *over the last one second.*
Long Term Cache Hits	The percentage of disk cache requests that were satisfied with cache blocks that were already in the file cache. *Long Term* means longer than a second.

continues

Table 8.6, Continued
Cache Utilization Parameters

Cache Parameter	Description
Long Term Cache Dirty Hits	The percentage of disk cache requests that were satisfied with cache blocks that were already in the file cache, but the disk block was *dirty* (not yet flushed to disk). This parameter indicates how often a request was made for a block that was just recently written to the cache. Blocks written to the cache are written to the disk in a time interval controlled by the SET the Dirty Disk Cache Delay Time, whose default value is 3.3 seconds. *Long Term* means longer than a second.
Too Many Dirty Blocks	The number of times a write request was delayed because there were too many dirty blocks.
Cache ReCheckBlock Count	The number of times disk cache requests had to be retried, because the target block was being used.

If the Long Term Cache Hits fall below 90 percent, you can improve performance by adding more server RAM. Meanwhile, you can make more RAM available to the system by unloading NLMs that are not needed. You can also remove DOS (used to boot the server machine) by using the REMOVE DOS command. However, this typically frees up only 104 KB of server RAM.

 The Cache Utilization option in MONITOR can be used to examine the Long Term Cache statistics. If this value falls below 90 percent, you can improve performance by adding more server RAM. Short-term solutions include unloading non-critical NLMs and using the REMOVE DOS console command.

You can also improve cache utilization by making the cache buffer size and the volume block size the same. NetWare requires that the cache block size be equal to the smallest volume block size. If you are using volumes with different volume block sizes, you cannot make the cache buffer and volume block size the same.

 You can optimize cache utilization by making the cache buffer size and the volume block size the same.

Novell makes the following recommendations for the SET parameters for improving speeds of disk reads and writes. These changes can be made by the SET command or by the SERVMAN.NLM.

To change disk and directory caching for faster writes, when there are many small write requests, set the Dirty Disk Cache Delay Time to 7 seconds, Maximum Concurrent Directory Cache Writes to 25, Dirty Directory Cache Delay Time to 2 seconds, and Maximum Concurrent Disk Cache Writes to 50.

```
SET DIRTY DISK CACHE DELAY TIME = 7 SECONDS
SET MAXIMUM CONCURRENT DIRECTORY CACHE WRITES
➥= 25
SET DIRTY DIRECTORY CACHE DELAY TIME = 2
➥SECONDS
SET MAXIMUM CONCURRENT DISK CACHE WRITES = 50
```

To change disk and directory caching for faster reads, set the Maximum Concurrent Disk Cache Writes to 10, Maximum Concurrent Directory Cache Writes to 5, and Dirty Directory Cache Buffer NonReferenced Delay to 60 seconds.

```
SET MAXIMUM CONCURRENT DISK CACHE WRITES = 10
SET MAXIMUM CONCURRENT DIRECTORY CACHE WRITES
➥= 5
SET DIRTY CACHE BUFFER NONREFERENCED DELAY
➥=60 SECONDS
```

The Dirty Disk Cache Delay Time has a default value of 3.3 seconds and can range from 0.1 to 10 seconds. This is the minimum amount of time the system waits before writing a dirty file cache buffer to server disk.

The Maximum Concurrent Directory Cache Writes has a default value of 10 and can range from 5 to 50. This is the maximum number of simultaneous writes of the directory cache buffers.

The Dirty Directory Cache Delay Time has a default value of 0.5 seconds and can range from 0 to 10 seconds. This is the minimum time the system waits before flushing a dirty cache buffer to disk.

The Dirty Cache Buffer NonReferenced Delay Directory Cache Delay has a default value of 5.5 seconds and can range from 1 second to 5 minutes. This is the time to wait after a directory cache buffer was referenced before reusing it.

 To change disk and directory caching for faster writes, set the Dirty Disk Cache Delay Time to 7 seconds, Maximum Concurrent Directory Cache Writes to 25, Dirty Directory Cache Delay Time to 2 seconds, and Maximum Concurrent Disk Cache Writes to 50.

To change disk and directory caching for faster reads, set the Maximum Concurrent Disk Cache

Writes to 10, Maximum Concurrent Directory Cache Writes to 5, and Dirty Directory Cache Buffer NonReferenced Delay to 60 seconds.

Controlling Turbo FAT Reuse Time

NetWare 4 uses the Turbo FAT feature to improve access to large, randomly accessed files. Normally, files are accessed by the FAT (File Allocation Table). The FAT is shared by all files on a NetWare volume and is cached in server RAM to provide faster access to its contents. The FAT contains a chain of pointers to data blocks for files. When a file needs to be accessed, the server finds the start in the chain in the Directory Entry Table (DET), and follows the chain in the FAT table.

For files that have more than 64 FAT entries that are randomly accessed, NetWare 4 builds a special FAT for that file in the server RAM. This special table is called the Turbo FAT (also called *index table*), and contains an index of blocks for that specific file only. This makes it possible to quickly find data blocks for the indexed file.

The system has built-in heuristics to determine whether a file is accessed randomly, and only uses Turbo FATs for files that are randomly accessed. Files that are accessed sequentially do not have Turbo FATs built for them.

 Files that have more than 64 FAT entries, and that are randomly accessed, are given a Turbo FAT that contains an index of blocks for that specific file only.

When an indexed file is closed, its Turbo FAT is not immediately released (in case that file is to be reused again). This delay is controlled by the SET Turbo FAT Reuse Wait Time parameter, which

has a default value of 5 minutes, 29.6 seconds. Indexed files that are reused within this SET parameter value will find their Turbo FATs in RAM and be able to reuse them. If the indexed file is used after this time, the Turbo FAT will have to be rebuilt again. You can increase the value of this parameter if you expect that there will be longer delays in the reuse of a file.

 When an indexed file is closed, its Turbo FAT is released after the value in SET Turbo FAT Reuse Wait Time parameter.

Examining Processor Utilization and Scheduling Information

The general MONITOR and SERVMAN statistics show the overall processor utilization. The MONITOR in NetWare 4 can be used to see processor utilization on a per-process basis. This allows you to determine where most of the processor time is being spent. Under continuous heavy processor loads, it is usually just a few processes that contribute to most of the processor load. You can use MONITOR to quickly identify which processes use most of the processor cycles. You may then decide to load these applications on separate servers dedicated to running them.

To view Processor Utilization using MONITOR, select Processor Information from Available Options. You can highlight any process and press Enter to see its processor utilization statistics. To see several processes together, you can mark them with the F5 key and press Enter. Alternatively, you can select all the processes by pressing the F3 key. Figure 8.51 shows the processor utilization for processes selected using the F3 key. You can also see

process utilization when you select Scheduling Information from Available Options (see fig. 8.52).

 To see processor utilization of all processes in MONITOR, select the Process Utilization option and press the F3 key.

In figure 8.51, process utilization information is sampled, processed, and displayed every second, and for figure 8.52, information is sampled, processed, and displayed every 2 seconds.

The Name column displays the name of the process being displayed. The Time column indicates the time the CPU spent executing code in that process or interrupt service routine. The Count column shows the number of times the process or interrupt service routine ran during the sample period. The Load column indicates the percentage of time the CPU spent in this process or interrupt service routine. If you scroll through the screen, you will see an overhead summary at the bottom. The summary includes Total Sample Time, Histogram Overhead Time, and Adjusted Sample Time. All statistics are displayed relative to the Adjusted Sample Time, which is the difference between the Total Adjusted Time and Histogram Overhead Time. The statistics collection is turned to ON only when the screens in figures 8.51 and 8.52 are displayed, and turned to OFF when you exit these screens.

If the server is idle, it spends most of its time in the idle loop process. This indicates a low server utilization.

 The server utilization is in inverse relationship to the utilization of the polling process. When the polling process utilization is high, the server utilization is low. When the server utilization is high, the polling process utilization is low.

```
Process Name                          Time    Count    Load
*AES cleanup process resource            0        0    0.00%
*AES Events                            191        9    0.01%
*AES Events                              0        0    0.00%
*AES Events                              0        0    0.00%
*AES Processes Call-Backs              893       18    0.07%
*AES resource tag                        0        0    0.00%
*AES resource tag                        0        0    0.00%
*AES resource tag                        0        0    0.00%
*AES resource tag                        0        0    0.00%
*AES resource tag                        0        0    0.00%
*AES resource tag                        0        0    0.00%
*AES resource tag                        0        0    0.00%
*AES resource tag                        0        0    0.00%
*AES resource tag                        0        0    0.00%
*AES resource tag                        0        0    0.00%
```

Figure 8.51
Viewing processor utilization for all processes.

```
Process Name            Sch Delay    Time    Count    Load
Console Command             0           0        0    0.00%
Console Logger    0         0           0        0    0.00%
FILTSRV           0         0           0        0    0.00%
IPFLT             0         0           0        0    0.00%
IPXRTR I/O                  0           0        0    0.00%
IPXRTR LSP Flood            0         296        3    0.00%
IPXRTR Timer                0       2,510       54    0.07%
MakeThread                  0           0        0    0.00%
Media Manager               0           0        0    0.00%
MONITOR main                0           0        0    0.00%
NetSync Backgroun           0         289        3    0.00%
NetSync Event               0           0        0    0.00%
NetSync I/O                 0           0        0    0.00%
NetSync Inform              0           0        0    0.00%
NetSync Watchdog            0           0        0    0.00%
NPRINTER          0         0       3,167       54    0.09%
PServer           0         0           0        0    0.00%
```

Figure 8.52
Viewing scheduling information for all processes.

The Scheduling Information displays only processes whose scheduling delays can be adjusted. You can use the + or – keys to increase or decrease the scheduling delay of the highlighted process. If the server CPU utilization for a process is too high, you can reduce it by increasing the scheduling delay.

Another way to change the scheduling delay is to use the SCHDELAY.

The general syntax for this NLM is as follows:

```
LOAD SCHDELAY [processName = number]
```

where *processName* is the name of the process and *number* is the amount of delay.

Loading SCHDELAY without any parameters shows the list of processes that are running and their current delay. For example, to increase the delay of the Media Manager process to 5, the command would be as follows:

```
LOAD SCHDELAY MEDIA MANAGER=5
```

To change the delay for a particular process to 0 (no delay), use the following command:

```
LOAD SCHDELAY  processName = 0
```

To change the delay for all processes to 0 (no delay), use the following command:

```
LOAD SCHDELAY ALL PROCESSES = 0
```

Network Performance

Network performance is affected by a variety of factors:

■ Network type (Ethernet, Token Ring, FDDI, and so on)

■ Packet burst configuration

■ Large Internet Packet size

These factors are examined next.

Network Type

The network type, such as Ethernet, Token Ring, or FDDI, has an important influence on the network performance. These different network technologies have differences in data transfer rate, packet size, and *Media Access Control (MAC)* layer operation.

Standard Ethernet has an operating speed of 10 Mbps, Token Ring operates at 4 or 16 Mbps, and FDDI operates at 100 Mbps. Newer versions of Ethernet, such as 100 BASE-T, can operate at 100 Mbps. In general, the faster the operating speed of the network, the better the network performance. However, there are a number of other factors that influence network performance. One of these factors is *packet size*.

Packet Size Considerations

Data is transmitted on the network in units called *packets* that have a maximum size for a given network type. For example, the maximum size of the data packet for Ethernet (excluding Ethernet protocol overhead, which is 18 bytes including the CRC) is 1,500 bytes. For Token Ring, the packet size depends on the Token Holding Time (THT), but in practical networks is limited to a size of 4 KB for 4 Mbps operation and 16 KB for 16 Mbps operation. In general, the larger the packet size, the faster the transfer rate, because more data can be transferred in a given number of packets.

A network may not always use its maximum packet size, but instead may use the default packet size whose value is encoded in the network board driver. For instance, although it is possible to operate a 16 Mbps Token Ring with a packet size of 16 KB, the size that most drivers can sustain is a 4 KB packet. Table 8.7 shows Novell's published list for default packet size for different network types. The default packet size is encoded in the network driver and can range from 576 bytes to 6,500 bytes.

Table 8.7
Default Maximum Packet Size

Packet Network Type	*Default Maximum Size (bytes)*
ARCnet	576
Ethernet (10BASE-T, 10BASE-2, 10BASE-5)	1,514
Token Ring (IEEE 802.5) at 4 Mbps	4,202
Token Ring (IEEE 802.5) at 16 Mbps	4,202

When a workstation makes a connection to the server, it negotiates the largest packet size to be used for the communication session. Because the server and workstation use different drivers, they have a different understanding of what the largest packet size should be on the network. Packet size negotiation ensures a common packet size both the server and workstation can operate at. The smaller of the default maximum packet sizes of the workstation and the server is selected as the maximum negotiated size for the session. This means that if the server can handle a 1KB packet and the workstation a 4 KB packet, the negotiated packet size will be 1 KB. For this reason, you should select drivers and network boards that can operate at the maximum packet size or can be configured to operate at their maximum packet size. You should do this not just for the workstations and servers, but also for any intervening routers; otherwise you will be limited to the maximum packet size the router can handle.

At the server, you must set the SET Maximum Physical Receive Packet Size parameter to the largest workstation packet size that is in use on that network. This SET parameter must be entered in the STARTUP.NCF file. You can use INSTALL or EDIT.NLM to edit the STARTUP.NCF file, or use the SERVMAN.NLM to make this change.

Other parameters that can be configured are the SET Maximum Packet Receive Buffers, Minimum Packet Receive Buffers, and Maximum Service Processes. The actual number of Packet Receive Buffers and Service Processes can be monitored using the main screen of MONITOR.

 The SET Maximum Packet Receive Buffers parameter determines the maximum number of packet receive buffers that are allocated for handling packets arriving at the server. The default setting of this parameter is 100 buffers, which may be inadequate for heavily loaded servers that need a value between 300 to 500. This parameter is entered in the STARTUP.NCF file.

The SET Minimum Packet Receive Buffers parameter determines the minimum number of packet receive buffers that are allocated for handling packets arriving at the server. The default setting of this parameter is 10 buffers. When the server starts, it allocates this minimum number of buffers on booting. If the number reported by MONITOR is higher than 10 when the server boots up, and the server is slow to boot up, it means that the server is allocating additional packet receive buffers and you should increase the value of the Minimum Packet Receive Buffers parameter. The SET Minimum Packet Receive Buffers parameter must be set in the STARTUP.NCF file.

 The SET Minimum Packet Receive Buffers parameter determines the minimum number of packet receive buffers that are allocated for handling packets arriving at the server and has a default setting of 10 buffers. This value must be increased if the server is slow in booting up. The parameter must be set in the STARTUP.NCF file.

The SET Maximum Service Processes parameter limits the growth of the number of processes that handle incoming packets, and can be set to a value between 5 and 100. It has a default value of 40. If MONITOR indicates that the Service Processes value is close to its current maximum setting, you should increase the value of the SET Maximum Services Processes. You can also increase this parameter to decrease the need to allocate more receive packet buffers; as the number of service processes increases, fewer packets will have to wait in the packet receive buffers for their turn to be processed.

MONITOR can be used to monitor the network board statistics, and this can provide valuable insight into the operation of the network. For instance, network board statistics can reveal trends in network traffic that could lead to a potential problem. Statistics for each logical board attached to the server can be displayed. The statistics are collected by the network board driver at the server. The network board statistics are grouped into two categories: *generic statistics* and *custom statistics*. A network board driver typically provides 15 different generic statistics (see fig. 8.53) that include variables such as Total Packets Sent, Total Packets Received, No ECB Available Count, and so on. Table 8.8 shows generic statistics for a network board.

Figure 8.53

Generic statistics for Ethernet.

```
┌─────────────────────────────────────────────────────────────────────┐
│         NE2000_1_E82 [NE2000 port=300 int=F frame=ETHERNET_802.2]     │
│ Generic statistics                                                    │
│     Total packets sent:                                    413,362    │
│     Total packets received:                                361,231    │
│     No ECB available count:                                      0    │
│     Send packet too big count:                                   0    │
│     Reserved:                                         Not supported   │
│     Receive packet overflow count:                               0    │
│     Receive packet too big count:                                0    │
│     Receive packet too small count:                   Not supported   │
│     Send packet miscellaneous errors:                            0    │
│     Receive packet miscellaneous errors:                         0    │
│     Send packet retry count:                                     0    │
│     Checksum errors:                                             0    │
│     Hardware receive mismatch count:                             0    │
│     Total send OK byte count low:                      111,377,706    │
│     Total send OK byte count high:                               0    │
│     Total receive OK byte count low:                    83,750,924    │
└─────────────────────────────────────────────────────────────────────┘
```

Custom statistics refer to a particular board and network driver. Both the NE2000 and the SMC8000 Ethernet network board drivers, for example, display a custom statistic called Enqueued Sends Count. This statistic is displayed as EnqueuedSendsCount in figure 8.54, and indicates the number of packets that the server was ready to send but had to wait in a queue because the network board was busy performing other tasks, or was not immediately allocated processor time to send the packets. If this number increases regularly, it indicates that the driver is not able to keep pace with the network traffic generated by the server. You can correct this problem by replacing a slower 8-bit/16-bit/32-bit network board with a faster 32-bit network board. If the network board driver is still getting saturated despite the high performance 32-bit network board, consider splitting the network traffic using two network boards installed at the server.

 Study Note

If the custom statistic Enqueued Sends Count (that shows the number of packets the server was ready to send but had to wait in a queue) is high, you can improve network performance by using a high performance network board or splitting network traffic.

The generic statistic *No ECB Count* (see fig. 8.54) can be monitored to indicate whether you have sufficient communication buffers. If this variable increases steadily, it indicates that there are insufficient communication buffers to handle the network traffic. If the Packet Receive Buffers is close to its upper limit as indicated by the SET Maximum Packet Receive Buffers parameter, you should increase the upper limit.

Figure 8.54

Custom statistics for an Ethernet SMC8000 board.

```
┌─────────────────────────────────────────────────────────────────────┐
│         NE2000_1_E82 [NE2000 port=300 int=F frame=ETHERNET_802.2]     │
│     Send abort from excess collisions:                           0    │
│     Send abort from carrier sense:                               0    │
│     Send abort from excessive deferral:                          0    │
│     Receive abort from bad frame alignment:                      0    │
│                                                                       │
│ Custom statistics                                                     │
│     UnderrunErrorCount                                           0    │
│     TransmitTimeoutCount                                         0    │
│     RxPagingErrorCount                                           0    │
│     ReceiveFIFOOverrunErrorCount                                 0    │
│     ReceiverMissedPacketCount                                    0    │
│     GotNothingCount                                              0    │
│     UnsupportedFramePacketCount                                  0    │
│     UnsupportedMulticastCount                                    0    │
│     BackToBackSendCount                                     42,987    │
│     EnqueuedSendsCount                                      24,491    │
└─────────────────────────────────────────────────────────────────────┘
```

Table 8.8
MONITOR Generic Network Board Statistics

Network Board Statistic	Description
Total Packets Sent	The total packets sent through that LAN driver interface. It can be used to indicate which LAN driver interface is handling most of the packets that are sent by the server.
Total Packets Received	The total packets received through that LAN driver interface. It can be used to indicate which LAN driver interface is handling most of the packets received by the server.
No ECB Count Available	This counter increments when a packet receive buffer is not available for an incoming packet. Packet receive buffers are allocated on demand until they reach the value in the SET Maximum Packet Receive Buffers parameter.
Send Packet Too Big Count	This counter increments when the server transmits a packet that is too big to be handled by the receive buffers. This indicates a problem with the value of the SET Maximum Physical Receive Packet Size parameter. It could also indicate a problem with the NIC driver or server software.
Send Packet Too Small Count	This counter increments when the server transmits a packet that is too small. This indicates a problem with the NIC driver or server software.
Receive Packet Overflow Count	This counter increments when the server receives a packet that is too big to be handled by the receive buffers. This indicates a problem with the workstation software arriving at a packet size that is too large (after packet size negotiation that is done when a workstation connects to the server). It could also indicate a problem with the NIC driver or NIC card at the sender.
Receive Packet Too Big Count	This counter increments when the server receives a packet that is too big to be handled by the NIC. This indicates a problem with the value of the SET Maximum Physical Receive Packet Size parameter. It could also indicate a problem with the NIC driver, NIC card, or sender software.
Receive Packet Too Small Count	This counter increments when the server receives a packet that is too small. This indicates a problem with the NIC driver, NIC card, or sender software.
Send Packet Miscellaneous Errors	This counter increments when errors occur in sending a packet that does not fit into any other category. Large values indicate problems with network hardware or software.

continues

Table 8.8, Continued
MONITOR Generic Network Board Statistics

Network Board Statistic	Description
Receive Packet Miscellaneous Errors	This counter increments when errors occur in receiving a packet that does not fit into any other category. Large values indicate problems with network hardware or software.
Send Packet Retry Count	This counter increments when the server tries to resend a packet because of hardware errors, such as cabling and NIC hardware problems. If there are long delays experienced by the packet, such as going over WAN links or many intermediate routers, it could cause the packet to *time out.* Try adjusting the time delay or the retry count to solve this problem.
Checksum Errors	This counter increments when a data error is detected by the CRC checksum (or other hardware checksum) in the packet. This indicates a problem with LAN cabling, NIC hardware, or excessive signal interference.
Hardware Receive Mismatch Count	This counter increments when the packet length indicated by the length field in the packet does not match the size of the packet received by the NIC. This occurs for packets that use IEEE 802.3 framing that has a length field. This indicates a problem with the NIC or NIC driver.
Total Send OK Byte Count Low	This is the total number of bytes sent by this NIC including the packet header. If you divide this number by the Total Packets Sent, you can get an average packet size for packets sent from the server on your network.
Total Receive OK Byte Count Low	This is the total number of bytes received by this NIC including the packet header. If you divide this number by the Total Packets Received, you can get an average packet size for packets received by the server on your network.
Total Group Address Send Count	This counter is used to keep track of the number of multicast packets sent by the server.
	Multicasting refers to packets that can be sent to multiple destinations. The IEEE addressing mechanisms for the MAC layer supports an Individual/Group (I/G) bit in the data-link layer (OSI model) address that allows a grouping of nodes on the network. Examples of the use of group addressing are SAP (Service Advertising Protocol) and RIP (Routing Information Protocol). SAP and RIP packets are essential for the operation of a NetWare-based network, but if you see an unusually large number of packets sent by your server, it indicates a software or routing problem.

Network Board Statistic	Description
Total Group Address Receive Count	This counter is used to keep track of the number of multicast packets received by the server. *Multicasting* refers to packets that can be sent to multiple destinations. The IEEE addressing mechanisms for the MAC layer supports an Individual/Group (I/G) bit in the data-link layer (OSI model) address that allows a grouping of nodes on the network. Examples of the use of group addressing are SAP (Service Advertising Protocol) and RIP (Routing Information Protocol). SAP and RIP packets are essential for the operation of a NetWare-based network, but if you see an unusually large number of packets received by your server, it indicates a software or routing problem with other servers or routers on the network.
Adapter Reset Count	This indicates the number of times an adapter was reset because of an internal failure in the adapter or a call made by the network adapter driver to initialize the board. A high value for this counter usually indicates a hardware problem with the network adapter. This statistic is reset when you load or unload the driver.
Adapter Operating Time Stamp	This shows the last time the network adapter changed state. Events that can cause a network adapter to change state include loading or unloading the network adapter driver and resetting the adapter, among others.
Adapter Queue Depth	When a packet is ready to be sent, it is placed in a send queue that is processed by the network adapter driver. If the queue size is large and/or continues to grow, it indicates excessive traffic on the network, a problem with the network adapter or network cabling, or the inability of the network adapter to handle the packet traffic generated by the server. In the latter case, you should try replacing the network adapter with a higher performance network adapter.
Send OK Single Collision Count	This applies to CSMA/CD-based networks such as Ethernet. This is a count of the number of packets that were transmitted successfully despite a single collision. A high value indicates a failure in a network adapter, exceeding distance specifications for cabling, or an impedance mismatch.

continues

Table 8.8, Continued
MONITOR Generic Network Board Statistics

Network Board Statistic	Description
Send OK Multiple Collision Count	This applies to CSMA/CD-based networks such as Ethernet. This is a count of the number of packets that were transmitted successfully despite two or more collisions. A high value indicates a failure in a network adapter, exceeding distance specifications for cabling, or an impedance mismatch.
Send OK But Deferred	This statistic indicates the number of packets that had to wait to be sent, but were sent successfully after their wait period. A high number indicates that the network is busy, and you may want to consider splitting your network to reduce traffic load.
Send Abort From Late Collisions	This applies to CSMA/CD-based networks such as Ethernet. This is a count of the number of packet transmissions that were aborted because of a late collision. A *late collision* is a collision that occurs after a number of bytes equal to the minimum Ethernet packet size has been sent. The minimum Ethernet packet size including header and CRC is 64 bytes (512 bits). If a collision occurs after 12 bits, it is a late collision. If the packet size was 64 bytes, it would have been completely transmitted before the collision was detected. Late collisions indicate problems with network adapter hardware, impedance mismatch, or cables that exceed distance specifications.
Send Abort From Excess Collisions	This applies to CSMA/CD-based networks such as Ethernet. This is a count of the number of packet transmissions that were aborted because of excessive collision. This indicates problems with network adapter hardware such as generating random transmissions ("jabber" problem), impedance mismatch, or cables that exceed distance specifications.
Send Abort From Carrier Sense	This applies to CSMA/CD-based networks such as Ethernet. This is a count of the number of packet transmissions that were aborted because of loss of carrier sense. This indicates problems with the network adapter, a break in the cable from the NIC to the network, or a general problem with the cable.
Send Abort From Excessive Deferral	This applies to CSMA/CD-based networks such as Ethernet. This is a count of the number of packet transmissions that did not take place because the Ethernet NIC had to wait for another station to finish transmitting. Ethernet NICs use the Listen Before Talking technique where NICs defer to other NICs that are transmitting. If the deferral delay exceeds a

Network Board Statistic	Description
	certain amount, the transmission is aborted and the Upper Protocol Layers are informed of this fact. This usually indicates that the network is heavily loaded, but it could also mean problems with the NIC.
Receive Abort From Bad Frame Alignment	This is used to count the number of frames that were improperly aligned when they were received. This is usually caused by hardware problems with NICs, repeaters/concentrators, or collisions that cause the frame to appear misaligned.

Understanding Packet Burst

The normal operation of NCP requests and replies is that every NCP packet has to have its own acknowledgment packet. This makes NCP a *send-and-wait* protocol. Send-and-wait protocols can, at any one time, have only one outstanding packet to be acknowledged (also some times called *Ping-Pong* protocol). Modern protocol design allows protocols to have the option of sending several packets in sequence (called the *window*), and have the receiver acknowledge them with a single acknowledgment packet. The larger the size of the window, the greater the efficiency of data transfer. The window option for NCP is called *packet burst* by Novell. For a detailed analysis of the efficiency of packet burst, refer to the author's *NetWare: The Professional Reference,* from New Riders Publishing.

If the packet in a window is corrupted in transmission, the protocol should have mechanisms to retransmit the entire packet sequence or selectively transmit only the corrupted packet. The window size is usually limited by the amount of buffer space available at the receiver and by requirements for acknowledged data to be received within a certain interval of time by upper layer protocols.

In many large networks, NetWare servers are often connected by WAN links that typically operate at slower speeds than LANs, and have longer time delays. When using NetWare over WAN links that have long delays, it is important that a protocol have a window capability so it can transmit a number of packets before obtaining an acknowledgment. Without the packet burst capability, the efficiency of data transfer can be very low. This is because the WAN link is not in use while the sender is waiting for an acknowledgment of the last packet it has sent.

When large amounts of data are transmitted without packet burst, the data is spread across a number of packets, each of which has to be separately acknowledged. If the data is sent in 1,000 packets, there will be 1,000 separate acknowledgments, and a total of 2,000 data and acknowledgment packets are transferred. If an intervening router has a small packet size, such as 512 bytes, the negotiated packet size between workstation and server will be limited to the small router packet size, and this will result in even a larger number of data and acknowledgment packets that would need to be transmitted.

 Packet burst allows the NCP protocol to transfer data up to 64 KB in a single read or write request, without having to individually acknowledge each packet used to transfer the data.

The window size for packet burst protocol is variable, It is called the *burst window size* and is defined as the number of packets in a *burst* transaction. The maximum amount of data that can be sent in a burst window is 64 KB. Assuming a packet size of 512 bytes, a maximum of 128 packets can be sent in a packet burst. If the packet size is 1,024 bytes, a maximum of 64 packets can be sent in a packet burst. The following simple formula shows the relationship between the number of packets (burst window) in a packet burst (*N*), and the packet size (*P*) in KB.

$$N = 64/P$$

The preceding formula shows the maximum number of packets that are transmitted. The actual number of packets in a packet burst is dynamically adjusted and is based on factors such as buffer capacity at receiver and line capacity. The DOS Requester keeps track of the number of packets lost. If enough packets are lost, it assumes that the network is very busy, and reduces the burst window size. Packets that are lost are selectively retransmitted rather than transmitting the entire burst.

The maximum amount of data that can be sent in a packet burst window is 64 KB.

The packet burst windows size is dynamically adjusted based on factors such as buffer capacity at receiver and line capacity.

With packet burst, the number of acknowledgment packets that need to be transmitted are reduced. And since a single acknowledgment can be used to acknowledge a number of packets, the communication efficiency is improved. Using packet burst, a workstation can issue a single request to read or write up to 64 KB of data. To prevent the workstation from being overrun by large amounts of data sent by the server, a flow control mechanism is used. This flow control mechanism is called the *packet burst gap time. Flow control* refers to mechanisms that prevent a sender from exceeding the capacity of a receiver to handle large amounts of data sent too quickly. The packet burst gap time is the time delay requested by workstations between packet burst transmissions. The value of the packet burst gap time should be such that the workstation has enough time to process the data received in the last packet burst transmission.

To prevent the workstation from being overrun by large amounts of data sent by the server, packet burst uses a flow control mechanism called the packet burst gap time, which is is the time delay requested by workstations between packet burst transmissions.

Packet burst is set up on a connection basis. NetWare 4 client software is by default enabled for packet burst. Applications do not have to be specifically written to use packet burst. They will automatically have better response times for large data transfers between workstations and servers.

When the DOS Requester loads, it determines whether the workstation has enough memory for the requested number of packet buffers (controlled through PB BUFFERS statement in the NET.CFG file). If sufficient memory is available, the Requester makes a packet burst connection. In a packet burst connection, the DOS Requester negotiates the maximum packet burst window size, based on the maximum packet size negotiated and the buffer capacity at the workstation and server. Once a connection is set up for packet burst, it exists for the duration of the connection, and is used for all data transmissions that are more than 512 bytes. Applications do not have to be packet burst aware; they will automatically benefit from packet burst. If the Requester fails to make a packet burst connection during an attach/login, it uses a normal NCP connection that does not use packet burst.

If a workstation has several connections to different file servers, some of these connections could be packet burst-enabled while others may not be. For packet burst to work, both sender and receiver must be enabled for packet burst. If either the workstation or server is not enabled for packet burst, NCP transmissions operate in the standard mode using the send-and-wait protocol where an acknowledgment is sent for each NCP packet. NetWare 4 workstations and servers are automatically enabled for packet burst. Earlier versions of NetWare had to be explicitly enabled for packet burst.

A NetWare 4 server cannot be disabled for packet burst, but a NetWare 4 workstation can be disabled for packet burst by adding a statement PB BUFFERS=0 in the DOS Requester section of the NET.CFG file. The PB BUFFERS statement is used to set the number of packet burst buffers used at the workstation. Its general form is as follows:

```
NetWare DOS Requester
PB Buffers = n
```

The number of packet buffers (*n*) can be set to a value of 0 to 10 (default value is 3). A value of 0 disables packet burst. Increasing the number of packet buffers does not always improve network performance if the workstation cannot keep up with the amount of data sent in a packet burst. If the network hardware and the workstation drivers are unable to handle the packet burst, performance can degrade.

If packets are dropped because of heavy network traffic, the NetWare client requestor automatically decreases the window size to reduce further packet

loss. Packets that are lost are transmitted selectively, and the entire packet burst need not be retransmitted.

 NetWare 4 servers are always enabled for packet burst and cannot be disabled. To enable packet burst at the workstation, set the PB BUFFERS = *n* (where *n* is a value from 0 to 10) in the NetWare DOS Requester section of the NET.CFG file.

Novell claims that the packet burst can improve performance from 10 to 300 percent depending on availability of buffer memory, data speed, and size of file being transmitted.

Large Internet Packet Size

The packet size to be used for a connection between the workstation and the server is negotiated when the workstation opens a connection to the server. The packet size depends on the physical network type being used and the packet receive buffer size at the workstation and the server. If there is an intervening router, the default packet size for routers is used. Because IPX routers have a default packet size of 512 bytes, the connection uses a default size of 512 bytes, and this can lower the data transfer rates for the connection.

 If there is an intervening router between a workstation and a server, the default packet size for routers (usually 512 bytes) is used unless it is configured for a larger packet size.

NetWare 4 has a feature called Large Internet Packet (LIP) that can be enabled using the console SET Allow LIP parameter. Using this feature allows the server to use a larger Internet packet size regardless of any intervening routers. You must, however, still ensure that the routers can handle packet sizes larger than 512 bytes. If a NetWare-based router is being used, you can configure the router for a larger packet size by using the following:

```
SET MAXIMUM PHYSICAL RECEIVE PACKET SIZE =
➥packet size
```

You must set the previous parameter for all intervening NetWare-based routers. If you are using a hardware- or software-based router from a third-party vendor, you will have to refer to the manufacturer's documentation on configuring the router for a larger packet size. Novell documentation provides information on maximum physical packet size, as shown in table 8.9, even though many drivers and network adapters provide higher limits for maximum packet sizes. The maximum packet size for ARCnet cannot be adjusted, and therefore LIP does not work for ARCnet.

 For a NetWare-based router, you can configure the router for a larger packet size by setting the SET MAXIMUM PHYSICAL RECEIVE PACKET SIZE parameter.

Large Internet Packets cannot be used with ARCnet.

Table 8.9
Novell's Limits for Maximum Packet Sizes

Network Type	Maximum Packet Size (bytes)
Ethernet	1,514
Token Ring @ 4 Mbps	4,202
Token Ring @ 16 Mbps	4,202
ARCnet	576

To enable LIP on a NetWare 4 server, enter the following at the server console:

```
SET ALLOW LIP =ON
```

You can also set this parameter in the STARTUP. NCF file for the server. The default setting for SET ALLOW LIP is ON for NetWare 4.01 (and above).

To enable LIP at a NetWare 4 workstation, use the LARGE INTERNET PACKETS statement in the NET.CFG file, as shown here:

```
LARGE INTERNET PACKETS=ON
```

The default value of LARGE INTERNET PACKETS is ON. When the DOS Requester loads, the FIO.VLM module processes the LARGE INTERNET PACKETS statement.

 To enable LIP, do the following:

1. At the server use SET ALLOW LIP=ON.

2. At the workstation add LARGE INTERNET PACKETS=ON in NET.CFG.

When LIP is used in conjunction with packet burst, it provides the best transfer rates because fewer large-sized packets are used, and they can be sent in succession without waiting for acknowledgment of each packet.

Managing Disk Performance

One of the strengths of NetWare has always been a fast and efficient file system. This system is central to NetWare's popularity in its ability to act as a file server. In NetWare 4, the file system has been improved. Some of these improvements are because of block suballocation and compression.

The type of disk drive, disk driver, and controller used in a NetWare server strongly affects the file services performance. The disk driver, implemented as an NLM (*.DSK), acts as an interface between the NetWare OS and the disk controller. The disk controller controls the operation of the disk.

Disk controllers that use bus-mastering and 32-bit technologies will improve the server performance. For improved performance Novell recommends disk controllers and disk drives that use the SCSI interface. These can service multiple drives attached to the same controller.

 Significant improvement in file service performance is possible using a high-end device driver/disk controller combination.

Block Suballocation

NetWare 4 allows the disk block size selected at installation time to be 4 KB, 8 KB, 16 KB, 32 KB, or 64 KB (where 1 KB is 1,024 bytes). This capability also existed in NetWare 3; in NetWare 3, however, if a 200-byte file was created on a volume that had a disk block size of 4 KB, a 4 KB block of storage would be allocated and the remaining 3,896 bytes would not be available for use, representing 95 percent wasted space. If the disk block size was 64 KB, the wasted space would be even greater. Figure 8.55 shows how block suballocation in NetWare 4 works.

 NetWare 4 allows the disk block size selected at installation time to be 4 KB, 8 KB, 16 KB, 32 KB, or 64 KB.

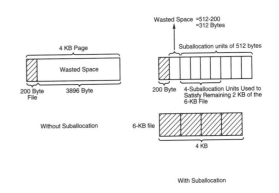

Figure 8.55
Block suballocation.

In NetWare 4, the unused disk block space is used in 512-byte suballocation units. This means that in the example of creating a file of size 200 bytes, a 512-byte suballocation within the 4 KB disk block would be used. The remaining seven 512-byte suballocation blocks would be available for sharing by the leftover fragments of other files. If all of these suballocation blocks were used, then in the NetWare 4 example there would be wasted space of only 312 bytes (512 – 200) out of a total of 4,096 bytes, which is only eight percent wasted space. Also, if the file sizes and leftover fragments were multiples of 512 bytes, there would be no wasted space.

 In NetWare 4, the unused disk block space can be shared by other files in 512-byte suballocation units.

Block suballocation can be defined as a mechanism in NetWare 4 that allows small files and files that are not multiples of the disk block size to share space in a disk block that would otherwise have gone wasted. The improved utilization in disk space is accompanied by the extra overhead in the operating system to maintain status of disk blocks that have been suballocated. Because disk writes are done in the background, however, the impact of this overhead is minimal.

The volume block size determines the number of suballocation units that it can hold. The default block size is determined for each volume and is a function of the size of the volume. Table 8.10 shows the default block size for a specific volume size. Remember that in block suballocation, a larger block size is not wasted for small files. Also, once selected, the block size cannot be changed.

Table 8.10
Default Block Size vs. Volume Size

Default Block Size (KB)	Volume Size (Range is in MB)
4	0 to 31
8	32 to 149
16	150 to 499
32	500 to 1,999
64	2,000 and above

 Block suballocation is enabled by default during NetWare volume installation, and is done at the server volume level. The decision to enable/disable suballocation is made at the time the volume is first created. You cannot enable or disable suballocation at a later point.

To examine volume suballocation, you can perform the following steps:

1. Run INSTALL at the server.

   LOAD INSTALL

2. Select Volume Options. A list of volumes mounted at the server appears.

3. Highlight a volume and press Enter.

   You see the Volume Information (see fig. 8.56), along with the volume file compression, block suballocation, and data migration status.

   If this is the first time the volume is being created, you can select Block Suballocation and set it to On or Off.

NetWare File System Compression

Studies have shown that the processor utilization of many NetWare servers in real-life networks does not often exceed 50 percent. In heavily loaded servers, it is not uncommon to see processor utilization higher than 90 percent, but such situations are relatively rare. The designers of NetWare 4 decided to use this un-utilized processor bandwidth for useful background tasks such as file system compression.

Figure 8.56
Volume information.

```
                        Volume Information
 Driver op
 Disk
 Volu    Vo    Volume Name:            SYS
 Lice
 Copy  NW     Volume Block Size:      64 KB Blocks
 Dire  SY
 NCF          Status:                 Mounted
 Prod
 Serv         File Compression:       On
 Exit
              Block Suballocation:    On

              Data Migration:         Off
```

In NetWare 4, file compression is done in the background. Certain parameters can be set at the file server to control the frequency at which compression can be done in the background. When a compressed file is retrieved, it is decompressed. The file blocks that are immediately decompressed are available for use, even as the rest of the file is being decompressed. Usually, the file remains in this decompressed state until a certain period of time has passed. The time frame for file recompression is controlled at the server.

It is helpful to understand how file compression takes place when answering such questions as: What happens if there is a server failure when a file is being compressed? Are the contents of the original, uncompressed file intact? During file compression, the following events take place:

1. The file compression process analyzes the file to be compressed and determines whether there is a minimum savings gain (the default setting is two percent) in compressing the file. In this process it creates a temporary file describing the original file.

2. In cases of no minimum savings gain, compression is not done.

   In cases of minimum savings gain, a temporary file is created to hold the compressed data.

3. Compression runs in the background, and the compressed file data is stored in the temporary file.

4. If the compression is successful, the temporary, compressed file replaces the original file. If an error such as a power failure occurs, the original file is kept intact.

Using the file compression feature, the effective disk space can be increased without adding new server drives. The amount of savings in disk space is called the *compression ratio,* and depends on the

nature of repeated characters or binary patterns in the file. Compression ratios are high for text files. The average compression ratio for a volume is 63 percent or more. This ratio means that 500 MB of files can take up as little as 185 MB (at 63 percent compression) of disk space. With disk space perennially at a premium on file servers, this feature is a great advantage.

Decompressing a file is very quick and has no noticeable effect on the performance of a file server. Compressing a file, on the other hand, can take up a significant amount of processor cycles. The processor utilization as reported through MONITOR can be high when compression is taking place. For this reason, compression usually is done at times when there is relatively little server activity (such as at midnight). Only files that have not been accessed for a specified period of time are compressed.

 Decompression of a file is very quick and has no noticeable effect on the performance of a file server, but compressing a file can increase server processor utilization.

Enabling Compression

The compression option can be disabled or enabled when running the INSTALL.NLM during installation of a volume on the NetWare server. The default is that compression is enabled. Once turned on, file compression cannot be disabled at the volume level unless you re-create the volume. Even if file compression is enabled at the volume level, you can disable file compression at an individual file or directory level by using the FLAG command. You can even disable file compression for the entire file server by setting the following at the file server:

```
SET ENABLE FILE COMPRESSION=OFF
```

Study Note Always enable file compression at the volume level. You can always use options to selectively disable compression for files and directories, or for the entire server.

The compression option can be disabled or enabled when running the INSTALL.NLM during installation of a volume on the NetWare server.

The default setting for file compression is ON. Once turned on, you cannot disable file compression at the volume level unless you re-create the volume.

To examine file compression for a volume, you can perform the following steps:

1. Run INSTALL at the server.

    `LOAD INSTALL`

2. Select Volume Options. A list of volumes mounted at the server appears.

3. Highlight a volume and press Enter.

    You see the Volume Information (see fig. 8.57), and the volume file compression, block suballocation, and data migration status.

If this is the first time the volume is being created, you can select File Compression and set it to ON or OFF.

If the file compression is Off, you can change the value to On, but if the file compression is On, you cannot change the file compression to Off without deleting the volume and re-creating it.

Controlling Compression

After file compression has been enabled at the volume level, you can make use of a number of SET parameters (see table 8.11) to control the behavior of file compression. These SET commands can be entered at the server console, in the AUTO-EXEC.NCF file, or through the SERVMAN NLM. To change these parameters using SERVMAN, use the following as a guideline:

1. Run SERVMAN at server console.

    `LOAD SERVMAN`

2. Select Console Set Commands from Available Options.

3. Select File System from Categories.

4. Scroll through the parameters until you see the compression parameters listed in figure 8.57.

Figure 8.57

Compression SET parameters in SERVMAN.

```
                         File system Parameters
 Compression Daily Check Stop Hour                    6
 Compression Daily Check Starting Hour                0
 Minimum Compression Percentage Gain                  2
 Enable File Compression                              On
 Maximum Concurrent Compressions                      2
 Convert Compressed To Uncompressed Option            1
 Decompress Percent Disk Space Free To Allow C...     10
 Decompress Free Space Warning Interval               31 Min 18.5 Sec
 Deleted Files Compression Option                     1

 The hour (0 = midnight, 23 = 11pm) when the file compressor ends scanning
 each enabled volume for files that need to be compressed (if Compression
 Daily Check Stop Hour is equal to Compression Daily Starting Hour then
 start checking every day at Compression Daily Starting Hour and run as
 long as necessary to finish all files meeting the compressible criteria.)
                        (also settable in STARTUP.NCF)
                               Setting: 6
                             Limits: 0 to 23
```

Table 8.11
File Compression SET Parameters

Compression Parameter	Description
Minimum Compression	Refers to the minimum gains in savings that a Percentage Gain compressed file must have to remain compressed. Value can range from 0 to 50, and has a default value of 2.
Enable File Compression	When this parameter is set to ON, the file compression process will run for volumes that have file compression enabled. If set to OFF, the file compression does not run, even though file compression has been enabled for a volume on the server. In other words, setting this value to OFF prevents file compression from running on the server volume. Immediate compress requests are queued and run when this parameter is set to ON. The default value is ON.
Compression Daily Check Starting Hour	The hour when file compression is activated and scan files on compression enable volumes to determine whether they can be compressed. Files that are open are not considered for compression. The value can range from 0 to 23 and has a default value of 0. A value of 0 is midnight and 23 is 11:00 p.m.
Compression Daily Check Stop Hour	The hour when the file compression process stops scanning for files to be compressed on compression enabled volumes. The value can range from 0 to 23 and has a default value of 6. A value of 0 is midnight and 23 is 11:00 p.m.
Days Untouched Before Compression	This specifies how many days the file compression should wait after a file has been accessed before attempting to compress it. The value can range from 0 to 100,000 days and has a default value of 7 days.
Maximum Concurrent Compressions	The number of simultaneous file compressions that can be taking place. This occurs if more than one volume is on the server The value can range from 1 to 8 and has a default value of 2.
Decompress Percent Disk Space Free To Allow Commit	Percentage of free disk space that should be on the volume before a file can be decompressed. This is used to prevent newly decompressed files from filling the volume. The default value is 10 percent and can range from 0 to 75.
Decompress Free Space Warning Interval	If free disk space is insufficient for decompressing the files, warning alerts are displayed on the console at the frequency specified by this parameter. The default value is 31 minutes, 18.5 seconds. The range is 0 to 29 days, 15 hours, 50 minutes, 3.85 seconds.

continues

Table 8.11, Continued
File Compression SET Parameters

Compression Parameter	Description
Deleted Files Compression Option	This parameter controls the way in which the server handles deleted files that have not been purged. The values have the following meanings: 0 = Don't compress deleted files. 1= Compress during next search interval. 2= Compress immediately. The default value is 1.
Convert Compressed To Uncompressed Option	This parameter controls how the server stores a compressed file that has been uncompressed. The values have the following meanings: 0 = Leave file in compressed state. 1 = Leave file compressed after a single access within the Days Untouched Before Compression. 2 = Leave file in the uncompressed state. The default value is 1.
Uncompress Percent Disk Space Free To Allow Commit	This is the percentage of free disk space that is required on a volume before an uncompressed file can be saved in the uncompressed state on the volume. This prevents newly uncompressed files from filling up the volume. The default value is 10 percent.
Uncompress Free Space Warning Interval	This is the time interval for displaying warning alerts when a volume has insufficient disk space for uncompressed files from filling up space on the volume. The default value is 31 minutes, 18.5 seconds.

Using the command FLAG or the utilities FILER and the NetWare Administrator, you can change the attributes of files and directories to control compression.

The Immediate Compress (IC) attribute can be applied to files only, and immediately starts the compression of the flagged file, unless the SET ENABLE FILE COMPRESSION is set to OFF. If the SET ENABLE FILE COMPRESSION is set to OFF, the file that is flagged with the IC attribute is queued for compression until the time when the SET ENABLE FILE COMPRESSION is set to ON.

To immediately compress the file SYS: ACCT\GLEDGER.DAT using the FLAG command, you would execute the following command:

```
FLAG  SYS:ACCT\GLEDGER.DAT  IC
```

The Don't Compress (DC) attribute can be applied to files and directories to prevent the flagged files from being compressed.

To prevent files in the SYS:CRITICAL\DATA directory and its subdirectories from being compressed, you can execute the following command:

```
FLAG  SYS:CRITICAL\DATA  DC  /S
```

 The Immediate Compress (IC) attribute can be applied to files only, and immediately starts the compression of the flagged file, whereas the Don't Compress (DC) attribute can be applied to files and directories, and prevents the flagged files from being compressed.

To change file attributes using FILER, use the following steps:

1. Run FILER.

2. Select Manage Files and Directories.

3. Use Directory Contents to browse the directory structure and highlight the file.

4. Press F10.

5. Select View/Set File Information from File options.

6. Highlight Attributes and press Enter to see the current file attributes.

7. Press Ins to see other file attributes that can be set.

8. Mark the attributes you want to assign (using the F5 key) and press Enter.

To change directory attributes using FILER, use the following steps:

1. Run FILER.

2. Select Manage Files and Directories.

3. Use Directory Contents to browse the directory structure and highlight the directory.

4. Press F10.

5. Select View/Set File Directory Information from Subdirectory options.

6. Highlight Directory Attributes and press Enter to see the current directory attributes.

7. Press Ins to see other attributes that can be set for the directory.

8. Mark the attributes you want to assign (using the F5 key) and press Enter.

To change file/directory attributes using the NetWare Administrator, use the following steps:

1. Double-click on the Volume object to see the directory contents

2. Highlight the file or directory, right-click, and select Details (or press Enter) to see file/directory details.

3. Select the Attributes page button.

4. For files, you see the form in figure 8.58 that can be used to change file attributes; and for directories, you see the form in figure 8.59 that can be used to change directory attributes.

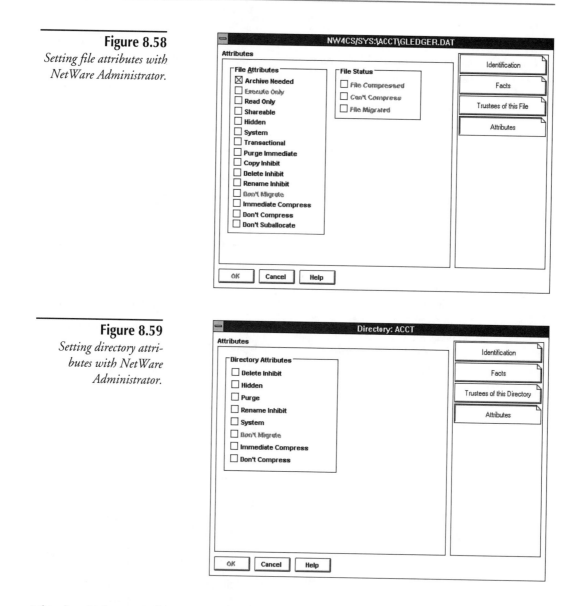

Figure 8.58

Setting file attributes with NetWare Administrator.

Figure 8.59

Setting directory attributes with NetWare Administrator.

Viewing Volume and Compression Statistics

After compression has been enabled, you can view compression ratios and statistics on the volume with NDIR, FILER, and NetWare Administrator.

To see compression statistics on the entire volume, use the following:

```
NDIR /VOL
```

The following is the output of the previous command:

```
Statistics for fixed volume NW4CS/SYS:
Space statistics are in KB (1024 bytes).

Total volume space:                         604,160  100.00%
Space used by 6,152 entries:                195,264   32.32%
Deleted space not yet purgeable:                  0    0.00%
                                            -------   ------
Space remaining on volume:                  408,896   67.68%
Space available to ADMIN:                   408,896   67.68%

Maximum directory entries:                   25,600
Available directory entries:                 11,108   43.39%

Space used if files were not compressed:    622,787
Space used by compressed files:             189,207
                                            -------   ------
Space saved by compressing files:           433,580   69.62%

Uncompressed space used:                      6,057
```

This output shows that the space saved by compressing the files is 69.62 percent. The space used by compressed files is 433,580 KB and the space used by uncompressed files is 6,057 KB.

To view compression ratios for a file or directory, you can use the following command:

NDIR *PathName*   /COMP

To see compression ratios for the SYS:SYSTEM directory, for example, use the following:

NDIR SYS:SYSTEM /COMP

Figure 8.60 shows the compression statistics that can be viewed from the volume statistics screen by using FILER. To observe these statistics, use the following steps:

1. Run FILER.

2. Select View volume information.

3. Select Statistics. You should see the volume statistics of figure 8.60.

4. To see the features of the volume (if suballocation, compression, or data migration have been enabled), select Features from View Volume Information. Figure 8.61 shows that compression and suballocation have been enabled for the volume, that only the DOS name space has been installed, and that the volume block size is 32 KB.

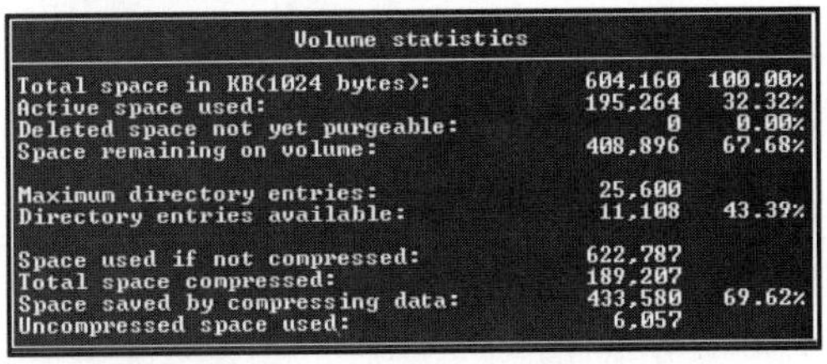

Figure 8.60
Volume statistics using FILER.

Figure 8.61

Volume features using FILER.

To view compression statistics using the NetWare
Administrator, use the following steps:

1. Start NetWare Administrator.

2. Highlight the Volume object. Press Enter to
   see the Detail properties (or right-click and
   select Details).

3. Select the Statistics page button.

4. You should see the compression statistics in
   the bottom left corner of the volume statistics
   screen (see fig. 8.62).

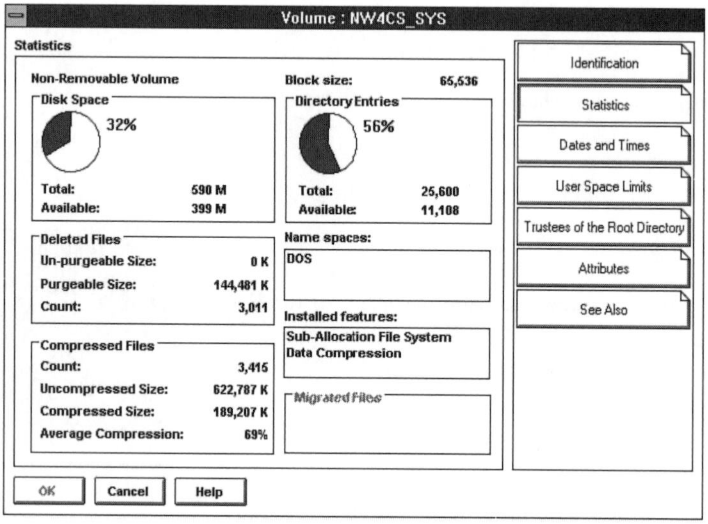

Figure 8.62

*Volume statistics using
NetWare Administrator.*

Study Guide for the Chapter

If you are preparing to pass exams, review the chapter with the following goals:

- Understand and remember the names of the new console commands and the new NLMs. Use the study tips as a quick review.

- Pay particular attention to the new commands for devices, language support, and the RTDM, TIMESYNC, SERVMAN, DOMAIN, and KEYB NLMs.

- After studying this chapter, attempt the sample test questions for this chapter. If you miss a question, review the appropriate topic until you understand the correct answer.

Chapter Summary

This chapter discussed the changes in NetWare 4 for managing the server. The new console commands for mirroring, magazine, and media support, listing and scanning for new devices, and restarting the server were discussed.

In addition, changes to the RCONSOLE and MONITOR NLM were discussed. Some of the new NLMs and how they are used in NetWare 4 also were discussed. Examples of these new NLMs are DOMAIN, DSREPAIR, DSMERGE, CDROM, NWSNUT, RTDM, SCHDELAY, and TIMESYNC.

Chapter Test Questions

Most of the test questions are multiple choice. Where a single answer is desired, they are indicated by a ○ (circle) notation that precedes the possible answers. Some questions require you to select more than one answer; these are indicated by a □ (box) preceding each answer. Not all the questions are multiple choice. Occasionally you will be asked for a short (usually one-word) answer. The answer is not case sensitive; you can type the answer in lower- or uppercase.

Certain questions will be repeated in different ways so that you can recognize them even when the wording is different. Taking practice quizzes will not only test your knowledge, but will give you confidence when you take your exam.

1. What is the NetWare 4 console command for obtaining help on server console commands?

   ○ A. ?

   ○ B. HELP

   ○ C. HELP CONSOLE

   ○ D. HELPCMD

2. Which console command allows the NLMs to use language-specific message files?

   ○ A. LANGSET

   ○ B. SET LANGUAGE

   ○ C. RESTART SERVER

   ○ D. REBOOT

   ○ E. LANGUAGE

   ○ F. KEYB

3. To restart a downed server and prevent execution of the STARTUP.NCF file, use which of the following commands?

   ○ A. RESTART SERVER -NA

   ○ B. RESTART SERVER -N=AUTOEXEC.NCF

   ○ C. RESTART SERVER -N=STARTUP.NCF

   ○ D. RESTART SERVER -NS

   ○ E. RESTART SERVER -I

   ○ F. RESTART SERVER -D

4. To restart a downed server and prevent execution of the AUTOEXEC.NCF file, use which of the following commands?

   ○ A. RESTART SERVER -NA

   ○ B. RESTART SERVER -N=AUTOEXEC.NCF

   ○ C. RESTART SERVER -N=STARTUP.NCF

   ○ D. RESTART SERVER -NS

   ○ E. RESTART SERVER -I

   ○ F. RESTART SERVER -D

5. To restart a downed server and enter the internal debugger, use which of the following commands?

   ○ A. RESTART SERVER -NA

   ○ B. RESTART SERVER -N=AUTOEXEC.NCF

   ○ C. RESTART SERVER -N=STARTUP.NCF

   ○ D. RESTART SERVER -NS

○ E. RESTART SERVER -I

○ F. RESTART SERVER -D

6. The Language Message files can be installed by using which NLM?

   ○ A. INSTALL NLM

   ○ B. MONITOR NLM

   ○ C. SERVMAN NLM

   ○ D. LANGUAGE NLM

   ○ E. ADDLANG NLM

7. The NetWare 4 RCONSOLE combines the functions of _____ and _____ for NetWare 3.

   ○ A. RCONSOLE, XCONSOLE

   ○ B. ACONSOLE, XCONSOLE

   ○ C. ACONSOLE, RCONSOLE

   ○ D. FCONSOLE, RCONSOLE

8. The RCONSOLE Workstation Address option enables you to see _____.

   ○ A. the workstation's node address

   ○ B. the workstation's network address

   ○ C. the workstation's connection number

   ○ D. the user name at the workstation

9. Which control key invokes the RCONSOLE menu?

   ○ A. Alt+F1

   ○ B. Alt+F2

   ○ C. Alt+F3

   ○ D. Alt+F4

○ E. Alt+F5

○ F. *

10. Which control key in the RCONSOLE program displays workstation address?

    ○ A. Alt+F1

    ○ B. Alt+F2

    ○ C. Alt+F3

    ○ D. Alt+F4

    ○ E. Alt+F5

11. Which control keys in the RCONSOLE program can be used to scroll through console screens?

    ○ A. Alt+F1

    ○ B. Alt+F2

    ○ C. Alt+F3

    ○ D. Alt+F4

    ○ E. Alt+F5

    ○ F. +

    ○ G. _

12. Which NLM creates a protected domain for running NLMs?

    ○ A. DSREPAIR

    ○ B. DOMAIN

    ○ C. DOMPROT

    ○ D. OSP

13. Which NLM supports the Real Time Data Migration feature?

    ○ A. MEMPOOL

    ○ B. MIGRATE

○ C. RTDM

○ D. RTM

14. Which NLM provides the User Utility Interface library for NetWare 4?

   ○ A. NWNUT

   ○ B. NUT

   ○ C. NUI

   ○ D. NWSNUT

15. Which NLM provides time synchronization across the network?

   ○ A. TIMESERV

   ○ B. SYNCTIME

   ○ C. TIMESYNC

   ○ D. TIMER

16. Which NLM can be used to merge roots of two NDS trees?

   ○ A. MERGEDS

   ○ B. DSMERGE

   ○ C. DSCOMB

   ○ D. DSCON

   ○ E. PARTMGR

17. Which NLM provides CD-ROM support?

   ○ A. CDROM

   ○ B. CD_ROM

   ○ C. CD-ROM

   ○ D. CDLIB

   ○ E. LIBCD

18. Which NLM provides international keyboard support?

   ○ A. KEYLIB

   ○ B. KEYLANG

   ○ C. KEYB

   ○ D. LANGUAGE

   ○ E. CODEPAGE

19. Which NLM can be used to view or modify SET parameters?

   ○ A. SERVMAN

   ○ B. MONITOR

   ○ C. INSTALL

   ○ D. KEYB

   ○ E. SET

20. Which of the following NLMs or console commands could be used to display SET parameters?

   ○ A. SERVMAN

   ○ B. MONITOR

   ○ C. INSTALL

   ○ D. KEYB

   ○ E. SET

21. Which NLM needs to be loaded to enable the DOMAIN commands?

   ○ A. DOMAIN

   ○ B. RING

   ○ C. DOMLIB

   ○ D. PROTECT

22. What command is used to list the NLMs loaded in the current domain?

    ○ A. DOMAIN LIST

    ○ B. DOMAIN DIR

    ○ C. MODULES

    ○ D. DOMAIN

    ○ E. DOMAIN=LIST

23. What command is used to change the protected domain to ring 2?

    ○ A. DOMAIN=2

    ○ B. DOMAIN PROTECT=2

    ○ C. DOMAIN PROTECT RING=2

    ○ D. DOMAIN RING=2

    ○ E. DOMAIN /R 2

24. What command is used to change the current domain to the operating system domain?

    ○ A. DOMAIN OS=ON

    ○ B. DOMAIN=OS

    ○ C. DOMAIN=OS_PROTECTED

    ○ D. DOMAIN=NW

    ○ E. DOMAIN=OS_PROTECT

25. What command is used to change the current domain to the protected domain?

    ○ A. DOMAIN OS=PROTECT

    ○ B. DOMAIN=OS

    ○ C. DOMAIN=OS_PROTECTED

    ○ D. DOMAIN=NW

    ○ E. DOMAIN=OS_PROTECT

26. Which NLM allows repair of problems with the NDS database?

    ○ A. NDSREPAIR

    ○ B. VREPAIR

    ○ C. DSREPAIR

    ○ D. DIBREPAIR

27. What command provides help on DOMAIN commands?

    ○ A. DOMAIN

    ○ B. DOMAIN /?

    ○ C. DOMAIN HELP

    ○ D. DOMAIN SYNTAX

28. The default error log file used by DSREPAIR is _____.

    ○ A. SYS:SYSTEM\DSLOG.TXT

    ○ B. SYS:SYSTEM\DS\DSLOG.TXT

    ○ C. SYS:SYSTEM\DS\DSREPAIR.LOG

    ○ D. SYS:SYSTEM\DSREPAIR.LOG

29. In the DSMERGE utility, _____.

    ○ A. the objects in the source tree become part of the target tree

    ○ B. the objects in the target tree become part of the source tree

    ○ C. containers in the source and target tree are merged

    ○ D. containers in the source and target tree are merged and if there are duplicate container names, the container in the target tree is renamed according to well-defined rules

30. In the DSMERGE utility, _____.

     A. the objects in the target tree become part of the source tree

     B. containers in the source and target tree are merged

     C. only the root objects are merged

     D. containers in the source and target tree are merged and if there are duplicate container names, the container in the target tree is renamed according to well-defined rules

31. In the DSMERGE utility, _____.

     A. the objects in the target tree become part of the source tree

     B. containers in the source and target tree are merged

     C. containers in the source and target tree are merged and if there are duplicate container names, the container in the target tree is renamed according to well-defined rules

     D. container object names for the same level of the NDS tree have to be unique in the source and target trees

32. If MONITOR reports the following:

    ```
    Total Cache Buffers = 1800
    Packet Receive Buffers = 50
    Current Disk Requests=5
    Open Files=13
    ```

    which statement is true?

   A. The number of cache buffers available when the server first booted is 1,800.

   B. The current number of packet receive buffers available to receive station requests is 50.

   C. The number of disk requests to other servers is 5.

   D. The number of TTS files that are opened is 13.

33. MONITOR reports NIC statistics that include the _____.

     A. total packets sent and received

     B. total packets that were lost

     C. total packets that were sent to the wrong address

     D. percentage of missed packets

34. The packet burst protocol _____.

     A. can send up to 64 KB in a single packet

     B. does not require an acknowledgment for each packet that is sent

     C. overflows packet receive buffers

     D. sends a reply for each packet

35. If MONITOR reports the following:

    ```
    Original Cache Buffers = 1772
    Total Cache Buffers = 1072
    Dirty Cache Buffers = 21
    Current Disk Requests = 0
    ```

    which statement is true?

☐ A. The total server memory is 1772 cache buffers.

☐ B. The system had 1772 blocks of cache memory.

☐ C. The system is currently using 1072 cache buffers.

☐ D. There is a large amount of disk write activity.

☐ E. There is a large amount of disk read activity.

36. If MONITOR reports the following:

```
Original Cache Buffers = 1772
Total Cache Buffers = 1072
Dirty Cache Buffers = 0
Current Disk Requests = 5
Open Files = 20
```

which statement is true?

☐ A. The total server memory is 1772 cache buffers.

☐ B. There are 5 packet requests waiting to be serviced.

☐ C. The system currently has 1072 cache buffers free.

☐ D. There is a large amount of disk write activity.

☐ E. There are 5 disk requests waiting to be serviced.

37. Which of the following can optimize cache utilization?

○ A. Making the cache buffer size less than the volume block size.

○ B. Making the cache buffer size and the volume block size the same.

○ C. Making the cache buffer size greater than the volume block size.

○ D. Enabling cache utilization only when the cache buffer size and the volume block size are the same.

38. If Long Term Cache Hits statistics are low, you can improve server performance by _____.

☐ A. adding more server disks

☐ B. adding more RAM

☐ C. loading more NLMs

☐ D. unloading NLMs

☐ E. removing DOS using the console command REMOVE DOS

39. Which MONITOR option can be used to obtain an approximate size of an NLM?

○ A. Cache Utilization

○ B. Processor Utilization

○ C. Memory Utilization

○ D. NLM Size Option

○ E. Module Information

Backup Services in NetWare 4

*T*his chapter discusses the native backup services available with NetWare 4. NetWare 4 backup uses the Storage Management Services (SMS). SMS is a hardware- and software-independent method for performing backups.

This chapter also discusses the different types of backup strategies available to NetWare 4 users, such as full backup, differential backup, and incremental backup. The principal tool for performing backups in NetWare 4 is SBACKUP. Use of this tool is discussed in length.

Understanding Backup Services

In NetWare 4, the backup services are consolidated in SBACKUP.NLM. Because SBACKUP is an NLM, it can only run on a NetWare server. The server on which the SBACKUP.NLM runs should have a backup device. This server is called the *host server*. The data source to be backed up and restored is called the *target*. The target could be file systems, databases on network nodes such as NetWare 3, NetWare 4, or DOS and OS/2 workstations (see fig. 9.1).

 NetWare 4 backup services are consolidated in SBACKUP.NLM.

The server on which SBACKUP runs is called the host server.

A number of backup strategies can be used with NetWare 4. These are as follows:

- Full backup
- Incremental backup
- Differential backup
- Custom backup

 SBACKUP supports full backup, incremental backup, differential backup, and custom backup.

Full Backup

In *full backup*, all data is backed up—for example, all directories and files in a volume, or all volumes on a file server. After the data is backed up, the archive bit is cleared for all files backed up.

The *archive bit* indicates whether the data should be backed up. When a file is modified, the archive

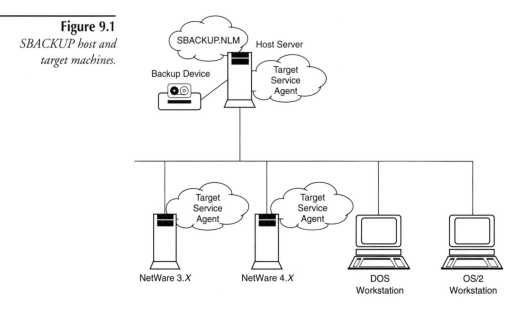

Figure 9.1
SBACKUP host and target machines.

bit is set, indicating that this file is a candidate for being backed up the next time because it has been modified. Backup programs clear the archive bit to indicate that the file is now backed up.

The full backup strategy is the most comprehensive of all backup strategies because it backs up all files regardless of whether they have been modified since the last backup. However, because of the large volume of data that may need to get backed up, full backup is the slowest of the backup strategies.

 In full backup

- All data is backed up regardless of the setting of the archive bit.

- The archive bits of all files backed up are cleared.

Full backup is the most comprehensive of all backup strategies but can take the longest time of all the backup strategies.

Incremental Backup

Incremental backup backs up all files that have been modified since the last backup (full or incremental). Files that have not been modified are not backed up. To obtain a complete record of the most updated versions of the files, you would have to start with the most recent full backup and add all the incremental changes recorded in each incremental backup session. That is,

```
Most Recent Backup = Last Full Backup + Δ1
➡+ Δ2 + .... Δn
     = Last Full Backup + Δi   (i =1 to n)
```

where each Δi is an incremental backup.

 The term Δd (pronounced delta, dee) and Δi (pronounced delta, eye), are used to represent changes, such as new files being backed up using incremental and differential backups. The symbol Δ is commonly used to represent changes.

The incremental backup contains a sequential history of the files that have been modified. This means that to restore data, you need the last full backup and every incremental backup after it. If the data on one of the backup tapes is corrupted, you might not be able to restore data. The exception to this is situations in which later incremental backups have the files that were inaccessible on the corrupted tape. In this case, you could restore the data from a later tape.

Because only the modified files are backed up, the incremental backup strategy tends to be very fast. If the number of files that are modified between incremental backups increases, the time required for doing an incremental backup also increases.

After performing an incremental backup, the archive bits of the files that have been backed up are cleared.

An incremental backup

- Only backs up modified files that have their archive bit set.

- Clears the archive bits of backed up files.

- Usually takes less time than full and differential backups.

- Contains a sequential history of the files that have been modified.

To restore data in incremental backup, you need the last full backup and every incremental backup after it.

Differential Backup

Differential backup is used to back up all files that have been modified since the last full backup. The archive bit is not cleared at the end of the backup, as is done in the case of full and incremental backups. This means that all files backed up in the first differential backup are also backed up in the second differential backup, together with any files that have been modified since the first differential backup. This process continues with each differential backup, and more files can be expected to be backed up with each differential backup.

To obtain a complete record of the most updated versions of the files, you would have to start with the most recent full backup and add to it the files in the most recent differential backup session. That is,

```
Most Recent Backup = Last Full Backup + Δd
```

where Δd is the most recent differential backup.

Because the differential backup contains all files that have been modified since the last full backup, you can restore data with just two tape backup sets: the backup set for the full backup and the backup set for the last differential backup.

If the data on one of the last differential backups is corrupted, you will have to fall back on the next-to-the-last differential backup. On the other hand, if any data in another differential backup tape is corrupt, it does not matter as long as the data in the most recent differential backup is good.

Because all modified files are backed up, the differential backup is the same as the incremental backup

for the first backup after the full backup. After that, the size of the data that needs to be backed up tends to grow with each differential backup. If all files have been modified, the differential backup session is the same as the full backup sessions. This tends not to be the case because most network volumes contain a mix of program and data, and program files are not usually modified.

It is best to use either a differential backup or incremental backup strategy. Mixing these two, although theoretically possible, can lead to potential confusion and therefore should be avoided.

 The following statements are true for differential backups:

- In differential backup the archive bits of the backed up files are not cleared.

- In differential backup all files modified since the last full backup are backed up.

- The first differential backup is the same as incremental backup in terms of speed and the files that are backed up.

- Successive differential backups usually take longer because more files are backed up.

- To restore data in differential backup, you need the last full backup and the most recent differential backup.

- If any data in a differential backup tape not belonging to the last differential backup set is corrupted, the data can still be recovered from the last full backup and the most recent differential backup.

- If the last differential backup is bad, you can only restore data up to the next-to-the-last differential backup.

Custom Backup

Custom backup gives you complete control over what files to back up. You can include or exclude parts of the directory structure to be backed up or select different types of data items to be backed up. Custom backup options are presented in detail in a later section in this chapter.

Custom backups are useful if you want to selectively back up a few files and directories, and not wait for a scheduled backup.

 Custom backup

■ Is useful if you want to selectively back up a few files and directories, and not wait for a scheduled backup.

■ Enables you to include or exclude parts of the directory structure to be backed up or to select different types of data items to be backed up.

Examining Storage Management Service

NetWare 4 implements backup services using Storage Management Service. SMS allows data to be backed up and restored independent of the backup hardware and file system. The Storage Management Service supports a variety of backup hardware devices, and it can back up file systems for DOS, OS/2, Macintosh, and UNIX. This capability to back up different file systems is particularly important because NetWare-based networks support a heterogeneous workstation operating system environment. SMS provides support for the following workstations and data representation:

■ DOS workstations

■ OS/2 workstations

■ Macintosh workstations (Macintosh name space)

■ Unix workstations (NFS name space)

■ NetWare Directory Service

■ NetWare File Systems (v2.2 to v4)

■ Btrieve (SQL) database

The primary tool that uses SMS is SBACKUP. SBACKUP runs as an NLM and relies on *target service agents* (TSAs) to communicate a data representation to it. The SBACKUP.NLM runs on the server that has the backup device. The SBACKUP.NLM is responsible for backup and restore operations. The NBACKUP functionality of earlier NetWare releases is now consolidated in SBACKUP.

 The NBACKUP functionality of earlier NetWare releases is now consolidated in SBACKUP.

The target service agents can run on NetWare servers and communicate with the workstations on the network. The target service agents have knowledge of different data representations. A target service agent called TSA410.NLM, for example, is used to back up/restore the NetWare 4 file system, and the target service agent TSA312.NLM does the same for NetWare 3. Table 9.1 contains a list of TSAs installed with NetWare 4. These TSAs can be found in the SYS:SYSTEM directory.

Table 9.1
Target Service Agents

Name	Description
TSA312.NLM	NetWare 3.11 file system TSA
TSA312.NLM	NetWare 3.12 file system TSA
TSA410.NLM	NetWare 4.1 file system TSA
TSA400.NLM	NetWare 4.0, 4.01, 4.02 file system TSA
TSA220.NLM	NetWare 2.2 file system TSA
TSADOS.NLM	TSA for backing up DOS files—runs at server
TSASMS.COM	TSA runs at DOS workstation to be backed up/restored; normally kept in the C:\NWCLIENT directory of the workstation
TSANDS.NLM	NetWare 4.1 TSA for backing up NDS
TSA_OS2.NLM	TSA for backing up OS/2 file system

 For each data or workstation type, there are special target service agents. Table 9.1 lists the more important TSAs. You should be aware of the names of these TSAs and their functions.

 The primary tool that uses SMS is SBACKUP.

SMS allows data to be backed up and restored independent of the backup hardware and file system.

SMS provides support for the following workstations and data representation:

■ DOS workstations

■ OS/2 workstations

■ Macintosh workstations (Macintosh name space)

■ Unix workstations (NFS name space)

■ NetWare Directory Service

■ NetWare File Systems (v2.2 to v4)

■ Btrieve (SQL) database

SMS Architecture

Besides SBACKUP.NLM and TSAs, SMS consists of a number of other support NLMs that work together to provide backup and restore operations. Figure 9.2 shows how this can be done.

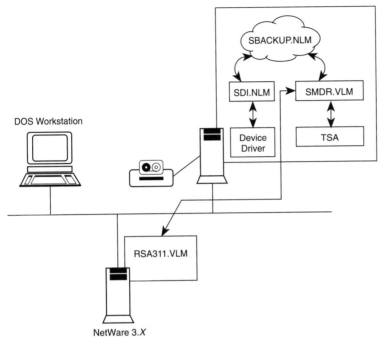

Figure 9.2
SMS components.

SMS consists of a number of other modules such as the *Storage Management Data Requester* (*SMDR*) used to pass commands between the SBACKUP and the TSAs, and device drivers that use the *Storage Device Interface* (*SDI*) to communicate between the SBACKUP program and the storage devices (see fig. 9.2).

The SBACKUP uses the SMDR to access the TSA. If the TSA is on the same server as the SBACKUP.NLM, then the data source is on the same server. An example of this would be using the TSA410.NLM on the host server to back up the host file system. Another example would be to use the TSANDS.NLM on the host to back up the NDS database on the host server.

> **Note** The term *host* refers to the server that has the backup device. The term *target* refers to the network device

(workstation or server) that has the data to be backed up or restored.

If the TSA is on a remote machine, such as a NetWare 3 server running TSA312.NLM, then the file system on the remote machine can be backed up. It is the responsibility of the TSA to obtain the requested data and pass it on to SBACKUP via the SMDR. The TSA is the agent *closest* to the source data being backed up and restored. It has knowledge of the file system or data representation of the source data.

SBACKUP backs up or restores the data by communicating with the backup device via the Storage Device Interface NLM (SDI.NLM) and the backup device drivers. The Storage Device Interface is used to detect the presence of the device and media and presents a list of devices available to the SBACKUP program. The backup operator can then select the appropriate backup device via the SBACKUP interface. The SMDR.NLM provides a high-level interface to the backup device drivers. The backup device drivers have knowledge of the backup device hardware and use commands for reading, writing, rewinding, and ejecting the storage media. The SDI.NLM, SMDR.NLM, STREAMS.NLM, CLIB.NLM, SPXS.NLM, and NWSNUT. NLMare autoloaded when SBACKUP loads.

To back up and restore workstations, a component called the *Workstation Manager* (WSMAN.NLM) must be loaded on the host server. WSMAN NLM is autoloaded when TSADOS or TSA_OS2 load. The Workstation Manager keeps an internal list of DOS TSRs (or OS/2 and Unix daemons) that have contracted it and are available for backup/restore operation.

 SBACKUP uses SDI and SMDR NLMs.

SBACKUP autoloads the SDI.NLM, SMDR.NLM, STREAMS.NLM, CLIB.NLM, SPXS.NLM, and NWSNUT.NLM if they are not already loaded.

 Storage Management Data Requester (SMDR) is used to pass commands between the SBACKUP and the TSAs.

 The Storage Device Interface is used to detect the presence of the device and media and presents a list of devices available to the SBACKUP program.

 To back up and restore workstations, another component, called the Workstation Manager (WSMAN.NLM), must be loaded on the host server.

 WSMAN NLM is autoloaded when TSADOS or TSA_OS2 load.

The SBACKUP Tool

The SBACKUP.NLM is loaded at the server. It is similar to the SBACKUP.NLM for NetWare 3 servers, but has been customized for the NetWare 4 operating system.

To use SBACKUP, you must first load all the necessary drivers and TSAs for the target being backed up. NetWare 4 ships with the tape drivers listed in table 9.2. The TAPEDAI.DSK can work with any tape device on a SCSI controller.

 To use SBACKUP, you must first load all the necessary drivers and TSAs for the target being backed up.

 The TAPEDAI.DSK can work with any tape device on a SCSI controller.

Table 9.2
Backup Device Drivers

Device Driver	Description
TAPEDAI.DSK	This is a generic ASPI-compatible tape driver for SCSI controllers. It is designed to use the Advanced SCSI Programming Interface (ASPI).
MNS16S.NLM and MNSDAT.DSK	These are device drivers for Mountain Network Solutions, Inc., SCSI controllers and tape devices.
PS2SCSI.DSK	These work with PS/2 SCSI controllers and IBM 2.2 GB 8mm tape devices.
AHA1540.DSK, AHA1640.DSK, AHA1740.DSK, ASPITRAN.DSK	These work with devices that use the Adaptec 1540, 1640, and 1740 controllers.

Steps for Using SBACKUP

The following steps guide you through the basics of performing a backup with the SBACKUP utility.

 Author's Note The actual screens presented using SBACKUP often depend on the selections you make from the SBACKUP menu for your network environment. For instance, you can select the Backup option, without logging in to the Target Service first. In this case, you will be presented with a screen to log in to the target service first before performing the backup operation. Another example is the writing of labels on tapes. If you are using a new tape or completely rewriting the tape and you have not written a new label on the tape, you will be presented with a screen to label the tape.

1. First load the appropriate backup device drivers on the server console. If you are using a SCSI controller, you may be able to use the generic TAPEDAI.DSK device driver.

```
LOAD TAPEDAI
```

Figure 9.3 shows the server console screen when this device driver loads. The version number of the TAPEDAI.DSK and its date of creation are displayed. In this particular version of the TAPEDAI driver, there were three outdated API calls, so a warning message was generated.

Study Note TAPEDAI uses the ASPI interface. ASPI does not provide sharing of tape devices between competing applications. You should not load any other device that uses ASPI when you are using the TAPEDAI driver.

Figure 9.3

LOAD TAPEDAI

messages.

```
NW4KS:load tapedai
Loading module TAPEDAI.DSK
    TAPE DRIVER
    Version 3.12    May 18, 1993
SERVER-4.00-30:    This module is using 3 outdated API calls
    You should upgrade to a newer module when it becomes available.
    Debug symbol information for TAPEDAI.DSK loaded
NW4KS:
```

2. Optional: Load any other device drivers required by the manufacturer's hardware.

3. Load the TSAs on the target. In this example, you want to back up the NetWare 4 file system and the NDS database. Therefore, you must load the TSA410.NLM and the TSANDS.NLM:

LOAD TSA410

Figure 9.4 shows the server console screen when the TSA for the NetWare 4 file system loads. The version number of the TSA and its date of creation are displayed.

Figure 9.5 shows the server console screen when the TSA for the NDS database loads. The version number of the TSA and its date of creation are displayed.

4. Before loading the SBACKUP.NLM, you must issue the command **SCAN FOR NEW DEVICES**. This ensures that the tape device recognized by TAPEDAI is registered by NetWare 4. The command **LIST DEVICES** can be used to see current devices.

Figure 9.6 shows the output of the LIST DEVICES command before the SCAN FOR NEW DEVICES is executed. Only one device, device # 0, is listed. This is the Micropolis 1528 hard disk with 1.2 gigabyte capacity.

Figure 9.7 shows the SCAN FOR NEW DEVICES command. No output is generated, but the command takes a few seconds.

Figure 9.8 shows the output of the LIST DEVICES command, after the SCAN FOR NEW DEVICES command recognizes the backup device. An additional device, device #1, is listed. This is the HP 35470A tape drive unit for DAT tapes.

5. Next, load the SBACKUP.NLM:

LOAD SBACKUP

After SBACKUP is loaded, you can use it to perform backups and restores.

To unload SBACKUP and the support NLMs, they should be unloaded in the reverse order of their load sequence; that is, you must unload SBACKUP first, and then the TSA NLMs, and finally the backup device drivers. An example of this unload sequence is shown here:

UNLOAD SBACKUP

UNLOAD TSA410

UNLOAD TSANDS

UNLOAD TAPEDAI

 The SIZE parameter for SBACKUP is the buffer size (K) used by SBACKUP. The value can be 16, 32, 64, 128, or 256 KB. The default value is 64 KB.

```
NW4KS:load tapedai
Loading module TAPEDAI.DSK
  TAPE DRIVER
  Version 3.12    May 18, 1993
SERVER-4.00-30:   This module is using 3 outdated API calls
  You should upgrade to a newer module when it becomes available.
  Debug symbol information for TAPEDAI.DSK loaded
NW4KS:load tsa400
Loading module TSA400.NLM
  NetWare 4.0 Target Service Agent
  Version 4.01    June 4, 1993
  Copyright 1993 Novell, Inc.  All rights reserved.
NW4KS:
```

Figure 9.4
LOAD TSA400 messages.

```
NW4KS:load tapedai
Loading module TAPEDAI.DSK
  TAPE DRIVER
  Version 3.12    May 18, 1993
SERVER-4.00-30:   This module is using 3 outdated API calls
  You should upgrade to a newer module when it becomes available.
  Debug symbol information for TAPEDAI.DSK loaded
NW4KS:load tsa400
Loading module TSA400.NLM
  NetWare 4.0 Target Service Agent
  Version 4.01    June 4, 1993
  Copyright 1993 Novell, Inc.  All rights reserved.
NW4KS:load tsa_nds
Loading module TSA_NDS.NLM
  NetWare Directory Target Service Agent 4.0
  Version 4.00    February 13, 1993
  Copyright 1993 Novell, Inc.  All rights reserved.
NW4KS:
```

Figure 9.5
LOAD TSA_NDS messages.

```
NW4KS:load tapedai
Loading module TAPEDAI.DSK
  TAPE DRIVER
  Version 3.12    May 18, 1993
SERVER-4.00-30:   This module is using 3 outdated API calls
  You should upgrade to a newer module when it becomes available.
  Debug symbol information for TAPEDAI.DSK loaded
NW4KS:load tsa400
Loading module TSA400.NLM
  NetWare 4.0 Target Service Agent
  Version 4.01    June 4, 1993
  Copyright 1993 Novell, Inc.  All rights reserved.
NW4KS:load tsa_nds
Loading module TSA_NDS.NLM
  NetWare Directory Target Service Agent 4.0
  Version 4.00    February 13, 1993
  Copyright 1993 Novell, Inc.  All rights reserved.
NW4KS:list devices
 1. Device #  0 MICROP   1528-15MD1076301 DD24 (5D000000).
NW4KS:
```

Figure 9.6
The LIST DEVICES command before scanning for new devices.

```
NW4KS:scan for new devices
NW4KS:
```

Figure 9.7
The SCAN FOR NEW DEVICES command screen.

Figure 9.8

The LIST DEVICES command after scanning for new devices.

```
NW4KS:scan for new devices
NW4KS:list devices
  8. Device #  1 HP - HP35470A (020000FF).
  1. Device #  0 MICROP   1528-15MD1076301 DD24 (5D000000).
NW4KS:
```

SBACKUP and the support NLMs should be unloaded in the reverse order of their load sequence; that is, you must unload SBACKUP first, and then the TSA NLMs, and finally the backup device drivers.

Using SBACKUP to Perform a Backup

The following steps show the sequence for performing a backup operation. The steps assume that all the necessary drivers have already been loaded.

1. The SBACKUP NLM must be loaded on the host server:

   LOAD SBACKUP

   After SBACKUP loads, you should see the SBACKUP Main Menu as shown in figure 9.9.

   The *Backup* option is used to specify a target to back up. It also asks you to specify the location of the session log, the device and media to use, and the type of backup to perform.

The *Restore* option is used to specify the target to which you want to restore. It asks you to specify what data you want to restore and the location to restore to. If a session log has been maintained, you can restore based on the session name. Alternatively, you can select the data directly from the tape. One reason for restoring directly from tape is if the session log file has been deleted or is corrupt. Restoring from a session log is convenient and quicker to do.

The *Log/error File Administration* option enables you to browse through the error log file that is created when a backup or restore session is done. This is a quick way to determine if any errors have occurred during backup or restore operations.

The *Storage Device Administration* option enables you to choose the device and media to be used for the backup or restore operation. This option is useful if you have more than one backup device. This option also can be used for checking the status of the media in the backup device.

The *Change Target to Back Up From or Restore To* option is used to display the names of the

Figure 9.9

The SBACKUP Main Menu.

```
                    Main Menu
 Backup
 Restore
 Log/error File Administration
 Storage Device Administration
 Change Target to Back Up From or Restore To
```

targets to which you are attached. You can select a target for performing an operation. When you do this, you are asked to specify a user name/password for logging in to the target.

2. Select the *Storage Device Administration* option to see the list of devices to which you can back up. You should see a list of devices that you can use. Using the Tab key displays the status of the device.

   The media in the device needs to be labeled. If the media has never been labeled, you can do this here or postpone it to a later point in the *Backup* option, when you are prompted to label the media. To label the media, highlight the backup device from the *List of devices* menu, and press Ins.

   Pressing the Tab key on the media that is listed shows the status of the media. If the media was written by an SMS application (such as SBACKUP), the media owner is not displayed. If the media was written by a non-SMS application, or if it was initially "blank," the media owner is listed as Unidentified.

3. Select the *Change Target to Back Up From or Restore To* option from the SBACKUP Main Menu. You only see the entries for the TSAs that have been loaded.

4. In this backup example, you select the NDS database for backing up. When you select an

option, you are prompted for the user name and password for the target device.

5. From the SBACKUP Main Menu, select *Backup*. You are asked to select the device and media to back up to, if you have not done this already.

   You are asked to select a location for the log and error file. If you have been using SBACKUP for some time and have already selected this option, this screen is bypassed. The default location is SYS:SYSTEM/TSA/LOG. You can, however, select any other location.

6. Next, you are asked if you want to perform a full backup or a custom backup. Generally, the choices are Full, Differential, Incremental, and Custom. For backing up the NDS database, you have a choice of Full and Custom only. The different backup types were explained earlier in the chapter.

7. In the example, select the Full backup method. You then are presented with backup options.

   Enter a description of what you want to back up. It is important to keep the description informative because when you select data to be restored, you are presented with a choice of the backup descriptions that you enter at this step.

8. To start the backup, press the F10 key. You are presented with a choice of when to start the backup (see fig. 9.10).

Figure 9.10
Proceed with Backup options.

If you want to start the backup later, you can select Start the Backup Later, and you are presented with a form to schedule a backup at a future date and time.

If you select the Backup Now option, you are presented with a status screen; press Enter to proceed to the next step. Enter the name of the label for the media set, if you are prompted for it. If the media is being completely overwritten, you are prompted for the label.

As the backup proceeds, you see a status window on the top right-hand corner of the screen that informs you of the status of the backup. Among other things, you are shown the elapsed time and the amount of data backed up. The data that is backed up is shown on the top left-hand corner of the screen.

At the end of the backup, you see a message informing you that the backup is complete. Press Enter to continue and exit SBACKUP.

 The Log/error File Administration option enables you to browse through the error log file that is created during a backup or restore session.

 The default location of the SBACKUP error log files is SYS:SYSTEM\TSA\LOG.

 The Storage Device Administration option enables you to choose the device and media to be used for the backup or restore operation.

 The Change Target to Back Up From or Restore To option is used to display the names of the targets to which you are attached.

Using SBACKUP to Perform a Restore

The following steps show the sequence for performing a restore operation. The steps assume that all the necessary drivers have already been loaded.

1. The SBACKUP.NLM must be loaded on the host server. Issue the following command:

   LOAD SBACKUP

   After SBACKUP loads, you should see the SBACKUP main menu. The different SBACKUP options are described in the preceding section.

2. Select the *Storage Device Administration* option to see the list of devices to back up to. You should see a list of devices that you can use.

   Press Ins to see the media in the device. Highlight the media and press Enter to select the media to restore from.

   Pressing the Tab key on the media that is listed shows the status of the media. Refer to the preceding section on performing backups using SBACKUP to see a description of the media status.

3. Select the *Change Target to Back Up From or Restore To* option from the SBACKUP Main Menu.

4. This procedure is described for restoring the NDS database. Selecting the NetWare 4.0 Directory TSA results in your being prompted for the user name for the target NDSTS (NDS target service) and the password.

5. From the SBACKUP Main Menu, select *Restore*. You are presented with a choice of restoring with session files or without session files.

Restoring with session files is simpler, but you may have to select restoring without session files if the log file has been deleted or has been corrupted.

If you select Restore a Session, you are asked to select a location for the log and error file. If you have been using SBACKUP for some time and have already selected this option, this screen is bypassed. The default location is SYS:SYSTEM/TSA/LOG. If you selected a different location at the time of performing a backup, you must specify this location.

Figure 9.11 shows the different backup sessions that have been performed. The most recent session is listed first. Highlight the session that you want to restore and press Enter.

6. Next, you are asked to select a device and media to restore from. This gives you an opportunity to insert the media in the device,

if you have not done so already. Press Enter to continue. You see a "Please wait" message as the media is read. You are shown the backup device and the media that you will be using. Press Enter and select an entire session.

You are then presented with Restore options (see fig. 9.12). Select Restore an Entire Session. You are asked to verify your choice; select Yes.

As the restore proceeds, you see a status window on the top right-hand corner of the screen that informs you of the status of the restore. Among other things, you are shown the elapsed time and the amount of data restored. The data that is restored is shown in the top left-hand corner of the screen.

At the end of the restore, you see a message informing you that the restore is complete. Press Enter to continue and exit SBACKUP.

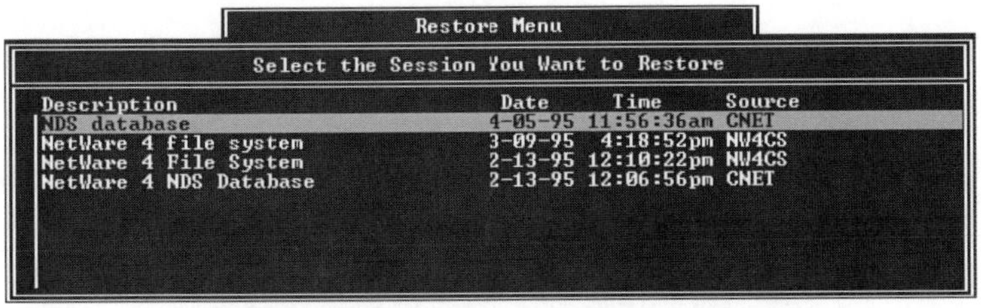

Figure 9.11

List of sessions to restore from.

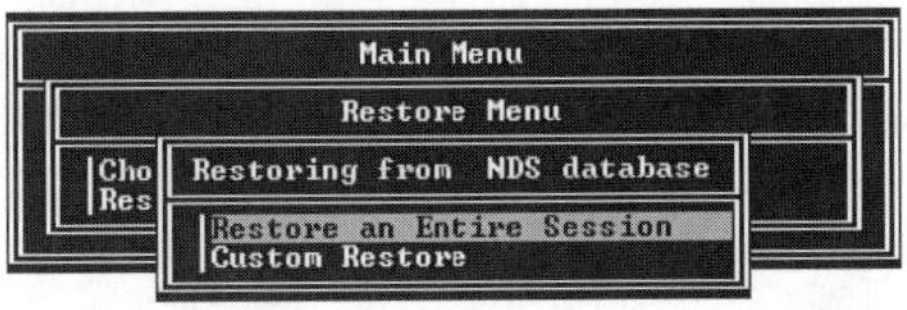

Figure 9.12

Restore options for NDS.

Restoring Without Session Files

Occasionally you may have a corrupt session log, or the session log may have been accidentally deleted. In this case, you must perform the restore without a session log. The following steps show you how this is done. These steps complement the steps outlined in the preceding section.

1. Perform steps 1-4 from the preceding section.

2. From the SBACKUP Main Menu, select Restore. You are then presented with a choice of restoring with session files or without session files. Select Restore Without Session Files if the session files are corrupted or have been deleted. You are shown a message that you have to select the device and media to restore from.

   `Press Enter to continue to the next step.`

   The SBACKUP program identifies the media you have inserted. Press Enter to continue.

   You then are presented with the restore options. Make the appropriate choices and press F10. Verify that you want to continue.

3. The SBACKUP program reads the sessions from the media. If this is not the session that you want to restore, you will have to select No, Go on to the Next Session on the Media. If there are many sessions on the media, this could take some time. If you found the session that you want to restore, select Yes, Restore This Session.

4. Proceed with the restore operations outlined in the preceding section, "Using SBACKUP to Perform a Restore."

Exploring Restore Options for Restoring a File System

The example of the restore operation was given in the context of restoring an NDS database. The restore options that are presented are quite different for restoring a file system. This section discusses the restore options that are peculiar to restoring a file system.

When you select the Restore A Session option from the Restore Menu for restoring a file system, you are asked to select the device/media and the name of the session to restore from. If you select Custom Restore, you see the restore options shown in figure 9.13.

Figure 9.13

Restore Options for a file system.

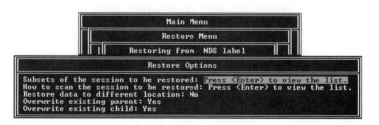

Selecting the Subsets o the session to be restored option from the Restore Options form shows you the data items (also called *data structure*) available for restoring (see fig. 9.14). This option classifies data items as Major TSA or Minor TSA resources. A *Major TSA resource* contains data that can be backed as a whole when selected. Examples of Major TSAs are the file server and the volume. When you select a Major TSA resource such as a volume, all directories and files within it are considered for restore operation. A *Minor TSA resource* is contained within a directory structure of a Major TSA resource. An example of this would be the directories and files within a volume.

In figure 9.14, if you want to include an entire volume for a restore operation, you would select Include Major TSA Resources and press Ins to see a list of major TSA resources available for selection (see fig. 9.15).

You can use the other options for excluding or including directories or files. If you want to include a specific directory for backup, you can select

Include Directories (full path) and press Ins to add a directory name.

Selecting the How to scan the session to be restored option from the Restore Options form shows you options for excluding different aspects of the file system (see fig. 9.16).

The group of data files and directories that you are restoring is called a *data set*. You can select the data sets that you want to exclude from the restore operation. If you want to restore a type of data from this list, select a value of No; otherwise select a value of Yes. By default all the Exclude options have a value of No. This means that all aspects of the data set should be scanned for the restore operation. The *data stream* refers to the data being restored. This option works with the other options Subsets of the session to be restored and the Overwrite option. It narrows the types of data sets that should be scanned for in the restore operation. For example, you can use this to exclude or include any of the following:

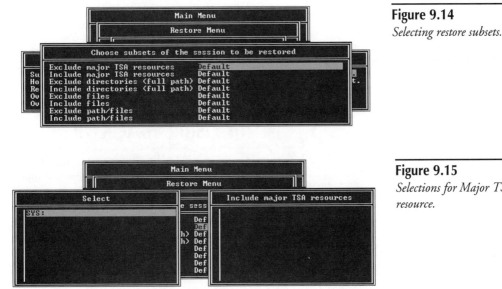

Figure 9.14
Selecting restore subsets.

Figure 9.15
Selections for Major TSA resource.

Figure 9.16

The How to Scan the Session to be Restored options.

```
NetWare Server Backup Utility  4.11          NetWare Loadable Module
                     Target: NW4CS

                          Main Menu
                         Restore Menu

           How to Scan the Session to be Restored
           Exclude data streams:                    No
Subsets of Exclude extended attributes:             No      the list.
How to scan Exclude directory trustees:             No     w the list.
Restore dat Exclude file trustees:                  No
Overwrite e Exclude volume restrictions:            No
Overwrite e Exclude directory space restrictions:   No
           Include file data from secondary storage: No
```

- Extended attributes

- Directory trustees

- File trustees

- Volume restrictions

- Directory space restrictions

If you want to restore data to a different location from where it was backed up, you should set the field Restore data to different location to Yes. The default value for this field is No, which means that data will be restored on top of existing data.

 Selecting the Subsets of the session to be restored option from the Restore Options form shows you the data items (also called *data structure*) available for restoring.

 Selecting the How to scan the session to be restored option from the Restore Options form shows you options for excluding different aspects of the file system.

 A Major TSA resource contains data that can be backed as a whole when selected. Examples of Major TSAs are the file server and the volume.

A Minor TSA resource is contained within a directory structure of a Major TSA resource. An example of this would be the directories and files within a volume.

Study Note While restoring files and directories, you can exclude/include any of the following:

- Extended attributes

- Directory trustees

- File trustees

- Volume restrictions

- Directory space restrictions

Understanding Guidelines for Using SBACKUP

There are a number of caveats to keep in mind when using SBACKUP. These are listed as follows for your reference.

- SBACKUP uses temporary files (SYS: SYSTEM\TSA$TMP.*) that can be as large as 7M. Make sure that you have enough free disk space on the server for these temporary files. The temporary files may become quite large especially if you have extended attributes or linked Unix files.

■ Switching to the system console when running SBACKUP and manually unloading the drivers is potentially dangerous. It could crash the server.

■ Do not mount/dismount volumes during an SBACKUP session. This could corrupt data and/or crash the server.

■ When backing up a system that has global compression enabled, wait for a period of time until the compression has been completed before backing up the file system. This allows a maximum number of files to be backed up in the compressed state.

■ In general, be aware of the name space formats supported by the file system being backed up. SBACKUP shows only DOS-type file names and paths. If you are using non-DOS file names for other types of name space support, use the DOS file-name equivalents. The error and backup log files, however, show the non-DOS file-name formats. SBACKUP currently supports name spaces for the following:

  ■ DOS

  ■ OS/2

  ■ NFS

  ■ Macintosh

  ■ FTAM

■ The NetWare server where SBACKUP is run requires a minimum of 3M of RAM in addition to other server RAM requirements.

■ If backing up other workstations (DOS, OS/2, and so on), you must know the workstation password, if it has been set.

■ SBACKUP logs out when the SBACKUP session finishes. If the SBACKUP session requires more than one media (tape), it waits for one to be inserted before continuing. If no one is on hand to feed another tape drive to the backup device, SBACKUP will be logged in to the target. This could pose a security weakness.

■ SBACKUP does not verify the data you have backed up. That is, it does not read what it has written and compare the data. You must perform an explicit restore if you are concerned about the accuracy of SBACKUP.

 The backup operator

■ Must be able to log in to NDS.

■ Must have Read and File Scan rights to the file system being backed up.

■ Must have the Browse object trustee right to the NDS tree, and the Read property right to All Properties.

 If you are performing an incremental or full backup, the archive bit is cleared at the end of the backup pass. To perform this, you must have the Modify right to the files being backed up.

Backing Up DOS Workstations

SBACKUP can be used to back up and restore DOS workstations. You can back up specific drives and directories at the workstation. To perform a backup/restore of the DOS workstation, you need to perform the following steps:

1. Load TSADOS.NLM at the server. This autoloads WSMAN.NLM, which is required to register the TSAs.

2. Load TSASMS.COM (TSR) at the workstation. This can be found in the C:\NWCLIENT

directory on the workstation. Table 9.3 shows the different options for the TSASMS command. For example, to allow the backup of the local drive C: from the host server NW4KS, and to set a password of shiv at the workstation, you can execute the following command:

```
TSASMS    /P=shiv /D=c   /SE=NW4KS
```

3. Load SBACKUP and select the DOS workstation's TSA. You can do this by selecting Change Target To Backup From Or Restore To. This shows a list of the TSA agents registered with SBACKUP running on the host server.

Table 9.3
TSASMS Options

TSASMS Option	Description
/H[elp]	Displays help screen. Using /? produces an ? error message, but the help screen is still displayed.
/B[uffers]=nbuf	Sets aside nbuf 1-KB buffers that will be used for backing up. The default is 1 buffer. Increasing this number increases the backup speed, at the expense of using more RAM at the workstation. Novell notes that the number of buffers does not seem to affect performance of restore functions. nbuf can be from 1 to 30.
/D[rives]=drives	Specifies a list of drive letters that can be backed up at the workstation. The list consists of a string of one-letter drive letters with no spaces or colons (:). For example, to backup drive C: only, you would use /D=C, and to back up drives A:, C:, and E:, you would use /D=ACE. The /DRIVES parameter is mandatory.
/N[ame]=wkstn_name	Sets the workstation's name. It must be specified to create the workstation name for the first time. This name is displayed in the SBACKUP menu. Once specified, the workstation name is created as a permanent entry in the emulated bindery of the host server specified in the /SE option. The network and node addresses are also stored in the emulated bindery entry. Any

TSASMS Option	Description
	attempt to back up this workstation with another name will fail. To remove the name, network, and node address information, you can use the /REMOVE option. If you move the workstation to another cable segment or change its network adapter address, you should use the /REMOVE option and use the /NAME option, again. You can use any name up to ten characters for the workstation. Because the name is registered with the host server, you should use a consistent logical scheme.
/R[emove]=host_server,wkstn_name	Deletes the workstation name, wkstn_name, that you originally specified with the /NAME parameter from the host server. The /REMOVE option removes the workstation name entry in the emulated bindery of the host_server. Use this option to register a different workstation name, network address, or node address.
/SE[rver]=host_server	Specifies the name of the host server on which the SBACKUP program runs. The TSASMS, on loading, connects to the specified host_server. The /SERVER parameter is mandatory.
/P[assword]=passwd	Used for security reasons so that only the backup operator who knows the registered workstation name and password can perform SBACKUP operations. You must use the /PASSWORD option or the /TRUST option, but not both. These options are mutually exclusive.
/T[rust]	Allows the backup operator to back up/restore the workstation without knowing the workstation password. As the name of the option suggests, this option requires you to trust the backup operator with the confidentiality of the files. You must use the /TRUST option or the /PASSWORD option, but not both. These options are mutually exclusive.
/ST[ack]=size	Specifies the size of the stack. The default stack size is 2,048 bytes, and can range from 512 to 4,096 bytes. Use this option if you get stack overflow error messages. When this error message occurs, you may want to increase the default value, by 128 bytes, until the error message disappears.
/U[nload]	Unloads the TSASMS from memory.

Study Guide for the Chapter

If preparing for exams, review the chapter with the following goals:

- Understand what SMS is and the principal tool used for performing SBACKUP. Use the Study Notes as a quick review.

- Pay particular attention to the different types of backup techniques. Review the SBACKUP operations that have been outlined in this chapter.

- After studying this chapter, attempt the sample test questions. If you miss the answers to a question, review the appropriate topic until you understand the reason for the correct answer.

Chapter Summary

This chapter discussed the native backup service for NetWare 4. NetWare 4 backup uses the Storage Management Services . The primary tool that uses SMS is SBACKUP.NLM.

You can use SBACKUP to support different types of backup strategies such as full backup, differential backup, and incremental backup. The advantages and disadvantages of each type of backup strategy were discussed.

The operation of SBACKUP for backup and restore operations was presented in detail.

Chapter Test Questions

Most of the test questions are multiple choice. Where a single answer is desired, it is indicated by a ○ (circle) notation that precedes the possible answers. Some questions require you to select more than one answer; these are indicated by the ☐ (box) preceding each answer. Not all the questions are multiple choice. Occasionally, you might get a question that asks you to type in an answer. The answer in this case is usually a one-word answer. The answer is not case-sensitive; you can type the answer in lower- or uppercase.

Certain questions will be repeated in different ways so that you can recognize them even when the wording is different. Taking practice quizzes not only tests your knowledge, but also gives you confidence when you take your exam.

1. NetWare 4 backup services are consolidated in _____.

   ○ A. SBACKUP.NLM

   ○ B. SBACKUP.EXE

   ○ C. NBACKUP.NLM

   ○ D. SBACKUP.NLM

2. The server on which SBACKUP runs is called the _____.

   ○ A. application server

   ○ B. target server

   ○ C. host server

   ○ D. backup server

3. Which of the following backup methods are supported by SBACKUP?

   ☐ A. Full backup

   ☐ B. Modified backup

   ☐ C. Fast backup

   ☐ D. Incremental backup

   ☐ E. Differential backup

4. In full backup, _____.

   ○ A. all data regardless of the setting of the archive bit is backed up

   ○ B. only modified files are backed up

   ○ C. all modified files since the last full backup are backed up

   ○ D. only the selected files are backed up

5. In full backup, _____.

   ○ A. the archive bits of all files that are backed up are cleared

   ○ B. only modified files that have their archive bit set are backed up

   ○ C. the archive bits of the backed up files are not cleared

   ○ D. the archive bits of the manually selected files are not cleared

6. In incremental backup, _____.

   ○ A. the archive bits of all files are cleared

   ○ B. only modified files that have their archive bit set are backed up

   ○ C. the archive bits of the backed up files are not cleared

   ○ D. the archive bits of the manually selected files are not cleared

7. In differential backup, _____.

   - A. the archive bits of all files that are backed up are cleared

   - B. only modified files that have their archive bits cleared are backed up

   - C. the archive bits of the backed up files are not cleared

   - D. the archive bits of the manually selected files are not cleared

8. In incremental backup, _____.

   - A. all data regardless of the setting of the archive bit is backed up

   - B. only modified files are backed up

   - C. all modified files since the last full backup are backed up

   - D. only the selected files are backed up

9. In differential backup, _____.

   - A. all data regardless of the setting of the archive bit is backed up

   - B. only modified files are backed up

   - C. all modified files since the last full backup are backed up

   - D. only the selected files are backed up

10. Which of the following statements for the full backup strategy is true?

   - A. It is the most comprehensive of all backup strategies.

   - B. It takes the shortest amount of backup time.

   - C. It allows files to be selectively backed up.

   - D. It takes more time than incremental backup but less time than differential backup.

11. Which of the following statements for the incremental backup strategy is true?

   - A. It takes the shortest amount of backup time.

   - B. It allows files to be selectively backed up.

   - C. It takes more time than differential backup but less time than full backup.

   - D. It takes the longest amount of backup time.

12. Which of the following backup methods has a sequential history of the files that have been modified?

   - A. Full backup

   - B. Incremental backup

   - C. Differential backup

   - D. Custom backup

13. To restore data in incremental backup, you will need _____.

   - A. the last full backup

   - B. the last full backup and last incremental backup

   - C. the last full backup and first incremental backup

   - D. the last full backup and every incremental backup after it

14. The first differential backup is _____.

    ○ A. the same speed as the last differential backup

    ○ B. the same as full backup in terms of speed and the files that are backed up

    ○ C. the same as incremental backup in terms of speed and the files that are backed up

    ○ D. slower than the last differential backup

15. To restore data in differential backup, you need _____.

    ○ A. the last full backup

    ○ B. the last full backup and the last differential backup

    ○ C. the last full backup and the first differential backup

    ○ D. the last full backup and every differential backup after it

16. If any data in a differential backup tape is corrupted, but is backed up correctly in the last differential backup set, _____.

    ○ A. the data cannot be recovered

    ○ B. the data can still be recovered from the last full backup and the first differential backup

    ○ C. the data can still be recovered from the last full backup

    ○ D. the data can still be recovered from the last full backup and the most recent differential backup

17. Custom backup is useful _____.

    ○ A. for backing up all files on the volume

    ○ B. for differential backups

    ○ C. if you want to selectively back up a few files and directories

    ○ D. for incremental backups

18. Custom backup enables you to _____.

    ○ A. include parts of the directory structure to be backed up, or select different types of data items to be backed up

    ○ B. include/exclude parts of the directory structure to be backed up, or to select different types of data items to be backed up

    ○ C. exclude parts of the directory structure to be backed up, or to select different types of data items to be backed up

    ○ D. include but not exclude parts of the directory structure to be backed up

19. Which of the following TSAs can be used for backing up a NetWare 4.1 file system?

    ○ A. TSA311.NLM

    ○ B. TSA411.NLM

    ○ C. TSA410.NLM

    ○ D. TSADOS.NLM

    ○ E. TSA_DOS.NLM

    ○ F. TSANDS.NLM

    ○ G. TSA_NDS.NLM

20. Which of the following TSAs can be used for backing up a NetWare 4.1 NDS database?

    ○ A. TSA311.NLM

    ○ B. TSA411.NLM

    ○ C. TSA410.NLM

    ○ D. TSADOS.NLM

    ○ E. TSA_DOS.NLM

    ○ F. TSANDS.NLM

    ○ G. TSA_NDS.NLM

21. SMS allows data to be backed up and restored _____.

    ○ A. independent of the backup hardware but dependent on the file system

    ○ B. independent of the backup hardware and file system

    ○ C. independent of the file system but dependent on the backup hardware

    ○ D. in an operating system-independent manner

22. The NBACKUP functionality of earlier NetWare releases is now consolidated in _____.

    ○ A. SBACKUP

    ○ B. SERVBACK

    ○ C. LBACKUP

    ○ D. DBACKUP

    ○ E. BACKNLM

23. SBACKUP makes use of _____.

    ☐ A. SDI.NLM

    ☐ B. DIBI.NLM

    ☐ C. SMDR.NLM

    ☐ D. VLMs

    ☐ E. SQRDR.NLM

24. Storage Management Data Requester (SMDR) is used to _____.

    ○ A. pass commands between SBACKUP and the SDI.NLM

    ○ B. pass commands between the SBACKUP and the TSAs

    ○ C. pass commands between the SDI and the device driver

    ○ D. communicate with the SDR.NLM

25. Which of the following are TSA NLMs that are needed to back up the NetWare 4.1 file system and the NDS database?

    ☐ A. SDI.NLM

    ☐ B. TSA_400.NLM

    ☐ C. TSA410.NLM

    ☐ D. TSANDS.NLM

    ☐ E. TSA_NDS.NLM

    ☐ F. TSA_UNIV.NLM

    ☐ G. TSA_NFS.NLM

    ☐ H. NWSNUT.NLM

26. The Storage Device Interface is used to _____.

    ○ A. detect the presence of the device and media and present a list of devices available to the SBACKUP program

    ○ B. communicate with the TSA

    ○ C. detect the presence of the correctly configured device driver

D. communicate with the
   SMDR.NLM

E. communicate with the SDR.NLM

27. To back up and restore workstations in
    NetWare 4.1, the _____ must be loaded on the
    host server.

    A. TSA_NDS.NLM

    B. TSA410.NLM

    C. WSMAN.NLM

    D. WS_MAN.NLM

28. To use SBACKUP, you must _____.

    A. have INSTALL.NLM running

    B. have MONITOR.NLM running

    C. load the necessary TSAs, but it is
       not necessary to load the backup
       device drivers because they can be
       loaded from within SBACKUP

    D. first load all the necessary drivers
       and TSAs for the target being
       backed up

29. The name of the generic driver that can work
    with any tape device on a SCSI controller is
    _____.

    A. TAPEDAI.DSK

    B. TAPEDISK.NLM

    C. TAPEASPI.DSK

    D. TAPEASPI.NLM

30. To unload SBACKUP and the support NLMs,
    _____.

    A. you must unload the TSA.NLMs
       first, then the SBACKUP program,
       and finally the backup device drivers

    B. you must unload SBACKUP first,
       then the backup device drivers, and
       finally the TSA.NLMs

    C. you must unload SBACKUP first,
       then the TSA.NLMs, and finally the
       backup device drivers

    D. you must unload device drivers first,
       then the TSA. NLMs, and finally
       the SBACKUP program

31. The Log/Error File Administration option in
    SBACKUP enables you to _____.

    A. browse through the error log file
       created in the backup session only

    B. browse through the error log file
       created during a backup or restore
       session

    C. browse through the error log file
       created during a backup or restore
       session and edit it

    D. edit the error log file created during
       a backup or restore session

32. The default location of the SBACKUP error
    log files is _____.

    A. SYS:SYSTEM\TSA\LOG

    B. SYS:PUBLIC\TSA\LOG

    C. SYS:SYSTEM\SBACKUP\LOG

    D. SYS:PUBLIC\SBACKUP\LOG

33. The Storage Device Administration option in SBACKUP enables you to _____.

    ○ A. show options for excluding different aspects of the file system

    ○ B. choose the device and media to be used for the backup or restore operation

    ○ C. display the names of the targets to which you are attached

    ○ D. show the data structures available for restoring

34. The Change Target To Back Up From or Restore To option in SBACKUP enables you to _____.

    ○ A. show options for excluding different aspects of the file system

    ○ B. choose the device and media to be used for the backup or restore operation

    ○ C. display the names of the targets to which you are attached

    ○ D. show you the data structures available for restoring

35. A Major TSA resource _____.

    ○ A. is the name of the TSA.NLM

    ○ B. contains data that can be backed as a whole when selected

    ○ C. consists of data such as files and directories contained in other resources

    ○ D. supports NLMs and programs required for the target host

36. A Minor TSA resource _____.

    ○ A. is the name of the TSA.NLM

    ○ B. contains data that can be backed as a whole when selected

    ○ C. consists of data such as files and directories contained in another resource

    ○ D. supports NLMs and programs required for the target host

37. The backup operator must have a minimum of _____.

    ○ A. Supervisor rights to the file system being backed up

    ○ B. Read rights to the file system being backed up

    ○ C. Read and Write rights to the file system being backed up

    ○ D. Read and File Scan rights to the file system being backed up

38. If you are performing an incremental or full backup, you must have _____.

    ○ A. Modify right to the files being backed up

    ○ B. Access Control right to the files being backed up

    ○ C. Supervisor right to the files being backed up

    ○ D. Delete right to the files being backed up

39. To back up the NDS database, the backup operator must have _____.

   ○ A. Read and Create object trustee right to the NDS tree, and the Read property right to All Properties

   ○ B. Rename object trustee right to the NDS tree, and the Supervisor property right to All Properties

   ○ C. Browse object trustee right to the NDS tree, and the Read property right to All Properties

   ○ D. Browse and Delete object trustee right to the NDS tree, and the Read and Write property right to All Properties

Managing NetWare 3 Servers Using NetWare 4 NetWare Directory Services

A large enterprise may have a mix of NetWare 3 and NetWare 4 servers. NetWare 3 servers represent their resource information such as user, group, and print objects in a local database called the bindery. Because the bindery is local to a NetWare server, the binderies are normally managed separately. NetWare 4, on the other hand, allows network resources to be represented in the global database called the NetWare Directory Services (NDS). This enables NetWare 4 servers to be managed through the global NDS.

To ease the management of a NetWare server environment, many organizations are in the midst of upgrading their NetWare 3 servers to NetWare 4. This migration may involve a transition phase when the NetWare-based LAN is running a mix of NetWare 3 and NetWare 4 servers. Novell created a set of NLMs, called NetSync, that enables many of the NetWare 3 server administration tasks to be performed from the NDS using NetWare 4 tools such as the NetWare Administrator and NETADMIN.

The NetSync Enterprise Tool

NetSync allows the management of NetWare 3 servers through the NDS. Because the NDS is supported on NetWare 4 servers, you must at least have one NetWare 4 server. The management of NetWare 3 servers, such as user and group account creation, is performed using the NetWare 4 tools NETADMIN or NWADMIN (NetWare Administrator). NetSync consists of the NETSYNC3 and NETSYNC4 NLMs that run on NetWare 3 and NetWare 4 servers, respectively. These NLMs permit the NetWare 3 user and group accounts to be synchronized using their bindery object representations on a NetWare 4 server.

Overview of Bindery Objects and Bindery Context in NetWare 4

The NetWare 4 server has the capability to allow objects in any NDS container to be seen as their equivalent bindery object representations. This is called *bindery emulation* and it provides backwards compatibility with NetWare 3 servers. The

container in which you set the server's bindery services is called the *bindery context*.

Users who log in to a NetWare server from a NetWare 3 client must have their user NDS object in one of the containers specified in the bindery context. If a NetWare 3 client tries to log in to a NetWare 4 server that does not have the bindery context set, it receives a bindery locked error.

The container in which you set the server's bindery services is called the *bindery context*.

Bindery services provide backwards compatibility with pre-NetWare 4 clients and services.

If a NetWare 3 client tries to log in to a NetWare 4 server that does not have the bindery context set, it receives a bindery locked error.

Bindery emulation, also called *bindery services*, creates a "flat" structure for the objects within an Organizational Unit or Organization container. The objects in these containers can be accessed by both NDS objects and by bindery-based clients and servers. Bindery services are applicable only to the leaves in the bindery context.

Bindery services

■ Create a flat structure within an Organization or Organizational Unit container

■ Apply only to leaf objects in the bindery context

Starting with NetWare 4.1, the bindery context can be set to up to 16 containers using the SET BINDERY CONTEXT console command. The NDS objects in these containers that can be emulated to a NetWare 3 bindery object are seen by bindery-based tools as a single bindery. In earlier versions of NetWare 4, the bindery context could be set to a single container only. This forced NetWare administrators to place all objects to be seen by bindery-based clients into a single container. When multiple containers are allowed in the bindery context, you have more flexibility in placing objects in containers and yet can view these objects as belonging to a single bindery.

By default, the NetWare 4 server's bindery context is set to the container in which the NetWare 4 server object is created during the server installation. If objects and clients in other containers need access to bindery services, you should set the bindery context to include these containers.

 You can change the bindery context containers using the SET BINDERY CONTEXT server console command.

The bindery context can be set to 16 containers.

By default, bindery services are enabled during NetWare 4 server installation, and the bindery context is set to the container in which the server is installed.

NetSync depends on the setting of a bindery context on the NetWare 4 server, and this bindery context cannot be changed without affecting NetSync operation. The default bindery context set for NetWare 4 is the container where the server is installed. However, you can set the bindery context for NetSync to any context, including a context that does not contain a NetWare 4 server.

The following shows the general format of the SET BINDERY CONTEXT command:

```
SET BINDERY CONTEXT=NDS container {; NDS
➡container}
```

This command can be issued from the server console, but it is generally placed in the AUTOEXEC.NCF file so that the bindery context is set whenever the server is started.

With bindery emulation, it is possible for workstation clients that use the older shell (NETX.EXE or NETX.COM) software to access the NetWare 4 server. The NetWare 4 server appears as a bindery-based NetWare 3 server, and the NDS objects in the containers in the bindery context appear as bindery objects. Bindery emulation is also important for NLMs that have been written to access bindery files. An example of this is the earlier version of the Norton Antivirus NLM that requires that you log in as the bindery user SUPERVISOR when making configuration changes. Other applications that depend on bindery-based objects are the following:

- UnixWare clients
- Windows NT and OS/2 clients
- DOS workstations logged in to an NDS tree and making an attachment
- Host access via NetWare for SAA
- Users using the MAP command to access a directory in another NDS tree

When specifying the bindery context containers, do not use a leading period in the container name. The server generates an error message if you use a leading period. For example, the following is illegal:

```
SET BINDERY CONTEXT = .OU=CORP.O=ESL;.O=ESL
```

Instead of the preceding command, use the following legal command that does not have a leading period before the container name:

```
SET BINDERY CONTEXT = OU=CORP.O=ESL;O=ESL
```

Because the bindery context is changed through the SET command, it can also be set using the SERVMAN.NLM that allows any SET parameter to be changed.

Issues Pertaining to Bindery Services

Generally, you should avoid having objects with the same name in containers in the bindery context. Consider two users Karen Smith and Kim Smith that are in the Corporate and Engineering departments of the organization Kinetics. Assume that the login name convention used in the organization is first name initial plus last name. Because these users are in different departments, they could both be assigned a login name of KSmith. For example the user Karen Smith could be described by the user object CN=KSmith.OU=CORP.O=KINETICS, and the user Kim Smith could be described by CN=KSmith.OU=ENG.O=KINETICS. There is no conflict when these users log in using NDS names because the two users are in different containers. Now, what would happen if the bindery context for the NetWare server used by Karen and Kim is set as indicated below?

```
SET BINDERY CONTEXT =
➥OU=CORP.O=KINETICS;OU=ENG.O=KINETICS
```

If user Kim Smith logs in from a bindery-based client with login name KSmith, the container OU=CORP.O=KINETICS is searched first for the bindery object KSmith. The KSmith user bindery object is found in the container

OU=CORP.O=KINETICS, and the user Kim attempts to log in as KSmith. But the bindery object found is for user Karen Smith, and not user Kim Smith. User Kim attempts to log in with her password thinking that she is being asked by the server to log in as herself. The server rejects the login if user Kim's password is different from user Karen's. In the unlikely event that user Kim and Karen have the same password, user Kim logs in to user Karen's account, and does not find the files and directories she expects in her home directory. In either case, the situation is ripe for chaos.

NetWare 4 searches the containers specified in the bindery context in the order in which they are specified. If there is more than one object with the same common name (CN), only the object in the first bindery context is visible; the remaining bindery objects in other containers are hidden by the first occurrence of an object with the same name.

 If you have the same common name in more than one container in the bindery context, you can have name conflicts. Only the first object specified in the container that responds to the client request is accessible.

Because only the common name of the leaf object is seen by bindery clients and bindery-based services, this name must be compatible with bindery names. For example, if the leaf object in the bindery context has the complete name of .CN=JohnD.OU=CORP.O=ESL, the bindery-equivalent name will be JOHND. You should, therefore, use common names that comply with bindery naming rules. For example, you should avoid using spaces in common names.

Use bindery-compatible common names for leaf objects in the bindery context. Avoid using spaces in common names.

NetWare 3 clients can only use bindery-emulated leaf objects that they can understand. NDS objects and properties such as profile objects and profile properties are not available through bindery-based services. Login scripts that are defined in the NDS objects are not available for use through bindery-based services. If you want to have bindery-based login to a NetWare 4 server, you must manage these through bindery-based system login scripts (kept in the SYS:PUBLIC\NET$LOG.DAT file) and user login scripts (kept in the SYS:MAIL directory).

 NDS objects and properties such as profile objects and profile properties are not available through bindery services.

The NetSync Cluster

A *NetSync cluster* consists of one NetWare 4 server and up to 12 attached NetWare 3 servers (see fig. 10.1). The NetWare 3 servers attach to the NetWare 4 server in the bindery emulation mode.

Whenever you update or create a user in the bindery context of the NetWare 4 server, that user is synchronized with all NetWare 3 servers in the NetSync cluster. If a new NDS user is created in the NetWare 4 bindery context, that user now exists as a bindery user on all NetWare 3 servers that are part of the NetSync cluster and that are attached to the NetWare 4 server. Similarly, if a property of the user such as the user's last name is changed, that change is replicated to all the NetWare 3 servers in the NetSync cluster. A practical benefit of this is that you do not have to update or create the user on each NetWare 3 server.

Figure 10.1
A NetSync cluster.

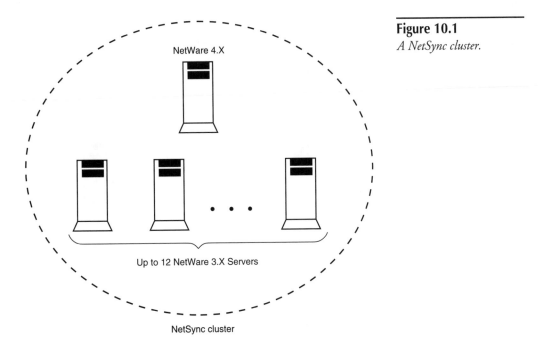

NetWare 4.X

Up to 12 NetWare 3.X Servers

NetSync cluster

A NetSync cluster consists of one NetWare 4 server and up to 12 attached NetWare 3 servers.

The updated bindery on each NetWare server is a superset of all the individual binderies at each NetWare server and is therefore called the *super bindery*. Any NetWare 3 user can access any other NetWare 3 server that is part of the same NetSync cluster.

The super bindery consists of the combined bindery and NDS users and group objects in the bindery context that is copied to all NetWare 3 servers that are part of the NetSync cluster.

Once a NetSync cluster is created, you must make all user and group account changes using the NetWare 4 administrative utilities such as the NETADMIN or NWADMIN. You should not use SYSCON for these tasks because SYSCON does not have knowledge of the NetSync cluster. Changes made through SYSCON result in the bindery objects on the servers being out of synchronization with each other. Synchronization in the NetSync cluster is achieved by the NETSYNC3.NLM that runs on each NetWare 3 server and the NETSYNC4.NLM that runs on the NetWare 4 server.

The NetWare 4 server acts as a repository for bindery objects copied from the NetWare 3 server into its bindery context. The NETSYNC4.NLM continuously monitors changes to objects in the NetWare 4 server's bindery context. Any changes made to the bindery objects in the NetWare 4 server's bindery context are downloaded to all the objects in the NetWare 3 servers in the NetSync cluster (see fig. 10.2).

Figure 10.2

NetSync synchronization.

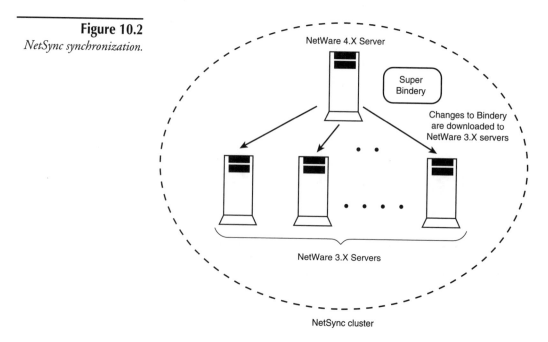

Once NetSync is installed, you should only use NetWare 4 administrative tools such as NETADMIN or NWADMIN to manage user and group accounts. Changes made to the NetWare 3 users and groups using SYSCON are not uploaded to the NetWare 4 host and other NetWare 3 servers in the cluster.

If you do not want the NetWare 3 servers to be managed from a central NetWare 4 server, you should not join the NetWare 3 server as part of the NetSync cluster. For example, if you plan to have a separate network supervisor for each NetWare 3 server and manage user and group accounts separately with SYSCON, you should not make the NetWare 3 server part of a NetSync cluster. Also, if you have only NetWare 4 servers on your network or intend to migrate all your NetWare 3 servers to NetWare 4 at the same time, there is no purpose in creating a NetSync cluster.

 You should use NetSync if

■ You want to make existing NetWare 3 users, groups, and print queues part of the NetWare 4 NDS without upgrading all NetWare 3 servers to NetWare 4.

■ You are running *NetWare Name Services* (*NNS*) and do not want to upgrade all servers in the NNS domain to NetWare 4 simultaneously.

■ You want to implement a temporary solution for central administration of a mixed NetWare 3/4 network before full migration to NetWare 4.

You should not use NetSync if

■ You intend to migrate all NetWare 3 servers to NetWare 4 simultaneously or in a short period of time.

■ You have only NetWare 4 servers on your network. That is, you do not have NetWare 3 servers.

■ You do not want to make NetWare 3 user and group accounts part of the NDS tree.

■ You plan to do administration using SYSCON or intend to have separate Supervisor passwords for administering the NetWare 3 servers.

Understanding Bindery Synchronization

Synchronization of the binderies in the NetSync cluster takes place from the NetWare 4 server bindery context to the NetWare 3 binderies (refer to fig. 10.2). Changes are made to the objects in the NetWare 4 bindery context first, and these are automatically copied as part of the bindery synchronization to the NetWare 3 binderies. These updates from the NetWare 4 bindery context to the NetWare 3 binderies are automatic, and the NetWare 4 bindery context is monitored continuously for changes.

If a NetWare 3 server that is part of a NetSync cluster is down when an update is sent out by the NetWare 4 server, the NetWare 3 server's bindery will be out of synchronization. When the NetWare 3 server is brought on-line again, the NetWare 4 server detects this event and downloads its bindery context to the NetWare 3 server so that the NetWare 3 server's bindery is now synchronized.

Ordinarily, the only time a NetWare 3 server's bindery is copied to the NetWare 4 bindery context is when the NetWare 3 server is first made part of the NetSync cluster. If inadvertent changes are made using SYSCON to the users and groups on a NetWare 3 server that is part of a NetSync cluster, these changes are not copied to the other binderies in the NetSync cluster, and this causes the bindery objects to be out of synchronization. In this case, an explicit copy must be made of the changed object on the NetWare 3 server to the NetWare 4 bindery context.

After a NetWare 3 server joins a NetSync cluster, you must make all changes to users, groups, and print services on the NetWare 3 servers using either the NETADMIN or NetWare Administrator in the NetWare 4 server. Changes made using these utilities are automatically sent to all servers in the NetSync cluster. Remember that one of the benefits of joining a NetSync cluster is central administration of the NetWare 3 servers. If you do not want central administration and prefer to manage users and groups using SYSCON, you should not join the NetSync cluster.

SYSCON must still be used for managing accounting charge rates on each NetWare 3 server. This is because accounting charges represent service and disk block usage and are always for a specific server. Therefore, by definition, the account charges are local to a server, and it makes little sense to synchronize this information across the servers in the NetSync cluster.

 Study Note The NETSYNC NLMs should be run continuously. You should, therefore, place the LOAD NETSYNC4 and LOAD NETSYNC3 commands in the AUTOEXEC.NCF files of the NetWare 4 and NetWare 3 servers, respectively.

 Study Note Accounting charges are local to a server and are not synchronized within the NetSync cluster.

Figures 10.3 and 10.4 illustrate bindery synchronization by showing the bindery objects on NetWare servers before joining a cluster and after joining a cluster.

Figure 10.3
Bindery objects before joining a NetSync cluster.

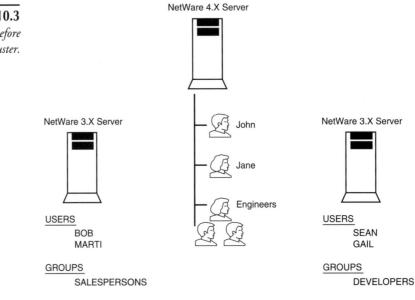

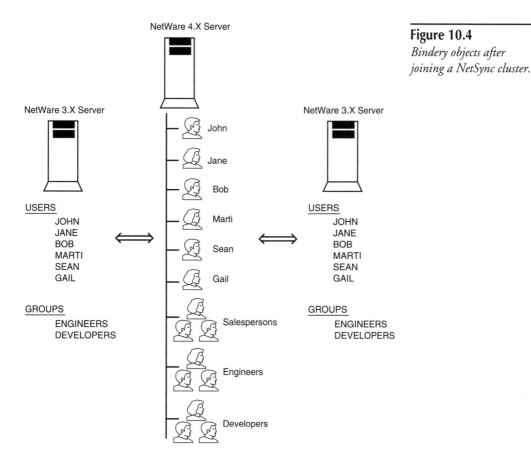

Figure 10.4
Bindery objects after joining a NetSync cluster.

Understanding NetSync Synchronization Problems

If a NetWare 3 server is down, it does not receive the synchronization information sent by the NetWare 4 server. This causes the NetWare 3 server to be out of synchronization with the NetSync cluster. When the NetWare 3 server is brought back up, the super bindery on the NetWare 4 server is downloaded to the NetWare 3 server. This resynchronizes the NetWare 3 server.

Generally, you should avoid deleting or renaming objects unless all servers in the NetSync cluster are

online. If you delete or rename user or group objects in the NetWare 4 bindery context while the NetWare 3 servers are down, these servers will be out of synchronization. When the downed NetWare 3 servers are brought online again, you must manually remove the objects deleted from the NetSync cluster. Otherwise, the deleted objects will be re-created if you manually upload the NetWare 3 bindery to the NetWare 4 host. Remember that if a new object is added to the super bindery, it is synchronized to all the NetWare 3 servers in the cluster.

If the NetWare 4 host in the NetSync cluster goes down while the binderies of one or more NetWare 3 servers are being uploaded to the NetWare 4 server, you should restart the synchronization when the NetWare 4 server comes back up.

If a NetWare 3 or NetWare 4 server runs out of disk space during bindery synchronization information, an error message is displayed on each server. You should add more disk space or make room for the bindery objects; then reload NETSYNC3.NLM or NETSYNC4.NLM.

Effect of Unloading NetSync

If you unload NETSYNC4 from the NetWare 4 server, the NETSYNC3 NLMs on the NetWare 3 servers in the NetSync cluster are automatically unloaded. To reload NETSYNC3 on the NetWare 3 servers, you must first load NETSYNC4 on the NetWare 4 server and then load NETSYNC3.

The REMAPID.NLM used for password synchronization must always remain loaded on the NetWare 3 server. If you unload REMAPID, you must assign new passwords to all bindery users in the system.

 Unloading NETSYNC4 from a NetWare 4 host causes NETSYNC3 NLMs on the NetWare 3 servers in the NetSync cluster to be automatically unloaded.

 To restart NetSync, first load NETSYNC4 on the NetWare 4 host; then load NETSYNC3 on the NetWare 3 servers in the NetSync cluster.

Understanding the NetSync Modules

NetSync consists of the following three primary NLMs (see fig. 10.5):

- NETSYNC4 that runs on NetWare 4 servers

- NETSYNC3 that runs on NetWare 3 servers

- REMAPID that runs on NetWare 3 servers and is used for password synchronization

Figure 10.5
NetSync NLMs.

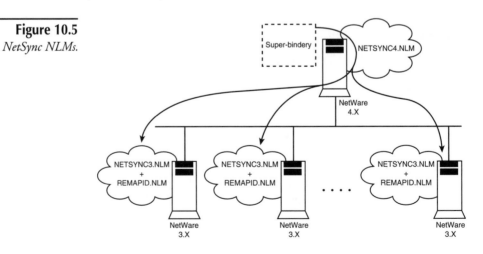

This section discusses these modules in further detail.

The NETSYNC4.NLM runs on a NetWare 4 server and is used to control the NetSync cluster. You can use NETSYNC4 to authenticate NetWare 3 servers that are reachable through the network and copy necessary files to the 3.x servers. Once NetWare 3 servers are synchronized to the bindery on the NetWare 4 server, NETSYNC4 monitors the super bindery for changes and downloads updated bindery information to all NetWare 3 servers in the NetSync cluster. For the NetSync cluster to work, the NETSYNC4 should run continuously. It is therefore best to place the following command in the NetWare 4 server's AUTOEXEC.NCF file:

LOAD NETSYNC4

 The NETSYNC4.NLM is loaded on the NetWare 4 host and controls the NetSync cluster.

The NETSYNC3.NLM runs on each NetWare 3 server that is part of the NetSync cluster. On joining the cluster, NETSYNC3 uploads the 3.x server's bindery information to the NetWare 4 server's bindery context. The NetWare 3 server then establishes a connection to the NetWare 4 server to receive updates to its bindery. In addition to synchronizing the server bindery, NETSYNC3 converts the 3.x PRINTDEF and PRINTCON databases to a NetWare 4 compatible database format, and it can move NetWare 3 print servers and their associated queues and printers to NetWare 4.

 The NETSYNC3.NLM is loaded on NetWare 3 servers and is used to copy (upload) the NetWare 3 server's bindery information to the NetWare 4 server's

bindery context. The NETSYNC3.NLM communicates with the NetWare 4 host to receive updates to the bindery.

 NETSYNC3 converts the 3.x PRINTDEF and PRINTCON databases to a NetWare 4 compatible database format, and it can move NetWare 3 print servers and their associated queues and printers to NetWare 4.

Both NETSYNC4 and NETSYNC3 log their activity in the SYS:SYSTEM\NETSYNC working directory on their respective servers, under the file name NETSYNC.LOG. The log file is in ASCII format and contains the messages displayed by NETSYNC3 on the server console. These messages describe the occurrence of events such as uploads and downloads of bindery information. The SYS:ETC\NETSYNC directories are created as part of the NetSync installation. The default log file maximum size is 0.5 MB. If the NETSYNC.LOG file is not cleared before it reaches its maximum size, NetSync automatically closes this file and renames it to NETSYNC.OLD. A new NETSYNC.LOG is then created. You can have only two NETSYNC files, NETSYNC.LOG and NETSYNC.OLD, at any time; older NetSync log files are automatically deleted.

 Both NETSYNC4 and NETSYNC3 log their activity in the SYS:SYSTEM\NETSYNC working directory on their respective servers, under the file name NETSYNC.LOG.

You should run NETSYNC3 continuously so that the NetWare 3 server can receive updates. But NETSYNC3 can only receive updates if

NETSYNC4 has been loaded on the NetWare 4 server. You must, therefore, load NETSYNC4 first on the NetWare 4 server; then load NETSYNC3 on the NetWare 3 servers. Add the following command to the NetWare 3 server's AUTOEXEC.NCF file:

LOAD NETSYNC3

The REMAPID.NLM is automatically loaded when NETSYNC3.NLM loads. REMAPID performs password synchronization for the bindery objects and should remain loaded even if the NETSYNC3 module is unloaded.

The REMAPID.NLM is autoloaded by NETSYNC3 and is used for password synchronization. If you unload REMAPID, you must assign new passwords to all bindery users in the system.

When you install NETSYNC3 on a NetWare 3 server, certain support NLMs are also installed. These support NLMs are the CLIB, STREAMS, NWPSRV3X, NWSNUT, AFTER311, A3112, and PBURST. The latest versions of these NLMs replace older versions on all NetWare 3 servers in the NetSync cluster.

NetSync has the following hardware requirements:

■ At least one NetWare 4 server to act as the host

■ Up to 12 NetWare 3 servers per NetWare 4 host

■ Necessary NetSync files

■ One unused license on the NetWare 4 server

Installing NetSync

To install NetSync, you must have at least one NetWare 4 server and up to 12 NetWare 3 servers per NetWare 4 server. You should also keep in mind the fact that NetSync is memory- and CPU-intensive on the NetWare 4 server, and CPU-intensive on the NetWare 3 server. Novell recommends that when NetSync is running, you should not let the cache buffer count drop below 200 or server utilization rise above 80 percent.

The NetWare 4 NetSync files are copied into SYS:SYSTEM directory during the NetWare 4 server installation. After installing NetSync on a NetWare 3 server, NetSync files exist in the SYS:SYSTEM\NETSYNC directory on the NetWare 3 server.

Before commencing the NetSync installation, perform the following tasks:

1. Resolve duplicate names.

2. Set the correct bindery context.

The following is an outline of the steps to install NetSync:

1. Load NETSYNC4 on a NetWare 4 server.

2. Enter the NetWare 3.1x server name.

3. Set the NetSync password. Do not use the same password as the Admin user's or bindery user SUPERVISOR's password. Use this password exclusively for synchronizing the servers.

4. Copy the NetWare 3 NetSync files to the NetWare 3.1x server.

5. Upload NetWare 3.1x bindery to the NetWare 4 server.

6. Enter the Supervisor user's name and password, and see the NetWare 3.1x server name appear on the authorized list.

7. Accept the option to add the NetSync3 commands to the AUTOEXEC.NCF file.

Installing NetSync on NetWare 3

You can install NetSync on NetWare 3 servers using the following procedure:

1. Restart the NetWare 3.1x server and load the NetWare 4 files. When you restart the server, the commands in the AUTOEXEC.NCF file start the NETSYNC3.NLM and the REMAPID.NLM.

2. Enter the NetWare 4 host name.

3. Enter the NetSync password you set in the preceding section.

Verifying NetWare 3.1x Synchronization

To verify that the NetWare 3.1x server is synchronized, perform the following steps:

1. Run NetWare Administrator from a workstation. Verify that the NetWare 3.1x objects have been added in the NetWare 4 host server bindery context.

2. Create a test user on the NetWare 4 host server. Verify that this user is created on each NetWare 3.1x server in the NetSync cluster.

Removing a NetWare 3 Server from a Cluster

Earlier, you learned how to add a NetWare 3 server to a NetSync cluster. On occasion, you may want to remove a NetWare 3 server from a NetSync cluster. For example, if you want to upgrade a NetWare 3 server to a NetWare 4 server, you should first remove the NetWare 3 server from the NetSync cluster.

You can remove a NetWare 3 server from a NetSync cluster using the NETSYNC4.NLM. This is done by deleting the server name from the list of authorized servers. This automatically removes the NetWare 3 server from the NetSync cluster. You can remove the servers only one at a time.

Removal of a NetWare 3 server from a NetSync cluster can be performed using the following steps:

1. Make sure that NETSYNC4 is running on the NetWare 4 server.

2. From NETSYNC4's Options menu, select Edit Server List.

3. Highlight the NetWare 3 server you want to delete and press the Del key.

Synchronizing Printing Functions Using NetSync

During NetSync installation on the NetWare 3 servers, all NetWare 4 workstation print utilities are copied to the NetWare 3 servers that join the NetSync cluster. The utilities that are copied are CAPTURE, NPRINT, NPRINTER (.NLM and .EXE), PCONSOLE, PRINTCON, PRINTDEF, PSC, PSERVER.NLM, and PUPGRADE.NLM. All support files needed for these utilities are copied as well.

After NetSync installation on the NetWare 3 server, you should replace the use of the NetWare 3 RPRINTER.EXE in NetWare 3 workstations with the equivalent NPRINTER.EXE utility. Replacing RPRINTER with NPRINTER can improve the printing performance on remote printers.

During NetSync installation on the NetWare 3 servers

■ All NetWare 4 workstation print utilities are copied to the NetWare 3 servers that join the NetSync cluster.

■ Databases for PRINTCON and PRINTDEF are upgraded to NetWare 4.

If you are running the NetWare 3 PSERVER.NLM on NetWare 3 servers, you should unload them and run the NetWare 4 PSERVER.NLM that was installed as part of the NetSync installation on the NetWare 3 server. When the NetWare 4 PSERVER loads, it automatically loads the NetWare 4 NPRINTER.NLM.

The NetWare 4 print utilities can operate in a bindery mode, and their behavior in the NetWare 3 server is similar to what can be expected from the NetWare 3 counterpart. The print job configurations and print databases created with PRINTCON and PRINTDEF are converted to a NetWare 4 format and copied to the NetWare 4 print databases.

To simplify administration of the NetWare 3 print servers, you can merge them into a single print server object in the NDS. This merging also results in the NetWare 3 printers being placed in the NDS where they can be managed from the single NetWare 4 print server.

When you run NETSYNC3 on a NetWare 3 server, you must confirm that you will be using the NetWare 4 print databases and utilities. If you do not confirm this change, NETSYNC3 will unload itself.

If you have a complex printing environment under NetWare 3, you can simplify it by moving it to a

NetWare 4 environment. NetSync does much of the necessary synchronization, but you may still have to perform some manual configuration.

You can use NetSync to move the NetWare 3 print servers to the NetWare 4 NDS so that these print servers can be administered from a central location. You can merge the print resources of all the NetWare 3 servers in the NetSync cluster (up to 12 NetWare 3 servers). As a result of this merging, configuration information for the NetWare 3 print servers and their associated printers and queues is transferred to a single NetWare 4 print server NDS object. Existing NetWare 3 print queues appear the same to the NetWare users, but are serviced by a NetWare 4 print server. The NetWare 3.1x printers are converted to NDS print objects and are available to NetWare 4 users.

If you have a complex printing environment under NetWare 3, you can simplify it by moving it to a NetWare 4 environment.

You can merge the print resources of all the NetWare 3 servers to a single NetWare 4 print server NDS object that can support up to 256 printers.

During NetSync print synchronization

■ Existing NetWare 3 print queues appear the same to the NetWare users but are serviced by a NetWare 4 print server.

■ The NetWare 3.1x printers are converted to NDS print objects and are available to NetWare 4 users.

The following is a guided tour of how to perform the print merge administration tasks:

1. Load NETSYNC4 on the NetWare 4 host server.

2. Load NETSYNC3 on the NetWare 3 host server.

3. Select Move a Print Server and specify the name of the print server to be moved.

4. In the NetWare 4 directory, enter the name of the print server you want to use.

 During NetWare 3.1x printer upgrade using NetSync

■ If you type an existing NetWare 4 print server name, the NetWare 3 print server is merged to the existing NetWare 4 print server.

■ If you type in a new NetWare 4 print server name, the NetWare 4 print server is created without a password.

To complete the print configuration, you must make sure that the printers are connected as indicated in the NetWare 4 printing environment. NetSync does not know about the physical printer configuration or to which device or printer port the printer is supposed to be connected. You must also load the PSERVER NLM and specify the merged print server to activate the NetWare 4 printing environment. Because NetWare 4 print server functions are more efficient than NetWare 3 print server functions, NetWare 3 users may notice an improvement in speed and performance over the NetWare 3 printing environment.

Some print environments use third-party direct network attached print devices. These devices either connect to a printer and then to the network, are installed in a port at the printer, or placed in a slot inside the printer itself. These print devices emulate a NetWare 3 print server and are designed to look in the NetWare 3 bindery for network printing information. Therefore, you should not move the queue server configurations used by these print devices unless you plan to reconfigure these print devices to the NetWare 4 environment. The third-party print devices can work with the NetWare 4 printing environment if you are using the bindery emulation mode at the NetWare 4 print server.

Study Guide for the Chapter

If preparing for exams, review the chapter with the following goals:

1. Understand the components of NetSync. Use the Study Notes as a quick review.

2. After studying this chapter, attempt the sample test questions. If you miss the answers to a question, review the appropriate topic until you understand the reason for the correct answer.

Chapter Summary

Large enterprises that are transitioning from NetWare 3 to NetWare 4 often have a mix of NetWare 3 and NetWare 4 servers. NetWare 3 servers do not have any inherent central management capability. By using bindery synchronization, it is possible to manage NetWare servers from the NDS of a NetWare 4 host. Users, groups, and print environments of a NetWare 3 server can be managed from the NetWare 4 NDS. This is accomplished by the NetSync tool.

Chapter Test Questions

Most of the test questions are multiple choice. Where a single answer is desired, it is indicated by a ○ (circle) notation that precedes the possible answers. Some questions require you to select more than one answer; these are indicated by a □ (box) preceding each answer. Not all the questions are multiple choice. Occasionally, you might get a question that asks you to type in an answer. The answer in this case is usually a one-word answer. The answer is not case-sensitive; you can type the answer in lower- or uppercase.

Certain questions are repeated in different ways so that you can recognize them even when the wording is different. Taking practice quizzes not only tests your knowledge, but also gives you confidence when you take your exam.

1. The container in which you set the server's bindery services is called the _____.

   ○ A. server context

   ○ B. bindery context

   ○ C. server location

   ○ D. bindery location

2. Bindery services provide _____.

   ○ A. the ability for NetWare 3 servers to be synchronized to NetWare 4 servers

   ○ B. forward compatibility with NetWare 4 clients and services

   ○ C. backwards compatibility with pre-NetWare 4 clients and services

   ○ D. bindery emulation for NetWare 4 clients

3. If a NetWare 3 client tries to log in to a NetWare 4 server that does not have the bindery context set, _____.

   ○ A. they are able to log in using the default bindery context

   ○ B. they receive a bindery synchronization error

   ○ C. they are able to log in if the BINDERY.CFG file contains a default bindery context

   ○ D. they receive a bindery locked error

4. Bindery services _____.

   □ A. create a flat structure within an Organization or Organizational Unit container

   □ B. apply only to leaf objects in the bindery context

   □ C. apply to all leaf and container objects in the bindery context

   □ D. create a flat structure within an Organization, Organizational Unit, or Country container

5. You can change the bindery context containers using the _____.

   ○ A. BINDERY_CONTEXT environment variable at the workstation

   ○ B. SET BINDERY CONTEXT server console command

   ○ C. SET CONTEXT server console command

   ○ D. CONTEXT environment variable at the workstation

6. The bindery context can be set to _____ containers.

   ○ A. 4

   ○ B. 8

   ○ C. 12

   ○ D. 16

   ○ E. 32

7. In NetWare 4, by default, _____.

   ☐ A. bindery services are enabled during NetWare 4 server installation

   ☐ B. bindery services are not enabled during NetWare 4 server installation

   ☐ C. The bindery context is set to the container in which the server is installed

   ☐ D. The bindery context is set to the parent of the container in which the server is installed

8. If you have the same common name in more than one container specified in the bindery context, _____.

   ☐ A. it does not pose any problem

   ☐ B. it can cause name conflicts

   ☐ C. only the first object specified in the container that responds to the client request will be accessible

   ☐ D. all objects that respond to the client request will be accessible for client operations

9. In specifying common names of leaf objects in the bindery context you can _____.

   ☐ A. use any NDS-compliant name

   ☐ B. comply with bindery naming rules

   ☐ C. use only uppercase names

   ☐ D. avoid using spaces in names

10. Which of the following is true for bindery services?

    ☐ A. All leaf objects in the bindery context are available through bindery emulation.

    ☐ B. All leaf and container objects in the bindery context are available through bindery emulation.

    ☐ C. NDS objects and properties such as profile objects and profile properties are not available through bindery services.

    ☐ D. Objects created through bindery services are placed in the bindery context.

11. Which of these is a valid method for setting the bindery context?

    ☐ A. SET BINDERY CONTEXT = .O=ICS

    ☐ B. SET BINDERY CONTEXT = O=ICS;OU=OPS;O=ICS

    ☐ C. SET BINDERY CONTEXT = O=ICS:OU=OPS:O=ICS

    ☐ D. SET BINDERY CONTEXT = .O=ICS;OU=OPS;O=ICS

    ☐ E. SET BINDERY CONTEXT = O=ICS

    ☐ F. SET BINDERY CONTEXT = .O=ICS:OU=OPS:O=ICS

12. You should set the bindery context in the
    _____.

    ○ A. STARTUP.NCF file

    ○ B. AUTOEXEC.NCF file

    ○ C. BINDERY.CFG file

    ○ D. NET.CFG file

13. Which of the following console commands
    can be used to determine the bindery context
    at a NetWare 4 server?

    ☐ A. SHOW BINDERY

    ☐ B. CONFIG

    ☐ C. SET BINDERY CONTEXT

    ☐ D. SET BINDERY CONTEXT =

14. NetSync cluster consists of _____.

    ○ A. one NetWare 4 server and up to 12
          attached NetWare 3 servers

    ○ B. one primary and one secondary
          NetWare 4 server and up to 16
          attached NetWare 3 servers

    ○ C. one NetWare 4 server and up to 16
          attached NetWare 3 servers

    ○ D. one primary and one secondary
          NetWare 4 server and up to 12
          attached NetWare 3 servers

15. In a NetSync cluster, _____.

    ☐ A. the super bindery consists of the
          combined bindery and NDS users
          and group objects in the bindery
          context

    ☐ B. objects in the super bindery are
          copied to all NetWare 3 servers that
          are part of the NetSync cluster

    ☐ C. the super bindery consists of the
          combined bindery of only NetWare
          3 servers

    ☐ D. objects in the super bindery are
          copied to all NetWare 3 and
          NetWare 4 servers that are part of
          the NetSync cluster

16. You should use NetSync if _____.

    ☐ A. you want to make existing NetWare
          3 users, groups, and print queues
          part of the NetWare 4 NDS without
          upgrading all NetWare 3 servers to
          NetWare 4

    ☐ B. you are running NetWare Name
          Services (NNS) and do not want to
          upgrade all servers in the NNS
          domain to NetWare 4 simulta-
          neously

    ☐ C. you intend to migrate all NetWare 3
          servers to NetWare 4 simultaneously
          or in a short period of time

    ☐ D. you have only NetWare 4 servers on
          your network. That is, you do not
          have NetWare 3 servers

    ☐ E. you want to implement a temporary
          solution for central administration
          of a mixed NetWare 3/4 network
          before full migration to NetWare 4

17. You should *not* use NetSync if _____.

    ☐ A. you intend to migrate all NetWare 3
          servers to NetWare 4 simultaneously
          or in a short period of time

    ☐ B. you are running NetWare Name
          Services (NNS) and do not want to
          upgrade all servers in the NNS
          domain to NetWare 4 simulta-
          neously

☐ C. you want to make existing NetWare 3 users, groups, and print queues part of the NetWare 4 NDS without upgrading all NetWare 3 servers to NetWare 4

☐ D. you have only NetWare 4 servers on your network. That is, you do not have NetWare 3 servers

☐ E. you do not want to make NetWare 3 user and group accounts part of the NDS tree

☐ F. you plan to do administration using SYSCON or intend having separate Supervisor passwords for administering the NetWare 3 servers

18. Which of the following is true for bindery synchronization?

☐ A. The NETSYNC NLMs should be run continuously.

☐ B. Only the NETSYNC3 NLMs should run continuously.

☐ C. Only the NETSYNC4 NLMs should run continuously.

☐ D. You should place the LOAD NETSYNC4 and LOAD NETSYNC3 commands in the AUTOEXEC.NCF files of the NetWare 4 and NetWare 3 servers, respectively.

☐ E. Accounting charges are synchronized within the NetSync cluster.

☐ F. Accounting charges are not synchronized within the NetSync cluster.

19. Unloading NETSYNC4 from a NetWare 4 host will _____.

○ A. cause NETSYNC3 NLMs on the NetWare 3 servers in the NetSync cluster to automatically unload

○ B. have no effect on the NETSYNC3 NLMs on the NetWare 3 servers

○ C. can cause the host server to crash

○ D. can cause a corruption in the supervisor password settings on the NetWare 3 servers

20. To restart NetSync, _____.

○ A. first load NETSYNC4 on the NetWare 4 host, and then load NETSYNC3 on the NetWare 3 servers in the NetSync cluster

○ B. first load NETSYNC3 on the NetWare 3 servers, and then load NETSYNC4 on the host NetWare 4 server in the NetSync cluster

○ C. first load REMAPID, then the NETSYNC4 on the NetWare 4 host, and then load the NETSYNC3 on the NetWare 3 servers in the NetSync cluster

○ D. first load BINDSYNC, then the NETSYNC4 on the NetWare 4 host, and then the load NETSYNC3 on the NetWare 3 servers in the NetSync cluster

21. The NETSYNC3 NLM is loaded on NetWare 3 servers and is used to _____.

    □ A. upload the NetWare 3 server's bindery information to the NetWare 4 server's bindery context

    □ B. upload the NetWare 4 user object information to the NetWare 4 bindery

    □ C. communicate with the NetWare 4 host to receive updates to the bindery

    □ D. for consolidating NetWare 4 print environment onto NetWare 3 servers

22. NETSYNC3 does the following:

    □ A. converts the NetWare 3 PRINTDEF and PRINTCON databases to a NetWare 4 compatible database format

    □ B. moves NetWare 3 print servers and their associated queues and printers to NetWare 4

    □ C. converts the NetWare 4 PRINTDEF and PRINTCON databases to a NetWare 3 compatible database format

    □ D. moves NetWare 4 print servers and their associated queues and printers to NetWare 3

23. Both NETSYNC4 and NETSYNC3 log their activity in the _____ working directory on their respective servers, under the file name _____.

    ○ A. SYS:SYSTEM\NETSYNC, BINDSYNC.LOG

    ○ B. SYS:PUBLIC\NETSYNC, BINDSYNC.LOG

    ○ C. SYS:SYSTEM\NETSYNC, NETSYNC.LOG

    ○ D. SYS:PUBLIC\NETSYNC, NETSYNC.LOG

24. Which of the following is true for NetSync?

    □ A. The REMAPID.NLM is autoloaded by NETSYNC3.

    □ B. The REMAPID.NLM is autoloaded by NETSYNC4.

    □ C. The REMAPID.NLM is used for password synchronization.

    □ D. The REMAPID.NLM is used for mapping user and group accounts between NetWare 3 and NetWare 4 servers.

    □ E. If you unload REMAPID.NLM, you must assign new passwords to all bindery users in the system.

    □ F. If you unload REMAPID.NLM, you must assign new mappings for mapping NetWare 3 user and group accounts to NetWare 4 servers.

    □ G. The SYS:SYSTEM\NETSYNC directory is automatically created during NetWare 4.1 server installation and contains NetSync log files and NetWare 3 NetSync files.

25. NETSYNC4 autoloads the following NLMs:

    □ A. CLIB

    □ B. NETAPI

    □ C. SYNCAPI

   ☐ D. STREAMS

   ☐ E. NWPSRV

   ☐ F. NWSNUT

   ☐ G. DSAPI

26. During NetSync installation on the NetWare 3 servers, _____.

   ☐ A. all NetWare 4 workstation print utilities are copied to the NetWare 3 servers that join the NetSync cluster

   ☐ B. NetWare 3 workstation print utilities are copied to the NetWare 4 host server

   ☐ C. NetWare 3 databases for PRINTCON and PRINTDEF are upgraded to NetWare 4

   ☐ D. NetWare 3 databases for PRINTCON and PRINTDEF are consolidated and stored on NetWare 3 servers

Designing and Troubleshooting the NDS Tree

This chapter discusses the issues involved in designing an effective NDS tree. Although NetWare 4 provides tools you can use to change the structure of an NDS tree, designing the tree correctly in the first place is much easier. You then can easily make incremental changes to the NDS tree to adapt it to meet the changing needs of your organization.

This chapter also discusses procedures and tools to help you troubleshoot NDS-related problems. This chapter assumes that you are familiar with the NDS concepts described in Chapters 2 and 4.

Designing the NDS Tree

A properly designed NDS tree offers the following benefits:

- Provides fault tolerance for the network

- Decreases unnecessary traffic

- Simplifies network administration and maintenance

- Enables users to access resources easily

- Minimizes the impact on users and reduces the need for training

The design for the NDS tree depends on design criteria relevant to your organization's needs. You also must take into account the fact that an organization's needs can change over time. The NDS design, therefore, should be flexible and easily accommodate changes.

Novell recommends that NDS design be accomplished in two phases:

- Structural design

- Detailed design

The *structural design phase* determines the overall NDS tree structure without going into too much detail about the NDS objects that populate the NDS tree.

The *detailed design phase* focuses on how users access the NDS tree, how the NDS tree is stored on servers, and how the common network time you need for Directory operations is implemented. The detailed design issues are discussed in Chapter 2 and Chapter 4, which discuss partition and replication, and NDS security. This chapter discusses the structural design of the NDS tree.

Creating a Structural Design for the NDS Tree

The method for creating a structural design is described in figure 11.1. The following list gives the three broad elements of the structural design method:

1. Determine the structural model

2. Establish naming conventions

3. Select implementation method

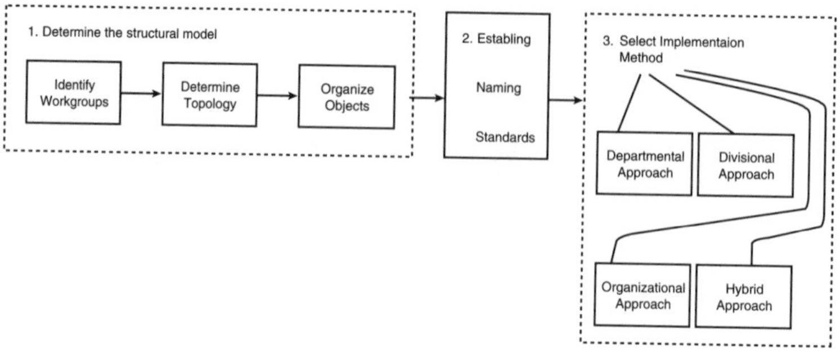

Figure 11.1

A flow chart describing the structural design method.

Determine the Structural Model

To determine the structural model, you need to identify the workgroup needs, determine the network topology, and organize the NDS objects.

You should consider the following factors as you identify the workgroup needs:

- How a group of individuals typically accesses network resources

- How the users of an organization see themselves in relation to a workgroup or larger administrative domain within the organization

- How users perceive the network resources that they access; for example, do the users think that the network resources they access belong to their workgroup or do they share it with other workgroups

The purpose of identifying the proper level of workgroup structure is to assist users in accessing the resources that they need and sharing information with others in their workgroup in a collaborative manner. The network should be easy to use for the users, and easy to administer and maintain by the network administrators.

You can use the following methods to arrange your workgroups:

- Administrative division

- Workgroups across divisions

- Geographical locations

In the administrative division method, you identify the workgroups by the company's organization chart. This approach emphasizes the organization's administrative and management structure. This method is particularly appropriate if the work the users perform is strictly along the organization charts for the organization. The divisions Engineering, Accounting, Marketing, Sales, and Corporate form a natural workgroup (see fig. 11.2).

In the workgroups across divisions method, you identify the workgroups according to the common projects and functions each division of the company performs. This approach emphasizes the project-oriented nature within an organization, and is particularly appropriate if the work users do is strictly along project lines and users from more than one division work on common projects or perform similar tasks and access the same resources. Figure 11.3 illustrates this approach.

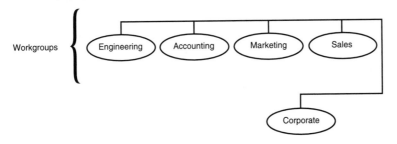

Figure 11.2

The administrative division workgroup.

Figure 11.3

Workgroups across divisions.

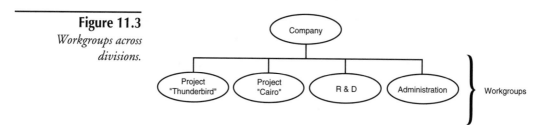

In the geographical location method, you identify the workgroups based on their physical location. This method is particularly appropriate if the work the users at each location do is distinct and users in a particular location need to perform similar tasks. Figure 11.4 illustrates this approach.

Some organizations might do best to combine these methods. Workgroups that use a combination of methods are called *hybrid* or *mixed environment workgroups*. Figure 11.5 illustrates the hybrid approach for workgroups.

After you identify the workgroups, you can start to determine your network topology. You need to understand network topology before you can understand how the resources are accessed. For example, you need to determine how many WAN links you need as well as their cost and bandwidths. If the users and the resources they need to be able to access are far apart and separated by expensive and slow links, the network might seem slow to the user, and might be expensive to use.

After you determine the network topology, you should determine the number of container levels your NDS tree needs. The number of container levels you can have in an NDS tree is practically unlimited. You cannot enter more than 256 characters for the NDS object path name: that is the only limit. You should decide on the number of levels that suit your needs.

You also should provide bindery services for those clients that need them.

Author's Note Novell documentation states that the Directory tree works well with approximately five to eight levels. Realistically speaking, two to five levels are adequate for most organizations.

Figure 11.4

Workgroups based on geographical location.

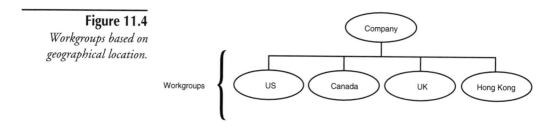

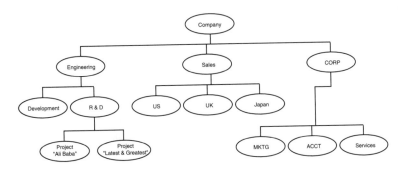

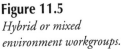

Figure 11.5
*Hybrid or mixed
environment workgroups.*

Establish Naming Conventions

Before you create the Directory tree, you should have a naming standard that describes rules for naming objects. You should include the naming standards in a written document. The NDS naming standard should account for the following:

- Conventions used for NDS objects, such as containers and leaf objects

- Property values that will be defined for NDS objects, such as a user's telephone number, fax number, postal address, and so forth

Here is a partial example of a naming standard for user objects:

1. Login names are eight characters so that DOS name home directories can be set up for users.

2. Login names should consist of first letter of first name plus first seven characters of last name (for example, BFRANKEN for Bob Frankenburger) (other naming conventions also possible).

3. Given Name property should have the user's first name.

4. Last Name property should have the user's full last name.

5. Title property should have the name of the user's title.

When you devise naming conventions, try to keep the names short, descriptive, and easy to remember and identify. Easy to remember names makes Directory searches easier.

To ensure adherence to the naming standards, apply the standards consistently. Consistency in naming NDS objects grants the following benefits:

- Provides a guideline for network administrators when they create, modify, and rename objects in the NDS tree

- Eliminates redundant planning for names during design of a new NDS tree or tree branch

- Helps users and administrators quickly identify network resources

For NDS operations, NDS names in different containers need not be unique. However, if these containers are placed in the bindery context defined by the SET BINDERY CONTEXT server console command that can have 16 containers, then the names that are to be visible to bindery clients should be unique. If duplicate names exist in the bindery context, only the first name will be recognized.

Plan the Implementation Method

After you determine what naming conventions to use, you must decide on the implementation method, which involves taking into account the following factors:

■ Whether you are upgrading from a NetWare 3.*x* network

■ Whether you are implementing NetWare 4 in one division and then upgrading the rest of the organization

■ Whether you plan to create individual NDS trees and then merge them

■ Whether you plan to create one NDS tree, and upgrade/add other servers to the NDS tree

The answers to the preceding considerations indicate which of the following implementation methods you should use:

■ Departmental approach

■ Divisional approach

■ Organizational approach

■ Hybrid approach

The *departmental approach* enables a group or department within an organization to implement NetWare 4 without waiting for the rest of the organization to agree on a networking goals and implementation strategy. This approach is useful under any of the following conditions:

■ No direct network communication links between the departmental networks

■ Coordination of planners, implementers, and administrators currently is difficult and impractical

The departmental approach gives you several NDS trees, one per department. When the time comes to link the departments using the network, you can use the DSMERGE tool to merge the NDS trees. DSMERGE requires unique tree names. If the trees do not have unique names, you can use DSMERGE to rename one or more of the trees. The departmental approach enables smaller groups within an organization to reap the benefits of NetWare 4 networks while leaving open the option of having a combined NDS tree with other departments in the future.

If one of the NDS trees to be merged has only an Organization container, you should consider adding an extra Organizational Unit container so that the leaf objects have their own separate container.

The *divisional implementation approach* is used for a large organization that has a separate division implemented by a separate tree in each location. Should the organization's needs require the divisions to share network resources, you can merge the separate trees. You could use the divisional implementation approach with any of the previously discussed workgroup models (administrative division, workgroups across divisions, geographical locations, hybrid or mixed environment). The divisional approach is similar to the departmental approach, but is bigger in terms of the larger size and complexity of the divisional trees that are implemented.

The *organizational implementation approach* is a top-down approach in which a single NDS tree serves for the entire organization. This approach assumes that you have a clear understanding of the organizational wide approach and a common agreement on implementing the NDS tree.

To summarize, for the organizational implementation approach:

- A single NDS tree is desired.

- All NetWare 4 servers are connected to each other using LAN/WAN links.

- A central group of administrators, such as the IS department, can manage the upgrade and implementation of the NetWare 4 network.

- The network is small enough that you can perform a near simultaneous upgrade of the network without adversely affecting business.

If you use the administrative model for identifying the workgroups, along with the organizational implementation, identifying workgroups might not be readily apparent to the central IS department. Identification of the workgroups requires an understanding of the organizational structure of a company down to the workgroup level, which is not an easy task in a large company. To assist you with this endeavor, you need working organizational charts for the company, network layout maps, and key personnel to help you identify the workgroups. One approach is to identify the workgroups by the applications they use, which results in workgroups such as NFS, Unix, SAA, and so on. You also might analyze the way information flows in the company to identify the different functional roles. You can use the hybrid workgroup model, with geographic locations at the top of the NDS tree, to preserve the workgroup characteristics of each location. That would prove easier than defining a workgroup that combines the characteristics of all the geographic locations.

Understanding NDS Design Criteria

Proper design of an NDS tree must take into account the following design criteria:

- Security of the NDS tree

- Partitioning and replication of the NDS tree

- Synchronizing time in the NDS tree

These design criteria are discussed in the sections that follow.

Security of the NDS Tree

Because the NDS tree is a repository of the descriptions of sensitive network resources, you must ensure that the network resources, represented by NDS objects, are properly protected. Users must have the necessary security permissions to access the network resources they need to perform their jobs. However, they should not have excessive rights to network resources (files, applications, printers, and so on) that would constitute a violation of other users' rights or compromise the organization.

You must consider, therefore, the following design issues that relate to the security of the NDS tree:

- Decide between a centralized versus distributed network administration approach.

- Determine the proper placement of groups in the NDS tree.

- Properly plan inheritance and security equivalencies.

- Assign appropriate rights to NetWare server objects.

- Provide appropriate access for traveling users.

Many of these issues summarized here for your reference also are discussed in Chapter 4.

 Be familiar with the main points for designing a secure NDS tree as listed above.

Centralized Versus Distributed Network Administration

The centralized approach is adequate for a small organization. In this approach, a single Administrator user can manage the NDS tree—the Admin user object created during installation of the first server in the NDS tree.

Larger organizations find it more practical for a number of administrators, called the *container administrators*, to carry out the functions of network administration. This is known as the distributed approach to network administration. In the *distributed approach*, the network administration tasks are divided among several network administrators. One way to do this is to assign one administrator per tree branch, by giving the administrator appropriate NDS rights to the root container (top-most container) of the tree branch.

Determining the Proper Placement of Groups in the NDS Tree

For small workgroup users who share the same needs, you can place them in an appropriate container object, and use the natural grouping of the

container objects to assign rights to the users. Remember that if you make a container a trustee, all user objects in that container and subcontainers inherit any rights assigned to that container.

In larger networks, user objects in the same container might require different sets of rights. If so, consider using the NDS group object. The NDS group object is particularly useful for users who are in different containers, and yet need the same permissions. Users working on a common project but who are in different departments, for example, might need a common set of rights. When you assign members to group objects, take into account the situation in which WAN links separate members of the group object and the resources they access. In this case, authentication occurs across the WAN links and might lead to undesirable network traffic across the WAN link.

You also might consider using the Organizational Role object to assign permissions for well-defined tasks, such as backup operators.

Properly Plan Inheritance and Security Equivalencies

The placement of User objects in groups and containers affects the rights that these objects inherit. User objects that are members of Group objects are security equivalent to the Group object. The Group object in which the User object is a member is listed explicitly in the Security Equal To property of the User object. Membership in a Group object, therefore, is called *explicit security equivalence*. Figure 11.6 shows that the Group object CN=Students.O=IBL is listed in the Security Equal To property of the User object Lisa. Figure 11.7 shows that Lisa is a member of the Group object CN=Students.O=IBL.

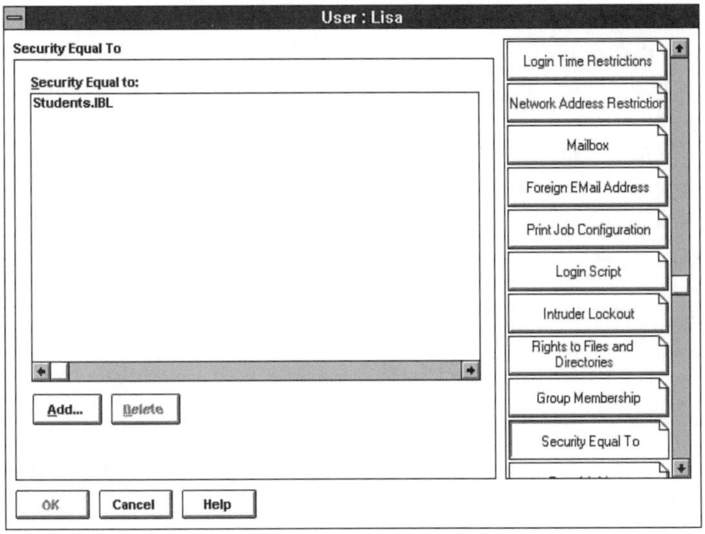

Figure 11.6
The explicit security equivalence of User to Group object.

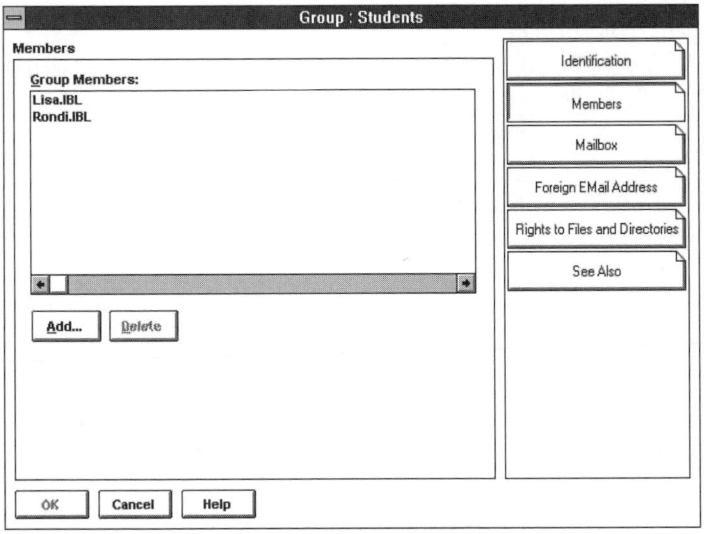

Figure 11.7
User membership to Group object.

Each container above the user, all the way up to the [Root], can contribute to the rights that accrue to the user, even though these rights do not show up in the Security Equal To property of the user object. Figure 11.6 shows that the Security Equal to property of the user Lisa does not contain its parent O=IBL. Because the containers do not show up in the Security Equal To property of the User object, the User object has an *implied security equivalence* to its parent containers. For example, all users in an NDS tree have an implied security equivalence to the [Root]. Any right assigned to the [Root] is implied for all users in the NDS tree.

Assign Appropriate Rights to NetWare Server Objects

Be careful how you assign NDS rights to NetWare Server objects. The Write Property right to the ACL of the Server object gives the user the Supervisor file system right to the root of all volumes attached to the server. If you assign a user the Supervisor object right to the Server object, for example, the user then has Supervisor file system rights in the server's volumes, because assigning a user the Supervisor object right to the Server object gives the user the All Properties right to the Server object. The All Properties Supervisor property right to the Server object gives the user the Write property right to the ACL of the Server object. The Write Property right to the ACL of the Server object gives the user the Supervisor file system right to the root of all volumes attached to the server.

Providing Appropriate Access for Traveling Users

Traveling users try to use their time more efficiently by accessing their organization's network from remote locations; you need to give such users special considerations for NDS rights. The following discussion is based on Novell's classifications of traveling users:

- Users who divide their work time between home and office

- Users who need access from a temporary location while they work on special projects

- Users who spend a considerable amount of their work time traveling and regularly need access to the network from remote locations

For each type of traveling user you should consider the following issues:

- Access to files on server volumes

- Access to applications

- Access to files from several remote locations

- Access to resources such as printers and e-mail accounts

- Authenticating NDS objects

- Number of traveling users

- Type of computer used by traveling users (portable versus desktop)

Partitioning and Replicating the NDS Tree

If you have a centralized database, a failure in the network at the central location makes the NDS database unavailable to the entire network. Centralization is not as much of a concern for small LANs. Centralization can become a serious reliability problem, however, for large networks separated by WAN links.

What you want to do, then, is distribute the database so that a single failure does not disable the entire NDS service. The logical division of an NDS database is called a *partition*. A duplicate image of the partition on another server is called a *replica* of the partition.

Consider the following design issues for partitioning and replication:

◼ Plan partition boundaries.

◼ Determine the appropriate replica assignment.

◼ Determine accessibility and fault tolerance versus network traffic and performance.

◼ Determine the effect of WAN links.

◼ Assign administrators of partitions and replicas.

> **Study Note**
> Be familiar with the main points for partitioning and replicating an NDS tree.

These design issues are discussed briefly, next. For additional information on partitions and replicas, see Chapter 2.

Plan Partition Boundaries

The logical subdivisioning of the NDS tree into partitions should be based on the following factors:

◼ Geographic location

◼ WAN topology

◼ Access to Directory information

◼ Number of objects in containers

◼ Needs of workgroups of users

◼ Access to information on network

◼ Reduction of unnecessary traffic on network

◼ Elimination of single point of failure

Determine the Appropriate Replica Assignments

During the installation of a server in an NDS tree, a default number and type of replica is created. These defaults are designed to prevent single points of failure. You might want additional replicas so that information in the replica is more easily accessible.

Determine Accessibility and Fault Tolerance Versus Network Traffic and Performance

To improve accessibility of information in the NDS tree, and the fault tolerance of a partition, you might want to create additional replicas. Creating additional replicas ensures that the NDS information is available even if the Master replica and replicas in other locations become corrupted.

Easy access of information also requires that replicas be kept on local servers. However, as the number of replicas increase, so does the amount of network traffic and the time necessary for keeping the replicas synchronized. The additional network traffic affects network performance adversely, so you need to balance the requirements for accessibility and fault tolerance against the requirements of minimizing network traffic and not degrading network performance.

Determine the Effect of WAN Links

If replica synchronization on the WAN links produces excessive network traffic, the network performance of the WAN link decreases. Many WAN links have relatively low bandwidths and are costly, and so you might want to avoid saturating these links.

 Consider using smaller partitions on fewer servers to reduce network traffic across WAN links.

Assign Administrators of Partitions and Replicas

Partitioning changes cause network traffic, particularly several partition changes over a short time span. Before you can make partition changes, such as splitting or merging partitions, you need Supervisor object rights to the roots of the affected trees. You therefore must assign the administrators responsible for making these changes. If the changes will propagate to servers in different geographical locations, you must coordinate your efforts more closely.

Synchronizing Time in the NDS Tree

Replica synchronization needs an accurate time reference that should be consistent across the network. This ensures accurate time-stamping of the NDS operations, regardless of the location on the network at which the operations are performed. *Time-stamps* are a unique code that records when an event takes place and the replica that originates it.

Accurate time-stamps on NDS operations are essential for an updated and properly synchronized NDS database. A change to a replica of a partition propagates to all servers within the replica ring. The time-stamps serve to keep the directory events that occur in order.

The following are design issues you should consider when you assign time synchronization:

- Determine the time server types for the NDS tree.

- Coordinate time sources.

- Reduce WAN traffic for synchronizing time.

- Determine the effect on time synchronization in case of directory tree merges.

 Be familiar with the main points for time synchronization in an NDS tree as specified in the preceding list.

Determine the Time Server Types for the NDS Tree

You must decide which time server types best suit your network needs. For small networks and for workgroup applications, the default time server type setting is adequate. The first NetWare server installed in the NDS tree is set up as a Single Reference Time Server by default. Additional servers are set up as Secondary Time Servers.

The Single Reference Time Server represents a single point of failure, and on larger networks you should increase the fault tolerance of the time source by providing multiple time sources. For example, you might want to select a combination of Primary Time Servers and Reference Time Servers as time sources. In any case, you must have a proper plan to coordinate the deployment of different server types.

Coordinate Time Sources

A design for large networks should take time provider groups into account. The time provider groups should be designed to provide local access to time sources and increase fault tolerance of the time sources. You also should try to minimize time synchronization traffic's effect on the network.

If you use a distributed network management strategy, you must coordinate the addition or changes to the time provider groups with other container administrators.

Reduce WAN Traffic for Synchronizing Time

If your network design includes WAN topologies, you should do your best to prevent the emergence of situations that force secondary time servers to communicate with a time source across a WAN link. Secondary Time Servers should obtain network time from a local time source.

Effect on Time Synchronization of Directory Tree Merges

Each NDS tree has its own sets of time sources. If you have to merge NDS trees (using the DSMERGE NLM), you must plan for the resulting tree to have appropriate time sources. For example, if each NDS tree has their own Single Reference Time Server, you cannot have two Single Reference Time Servers in the resulting tree because an NDS tree can have only a Single Reference Time Server.

Designing the NDS Tree

This section presents several case studies that explain ways to design a proper NDS tree. Designing an NDS tree includes consideration of the relevant design issues discussed in the previous section.

NDS Design—Case Study 1

Sita Corporation's corporate headquarters are in New York. The New York headquarters also house the Finance, Marketing, and Administration departments for the entire organization. Each department in New York has its own NetWare 4 server, and the Administration department has an additional server, giving it two. All divisions of the organization use a common corporate server, also located in New York.

Sita Corp. has additional sales offices in London and Paris, each of which has its own server and at least one network printer.

Users in the various locations need to share information with the rest of the company, so network connections exist between each location.

Draw a directory tree for Sita Corp. and show the partition boundaries, replica assignments to servers, and time server types.

Solution: One requirement for the case study is that users in each location need to share information with the rest of the company. This need is best served by placing the network resources in a single NDS tree, because network connections exist between each location.

The different locations suggest using the geographical location model to assign workgroups. The workgroups can correspond to organizational units under the Organization object named SITA. You could name the workgroups in London and Paris after those locations. Because each of these locations houses only a Sales office, you do not need additional subcontainers at these offices. New York, on the other hand, has three departments: Finance, Marketing, and Administration. You could model each of these as an Organizational Unit object under the New York container. Figure 11.8 shows a possible NDS tree for this case study. The NDS tree shows the partial resources described in the case study. Because all the departments share the Corporate server, it goes directly under the O=SITA container.

The partition boundaries for this NDS tree are shown in figure 11.9. Each location has its own partition boundary that represents the subtree for that location. Because New York serves as home base for the corporate headquarters, the [Root] partition is kept there.

Figure 11.10 shows the replica assignments for the NDS tree. Notice that two Read/Write replicas of the OU=LONDON and OU=PARIS partitions are kept in New York and another location. Because the [Root] partition is the most critical, two replicas of it are kept in New York, and one Read/Write partition on the servers in London and Paris. Each location has a replica of the Master partitions in other locations. The Master replica for a partition is kept on a server at that location. If you want extra redundancy, you might keep an additional Read/Write replica of the OU=LONDON and OU=PARIS partitions on servers MKTG_FS and ADM_FS2, respectively.

Figure 11.8

NDS tree for case study 1.

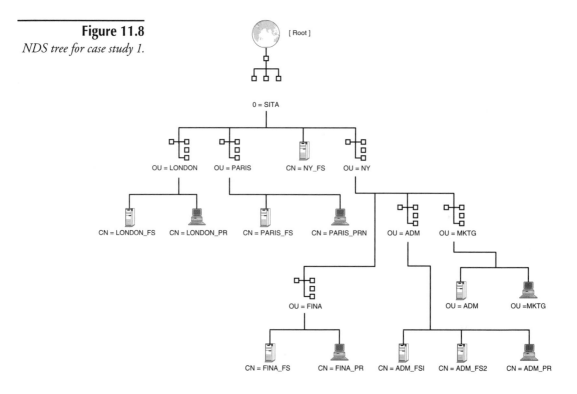

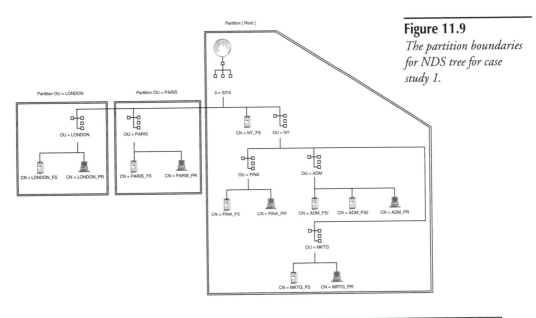

Figure 11.9

The partition boundaries for NDS tree for case study 1.

Servers	Partitions		
	[Root]	OU = LONDON	OU = PARIS
NY_FS	Master	Read/Write	Read/Write
FINA_FS	Read/Work		
MKTG_FS			
ADM_FS1	Read/Write		
ADM_FS2			
LONDON_FS	Read/Write	Master	Read/Write
PARIS_FS	Read/Write	Read/Write	Master

Figure 11.10

The replica assignments for NDS tree for case study 1.

Servers	Time Server Type
NY_FS	Reference Time Server
FINA_FS	Secondary Time Server
MKTG_FS	Secondary Time Server
ADM_FS1	Secondary Time Server
ADM_FS2	Secondary Time Server
LONDON_FS	Primary Time Server
PARIS_FS	Primary Time Server

Figure 11.11

The Time server types for NDS tree for case study 1.

Figure 11.11 shows each server's time server types. Each location has its own time source. New York has a Reference Time Server, and the other locations (Paris and London) have a Primary Time Server. All other servers are Secondary Time Servers.

NDS Design—Case Study 2

Rama Corporation's corporate headquarters are in Livingston, Montana, housed in a single building that includes the Finance, Marketing, Sales, and Production departments. Each department has its own NetWare 4 server and at least one printer.

Users in each location need to share information with the other departments and network connections exist between each department.

Draw a directory tree for Rama Corp. and show the partition boundaries, replica assignments to servers, and time server types.

Solution: One requirement for the case study is that users in each location need to share information with the rest of the company. You can accomplish this most efficiently by placing the network resources in a single NDS tree, which you can do because network connections exist between each location.

The different workgroups would suggest that you use the administrative division model to assign workgroups. The workgroups can correspond to

departments which are implemented as organizational units under the Organization object named RAMA. Figure 11.12 shows a possible NDS tree for this case study. The NDS tree shows the partial resources described in the case study.

The partition boundaries for this NDS tree are shown in figure 11.13. The simplest partition solution is shown that has only one partition: the [Root] partition.

Figure 11.14 shows the replica assignments for the NDS tree. Notice that there are two Read/Write replicas of the [Root] partition.

Figure 11.15 shows the time server types of each server. The server on which the Master replica of [Root] is kept acts as a Single Reference Time Server. All other servers are Secondary Time Servers.

Figure 11.12

NDS tree for case study 2.

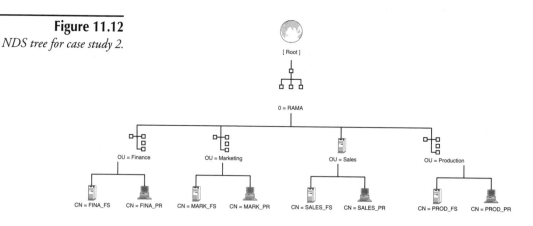

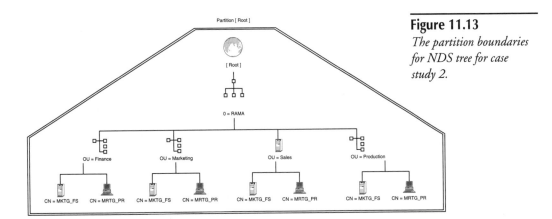

Figure 11.13

The partition boundaries for NDS tree for case study 2.

Servers	Partition
	[Root]
FINA_FS	Master
MARK_FS	Read/Write
SALES_FS	Read/Write
PROD_FS	Read/Write

Figure 11.14

The replica assignments for NDS tree for case study 2.

Servers	Time Server Type
FINA_FS	Single Reference Time Server
MARK_FS	Secondary Time Server
SALES_FS	Secondary Time Server
PROD_FS	Secondary Time Server

Figure 11.15

The time server types for NDS tree for case study 2.

Merging NDS Trees

Earlier in this chapter the departmental and divisional approaches of implementing the structural design were mentioned. Both of these approaches require that you use DSMERGE when you need to merge the trees. This section discusses using DSMERGE.

Ideally, when you design an NDS tree for an organization, you should agree on a top-level design of the NDS tree so that you can add departments within the organization as subcontainers of the tree. Therefore, the organization should have a high level of coordination and agreement between the departments on the top-level structure of the NDS tree. Few large organizations have this level of coherence and agreement on the top level NDS design. The main objectives can easily become submerged in political turf-war issues. Using DSMERGE enables you to design departmental networks independently, and later merge them into one NDS tree. You can have multiple NDS trees, but the only way to access resources in the separate NDS tree is to use separate logins to the NDS tree, or bindery emulation—a process that circumvents the many advantages of NDS.

If you start your NDS design implementation with a departmental approach, you can change to a divisional or organizational approach by using DSMERGE to merge the trees.

Understanding the DSMERGE Tool

You can use the DSMERGE NLM to merge the roots of two separate NDS trees. The [Root] objects of the separate NDS trees are merged. The container objects and their leaf objects can maintain separate identities within the newly merged root. When you merge NDS trees, you basically have two types of NDS trees: a *source NDS tree* and a *target NDS tree*. You merge the source NDS tree into the target NDS tree. The root of the target NDS tree becomes the new root of the *consolidated tree*. Objects in the source NDS tree move to the target NDS tree. In actual practice, this movement is accomplished by deleting the [Root] of the source NDS tree and making it a child partition to the [Root] of the target NDS tree. The source NDS tree becomes a branch of the target NDS tree, which means that the objects in the source NDS tree become part of the target NDS tree. The target [Root] object becomes the new root for objects from the source tree.

The DSMERGE tool does not change NDS names or the context of objects within the containers. Therefore, the complete names for objects in the consolidated tree are the same as the names before you merged the trees.

You must decide which NDS tree is the source tree and which NDS tree is the target tree. Because you merge the source NDS tree with the target NDS tree, the source NDS tree usually is smaller, although this need not be the case. Sometimes, political factors intervene and decide who merges with whom. Merging a smaller tree with a larger tree is faster than merging a larger tree with a smaller tree. After the merge, the target tree name is retained; the source target tree name is lost.

The objects that were subordinate to the local root object become subordinate to the target root object.

To merge the two NDS trees, you must have Supervisor object rights to the roots of both NDS trees. You are asked to supply NDS login names and passwords for both trees.

DSMERGE enables you to merge only the roots of two separate NDS trees. The top level organizations are immediately placed beneath the [Root]. Container objects and leaf objects maintain their identity under the newly merged root, which means complete names of objects in the source and target trees should not change in the merged tree. You must make sure that containers at the same level in the source and target trees have unique names. If you have two containers in the separate trees that have conflicting names (same names) for a level of the tree, you cannot merge the trees; DSMERGE asks you to change the name of the source Organization (O) object that conflicts with the target Organization (O) name. You can use NWADMIN or NETADMIN to rename the source Organization object.

Figure 11.16 shows examples of the source and target trees used in tree merging. The O=KINETICS tree branch merges with the target NDS tree. The consolidated NDS tree has the [Root] of the target tree with O=KINETICS added as a tree branch directly under [Root]. The Organization O=SCS in the source NDS tree has the same name as the Organization O=SCS in the target NDS tree.

During the merge, DSMERGE detects the duplicate name and asks you to rename the source Organization name O=SCS. In the example in figure 11.16, O=SCS is renamed to O=KSCS in the consolidated tree. If you do not want to change the name, your only choice is to move the duplicate name container O=SCS under another tree level. It is possible to have duplicate Organizational Unit (OU) objects as seen by the OU=CORP in figure 11.16 that exists in containers O=ESL and O=KINETICS. The problem with duplicate names exists for objects that are immediately below the [Root] objects. These objects are the Country (C) and Organization (O) container objects.

Preparing for DSMERGE

Before you can merge the NDS trees, you must prepare both source and target trees. Merging is a single transaction and according to Novell is not subject to catastrophic failure caused by power outages or hardware failure. You should, however, for your own assurance, back up the NDS database in both the source and target trees. You can use SBACKUP for this.

The following is a list of preparation tasks that you should perform before you merge two NDS trees:

■ Ensure that you have unique names for Organization and Country objects under [Root]. You can resolve duplicate names during the tree merge operation or by using NETADMIN or NWADMIN in a separate step.

■ Obtain login names and passwords for a user account in each tree that has Supervisor object rights to the [Root] of the NDS tree.

■ Back up each NDS tree. You can use SBACKUP or a third-party backup utility to do the backup.

■ Establish time synchronization in each NDS tree.

■ Change time synchronization at each server so that all servers in the source and target trees have one Single Reference or Reference Server for a time source.

■ If both NDS trees have the same name, rename one of them so that the NDS tree names are unique.

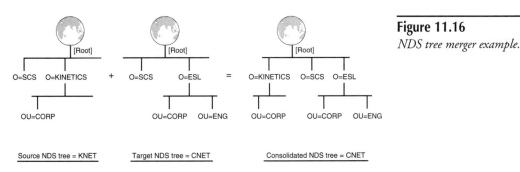

Figure 11.16

NDS tree merger example.

- Locate the servers on which DSMERGE should run. These are servers that have a Master replica of the [Root] partition for each NDS tree.

- Run DSREPAIR on source and target NDS trees to clean up any NDS database problems.

Some of the more important issues mentioned in the preceding list are discussed next.

Time Synchronization before the Merge

Before NDS can work correctly, each tree should contain only one Reference Time Server or one Single Reference Time Server in a tree. After the merge, the tree should contain only one Reference or one Single Reference Time Server. If the source and target trees each have a Single Reference Time Server or a Reference Time Server, then after the merge, the consolidated tree will have too many Single Reference or Reference Time Servers. To avoid this, you must change the Time Server types so that you have a maximum of one Single Reference Time Server and one Reference Time Server in both the trees to ensure that the consolidated tree contains only one Reference or one Single Reference Time Server.

You can use the SET TIME SERVER TYPE command to change the time server type, or SERVMAN.NLM to change this parameter. You also can edit the TIMESYNC.CFG file.

If you make time synchronization changes on a server, you should bring it down and restart it. You can use the following console command to force time synchronization:

```
SET TIMESYNC RESTART FLAG = ON
```

This flag activates the TIMESYNC.NLM, after which the flag value is set to OFF. After the time synchronization has been established, you see messages similar to the following:

```
NW4CS: SET TIMESYNC RESTART FLAG = ON
TIMESYNC Restart Flag action was SUCCESSFUL.
12-24-94: 5:12:33 pm: TIMESYNC-4.10-138
    Time Synchronization has been established.
NW4CS:
```

Wait until all the servers report that time synchronization has been established. On a large network, this can take as long as or longer than an hour.

Renaming an NDS tree

The source and target trees should have different tree names. The tree name of the target tree becomes the consolidated tree's name. If the source and target trees have the same name, you should change one of the tree names, preferably the tree name of the source tree, because it is the one that disappears after merging.

You use DSMERGE to change the name of a tree. To find out the NetWare server on which you must run DSMERGE, you use the Partition Manager to find the server that has a replica of the [Root] partition. The following is an outline of the procedure for changing the name of a tree.

1. Log in to the source NDS tree with Supervisor object rights to [Root].

2. You can use the Partition Manager from the NetWare Administrator or use the PARTMGR.EXE DOS-based tool.

   The steps that follow assume that you are using the Partition Manager.

3. Run NetWare Administrator and change the context to [Root]. If you do not change your context to [Root] at this point, you will have to

do so from within Partition Manager. Either method is fine.

To change context to [Root] from the NetWare Administrator:

■ Select the **V**iew menu.

■ Select Set C**o**ntext.

■ Enter the new context [Root].

4. Run Partition Manager from the NetWare Administrator:

■ Select the **T**ools menu.

■ Select **P**artition Manager.

If you change your context to [Root], you will examine the [Root] partition; otherwise, you need to change your context to [Root] from within Partition Manager. From the Partition Manager screen for the [Root] partition, select the Replicas button. You should see a screen similar to figure 11.17, showing the replicas of

the master partition and the server that contains the master partition. Note the name of this server. You must run DSMERGE on the server that has the Master replica of the root partition.

5. Exit Partition Manager.

6. Run the DSMERGE.NLM on the server that you noted in step 4.

   LOAD DSMERGE

7. You should see the DSMERGE Available Options screen (see fig. 11.18).

   Select the Rename this tree option.

8. The Rename Tree Information dialog box appears (see fig. 11.19). Enter the administrator name, the administrator password, and the new name of the tree. The administrator name and password is for the user that has Supervisor object rights to the [Root].

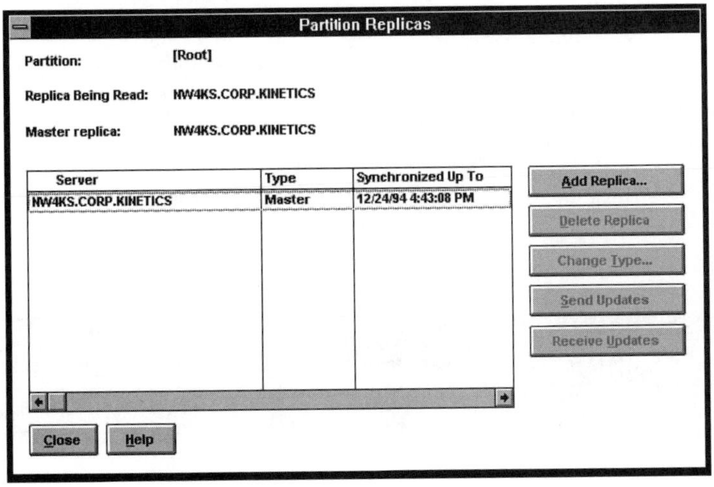

Figure 11.17
Replicas of [Root] partition.

Figure 11.18
The DSMERGE Available Options menu.

9. After you make your entries in the Rename Tree Information dialog box, press F10 for the changes to take effect.

   A warning message appears (see fig. 11.20), advising you of the serious consequences of changing a tree name and that you might have to change the PREFERRED TREE statement in the NET.CFG file of NetWare workstations. You do want to change the tree name, so press Enter to continue.

   You are prompted to confirm renaming the tree. Select Yes.

   You see status messages as DSMERGE collects information about servers in the tree and updates all servers in the tree. On a large network with slow WAN links, this can take quite a while. If the tree renaming is successful, you see a message informing you of the success of the operation. Press Enter.

You return to the Available Options of the DSMERGE screen. However, now you should see the changed tree name at the top of the screen.

Understanding DSMERGE Options

Figure 11.18 shows the DSMERGE options. You can use these options to perform a number of useful checks and operations.

The Check servers in this tree option enables you to verify that each server in the tree has the correct name. This option requires that the server on which you run DSMERGE has a replica of the Root partition; it need not be a Master replica. If you select this option, DSMERGE verifies the status of servers in the tree and reports a list of the servers and their status. Figure 11.21 shows a sample screen report for a tree that has only one server.

You use the Check time synchronization option to check each server in the tree for proper time synchronization. This option requires that the server on which you run DSMERGE have a replica of the Root partition; it need not be a Master replica. If you select this option, DSMERGE verifies the status of time synchronization and time sources on all servers in the tree. Figure 11.22 shows a sample screen report for a tree that has only one server.

Figure 11.19
The DSEMERGE Rename Tree Information dialog box.

```
┌─────────────────────────── Rename Tree Information ───────────────────────────┐
│ Local tree:          KNET                                                      │
│ Administrator name:  _____ │
│ Password:                                                                      │
│ New tree name:                                                                 │
└────────────────────────────────────────────────────────────────────────────────┘
```

```
  Renaming a Directory Services tree has significant repercussions.
  You should carefully plan and prepare before you rename a tree.

  After renaming a tree, you may need to change the "Preferred Tree"
     statement in each NET.CFG file on each client's workstation.

  The new tree name must be unique to avoid confusing the clients.

                    <Press ENTER to continue>
```

Figure 11.20
The DSMERGE warning message about the consequences of changing a tree name.

The Rename trees option was discussed in the previous section. The Merge two trees option is used for merging the NDS tree and is described in the next section.

Merging NDS Trees Using DSMERGE

You must load DSMERGE on a server that contains the Master replica. You can use Partition Manager to find the name of this server. If you do not know the server on which the Master replica is stored, you are prompted with the correct server name when you attempt an operation that requires the Master replica.

Merging many trees operates faster if you designate the source tree as the tree with fewer objects. Each tree you add to the target tree has its own NDS partition. You might want to use Partition Manager if you want to combine separate partitions into a single NDS partition.

After the merge, the source tree name no longer exists. You must, therefore, update the PRE-FERRED TREE statement in the NET.CFG file on NetWare workstations. If you want to minimize the number of NET.CFG files to update, designate the tree with the most clients as the target tree because the final tree retains the name of the target tree. You also can rename the tree after the merge operation so that the majority of the NetWare workstations NET.CFG file reference the consolidated tree's name.

To perform the NDS tree merge operations, you must have Supervisor object right to the [Root] of the source and target trees, and the servers in the tree should be synchronized to the same time source. The following is an outline of the tree merge operation.

1. Load DSMERGE on the server that contains the Master replica of the source tree.

   LOAD DSMERGE

2. Select the Merge two trees menu option from the Available Options menu.

3. The Merge Trees Information dialog box should appear (see fig. 11.23).

```
               Status Of Servers In The Tree
  Server Name            | Version       | Status
  NW4KS.CORP.KINETICS     | 4.1 (443)     | Up
```

Figure 11.21
The status of servers in the tree.

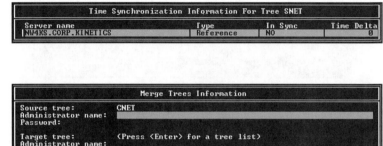

Enter the values for the fields in the dialog box, then press F10 to start the merge. The meanings of these fields are explained in the following list, in the order in which they appear in figure 11.23.

- **Source Tree.** This is the name of the tree on the source server.

- **Administrator Name.** This is the name of the user who has Supervisor object rights to the [Root] of the NDS *source* tree. You should enter the complete NDS name of the user (example: .CN=CORP.O=KINETICS or .CORP.KINETICS).

- **Password.** Enter the password of the user account for the source tree that was entered in the previous Administrator Name field.

- **Target Tree.** This is the name of the NDS tree into which the source NDS tree is to be merged. This name becomes the name of the consolidated tree.

- **Administrator Name.** This is the name of the user with Supervisor object rights to the [Root] of the NDS *target* tree. You should enter the complete

NDS name of the user (example: .CN=CORP.O=KINETICS or .CORP.KINETICS).

- **Password.** Enter the password of the user account for the target tree entered in the previous Administrator Name field.

4. After you enter the information in the Merge Trees Information box, press F10 to start the merge. A message screen informs you of the different phases of the merge process. DSMERGE has four merge phases. You can back out of the merge process any time during the first three phases (the check, preparation, and merge phases). After you reach the completion phase, however, the changes become permanent. The different DSMERGE phases are explained in the next list:

- **Check phase.** Checks the source and target NDS trees for problems that could prevent a successful merge.

- **Preparation phase.** Prepares the source NDS tree for merging; consists of creating a separate partition for each organization and country object and deleting all replicas of the [Root] partition except the Master replica.

- **Merge phase.** Modifies the source NDS tree so that the Master replica of the [Root] of the source tree changes to a Read/Write replica of the [Root].

- **Completion phase.** Completes merging. At this point the process is not reversible. DSMERGE waits for NDS synchronization to finish and for all servers to recognize the new replica of the [Root].

Press F10 to start the execution of the DSMERGE phases.

5. After you move beyond the check phase, a dialog box appears asking you to confirm that you want to merge the NDS trees.

Select Yes to continue.

If the time is not synchronized, or the NDS database needs repair, DSMERGE does not continue. You must synchronize the servers and repair any problems in the NDS database before you can complete the tree merging.

6. As the merge process continues, the server addresses are collected and processed. When the merge process completes, a a message appears, informing you accordingly.

Detecting NDS Problems

NDS is a global distributed database. If part of the database (replica) becomes corrupted, you should be able to detect and correct the problem. As any number of problems can arise with any distributed database, so can they in connection with NDS. This section discusses these problems and their solutions.

The following types of problems can arise with NDS:

- Inconsistencies in the NDS database

- Unsynchronized replicas

- Problems with synchronization when servers are down

Inconsistencies in the NDS Database

NDS is a distributed, global, replicated database that is "loosely consistent." The loose consistency property of the NDS database implies that replicas can be out of synchronization for short periods of time, because synchronization can take a few seconds. NDS operations can tolerate a few seconds of inconsistency during synchronization of the replicas. This inconsistency during the synchronization process does not imply a problem with the NDS database.

Understanding Time to Synchronize

Knowing the amount of time required for a change in a replica to be propagated to other servers in the replica ring is useful. Remember that the replica ring is the set of servers that have replicas of the partition. The synchronization time depends on the nature of the change, the partition size, and the number of servers in the replica ring.

The change to the NDS database can be simple or complex. *Simple changes* affect only a single NDS object, such as a change to the Fax number property of a user object. Simple changes are performed relatively quickly on the replica, and then the replica changes are synchronized to only those servers that contain the replicas of that partition (that is, the replica ring). Another example of a simple change is the creation of a partition, which takes very little time. The NDS adds partition attributes that describe the subtree, now a new partition.

Complex changes take more time, and require more careful planning. Merging and splitting partitions are examples of complex changes. If partitions are to be merged, NDS performs the following tasks:

1. Locates the servers that contain the replica of the partition.

2. Forces the servers that have a replica of the partitions to be joined to have a copy of the replica of both partitions that are to be merged.

3. Ensures that after the partition merger is completed, the servers have the combined information of both partitions.

NDS Fault Tolerance

If the NDS database has serious inconsistency problems, having replicas of the partitions can prove useful. For redundancy purposes, you might want to have two to three replicas of a partition. Novell documentation recommends three replicas per partition. However, as the number of replicas increases, so does the amount of synchronization time. As part of your NDS design, you should make sure that the replicas are both on-site (local to your network), and off-site (on a remote network), to ensure preservation of at least one replica in case of major catastrophes (floods, earthquakes, and so forth).

You should treat backing up of the NDS database the same way you do backing up other critical resources, such as files and directories. You should implement a schedule for backing up the NDS database on a daily, weekly, or monthly basis. You can restore the Directory from the backup, if other means of restoring the NDS database fail. For example, if a merge or split operation fails because of a power failure or other interruption, the Master replica can become corrupted and propagate errors to other replicas. Your first recovery option is to check for an unaffected Read/Write replica of the partition, and if so, to make it the Master partition. If such a replica does not exist, your second recovery option is to restore the Directory from the latest backup.

During partition operations, such as a merge, split or move, the affected partitions are locked to prevent simultaneous partitions on these operations from being performed. Novell recommends that you should perform partition operations from only one station at a time to enable you to help track the partition operations.

NDS Database and the SYS: Volume

The NDS database is stored on the SYS: volume, and to maintain the consistency of this database, NetWare uses the TTS (Transaction Tracking System) feature, which is automatically enabled for a volume when the volume is mounted. TTS is used in NetWare to ensure that critical system files are restored to a consistent state upon failure within the server. If the TTS is disabled or shutdown, interrupted changes to the NDS database can lead to a corrupted NDS database. The TTS is disabled if the volume becomes full, so you should monitor the storage space on the SYS: volume and prevent the volume from becoming full. The following are guidelines for preventing the volume from becoming full:

■ Set minimum space requirements so that you receive a warning if the SYS: volume is running out of space.

■ Store print queues on other volumes besides the SYS: volume.

■ Store applications and data likely to grow in size on other volumes besides the SYS: volume.

■ Do not add replicas to servers that are low on space in the SYS: volume.

■ Do not use extended schemas if the space on the SYS: volume is low. Extended schemas allow the creation of new types of NDS objects, and additional properties for existing objects.

■ Use the following statement in the STARTUP.NCF file to backout any incomplete transactions in the database:

```
SET AUTO TTS BACKOUT FLAG=ON
```

By default, this parameter value is ON.

If TTS is disabled on a server that contains active replicas, the replicas can become corrupted. TTS can become disabled if the SYS: volume becomes full.

Unsynchronized Replicas

Because the NDS database has loose consistency, the replicas might not be synchronized during synchronization, which is perfectly normal. However, persistent problems in NDS operations can indicate synchronization problems. The symptoms of nonsynchronization can appear at the client of the server.

Any of the following symptoms at the client can indicate replica synchronization problems:

■ NDS object modifications made to the Directory seem to disappear unexpectedly.

■ Changes made to NDS rights seem to disappear unexpectedly.

■ Errors at clients cannot be duplicated.

■ Client performance is inconsistent.

■ Clients prompt for passwords when none have been assigned.

You can detect synchronization occurrences at the server by turning the DS trace screen ON, using the following server console command:

```
SET DSTRACE = ON
```

The DS trace screen shows the replica synchronization operations (see fig. 11.24). The messages are of the following type:

```
SYNC: Start sync of partition name state: xx
➥type: yy

SYNC: End sync of partition name. All
➥processes = YesNo
```

In the previous message, *name* is the name of the partition, and *YesNo* can be YES or NO. If you see NO for longer than 20 minutes, you have a synchronization problem and should take corrective action.

If the NetWare 4 server DS trace screen shows the following message, you have a synchronization problem:

```
SYNC: End sync of partition name. All
➥processes = NO
```

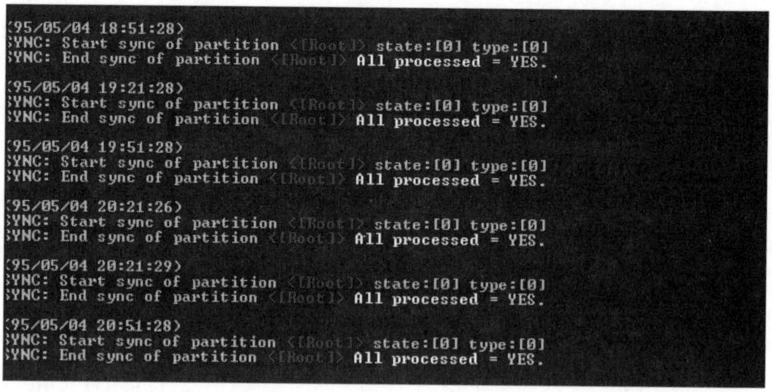

Figure 11.24

The DS trace screen.

Novell recommends the following actions if you detect server synchronization problems:

1. Let the systems run for a few hours. The replicas might synchronize and correct the problem. Bringing the servers down might prevent this self-correction.

2. Run DSREPAIR.

If you see several Unknown NDS objects in the NDS tree, it can indicate synchronization or other NDS problems. Unknown objects also can appear during partition operations (merge, split, create, move) when the system is in a state of flux.

Problems with Synchronization When Servers Are Down

If servers that belong to a replica ring are down, they do not receive replica synchronization information, and, therefore, will fall out of synchronization. Servers might be down because of planned maintenance or failure.

The NDS database was designed to take into account periods when the servers that hold replicas are not available. When the servers are brought online, the replicas on them automatically resynchronize and become available.

During the time a server is unavailable, the servers that send updates to the unavailable server use a back-off algorithm that tells them not to send changes to the unavailable server. The disconnected server periodically requests updates if it receives no changes over a period of time. The downed server uses the last time it received an update and other information to detect that it is out of synchronization when it comes back online, and requests an update.

Planned Shutdown of Server

If you plan to bring down a server that contains the only replica of a partition, you should move that partition to another server or create a replica of the partition.

Table 11.1 provides guidelines on how to manage planned shutdown of servers.

Table 11.1
Planned Server Shutdown

Server Shutdown Event	Planned Action
Make the server inaccessible permanently.	Back up NDS, and remove NDS from server.

Server Shutdown Event	Planned Action
Replacement of the hard disk that contains the SYS: partition.	Back up NDS, and remove NDS from server. Restore replicas on the server when server is online again.
Bring down a server temporarily for partition changes, relocation of server to another site, large number of changes/ additions/deletions of replicas.	Remove replicas from the server before bringing down the servers.

Unplanned Shutdown of Server— Server Failure

If a server that contains replicas fails unexpectedly, it could result in Directory loss, unless the replicas on the server exist on other servers that are still accessible.

If a server fails, you should use the Partition Manager tools to remove the server from the Directory tree. The explicit deletion of the server informs other servers in the replica ring that the failed server no longer belongs to the replica ring, and that they should not attempt to update the failed server's replicas. If a server fails, the back-off algorithm causes the server to send updates less frequently. However, the servers in the replica still continue to contact the failed server unless the server is deleted or comes back online. The failure to contact appears as server console messages of the type "Unable to contact server XXXXX."

Troubleshooting NDS Problems

This section discusses procedures for the following tasks:

- Determining synchronization status of a partition

- Restoring system software after NDS or SYS: volume failure

- Removing the NetWare server object from the NDS tree

- Updating corrupted replicas

Determining Synchronization Status of a Partition

Before you attempt any NDS operation, you should check the synchronization status of a partition to avoid potential problems and misunderstandings in your troubleshooting endeavors. You can use the DSREPAIR.NLM to determine the synchronization status of a partition. The following is an outline of the procedure:

1. Run the DSREPAIR NLM:

   LOAD DSREPAIR

2. Select Replica Synchronization.

3. Authenticate yourself by entering the complete name of the Admin user and the password.

4. Check the DSREPAIR log file for the status of the server (see fig. 11.25).

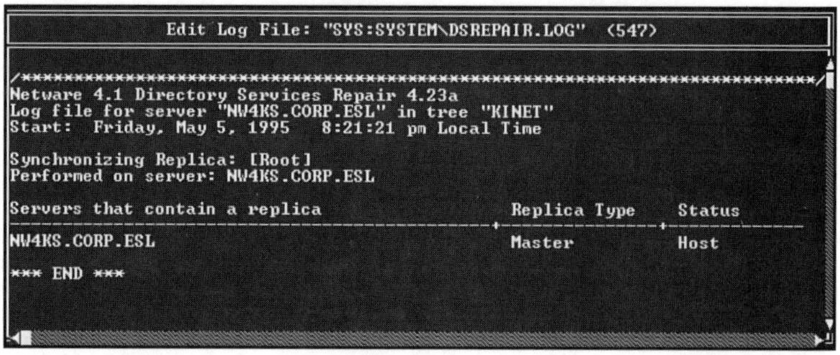

Figure 11.25
DSREPAIR log file.

```
┌─────────────────────────────────────────────────────────────────────────┐
│              Edit Log File: "SYS:SYSTEM\DSREPAIR.LOG"  (547)              │
├─────────────────────────────────────────────────────────────────────────┤
│/*****************************************************************************/│
│Netware 4.1 Directory Services Repair 4.23a                               │
│Log file for server "NW4KS.CORP.ESL" in tree "KINET"                      │
│Start:  Friday, May 5, 1995   8:21:21 pm Local Time                       │
│                                                                           │
│Synchronizing Replica: [Root]                                             │
│Performed on server: NW4KS.CORP.ESL                                       │
│                                                                           │
│Servers that contain a replica                  Replica Type    Status    │
│─────────────────────────────────────────────────────────────────────────│
│NW4KS.CORP.ESL                                   Master          Host      │
│*** END ***                                                                │
│                                                                           │
└─────────────────────────────────────────────────────────────────────────┘
```

Restoring System Software after NDS or SYS: Volume Failure

If the SYS: volume, which contains the hidden files that implement the NDS database, fails because of a disk crash or other problems, you must reinstall NDS. Because the disk file contains other system critical files, you might have to reinstall the server software.

If the SYS: volume also contains the Master replica of a partition, you have to take additional steps to recover the Master replica. You can use DSREPAIR or the Partition Manager, for example, to upgrade another replica of the partition to a Master replica. You need the Master replica to make partition changes. You still can use Read/Write replicas to do other administration functions.

Novell recommends the following general outline to restore replicas after you recover the SYS: volume.

1. Record the status of the replicas in each replica ring for a given partition. Note which server, if any, has the Master replica.

2. Delete the failed server and its associated volume objects.

3. Resolve NDS errors and remove replica pointers to nonexistent replicas.

4. Reinstall hard drive on server.

5. Place replicas back on server.

6. Restore the file system data from backup.

7. Set the correct bindery context.

Recording the Replica Status

You can use the following steps to record the status of replicas:

1. Use the Partition Manager and select server objects. Note the replicas on each server.

2. If a replica on the failed server shows a master status, you need to designate a new Master replica on an up-and-running server that has a properly synchronized Read/Write replica.

   You can use DSREPAIR for this task, as outlined next.

3. Run DSREPAIR.

   `LOAD DSREPAIR`

4. Select the Advanced options menu. You should see the screen shown in figure 11.26.

Figure 11.26
The DSREPAIR Advanced Options menu.

5. Select Replica and partition operations. You see a list of replicas.

6. Highlight a read/write partition and press Enter.

7. Select Designate this server as the new Master replica (see fig. 11.27).

8. Exit DSREPAIR.

Figure 11.27
The Replica Options menu.

Deleting the NetWare Server and Volume Objects

You need to use the Partition Manager to delete servers, because the servers contain replica and other partition information. Make partition changes

when you can reach all servers in the replica ring expected to be up.

You can use the following steps for deleting the NetWare server and volumes:

1. Run NetWare Administrator on a NetWare workstation.

2. From the Tools menu, select Partition Manager.

3. Navigate the Directory tree to find the server object you want to delete.

4. Select the server to be deleted, and select Delete Server. After you delete a server object, the change is synchronized to the other replicas.

5. Use NetWare Administrator or NETADMIN to delete the volume objects for the deleted server.

Resolving NDS Errors

Use the following as a guideline for resolving NDS errors and removing replica pointers.

1. Run DSREPAIR at the server console:

   ```
   LOAD DSREPAIR
   ```

2. Select Replica Synchronization to see all partitions that existed on the deleted server.

   You see the Collecting replica synchronization status screen (see fig. 11.28), and then the DSREPAIR log.

3. If you see error messages with code 625 (also called 625 errors), perform the following steps on all servers that contain the replica in question, until the errors disappear.

Figure 11.28

Collecting replica synchronization status screen.

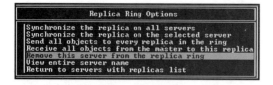

```
         Collecting replica synchronization status

 ┌──────────────────────────────────────────────────────────┐
 │                           100%                             │
 └──────────────────────────────────────────────────────────┘

 ┌──────────────────────────────────────────────────────────┐
 │->Start:  Friday, May 5, 1995   9:32:52 pm Local Time       │
 │->                                                          │
 │->Synchronizing Replica: [Root]                             │
 │->Performed on server: NW4KS.CORP.ESL                       │
 │->                                                          │
 │->Processing server: NW4KS.CORP.ESL                         │
 │                                                            │
 │                                                            │
 └──────────────────────────────────────────────────────────┘
```

a. From the DSREPAIR Available Options menu, select the Advanced Options menu (see fig. 11.26).

b. Select Replica and partition operations. A list of replicas appears.

c. Highlight the partition that has the errors and press Enter.

d. Select View replica ring. You see a list of servers that contain a replica of the partition.

e. From the list of servers in the replica ring, highlight the deleted server and press Enter. You see the Replica Ring Options menu (see fig. 11.29).

```
┌─────────────────────────────────────────────┐
│            Replica Ring Options               │
├─────────────────────────────────────────────┤
│Synchronize the replica on all servers    •   │
│Synchronize the replica on the selected server│
│Send all objects to every replica in the ring │
│Receive all objects from the master to this replica│
│Remove this server from the replica ring      │
│View entire server name                        │
│Return to servers with replicas list           │
└─────────────────────────────────────────────┘
```

Figure 11.29

The Replica Ring Options menu.

f. Select Remove this server from the replica ring and answer Yes to verify operation.

g. Exit DSREPAIR.

Reinstall Hard Drive on Server

To install the hard drive on the server, use the procedures recommended by the hardware vendor and that are appropriate for the hard disk. Now might be a good time to replace your hard drive with that higher capacity drive you have had your eye on for some time.

Use the INSTALL.NLM to reinstall the system software. Install the NetWare server object in the original context.

Place Replicas Back on Server

You can use the Partition Manager and the replicas you documented for the server to place the replicas back on the restored server.

The amount of time it takes to perform this operation depends on the size of the network and the speed of your LAN and WAN links.

Restore File System Data from Backup

If you had other applications on the SYS: volume, restore these application from backup media. This restore operation backs up data and ownership and trustee information for files and directories. Check for whether the ownership and trustee information restores properly. In a worst case scenario, you have to establish ownership and trustee information manually.

Set the Correct Bindery Context

The bindery context is important for bindery-based clients. The default value of the bindery context is the same as the server context. If the bindery-based clients require other containers for part of the bindery context, add these additional containers to the SET BINDERY CONTEXT command in the AUTOEXEC.NCF file.

Updating Corrupted Replicas

You can send updates from a Master replica to update other replicas. This procedure updates all other replicas, regardless of the accuracy of time stamps. You must, therefore, ensure that the Master replica has the correct time-stamps. Depending on the size of the replica and your network topology, this procedure can cause excessive network traffic.

You can use the following procedure with the Partition Manager to send updates:

1. Run Partition Manager from the Tools menu of NetWare Administrator.

2. Highlight the partition, and select the Replicas button (see fig. 11.30).

3. Select the Master replica (see fig. 11.31).

4. Select the Send Updates button and confirm the operation.

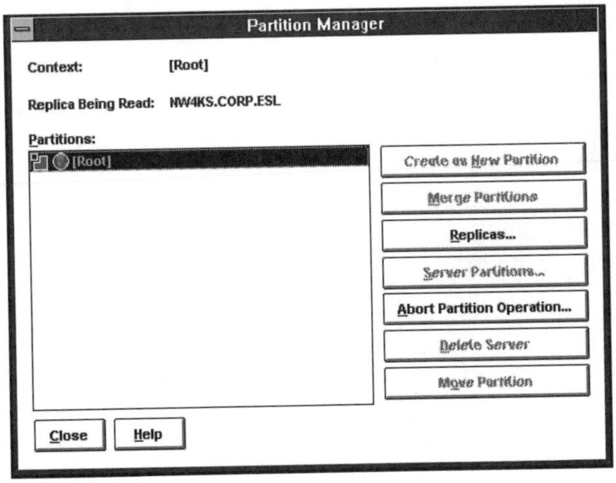

Figure 11.30

Viewing a specific partition using Partition manager.

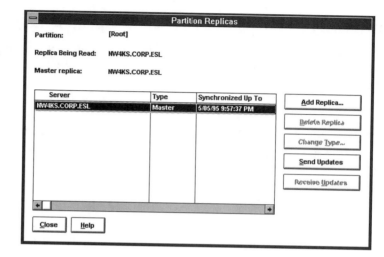

Figure 11.31

Using Master replica to send updates using Partition Manager.

Study Guide for the Chapter

If preparing for exams, review the chapter with the following goals:

- Understand the structural design of the NDS tree and the operations DSREPAIR performs.

- Pay particular attention to the tools used for NDS troubleshooting.

- After you study this chapter, attempt the sample test questions. If you miss the answer(s) to a question, review the appropriate topic until you understand the reason for the correct answer.

Chapter Summary

This chapter discusses the issues involved in designing an effective NDS tree. A proper design reduces the maintenance overhead of the NDS tree. You can then easily make incremental changes to the NDS tree, to adapt it to meet the changing needs of your organization.

This chapter also discusses the procedures and tools that you can use to troubleshoot NDS-related problems.

Chapter Test Questions

Most of the test questions are multiple choice. Where a single answer is desired, they are indicated by a ○ (circle) notation that precedes the possible answers. Some questions require you to select more than one answer; these are indicated by the □ (box) preceding each answer. Not all the questions are multiple choice. Occasionally, you might get a question that asks you to type in an answer. The answer in this case is usually a one word answer. The answer is not case-sensitive; you can type the answer in lower- or uppercase.

Certain questions will be repeated in different ways so that you can recognize them even when the wording is different. Taking practice quizzes will not only test your knowledge, but will give you confidence when you take your exam.

1. A properly designed NDS tree has the following benefits:

    □ A. Provides fault tolerance for the network

    □ B. Increases LAN speeds

    □ C. Decreases unnecessary traffic

    □ D. Simplifies network administration and maintenance

    □ E. Simplifies network administration and maintenance at the expense of increased network traffic

2. A properly designed NDS tree has the following benefits:

    □ A. Enables users to access needed resources easily

    □ B. Reduces network traffic but some objects are harder to access

    □ C. Minimizes the impact on users and reduces need for training

    □ D. Reduces cost of network administration but users need additional training

3. The elements of the structural design method are _____.

    □ A. determining the structural model

    □ B. determining the deterministic model

    □ C. establishing naming conventions

    □ D. planning the implementation method

    □ E. planning the detailed design phase

4. Determining the structural model consists of _____.

    □ A. identifying the workgroup needs

    □ B. identifying the LAN components

    □ C. determining the network topology

    □ D. assigning NDS rights

    □ E. organizing the NDS objects

5. You can base your workgroups using any of the following:

    □ A. Administrative division

    □ B. Network division

    □ C. Workgroups across divisions

    □ D. Geographical locations

    □ E. LATA divisions

6. The NDS naming document standard should take into account the following:

   ☐ A. Conventions used for naming containers

   ☐ B. Conventions used for naming the [Root] object

   ☐ C. Conventions used for naming leaf objects

   ☐ D. Property values that will be defined for NDS objects

   ☐ E. Conventions for naming LAN segments and assigning network numbers

7. Consistency in naming NDS objects has the following effects:

   ☐ A. Provides a guideline for network administrators when creating, modifying, renaming objects in the NDS tree

   ☐ B. Eliminates redundant planning for names when a new NDS tree or tree branch is to be designed

   ☐ C. Helps users and administrators quickly identify the network resources

   ☐ D. Can increase planning for names when a new NDS tree or tree branch is to be designed

   ☐ E. Users and administrators must be trained in the naming of objects, and this can add to the ability to quickly identify the network resources

8. The following are valid implementation methods for implementing the NDS tree:

   ☐ A. Departmental approach

   ☐ B. Container approach

   ☐ C. Divisional approach

   ☐ E. Organizational approach

   ☐ F. Country approach

   ☐ G. Hybrid approach

9. The following design criteria must be taken into account in NDS tree design:

   ☐ A. Security of the NDS tree

   ☐ B. Geographical location of the NDS tree

   ☐ C. Partitioning and replication of the NDS tree

   ☐ D. Synchronizing time in the NDS tree

   ☐ E. Synchronizing user access to the NDS tree

10. The departmental approach in implementing the NDS tree is useful when any of the following conditions are true:

   ☐ A. A single NDS tree is desired.

   ☐ B. All NetWare 4 servers are always connected to each other using LAN/WAN links.

   ☐ C. There is no direct network communication links between the departmental networks.

   ☐ D. Coordination of planners, implementers, and administrators is difficult and not practical at the moment.

11. The organizational approach in implementing the NDS tree is useful when any of the following conditions are true:

☐ A. A single NDS tree is desired.

☐ B. All NetWare 4 servers are connected to each other using LAN/WAN links.

☐ C. There is no direct network communication links between the departmental networks.

☐ D. Coordination of planners, implementers, and administrators is difficult and not practical at the moment.

☐ E. A central group of administrators such as the IS department can manage the upgrade and implementation of the NetWare 4 network.

☐ F. The network is small enough that you can perform a near simultaneous upgrade of the network without adversely affecting the organization's business.

12. Which of the following are design issues that relate to the security of the NDS tree?

☐ A. Deciding between a centralized versus distributed network administration approach

☐ B. Deciding between deterministic versus non-deterministic NDS updates

☐ C. Determining the proper placement of groups in the NDS tree

☐ D. Properly planning inheritance and security equivalencies

☐ E. Determining the placement of objects in the Country container

☐ F. Assigning appropriate rights to NetWare server objects

☐ G. Providing appropriate access for traveling users

13. Which of these are appropriate classifications for traveling users?

☐ A. Users who divide their work time between home and office

☐ B. Users who need access from a temporary location while they are working on special projects

☐ C. Users who need Admin privileges

☐ D. Users who spend a considerable amount of their work time traveling and need access to the network regularly from remote locations

☐ E. Users who spend most of their time at a fixed location

14. Which of these are design issues to consider for partitioning and replication?

☐ A. Planning partition boundaries

☐ B. Planning container boundaries

☐ C. Determining the appropriate replica assignments

☐ D. Determining replica assignments per user

☐ E. Determining accessibility and fault tolerance vs. network traffic and performance

☐ F. Determining country boundaries

☐ G. Determining the effect of WAN links

☐ H. Assigning administrators of partitions and replicas

15. Which of these are design issues to consider when assigning time synchronization?

   ☐ A. Determining the time server types for the NDS tree

   ☐ B. Determining CPU speed of servers

   ☐ C. Coordinating time sources

   ☐ D. Reducing WAN traffic for synchronizing time

   ☐ E. Determining number of users per container

   ☐ F. Determining the effect on time synchronization in case of directory tree merges

16. Which tool is used for merging NDS trees?

   ○ A. PARTMGR

   ○ B. DSREPAIR

   ○ C. DSMERGE

   ○ D. TREEMERG

   ○ E. TREEJOIN

17. You can rename a tree using _____.

   ○ A. PARTMGR

   ○ B. DSMERGE

   ○ C. DSREPAIR

   ○ D. TREENAME

   ○ E. NAMETREE

18. Which of these are problems that can arise with NDS?

   ☐ A. Inconsistencies in the NDS database

   ☐ B. Unsynchronized replicas

   ☐ C. Problems with internal network numbers

   ☐ D. Problems with synchronization when servers are down

   ☐ E. Unsynchronized users

19. Which of the following can lead to replicas becoming corrupted on a server?

   ☐ A. TTS is disabled on SYS: volume

   ☐ B. Non-SYS: volumes are full

   ☐ C. SYS: volume becomes full

   ☐ D. TTS is disabled on non-SYS: volumes

20. Which of the following symptoms at the client could indicate problems with replica synchronization?

   ☐ A. NDS object modifications made to the Directory seem to disappear unexpectedly.

   ☐ B. Changes made to NDS rights seem to disappear unexpectedly.

   ☐ C. Changes made to the NDS appear in all replicas.

   ☐ D. Errors at clients cannot be duplicated.

   ☐ E. Client performance is inconsistent.

   ☐ F. Client performance is improved.

   ☐ G. Clients prompt for passwords when none have been assigned.

21. At the server, you can detect synchronization problems by turning the DS trace screen ON using the server console command _____.

    ○ A. SET DSTRACE SCREEN = ON

    ○ B. SET DSTRACE = ON

    ○ C. SET DIRECTORY TRACE = ON

    ○ D. SET ENABLE DS TRACE = ON

    ○ E. SET ENABLE DSTRACE = ON

    ○ F. SET ENABLE DS TRACE = Yes

    ○ G. SET ENABLE DSTRACE = Yes

22. Which of these are tasks associated with NDS troubleshooting?

    ☐ A. Determining synchronization status of a partition

    ☐ B. Determining status of user objects

    ☐ C. Restoring system software after NDS or SYS: volume failure

    ☐ D. Removing the NetWare server object from the NDS tree

    ☐ E. Updating corrupted replicas

    ☐ F. Running PCONSOLE

Managing Supplementary Network Services

his chapter focuses on how you can use NetWare 4.x networks to provide messaging services, and how you can use the NetWare Multi-Protocol router with a NetWare server. In addition, you learn about the NetWare MHS mail services bundled with NetWare 4.x.

Applications such as e-mail use messaging services to provide message-based communications between applications that run on different nodes on a network. Message-based applications have become an important method for providing communications in an organization.

Components of Messaging Services

Messaging services transport data, called *messages*, between nodes on the network, using the network's underlying communications protocol. The method of transmitting messages is called *store-and-forward*, in which the message can be temporarily held at an intervening node on the network before eventually being delivered. The message is delivered and stored at the final destination node until the recipient is ready to read it and decide on its status (forward it, delete it, or store it). The types of messages include text, binary, graphic, audio, and video information.

For a simple LAN-based messaging application (see fig. 12.1), messaging services consist of the following components:

- Messaging Server (also called Messaging engine)
- User mailboxes
- Messaging applications

The messaging server accepts messages from an application, typically a user's e-mail client software, and delivers the message to the destination user's mailbox. In a larger network consisting of an interconnection of many different types of networks, the message might need to be routed to other messaging servers before eventual delivery.

 In a simple local message delivery you can expect the following messaging components:

- Messaging engine
- User mailboxes
- Messaging applications

User mailboxes are held on a machine local to the user, typically the server onto which the user is most frequently logged. A common method of implementing user mailboxes is to use a file system directory on the local server. Other methods, which treat the user mailboxes as abstract mail objects, also are available.

Figure 12.1
Simple LAN-based messaging services.

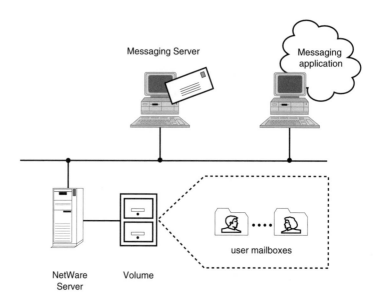

Messaging applications are e-mail client software and groupware software, such as Novell's GroupWise, calendaring software, scheduling programs, and so on.

Larger networks require other messaging service components, such as mail gateways and mail routers. Mail gateways allow the delivery of messages to a foreign e-mail system. Mail routers are store-and-forward computers that can temporarily store the message and then forward it to the final destination or an intervening destination. Some systems might implement the mail router as part of the messaging server.

NetWare 4 MHS Services

NetWare 4 server software comes bundled with a store-and-forward messaging engine for NetWare 4-based networks, implemented by the MHS.NLM installed on the server during the NetWare 4 MHS services installation.

NetWare 4 MHS services also include DOS and MS Windows versions of an e-mail client software, called FirstMail. FirstMail is an NDS-aware e-mail client from Novell.

 MHS.NLM, which runs on the NetWare 4 server, implements NetWare 4 Message Handling services.

NetWare 4 MHS services include the FirstMail e-mail client software for DOS and MS Windows.

NetWare 4 MHS Installation Requirements

The NetWare 4 MHS software is provided in the NetWare 4 CD-ROM. You can create an unlimited number of mailboxes per NetWare server. You are, however, limited by the NetWare server license, which limits the number of concurrent user sessions on the network.

The minimum hardware requirements of the NetWare server on which you install MHS are as follows:

- Intel 80386 processor or better

- 12 MB of RAM for server

- 65 MB of server hard disk

- CD-ROM drive required for installation

The NetWare MHS services take up the following server resources:

- 500 KB of RAM

- 2.5 MB disk space for program storage, plus additional disk space for user mailboxes (the amount of disk space for user mailboxes depends on the size and number of messages stored in the user's mailboxes)

Novell claims that the preceding minimum requirements are not sufficient to handle more than 10 users or more than 100 messages per day. For networks that need to process more than 100 messages per day, the following configuration is recommended:

- Intel 80386 processor or better

■ 16 MB of RAM for server, plus additional RAM to maintain more than 30% free cache buffers

■ 65 MB of server hard disk, plus an additional 5 MB per user mailbox

Installing NetWare 4 MHS Services

The following is a guided tour of installing NetWare 4 MHS services:

1. Mount the NetWare 4 Operating System CDROM:

   LOAD ASPICD (for ASPI for SCSI CDROM)

   LOAD CDROM

   CD MOUNT N

   You can obtain the value you need for *N* by typing the following command:

   CD VOLUME LIST

2. Load the INSTALL NLM at the NetWare server:

   LOAD INSTALL

   You should see a screen similar to fig. 12.2.

3. Select Product Options.

   You should see a screen similar to fig. 12.3.

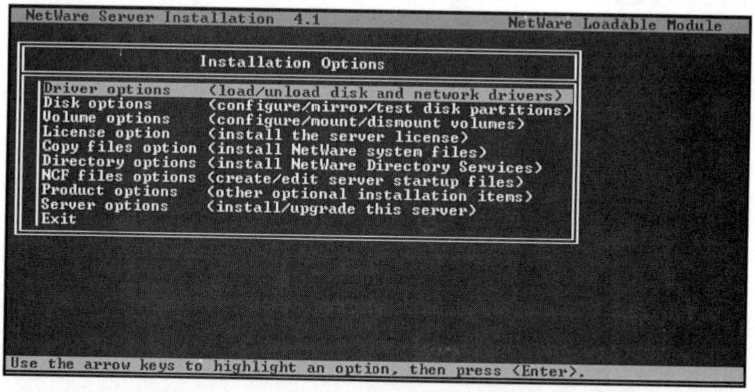

Figure 12.2
The Install NLM screen.

Figure 12.3
Other installation options.

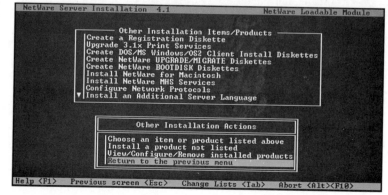

4. Select Choose an item or product listed above and highlight Install NetWare MHS (see fig. 12.4).

   Press Enter.

5. You should see the path name from which MHS Services will be installed (see fig. 12.5).

   Press Enter.

6. You see a status of messages reporting the files that are copied (see fig. 12.6).

7. You see a Postmaster General Authentication screen. Supply the Admin user name and password, then press Enter.

8. If the NetWare server on which MHS is being installed has multiple volumes, select the volume on which MHS services will be installed.

9. If this is the first install to the MHS tree, you are asked to verify your choice. Answer Yes.

10. You see a message that announces the completion of the MHS installation.

    Exit the INSTALL NLM.

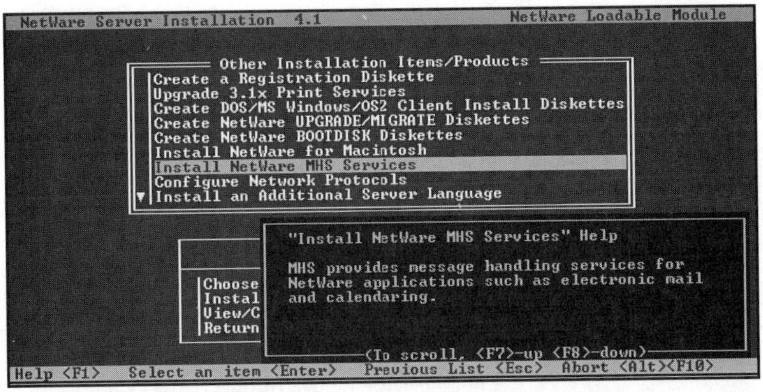

Figure 12.4

The Install NetWare MHS Service option.

Figure 12.5

Default source path name for NetWare MHS Services.

Figure 12.6

File Copy Status.

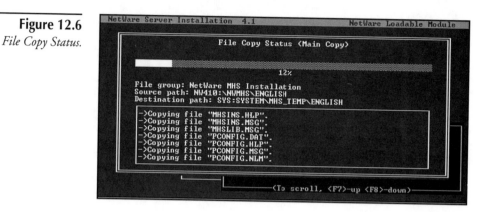

11. Load the MHS NLM:

    LOAD MHS

    Also, place this statement in the AUTO-EXEC.NCF file.

You also can install NetWare MHS services during the initial NetWare 4.*x* installation by completing the previously outlined steps after the initial NetWare 4.*x* server installation.

Post NetWare 4 MHS Installation Check

The Messaging Server and the Message Routing Group objects are created during the NetWare 4 MHS installation. This section describes these objects, their properties, and the changes they make to the NDS tree.

The Messaging Server enables the messaging services. This object defines the location of the message directory structure: the \MHS directory on the volume object in which MHS services was installed. The Messaging Server also identifies (through its NetWare Server property) the NetWare server on which the MHS services (MHS.NLM) runs.

The Message Routing Group serves to identify a cluster of Messaging Servers that communicate with each other for transferring messages. A default message routing group, called MHS_ROUTING-_GROUP, is created during the NetWare MHS services installation.

 The Messaging Server and Message Routing Group objects are created by default during the NetWare 4 MHS services installation.

The following is a list of the changes that occur to the NDS tree:

■ The default Messaging Server and Message Routing Group are created in the context in which the NetWare 4 server is installed. Figure 12.7 shows the Messaging Server (NW4CS_MSG) and the Message Routing Group (MHS_ROUTING_GROUP) objects created in the server context OU=CORP-.O=ESL.

■ A Postmaster General (default owner) user of the Message Routing Group is assigned. This user is the Admin user specified during the MHS installation. Figure 12.8 shows a Postmaster General of Admin.ESL.

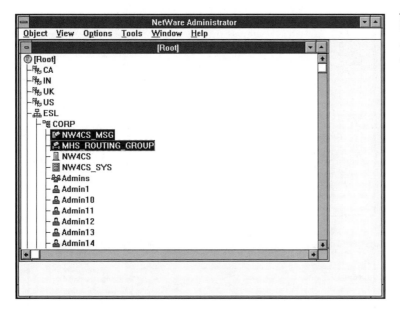

Figure 12.7
Newly created message objects in server context.

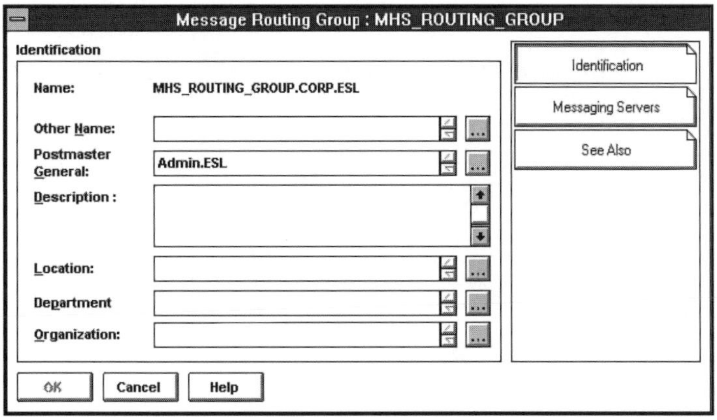

Figure 12.8
The Postmaster General owner of Message Routing Group.

■ The default Messaging Server object is added to the Messaging Servers property of the Message Routing Group (see fig. 12.9).

■ A Postmaster for the Messaging Server is assigned (see fig. 12.10). This is the Admin user specified during the MHS installation.

■ The Message Routing Groups property of the Messaging Server is set to the default Message Routing Group object (see fig. 12.11).

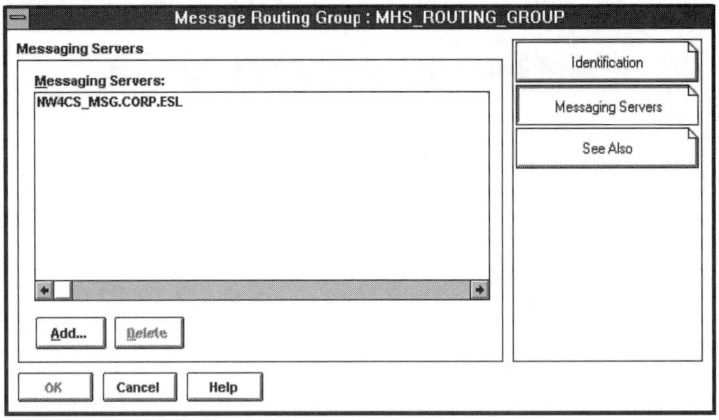

Figure 12.9

The Messaging Servers property of the Message Routing Group.

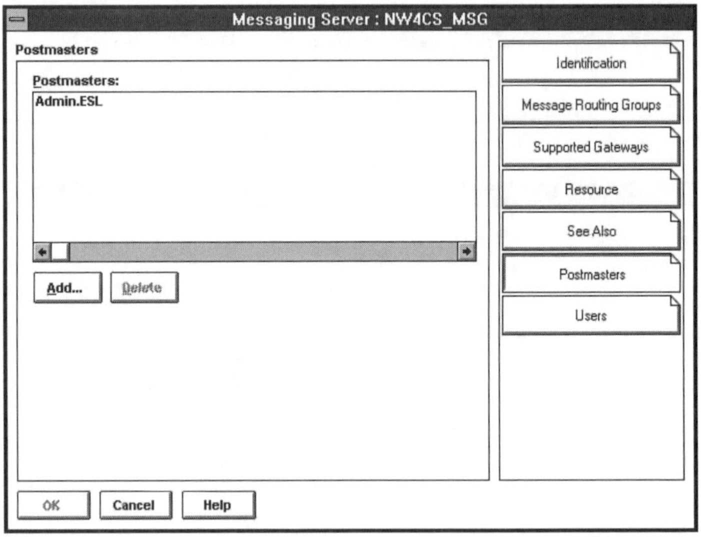

Figure 12.10

The Postmasters property of the Messaging Server.

■ The NetWare Server property of the Messaging Server is set to the NetWare server on which the MHS installation was done. Additionally, the MHS Database Location property of the Messaging Server is set to the volume on which MHS services was installed. Figure 12.12 shows examples of these property settings.

■ The Postmaster General (Admin) user's Mailbox Location and Mailbox ID properties are set. The Mailbox Location is set to the Messaging Server, and the Mailbox ID is set to Admin (see fig. 12.13).

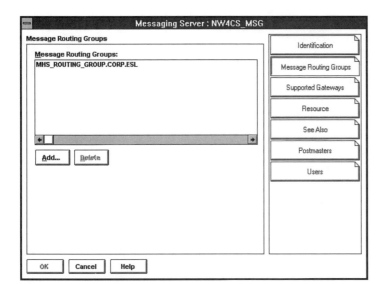

Figure 12.11
The Message Routing Groups property of the Messaging Server.

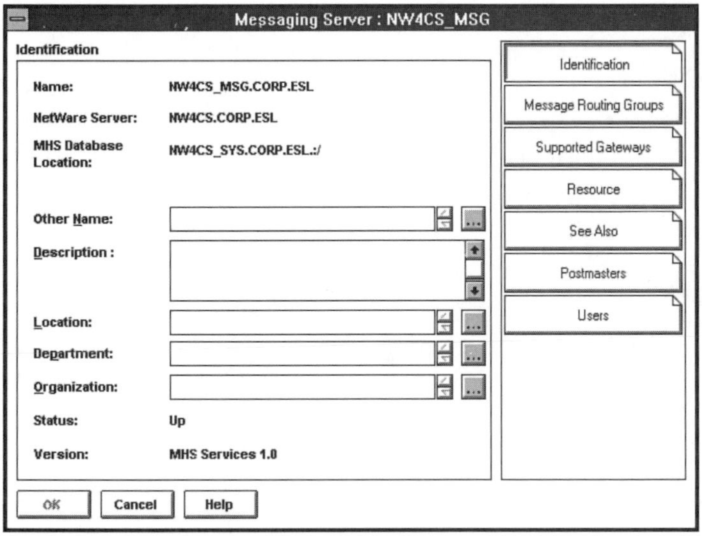

Figure 12.12
The NetWare Server and the MHS Database Location properties for a Messaging Server object.

■ First Mail program for DOS (MAIL.EXE) and MS Windows (WMAIL.EXE) are installed automatically in the SYS:PUBLIC directory of the NetWare server on which the installation was done.

If you delete or rename the Postmaster General user (Admin user), you must make changes to the Postmaster General properties of the Messaging Server and the Message Routing Groups. If you neglect to do this, the messaging services malfunction.

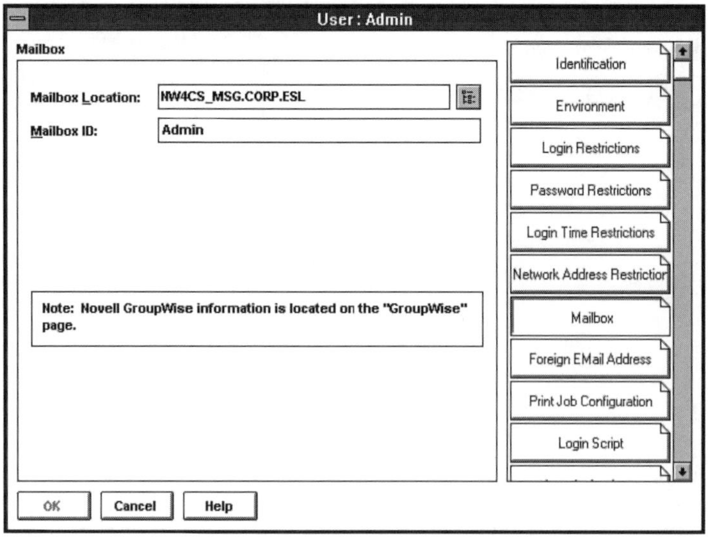

Figure 12.13
*The Mailbox Location
and Mailbox ID of
Postmaster General user.*

Assigning MHS-Related Properties to NDS Objects

The User, Group, Organizational Role, Organization, and Organizational Unit NDS objects all have MHS-related properties. You can use NWADMIN to assign these properties. You can use the Users page button of the Messaging Server object, or select the Mailbox page button of the object whose property you need to set.

The following list outlines how you can set these properties from the Messaging Server.

1. Double-click on the Messaging Server icon from within NWADMIN.

2. Select the Users property page button (see fig. 12.14).

3. Click on the Add button, and then use the ensuing Select Object dialog box (see fig. 12.15) to select the objects you need to assign to the Messaging Server. Any object you select has its Mailbox Location property set to the Messaging Server and the Mailbox ID set to the object's relative distinguished name (RDN).

The following steps outline how you can set these properties from the User, Group, Organizational Role, Organization, or Organizational Unit object. The example given here involves setting the mailbox properties for the organization O=SCS.

1. Right-click on the selected object from NWADMIN and select the Details option.

2. Click on the Mailbox page button (see fig. 12.16).

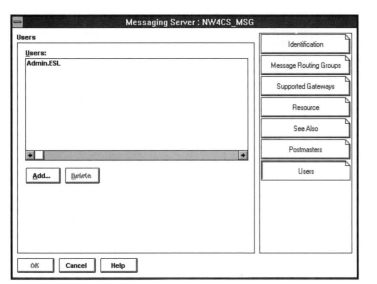

Figure 12.14
The Users property of Messaging Server.

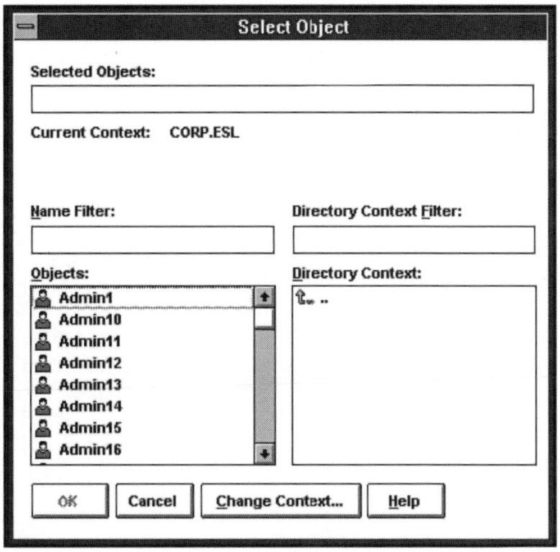

Figure 12.15
The Select Dialog box for assigning users to Messaging Server.

3. Select the Browse icon to the right of the Mailbox Location (see fig. 12.17).

4. Use the Select Object dialog box to navigate the NDS tree and find the messaging server you want to assign to the Mailbox Location property (see fig. 12.18), and click on OK.

You see the Mailbox properties set for the object (see fig. 12.19).

5. Select OK.

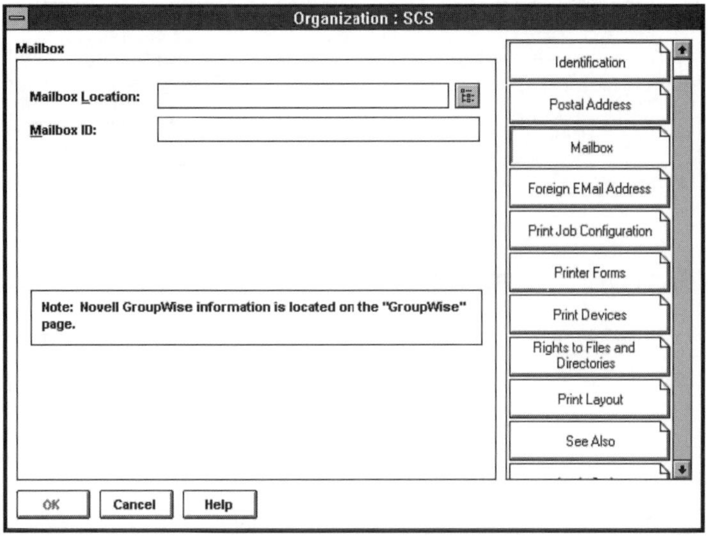

Figure 12.16
The Mailbox properties of Organization O=SCS.

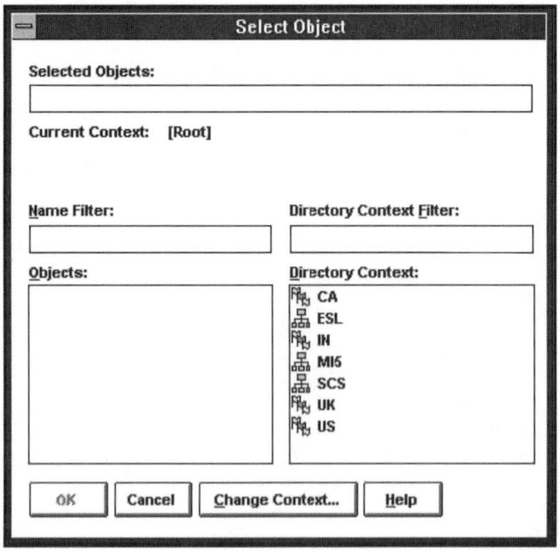

Figure 12.17
The Select Object dialog box for selecting the Messaging Server.

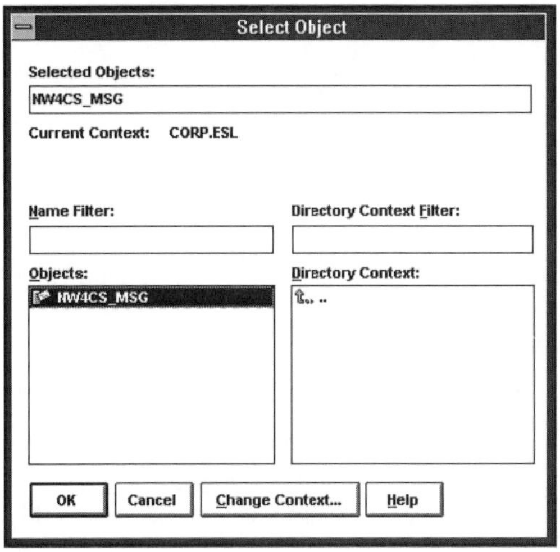

Figure 12.18
The Messaging Server object found using the Select Object dialog box.

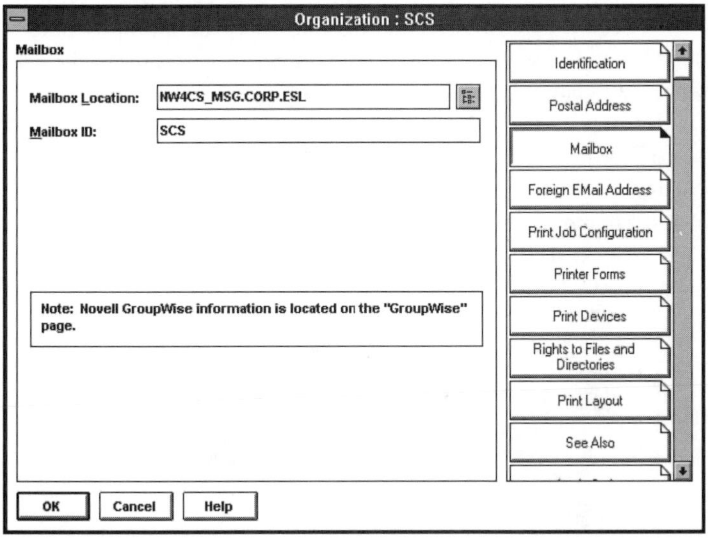

Figure 12.19
Mailbox properties set for O=SCS.

Other MHS-Related NDS Objects

Besides the Messaging Server and the Message Routing Group objects created during the installation of NetWare 4 MHS services, two other objects deal with messaging services: the External Entity object and the Distribution List object.

The External Entity Object

You use the External Entity object to refer to non-native NDS objects, such as e-mail addresses of foreign e-mail systems. The objects are created and configured during installation of the gateway software; they are not used for basic MHS services.

You can use the External Entity object as a placeholder that allows you to send messages to users not normally listed in the NDS tree because they are not part of the NDS-based network.

The Distribution List Object

You use the Distribution List to group multiple mailbox addresses. If the mailboxes are on the same servers, using Distribution List objects to send the same message to multiple recipients can reduce network traffic. You can deliver just one message to the Distribution List mailbox, for example, and then replicate the message for every mailbox on the Distribution List.

You also can use NDS group objects to distribute mail to the members of the group. Whereas a group's membership property cannot contain other groups, the Distribution List object can contain other Distribution Lists. In other words, you can *nest* Distribution Lists. Members of a Distribution List do not share login scripts or trustee assignments. The membership only serves for the convenience of sending messages to multiple recipients.

The following list outlines how you can create a Distribution List:

1. Right-click on the container object in which you want to create the Distribution List.

2. Select Create, and select the Distribution List from the list of objects. The dialog box for creating a distribution list appears (see fig. 12.20).

3. Enter the name of the Distribution List.

4. Click on the Browse button to the right of the Mailbox Location field to set its value. You should then see the Select Object dialog box (see fig. 12.21).

5. Use the Select Object dialog box to browse the NDS tree and select the appropriate messaging server on which you want to define the Distribution List.

6. Check the Define Additional Properties box and select Create. You should see the properties of the Distribution List object (see fig. 12.22).

Figure 12.20

The Create Distribution List dialog box.

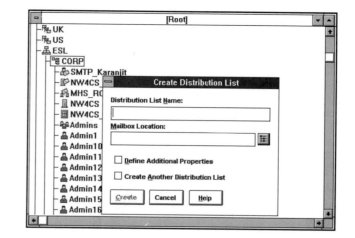

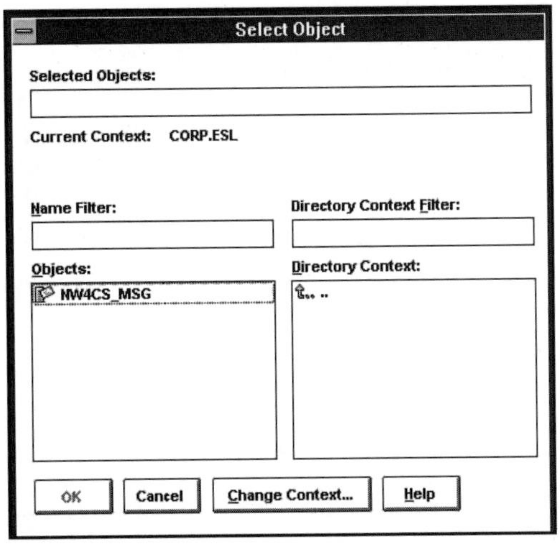

Figure 12.21

The Select Object dialog box for setting the Mailbox Location.

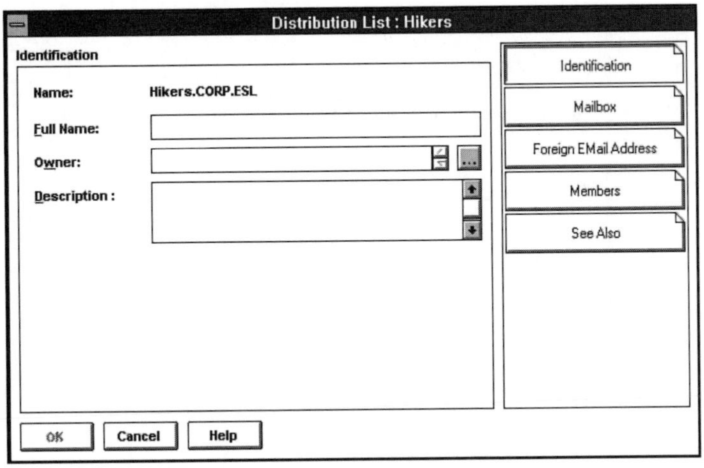

Figure 12.22

Distribution List properties.

7. Select the Members page button (see fig. 12.23).

8. Select Add, and then use the Select Object dialog box to assign members to the distribution list (see fig. 12.24).

9. Click on OK to save changes.

Figure 12.23
Members property of Distribution List object.

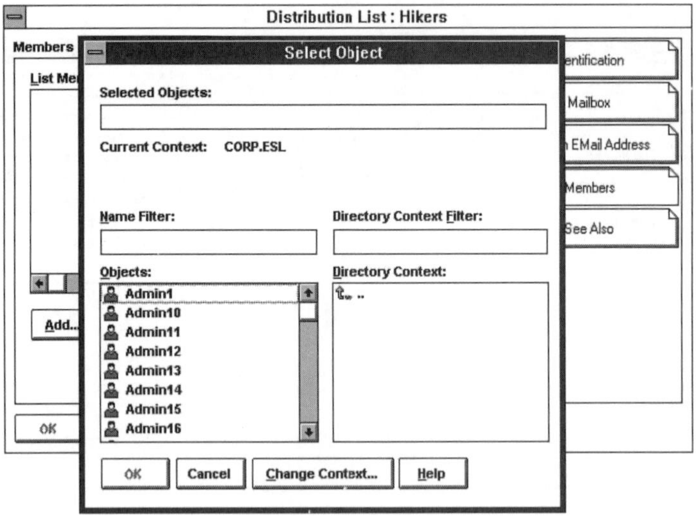

Figure 12.24
Adding members to the Distribution List.

Using FirstMail

FirstMail is available in MS Windows and DOS versions. The following guided tour outlines setting up and using FirstMail for MS Windows.

First, you must set up a program item to use FirstMail. Use the following as an outline for performing this for MS Windows:

1. Select **F**ile from Program Manager.

2. Select **N**ew.

3. Select Program **I**tem and choose OK.

4. In the Program Item Properties, enter the following:

   ```
   Description: FirstMail
   ```

   ```
   Command Line: Z:\PUBLIC\WMAIL.EXE
   ```

5. Save changes.

The following is a guided tour for using FirstMail to create, send, and receive e-mail messages:

1. Double-click on the FirstMail icon. You should see the FirstMail screen (see fig. 12.25).

2. Select New Message from the File menu, or click on the first icon (pen and paper). You should see the screen for creating messages (see fig. 12.26).

3. Enter the following information:

   ■ **To:** *Name of another MHS user*

   ■ **Subj:** *Enter name of subject*

   ■ **Cc:** *Optionally enter another MHS user*

   Click on the message area, then type a message.

4. Optionally, enable any of the following message options:

   ■ Confirm reading

   ■ Confirm delivery

   ■ Copy self

   ■ Urgent

   ■ No signature

5. Click on the Send button.

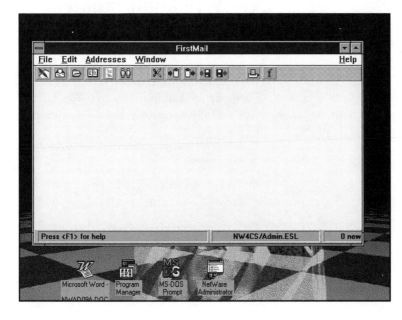

Figure 12.25
The FirstMail screen.

Figure 12.26

The Create message screen.

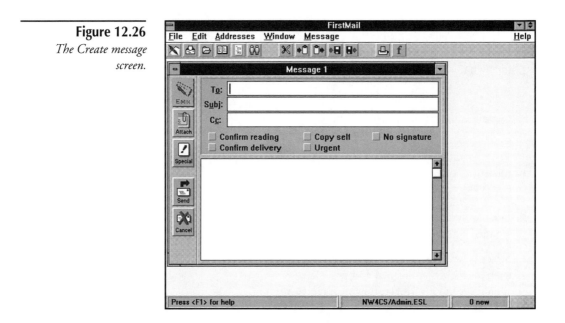

The recipient of the message should do the following tasks to read the message:

6. Log in to the network.

7. Start FirstMail.

8. Select Read New Mail from File menu or click on the second icon (envelope) on the toolbar.

9. Double-click on the message.

10. To save the message, highlight it.

    Click on the Move button in the New mail folder toolbar.

    Select the mail folder in which to save the message.

NetWare Multi-Protocol Router

You can use NetWare 4 with the NetWare Multi-Protocol Router (MPR) to enable the server to act as a router for multiple protocols. You can use NetWare MPR to perform the following services:

■ Off-load routing processing functions from busy servers

■ Provide security by isolating network segments

■ Connect dissimilar media, data-link layer functions (frame types), and transports at all levels in the ODI layers

You use a NetWare utility called the INETCFG-.NLM to configure the transport protocols. The following section outlines how to use INETCFG.NLM to manage the NetWare MPR.

 You use INETCFG.NLM to configure NetWare MPR.

NetWare MPR benefits include the following:

- Off-load routing processing functions from busy servers

- Provides security by isolating network segments

- Can be used to connect dissimilar media

The INETCFG.NLM Utility

You can run the INETCFG.NLM simply by typing the following command:

`LOAD INETCFG`

Another way to run INETCFG.NLM is to access the Configure Communication Protocols option from the INSTALL.NLM, using the procedure outlined here:

1. Type **LOAD INSTALL**

2. Select Product Options.

3. Select Choose an item or product listed above.

4. Select Configure NetWare Protocols.

The INETCFG.NLM program enables you to extract the LOAD and BIND statements for network board drivers to a separate file, called SYS:ETC\NETINFO.CFG. The extracted statements are removed (actually, commented out)

from the AUTOEXEC.NCF file and placed in the SYS:ETC\NETINFO.CFG file in a stylized format that the INETCFG.NLM understands. Any future modifications to the network communication settings are made to the NETINFO.CFG file. The INETCFG.NLM provides a friendly, menu-driven utility that you can use to configure the communication settings in the NETINFO.CFG file. Using the INETCFG.NLM helps avoid common syntax errors when you edit a text file, such as the AUTOEXEC.NCF file.

 The INETCFG.NLM can simplify configuring network boards, loading protocols, and binding protocols to specific network boards, as well as avoiding syntax errors when you edit the AUTOEXEC.NCF file.

When you load the INETCFG.NLM for the first time, you can extract the existing LOAD and BIND statements from the AUTOEXEC.NCF file to the INETCFG menu system (see fig. 12.27). After you press Enter, you are asked if you want to proceed with importing of LOAD and BIND statements from the AUTOEXEC.NCF file. If you select Yes, you are shown a status message that informs you about the actions that have been performed. You then are given a choice to modify AUTOEXEC.NCF to reflect the import process. If you do not select the option to modify AUTOEXEC.NCF, you must manually comment out the LOAD and BIND statements in the AUTOEXEC.NCF file. A specific LOAD or BIND statement can exist either in AUTOEXEC.NCF or in NETINFO.CFG file, but not in both.

Select the option to modify AUTOEXEC.NCF creates board and protocol entries in the NETINFO.CFG file corresponding to the

Figure 12.27

The First time option when INETCFG is run.

```
LAN driver, protocol or remote access commands in AUTOEXEC.NCF should be
transferred to the configuration files maintained by INETCFG.NLM. After
transfer, they may be configured by using the INETCFG.NLM menu system.
```

AUTOEXEC.NCF statements. If you do not extract these statements, you must select the individual options within INETCFG to make the conversion and comment out the extracted statements in the AUTOEXEC.NCF file. After you extract a LOAD or BIND statement to the NETINFO.CFG file, it cannot appear in the AUTOEXEC.NCF file.

 The INETCFG.NLM extracts LOAD and BIND statements for communication protocols out of the AUTOEXEC.NCF file and places them in the SYS:ETC\NETINFO.CFG file. A specific LOAD or BIND statement can be in either the AUTOEXEC.NCF or NETINFO.CFG file, but not in both.

The contents of the SYS:ETC\INITSYS.NCF file are shown next for your reference:

```
#! --- WARNING -- WARNING -- WARNING --
#! This file was created by the
➥Internetworking Configuration Console.
#! It is intended to be modified ONLY by the
➥configurator (INETCFG.NLM).
#! Tampering with this file may cause severe
➥malfunctioning of the system.
#! The configurator will check for tampering
➥and abort if it is detected.
#! ---------------------------------------
----------------------------
load snmp config=Sys:Etc
initialize system
```

The statement to load SNMP has not been extracted—it is placed in the SYS:ETC\INITSYS.NCF file, but the statements for loading the

board, the communications protocols, and binding of communication protocols to the boards are commented out. The new statements are LOAD CONLOG and INITIALIZE SYSTEM. LOAD CONLOG activates the CONLOG.NLM that captures system and error messages during initialization to the SYS:ETC\CONSOLE.LOG file. You can examine the CONSOLE.LOG file later for system messages. If you don't log console messages to a file, you might not notice the status and error messages because they scroll off the screen too quickly. Because CONSOLE.LOG captures important system and error messages, you can use it to troubleshoot system configuration problems.

 The CONLOG.NLM activates the capturing of system and error console messages to the SYS:ETC\ CONSOLE. LOG file.

The INITIALIZE SYSTEM command activates the processing of the configuration information in the NETINFO.CFG file. At the end, UNLOAD CONLOG unloads CONLOG.NLM, because the important status and error messages are captured to the CONSOLE.LOG file and the CONLOG.NLM no longer is needed.

 The INITIALIZE SYSTEM command activates the processing of the configuration information in the NETINFO.CFG file.

After you import LOAD and BIND statements to NETINFO.CFG, you must run INETCFG to make changes to these statements, rather than attempt to change NETINFO.CFG directly. You might want to change these statements, for example, when you add a new network board or change the setting for an old network board, or when you add new protocol support or change the existing protocol configuration.

 When you load INETCFG, it performs the following:

1. Creates a new AUTOEXEC.NCF file and stores the old file in SYS:SYSTEM\AUTOEXEC.BAK

2. Prompts you to import the LOAD, BIND, and remote access commands from the old AUTOEXEC.NCF file

3. Inserts the following commands in the AUTOEXEC.NCF file:

   a. LOAD CONLOG to begin a log file of console messages in SYS:ETC\CONSOLE.LOG

   b. INITSYS.NCF for server to initialize use of the configuration information in the INETCFG database

   c. UNLOAD CONLOG to stop console logging after startup is complete

Navigating the INETCFG Menus

To understand the main options for using INETCFG, run INETCFG:

```
LOAD INETCFG
```

You should see the Internetworking Configuration menu (see fig. 12.28).

- **Boards.** Use to configure LAN/WAN boards.

- **Network Interface.** Use to configure ports on a multiport network boards. You could, for example, configure each port on a multiport WAN board to use a different WAN protocol, such as PPP, frame relay, or X.25.

- **WAN Call Directory.** Use to define WAN call destinations for protocols such as PPP, frame relay, or X.25. You generally use this option to specify media-specific information to connect to remote sites.

- **Protocols.** Use to configure routing protocol operation for IPX, RIP, and NLSP.

- **Bindings.** Use to bind protocols that are enabled to the network driver interface. Protocols are bound per interface. You can bind the same protocol to the same interface several times using different frame type parameters.

- **Manage Configuration.** Use to configure network management parameters, edit system files, and copy configuration information to or from disks. You could use this option, for example, to configure SNMP parameters and remote access to the server.

- **View Configuration.** Use to display the commands INETCFG generates. You also can use this option to view console messages logged during system initialization.

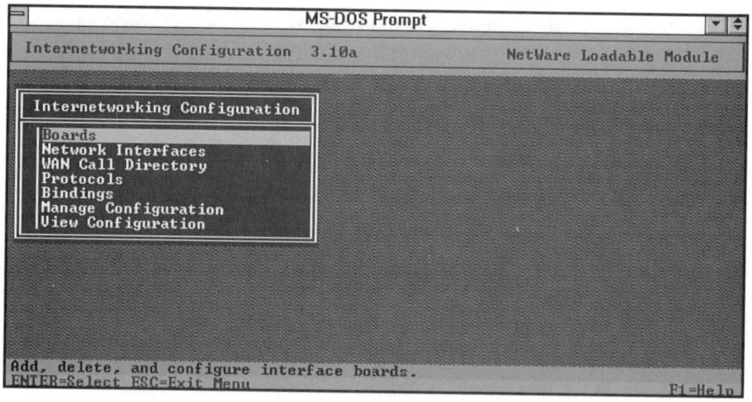

Figure 12.28

The INETCFG's Internetworking Configuration menu.

```
┌─                          MS-DOS Prompt                      ▼ ♦┐
│ Internetworking Configuration  3.10a          NetWare Loadable Module │
│                                                                       │
│   ┌─ Internetworking Configuration ─┐                                │
│   │ Boards                          │                                │
│   │ Network Interfaces              │                                │
│   │ WAN Call Directory              │                                │
│   │ Protocols                       │                                │
│   │ Bindings                        │                                │
│   │ Manage Configuration            │                                │
│   │ View Configuration              │                                │
│   └─────────────────────────────────┘                                │
│                                                                       │
│                                                                       │
│ Add, delete, and configure interface boards.                         │
│ ENTER=Select ESC=Exit Menu                                  F1=Help   │
```

Study Note You can display only the last 8 KB of information in the CONSOLE.LOG file when you use the INETCFG.NLM.

■ After you study this chapter, try to answer the sample test questions. If you make mistakes, review the appropriate topics until you understand the reasons for the correct answers.

Study Guide for the Chapter

If you are preparing for passing exams, review the chapter with the following goals:

■ Understand the different NDS objects for messaging services, and a brief overview of MPR configuration.

■ Know about the FirstMail MHS clients for DOS and MS Windows.

Chapter Summary

In this chapter you learned about how NetWare 4.*x* networks can be used to provide messaging services. You learned about the NetWare MHS mail services that are bundled with NetWare 4.*x*, and the procedures for installing, configuring, and using these services.

Chapter Test Questions

Test questions can have a single correct answer or multiple correct answers. Where a single answer is desired, a ○ (circle) notation precedes the possible answers. Some questions require you to select more than one answer. These questions are indicated by the □ (box) preceding each answer. Not all the questions are multiple choice. Occasionally, you may get a question that asks you to type in an answer. The answer in this case is usually a one-word answer. The answer is not case sensitive, so you can type the answer in lower- or uppercase.

Certain questions are repeated in different ways so that you can recognize them even when the wording is different. Taking practice quizzes not only tests your knowledge, it gives you confidence when you take your exam.

1. In a simple local message delivery you can expect the following messaging components:

   □ A. Messaging engine

   □ B. Database engine

   □ C. User mailboxes

   □ D. Messaging applications

   □ E. Routing engine

2. NetWare 4 Message Handling Services is implemented by the following NLM that runs on the NetWare 4 server:

   ○ A. MSG.NLM

   ○ B. MESSAGE.NLM

   ○ C. MHS.NLM

   ○ D. MHS4.NLM

   ○ E. MSG_SRV.NLM

3. NetWare 4 MHS services include the following e-mail client software:

   ○ A. MHSX client

   ○ B. Mail First

   ○ C. FirstMail

   ○ D. CC Mail

   ○ E. FirstClient

4. NetWare 4 MHS Services take up the following resources on the NetWare server:

   ○ A. 100 KB of RAM

   ○ B. 200 KB of RAM

   ○ C. 300 KB of RAM

   ○ D. 400 KB of RAM

   ○ E. 500 KB of RAM

5. NetWare 4 MHS Services take up _____ MB for program storage.

   ○ A. 1.5 MB

   ○ B. 2.5 MB

   ○ C. 3.5 MB

   ○ D. 4.5 MB

   ○ E. 5.5 MB

6. After the NetWare 4 MHS services installation the following objects are created by default:

   □ A. Messaging Server

   □ B. Distribution List

   □ C. Message Routing Group

   □ D. External Entity

7. The Messaging Server object is used to represent the _____.

   ○ A. Routing server

   ○ B. Messaging engine

   ○ C. User mailbox

   ○ D. E-mail client server

8. The Messaging Routing Group is a cluster of _____.

   ○ A. users that transfer messages to each other

   ○ B. messaging servers that transfer messages to each other

   ○ C. mailboxes that receive the same messages

   ○ D. NetWare 4 servers used for licensing

9. The External Entity is used to represent an external _____.

   ○ A. mail server

   ○ B. mailbox

   ○ C. NetWare server

   ○ D. mail application

10. Which of the following is true for Distribution List objects?

   ☐ A. A distribution list can contain only User objects.

   ☐ B. Distribution list members do not share login scripts or trustee rights.

   ☐ C. Distribution list members share login scripts or trustee rights.

   ☐ D. Distribution lists can contain other distribution lists.

   ☐ E. Distribution lists cannot contain other distribution lists.

11. NetWare MPR provides which of the following services?

   ☐ A. It can be used to off-load routing processing functions from busy servers.

   ☐ B. It provides security by isolating network segments.

   ☐ C. It provides security by performing application level filtering.

   ☐ D. It provides a routing function that can be used to connect dissimilar media.

   ☐ E. It can provide limited file and print services.

12. NetWare MPR configuration is done using _____.

   ○ A. INETC.NLM

   ○ B. MPRCFG.NLM

   ○ C. INETCFG.NLM

   ○ D. PRODUCT.NLM

   ○ E. INSPROD.NLM

   ○ F. MPR.NLM

13. The INETCFG.NLM can _____.

   ☐ A. simplify the configuration of network boards

   ☐ B. be used for the loading of protocols

☐ C. be used for binding of protocols to specific network boards

☐ D. be used for configuring PSERVER

☐ E. be used for configuring time synchronization

14. The INETCFG.NLM program enables you to extract the _____.

○ A. LOAD and BIND statements for network board drivers to a separate file called SYS:ETC\NETINFO.CFG

○ B. LOAD and BIND statements for network board drivers to a separate file called SYS:ETC\INETCFG.CFG

○ C. LOAD statements for network board drivers to a separate file called SYS:ETC\NETINFO.CFG

○ D. LOAD statements for network board drivers to a separate file called SYS:ETC\INETCFG.CFG

15. The CONLOG.NLM _____.

○ A. activates the capturing of system and error console messages to the SYS:ETC\CONSOLE.LOG file

○ B. activates the capturing of system and error console messages to the SYS:PUBLIC\CONSOLE.LOG file

○ C. starts a virtual console, and logging capability for system console messages to the SYS:ETC\CONSOLE.LOG file

○ D. starts a virtual console, and logging capability for system console messages to the SYS:PUBLIC\CONSOLE.LOG file

16. Which command activates the processing of the configuration information in the NETINFO.CFG file?

○ A. START SYSTEM

○ B. START INETCFG

○ C. INITIALIZE SYSTEM

○ D. INITIALIZE INETCFG

Answers to Chapter Test Questions

Chapter 1

1. B
2. C
3. A B
4. A B D
5. B C
6. B E
7. B
8. C
9. A
10. C
11. A C
12. A
13. A B
14. B E
15. C

16. E
17. D
18. B
19. D
20. B
21. C
22. D
23. C
24. D
25. C
26. C
27. C
28. B D E
29. B C E F G
30. C
31. B

32. B
33. A
34. A
35. B
36. D
37. C
38. A
39. B
40. C
41. C
42. A
43. C
44. D
45. D
46. B C D F
47. D
48. D
49. A B
50. A C
51. A B C
52. D
53. B
54. C
55. B
56. C E
57. A
58. C

59. A C
60. C
61. E
62. A B E
63. B D
64. B
65. A D

Chapter 2

1. C
2. B
3. A D
4. A C
5. A
6. D
7. B
8. C
9. C
10. C
11. B
12. C
13. B
14. A
15. D
16. C
17. A

18. [partition]
19. C E
20. F
21. A C
22. A C
23. A D
24. D
25. A B
26. C
27. C
28. D
29. A D
30. A B F
31. A F
32. B E
33. E
34. B
35. E
36. A C E F
37. A B D
38. B D
39. D
40. C
41. A B
42. C
43. D
44. D
45. B C D

46. B
47. B
48. A
49. D
50. C F
51. B D
52. C
53. A
54. C
55. A C D
56. A
57. C
58. C E
59. B C
60. B
61. C
62. B
63. E
64. F
65. A
66. E
67. F
68. A D
69. B
70. B C E G
71. A B C E
72. [context]
73. [replica]

Chapter 3

1. A C E
2. C
3. A
4. C
5. D
6. A C E
7. A
8. A C
9. C
10. D
11. D
12. B C
13. C
14. B C D E
15. C
16. D
17. C
18. B
19. D
20. D
21. D
22. D
23. B
24. C
25. C
26. D
27. A
28. D
29. D
30. A B C E
31. A B D E
32. A D
33. C D
34. B C D
35. E
36. C
37. A
38. A
39. C
40. C
41. B
42. D
43. C
44. A
45. C
46. B
47. B E F
48. A C D
49. A
50. C
51. A
52. B
53. C

54. D

55. E

56. F

57. B

58. B

59. E

60. B

Chapter 4

1. A

2. A B

3. A B

4. C D F

5. D

6. A

7. B

8. C

9. B

10. B

11. C

12. A

13. B

14. C

15. D

16. D

17. B

18. B

19. C D

20. B C F

21. A

22. A C

23. D

24. A B C E

25. G

26. B

27. A

28. C

29. D

30. E

31. B

32. C

33. D

34. E

35. F

36. A D

37. A C

38. D

39. A

40. B

41. C D

42. B D

43. E

44. D

45. B

46. B

47. A
48. B
49. C
50. B F
51. C D G
52. D
53. D
54. A C E
55. C
56. A
57. D
58. B
59. A C D
60. B C
61. B D
62. B D E

Chapter 5

1. A C D
2. A B E
3. D
4. E
5. A
6. D
7. D

8. D
9. C
10. D
11. A C D F
12. B
13. D
14. A
15. A
16. D
17. A D
18. C
19. A C E
20. B
21. B
22. B
23. B
24. C
25. A D
26. D
27. C
28. D
29. B
30. C
31. B
32. D

33. C

34. A B

35. C

36. B

37. A

38. D

40. D

41. A

42. F

43. D

44. D

45. A

46. B

47. C

48. A

49. B

50. B

51. C

52. E

53. A

54. D

55. D

Chapter 6

1. C

2. A

3. B

4. C

5. D

6. C

7. A

8. B

9. A

10. C

11. D

12. B C E

13. D

14. C

15. A

16. B

17. D

18. C

19. B

20. C

21. B D E F

22. A C E

23. A

24. C

25. B

26. D

27. A

28. D

29. C

30. B

31. D

32. A
33. C
34. D
35. C
36. B
37. C
38. B
39. A B D
40. A B
41. B
42. C
43. A
44. A C E F
45. C
46. E
47. E

Chapter 7

1. A E
2. C E F
3. B D
4. A
5. A C
6. B
7. B
8. C
9. D
10. C
11. D
12. A
13. B
14. C
15. D
16. F
17. C
18. B
19. A C D
20. B
21. A
22. A
23. B
24. A
25. B
26. B E
27. B
28. E
29. C
30. D
31. C
32. B
33. C
34. C
35. B
36. A B
37. B C D
38. A C

39. B

40. B

41. E

42. A C D

43. C

44. A

45. C

46. B C

Chapter 8

1. B

2. E

3. D

4. A

5. F

6. A

7. C

8. A

9. A

10. E

11. C D

12. B

13. C

14. D

15. C

16. B

17. A

18. C

19. A

20. A E

21. A

22. D

23. E

24. B

25. C

26. C

27. C

28. D

29. A

30. C

31. D

32. B

33. A

34. B

35. B D

36. C E

37. B

38. B D E

39. C

Chapter 9

1. A

2. C

3. A D E

4. A

5. A

6. B

7. C

8. B

9. C

10. A

11. A

12. B

13. D

14. C

15. B

16. D

17. C

18. B

19. C

20. F

21. B

22. A

23. A C

24. B

25. C D

26. A

27. C

28. D

29. A

30. C

31. B

32. A

33. B

34. C

35. B

36. C

37. D

38. A

39. C

Chapter 10

1. B

2. C

3. D

4. A B

5. B

6. D

7. A C

8. B C

9. B D

10. C D

11. B E

12. B

13. B C

14. A

15. A B

16. A B E

17. A D E F

18. A D F

19. A

20. A

21. A C

22. A B

23. C

24. A C E G

25. A D E F G

26. A C

Chapter 11

1. A C D

2. A C

3. A C D

4. A C E

5. A C D

6. A C D

7. A B C

8. A C E G

9. A C D

10. C D

11. A B E F

12. A C D F G

13. A B D

14. A C E G H

15. A C D F

16. C

17. B

18. A B D

19. A C

20. A B D E G

21. B

22. A C D E

Chapter 12

1. A C D

2. C

3. C

4. E

5. B

6. A C

7. B

8. B

9. B

10. B D

11. A B D

12. C

13. A B C

14. A

15. A

16. C

Preparing for and Taking the Exams

The purpose of taking an exam is to test your knowledge of a subject area. The outcome of taking the exam, the exam results, is supposed to indicate the degree to which you have mastered the subject.

Most of us who have taken exams in school know that while quite often the exam results indicate the degree to which you have mastered the subject, the exam results don't always reflect how much you know or don't know. There are some students who understand the subject matter extremely well, but are poor "test takers." Others have a superficial knowledge of the subject area, yet seem to do very well on the exams.

And there are, of course, those who know the subject area and also do well on an exam in that subject area. The purpose of this book is to train you to fall into the latter category.

How This Book Can Help You

As part of your preparation for taking the exams, study the information in this book so that you have a good understanding of the subject area. The sample test questions that follow each chapter will help test your basic understanding of the subject matter. But no matter how well a test is designed, it cannot test all that you know or don't know. The key to doing well on an exam is to build your knowledge of the subject area so that you are confident about it. There is no harm in over-preparing for an exam. You not only will be able to pass the exam, but as an important side effect, you will have a superior knowledge base that will help you in your career.

This book and the sample questions are designed with this goal in mind. They go into details that you will probably never be asked in an exam. Also, some of the questions, in the author's opinion, are more difficult and detailed than those you will find in the exams. For questions that have multiple correct answers, currently the Novell tests will tell you the number of correct answers. This makes it easier to guess an answer when you are not sure. For questions with multiple correct answers in this book, no attempt has been made to give you this hint. This makes answering the questions a little harder and

has been done to help you increase your confidence on the subject, once you understand the reason for the right answer.

Also, when you take your test, read the questions carefully. Many a question has been answered incorrectly, not because of lack of knowledge, but because of misreading the question. You should also consider the choice of answers to each question carefully. Usually one or two choices can be eliminated easily, but you may see some choices that are quite close. In this case, you should select the answer that is more correct or applicable.

As you go through this book, it would be best if you have at least one NetWare 4.x server and a workstation on a network that you can experiment with. The author realizes that you might not have access to such a system at all times of the day, and even if you do, you might not be near one when you are reading this book and preparing for your exams. To help you out, many network administration tasks are presented in a guided-tour manner with plenty of screen shots so that you can see how a task is performed. This is the next best thing to doing hands-on network administration tasks on the network.

Author's Technique on Memorization

You need very little rote memorization for the NetWare 4.x exams, but if you feel that you need to memorize some facts and have a hard time recalling them, you may want to try the following:

Before going to sleep, mentally go over the facts that you want to remember (use the book to review the facts, if you cannot remember them). On waking up, try to remember the facts and write them down. In general, writing down facts that are difficult to remember will help you remember them. The author has had great personal success from using this technique—especially when dealing with the hard-to-remember details of high school history—before an exam. Many people also find using flash cards (or cue cards) to be a very helpful study aid.

Using the Test Questions in the Book

After going through each chapter in the book, answer the questions at the end of each chapter. Progress through the book until you finish the last chapter.

Registering for the Test

When you are ready, you can register to take a test. The certification tests currently are given by Drake Prometric which can be reached at the following address:

Drake Prometric
8800 Queen Avenue South
Bloomington, MN 55431
U.S.A.

In the U.S. and Canada the phone number for Drake Prometric is 800-RED-EXAM. Table B.1 lists the phone numbers for other countries. Should you have difficulty in calling any of the numbers listed in the table, you can call Drake directly at 612-921-6807 in the U.S. (The country code for North America is 1.)

You can register for a test in any one of the many places that offer Drake Testing. Your information is registered under an identification number. In the U.S., this is your Social Security number. You can use this identification number to track your exam status. You can register for the test from either three hours or three days before taking the exam. The three hour option is currently available on what is called a "fast site" in North America—if an exam time slot is available. You have to know the test number of the test you are taking. Because the test numbers can change, they are not listed in this book.

You can obtain the test number by calling 800-NETWARE (or 801-429-7000 outside North America) and asking for the test number for "NetWare 3.*x* to 4.*x* Update Exams," or "NetWare 4.*x* Administration," or "Advanced NetWare 4.*x* Administration." The fee for taking a test is $85 (U.S. currency) at the time of this book's publication, and is payable at registration (through credit card). After you pay your fee, you can take the test within one year. After that, you forfeit your test fee. The test price may fluctuate, and there might be special promotional offers that you can take advantage of. The test fee for sites outside the U.S. is likely to be higher. After you register, you should receive a confirmation for your test through your postal service.

Table B.1
Drake Prometic Phone Numbers

Country	Phone Number
U.S. and Canada	800-RED-EXAM (733-3926) 612-921-6807
Great Britain	44 344860400
France	33147750909
Germany	4921159730
Italy	39248013554
Spain	3415774941
Belgium	3227250200
Australia	6124133077
Singapore	653228503
Taiwan	8662775383
Hong Kong	852827223
Japan	81354811141

Taking the Test

If you have never taken a Drake test, it is advisable that you come at least 15 minutes before your exam appointment. When you register at the exam site, you will be asked to prove your identity. This is usually done through a photo identification such as a driver's license and a credit card.

The exams are computer-based, and a Drake employee will administer your exam. You will be given an ID to sign on to the computer, and you will take a practice multiple-choice test to get the feel of what the exam is like. Testees interact with their computers using an MS Windows-based application; you can use either the mouse or the function keys. At some sites, in the author's experience, the mouse pointing device is not particularly good. If you have this problem, be prepared to use the function keys instead. During the exam you can take notes on writing paper provided by the exam site, but you cannot take the paper out of the room. Some sites explain these rules quite well; other sites do not.

Form Test Versus Adaptive Test

Novell currently favors the adaptive method of testing. When a test is first developed, however, it is offered as a form test.

A form test has a certain number of fixed questions. The number of questions varies anywhere from 50 to 80 (or more). You can spend as long as you want on a question, but obviously not too long, because you should leave time to answer all the questions. With a form-based test, you can go back and review the questions you have already answered. If you find a particular question difficult, you can mark it and come back to it later.

After Novell has given an exam a number of times, it gathers the test results and generates an adaptive test based on those results. It is Novell's intention that all the tests will eventually be adaptive tests. Having said this, some of the CNE elective tests on TCP/IP and NFS are still form-based, even though they have been offered for a long time, and many people have taken these popular tests.

In an adaptive test, each question depends on the way you answered a previous question. The test is supposed to start out with a simple question on a particular topic. It is programmed to ask a minimum number of questions on each topic to be tested. If you answer all (or nearly all) of the questions correctly, it will ask you a minimum number of questions. This minimum number depends on the test, but is usually in a range from 10 to 15. The maximum number of questions can be from 20 to 25. If you answer a question incorrectly, the test may ask you a similar question again. In general, if you answer a question incorrectly, you will see more than the minimum number of questions on a topic.

Some test takers have assumed that if they see a similar question asked again, they must have answered the previous question incorrectly. This is not always so. You should always rely on your own certainty of the right answer. If you answer too many questions incorrectly overall, or answer too many questions incorrectly on an important topic (such as directory services), then you will fail the test. In an adaptive test, after you answer a question, you cannot go back and modify your previous answer. An adaptive test lasts about 20 to 30 minutes, though you can finish it in much less time.

The intention behind the adaptive test is to make the testing period shorter and less painful than with the form-based test. Opinion is divided as to whether this is true. Some people feel that the shortness of the test is a worthwhile feature. Others prefer the form-based tests because they are more comprehensive and testees can walk away from it feeling as if they have demonstrated more of their knowledge. They can also review their answers in case they made a simple mistake in reading a question.

This book prepares you to take both types of tests. You should check with Drake Prometric to learn whether the test is form-based or adaptive. If the test is one hour or longer, you can conclude it is form-based. Adaptive tests are usually 30 minutes or less.

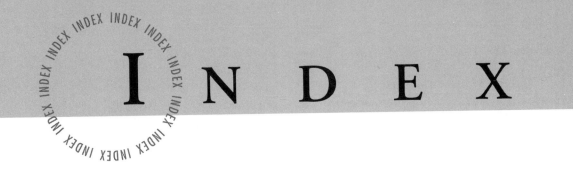

I N D E X

PLUG YOURSELF INTO...

THE MACMILLAN INFORMATION SUPERLIBRARY™

Free information and vast computer resources from the world's leading computer book publisher—online!

FIND THE BOOKS THAT ARE RIGHT FOR YOU!

A complete online catalog, plus sample chapters and tables of contents give you an in-depth look at *all* of our books, including hard-to-find titles. It's the best way to find the books you need!

● STAY INFORMED with the latest computer industry news through our online newsletter, press releases, and customized Information SuperLibrary Reports.

● GET FAST ANSWERS to your questions about MCP books and software.

● VISIT our online bookstore for the latest information and editions!

● COMMUNICATE with our expert authors through e-mail and conferences.

● DOWNLOAD SOFTWARE from the immense MCP library:
   - Source code and files from MCP books
   - The best shareware, freeware, and demos

● DISCOVER HOT SPOTS on other parts of the Internet.

● WIN BOOKS in ongoing contests and giveaways!

TO PLUG INTO MCP: → **WORLD WIDE WEB: http://www.mcp.com**

GOPHER: gopher.mcp.com
FTP: ftp.mcp.com

WANT MORE INFORMATION?

CHECK OUT THESE RELATED TOPICS OR SEE YOUR LOCAL BOOKSTORE

CAD and 3D Studio

As the number one CAD publisher in the world, and as a Registered Publisher of Autodesk, New Riders Publishing provides unequaled content on this complex topic. Industry-leading products include AutoCAD and 3D Studio.

Networking

As the leading Novell NetWare publisher, New Riders Publishing delivers cutting-edge products for network professionals. We publish books for all levels of users, from those wanting to gain NetWare Certification, to those administering or installing a network. Leading books in this category include *Inside NetWare 3.12*, *CNE Training Guide: Managing NetWare Systems*, *Inside TCP/IP*, and *NetWare: The Professional Reference*.

Graphics

New Riders provides readers with the most comprehensive product tutorials and references available for the graphics market. Best-sellers include *Inside CorelDRAW! 5*, *Inside Photoshop 3*, and *Adobe Photoshop NOW!*

Internet and Communications

As one of the fastest growing publishers in the communications market, New Riders provides unparalleled information and detail on this ever-changing topic area. We publish international best-sellers such as *New Riders' Official Internet Yellow Pages, 2nd Edition*, a directory of over 10,000 listings of Internet sites and resources from around the world, and *Riding the Internet Highway, Deluxe Edition*.

Operating Systems

Expanding off our expertise in technical markets, and driven by the needs of the computing and business professional, New Riders offers comprehensive references for experienced and advanced users of today's most popular operating systems, including *Understanding Windows 95*, *Inside Unix*, *Inside Windows 3.11 Platinum Edition*, *Inside OS/2 Warp Version 3*, and *Inside MS-DOS 6.22*.

Other Markets

Professionals looking to increase productivity and maximize the potential of their software and hardware should spend time discovering our line of products for Word, Excel, and Lotus 1-2-3. These titles include *Inside Word 6 for Windows*, *Inside Excel 5 for Windows*, *Inside 1-2-3 Release 5*, and *Inside WordPerfect for Windows*.

Orders/Customer Service **1-800-653-6156**   Source Code **NRP95**

New Riders Publishing   201 West 103rd Street ◆ Indianapolis, Indiana 46290 USA

REGISTRATION CARD

CNE Training Guide: NetWare 4.1 Update

Name _____ Title _____

Company _____ Type of business _____

Address _____

City/State/ZIP _____

Have you used these types of books before? ☐ yes ☐ no

If yes, which ones? _____

_____

How many computer books do you purchase each year? ☐ 1–5 ☐ 6 or more

How did you learn about this book? _____

Where did you purchase this book? _____

Which applications do you currently use? _____

_____

Which computer magazines do you subscribe to? _____

_____

What trade shows do you attend? _____

_____

Comments: _____

_____

_____

Would you like to be placed on our preferred mailing list? ☐ yes ☐ no

☐ **I would like to see my name in print!** You may use my name and quote me in future New Riders products and promotions. My daytime phone number is: _____

New Riders Publishing   201 West 103rd Street ◆ Indianapolis, Indiana 46290 USA

Fax to **317-581-4670**   Orders/Customer Service **1-800-653-6156**   Source Code **NRP95**

Fold Here

- -

‖‖‖‖

NO POSTAGE
NECESSARY
IF MAILED
IN THE
UNITED STATES

BUSINESS REPLY MAIL

FIRST-CLASS MAIL PERMIT NO. 9918 INDIANAPOLIS IN

POSTAGE WILL BE PAID BY THE ADDRESSEE

NEW RIDERS PUBLISHING
201 W 103RD ST
INDIANAPOLIS IN 46290-9058